The Philosophy of William of Ockham in the Light of Its Principles

Every philosophy is sustained by a number of elemental principles that give it cohesion and unity. Ockham's is no exception. The principles of the divine omnipotence and the rule of parsimony of thought known as Ockham's razor, and others like the principle of non-contradiction, help to shape the entire range of his thought. Many of his conclusions on matters as diverse as God's knowledge, will, and power, on creation and the causality of natural things, and on human intuition and morality are reducible to them.

These principles are not unique to Ockham but were common to all the scholastics. Yet it is precisely in confrontation with the views of his predecessors and contemporaries such as Scotus, Henry of Ghent, Aquinas, and Chatton that the particular force and character of his thought are revealed. Over and again he sets each principle to powerful use, but allows no single one to dominate, or to yield all its consequences.

Martin Heidegger once declared, "Every thinker thinks but one single thought." The original and focal point of Ockham's thought is the singular or individual thing (*res singularis*), as common nature (*natura communis*) is the central conception of Scotism and the act of existing (*esse*) is of Thomism. With Ockham the traditional conjugations of being come to signify the thing itself in its ineluctable unity. The concept of being is univocal, standing for and signifying individuals. A being is radically diverse and incommunicable, differing from every other being not only in number but in essence. Indeed, an individual thing can no longer be said to *have* an essence; it *is* an essence.

Ockham takes his place among the great philosophers because, like them, he drew out all the implications of his insight. He remains a seminal thinker: his denial of common essences, his emphasis on language in philosophical discourse, all anticipate significant developments in modern philosophy.

Studies and Texts 133

The Philosophy of William of Ockham

in the Light of Its Principles

ARMAND MAURER

Toronto

PIMS

Pontifical Institute of Mediaeval Studies

CANADIAN CATALOGUING IN PUBLICATION DATA

Maurer, Armand A. (Armand Augustine), 1915–
  The philosophy of William of Ockham in the light of its
  principles.

(Studies and texts, ISSN 0082–5328 ; 133)
Includes bibliographical references and index.
ISBN 0–88844–133–9

1. William, of Ockham, ca. 1285–ca. 1349.   2. Philosophy,
Medieval.   I. Pontifical Institute of Mediaeval Studies.
II. Title.   III. Series: Studies and texts (Pontifical Institute
of Mediaeval Studies) ; 133.

B765.O34M386 1999   189'.4   C99–931222–7

© 1999

Pontifical Institute of Mediaeval Studies
59 Queen's Park Crescent East
Toronto, Ontario, Canada M5S 2C4

PRINTED IN CANADA

for JOSEPH C. WEY

Contents

Abbreviations

Primary sources are cited using the conventional internal reference, followed by the modern edition (abbreviated where necessary) in parentheses, and the translation, where relevant. Frequently cited works by Ockham, Aristotle, Scotus, and Aquinas use the abbreviations listed below. Detailed information about editions and translations cited can be found in the bibliography of primary sources on pp. 548–557.

SERIES

CCL   Corpus Christianorum, Series Latina (Turnhout: Brepols, 1953–)
CSEL   Corpus scriptorum ecclesiasticorum latinorum (Vienna: F. Tempsky, and various imprints, 1866–)
PG   Patrologiae cursus completus: Series Graeca, ed. J.-P. Migne, 161 vols. (Paris: Migne, 1857–1866)
PL   Patrologiae cursus completus: Series Latina, ed. J.-P. Migne, 221 vols. (Paris: Migne, 1844–1864)

WILLIAM OF OCKHAM

The works of Ockham are cited from the three principal modern collections listed below. For bibliographical details, see pp. 548–549.

OP   *Opera Politica*
OPh   *Opera Philosophica*
OTh   *Opera Theologica*

Individual works are cited by the following abbreviations:

Brevis sum. Phys.	*Brevis summa libri Physicorum*
Expos. Elench.	*Expositio super libros Elenchorum*
Expos. in Periherm.	*Expositio in librum Perihermenias*
Expos. in Phys.	*Expositio in libros Physicorum*
Expos. in Praedicab.	*Expositio in librum Porphyrii de Praedicabilibus*

Expos. in Praedicamen.	*Expositio in librum Praedicamentorum*
Opus nonag. dierum	*Opus nonaginta dierum*
Ord.	*Ordinatio*
Quaest. in Phys.	*Quaestiones in libros Physicorum*
Quaest. variae	*Quaestiones variae*
Quodl.	*Quodlibeta septem*
Rep.	*Reportatio*
Sum. log.	*Summa logicae*
Sum. phil. nat.	*Summa philosophiae naturalis*
Tract. de corp. Christi	*Tractatus de corpore Christi*
Tract. de praedes.	*Tractatus de praedestinatione*
Tract. de quant.	*Tractatus de quantitate*

ANONYMOUS

Tract. de prin. theol.	*Tractatus de principiis theologiae*

ARISTOTLE

Anal. Prior.	*Analytica Priora*
Anal. Post.	*Analytica Posteriora*
Eth. Nic.	*Ethica Nicomachea*
Metaph.	*Metaphysica*
Phys.	*Physica*
Top.	*Topica*

JOHN DUNS SCOTUS

Metaph.	*Quaestiones super libros Metaphysicorum*
Ord.	*Ordinatio*
Quodl.	*Quaestiones quodlibetales*
Rep. Paris.	*Reportata Parisiensia*

THOMAS AQUINAS

De pot.	*De potentia*
De ver.	*De veritate*
In Metaph.	*Commentaria in Metaphysicam*
In Phys.	*Commentaria in octo libros Physicorum*
In Sent.	*Scriptum super libros Sententiarum*
SCG	*Summa contra Gentiles*
ST	*Summa theologiae*

Introduction

> If you say, I don't want to talk about words but only about things, I say that, although you only want to talk about things, you can only do it with words or concepts or other signs.
> Ockham, *Ordinatio* 1.2.1 (*OTh* 2:47.3–6)

L IKE ALL SCHOOLMEN OF the high Middle Ages, William of Ockham is best known to us through his writings. Ockham the man remains shrouded in obscurity; only briefly, at important moments of his life, does he emerge in history. The details of his life, and even of his death, are largely conjectural.[1]

It is generally agreed that he was born about 1285, probably in the village of Ockham, in the county of Surrey, southwest of London. He entered the Franciscan Order before the age of fourteen and was educated in philosophy probably at the Franciscan school in London. It is noted in the register of Bishop Robert Winchelsey, Archbishop of Canterbury, that a certain "Gulielmus de Okham" was ordained subdeacon in the conventual church of

---

1. For Ockham's life see Léon Baudry, *Guillaume d'Occam. Sa vie, ses oeuvres, ses idées sociales et politiques* 1: *L'homme et les oeuvres* (Paris, 1949); Philotheus Boehner, introduction to Ockham, *Philosophical Writings*, rev. Stephen F. Brown (1957; Indianapolis/Cambridge, 1990), pp. xi–xvi,; James A. Weisheipl, "Ockham and Some Mertonians," *Mediaeval Studies* 30 (1968): 164–174; William J. Courtenay, *Schools and Scholars in Fourteenth-Century England* (Princeton, 1987), pp. 194–196, "Ockham, Chatton, and the London *Studium:* Observations on Recent Changes in Ockham's Biography," in *Die Gegenwart Ockhams*, ed. Wilhelm Vossenkuhl and Rolf Schönberger (Weinheim, 1990), pp. 327–337; Francis E. Kelley, "Ockham: Avignon, Before and After," in *From Ockham to Wyclif*, ed. Anne Hudson and Michael Wilks (Oxford, 1987), pp. 1–18. Regarding Ockham's death see C.K. Brampton, "Traditions Relating to the Death of William of Ockham," *Archivum Franciscanum Historicum* 53 (1960): 442–449; Gedeon Gál, "William of Ockham Died 'Impenitent' in April 1347," *Franciscan Studies* 42 (1982): 90–95.

St. Mary, Southwark, in greater London, in 1306. As the canonical minimum of age for receiving the subdiaconate was twenty, he would have been born before 1286, unless he obtained a dispensation. He must have been ordained a priest before 19 June 1318, when he received a licence to hear confessions.

Around 1309 he was sent to Oxford to study theology. After five years there he would have lectured cursorily on the Bible for two years. Then, between 1317–1319 he commented on the *Sentences* of Peter Lombard, receiving the degree of Bachelor of the *Sentences*. With two more years of studies he completed the requirements for the degree of Master of Theology, even giving his inaugural lecture or *inceptio*; but he did not become a Regent Master of Theology, occupying the Franciscan chair at Oxford. He was probably waiting for his turn to arrive; but he was also opposed by John Lutterell, the chancellor of the university, who suspected him of heresy. In the interval he was sent to the Franciscan house of studies in London, where he lectured and wrote extensively. He revised the first book of his *Sentences* (known as his *Ordinatio*), commented on Aristotle's logic and physics, and wrote his monumental *Summa logicae* and *Quodlibeta*, though these works may have been finished in Avignon. At London he lived with his confreres Walter Chatton who became a staunch critic, and Adam of Wodeham who became a follower.

A new period began in Ockham's life in July 1324, when he was summoned by Pope John XXII to Avignon to answer the charge of heresy brought against him by John Lutterell. He remained there four years while his case was being examined by a papal committee. The committee censured some of Ockham's doctrines in his *Sentences*, but its inquiry was not completed and none of the disputed doctrines was formally condemned.

While at Avignon Ockham became embroiled in a controversy over apostolic poverty. Michael of Cesena, the Franciscan Minister General, whom the pope had also summoned to Avignon, opposed John XXII's opinion that even though Christ himself owned no property, he and his apostles had possessions in common. The dispute had implications for the Franciscan Spirituals, led by Michael of Cesena, who wanted to return to St. Francis' ideal of absolute poverty.[2] Convinced that the pope had fallen into heresy and hence was not truly pope, Ockham with Michael of Cesena and several other Franciscans fled from Avignon on 26 May 1328. Making their way down the Rhône, they then sailed from Aigues Mortes to Genoa and from there travelled to Pisa, where they met the German Emperor Louis of Bavaria, who was also at enmity with the pope over political matters. Under the protection of the emperor, the Franciscans went to Munich, where they took refuge in the Franciscan convent. After the flight of the Franciscans the pope excommunicated them, and the Franciscan Order expelled them from its ranks.

Ockham spent his last twenty years in Munich, writing on apostolic and Franciscan poverty and the relations between the Church and Empire. It has been the general opinion of historians that shortly before his death he took steps to be reconciled with the Church and his Order. A recent study indicates that it was not he, but one of his *socii*, named William of England, who returned the ancient seal of the Order (taken to Munich by Michael of Cesena) to the new Minister General, asked to be reconciled to the Church, and was absolved in 1349. As far as is known, Ockham died without reconciliation. A plaque once attached to his tomb gives the date of his death as 10 April 1347. It has been thought that he died of the plague which was then raging in Europe, but in 1347 it had not yet reached southern Germany. He was buried in the Franciscan church in Munich, but the body has since been removed and its location is unknown.

Ockham can best be seen as a Franciscan theologian, following in the tradition of his Order initiated by Alexander of Hales and John of la Rochelle in the first half of the thirteenth century, and carried on and developed by the illustrious theologians Bonaventure and Duns Scotus. Among his fellow Franciscans Ockham

---

2. See John Moorman, *A History of the Franciscan Order: From Its Origin to the Year 1517* (Oxford, 1968), pp. 307–319; Léon Baudry, "L'Ordre franciscain au temps de Guillaume d'Occam," *Mediaeval Studies* 27 (1965): 184–211.

was especially preoccupied with the thought of Scotus, who died in Cologne in 1308, while Ockham was still a student. He borrowed many philosophical and theological notions from his predecessor, such as the distinction between intuitive and abstractive knowledge, the distinction between the absolute and ordered power of God, the principle of parsimony or the razor, and the conviction that the individual, and not an essence or common nature, is the ultimate perfection of reality. Yet all of these ideas took on new meaning in Ockham's own works, becoming part of a revolutionary philosophy that was to shake scholasticism to its depths, point it in new directions, and influence the course of Western philosophy up to the present.

There is good reason, then, to call Ockham a philosopher; and yet he would undoubtedly have been surprised to receive the title. To him, a philosopher (*philosophus*) was a man like Aristotle or Averroes, who based his conclusions on empirical and rational evidence. Ockham laid claim to the more prestigious title of Master of Theology (*magister theologiae*), and it was from this position that he surveyed the philosophical scene and enthusiastically entered into it. His main works are professedly theological, but they often engage philosophical themes with rational arguments. His monumental *Summa logicae* and commentaries on Aristotle profess to explain the thought of the Greek philosopher, but Ockham makes it his own, at least as a probable opinion and when corrected by "the truth of the theologians." In these philosophical works Ockham never forgets that he is a theologian, to the point of sometimes introducing his favorite revealed principle of the divine omnipotence into philosophical discussions.[3] This makes it difficult to assess his status as a philosopher. We shall try to throw some light on this subject when we examine his views on theology and philosophy in Chapter 2.

In the late Middle Ages Ockham was seen as the initiator of a new way of doing theology and philosophy called the *via mo-*

---

3. See, for example, the index of the *Sum. log.* under the heading "Deus, potentia" (*OPh* 1: 867), and the index of the *Quaest. in Phys.* under the same heading (*OPh* 6: 842).

derna, in contrast to the *via antiqua* (although, as historians are quick to point out, these terms seem to have originated a century after Ockham, when rivalry between the two factions of the *moderni* and *antiqui* became fierce in the universities of Western Europe.) The *moderni* followed the nominalism of the Ockhamists and the terminist logic that flourished especially at Oxford in the thirteenth century and was developed by Ockham in the fourteenth. The *antiqui,* who favored the older modist or realist logic based on the philosophy of Aristotle and Averroes and their thirteenth-century commentators, dominated Paris. Already in the thirteenth century, however, there was a growing conflict between the advocates of the newer terminism and the older logic.[4] It should be noted that to Ockham himself the term *modernus* simply meant a contemporary, and *antiquus* or *antiquus doctor* an older writer like Aristotle, Augustine, Damascene and Anselm. Moreover, he did not align himself with the *moderni* but with the *antiqui.* Clearly, he did not regard himself as breaking away from the traditional teachings of the Church in either theology or philosophy, but rather as continuing that tradition and furthering its development.[5]

This book aims to examine Ockham's basic philosophical views in confrontation with the opposing views of his scholastic

---

4. There is an extensive bibliography on the subject conveniently brought together by Walter L. Moore, "Via Moderna," in *Dictionary of the Middle Ages,* ed. in chief, Joseph R. Strayer (New York, 1989), 12: 406–409. See especially William J. Courtenay, "*Antiqui* and *moderni* in Late Medieval Thought," *Journal of the History of Ideas* 48 (1987): 3–10; Astrik L. Gabriel, "*Via Antiqua* and *Via Moderna* and the Migration of Paris Students and Masters to the German Universities in the Fifteenth Century," in *Antiqui und Moderni: Traditionsbewußtsein und Fortschrittsbewußtsein im späten Mittelalter,* ed. Albert Zimmermann (Berlin/New York, 1974), pp. 439–483; Neal W. Gilbert, "Ockham, Wyclif, and the 'via moderna,' ibid., pp. 85–125.

On British logic and Ockhamist logic in particular see Courtenay, *Schools and Scholars,* pp. 193–249; the essays in *The Rise of British Logic,* ed. Osmund Lewry (Toronto, 1983); and appropriate chapters in *The Cambridge History of Later Medieval Philosophy,* ed. Norman Kretzmann et al. (Cambridge, 1982).

5. For Ockham's use of the terms *modernus* and *antiquus* see *Quodl.* 3.2, 5.22 (*OTh* 9: 208–209, 564–569).

predecessors and contemporaries. It has already been said that he was first and foremost a theologian, but his works contain a philosophizing of striking originality and genius. This is true of his philosophical writings, notably his monumental *Summa logicae*, but it is perhaps even truer of his theological works, chief among which are his commentary on the *Sententiae* of Peter Lombard and his *Quodlibeta*. Like all the great masters of the Middle Ages – Bonaventure, Thomas Aquinas, Henry of Ghent and Duns Scotus to mention only a few – he believed that his theological inquiries demanded the aid of rigorous philosophical activity. He philosophized not only for philosophical ends, but also, and especially, to provide a finely honed instrument for theological investigation. In the Letter introducing his *Summa logicae* he says that he wrote it as an aid to theology and the other sciences. He complains that young members of the faculties of theology and the other disciplines were delving into the subtleties of their sciences before acquiring a mastery of logic, with the result that they made many mistakes and became entangled in difficulties that offer little or no problem to experts in logic.[6]

Of course, Ockham was not recommending to these young scholars just any logic, but his own! From his *Summa logicae* they would learn the elements of his innovative logic, as well as other essentials of his general nominalist reform of philosophy. This work, and his lengthy commentaries on Aristotle's logic, also introduced them to Aristotelian logic, and the need to modify it when confronting Christian revelation. After becoming an expert in logic, they could proceed to study his works in physics and his vast theological tomes, which throw further light on his philosophical views in a theological setting.

---

6. "Et quia plerumque contingit ante magnam experientiam logicae subtilitatibus theologiae aliarumque Facultatum iuniores impendere studium, ac per hoc in difficultates eis inexplicabiles incidunt, quae tamen aliis parvae sunt aut nullae, et in multiplices prolabuntur errores, veras demonstrationes tamquam sophismata respuentes et sophisticationes pro demonstrationibus recipientes, tractatum hunc duxi scribendum, nonnumquam in processu regulas per exempla tam philosophica quam theologica declarando" (*Sum. log.* epist.prooem. [*OPh* 1: 6.21–28]).

The present inquiry aims to discern the principles and primary notions from which Ockham's philosophy flows. Every philosopher or philosophically-minded theologian who aspires to any degree of systematic thought relies on certain explicit or implicit principles to give his thought shape and cohesion. Ockham leaves us in no doubt what his principles are and how he understands them. Chief among them is his belief in the absolute power and freedom of God and the complete contingency of the created world. God alone is absolutely necessary; even the physical and moral laws of our world are contingent. Scotus had already emphasized the contingency of creation, but we shall see that in this regard Ockham went even further than his Franciscan predecessor, for example in the interpretation of the decalogue.

An allied principle pervading Ockham's thought is the distinction between God's power considered in itself and absolutely (*potentia absoluta*) and the same power considered from the perspective of what God has actually willed to happen (*potentia ordinata*). The distinction was in general use among theologians since the thirteenth century, but they did not always understand it in the same way. Ockham offers his own interpretation of the distinction in the divine power, which will occupy our attention in Chapter 5. He makes frequent use of the Christian belief in the divine omnipotence not only to settle questions in theology but also in philosophy.

Another principle in general use by the schoolmen is the rule of economy or simplicity of thought: a plurality should not be posited without necessity. Schoolmen in the thirteenth century occasionally appealed to this rule, whose origin can be traced to Aristotle. Duns Scotus invoked it much more frequently; Ockham, for his part, resorts to it so often that it came to be known as Ockham's razor.[7] He leaves his mark on this principle, just as he does on the others. Examining the role it plays in his philosophy,

7. Thus, in the index of the *Quodlibeta*, under the heading "Pluralitas non est ponenda sine necessitate," the excellent editor simply notes *passim* (everywhere). For the meaning of this principle see below, pp. 121–129.

we shall see that it features in dialectical reasoning, leading to conclusions that are not strictly demonstrated but only persuasive or highly believable. This prompts us to an examination of Ockham's (often neglected) notion of dialectics and the pervasive role this kind of reasoning plays in his thought.

The importance of the principles of the divine omnipotence and the razor in Ockham's thought was given prominence by an anonymous disciple in a treatise entitled *De principiis theologiae*, written between 1328 and 1350. From these two principles the disciple was able to derive two hundred and forty-eight theological and philosophical conclusions of his master.[8] There is a precedent, then, for presenting Ockham's thought in the light of his principles. His interpretation and use of these principles will be examined in conjunction with other principles, like the principle of noncontradiction, along with basic logical, epistemological, and metaphysical notions. It is to be hoped that this will enable the reader to understand not only what Ockham taught but also why he taught it.

While examining Ockham's philosophy it will become evident that it is not dominated by one single principle – not even by the powerful principle of the divine omnipotence. Like all philosophies of note – and here Kantianism with its balance of pure and practical reason readily comes to mind – Ockhamism is the consequence of a number of principles that tend to balance each other (but not without tension), and thus prevent the conclusions of any one of them from disrupting the unity of the whole synthesis. We shall see Ockham restraining the consequences of the principle of the divine omnipotence with other principles, such as the truth of evident intuition in his doctrine of the intuition of a nonexistent, and the veracity of right reason in his moral doctrine.

This study begins with a sketch of Ockham's basic notions in logic and metaphysics which are operative throughout his whole philosophy. His conception of language and its relation to reality, notably his interpretation of how words can stand for things in propositions (*suppositio terminorum*) determines in advance his

8. See *Tract. de prin. theol.* (*OPh* 7: 507–639).

positions on many disputed issues. His analysis of abstract words leads him to the conclusions that only individual things *(res)* are real, and that individuals are such by nature and have no essences in common. Each individual is an individual of itself and by essence. This new conception of reality as radically individual has repercussions throughout the doctrine, and its influence will remain in Western philosophy.

All the theologians of the Middle Ages professed the same Catholic faith, but they differed in their understanding of it because of the divergent philosophies they brought to bear upon it. They all accepted the same canonical books of scripture and their revelation of truths necessary for salvation, but they did not always see eye to eye on how these truths are to be understood. Duns Scotus used a rational philosophy different from that of Thomas Aquinas, and Ockham in his turn devised a philosophy deeply at variance with both Thomism and Scotism. Even when he used the same language as they did, he usually gave it his own meaning. It is true that medieval theologians shared common outlooks and problems, especially if they belonged to the same religious order or school. In this connection we cannot forget that Ockham was a Franciscan. Though he was somewhat of a maverick in the Franciscan school, he maintained deep ties with his Franciscan predecessors, especially Duns Scotus. This is so true that without an acquaintance with Scotus' thought one cannot appreciate Ockham's critical and revolutionary ideas in both theology and philosophy. The historian is faced with the twofold task of seeing Ockham in continuity with his predecessors and in critical reaction to them. Ockham facilitates the task by frequently presenting the views of his immediate predecessors and contemporaries before criticizing them and giving his own positions. This enables the historian to see his philosophy in all its originality, and at the same time to view the panoply of opinions current in his day.

The book is devoted to Ockham's philosophy. At times it ventures into the domain of his theology, but only insofar as this helps to illuminate his philosophy. It would be difficult, and even impossible, to avoid his theology entirely in an exposition of his philosophy, given the close connection between them. The book does not include Ockham's political ideas, which date from the post-Avignon period, when he was engaged in controversies over the relations between Church and Empire and the evangelical vow of poverty. This would demand a better acquaintance with the political and legal issues involved than the author can claim.

The book aims to introduce students and other interested readers to Ockham's philosophy. The author is not a devotee of that philosophy; but he wrote the book in the first place not to criticize it but to elucidate it. However, he could not refrain from pointing out serious tensions and unresolved conflicts that appear at crucial moments in the philosophy. It is suggested that these are inevitable, given the impact of different principles at work in it. For the most part the author remains a concerned observer, watching with fascination as the Franciscan weaves his philosophical and theological threads into a new doctrinal synthesis.

I am grateful to my colleagues and friends who encouraged and helped me to write the book, especially Joseph C. Wey, the late Edward A. Synan, James P. Reilly, and Ronald Tacelli. I am also grateful to Fred Unwalla, the editor of the book who guided it through publication, and to Caroline Suma for her library assistance. I thank the late Gedeon Gál who, with his usual kindness and generosity, read the first draft of the manuscript and made corrections and improvements in it. The book would be the poorer without his aid. I owe a special debt of gratitude to James K. Farge for his untiring computer and editorial help.

I wish to thank the Franciscan Institute of St. Bonaventure University for permission to reprint the substance of my article "The Role of Divine Ideas in the Theology of William of Ockham," which appeared in *Studies Honoring Ignatius Charles Brady, Friar Minor*, edited by Romano S. Almagno and Conrad L. Harkins (1976). Finally, thanks to the State University of New York Press for permission to adapt my chapter "William of Ockham," printed in *Individuation in Scholasticism*, edited by Jorge J.E. Gracia (1994).

PART I

Principles

CHAPTER 1

Logic and Reality

LIKE ALL MEDIEVAL LOGICIANS who took Aristotle as their mentor, Ockham conceived of logic as an art whose rules govern the advancement of all the sciences.[1] It is the art of discerning the true from the false. Thus it concerns the formal rules of reasoning and other elements of thought that assist us in right thinking. It does not exclude, however, the consideration of problems bearing upon reality itself, at least insofar as thought is related to reality. Unlike modern types of logic, Ockham's, like Aristotle's, is a philosophical logic. In his works on logic he does not hesitate to express his views on philosophical issues that go beyond the limits of formal logic, such as the nature of reality and its relation to the mind. Thus his logic is closely tied up with his metaphysics, without however being confused with it. That is why we shall treat not only of Ockham's purely logical notions but also some of his basic ideas about the nature of reality and its relation to conceptual and linguistic forms.

No attempt will be made to cover all the elements of Ockham's logic. Others have written at length on the subject, and the reader is directed to their works for a more complete account of the subject.[2] We shall simply explain a few of the more basic notions in his logic of terms and propositions. We shall often meet these notions as we proceed, and readers must grasp their meaning if they are to follow Ockham's argument.

---

1. *Sum. log.* epist.prooem. (*OPh* 1: 5–6); *Expositio in librum artis logicae* prooem (*OPh* 2: 3–7).
2. See Marilyn McCord Adams, *William Ockham* (Notre Dame, IN, 1987), 1: 317–492; Ernest A. Moody, *The Logic of William of Ockham* (New York, 1935; 2nd ed. 1965).

1 The Logic of Terms

Terms in General

Ockham begins his major work in logic, the *Summa logicae*, with the definition of a term (*terminus*), the distinction between the various kinds of terms, and their respective values as signs. "It is the mind of all practitioners of logic," he writes, "that arguments are made up of propositions and propositions of terms." Thus Aristotle calls a term a component part of a proposition, that is, both the predicate and that of which it is predicated (namely, the subject), either joined by "is" or separated by "is not."[3] In a broader sense a term is any proximate part of a proposition, including not only its subject and predicate, but also the copula or verb, and all the qualifiers of these linguistic elements, such as adjectives and adverbs. Even a proposition can be a term in this wide sense, as when a proposition is used as the subject of a proposition; for example, "That man is an animal is a true proposition." In a narrower sense a term, in contrast to a proposition, is an incomplex or simple expression. In a more precise and exact sense, a term is or can be the subject or predicate of a proposition, but only when it functions as a sign of something. This excludes verbs, conjunctions, adverbs, interjections and the like. Of course these can also be subjects or predicates (as when we say "'To read' is a verb," or "'If' is a conjunction"), but here they do not function as signs of anything but simply stand for a word or concept.[4]

Terms of whatever sort constitute language (*oratio*).[5] Following Boethius, Ockham describes three kinds of language: written,

---

3. "Omnes logicae tractatores intendunt astruere quod argumenta ex propositionibus et propositiones ex terminis componuntur. Unde terminus aliud non est quam pars propinqua propositionis" (*Sum. log.* 1.1 [*OPh* 1: 7.3–5]). See Aristotle, *Anal. Prior.* 1.1, 24b16–18. For the logic of terms see Marilyn Adams, *William Ockham* (Notre Dame, IN, 1987), 1: 317–382; and Paul Spade, "The Semantics of Terms," in *The Cambridge History of Later Medieval Philosophy*, ed. Norman Kretzmann et al. (Cambridge, 1982), pp. 188–196.

4. *Sum. log.* 1.2 (*OPh* 1: 9.3–10.25).

5. *Oratio* in the wide sense is any meaningful group of words, even if it does not include a verb, such as "white man" or "rational animal." In the strict sense an *oratio* is a suitable arrangement of words with a noun or pronoun and a verb, in short a sentence, which may be declarative, imperative or optative; see *Expos. in Periherm.* 1.3 (*OPh* 2: 390.8–17).

spoken, and mental. Written language is composed of terms or words inscribed on some material and visible to the eye. Spoken language is made up of words uttered by the mouth and audible to the ear. Mental language is different from both of these because, as Augustine says, it remains in the mind and is incapable of outward expression, except through words which are signs subordinated to it. A mental term is called a concept or "intention" (*intentio*) of the mind; by its nature it is a part of a mental proposition.[6]

All terms or words (*voces*) are signs but they do not have the same value as signifiers. Concepts are the primary and natural signs of things; oral and written terms are secondary and conventional signs of the same things. The terms of written and spoken language are conventional signs, varying from people to people, and having no natural likeness to the things they signify. The terms of mental language are signs of an entirely different sort: they are concepts or intentions functioning as natural signs of things. As Augustine says, they "belong to no tongue," and therefore they cannot change their meaning at someone's pleasure. In this respect they differ from written and spoken terms, which have their meaning by human convention.[7]

---

6. *Sum. log.* 1.1 (*OPh* 1: 7.13-25). Boethius, 'De signis,' *In librum Aristotelis De interpretatione*, ed. secunda, 1 (PL 64: 407B). For Ockham's notion of mental language see John Trentman, "Ockham on Mental," *Mind* 79 (1970): 586-590; Calvin Normore, "Ockham on Mental Language," *Historical Foundations of Cognitive Science*, ed. J.C. Smith (Dordrecht, 1990), pp. 53-70; Claude Panaccio, *Les mots, les concepts et les choses* (Montréal and Paris, 1991), pp. 24-26, 69-164, "From Mental Word to Mental Language," *Philosophical Topics* 20 (1992): 125-147, and "Intuition, abstraction et langage mental dans la théorie occamiste de la connaissance," *Revue de métaphysique et morale* 97 (1992): 61-81; Hester G. Gelber, "I Cannot Tell a Lie: Hugh of Lawton's Critique of Ockham on Mental Language," *Franciscan Studies* 44 (1984): 141-179; Wolfgang Hübener, "*Oratio mentalis* and *oratio vocalis* in der Philosophie des 14. Jahrhunderts," in *Sprache und Erkenntnis im Mittelalter*, ed. Jan P. Beckmann et al. (Berlin/New York, 1981), 1: 488-497; Paul Spade, "Synonymy and Equivocation in Ockham's Mental Language," *Journal of the History of Philosophy* 18 (1980): 9-22.

7. *Sum. log.* ibid. (*OPh* 1: 7-9); cf Augustine, *De Trinitate* 15.10 (CCL 50A: 485-486). In one sense a sign is anything that on being perceived makes us think of something previously known; for example, an effect is the sign of its cause or a circle is the sign of wine in a tavern. In this sense an utterance (*vox*) is a natural sign. In another sense a sign is something that makes us think of something and

Spoken words are the primary conventional signs; written words are subordinate to them. It may seem questionable to us today that written words are inferior as signs to spoken words, but Ockham lived in an oral culture that placed greater value on spoken than on written language. What Marshall McLuhan called the "Gutenberg Era" was still to come.

While Ockham subordinates words to concepts in their function as signs, he insists that words are intended primarily to signify the same things as concepts. Words are not first and properly signs of concepts but of things.[8] In making this decision he takes sides in a lively debate in his day over the question whether words first signify concepts or things.[9] According to Aristotle spoken words are first of all symbols of the "affections" (*passiones*) of the soul, and written words are symbols of spoken sounds.[10] Boethius understood Aristotle to mean that a spoken word signifies both the concept of a thing and the thing itself, but primarily it signifies the concept and only secondarily the thing.[11] Aquinas followed Boethius, contending that general words like "man" cannot immediately signify things but natures in abstraction from individual things. He thought it clear from their abstract mode of signifying that they first signify concepts and things only through concepts.[12] Scotus, on the contrary, took the position that what is first signified by a general word that is a sign of something real is

---

it can be used as a substitute for it in a proposition, or be added in the proposition (for example, an adjective or adverb), or that can be composed of such words (for example, a phrase or sentence). In the latter sense a word is not a natural but a conventional sign; see *Sum. log.* ibid. (*OPh* 1: 8.53–9.65).

8. Ibid. (*OPh* 1: 7.26–8.34).

9. For this debate see Stephen F. Brown, "A Modern Prologue to Ockham's Natural Philosophy," in *Sprache und Erkenntnis im Mittelalter*, ed. Beckmann, pp. 107–129; Armand Maurer, "William of Ockham on Logic and Reality," ibid., pp. 795–802, repr. *Being and Knowing* (Toronto, 1990), pp. 423–430; Panaccio, *Les mots, les concepts et les choses*.

10. Aristotle, *De interpretatione* 1, 16a3–4.

11. Boethius, *In librum De interpretatione*, ed. prima 1 (PL 64: 298D–299A), ed. secunda (PL 64: 409B).

12. *Expositio libri Peryermenias* 1.2 (Leonine ed. 1.1: 10.88–112).

not the individual but its essence or *quod quid est*. This is consistent with his view that an essence has a real entity, formally distinct *a parte rei* from the individuals in which it exists. Since the essence is real, it can serve as the primary significate of the word.[13] Ockham, for his part, agreed with Scotus that general words like "man" are not directly signs of concepts but of realities; by realities, however, he means individual things, not real essences or natures as conceived by Scotus.[14] What is at stake in this dispute over words, concepts, and things is the fundamental issue of what counts as real. We shall return to this subject when we take up the problem of universals.

Categorematic and Syncategorematic Terms

Ockham follows the usual practice of thirteenth-century logicians of dividing terms into categorematic and syncategorematic. The former have a definite and determinate meaning, as "man" designates all (actual and possible) humans. Examples of syncategorematic terms are "all," "none," "some," "whole," "except," "so much," and "insofar as." Terms of this sort have no definite meaning by themselves, but in some way they modify or affect categorematic terms. They are like zero in arithmetic, which means nothing in itself but which gives meaning to the number to which it is added. When we say "some men" we restrict the number of individuals the word "man" stands for. When "all" is added to "whiteness" it makes "whiteness" stand for all whitenesses. Both categorematic and syncategorematic terms are found in spoken, written and mental language.[15]

---

13. Scotus, *Ord.* 1.27 (Vatican ed. 6: 97, n. 83), *Expositio in Perihermenias, opus secundum* 1 (Vivès ed. 1: 582–585). Scotus presents both sides of the *magna altercatio* in his commentary on the *Perihermenias* (that is, on the *De interpretatione*) 1.2 (Vivès ed. 1: 540ff). The "great debate" concerned general words used in science; it had nothing to do with the naming of individuals.

14. *Expos. in Periherm.* 1.prooem (*OPh* 2: 347–348); *Ord.* 1.22.un. (*OTh* 4: 48–49).

15. *Sum. log.* 1.4 (*OPh* 1: 15.4–16.34). In a broad sense syncategorematic terms may be said to be meaningful; indeed, this is true of all parts of language: see *Expos. in Periherm.* 1.1 (*OPh* 2: 378.38–379.63).

Concrete and Abstract Terms

Because of the philosophical and theological importance of this distinction Ockham treats of it at length in the *Summa logicae* and *Quodlibeta*.

Following the ancient grammarians, he distinguishes between concrete and abstract terms as having the same beginning but not the same ending; for example, "just" and "justice," "white" and "whiteness," "animal" and "animality." As in these examples, the concrete term is often adjectival in form whereas the abstract is substantive.[16]

Sometimes concrete and abstract terms signify and stand for different things; in other words they are not synonyms. "Just" stands for persons in the proposition "The just are virtuous," for it is persons who are just. Justice itself is a virtue but it is not virtuous. "Justice" stands for the quality of justice. Here the concrete term cannot be predicated of the abstract term; we cannot say "Justice is just." In this case the abstract term stands for an accident or form really inhering in a subject, and the concrete term stands for the subject possessing that accident or form. Similarly "The knower" is the concrete subject in which the accidental form "knowledge" is present.[17]

In some cases, however, a concrete and abstract term are said to be synonyms. For example, according to Aristotle the terms "God" and "Godhead," "man" and "humanity," "animal" and "animality," "horse" and "horseness," have the same meaning and stand for the same thing.[18] And if this is so, Aristotle must grant that the following propositions are true: "A man is humanity" and "Humanity runs." This is because in his philosophy he recognizes nothing as real except matter, form, the composite of the two, and accidents. In the above propositions the subject and predicate signify and stand for exactly the same thing, namely the human composite of form and matter, and consequently they are synonyms. Ock-

---

16. *Sum. log.* 1.5 (*OPh* 1: 16.5–12).

17. Ibid. (*OPh* 1: 16.13–17.23).

18. At *Sum. log.* 1.6 (*OTh* 1: 19.16–19) Ockham says that this is the mind of Aristotle (*Categories* 1, 1a8–12).

ham protests, however, that it is inappropriate to say "A man is humanity," because "humanity" is used as equivalent to the reduplicate phrase "man insofar as he is man." The syncategorematic expression "insofar as" indicates that "humanity" is taken as equivalent to "man in his essential definition," and man is not the same as his definition. Similarly it is correct to say "Man runs" but not "Humanity runs," for it is not man as man , but an individual man, who runs.[19]

However, if we speak, not with Aristotle, but "according to the truth of the theologians" we should not say that "man" and "humanity" are synonymous terms, for in speaking of Christ we can say "The Son of God is man" but not "The Son of God is humanity." This is because, according to the theologians, "humanity" signifies a nature composed of a body and an intellectual soul without connoting whether or not this nature subsists, whereas "man" implies human nature as *per se* subsistent. Now in Christ human nature subsists by the divine Person, and hence it is correct to say "The Son of God is man"; but since "humanity" abstracts from subsistence it is incorrect to say "The Son of God is humanity."[20]

Consequently the theological interpretation of concrete and abstract terms, which expresses the truth of faith, is in conflict with Aristotelian logic. This is the first of several occasions when Ockham finds it difficult, if not impossible, to bring Aristotelianism into harmony with Christian faith. We shall return to this topic in the next chapter.

Ockham remarks that in ordinary language we rarely or never find abstract terms used as equivalent to a name along with a syncategorematic expression, for example "humanity" meaning "man insofar as he is man"; yet this is common among philosophers and theologians and it can lead to misunderstandings. As an example Ockham gives the oft-quoted saying of Avicenna: "Horseness is nothing else than horseness; for of itself it is neither one nor many, nor does it exist in sensible things or in the mind." Ockham

---

19. *Sum. log.* 1.8 (*OPh* 1: 30.15–32).
20. Ibid. 1.7 (*OPh* 1: 24.55–25.67); *Quodl.* 5. 10–11 (*OTh* 9: 518–528).

cautions the reader that it was not Avicenna's intention that "horseness" signifies some entity that is neither one nor many and neither existing outside the mind nor in it. All he meant is that none of these notions is included in the definition of "horse" or "horseness."[21] We shall return to Ockham's views on abstract terms when we treat of his doctrine of universals.

Absolute and Connotative Terms

Purely absolute terms do not signify one thing primarily and another thing, or the same thing, secondarily; rather, everything they signify is signified equally primarily. "Animal," for example, equally signifies cattle, donkeys, humans, and other animals, no one before another. In contrast, connotative terms signify one thing primarily and another secondarily. An example is "white" (*album*), which primarily signifies something (a substance) and secondarily the quality or form of whiteness. Like all connotative terms it can be given a nominal definition (*quid nominis*): "something having whiteness," or "something with the form of whiteness." On the contrary, absolute names strictly speaking do not admit of nominal definitions of this sort, for they do not have several significates. Connotative terms, however, do not have real but only nominal definitions; as "cause" means "something upon whose existence something else follows," or "something capable of producing something else." In these definitions what is primarily signified is (in Latin) in the nominative case and what is secondarily signified is in one of the inflected cases.

All relative terms are connotative, for their definitions include different things or the same thing in different ways. Thus we define "similar" as "that which has a quality of the same sort as another thing." But "connotative" is a broader term than "relative," for as we have seen above some absolute terms, like "white," are also connotative. Ockham specifies that those who maintain that

21. *Sum. log.* 1.8 (*OPh* 1: 31.51–72). For the quotation from Avicenna see *Liber de philosophia prima* 5.1 (ed. Van Riet 2: 228.29–33).

quantity is not something distinct from substance and quality must hold that all names in the category of quantity are connotative. As we shall see, this is in fact Ockham's own position. For example, a body is a thing whose parts are distant from each other in length, breadth, and depth. The terms "true" and "good" are also connotative. "True" means the same as "intelligible," namely "something that can be apprehended by the intellect." "Good" means "something that can be willed and loved according to right reason."[22]

In an effort to clarify the nature of mental language, Ockham raises the question whether the features of spoken and written language are also found in mental language. He replies that there are nouns, verbs, pronouns, participles, adverbs, conjunctions, and prepositions in mental language, just as there are in spoken and written language. This is necessary for the truth and falsity of propositions. Thus the proposition "Socrates is a man" is true, but "Socrates is of a man" is false because of the different cases of the predicates. Hence the variation of the predicate's case in spoken language must have a corresponding variation in mental language if that language is true. Case and number are common features of both languages. So too, among verbs there are mode, number, time, and person. "Socrates loves" has a different meaning than "Socrates is loved." Hence this grammatical difference must be reflected in the mental proposition. But if the grammatical feature does not affect the sense of the proposition, or if it is not necessary for its expression but only makes it more suitable or graceful, it need not be matched in mental language.[23]

---

22. *Sum. log.* 1.10 (*OPh* 1: 35–38). See Paul Vincent Spade, "Ockham's Distinctions between Absolute and Connotative Terms," *Vivarium* 13 (1975): 55–76.

23. *Quodl.* 5.8 (*OTh* 9: 508–513); *Sum. log.* 1.3 (*OPh* 1: 11–14). Adams (*William Ockham* 1: 289–305) discusses at length the relations between conventional and mental languages. She concludes that in principle Ockham could have dispensed with all terms in mental language except absolute terms in the categories of substance and quality. Connotative terms in particular could be reduced to absolute terms. For a convincing criticism of this opinion see Martin Tweedale, "Ockham's Supposed Elimination of Connotative Terms and His Ontological Parsimony," *Dialogue* 31 (1992): 431–443.

Terms of First and Second Imposition

The previous divisions of terms apply both to those that naturally signify and those that signify only by convention, that is, they apply both to concepts and to spoken or written words. The present division occurs only between conventional signs, or spoken and written words.

Grammarians use words like "noun," "verb," "case," "number." These are names applied to parts of speech as they function as signs. In short, they are names of names. For example, if we call "man" a noun, "noun" is a word of "second imposition." In this case there is a concept in the mind corresponding to the word "man." More strictly, words of second imposition have no corresponding concept, like "figure" or "conjugation."

Terms of first imposition are all those that are not of second imposition. In the wide sense they include syncategorematic terms like "every," "none," "some." Strictly, however, only categorematic terms are names of first imposition. These include terms of first intention (to be explained below), like "man," "animal," "Socrates," and "being"; also terms of second intention, for example "genus," "species," and "universal."[24]

Terms of First and Second Intention

An "intention" in the present context is a being in the mind that can naturally be the sign of something else.[25] It is also called a concept of the mind or likeness of a thing. Mental propositions are made up of intentions or concepts, as spoken or written propositions are made up of words. Mental propositions are prior to their oral or written counterparts. Before uttering or writing a proposition, we form a mental proposition within our mind. Indeed, sometimes we form a mental proposition that we do not know how to express outwardly because we lack the appropriate words. As for the nature of the concept, that will be the subject of a later chapter.[26]

24. *Sum. log.* 1.11 (*OPh* 1: 38–41).
25. The Latin *intentio*, with the literal meaning of "a stretching out," was used to translate the Arabic word for concept in the works of Avicenna.
26. See below, pp. 496–510.

In the wide sense any concept is a first intention if it is a sign of something that is not itself a sign; for example, the concept "man," which signifies all humans. In this broad sense even mental verbs, syncategorematic concepts, and conjunctions are names of first intention. Strictly, however, a first intention is a mental noun (*nomen mentale*) that naturally stands for what it signifies in a proposition.

A second intention is a sign of a first intention. Examples are the logical notions of "genus," and "species." "Genus" is a common concept predicable of all genera, as when we say "Stone is a genus," "Animal is a genus," and so on. Similarly we can predicate the concept "species" of many species. We are then predicating one concept of several other concepts. Concepts of second intention naturally signify concepts of first intention, as names of second imposition conventionally signify names of first imposition.[27]

Terms as Having Meaning (Significatio)

Meaning (*significatio*) and supposition (*suppositio*) are the two most important functions of terms, whether they are words or concepts. Though these functions are closely related, they are nevertheless distinct. As we shall see, supposition is the use of a term standing for something in a proposition, but it does not always stand for what it signifies. Moreover, terms never have supposition outside of their use in propositions, whereas they can have meaning or signification by themselves apart from propositions. As signs, however, they can always become parts of a proposition.[28]

There are two meanings of "sign." In the widest sense a sign is anything which, when known, brings something else to mind. A sign cannot give us our first knowledge of a thing, but it makes us actually know something we retain in our memory. In this sense an effect is

27. *Sum. log.* 1.12 (*OPh* 1: 41–44).

28. For the notion of signification see *Sum. log.* 1.33 (*OPh* 1: 95–96); *Quodl.* 5.16 (*OTh* 9: 542–545). Philotheus Boehner, "Ockham's Theory of Signification," *Franciscan Studies* 6 (1946): 143–170, repr. in his *Collected Articles on Ockham* (St. Bonaventure, NY, 1958), pp. 201–232; Marilyn McCord Adams, "Ockham's Theory of Natural Signification," *The Monist* 61 (1978): 444–459.

the sign of its cause, a circle is the sign of a tavern, and a vocal utterance (like a groan) naturally signifies something. In a stricter sense, a sign brings something to mind and it can substitute or stand for it in a proposition. This includes both categorematic and syncategorematic expressions, verbs, and other parts of speech lacking a determinate meaning. Taken in this sense an utterance is not a natural sign of anything. Concepts, however, are natural signs.[29]

"Signify," in the second sense, also has several meanings. In one sense a term is said to signify something when it stands for, or is able to stand for, that thing in a proposition in which the term is predicated of the pronoun referring to that thing by the verb "is." For example, "white" signifies Socrates if it is true to say "He is white," pointing to Socrates. Signifying is here the same as referring to an actually existing individual.

In a wider sense terms can signify past, future, and possible things. An example is "white" in the proposition "What is white can run." In still another sense a thing is signified if it is the basis on which a name is given. Thus the term "rational" signifies man's intellectual soul, for it is given to signify that soul.

In the broadest sense of all, signification or meaning applies to any term that can be a part of a proposition, and even to a whole proposition, as long as it designates something in one way or another. Even a negative term like "blind" or "immaterial" has meaning in this wide sense.

As we shall see when treating of universals, universal or general terms do not signify essences or natures in some way distinct from individuals. Rather, they signify individuals themselves, as "man" signifies nothing but individual men, and not one man more than another.[30] Indeed, in a wide sense "man" signifies all humans, whether they actually or possibly exist. Walter Burley, a

---

29. *Sum. log.* 1.1 (*OPh* 1: 8.53–9.65). "[C]onceptus seu passio animae naturaliter significat quidquid significat, terminus autem prolatus vel scriptus nihil significat nisi secundum voluntariam institutionem" (*OPh* 1: 8.47–49).
30. Ibid. 1.33 (*OPh* 1: 95–96); *Quodl.* 5.16 (*OTh* 9: 543–544).

contemporary of Ockham, raised the objection that, since we only name what we know, a general term like "man" cannot signify unknown humans.[31] The reply to Burley is contained in the Ockhamist *Elementarium logicae*: "A name is given distinctly to something known and it is given indistinctly and confusedly to what is like it. In this way every man was known to the one giving this name to signify all men, because their like was known to them."[32] In fact, Burley thought that general words do not signify individuals but real common natures or universals.[33]

Terms as Standing for Things (Suppositio)

Terms not only have the function of signifying things but also of standing for them (*suppositio*). This function of terms was a medieval innovation in logical theory, having its origin in the twelfth-century works of Abelard. It was developed at great length by late medieval logicians and in part it was given an original interpretation by Ockham.[34] We shall not be concerned with all the elements of the theory, but only with those we shall meet in subsequent chapters of our book.

31. Walter Burley, *De puritate artis logicae tractatus longior* (ed. Boehner p. 8.12–18).

32. "Ad quartum dicendum est quod nomen non imponitur nisi noto distincte et indistincte seu confuse in suo simili. Et isto modo quilibet homo fuit notus imponenti hoc nomen 'homo' ad significandum omnes homines, quia suum simile fuit notum sibi" (*Elementarium logicae* 3.5 [*OPh* 7: 104.31–105.34]). The authenticity of this work is doubtful but not the doctrine.

33. Walter Burley, *De puritate artis logicae* (ed. Boehner p. 3.6–25).

34. For the history of the notion of *suppositio* see William and Martha Kneale, *The Development of Logic* (Oxford, 1962), pp. 209, 246–274. For Ockham's doctrine of supposition see Adams, *William Ockham* 1: 327–382, and "What Does Ockham Mean by 'Supposition'?" *Notre Dame Journal of Formal Logic* 17 (1976): 375–391; Paul Vincent Spade, "Ockham's Rule of Supposition: Two Conflicts in His Theory," *Vivarium* 12 (1974): 63–73; John Swiniarski, "A New Presentation of Ockham's Theory of Supposition with an Evaluation of Some Contemporary Criticisms," *Franciscan Studies* 30 (1970): 181–217; Stephen F. Brown, "Walter Burleigh's Treatise *De Suppositionibus* and Its Influence on William of Ockham," *Franciscan Studies* 32 (1972): 15–64.

Ockham defines *suppositio* in the usual fashion as the substitution of a term for something else: *Dicitur autem suppositio quasi pro alio positio*.[35] *Suppositio* differs from *significatio* in that terms can have meaning by themselves, whereas they substitute for things only in propositions. For example, by itself the term "dog" means all actual and possible individual dogs, but it has a substitutive function only as it is used in a proposition. Moreover, this function will differ according to the kind of proposition in which it occurs. If I say "'Dog' is a word" the term "dog" does not have the same substitutive value as when I say "Dog is an animal." In the first case "dog" stands for the word "dog"; in the second it stands for all individual dogs.

The property of *suppositio* belongs to spoken, written, and mental terms. It applies, moreover, to both the subject and the predicate of a proposition. Suppose the term is the subject of a proposition; for example, "man" in the proposition "Man is an animal." The proposition denotes that any man is truly an animal, so that it would be true to say that Socrates is an animal, while pointing to Socrates. In this case "man" stands for Socrates. However, the proposition "'Man' is a noun" denotes that the word "man" is a noun, and "man" stands for the word.[36]

Other schoolmen showed great virtuosity in distinguishing between different kinds of *suppositio*. Ockham limits himself to describing the three principal ones: personal, simple, and material, and several subdivisions of personal supposition.

A term has personal supposition when it stands for what it signifies, whether its significate is an extramental thing, a spoken or written word, or a mental concept.[37] Thus, whenever the subject

---

35. *Sum. log.* 1.63 (*OPh* 1: 193.11). For the supposition of terms see *Expos. Elench.* 1.2 (*OPh* 3: 24–30); *Ord.* 1.2.4 (*OTh* 2: 134.22–138.21).

36. *Sum. log.* 1.63 (*OPh* 1: 194.16–32).

37. "Suppositio personalis, universaliter, est illa quando terminus supponit pro suo significato, sive illud significatum sit res extra animam, sive sit vox, sive intentio animae, sive sit scriptum, sive quodcumque aliud imaginabile; ita quod quandocumque subiectum vel praedicatum propositionis suppo-

or predicate of a proposition is used with its function of signification it has personal supposition. For example, when we say "Every man is an animal," "man" stands for what it signifies, namely all actual or possible humans. Ockham denies that the term stands for anything common to them, citing John Damascene in support of his nominalist interpretation of personal supposition. As we shall see, Ockham insists that there is no nature or essence signified by the term "man," but only individual human beings. True, Damascene says that the substantive word "man" signifies all individual humans, but Ockham neglects to mention that Damascene immediately adds that all humans are so called because they do not differ in species or nature. This would suggest a realist interpretation of personal supposition rather than Ockham's nominalist one.[38]

Ockham warns the reader that personal supposition is not so called because in it a term necessarily stands for a person.[39] In the propositions "Every spoken word is a part of speech," and "Every species is a universal," both subjects have personal supposition because they stand for what they signify.

Only categorematic terms can have personal supposition. This excludes all syncategorematic terms, whether they are nouns, conjunctions, adverbs, prepositions, etc. It also excludes all verbs, for a verb cannot be a subject or predicate when it is taken as a sign. It is true that a verb like "to read" can be a subject, as when it is said "To read is good." But here "to read" is not used as a verb but as a noun.[40]

Personal supposition is the only one among the three main types for which Ockham gives subdivisions. The first of these is the distinction between discrete and common supposition. Personal supposition is called discrete when the term signifies one individual by its proper name or pronoun, as in the particular propositions

nit pro suo significato, ita quod significative tenetur, semper est suppositio personalis" (*Sum. log.* 1.64 [*OPh* 1: 195.4–9]).

38. Ibid. (*OPh* 1: 195.9–13). John Damascene, *Dialectica* 10 (PG 94: 571A). See Kneale, *Development of Logic*, p. 267 n2.

39. Ibid. (*OPh* 1: 197.60–61).

40. Ibid. 1.69 (*OPh* 1: 208.3–14).

"Socrates is a man," and "This man is a man." In common personal supposition the term is common, as in the proposition "Man runs," and "Every man is an animal."

Common personal supposition is further divided into confused and determinate. It is called determinate when the proposition allows us to pass by disjunction to particular propositions. Thus "Man runs," entails "This man runs," or "That man runs," and so on. The supposition is called determinate because it denotes that a common proposition is true for some determinate individual, and its truth is assured even if it holds good for that individual alone. In the proposition "Man is an animal," both the subject and predicate terms have determinate supposition; it follows that if man is an animal therefore this man or that man is an animal, and man is this or that animal.

If the personal supposition of a term is not determinate it is common. It is called simply confused when it entails particular propositions with a disjunction bearing exclusively on the predicate. For example, in the proposition "Man is an animal" the word "animal" has simply confused supposition because we can infer from it that every man is this or that animal. But it does not follow that every man is this animal, or that every man is that animal.

Supposition is confused and distributive when it entails a series of particular propositions united by the conjunction "and." For instance, in the proposition "Every man is an animal" the word "man" has confused and distributive supposition because we can infer from it the following connected propositions: "This man is an animal, and this other man is also an animal, and so on." Confused and distributive supposition is called "mobile" when it admits of an exception, as in the proposition "Every man except Socrates runs." It is called "immobile" if no exception is possible.[41]

---

41. *Sum. log.* 1.70 (*OPh* 1: 209–212). For a discussion of types of personal supposition and attempts to correlate them with modern logic see Adams, *William Ockham* 1: 352–382. It is pointed out on p. 382 that Ockham's interest in the elaborate treatment of these types of supposition and the rules governing them is not a useless exercise but is useful in detecting fallacies.

Simple supposition is the standing of a term for a mental concept when the term does not function as a sign. For example, in the proposition "Man is a species" "man" stands for a concept, for that concept is the species. Strictly speaking the term "man" in this context does not signify the concept but only substitutes for it. When it is used as a sign, the concept and corresponding word signify individual humans, the word signifying them in subordination to the concept.[42] In the above example of simple supposition the term "man" stands for itself, that is, for the universal concept that is the species "man." It is also possible for a term in simple supposition to stand, not for itself, but for another mental intention, though without signifying it. An example is "'Man is an animal' is a true proposition." Here "man" does not stand for itself but for the subject of the true proposition.[43]

Ockham realized that his definition of simple supposition differed from the usual one, which was "the standing of a term for that which it signifies." This was the teaching of the influential logician William of Sherwood (c. 1240). William taught that in the proposition "Man is a species" the term "man" stands for what it signifies, but without a relation to individual humans. In the proposition "Man is the most noble creature," "man" stands for its significate but in relation to individual humans.[44] Peter of Spain (d. 1277) described simple supposition as "the taking of a common term for a universal reality represented by it."[45] These logicians

---

42. "Suppositio simplex est quando terminus supponit pro intentione animae, sed non tenetur significative. Verbi gratia sic dicendo 'homo est species' iste terminus 'homo' supponit pro intentione animae, quia illa intentio est species; et tamen iste terminus 'homo' non significat proprie loquendo illam intentionem, sed illa vox et illa intentio animae sunt tantum signa subordinata in significando idem, secundum modum alibi expositum" (ibid. 1.64 [*OPh* 1: 196.26–32]).

43. Ibid. 1.68 (*OPh* 1: 207.7–208.3).

44. *William of Sherwood's Introduction to Logic* 5.7.2, trans. Norman Kretzmann (Minneapolis, 1966), p. 111.

45. "Simplex suppositio est acceptio termini communis pro re universali significata per ipsum" (*Summulae logicales* 6.5, ed. L.M. de Rijk [Assen, 1972], p. 81).

understood simple supposition as realists, claiming that universal terms both stand for and signify real common natures. As we shall see when considering Ockham's doctrine of universals, he was convinced that individual things do not have natures in common. Universals are only terms, either spoken, written, or mental. So general terms, like "man," cannot signify real common natures but only individuals. In accord with his opinion of reality as radically individual, Ockham offers a new definition of simple supposition as the standing of a term for a mental concept, without signifying it or a real common nature.

Walter Burley, a contemporary critic of Ockham, held a realist view of universals, claiming that "there is a common reality outside the mind in which two stones are united and in which a stone and an ass are not united."[46] Consistent with his belief in the reality of common natures, he opposed Ockham's notion of simple supposition, defining it in the older fashion as the standing of a common term for what it signifies absolutely (that is, a real nature), not in relation to individuals in which it exists or to the terms of which it is predicated.[47] Another critic of Ockham, the Pseudo-Richard of Campsall, dissented from him for precisely the same reason. Ockham was mistaken, he contends, in defining simple supposition as the standing of a term for a mental concept without its functioning as a sign. In fact, this type of supposition occurs when a term substitutes for its natural significate, which is a reality precisely

---

46. "Quia si nullus intellectus esset, adhuc duo lapides magis convenirent quam unus lapis et asinus. Sed omnis convenientia est in aliquo uno. Nam omnis convenientia est unitas fundata supra multitudinem quia quecunque conveniunt, in aliquo conveniunt, ergo est aliqua res communis extra animam in qua duo lapides conveniunt et in qua lapis et asinus non conveniunt" (*Super artem veterem Porphirii et Aristotelis* [Venice, 1497; repr. Frankfurt, 1967], f. a4vb). See Ivan Boh, "Walter Burley," in *Individuation in Scholasticism: The Later Middle Ages and the Counter-Reformation (1150–1650)*, ed. Jorge J.E. Gracia (Albany, NY, 1994), pp. 347–372.

47. Walter Burley, *De puritate artis logicae* 1.3 (ed. Boehner p. 11). For Burley's relations to Ockham see Brown, "Walter Burleigh's Treatise *De Suppositionibus*," pp. 15–64.

as conceived, such as humanity. A term like this does not stand for a real individual or a universal concept in the mind, but for a nature formally, but not really, distinct from the individual. Campsall's citation of Duns Scotus in this context is proof of his sympathy for his metaphysics of the common nature and universals.[48]

The lively controversy over simple supposition in the later Middle Ages is understandable, for it engaged a philosopher's basic views on reality and knowledge. This will be clearer when we treat of the problem of universals later in the chapter.

Material supposition is the standing of a term for a spoken or written word, but the term is not used as a sign. An example is "man" in the proposition "Man is a noun," or "Man is a written word." Here the term "man" stands for itself, but it does not signify itself. The proper meaning or signification of "man" is the totality of individual humans. Similarly, in the proposition "'Man' is written," "man" has material supposition for it stands for a written word.[49] Verbs, adverbs, participles, pronouns, conjunctions, prepositions and interjections can feature in material supposition, as in the propositions "'If' is a conjunction" and "'Reading' is a participle."[50]

Besides the above kinds of supposition in which a term is taken in its proper sense, Ockham describes others in which a term has an unusual meaning; for example, when it stands antonomastically for that to which it especially belongs, as when we say "The Apostle says this," referring to St. Paul, or "The Philosopher denies this," referring to Aristotle. This use of terms and all metaphorical expressions are instances of what Ockham calls "improper supposition."

48. *Logica Campsale Anglicj, valde utilis et realis contra Ocham* 51 (ed. Synan 2: 351–353); see the editor's introduction 2: 64–65.

49. "Suppositio materialis est quando terminus non supponit significative, sed supponit vel pro voce vel pro scripto" (*Sum. log.* 1.64 [*OPh* 1: 196. 38–39]).

50. Ibid. 1.67 (*OPh* 1: 206.9–15).

Ockham adds that it is important to know when a term or proposition is to be taken in its proper sense (*de virtute sermonis*), when its meaning is expressed in ordinary language (*secundum usum loquentium*), and when it agrees with the intention but not necessarily with the letter of an author (*secundum intentionem auctorum*). He warns that many mistakes are made by failing to make these distinctions and always taking an expression with its proper meaning.[51]

Ockham finds that logicians have often made mistakes because of their ignorance of the supposition of terms and its various forms, especially simple supposition. The cause of many of these errors is the philosophical notion that there are essences or natures common to several individuals and distinct from them, whereas in fact there is nothing in reality but individuals. Ockham recognizes that it is beyond the scope of the logician to settle the question of the nature of reality. In his *Isagoge* (an introduction to Aristotle's *Categories*), Porphyry refused to say whether universals are real or only concepts, reserving this for a higher science. Ockham agrees with this limitation of logic.[52] The question of universals belongs to sciences of reality, like metaphysics, and not to logic, which is a science of signs. And yet, as we shall presently see, he feels no compulsion to restrict himself to the study of signs in his logical works, but delves into the metaphysical question of the nature of reality itself.

51. *Sum. log.* 1.77 (*OPh* 1: 236–238).

52. "Unde error istorum omnium qui credebant aliquid esse in re praeter singulare et quod humanitas, quae est distincta a singularibus, est aliquid in individuis et de essentia eorum, induxit eos in istos errores et multos alios logicales. Hoc tamen ad logicum non pertinet considerare, sicut dicit Porphyrius in prologo, sed logicus tantum habet dicere quod suppositio simplex non est pro suo significato; sed quando terminus est communis habet dicere quod suppositio simplex est pro aliquo communi suis significatis. Utrum autem illud commune sit in re vel non, ad eum non pertinet" (ibid. 1.66 [*OPh* 1: 204.128–205.136]). See Porphyry, *Isagoge*, trans. Boethius (ed. Minio-Paluello p. 5).

2 Categories

Aristotle classified the most general genera or kinds of things in ten categories: substance, quantity, quality, relation, place, time, position, state, action, and passion.[53] Ockham devotes considerable attention to the meaning of this classification, for it is of vital importance for both philosophy and theology.[54]

The Latin term for "category" is *praedicamentum*, that is, something predicated or said of a subject. Now what is predicated or said of something is not a thing but a word(s) or concept(s).[55] So the division of the categories is not a division of extramental things but first of all of incomplex words and then of corresponding mental concepts. We should not think that the categories are things outside the mind and really distinct from each other, but that they are distinct words and concepts signifying extramental things. Neither should we imagine that corresponding to the distinction between words and concepts there is always a similar distinction between the things signified.[56]

This is clear enough, for sometimes the same thing is signified through several categories, though not in the same way. For example, when we say "Man is a substance," "substance" signifies an individual human being without connoting anything else. When we say "Man is a father," "father," which is in the category of relation, signifies the same human being but connoting his child. So we should not imagine that there is a "small thing" (*parva res*) in reality corresponding to the category of relation and distinct from the individual in the category of substance. As we shall see, this is true of all the categories of accidents except quality. There are

53. Aristotle, *Categoriae* 4, 1b25–27. Porphyry and Boethius assumed that Aristotle intended the categories to be a classification of things. This is also the interpretation of some modern scholars such as J.L. Ackrill, *Aristotle's "Categories" and "De Interpretatione"* (Oxford, 1963), pp. 71–73, 75–76.

54. *Expos. in Praedicamen.* 7–17 (*OPh* 2: 157–303); *Sum. log.* 1. 40–62 (*OPh* 1: 111–193); *Quodl.* 5.21–23 (*OTh* 9: 559–574).

55. *Quodl.* 5.23 (*OTh* 9: 569.12–14).

56. *Expos. in Praedicamen.* 7 (*OPh* 2: 157.11–158.43); *Expos. in Phys.* 3.2 (*OPh* 4: 418.32–35).

distinct realities corresponding to distinct categories only in the case of substance and quality.[57] We shall return to this subject when treating of the individual categories.

Ockham probes more deeply into the relation between categories and reality when he raises the question: what does it mean to be in a category? His answer is not simple, for he distinguishes between two meanings of "being in a category." In one sense something may be said to be in a category if the category can be truly predicated of the pronoun referring to it. In this sense, all individual substances outside the mind are in the category of substance, for "substance" can be truly predicated of the pronoun referring to each of them, as when we say of an animal "It is a substance." So too, all universals, such as genera, species, and differences, are most certainly in the category of quality, for no matter what universal is referred to, it is true to say "It is a quality." (This is understandable, for in his later works Ockham describes all universals, and concepts in general, as qualities of the mind).[58] In another sense some universals are in the category of substance and some in the category of quality. For example, in the proposition "Man is a substance," the term "man" does not stand for itself, but it stands for and signifies all individual humans. So the universal "man" may be said to be in the category of substance. In the proposition "'Man' is a quality," the term "man" stands for itself, namely a concept of the mind. So the term is in the category of quality.[59] In neither of these two meanings of "being in a category" is a reality *in* a categorical concept. One concept can exist in another, as the genus "animal" exists in the species "man," for "man" is a "rational animal." But realities outside the mind cannot enter mental

57. *Expos. in Praedicamen.* 7 (*OPh* 2: 159.44–97); *Quodl.* 5.22 (*OTh* 9: 569. 125–130; 565.31–36). Ockham is here taking issue with "moderns" like Walter Burley. Notice that Ockham does not count himself among the moderns.

58. See below, pp. 508–509.

59. *Quodl.* 5.23 (*OTh* 9: 570.27–571.44); *Sum. log.* 1.42 (*OPh* 1: 119.50– 120.70).

concepts or be a part of them, nor can mental categories be composed of extramental realities. The two orders of categorical concepts and extramental reality must be kept rigorously separate. As a category written in a book is composed of written words, and a spoken category is composed of spoken words, so a mental category is composed of concepts and in no sense of extramental things.[60]

As for the number of the categories, Aristotle lists ten, but Ockham thinks it is difficult to prove this is the exact number.[61] However this may be, he favors Averroes' suggestion that their distinction is based on the various questions that can be asked about an individual substance. What (*quid*) is it? The concepts given in reply: "man," "animal," and so on, are in the category of substance. Of what sort (*quale*) is it? The replies "white," "hot" are in the category of quality. How much or how great (*quantum*) is it? The replies "two cubits" or "three cubits" are in the category of quantity. A question like "whose child is this?" brings the reply "Socrates'," indicating the category of relation. Similarly, replies to where?, when?, what did he do?, how was he affected? and so on, are in the remaining categories. Only words and concepts are in a category that can be suitable replies to some question asked about an individual substance. This includes nouns, verbs, adverbs, and prepositions, with their cases. But conjunctions and syncategorematic terms are not in a category, for we do not reply to any question about an individual substance if we say "if" or "and" or "every."[62]

Substance

Substance is the first category. In a broad sense Ockham defines it as any thing (*res*) distinct from others. This even includes accidents (at least the accident of quality). Thus philosophers speak of the

---

60. *Quodl.* 5.23 (*OTh* 9: 573.114–574.119).
61. *Expos. in Praedicamen.* 7 (*OPh* 2: 161.119–121).
62. *Quodl.* 5.22 (*OTh* 9: 567–569); *Sum. log.* 1.41 (*OPh* 1: 116.64–117.96).

"substance of color." More strictly substance is any thing that is not an accident really inhering in a substance. This applies to matter and form and the composite of the two. Most strictly it is that which is neither an accident inhering in something else nor an essential part of something else, like matter and form.[63]

Aristotle divided substances into primary and secondary, the former being individuals, the latter universals.[64] For Ockham, this is not a distinction between things or realities but between names denoting or signifying substances outside the mind. First substances are names proper to one substance, like "Socrates"; second substances are names common to many substances, like "man."[65] The only true substances in the category of substance are individual things (*res*) existing outside the mind. Second substances are only mental concepts or words signifying first substances. As concepts, they are mental qualities, located in the category of quality. Referring to any one of them, it can be said "It is a quality." They can be said to be in the category of substance in the sense that "substance" can be predicated of them when they are taken with personal supposition, standing for what they signify. Thus we can say "Man is a substance," taking "man" as signifying and standing for individual humans.[66]

As we shall see, a second substance or universal, like "man," does not signify a nature or essence common to many individuals, as the realists held, but it is a sign of individuals. Moreover, it signifies each of them with exactly the same sense; in short, they are univocal terms. In propositions, first substances function as sub-

---

63. *Sum. log.* 1.42 (*OPh* 1: 118.5–14). Ockham also treats at length of substance in *Expos. in Praedicamen.* 8–9 (*OPh* 2: 162–202).

64. Aristotle, *Categoriae* 5, 2a11–17.

65. "Et ideo dicendum est quod ista divisio non est nisi divisio unius nominis communis in nomina minus communia, ut sit aequivalens isti divisioni: nominum importantium seu significantium substantias extra animam quaedam sunt nomina propria uni substantiae, et illa nomina vocantur hic primae substantiae; quaedam autem nomina sunt communia multis substantiis, et illa nomina vocantur secundae substantiae" (*Sum. log.* 1.42 [*OPh* 1: 119.50–55]).

66. Ibid. (*OPh* 1: 119.56–120.70).

jects while second substances function as predicates; first substances are never predicates.[67]

Primary substances are the main constituents of Ockham's universe. They are individual things (*res*), each of which is one in number and self-identical. The only other things in Ockham's world are the parts that go to make up substances, like form and matter in the case of material substances, and certain kinds of qualities, which are accidents inhering in substances. For a while he entertained the notion of the concept as a fictive being (*fictum*), with a noncategorical kind of being called "objective" being, but he seems to have abandoned the notion in later works.[68]

Another name for first substance is "suppositum," but this term has special connotations. Ockham defines a suppositum as a complete being, incommunicable by identity, not suited to inhere in anything, and not sustained by anything. It is something existing through itself (*per se*). If a suppositum is a substance with a intellectual nature, it is a person. As a complete being, a suppositum excludes both essential and integral parts of a substance. As incommunicable by identity it excludes the divine essence, which, though a complete being, is communicable by identity to the divine Persons. As not suited to inhere in anything it excludes all accidents. As not sustained by anything it excludes the human nature assumed by the divine Word.[69]

As a theologian Ockham held the orthodox position that in the Incarnation the second Person of the Trinity assumed a human nature and not, as the Nestorians claimed, a human suppositum or person. In other words, in Christ there is but one Person – the second Person of the Trinity – with two natures, divine and human, the human nature being taken up and sustained by the

---

67. Ibid. 1.43 (*OPh* 1: 123.33–124.51). The editors cite Pseudo-Richard of Campsall's claim, against Ockham, that properly speaking a univocal term like "man" primarily denotes human nature and only secondarily individual humans: *Logica Campsale Anglicij* 40.06 (ed. Synan 2: 223–224).

68. See below, pp. 504–510.

69. *Quodl.* 4.7 (*OTh* 9: 328.11–21); *Sum. log.* 1.7 (*OPh* 1: 29.185–188). On the person see *Sum. log.* 1.66 (*OPh* 1: 204.112–120); *Ord.* 1.23.un. (*OTh* 4: 62.5–65.2).

divine Person.[70] But Ockham was clearly aware of the difficulty of reconciling this truth of faith with the Aristotelian view that a concrete term and its abstract equivalent (for example "man" and "humanity") signify entirely the same thing. Strictly speaking, an Aristotelian can say "Man is humanity" or vice versa. The only reason for denying this would be the adding of a syncategorematic term to the subject or predicate; for instance, if "humanity" meant "man insofar as he is man," or "man as such." Clearly, "man" is not "humanity as such"; otherwise it would be true that humanity as such runs when Socrates runs.[71]

According to "the truth of the theologians," however, the terms "man" and "humanity" are not synonyms, whether or not syncategorematic terms are added. They can stand for different realities, and one term can signify or consignify a reality that the other does not. The theologians say that the term "man" truly stands for the Son of God, and thus it signifies or denotes him, but this is not true of the term "humanity." Since Christians can say that the Son of God is man, but not that he is humanity, these terms are not synonymous. However, Ockham's philosophy allows him to say that in the Incarnation in a certain sense a human suppositum was assumed by the divine Person. This is because in Ockham's view the terms "this human nature" and "this suppositum" stand for entirely the same reality. Consequently if it is true to say that "this nature is assumed" it will also be true to say "this suppositum" is assumed.[72]

In order to avoid this embarrassment Ockham has recourse to a logical distinction. While it is true to say that the terms "individual human nature" and "individual suppositum" stand for and

---

70. *Quodl.* 4.7 (*OTh* 9: 328–337); *Rep.* 3.1 (*OTh* 6: 3–42). The Council of Chalcedon (451) declared that in Christ there is a real union of his divine and human natures in one Person or suppositum; see *Enchiridion Symbolorum*, ed. H. Denzinger and A. Schönmetzer, 36th ed. (Freiburg-i.-Br., 1976), pp. 106–109, §300–303.

71. *Sum. log.* 1.7 and 1.8 (*OPh* 1: 23–24 and 1: 29.8–30.32).

72. *Quodl.* 4.7 (*OTh* 9: 333.117–125).

signify entirely the same reality, they have different nominal definitions. A human nature is defined simply as a nature composed of a body and intellectual soul, without connoting that it exists by itself or is assumed by another, whereas a suppositum adds that the nature is not assumed by anything else. Since these terms have different meanings, they are not synonyms and so they cannot be used interchangeably. Because of their difference in definition it is possible to say "this individual nature is assumed," but it is impossible to say "this suppositum is assumed."[73]

The gist of Ockham's involved argument seems to be that the Son of God can assume a human suppositum, but when it is actually assumed it loses its status as a suppositum or person, so that in fact only a human nature is assumed. If the Son of God abandoned the assumed human nature, that nature would at once regain its condition of a human suppositum. The individual human nature, or humanity in itself, is neutral to being its own suppositum or to depend for its *per se* existence on an extrinsic suppositum like the Son of God. Its dependence on the Son of God is not due to the active bent of the nature itself but presumably to the divine agency.[74]

To show how the human nature of Christ could first be a suppositum and then, when assumed by him, not a suppositum but simply a nature, Ockham gives the example of food, which is a suppositum but, when eaten, is not a suppositum existing *per se* but becomes part of the eater. The example, however, is ineffective, because the eaten food takes on our nature, whereas the Son of God assumes human nature. No realistic example would be helpful, because Ockham's explanation of the Incarnation is on the level of terms and their definitions and not on the level of reality. The neutral individual human nature that Ockham supposes can indifferently enter a human

---

73. Ibid. (*OTh* 9: 334.132–145).
74. Ibid. (*OTh* 9: 336.173–185; 337.195–204). For conflicting views of Ockham's doctrine of the Incarnation see Peter Geach, "Nominalism," in *Aquinas: A Collection of Critical Essays,* ed. Anthony Kenny (Garden City, NY, 1969), pp. 139–154; and Adams, *William Ockham* 2: 980–996.

or divine *suppositum* appears to be a remnant of the Avicennian essence, reduced to the status of a term or definition.

Quantity and Quality

Following Aristotle, Ockham describes the nine categories that follow upon substance as accidents, but in his interpretation only certain kinds of quality are realities (*res*) really distinct from substance and really existing in it. The other accidents are only names or concepts signifying substance in various ways.[75]

Quantity is either continuous or discrete.[76] If quantity is permanent and continuous, its concept signifies material substance with the connotation that it has parts, one of which is at a distance from another in place. The parts make up a whole that is one in number and without anything in between; otherwise it would not be continuous. Discrete quantity or number need not have parts occupying different places and combined to form something one in number.

It was the general opinion of the "moderns," like Giles of Rome and Scotus, that a particular continuous quantity is a thing (*res*) really and completely distinct from substance and quality, existing in substance as in a subject. Lying between substance and quality, the latter exists in substance through quantity.[77]

In opposition to this widespread notion of quantity, Ockham contends that quantity is really identical with corporeal substance. A material substance is quantified of itself and not through an added accident. Ockham argues that if quantity were a distinct reality, God could produce it without substance, for he can pro-

---

75. On the subject of quantity and quality see *Expos. in Praedicamen.* 10, 11 (*OPh* 2: 203–238); *Expos. in Phys.* 1.4 (*OPh* 4: 54–63); *Sum. log.* 1.44 (*OPh* 1: 132–139); *Quodl.* 4.27 (*OTh* 9: 433–440); *Tract. de quant.* 3 (*OTh* 10: 51–85).

76. *Quodl.* 4.27 (*OTh* 9: 439.127–144).

77. *Sum. log.* 1.44 (*OPh* 1: 132.3–9). For the "moderns," who include, besides Giles and Scotus, Aquinas, Richard of Middleton, Walter Burley, Francis of Marchia, and John Buridan, see Anneliese Maier, "Das Problem der Quantität oder räumlichen Ausdehnung," in her *Metaphysische Hintergründe der Spätscholastischen Naturphilosophie* (Rome, 1955), pp. 141–223; Adams, *William Ockham* 1: 172.

duce and conserve one absolute reality without another. Ockham uses the same theological argument to prove that a point, line or surface cannot be a reality different from a material substance or body. They differ from it only in concept. Neither are there realities corresponding to numbers; discrete quantity adds nothing real to numbered things. Quantity, however, is a category distinct from substance, for, unlike substance, continuous quantity connotes the separation of parts of substance in place and discrete quantity connotes its division in number.[78]

Ockham offers this as the doctrine of Aristotle. Sensitive to its possible opposition to the Church's teaching on the eucharist, Ockham does not say it is true or false, Catholic or heretical.[79] However, he will show its agreement with the mind of Aristotle, and he will argue in support of it.

According to Aristotle accidents immediately exist in substance and not one accident through another, as would be the case if quality existed in substance through quantity.[80] In particular, contrary qualities, like black and white, do not first exist in quantity and then through quantity in substance. Substance alone is the immediate subject of contrary qualities.

Ockham gives several philosophical and theological arguments in support of this interpretation of Aristotle. Though he does not think they are conclusive, he gives them for what they are worth.[81]

Perhaps his most telling argument is based on the theological principle of the divine omnipotence: God can conserve every absolute thing and destroy anything by nature posterior to it. Now it is the general opinion that a substance, like a piece of wood, has parts outside of parts through the added reality of quantity. But if this were so, God could conserve the substance without the added quantity. The substance would then have parts outside of parts through itself and not through an added reality of quantity. This argument, which Ock-

78. *Sum. log.* 1.45 (*OPh* 1: 145.163–174).
79. Ibid. 1.44 (*OPh* 1: 132.14–16; 136.128–133).
80. Ibid. 1.43 (*OPh* 1: 126.99–133); Aristotle, *Categoriae* 5, 4a10–22.
81. Ibid. (*OPh* 1: 134.69–71).

ham finds very congenial to theology, equally applies to quality. The quantification of quality can be explained by substance and not by quantity lying between itself and substance. Calling upon the principle of the razor, which states that a plurality is not to be posited without necessity, Ockham concludes that it is superfluous to admit quantity as a reality distinct from substance.[82]

Ockham finds reasons to hold that, unlike quantity, certain qualities are real accidents, really distinct from substance and directly inhering in it. According to Aristotle, a substance through its qualities is said to be such and such (*quale*). Ockham specifies that this excludes a substantial difference like "rational," which denotes that a human being is such and such, but in the order of substance.[83] The qualities Aristotle has in mind are accidents, and these are of four kinds: (1) dispositions that are more or less permanent (*habitus, dispositio*), like justice and health; (2) Natural abilities or inabilities (*naturalis potentia et impotentia*), like fighting or running; (3) affective qualities (*passibilis qualitas et passiones*), like whiteness and sweetness; (4) shape and figure (*forma et figura*), like triangle.[84]

Though some "moderns" like Walter Burley and Pseudo-Richard of Campsall believed that every quality is a reality really distinct from substance and quantity,[85] Ockham was more parsimonious, contending that some are really identical with substance and others are not. His general rule for making this distinction is that "when some predicables can be verified of the same thing successively, but not at the same time, solely because of local motion, it is

---

82. *Sum. log.* 1.44 (*OPh* 1: 134.69–135.91; 137.148–155); *Quodl.* 4.27 (*OTh* 9: 433.7–9).

83. *Expos. in Praedicamen.* 14 (*OPh* 2: 268.4–269.20); see Aristotle, *Categoriae* 8, 8b25.

84. Ibid. (*OPh* 2: 274–286); *Sum. log.* 1.35 (*OPh* 1: 181.36–182.67); see Aristotle, *Categoriae* 8, 8b25–10a24.

85. *Sum. log.* 1.56 (*OPh* 1: 182.3–183.18). Among the 'moderns,' the editors cite (p. 182n) Walter Burley, "De qualitate," in *Super artem veterem* (Venice ed. ff. f4ra–g1va) and Pseudo-Richard of Campsall, *Logica Campsale Anglicj* 44.08 (ed. Synan 2: 294).

not necessary for these predicables to signify distinct things."[86] Thus qualities of the fourth kind, such as "curved" or "straight," are not really distinct from material substance, because it is only through local motion that they can be asserted successively of the same thing. A body is said to be curved after being straight because its parts have been moved closer together. Other examples are rarity and density. But qualities of the third kind are really different from substance, for something cannot change from one contradictory to another without acquiring and losing something, at least when the change cannot be accounted for simply by the passage of time or by local motion. This is the case with someone's first being white and then not white. So whiteness is a quality really distinct from the person. Some dispositions are not really different from substance and other qualities, such as health or beauty. Virtue, knowledge and happiness, however, are realities distinct from the person, for we experience our gaining or losing them. The same would seem to be true of abilities and lack of abilities.[87]

Ockham's opinion that quantity is not a reality distinct from substance and quality was opposed by most theologians as contrary to the Church's doctrine of the eucharist. The commission appointed by Pope John XXII at Avignon to examine Ockham's teaching censured his views on the eucharist as incompatible with the Catholic faith, which holds that in the eucharist the substances of the bread and wine are changed into the body and blood of Christ. The substances of bread and wine do not remain but their quantity does, for they retain their appearances (*species*), one of which is their extension in space.[88]

---

86. Ibid. 1.55 (*OPh* 1: 180.20–24); *Quodl.* 7.2 (*OTh* 9: 708.38–41).

87. Ibid. (*OPh* 1: 180.24–29); *Quodl.* 7.2 (*OTh* 9: 707–708); *Expos. in Praedicamen.* 14 (*OPh* 2: 271.29–40).

88. There was no formal condemnation of Ockham's doctrine of the eucharist or other opinions, but some of them were censured by the examining committee. See A. Pelzer, "Les 51 articles de Guillaume Occam censurés en Avignon en 1326," *Revue d'histoire ecclésiastique* 18 (1922): 240–270; J. Koch, "Neue Aktenstücke zu dem gegen Wilhelm Ockham in Avignon geführten Prozess," *Recherches de théologie ancienne et médiévale* 7 (1935): 353–380 and 8 (1936): 79–93, 168–197.

It is beyond the scope of the present work to consider Ockham's eucharistic doctrine, but a word about it is in order, for it throws light on his notions of the categories of quantity and quality in their relation to substance.[89]

Ockham firmly asserts his solidarity with the Church's teaching on the eucharist. It is my faith, he says, because it is the Catholic faith, that the body of Christ is truly and really contained under the appearance of bread. Moreover, he believes that the substance of the bread is transubstantiated or changed, so that the substance of bread does not remain but only accidents subsisting *per se* without a subject.[90] He points out that scripture does not expressly teach that the substance of the bread does not remain after consecration, but he believes this to be divinely revealed on the authority of the Church fathers or proved by authoritative biblical scholars.[91] It is a moot point, however, whether God could preserve the substance of bread along with the body of Christ. Thomas Aquinas thought this to be contradictory, but Duns Scotus disagreed with him. In Scotus' view, the substance of bread in fact does not remain, but it is not contradictory that through the divine power it could remain with the body of Christ. Ockham favors the Scotist opinion as more probable and more exalting the divine omnipotence.[92]

Ockham has no doubt that God can conserve the appearances of the bread without its substance, for he held it as a principle of theology that God, being omnipotent, can make an absolute thing, such as an accident, exist without another really distinct thing, such as a substance.[93] But Ockham's critics were quick to point

---

89. For Ockham's doctrine of the eucharist see Gabriel Buescher, *The Eucharistic Teaching of William Ockham* (St. Bonaventure, NY, 1950); David Burr, "Quantity and Eucharistic Presence: The Debate from Olivi through Ockham," *Collectanea Franciscana* 44 (1974): 5–44.

90. *Tract. de corp. Christi* 2 (*OTh* 10: 91–92).

91. Ibid. 4 (*OTh* 10: 95.3–9).

92. Ibid. 6 (*OTh* 10: 99–101); for Ockham's references to Aquinas and Scotus see *OTh* 10: 101 n8.

93. Ibid. 13 (*OTh* 10: 115–116).

out a difficulty in his application of this principle. Though God can make the other accidents exist without substance, he cannot make quantity exist without it, if Ockham is correct in holding that material substance and quantity are really the same. On this supposition, if the substance of bread does not remain in the consecrated host, neither does quantity; and yet the host appears as extended in space and capable of being broken, which are properties due to quantity.

In reply to this criticism Ockham distinguishes between two meanings of "quantity." There is quantity that is identical in reality with substance, and this quantity passes away with substance in the eucharist. However, there is another quantity that is not distinct from quality, and this remains along with the qualities of the bread and quantifies them. Continuous quantity, he explains, is only the condition of having parts outside of parts in place, and this condition is found in both substance and qualities.[94] In the eucharist the qualities of the bread subsist by themselves and not in a subject. In fact, they constitute a body, in the sense of having three dimensions. This is a different meaning of body from body as an individual substance, such as an animal. Ockham says that the meaning of body as something that is three dimensional is rare or never used, but it was well known to the schoolmen, such as Aquinas, though they did not apply it to quality as Ockham does.[95]

This theology of the eucharist is different from the one commonly accepted at the time. Both Aquinas and Scotus taught that after consecration the quantity of the bread subsists through the divine agency and functions as the one subject of the qualities that appear in the host. Ockham offers a more parsimonious account of the eucharist. In his view it is superfluous to posit quantity as the subject of qualities in the eucharist. God can make the host's individual qualities subsist by themselves, each with its own quantity, with which it is really identical, and which gives the quality its tridimensional extension in space. In this case, all the

94. Ibid. 42 (*OTh* 10: 234.207–210). For the two meanings of quantity see *Tract. de quant.* 3 (*OTh* 10: 53–54).
95. Ibid. 41 (*OTh* 10: 222.5–23). See Aquinas, *ST* 1.7.3; 1.18.2.

qualities are not unified by one quantity in which they reside; they have only the unity of an aggregate.[96]

Though the philosophy Ockham uses in his theology of the eucharist is new and original, the theology is not contrary to the doctrine of the Church. It accepts the reality of the body of Christ under the appearance of bread through the conversion or transubstantiation of the substance of the bread into the body of Christ, while acknowledging that this is a mystery beyond the power of reason to explain.[97] According to Ockham, in the eucharist the body of Christ is not quantified as it is in heaven, with part outside part. In technical language it is not there "circumscriptively." However, it is there "definitively," that is, as a whole in a whole place and in each part of the place. This is how an angel exists in place or an intellectual soul exists in the body. With the latter mode of being in place, the body of Christ (indeed, the whole Christ, both God and man) by the divine power can exist entirely and simultaneously in many places and in each part of these places.[98]

In Chapter 2 we shall consider the relation of Ockham's philosophy to that of Aristotle. However, it is already apparent from Ockham's treatment of the categories of substance, quantity, and quality that he offers – always in the name of Aristotle – a highly original philosophy that the latter would not recognize. To speak, as Ockham does, of "some quantity that is substance" and "the quantity that is quality" is hardly Aristotelian.[99] Indeed, to the true Aristotelian Ockham makes blatant category mistakes; but he would not let us forget that, after all, the categories are human concepts that must give way before the divine omnipotence and the stricture of the razor.

---

96. *Tract. de corp. Christi* 19 (*OTh* 10: 129–131). Using the razor, Ockham offers a persuasive argument that both substance and quality can be quantified without a quantity really distinct from them (ibid. 29 [*OTh* 10: 157.9–158.16]).

97. Ibid. 1 (*OTh* 10: 89.10–14).

98. For the distinction between these ways of being in place see *Rep.* 4.6 (*OTh* 7: 65.6–11); *Quodl.* 1.4 and 4.21 (*OTh* 9: 25.47–54 and 9: 400.14–401.19). See below pp. 358–444.

99. *Tract. de quant.* 3 (*OTh* 10: 52.3–10).

Relation

Terms in the category of relation have a different mode of signifying from those in the categories of substance and quality. Terms in these categories signify really distinct things, as the term "man" in the category of substance signifies all humans just in themselves, and the term "white" in the category of quality signifies all whitenesses just in themselves. Terms in the category of quantity do not signify things different from substances and qualities, but they signify them as having parts outside of parts.

Terms in the category of relation, however, do not signify distinct things, but they are names signifying things, not absolutely but in relation to something else.[100] Thus the relative terms "father" and "double" do not signify distinct realities existing in someone who is a father or in something that is twofold. In short, relations are not absolute things (*res*) but only names. A relative name (either word or concept) signifies several absolute things, as "father" denotes conjointly a man and his offspring; or it can denote several absolute things, as the term "people" denotes several humans.[101] Ockham says that many theologians hold that a relation is a thing (*res*) really and entirely distinct from an absolute thing, and that he himself at one time thought this was Aristotle's doctrine. When he wrote the *Summa logicae*, however, he had changed his mind and was now persuaded that Aristotle's principles lead to the opposite opinion: that a relation is not an extra-

100. Ockham treats of the category of relation in many works: *Expos. in Praedicamen.* 12, 13 (*OPh* 2: 238–268); *Ord.* 1.30.1–5 (*OTh* 4: 281–395); *Sum. log.* 1.49–54 (*OPh* 1: 153–179); *Expos. in Phys.* 3.2 (*OPh* 4: 417–418); *Quodl.* 6.8–30 (*OTh* 9: 611–701). The *Tractatus de relatione* (*OPh* 7: 335–369) formerly attributed to Ockham is not authentic.

101. *Expos. in Praedicamen.* 12 (*OPh* 2: 239.30–240.46); *Ord.* 1.30.1 (*OTh* 4: 314.14–18); *Quodl.* 5.15 (*OTh* 9: 639.70–73). Some relative names signify a thing which connotes another existing thing; for example the name "father" can only be applied to a man if he has an existing son or daughter. Other relative names signify a thing without connoting whether another thing exists or not; for example, the term "creative" relative to "creatable"; see *Quodl.* 6.20 (*OTh* 9: 656.21–657.28).

mental reality really distinct from absolute realities and existing in them.[102] Similarity or dissimilarity, for example, is not "a small thing" (*parva res*) between similar or dissimilar things.[103] Because the name or concept "relation" does not signify a thing but a name or concept, Ockham believes that according to Aristotle the terms "relation" and "relative" are names of second imposition and concepts of second intention, unlike terms in the categories of substance and quality, which are names of first imposition and concepts of first intention.[104]

Ockham's notion of relation as only a name or concept does not lead him to conclude, as we might expect, that all relations are made by the mind (*relationes rationis*). Linguistic and conceptual relations are indeed the work of the mind, but there are also real relations (*relationes reales*), which do not depend on the mind or will.[105] Thus it is not owing to the mind or will that Socrates is like Plato in being white. Socrates is really related to Plato in this respect. The mind has no more to do with this fact than it has with Socrates' being white. Rather, from the fact that Socrates is white and Plato is white, Socrates is like Plato. But the two men are not related in being white because of some third thing that relates them; *they are related only by themselves*. And since they are absolutes, Ockham paradoxically concludes that Socrates is like

102. *Sum. log.* 1.49 (*OPh* 1: 153.2–154.16).

103. *Quodl.* 6.8 (*OTh* 9: 612.14–15).

104. According to Aristotle, Ockham says, when relation is taken as one of the widest categories (*genus generalissimum*), it is a concept of second intention, for it does not signify or stand for an extramental reality that is not a sign; it only signifies and stands for names that are either of first or second intention. You can't say "Socrates is a relation" or "Whiteness is a relation." But you can say "Father is a relation" or "Likeness is a relation." The genus "relation" can be predicated of the concept of "father" and "likeness," which are species of relation. Species of relations can be names of first intention, signifying and standing for extramental things. Thus "father" designates conjointly a man and his offspring; see *Quodl.* 6.22 (*OTh* 9: 666–669).

105. For the distinction between real and conceptual or mental relations see *Ord.* 1.30.5 (*OTh* 4: 385.16–386.20 and 387.10–24); *Ord.* 1.35.4 (*OTh* 4: 472.4–473.5); *Quodl.* 6.25 and 6.30 (*OTh* 9: 680.49–58 and 698–701).

Plato *because of absolutes!*[106] It should be noted, however, that the paradox is only linguistic, for in Ockham's view the distinction between relative and absolute is not, properly speaking, between beings but names.[107] In the strict sense a thing (*res*) is not absolute, though Ockham often speaks of it as such. He uses this language when he asserts that if only one absolute thing existed there would be no real relation; but because there are several the mind can express them in different ways. First, it can express precisely that Socrates is white; and then it has absolute concepts. Second, it can also express that Plato is white. Third, it can express that both Socrates and Plato are white, and it can do this by a relative concept or intention, affirming "Socrates is like Plato in whiteness"; for the proposition "Both Socrates and Plato are white" means entirely the same as "Socrates is like Plato in being white." We could not wish for a more radical elimination of relation as a reality.[108]

In Ockham's day it was usual to maintain that many real relations were things (*res*) really distinct from the things related. To cite an eminent example, this was the position of Duns Scotus. The Scotist doctrine of real relation implies the existence of really distinct things as the "ends" (*extrema*) of the relation. It also implies that the things related are united in having a nature or essence in common. From the very nature of this foundation a real relation arises between the things without the mind's relating one to the other. In this case there is a real distinction between the relation and the foundation of the relation, for the foundation can exist without the relation. In contrast, a "relation of reason" is only a "thing of reason," conceptually distinct from its foundation.[109]

---

106. *Ord.* 1.30.1 (*OTh* 4: 316.3–24).

107. "Similiter distinctio entis per absolutum et respectivum non est entis in quantum ens sed terminorum" (*Sum. log.* 1.51 [*OPh* 1: 167.148–150]).

108. *Ord.* 1.30.1 (*OTh* 4: 316.3–24).

109. Scotus, *Ord.* 1.31.un (Vatican ed. 6: 204, n. 6) and 2.1.4–5 (Vatican ed. 7: 102, n. 200). Ockham presents this as the common opinion; see *Ord.* 1.30.2 (*OTh* 4: 321.14–322.2).

Ockham takes obvious pleasure in spelling out the absurdities he finds in the Scotist doctrine of relation. To mention but a few: If the relation were a reality really distinct from the things related, God, being omnipotent, could make two absolute white things without a relation between them, and still they would be alike.[110] Again, if Socrates were like Plato, their likenesses would also be alike by another relation of likeness, and so on to infinity.[111] Again, if fatherhood were a different reality from a father and his son, God could conserve it in existence without the father's begetting his son, and a man would be the father of a son he did not beget.[112] Further, when a donkey moved on the earth every heavenly body would also be moved and receive a new reality, for it would be at a different distance from the donkey than before.[113] Another absurdity: Every time I move my finger I would fill the universe with an infinity of new accidental realities, because my finger would have a different location in relation to the heavens and the earth and each of their parts.[114]

In support of his position Scotus argued that a thing cannot change from one contradictory to another without acquiring or losing something in the process. For example, if something that is not active becomes active, or something that is not acted upon becomes acted upon, it must acquire or lose something: through the change something must be produced or destroyed. But what is acquired or lost is not something absolute but relative, namely a new relation of agent to patient or patient to agent. Hence, there are real relations distinct from absolute things.[115]

The argument of Scotus, and others like it, do not convince Ockham of the reality of relations. Scotus believes that when an

---

110. *Ord.* 1.30.1 (*OTh* 4: 291.21–292.2).

111. Ibid. (*OTh* 4: 293.17–19).

112. *Sum. log.* 1.50 (*OPh* 1: 161.68–74).

113. Ibid. (*OPh* 1: 159.9–12).

114. *Quodl.* 7.8 (*OTh* 9: 728.48–55).

115. Scotus, *Ord.* 2.1.4–5 (Vatican ed. 7: 101–110, nn. 200–222). See Ockham, *Ord.* 1.30.2 (*OTh* 4: 321.14–322.2).

agent begins to act it undergoes a change and acquires a new relative reality called "action." But it is unnecessary to posit a reality of this sort to account for an agent or patient. Reminding his opponent that "a plurality should not be posited without necessity," he contends that all the facts can be explained without it. Nothing more is needed than the agent and patient and the absolute effect in the patient at the presence of the agent.[116]

Although Ockham considered this to be the more probable view of Aristotle and indeed of human reason itself, when he treats of the divine Trinity he grants that in God there are real relations that are not simply names or concepts but distinct realities. Since the time of the Church fathers the three divine Persons have been thought to be different from each other by their relation of origin. The Father is the source of the whole Trinity, the Son proceeds from the Father, and the Holy Spirit from both the Father and the Son. Each Person is a relative reality: the Father is Fatherhood, the Son Sonship, and the Holy Spirit Spiration. Yet, the Persons are really one in their absolute nature or essence. In short, they are one God.[117]

Thus, even though experience and reason persuade Ockham that every thing is absolute and that there are no relative things or realities, his faith obliges him to acknowledge relative realities in God. This conflict between reason and faith does not disturb him, for he expects to find marvels in God that are not in creatures. He is perturbed, however, that so many theologians, like Scotus, believing in the existence of relative realities in God, should transfer the notion to creatures, where the Philosopher does not find it.

The central notion in the opposing doctrines of Ockham and Scotus on the nature of relations is "thing" (*res*). While Scotus contends that a real relation in creatures is an accidental thing really in-

116. Ockham, *Ord.* 1.30.2 (*OTh* 4: 322.4–19). Peter Aureol preceded Ockham in holding this doctrine of relation: see Aureol, *Commentaria in Sent.* 1.30.1 (Rome ed. 1: 667); cf. Ockham, ibid. (*OTh* 4: 328.13–24) and the editor's note *OTh* 4: 328 n1.

117. For Ockham's doctrine of the Trinity see *Ord.* 1.30.4 and 1.31.5 (*OTh* 4: 366–374 and *OTh* 4: 395–407); *Quodl.* 6.26–27 (*OTh* 9: 683–689).

hering in the things related, Ockham insists that it is not a thing at all but a name or concept signifying several things. In the perspective of philosophy there are no relative things but only absolutes.

Ockham's predecessors found still other ways of accounting for relations. Henry of Harclay, a near contemporary of Ockham, agreed with him that a real relation is not a real thing, inhering in the foundation of the relation; neither is it something dependent on the mind. Since a relation does not inhere in the related thing, it does not have the property of "in-ness" (*initas*) but rather "towardness" (*aditas*). This is not a real thing (*res aditatis*), though it can be called a thing if the term is extended to everything that is not dependent on the mind. A real relation brings to something a new condition (*habitudo*), or the fact of being associated (*societas*), or existing together (*simultas, coexistentia*). Thus Harclay seems to have adopted a notion of relation opposed to the strongly realist view of Scotus, but also unlike the nominalist or conceptualist position of Ockham.[118]

Aquinas' doctrine of relation gives a central role to the metaphysical notion of being (*esse*).[119] Like all the nine categories of accidents, he remarks, a relation is a being, but its being is more properly called a "being in" a subject (*inesse subjecto*). However, relation is different from the other accidents in that its nature (*ratio*) does not imply its inherence in a subject but only its being toward something outside. In categories such as quantity and quality their natures include a reference to the substance in which they

---

118. See Mark G. Henninger, "Henry of Harclay's Question on Relations," *Mediaeval Studies* 49 (1987): 76–123. In his earlier commentary on the *Sentences* Harclay adopted the Scotist doctrine of relation. See M.G. Henninger, "Henry of Harclay's *Quaestio* on Relations in his *Sentences* Commentary: An Edition," in *Greek and Medieval Studies in Honor of Leo Sweeney, S.J.*, ed. William J. Carroll and John J. Furlong (New York, 1994), pp. 237–254, and "Some Late Medieval Theories of the Category of Relation" (PhD dissertation, University of California, Los Angeles, 1984).

119. For Aquinas' notion of relation see *In Sent.* 1.8.4.3, sol. ad 4 and 1.26.2.1 (ed. Mandonnet–Moos 1: 224–225 and 628–632); *ST* 1.28.1–2; *Quodl.* 9.4. See Clifford Kossel, "Principles of St. Thomas's Distinction between *Esse* and *Ratio* of Relation," *The Modern Schoolman* 24 (1946): 19–36; 25 (1947): 93–107.

exist, quantity being the measure of substance, quality its disposition. But by its special nature relation is only a relatedness to another. It is not something, but toward something (*non aliquid, sed ad aliquid*). Hence among all things it has the weakest being (*debilissimum esse*). This accounts for the fact, Aquinas adds, that Gilbert of Poitiers (d. 1154) and his followers thought of relations as existing only in the mind and hence as concepts of second intention. But Aquinas insists that this is true only of conceptual relations, like the relation of a thing to itself, and not of real categorical relations, which have a foundation in reality. In conceiving a real relation as a special way of existing and not only as a name or concept (Ockham), or as a thing (*res*) (Scotus), or as a "towardness" or co-existence (Harclay), Aquinas is true to his existential approach to metaphysical questions.

We shall meet these philosophers and their personal ways of philosophizing again when we take up the problem of universals.

The Other Six Categories

Ockham treats more briefly the remaining six categories: action, acted upon (*passio*), time, place, posture, and state. These categories do not imply things distinct from substance and quality; they are only names designating these absolute things in various ways. A verbal account is all that is needed to explain them. Scotus thought that action is a reality existing in the agent and both action and *passio* are realities existing in the patient. According to Aristotle, however, the noun "action" stands for the same thing as "agent," and "acted upon" for the patient. The meaning is that something really acts and something is really acted upon. "Action" is only an arrangement of words (*ordinatio verborum*) implying that something makes or does something. It is superfluous to posit anything more.[120]

120. *Sum. log.* 1. 57, 58 (*OPh* 1: 183–188); *Expos. in Praedicamen.* 16 (*OPh* 2: 296–303). See Scotus, *Quaestiones super libros Aristotelis De anima* 7 (Vivès ed. 3: 503, n. 3). This was also the opinion of Peter Aureol, *Commentaria in Sent.* 1.27.1 (Rome ed. 1: 600b).

The category of time (*quando*) does not designate a reality distinct from substance and quality; it simply denotes them adverbially instead of nominally. It answers the question "when," as "place" (which, like time, has no distinct reality) answers the question "where" (*ubi*).[121] Posture (*positio*) signifies the arrangement of a thing's parts in place, like "sitting" or "standing." State (*habitus*) designates the relation of a thing to something external that it possesses; for example, being armed or shod.[122] Walter Chatton interpreted Aristotle to mean that these categories denote relative realities grounded in absolute things; for example, time is the relation of "whenness" (*quandalitas*) and place is the relation of "whereness" (*ubitas*).[123] But Ockham preferred Peter Olivi's reading of the Philosopher, that these categories do not correspond to distinct essences, but they are different verbal or conceptual descriptions of absolute things.[124]

Although Ockham finds the discussion of these six categories somewhat tedious, he does see some value in it.[125] It is helpful for us to form a better notion of his program of using the razor and other arguments to show that certain supposed realities are nothing but names.

3 Predicables

As we have seen, the categories are ten universal words or concepts that directly signify things either absolutely or as connoting other things. There is another set of five universals, called "predicables," that must be clearly distinguished from them. Ockham lists them

---

121. *Sum. log.* 1.59, 60 (*OPh* 1: 188–191). Note that God by his absolute power could make all the places in the world in a body existing in the same place: *Quaest. in Phys.* 14 (*OPh* 6: 430.23–24).

122. *Sum. log.* 1.61, 62 (*OPh* 1: 191–193).

123. Chatton, *Sent. (Reportatio)* 1.30.3 (Paris, BNF, MS. lat. 15887, ff. 65rb–66v). Pseudo-Richard of Campsall criticized Ockham's doctrines of the categories of time, place, position and habit contending, with Chatton, that they designate relative realities; see *Logica Campsale Anglici* 46–49 (ed. Synan 2: 325–348).

124. Olivi, *Quaestiones in secundum librum Sententiarum* 58 (ed. Jansen 2: 446–448).

125. *Expos. in Praedicamen.* 16 (*OPh* 2: 303.147–150).

as "species," "genus," "difference," "property," and "accident." These do not signify things but rather denote various ways in which predicates may be attributed to subjects. Thus, in the proposition "Socrates is a man," "man" denotes a species. In "Man is an animal," "animal" denotes a genus. In "Man is rational," "rational" denotes a difference. In "Man is capable of laughter," "capable of laughter" denotes a property. In "Man is white," "white" denotes an accident. Because categorical terms signify things, either absolutely or connotatively, they are concepts of first intention or words of first imposition. Predicables, in contrast, denote other universals, and hence they are concepts of second intention or words of second imposition.[126]

The notion of predicables goes back to Aristotle's *Topics*, where they are listed as definition, property, genus, and accident.[127] In his commentary on Porphyry's *Isagoge*, Boethius adopted Porphyry's listing of genus, species, difference, property, and accident.[128] This became standard in the Middle Ages, and it was accepted by Ockham. There was little agreement, however, on the meaning of the predicables and their relation to reality. Like the categories, they are universals, and it was widely debated what status universals might have in words, concepts or reality. As this will be the subject of a later section of the chapter, we shall pass over it here. It is enough to say that Ockham considers universals to be nothing but words or concepts. He resists every effort to locate them in individual things.[129] Thus, when Porphyry speaks of many individual men "being contained in" the human

126. The main source of Ockham's doctrine of the predicables is *Expos. in Praedicab.*, especially the prooem. (*OPh* 2: 8–16); see also *Sum. log.* 1.18 (*OPh* 1: 62–84).

127. Aristotle, *Top.* 1.5, 101b38.

128. Boethius, *In Isagogen Porphyrii commenta*, editio secunda, 1.5 (CSEL 48: 151, n. 6); trans. Richard McKeon as "The Second Edition of the Commentaries on the Isagoge of Porphyry," in *Selections from Medieval Philosophers*, ed. McKeon (New York, 1929–1930), 1: 70–99, at p. 84.

129. The division into the five predicables is not between things but between names or concepts or intentions in the mind: "divisio nominum vel conceptuum vel intentionum in anima" (*Expos. in Praedicab.* 1 [*OPh* 2: 24.9–10]).

species, Ockham takes this to mean that "man" is predicated of many individual men. Porphyry's statement that human properties "exist in" all individual men precisely because they are human, means that they are predicated of all of them. Ockham adds that through ignorance of the equivocal meaning of "to be in" many mistakes are made in understanding the sayings of the philosophers, among others.[130]

It was said above that the predicables differ in the way a predicate is attributed to a subject. A species and a genus are alike in that they are predicated essentially (*in quid*) of a subject. They differ, however, because a genus is predicated essentially of many things differing in species; for example "animal" predicated of "man" and "horse." A species is predicated essentially of many things differing only in number, for example "man" predicated of "Socrates" and "Plato." ("Species" is here taken as an ultimate species [*species specialissima*], that is, one that cannot be divided into more general species and thus function as a genus; for example "man.") Both the species and genus denote the whole subject of which they are predicated essentially (*in quid*) and not only a part of it. They differ in that a genus is predicable of more subjects than a species, as "animal" extends to more individuals than "man" and also to other species than man.

The predicable "difference" (understood as "essential difference") is like "genus" or "species" in that it denotes something intrinsic to that for which it stands in a proposition; for example "rational" in the proposition "Socrates is rational," or "Man is rational." But it does not primarily denote the whole of Socrates or man but a definite part, namely his intellectual soul. The abstract term "rationality" means the same as the part of man that is his intellectual soul, unlike the abstract term "animality," which denotes the whole of man and not just a part. An essential difference is not predicated *in quid*, for in

---

130. "Et ideo est advertendum quod frequenter 'esse in' accipitur pro 'praedicari,' et ita accipitur hic. Quando dicit auctor quod proprietates hominis sunt in omnibus hominibus particularibus, eo quod sunt homines, intelligit per 'esse in hominibus particularibus' praedicari de hominibus particularibus. Et ignorantia istius aequivocationis de 'esse in' est causa multorum errorum in exponendo auctoritates philosophorum et aliorum" (*Expos. in Praedicab.* 2 [*OPh* 2: 53.56–62]).

reply to the question "What is Socrates?" it is not appropriate to say "He is rational," as it is to say "He is a man" or "He is an animal." This is because "rational," unlike "man" and "animal," does not express the whole of Socrates. A difference is predicated *in quale*; that is, it is given as a reply to the question "Of what sort is this?"

Some properties belong to everything in a species, as "capable of laughter" belongs to all humans; others only belong to an individual, as "being a doctor." But "capable of being a doctor" is a property of every human, unless there is a natural impediment. Ockham cautions us not to think of a property as a sort of reality formally distinct from the subject in which it exists. In fact, to say that a man is "capable of laughter" simply means that he can laugh.

Unlike a property, an accident can either belong or not belong to an existing subject. Some accidents are separable, like sleep; others are inseparable, like the blackness of a crow. True, a crow cannot be white, but at least it can be thought of as white, for there is nothing about whiteness to prevent a crow's being white. The reason why it cannot be white lies elsewhere, for instance in the crow's nature or the nature of its causes. On the contrary, a human being cannot even be conceived as incapable of laughter.[131]

4 Transcendental Terms

The categories are the most general genera of things, under which are arranged subgenera and species. For example, under the category of substance are placed the genus "animal" and the species "man." Some names are more general than these and indeed apply to everything. Because these names go beyond the categories, the medieval schoolmen called them "transcendent" (*transcendentia*). Since the sixteenth century they have been known as "transcendentals."[132] These terms signify and stand for all things, even for

131. Ockham treats of each of the predicables and their relations in *Expos. in Praedicab.* (*OPh* 2: 16–131); *Sum. log.* 1.20–25 (*OPh* 1: 67–84).

132. "Transcendental" (*transcendentalis*) first appears in the sixteenth century in the works of Suárez, who attributed it to Chrysostom Javelli (Joseph Owens, *An Elementary Christian Metaphysics* [Milwaukee, 1963], p. 111n1).

signs, such as words and concepts, insofar as they are also things. They are, moreover, terms of first intention, predicable of everything essentially (*in quid*).[133]

Ockham does not give us a full account of transcendental terms, though no doubt he intended to do so in his projected commentary on Aristotle's *Metaphysics*, which unfortunately he did not write or complete. In his *Summa logicae* he devotes a chapter to each of the transcendentals "being" and "one";[134] and in a list of transcendentals that was traditional in his day he includes "thing," "something," "true," and "good."[135] He also speaks of a transcendental concept of substance that is predicable of God, and a concept of the quality of wisdom that, applied to God, is like a transcendental name.[136] Scotus described the transcendentals as absolute perfections that apply to God in the highest possible way, and Ockham shows no reason to disagree with Scotus. He would only insist that they are not in any way distinct in God himself, but only different terms predicated of him.[137]

The other transcendental terms signify the same thing as being, but they differ from it and from each other in concept. They do not designate something other than being but only different properties (*passiones*) or modes of being. Thus they are not synonyms but differ in their nominal definitions. "One" is defined as "a being insofar as it is undivided in itself and divided or distinct from others."[138] "True" is defined as "being as knowable by a mind,"

---

133. *Sum. log.* 1.11 and 1.38 (*OPh* 1: 40.65–71 and 106.8–10).

134. *Sum. log.* 1.38, 39 (*OPh* 1: 106–111).

135. *Sum. log.* 1.11 (*OPh* 1: 40.65–41.78). Aquinas, *De ver.* 1.1, lists as transcendentals: "being," "thing," "one," "something," "good," and "true."

136. *Quodl.* 7.13 (*OTh* 9: 750.35–39, 752.68–75).

137. Scotus, *Ord.* 1.3.1.3 (Vatican ed. 3: 84, n. 135), cited by Ockham, *Ord.* 1.2.9 (*OTh* 2: 297.9–20).

138. *Ord.* 1.2.1 (*OTh* 2: 23.2–3); *Sum. log.* 1.39 (*OPh* 1: 109–111). The term "one" has many meanings. Some things are one that do not include a multiplicity of really distinct parts, such as an angel or human soul. Other things are one that do include such a multiplicity of parts, either of the same or different nature. An example of the first is the quantity of a mass and a form that can be augmented

and "good" as "being as desirable by a will," or more adequately as "something desirable and lovable according to right reason."[139] These transcendental terms are convertible with being. They are, moreover, connotative names, for they designate one thing directly and another obliquely; for example, "true" denotes a being while connoting a mind that can know it. As transcendentals, truth and goodness are metaphysical terms. In another sense, truth is a property of propositions and goodness a property of moral actions.

Finally, a word should be said about Ockham's notion of beauty. Like most of the schoolmen (with the exception of Bonaventure) he does not include it among the transcendentals but places it in the categories in the first species of quality, as something possessed (*habitus*). An example is the beauty of a living body, characterized by an appropriate size and color of its bodily parts, their due proportion and health.[140] As we reflect on the beauty of creatures, we can abstract the notion of beauty from them and apply it to God, recognizing creaturely beauty as a vestige of the divine beauty. Beauty as a quality, like the quality of wisdom, is then used like a transcendental.[141]

Ockham uses the terms *ens*, ("being"), *entitas* ("entity"), and *res* ("thing") as synonyms. The term *esse* ("to be") also signifies *res*, but it has a different function in language: as a verb *esse* can be used as a copula between two terms, as when we say "Man is an animal"; the noun *res* or *entitas* cannot have this function. The term *esse* can also be used as a noun, and then it means the same as *res*. In this usage *esse*

---

by adding part to part; an example of the second is a substance composed of form and matter. All these are one in the strict sense. In an improper and less strict sense a kingdom, people or world can be called one; see *Ord.* 1.24.1 (*OTh* 4: 76.17–77.17). The latter have only the unity of an aggregate; a whole composed of essential parts, like form (which is actual) and matter (which is potential) are one *per se*; see *Quaest. variae* 6.2 (*OTh* 8: 212.130–213.140).

139. *Ord.* ibid. (*OTh* 2: 23.13–15); *Sum. log.* 1.10 (*OPh* 1: 38.90–94).

140. *Expos. in Praedicamen.* 14 (*OPh* 2: 271.29–40, 283.13–20).

141. *Expos. in Phys.* 14 (*OPh* 2: 271.29–46); *Sum. phil. nat.* 3.17 (*OPh* 6: 304.5–21); *Ord.* 1.3.9 (*OTh* 2: 549.3–14).

can be applied to God, the first cause, meaning that he does not depend on anything else; but when it is applied to creatures it signifies them as dependent on and directed to the first cause. In fact, they have no being except as thus dependent and directed.[142]

Apart from God, then, creatures have no being of their own. In Ockham's words: "When a man is not dependent on God he does not exist, and then neither is he a man. And so we should not imagine that an essence is indifferent to being and non-being, any more than it is indifferent to essence and non–essence, for just as essence can either be or not be, so essence can be essence or non-essence."[143] An essence has only the logical indifference of being the subject of two contradictory propositions that can be true at different times, as we can say of the essence "man," "Man exists" or "Man does not exist."

The logical indifference of an essence to being or non-being led some philosophers, notably Giles of Rome, to believe that the essence of a creature is really indifferent to existence or non-existence, so that its essence and existence are two really distinct entities (*duae res*). For example, the essence of an angel can either exist or not exist, and so its existence is separable and distinguishable from its essence. Hence its essence and existence must be two really distinct entities. To this, Ockham replies that there is no more reason to think that essence and existence are two distinct entities than that essence and essence are two distinct entities. In fact, the terms "essence" and "existence" signify and consignify exactly the same thing.[144]

Let us suppose for the moment that a creature's existence is really distinct from its essence. Existence would be either a substance or an accident. If it were an accident, it would be either a quality or a quantity, which is clearly false. Neither can existence be a substance, for every substance is either matter, form, or their

142. *Sum. log.* 3–3.27 (*OPh* 1: 554.22–33. For *esse* as a verb and noun see *Quodl.* 2.7 (*OTh* 9: 143.56–144.67).

143. Ibid. (*OPh* 1: 554.32–36).

144. Ibid. 3–2.27 (*OPh* 1: 554, 33–43); *Quodl.* 2.7 (*OTh* 9: 143.47–144.67).

composite. But it is obvious that neither of these is existence, if existence is reality distinct from a thing's entity. Moreover, if essence and existence were two things, their union would be either substantial or accidental. If it were substantial, one would be act and the other potency, and so they would be related as form and matter, which is absurd. If their union were accidental, they would be a mere aggregate and one would be the accident of the other. What is more, if they were two things, it would not be contradictory for God to conserve the entity of a thing without existence, or its existence without entity, both of which are impossible. The conclusion is obvious: thing (*res*) and being (*esse*), are not two things, but rather two concepts or words signifying the same thing.[145]

Proponents of the real distinction between essence and existence appeal to the traditional distinction in a thing between "that which is" (*quod est*) and "that whereby it is" (*quo est*). Its essence is that which is, its existence is that whereby it is. Hence the existence of a creature is really other than its essence. But in Ockham's view the distinction between *quod est* and *quo est* should rather be understood as the difference between the creature (that which is) and God (that whereby the creature is). Of course this distinction does not apply to God, for he does not exist by something: he alone is being or existence itself (*ipsum esse*), the absolutely necessary being.[146]

---

145. *Sum. log.* ibid. (*OPh* 1: 553.3–21); *Quodl.* ibid. (*OTh* 9: 141–145). Ockham's criticism of the real distinction between essence and existence seems to be mainly directed against Giles of Rome, who taught that essence and existence in creatures are two really distinct realities (*res*), especially in his *Theoremata de esse et essentia*, ed. Edgar Hocedez (Louvain, 1930). According to Aquinas essence and *esse* in creatures are really distinct, not as two things or realities, but as two principles or constituents of a created being. For the controversy over this question see Etienne Gilson, *A History of Christian Philosophy in the Middle Ages* (New York, 1955), pp. 420–427.

146. *Sum. log.* ibid. (*OPh* 1: 555.51–58). The terms *quod est* and *quo est* originated with Boethius, *De hebdomadibus* (PL 64: 1311C), and Gilbert of Poitiers' commentaries on Boethius; see *The Commentaries on Boethius by Gilbert of Poitiers*, ed. Nikolaus M. Häring (Toronto, 1966).

In the *Summa logicae* Ockham quotes Robert Grosseteste's saying, that when the first cause or God is called *esse* the term denotes
his absolutely simple essence; but when the term is applied to creatures it designates nothing but their relation of dependence on God
– a relation that brings about no diversity in creatures.[147] In his
Quodlibets, however, Ockham denies that the existence of a creature is a relation of dependence on God, for the simple reason that
a relation of this sort is superfluous. As we have seen, relations are
not realities but only names or concepts. An effect does not
depend on a relation to its cause, nor an accident to its subject, nor
form to matter. Indeed, God can make one of these exist without
the other. Much less, then, does a creature, such as an angel,
depend on a relation to the creator.[148] Ockham is not denying
that creatures depend on God for their existence, but only that
this involves a relation by which they are dependent. Like all
related things, God and creatures are related by themselves and not
by an added relation.

5 Universals

All the terms described above are general or universal. It is time to
ask what a universal term is and how it differs from an individual
term. This will bring us to the controversial question of the relation of universal terms to reality, or the problem of universals.

Ockham accepts Aristotle's definition of a universal as "that
which is of such a nature as to be predicated of many subjects,"
while an individual is "that which is of such a nature as not to be
predicated of many subjects." Thus "man" is universal but "Plato"
is individual or singular.[149] Ockham adds the precision that a

---

147. *Sum. log.* 3-2.27 (*OPh* 1: 554.44–555.50). See Robert Grosseteste, *In
Aristot. Anal. Poster.* 2.1 (ed. Rossi p. 291.80–84).

148. *Quodl.* 2.7 (*OTh* 9: 142.13–19).

149. "Divisio est quod propositionum quaedam sunt singulares, quaedam
non. Dicit igitur [Aristoteles] quod rerum subicibilium quaedam sunt universales, quaedam singulares. Et exponit, dicens quod universale est illud quod
de pluribus natum est praedicari. Singulare vero est quod non est natum prae-

universal may be that which is actually predicable of many subjects or that which can be predicated of many subjects, though in fact it is not. Suppose there were only one white thing, then "white" would not be universal in the first sense but only in the second. Nevertheless it can be universal in the first sense if more white things are added.[150]

What exactly is meant by saying that a universal is "that which" is predicated of many subjects? *What* precisely is predicated? In short, what is a universal? Is it only a term or name, spoken, written, or conceived, or is it in some way also a reality? This is the famous problem of universals that exercised the minds of philosophers in antiquity and the Middle Ages and is still debated today. There is no doubt what Ockham's answer is. He insists that the worst mistake in philosophy is to hold that, over and above individual things, there are universal realities (*res universales*) which, when conceived, are parts of universal propositions.[151] One of his most intensive efforts is to eradicate this idea from philosophy. His own position is clear cut: universals are nothing but terms or names (*nomina*), either spoken, written, or conceived. Universal concepts are themselves mental names (*nomina mentalia*). This is why he and his followers were called nominalists or terminists in the Middle Ages. Nominalists (*nominales*), as distinct from realists (*reales*), were described by Albert the Great as those who claimed that universals, and the community among particulars referred to by them, exist only in the mind.[152] This perfectly fits Ockham's doctrine. In our day nominalism usually (but not always) means the doctrine that universals

dicari de pluribus, sicut 'homo' est universale, sed 'Plato' est de numero eorum quae sunt singularia" (*Expos. in Periherm.* 1.5 [*OPh* 2: 398.10–399.15]). See Aristotle, *De interpretatione 7*, 17a38–17b3.

150. Ibid. (*OPh* 2: 405.33–39).

151. Ibid. (*OPh* 2: 362.9–363.19).

152. "Et tale esse in intellectu universalia habere dixerunt illi qui vocabantur Nominales, qui communitatem (ad quam particularia universalium, de quibus dicuntur ipsa universalia, referuntur) tantum in intellectu esse dicebant" (*Liber de Praedicabilibus* 2.2 (*Opera omnia* 1: 19).

are words, in contrast to conceptualism, which identifies universals with concepts. In these terms he is more aptly called a conceptualist, for he thought a universal is primarily a concept.[153]

Ockham takes up the problem of universals in many works,[154] but his most extensive and systematic treatment of the subject is in his *Ordinatio*, distinction 2, questions 4 to 8.[155] This is a veritable treatise on universals inserted by Ockham into his commentary on the *Sentences* in order to lay the groundwork for the resolution of theological issues, such as the possibility of predicating univocal concepts of God and creatures, and the knowability of the divine essence. The questions present and criticize positions on universals arranged according to the degree of reality they ascribe to a universal, beginning in question 4 with the most realistic view and ending in question 7 with the least realistic. Question 8 contains Ockham's own nonrealist position on the subject.

The Opinion of Walter Burley

The first opinion regarding universals, described in question 4, is that a univocal universal is a reality (*res*) existing outside the mind in every individual in a genus or species and belonging to the individual's essence. The universal is really distinct from the individuals and from all other universals existing in them. For example, universal humanity is a true reality, existing outside the mind in

153. See Philotheus Boehner, "The Realistic Conceptualism of William Ockham," *Franciscan Studies* 4 (1946): 307–335; repr. in his *Collected Articles on Ockham*, pp. 156–174.

154. Ockham treats of universals in: *Expos. in Praedicab.* prooem. 2 (*OPh* 2: 10–15); *Expos. in Praedicamen.* 8 (*OPh* 2: 162–171); *Expos. in Periherm.* 1.prooem. (*OPh* 2: 348–376); *Ord.* 1.2.4–8 (*OTh* 2: 99–292); *Sum. log.* 1.14–19 (*OPh* 1: 47–67); *Quodl.* 5.12–13 (*OTh* 9: 528–536). For Ockham's treatment of the problem of universals see Adams, *William Ockham* 1: 3–141 and "Universals in the Early Fourteenth Century," in *Cambridge History of Later Medieval Philosophy*, ed. Kretzmann et al., pp. 411–439; Gordon Leff, *William of Ockham* (Manchester, 1975), pp. 78–123. In this section I have drawn upon my chapter "William of Ockham," in *Individuation in Scholasticism*, ed. Gracia, pp. 373–396.

155. Ockham, "Five Questions on Universals from his *Ordinatio*, d. 2, qq. 4–8," trans. Paul Vincent Spade, in *Five Texts on the Mediaeval Problem of Universals*, ed. Spade (Indianapolis/Cambridge, 1994), pp. 114–231.

all humans and really distinct from them and from universal animal and substance. Moreover, the universal realities existing in each individual in a genus or species are in no way diversified or multiplied in the different individuals.[156]

Ockham does not say who, if anyone, was of this opinion. He remarks that it has been falsely attributed to Duns Scotus,[157] and he hints at the Platonic basis of the position, without ascribing it to Plato himself.[158] It bears some resemblance to the doctrine of William of Champeaux, at least as it was interpreted by Abelard.[159] Ockham appears to have in mind his contemporary, Walter Burley, as the author of this opinion, and to have drawn upon Henry of Harclay's criticism of it.[160]

The theory was devised, Ockham says, to account for the essential predication of one thing of another and for our definitions and sciences of reality. As Aristotle showed, the object of a definition is not primarily an individual but a universal substance distinct from the individual, and yet intrinsic to it and belonging to its essence. It is this universal substance that is predicated essentially of an individual, as when we say "Socrates is an animal." Moreover, a science of reality (*scientia realis*) must have a universal substance as its object, for science treats primarily of the universal and not of the individual.[161]

156. *Ord.* 1.2.4 (*OTh* 2: 100.17–101.11). Ockham criticizes the view that a substance is composed of several extramental universal realities in his *Sum. log.* 1.15 (*OPh* 1: 50–54).

157. *Ord.* 1.1.5 (*OTh* 2: 154.2–7).

158. Ibid. (*OTh* 2: 122.7–12).

159. See Martin Tweedale, *Abailard on Universals* (Amsterdam, 1976), p. 97 and n10.

160. Walter Burley, *Super artem veterem* (Venice ed. 4rb–va); *Circa Tertium De Anima*, in *Questions on the De Anima of Aristotle by Magister Adam Burley & Dominus Walter Burley* 2.60 and 3.65, ed. Edward A. Synan (Leiden/New York, 1997), pp. 105–106 and 124. See Boh, "Walter Burley," *Individuation in Scholasticism*, pp. 347–372; Adams, "Universals in the Early Fourteenth Century," pp. 411–439; Agustin Uña Juárez, *La filosofia del siglo xiv: contexto cultural de Walter Burley* (Madrid, 1978). For Henry of Harclay see Gál, "Henricus de Harclay," pp. 178–234.

161. *Ord.* 1.2.4 (*OTh* 2: 101.12–103.18).

This opinion of universals receives Ockham's harshest disapproval, calling it absolutely false and absurd.[162] If there were a universal reality existing in individuals and really distinct from them, God could by his absolute power create the universal without the individuals, or the individuals without the universal; he could, for example, create humanity without individual humans or individual humans without humanity. The theory holds that a universal is intrinsic to the individual and yet really distinct from it. It must, then, be a part of the individual. But a part cannot be essentially predicated of a thing; we cannot say, for example, that Socrates is his body or soul or hand. Nevertheless we do say "Socrates is an animal." Hence animal cannot be a part of Socrates. In fact, Ockham urges, in this proposition "animal" is only a term standing for Socrates, taking his place when we talk and think about him. There is no need, then, to suppose that there is a universal reality (res universalis) within the individual and predicable of it.[163]

Moreover, we do not have to assume universal or common realities to provide objects of our general definitions. We define man as a rational animal, but this primarily defines the term "man," not some common reality. Nevertheless the definition may be said to express the individuals in the species, because in a way it can be said of them and it stands for them when used in propositions. Thus we can say that Socrates or Plato is a rational animal (but not simply "rational animal"), and the term "rational animal" stands for them and other individual humans.[164]

As for sciences dealing with the real world, Aristotle showed that their primary objects are not individuals but universals,[165] although the universals in question are terms of propositions and not common realities. Indeed, for Ockham, "every science, whether it be a science of reality or rational science [that is, logic], is concerned only with

---

162. *Ord.* 1.2.4 (*OTh* 2: 108.2).
163. Ibid. (*OTh* 2: 122.7–123.24).
164. Ibid. (*OTh* 2: 127.5–129.20).
165. Aristotle, *Anal. Post.* 1.4–5, 73b26–74a13; *Metaph.* 7.15, 1039 b20–1040a8.

propositions as with what is known, for propositions alone are known."[166] He is not denying that we know individuals; they are the first objects of the intuitive cognition of the senses and intellect. Neither is he denying that science in its own way treats of individuals. The point he is making is that universal propositions are the immediate and direct objects of scientific knowledge. Science deals with individuals insofar as the terms of its propositions stand for them. In a science of reality (*scientia realis*) the terms of its propositions have personal supposition, standing for what they signify, namely individual extramental realities. This is the case with the propositions of physics, mathematics, and metaphysics. In order to account for sciences of this sort, then, it is not necessary to assume that there are universal realities, really distinct from individual things.[167]

The Opinion of an Unknown Author

Having disposed of this rather crude form of realism of universals, in question 5 Ockham turns to a lesser form of realism. This opinion agrees with the one preceding that the universal is a reality (*res*) existing outside the mind in individual things and really distinct from them; but the universal is now said to enter into composition with the individual and to be "contracted" by an individuating difference rendering it individual. Thus the universal is really multiplied and varied in individuals. For example, Plato and Socrates have in common the reality of humanity, but owing to their individual differences Plato's humanity is really not Socrates.'[168]

Ockham notes that this opinion of universals, like the one preceding, has been mistakenly ascribed to Duns Scotus. The editors of Ockham's *Ordinatio* point out that William of Alnwick

---

166. "[E]st sciendum quod scientia quaelibet sive sit realis sive rationalis est tantum de propositionibus tamquam de illis quae sciuntur, quia solae propositiones sciuntur" (*Ord.* 1.2.4 [*OTh* 2: 134.7–9]). See *Expos. in Phys.* prol. (*OPh* 4: 11.9–26).

167. *Ord.* 1.2.4 (*OTh* 2: 134.3–138.21). For the notion of supposition of terms see above, pp. 25–32.

168. Ibid. 1.2.5 (*OTh* 2: 154.2–7).

was likely guilty of this misinterpretation.[169] In the twelfth century Gilbert of Poitiers defended a similar theory of universals.[170] Like the one preceding, this opinion explains universals and their relation to individuals in terms of things (*res*) and their real distinction. It is a mitigated form of realism, however, for it introduces the notion of an individuating difference that diversifies a universal reality when existing in individuals. For this reason Ockham regards the opinion as moving in the right direction but still far from the truth. He argues that if the nature of an individual is really distinct from the individual difference that renders it individual, they are separable, at least by the divine power. There would be no contradiction in a nature's being separated from the various differences it has in individuals. For example, the humanities of Socrates and Plato, being really distinct, could exist in separation from their individuating differences. They would then be really distinct by themselves (*seipsis*) and not through individual differences really distinct from them.[171] This is the position Ockham himself will defend, but first he meets the challenge of several less realistic doctrines of universals.

The Opinion of Duns Scotus

In question 6 Ockham describes and criticizes a third, mitigated realistic conception of universals. It is realistic, for it maintains that universals really exist outside the mind in individual things; but the universal is not conceived as a thing (*res*), but as a nature that is incompletely universal in its real existence and completely universal only as it exists in the mind. In itself a nature is neither universal nor particular; it is universal when it exists in the mind and individual when

169. See the editor's note *OTh* 2: 154 n1. Alnwick's question to which the editors refer has been edited by P.T. Stella, "Illi qui student in Scoto: Guglielmo di Alnwick e la "haecceitas" scotista," *Salesianum* 30 (1968): 614–637.

170. See Jorge J.E. Gracia, *Introduction to the Problem of Individuation in the Early Middle Ages* (Munich, 1984; 2nd rev. ed. 1988), pp. 155–193; Gilson, *History of Christian Philosophy*, pp. 140–144.

171. *Ord.* 1.2.5 (*OTh* 2: 154.9–17, 159.3–6).

it exists outside the mind in things. In the latter case it is "contracted" by an individual difference that renders it individual. Unlike the former opinion, the "contracting" difference is held to be really the same as, and only formally distinct from, the nature it individuates.

Ockham identifies this as the opinion of Duns Scotus, "the Subtle Doctor, who surpassed the others in keenness of judgment."[172] To ensure that he is not misinterpreting Scotus' opinion, as others have done, he bases it mainly on quotations from Scotus' Oxford commentary on the *Sentences* (*Opus Oxoniense*), "without changing the words he uses in different places." His great respect for Scotus is clear from the fact that he alone is identified by name and his opinion on universals is given most careful attention.

Ockham correctly places the Scotist doctrine between the ultrarealism of question 5, which posits a real distinction between the universal and the individual, and the lesser realism of question 7, which (as we shall see) denies the reality of the distinction and places it on the side of the mind.

The keystone of Scotus' doctrine is rightly identified by Ockham as the notion of a common or "contractible" nature. In Scotus' view a nature is not a thing (*res*), like the universals of questions 4 and 5, but nonetheless it is a reality (*realitas*) that can exist in many individuals and that is one with a unity less than numerical unity. Since a nature is common of itself, it needs an additional factor to render it individual. For example, something must be added to the common nature of humanity to individuate it in this or that human being. Scotus argues that the additional factor is not a negation, accident, actual existence, or matter. Rather, it is an

---

172. "[I]sta opinio est, ut credo, opinio Subtilis Doctoris, qui alios in subtilitate iudicii excellebat" (ibid. 1.2.6 [*OTh* 2: 161.6–8]). The editors refer to the works of Scotus cited by Ockham (*OTh* 2: 161–173). For Scotus' doctrine of universals see Gilson, *Jean Duns Scot*, pp. 84–115, 444–477; Allan B. Wolter, "John Duns Scotus," in *Individuation in Scholasticism*, ed. Gracia, pp. 271–298, and *The Philosophical Theology of John Duns Scotus*, ed. Marilyn M. Adams (Ithaca, NY, 1990), pp. 42–53, 64–65, 73–83. See also Olivier Boulnois, "Réelles intentions: nature commune et universaux selon Duns Scot," *Revue de métaphysique et morale* 97 (1992): 3–33.

entity called an "individual difference," or "thisness" (*haecceitas*), belonging to the category of substance but not to the quidditative or essential order, for it adds no new essential note to the nature but simply renders it individual. It can individuate the nature because it itself is particular and one in number. A principle of individuation is required not only for the nature as a whole, but for each of its essential parts. Thus both the matter and form of a composite material nature require their own individual differences, as the whole composite requires its own. The individual difference is an entity in its own right: it is not matter or form or the composite of the two; rather, it is the ultimate reality (*ultima realitas*) of the being of matter, form, and the composite. The entity of the common nature and that of the individual difference are not really distinct, in the sense of being two things (*res et res*), but they are two realities or formalities, formally distinct in one and the same individual.

As the common nature of Scotus is not of itself individual, neither is it of itself completely or actually universal. If it were, it could not be numerically one and individual in reality. Again, the nature is not completely universal as it exists in a real individual, because in this condition it is not predicable of every individual possessing the nature. For this to be possible, the nature must be abstracted from individuals, released so to speak by the mind from the individual differences that contract it in reality, and given a numerical unity in the concept of the mind. The nature, so conceived, can then be predicated of each individual with the nature, saying "Socrates is a man," "Plato is a man," etc.[173]

The Scotist notion of a common nature comes under Ockham's sharp criticism. It is not a real thing (*res*) nor a mental being (*ens rationis*), but a reality situated somewhere between them. To Ockham, who always looked for explanations in philosophy as simple and uncluttered as possible, the reality of the common nature appears to be superfluous. If universals and individuals can

173. *Ord.* 1.2.6 (*OTh* 2: 161.2–167.3).

be accounted for without assuming a common nature, it should be expunged from philosophy.

Scotus contends that because a nature or essence can be defined in itself it must have some being and unity in itself; otherwise the definition would have no object. Moreover, because a nature can be individual in the real world and universal in the mind it must be really indifferent to these various modes of being. But Ockham retorts that a definition is a concept, and like all concepts it signifies individual things. Thus the definition "rational animal," like the simple concept "man," signifies all humans; it does not signify a nature common to all of them. The alleged indifference of the nature to individual and universal being is in fact a logical indifference to two ways a term can be used in a proposition. The proposition "Humanity of itself is indifferent to being universal or particular" means that the terms "universal" and "individual" can be predicated indifferently of humanity. We can say "Humanity is universal" or "Humanity is individual." In the first case the term "humanity" has simple supposition because it stands for the concept "humanity." In the second case "humanity" has personal supposition because it stands for and signifies all individual humans. Thus, with an adroit use of his theory of the supposition of terms, Ockham banishes common natures from the real world.[174]

Scotus was convinced that corresponding to abstract terms like "humanity" or "horsenesss" there were specific natures formally distinct from the individuals in which they existed. The abstract term signifies only the specific nature; the concrete term (for example, "man," "horse") adds over and above this the individual difference. Thus, the distinction between abstract and concrete terms indicates a distinction in things themselves.

Ockham, following in the spirit of Aristotle, can find no philosophical justification for this conclusion. He sees Scotus and his

174. Ibid. (*OTh* 2: 219.1–220.16). Ockham's argument against Scotus reveals Avicenna's metaphysical notion of essence as underlying the Scotist conception of a common nature. For Avicenna's doctrine and its influence on Scotus, see Etienne Gilson, *Being and Some Philosophers*, 2nd ed. (Toronto, 1952), pp. 76–87.

followers bewitched by abstract terms; but a simple analysis will dissipate their power to deceive. The only difference between abstract and concrete terms is that they have different endings, and abstract terms usually have more syllables, as is clear in the examples, "just" and "justice," or "animal" and "animality." When it is a question of absolute terms in the category of substance, the abstract and concrete forms are synonyms. "Humanity" and "man" signify the same individual men. However, this does not mean that they can be used in the same way in sentences. "Humanity" is the equivalent of the reduplicative phrase "man insofar as he is man," or "man *qua* man." Accordingly "humanity" cannot be used wherever "man" is used: we can say "Socrates is a man" but not "Socrates is humanity." This would be to say that he is man *qua* man, or man as defined. Could the abstract form of the word signify the specific nature of man as formally distinct from the individual? If so, it would be equally reasonable to say that "Socrates" and "socrateity" denote items formally distinct in him, for the first term is concrete and the second abstract.[175]

In this as in similar matters, such as the distinction between the divine essence and its attributes, Ockham observes that the problem is verbal rather than real, and logic offers the solution. "Those ignorant of logic," he complains, "uselessly fill up pages about these subjects, making a problem where there is none, and passing over the problem they should be investigating."[176]

Though Ockham admired Scotus for his logical skill, he could have had him in mind when he wrote these lines. What else is Scotus' doctrine of essence but a confusion of logic and metaphysics? Scotus liked to quote Avicenna's dictum that "Horseness is nothing else than horseness; of itself it is neither one nor many,

175. *Sum. log.* 1.7 (*OPh* 1: 23–24). This analysis of terms is meant to be Aristotelian and philosophical. According to the "truth of the theologians," however, "man" and "humanity" can stand for and signify the same thing. This is to accommodate propositions regarding the Incarnate Word; see ibid. (*OPh* 1: 25).

176. "Propter quod nescientes logicam quaternos innumeros circa talia inutiliter replent, facientes difficultatem ubi nulla est, et deserentes difficultatem quam investigare deberent" (ibid. 1.8 [*OPh* 1: 31.48–50]).

neither existing in the sensible world nor in the mind."[177] Scotus interpreted this to mean that a specific essence or nature has an entity of its own which is indifferent to being in the mind or in reality; in the former it is universal, in the latter individual. Of itself, however, it is neither of these, but the simple essence that is captured in a definition.[178]

Ockham sees this as a rank confusion between two kinds of acts clearly distinguised by the logician.[179] There is an exercised act (*actus exercitus*) expressed by the verb "is" or a similar verb. For example, when we say "Man runs," "Man disputes," we mean that he is actually exercising an act. There is also a signified act (*actus signatus*) expressed by verbs like "to be predicated of," "to be the subject of." These verbs do not indicate that something performs an act, but that a predicate is attributed to a subject. Had Scotus kept this distinction in mind he would not have misinterpreted Avicenna. When Avicenna said that horseness is nothing else than horseness, he simply meant that the definition of horse does not include the notions of one or many, existence in the mind or in reality. He did not intend the absurdity that horseness is a reality that *is* actually neither one nor many, neither existing in nature nor in the mind.

While dismissing Scotus' notion of the common nature, Ockham at the same stroke eliminates his formal distinction or nonidentity from philosophy.[180] According to Scotus the distinc-

177. Scotus, *Ord.* 2.3.1.1 (Vatican ed. 7: 402–404).

178. *Sum. log.* 1.8 (*OPh* 1: 31.51–72).

179. Ibid. 1.66 (*OPh* 1: 202–203).

180. For Scotus' doctrine of the formal distinction see Gilson, *Jean Duns Scot*, pp. 244–246, 498–500; Maurice Grajewski, *The Formal Distinction of Duns Scotus* (Washington, DC, 1944); Allan B. Wolter, "The Formal Distinction," in *John Duns Scotus, 1265–1965*, ed. John K. Ryan and Bernardine M. Bonansea (Washington, DC, 1965), and "The Realism of Scotus," *The Journal of Philosophy* 59 (1962): 725–736, both repr. in his *Philosophical Theology of John Duns Scotus*, pp. 27–41, pp. 42–53; Hester G. Gelber, "Logic and the Trinity: A Clash of Values in Scholastic Thought, 1300–1335" (PhD dissertation, University of Wisconsin, 1974), pp. 71–102. Gelber traces the development of the distinction in Scotus' works, studies its origin in the early Franciscan School, and sketches Ockham's understanding and criticism of it (pp.

tion between a nature and its individuating difference is not real, in the strong sense of a distinction between two things (*res*) one of which can exist without the other. Rather, the distinction is said to be formal, meaning a distinction between two realities or formalities, one of which is not contained in the essential definition of the other. By this criterion there is a formal distinction between the divine attributes, for one can be defined without the other. Similarly a created nature, such as humanity, is formally distinct from the individuality of a particular man because the nature can be defined without the difference.[181]

In rebuttal Ockham argues that the best way to prove a distinction between any two items is by means of the principle of noncontradiction. In the world of our experience, if it is true that A is and B is not, it follows that B is not A. Now, according to Scotus something can be truly affirmed of a nature and denied of an individual difference: a nature of itself is common to many individuals but an individual difference is not. Therefore, if these are distinct in reality, as Scotus believes, they must be really and not only formally distinct.[182]

To Scotus, this only proves that the nature and individual difference are formally distinct. Contradiction, as he sees it, does not always prove a real distinction; sometimes it reveals only a formal distinction. If the contradictories are primary and unqualified, as in the example: A is and B is not, one can conclude that the items in question are really distinct. But if a qualification is added,

---

172–185). She shows (p. 182) that Desmond P. Henry's criticism of Ockham's critique of Scotus ("Ockham and the Formal Distinction," *Franciscan Studies* 25 [1965]: 285–292) is taken out of context. For Ockham's reformulation and use of the formal distinction in the Trinity see Michael Jordan, "What's New in Ockham's Formal Distinction?" *Franciscan Studies* 45 (1985): 97–110. For Ockham's criticism of the formal distinction see Rolf Schönberger, "Realität und Differenz: Ockhams Kritik an der *distinctio formalis*," in *Die Gegenwart Ockhams*, ed. Wilhelm Vossenkuhl and Rolf Schönberger (Weinheim, 1990), pp. 97–122.

181. Scotus, *Ord.* 2.3.6 (Vatican ed. 7: 483–484, nn. 187–188), cited by Ockham, *Ord.* 1.2.6 (*OTh* 2: 162.3–163.2).

182. *Ord.* 1.2.6 (*OTh* 2: 173.11–174.23).

such as "of itself" or "formally," then contradictories prove only a formal distinction. If one can say, for example, that A is formally A, and B is not formally A, one can conclude that they are formally, and not really, distinct.[183]

Ockham replies:

> It is impossible for some items in creatures to differ formally unless they are really distinct. Consequently, if a nature is in any way distinct from that contracting difference, they must be distinct as two things (*res et res*), or as two beings of reason (*ens rationis et ens rationis*), or as a real being and a being of reason (*ens reale et ens rationis*). But the first is denied by him [i.e. Scotus] and so too the second. Therefore the third must be granted.[184]

In short, a nature must be distinguished from an individual as a concept from a reality.

Scotus' appeal to degrees of contradiction is to no avail, Ockham insists, for all contradictories are equally contradictory. It is just as contradictory, for example, to say, "to be formally A and not to be formally A" as it is to say, "to be A and not to be A." The addition of the qualifier "formally" does not weaken the contradiction. If this is denied, Ockham says, there is no way of proving a real distinction among really existing things. If Scotus should argue that a donkey is not rational and a man is rational, therefore a man and a donkey are really distinct, Ockham could equally well conclude that they are only formally distinct.[185]

---

183. Ibid. (*OTh* 2: 175.11–17).

184. "[I]mpossibile est in creaturis aliqua differre formaliter nisi distinguantur realiter; igitur si natura aliquo modo distinguitur ab illa differentia contrahente, oportet quod distinguantur sicut res et res, vel sicut ens rationis et ens rationis, vel sicut ens reale et ens rationis. Sed primum negatur ab isto, et similiter secundum, igitur oportet dari tertium" (ibid. [*OTh* 2: 173.12–17]). Cf. Scotus, *Ord.* 2.3.6 (Vatican ed. 7: 484, n. 188). Ockham limits his argument to creatures because he holds the validity of the formal distinction in the Trinity.

185. *Ord.* 1.2.6 (*OTh* 2: 174.8–23); cf. ibid. 1.2.1 (*OTh* 2: 14.8–17.7). See Marilyn M. Adams, "Ockham on Identity and Distinction," *Franciscan Studies* 36 (1976): 5–74.

Thus Ockham's univocal interpretation of the principle of noncontradiction compels him to eliminate the formal distinction from philosophy. There remain only the real distinction between things, the mental distinction between beings of reason, and an unnamed distinction between a real being and a being of reason. Ockham accepts the formal distinction only in theology, though it leads to a logical fallacy. The Christian faith teaches that in the Trinity there are three really distinct Persons who are identical with the one divine essence. Using the principle of noncontradiction, we should say:

> The divine essence, one in number, is the Son;
> The Father is not the Son;
> Therefore the Father is not the divine essence.

The Christian faith, however, assures us that this is incorrect: the Father, like the Son, is identical with the one divine essence. But Ockham argues that this is a unique case beyond our comprehension, to be admitted only because sacred scripture compels us to. In the created world no one thing is several things and each of them.[186]

Scotus tried to throw some light on the mystery of the Trinity by introducing a formal distinction between the Persons and the divine essence: though really identical with the divine essence, he contended, the Persons are formally nonidentical with it.[187] Ockham agrees with Scotus for linguistic reasons: There must be some distinction in reality (*ex natura rei*) between the Persons and the divine essence, he reasons, because these nouns do not signify

---

186. "Haec responsio [scil. Scoti] non sufficit, quia sicut est singulare in Deo quod tres res sunt una res numero, et ideo illa res una numero est quaelibet illarum trium rerum, et tamen una illarum trium rerum non est reliqua, ita est singulare et excedens omnem intellectum quod non sequitur: essentia una numero est Filius, Pater non est Filius, igitur Pater non est essentia. Et ideo illud singulare non debet poni nisi ubi auctoritas Sacrae Scripturae compellit. Et ideo talis consequentia nunquam debet negari in creaturis, quia ibi nulla auctoritas Sacrae Scripturae compellit, cum in creaturis nulla una res sunt plures res et quaelibet earum" (*Ord.* 1.2.6 [*OTh* 2: 175.1–10]).

187. Scotus, *Ord.* 1.2.2.4 (Vatican ed. 2: 349–361).

the same thing in the same way, and consequently they are not synonyms. And since the distinction between them cannot be real, in the strong sense of being two things (*res*), Scotus is very probably correct in calling their distinction or nonidentity real in the lesser sense of formal. However, it cannot be formal in the Scotist sense of a distinction between several formalities in a thing, for these have already been eliminated from things. It remains that the formal distinction, thus reinterpreted, should be posited in God only because faith compels us to do so. It cannot be found in creatures, in whom there is never three really distinct realities that are really one.[188]

With the elimination from his metaphysics of formalities as distinct from things (*res*), Ockham was unable to develop a theology of the Trinity with the logical consistency and depth of Scotism. Verbally he agreed with Scotus that the Persons are formally distinct from the divine essence, but when this is rightly understood, he adds, it simply means "that the [divine] essence is three Persons and that a Person is not three Persons"; moreover, "that the [divine] essence is Sonship, and Fatherhood is not Sonship, and nevertheless the [divine] essence is Fatherhood."[189] In other words the formal distinction, "which seems to be contrary to reason," expresses a mystery held on faith.

In question 7 Ockham opposes three doctrines ascribing the least possible reality to universals. They are alike in claiming that a universal and individual (say, humanity and Socrates) are really identical, with only a mental distinction between them. In this respect they differ from the preceding opinions on universals, all of which posit some distinction in reality between the universal and the individual. Nevertheless they agree that universals are in some way extramental and really exist in individuals.[190] Ockham here expunges the last trace of realism from the doctrine of universals, preparing the way for his own nominalist or conceptualist position, that universals exist in the mind and in no way in reality.

188. *Ord.* 1.2.11 (*OTh* 2: 364–376).
189. *Sum. log.* 2.2 (*OPh* 1: 254.130–138); *Ord.* 1.2.1 (*OTh* 2: 17.9–19.2).
190. *Ord.* 1.2.7 (*OTh* 2: 229.1–6).

Following the plan of his exposition of doctrines of universals, Ockham places the opinions of question 7 in an order of decreasing realism, with the last (Henry of Harclay's) closest to his own.

The first opinion holds that both generic and specific forms subsist in individuals but in different ways. A generic form, like animality, in itself has absolutely no real unity but only a unity due to the mind. It exists in individuals only when divided by formal differences, like rational and irrational. However, an ultimate specific form, like humanity, has a real and natural unity just in itself, and as such it is universal, but it is individual when particularized in a given thing.[191]

The author of this opinion is unknown.[192] It is not Aquinas, for he denies that either a generic or specific form, considered just in itself, has any unity. It can be one as it exists in the mind as a universal, and it can be many as it exists in reality; but unity and plurality belong to an essence, not in itself, but only as it exists. Of itself a nature or essence has no being or unity.[193]

Whoever the author of the opinion under consideration may have been, it does not escape Ockham's critical analysis. He queries the nature of the distinction between a specific form and its status as an individual. If they do not differ in any way, the form by itself is no more universal than the form in its individual state. If they do differ in some way, they do so either in reality (*secundum rem*) or according to reason (*secundum rationem*). The first alternative has been disproved in questions 4–6. The second is also

191. *Ord.* 1.2.7 (*OTh* 2: 226.5–227.7).
192. The editors suggest that this is the doctrine of Aquinas and Hervaeus Natalis, while conceding that it is not found literally in their works; see *OTh* 2: 226 n1. They refer to the pseudo-Thomistic treatise *De universalibus* as a possible source of this opinion. The treatise is not authentic, although it borrows from Aquinas' *De ente et essentia*, and is published among the works in the Vivès edition (Paris, 1875), 28: 177–178.
193. *De ente et essentia* 3 (Leonine ed. 43: 374–375). See Joseph Owens, "Common Nature: a Point of Comparison between Thomistic and Scotistic Metaphysics," *Mediaeval Studies* 19 (1957): 5–6, and "Unity and Essence in St. Thomas Aquinas," *Mediaeval Studies* 23 (1961): 240–259.

ruled out, because a distinction of reason in Ockham's view is present only between beings of reason (*entia rationis*), for example between concepts.[194] In an earlier question he discussed this type of distinction at length and concluded that it has no bearing on a real thing: no thing is the same as, or distinct from, itself because of a distinction made by the mind.[195] This implies that there is no distinction of reason with a foundation in any one thing – a point to which we shall have occasion to return. The only other possible distinction between a form and an individual is that between a concept and a real thing. In this case the form of a species, such as humanity, would have no real unity at all, but only the unity of a concept, and this cannot be said to exist in real individuals. As we shall see, this is Ockham's own answer to the question of universals.

The Opinion of Thomas Aquinas

The second opinion on universals seems to be that of Aquinas or one of his followers. Ockham describes it thus:

> Others hold that a thing (*res*) is individual as it actually exists, and the same thing is universal as it exists in the mind. Thus the same thing is universal with respect to one being (*esse*) or according to one consideration, and individual with respect to another being (*esse*) or according to another consideration.[196]

This appears to be gleaned from a page of Aquinas' *De ente et essentia*,[197] though Ockham couches the doctrine of universals in his own language of things (*res*) instead of Thomas' language of essences or natures. According to Aquinas, a nature or essence, con-

194. *Ord.* 1.2.7 (*OTh* 2: 240.10–16).
195. Ibid. 1.2.3 (*OTh* 2: 75.5–11); *Quodl.* 3.2 (*OTh* 9: 208–211).
196. "Alii autem ponunt quod res secundum esse suum in effectu est singularis, et eadem res secundum esse suum in intellectu est universalis, ita quod eadem res secundum unum esse vel secundum unam considerationem est universalis, et secundum aliud esse vel secundum aliam considerationem est singularis" (ibid. 1.2.7 [*OTh* 2: 227.9–13]).
197. *De ente et essentia* 3 (Leonine ed. 43: 374.26–90), trans. Armand Maurer, as *On Being and Essence*, 2nd ed. (Toronto, 1983), pp. 46.2–48.6.

sidered just in itself, has no being or unity; but it can acquire a twofold being (*esse*) when considered in relation to individual things and to the mind. In individuals the nature has a multiple being (*multiplex esse*) corresponding to the diversity of individuals; as it exists in the mind the nature takes on the character of a universal, being the likeness of many things. A nature is completely and actually universal only through an act of the mind abstracting the nature from the individuals in which it exists. In his *Summa contra Gentiles* Aquinas writes:

> What is common to many is not anything over and above the many except through the mind alone. For example, animal is not something besides Socrates and Plato and other animals except through the mind's apprehending the form of animal stripped of all its individuating and specifying characteristics.[198]

Ockham's criticism of this opinion does not come to grips with its metaphysical notions of a nature and its possible ways of existing. To him, a nature's acquiring the being of a universal only means its receiving a new name because it is thought of in a new way. He argues that when a thing is given another name because of something extrinsic to it, such as a new existence in thought, everything to which that extrinsic factor applies can receive the name. It follows that if a thing that is really individual is universal through the existence it has in thought, we come to the absurd conclusion that every object of the mind can be universal simply by being thought. Thus Socrates, by existing in thought, can be universal and common to Plato. So too, the divine essence can be universal through its existing in thought, though it is at the peak of singularity.[199]

---

198. "Quod est commune multis non est aliquid praeter multa nisi sola ratione, sicut animal non est aliud praeter Socratem et Platonem et alia animalia nisi intellectu, qui apprehendit formam animalis exspoliatam ab omnibus individuantibus et specificantibus" (*SCG* 1.26 §5 [Leonine ed. 13: 81]).

199. *Ord.* 1.2.7 (*OTh* 2: 241.2–13).

The conclusion is confirmed by the fact that what is contradictory to something's nature cannot belong to it through an extrinsic factor. Now, it is contradictory to the nature of one thing to be common to another. Hence community cannot belong to a thing through an added extrinsic factor such as existence in thought. It follows that, whether or not an individual thing is thought, it could not be common or universal by receiving a certain mode of existing.[200]

These arguments throw significant light on Ockham's notion of the individual and its relation to existence or being. His reasoning is dominated by the notion of a thing (*res*) as individual of itself and by its essence. A thing is so radically individual in his view that it has nothing in common with any other thing. We have yet to examine Ockham's solution of the problem of universals, but we can already surmise that it will not admit of real community or universality. We are forewarned that for him existence or modes of existence will not play a role in solving the problem, as they do for Aquinas. In that doctrine the essence of a creature is really distinct, or other than, its act of existing (*actus essendi*). An essence of itself has no reality: it is not a thing, but the possibility of a thing existing when actualized by an act of existing. It can be actualized in reality, and then the essence can exist in one or more individuals. The same essence can exist in the mind, abstracted from individuals, and then it is a universal, being the likeness of many individuals and able to be predicated alike of all of them. Thus in Aquinas' view the problem of individuality and universality is insoluble without reference to the act of existing or being (*esse*).[201]

---

200. Ibid. (*OTh* 2: 241.14–19).

201. For Aquinas' notion of being see Etienne Gilson, *Le thomisme*, 6th ed. (Paris, 1965), pp. 169–189 (5th ed. trans. L.K. Shook as *The Christian Philosophy of St. Thomas Aquinas* [New York, 1956], pp. 29–45); Owens, "Common Nature: A Point of Comparison," *Mediaeval Studies* 19 (1957): 1–14, and "Diversity and Community of Being in St. Thomas Aquinas," *Mediaeval Studies* 22 (1960): 257–302.

The Thomistic doctrine does not come within Ockham's purview, being alien to his basic insight into being as an individual thing. For a while he entertained the notion of a *fictum*, whose being was not real but phenomenal or "objective"; but out of regard for the principle of parsimony he seems to have eventually abandoned the notion.[202] With utter simplicity he built his philosophy around the fundamental notion of being as a real individual (*res*). For Aquinas, the distinction between an individual and a universal demands a real otherness of a communicable essence and a being (*esse*) proper to the individual.[203]

But Ockham argues that this real distinction is neither required nor possible to account for universals. If essence and being were really distinct, they would be two things (*res*), and God could preserve one without the other and an essence could exist without existence – an obvious absurdity! For Ockham, there is only a verbal distinction between the terms *res* and *esse*, both signifying the same thing, the former as a noun and the latter as a verb.[204] In any case, existence could not account for an individual if it comes to an essence from without, as Aquinas thought, for individuality is a property immediately belonging to a thing, and not a factor received from without.

The Opinion of Henry of Harclay

The third and least realist opinion of universals described by Ockham is that of Henry of Harclay, who has recently received more attention as an original thinker and a precursor of Ockham. Professor of theology at Oxford and Chancellor of the University in 1312, he became Bishop of Lincoln and died in 1317.[205]

202. See below, pp. 508–509.

203. "Ad hoc enim quod sit universale et particulare, exigitur aliqua diversitas realis, ut supra dictum est, quidditatis communicabilis, et esse quod proprium est" (*In Sent.* 1.13.1.3, sol. [ed. Mandonnet-Moos 1: 307]).

204. *Sum. log.* 3–2.27 (*OPh* 1: 553–555). See above, p. 59.

205. See *Cambridge History of Later Medieval Philosophy*, ed. Kretzmann et al., pp. 423–435, 575–578, 583–584; Mark G. Henninger, "Henry of Harclay," in *Individuation in Scholasticism*, ed. Gracia, pp. 333–346.

Like Ockham, Harclay holds that the individual and universal are really one and the same thing and distinguisable only by the mind. He parts company with Ockham, however, in following the common opinion that universals in some way exist in individual things. This places him, however narrowly, on the side of realism, thus meriting Ockham's criticism.

Ockham places Henry among the "moderns" who maintain that one and the same thing is either individual or universal depending on the way the mind conceives it. In a passage from Harclay's *Disputed Questions* cited by Ockham, he contends that an individual can be conceived either distinctly or confusedly, resulting in two different concepts of it. One is a distinct notion representing the individual alone; the other is a vague notion equally representing more than one individual. For instance, we can form a distinct concept of Socrates that applies only to him and a confused concept of man that applies to both Socrates and Plato.[206]

One of the first disciples of Scotus, Harclay initially adopted the Scotist notion of a common nature as the foundation of a universal concept. In his later *Disputed Questions* he abandoned the idea that individuals have natures or essences in common and taught that the only basis of universal concepts is the similarity among things. For example, because two white things are similar the mind can form a common concept that represents both.

Harclay was on the way to Ockhamism in his conviction that everything outside the mind is individual by itself, but Ockham criticizes him for failing to see all the implications of this notion of an individual.[207] Had he done so, he would not have written: "Though a thing in itself is individual, *it is universal* insofar as it

206. *Ord.* 1.2.7 (*OTh* 2: 227.15–228.20). Harclay's question on universals has been edited by Gál, "Henricus de Harclay: Quaestio de significato conceptus universalis," *Franciscan Studies* 31 (1971): 178–234.

207. "[D]ico quod omnis res posita extra animam est singularis eo ipso" (Henry of Harclay, ibid. [ed. Gál p. 216, n. 79]); cited by Ockham, *Ord.* 1.2.7 (*OTh* 2: 228.4–5).

is passively represented, which is nothing else than that it is confusedly and indistinctly knowable."[208]

Ockham dismisses this as absolutely false and unintelligible. Let us suppose that A indistinctly conceived is universal. It follows that A indistinctly conceived is common to B. We can say, then, that B is A indistinctly conceived; for instance, that Socrates indistinctly conceived is Plato, or that God indistinctly conceived is a creature.[209]

In calling an individual in a sense universal, Ockham sees Harclay making the error of attributing contradictories to one and the same thing. To be predicable of many subjects, and not to be predicable of many subjects, are contradictory properties, the first belonging to a universal and the second to an individual, and hence they cannot without contradiction be ascribed to one and the same thing.[210]

Ockham's Own Opinion

Having criticized in questions 4–7 doctrines of universals in decreasing degrees of realism, in question 8 Ockham gives his own nonrealist position on the subject. He is fully aware of the radical step he is taking in leaving the common opinion in all its varieties and marking out his own stand on universals:

> In coming to a conclusion on this question, all those I have seen agree in saying that the nature that is somehow universal (at least in potency and incompletely) is really in the individual, although some say it is distinguished really from the individual, some only formally, some that it is in no way distinguished on the side of

208. "[L]icet [res] in se sit singularis, quantum ad repraesentationem passivam est universalis. Quod non est aliud nisi quod confuse et [in]distincte est cognoscibilis" (Henry of Harclay, ibid. [ed. Gál p. 218, n. 83]); I have added [res] and [in].

209. *Ord.* 1.2.7 (*OTh* 2: 241.21–242.6). Ockham also criticizes Harclay for holding that a universal concept always results from indistinct knowledge. On the contrary, Ockham argues that in the case of a simple object a universal concept can result from distinct knowledge: "No incomposite reality can be confusedly understood if it is understood, and yet there is truly a universal respecting incomposite items" (ibid. [*OTh* 250.10–12]).

210. *Ord.* 1.2.7 (*OTh* 2: 236.9–17).

the nature of the thing, but only according to reason or through the consideration of the intellect.[211]

Contrary to the consensus of his predecessors, Ockham argues that in no sense is a universal in an individual. By its nature a universal is a sign of many things, and a sign does not exist in the thing it signifies. We cannot say that the word "man" is in Socrates or Plato or any other human being. It is just as absurd to say that a universal concept is in the things it signifies and stands for in discourse. Neither is a universal a part of an individual, whether the universal is a written or spoken word or a concept.[212]

Given that a universal is a sign of many things and predicable of them in propositions, the question remains: Is it something real, and if so, what reality does it have?

In his *Ordinatio* Ockham presents several nonrealist opinions regarding universals, one of which he rejects out of hand and the others he considers more or less defensible and probable, without choosing any one as truer than the others. Any one of them, however, he regards as preferable to the opinions disproved in the previous questions.

The opinion rejected by Ockham claims that universals are not natural but conventional signs, like a word (*vox*). They are said to be universal not by nature but by "voluntary institution," so that their meaning could be changed or lost "at the pleasure of those who use the language." A natural sign, by contrast, does not depend on the will for its meaning, and its meaning does not change at anyone's

211. "In conclusione istius quaestionis omnes quos vidi concordant, dicentes quod natura, quae est aliquo modo universalis, saltem in potentia et incomplete, est realiter in individuo, quamvis aliqui dicant quod distinguitur realiter, aliqui quod tantum formaliter, aliqui quod nullo modo ex natura rei sed secundum rationem tantum vel per considerationem intellectus" (ibid. [*OTh* 2: 225.17–226.3]). I have used the Spade translation.

212. "Ideo dico quod universale non est in re ipsa cui est universale nec realiter nec subiective, non plus quam haec vox 'homo,' quae est una vera qualitas, est in Sorte vel in illo quod significat. Nec universale est pars singularis respectu cuius est universale, non plus quam vox est pars sui significati" (ibid. [*OTh* 2: 252.1–5]).

good pleasure.[213] According to John of Salisbury, Roscelin in the eleventh century proposed a similar nominalist version of universals, holding that they are nothing but vocal utterances (*voces*).[214]

Ockham dismisses this conception of universals with the remark that if it were true, genera and species would not be natural, but only signs whose meaning would be established by convention.[215] He does not deny that spoken and written words are universals; they are indeed signs of many things and predicable of them. What he wants to stress is the essential difference between the universality of words and concepts. Concepts, both individual and universal, are natural and primary signs of things; words, both spoken and written, are conventional signs, and their signification is subordinate to that of concepts.[216]

Among the opinions that universals are natural mental signs of many things, Ockham lists four as being probable: (1) The universal is a mental concept identical with the act of understanding (*intellectio*). (2) It is a likeness (*species*) in the mind preceding the act of knowing and equally representing many individuals. (3) It is a mental likeness of many things, or mental *verbum*, following the act of knowing. (4) It is not a real mental being but an "objective" being or *fictum*, formed in the mind as a likeness of a real or imaginary being.[217]

At this point Ockham does not definitely choose any one of these theories as his own. He finds reasons for and against them, without preferring one of them to the others. In Chapter 10, when treating of Ockham's doctrine of knowledge, we shall return to his

---

213. *Ord.* 1.2.8 (*OTh* 2: 271.2–7). On natural and conventional signs see *Sum. log.* 1.1 (*OPh* 1: 7.3–9.65).

214. John of Salisbury, *Metalogicon* 2.17, ed. Clemens C.I. Webb (Oxford, 1929), p. 92. Abelard also held that universals are names (*sermones, vocabula*), but names with meaning. In fact, the doctrine was well known in the eleventh century, as the *Dialectica* of Garlandus Compotista witnesses; see Tweedale, *Abailard on Universals*, pp. 135–136.

215. *Ord.* 1.2.8 (*OTh* 2: 271.9–12).

216. *Sum. log.* 1.1 (*OPh* 1: 7–9). See above, pp. 15–17.

217. *Ord.* 1.2.8 (*OTh* 2: 267.2–292.2).

We are now in a position to appreciate better the nature and central position of the individual in Ockham's philosophy.[219] From the logician's point of view, an individual differs from a universal in that the latter is a term predicable of many subjects while the former (at least according to Porphyry) is a term predicable of only one.[220] Again, an individual term is the name of only one thing. Thus defined, an individual term includes proper names and demonstrative pronouns when they denote an extramental thing; for example, when we say "This is a man." Also included are demonstrative pronouns joined to a general term, such as "this animal" or "this stone."[221]

From an ontological perspective there are two meanings of an individual or singular thing. In one sense it means whatever is one and not many. So defined, even a universal word or concept is an individual; it is universal insofar as it is the sign of many things and is predicable of them. A spoken or written word is an individual sound or character, used as a conventional sign of many things. A mental concept is also an individual: its universality is its function of being a natural sign of many things. In another sense an individual is something that is one in number and not many, and it is not its nature to be the sign of many things. In this sense

218. See below, pp. 496–510.

219. This is the theme of Pierre Alféri's excellent book, *Guillaume d'Ockham: Le singulier* (Paris, 1989), especially pp. 15–106. For a philosophical and historical account of the notion of an individual see Jorge J.E. Gracia, *Introduction to the Problem of Individuation,* and his *Individuality: An Essay on the Foundations of Metaphysics* (New York, 1988); see also Maurer, "William of Ockham," in *Individuation in Scholasticism,* ed. Gracia, pp. 387–389.

220. *Expos. in Praedicab.* 1 (*OPh* 2: 23.2–7).

221. *Sum. log.* 1.19 (*OPh* 1: 66.16–30); *Quodl.* 5.12 (*OTh* 9: 529.20–26).

no universal is individual, for it is the nature of a universal to nify many things and to be predicable of them.[222]

Ontologically, then, every universal is a particular thing: *quodlibet universale est una res singularis*. Functionally, universals are names, either spoken, written, or mental. Universals existing in the mind are mental names (*nomina mentalia*).[223] From the viewpont of distinguishing one individual from another, it can be said that an individual "consists of different properties which, taken all together at the same time, cannot be found in any other."[224]

Though Ockham calls a universal a singular thing, the adjective "singular" is redundant, for in his view every thing (*res*) is singular or individual. What is more, it is individual of itself (*de se haec*) and not through an individuating principle. Scotus thought that to be individual of itself was a prerogative of the divine nature; a created nature is "this" (*haec*) through an added haecceity.[225] Ockham extends the notion of a nature's being *de se haec* to the created order.

Individuals are also primarily diverse (*primo diversa*); that is to say, "There is nothing in [any two individuals] that is one and the same: whatever is in one simply and absolutely of itself is not something that exists in another." The only exception is the presence of numerically the same matter in two things, one of which begets the other.[226] We would not wish for a stronger statement of the radical incommunicability of individuals.[227] There

222. *Sum. log.* 1.14 and 1.19 (*OPh* 1: 48.13–52 and 1: 65–67).

223. Ibid. 1.3 (*OPh* 1: 11.27–12.33).

224. *Expos. in Praedicab.* 2 (*OPh* 2: 51.5–7).

225. Scotus, *Ord.* 1.1.1.2 (Vatican ed. 2: 30–31); *Metaph.* 7.13 (Vivès ed. 7: 402–403, n. 1).

226. "[D]ico quod aliqua esse 'primo diversa' potest intelligi dupliciter: vel quia nihil est unum et idem in utroque, sed quidquid est in uno simpliciter et absolute de se non est aliquid quod est in alio; et isto modo concedo quod omnia individua sunt se ipsis primo diversa, nisi forte aliter sit de individuis ex quorum uno generatur aliud propter identitatem numeralem materiae in utroque" (*Ord.* 1.2.6 [*OTh* 2: 212.18–23]).

227. Because individuals are what they are, they are not only incommunicable but also separable. John F. Boler ("Ockham's Cleaver," *Franciscan Studies* 45 (1985): 119–120) writes of a "principle of separability," as a basic intuition of

is nothing in the individual that is not individual, including its essence. There is no communication in essence between individuals: each is an essence in its own right.

An individual is so basically one by itself it cannot be the foundation of a conceptual distinction. There is a real distinction between real beings, and, if they are composed, between their parts. For example, two humans are really distinct, and so too are their forms and matters. The qualities of whiteness and sweetness in milk are also really distinct individual accidents. A distinction of reason is one made by the mind between several names or concepts. If they are concepts of the same thing, it cannot be said that the thing differs from itself because of the diversity of concepts we form of it. A distinction of reason has to do with descriptions and not with the individual described. However, in an improper sense something may be said to be distinguished conceptually (*ratione*) if distinct concepts or descriptions apply to it, but this does not imply a distinction in the thing itself. We shall see that this is the case with God and his attributes. It should now be clear that it is equally true of every individual and its properties.[228]

Does the notion of an individual apply only to real, actual beings such as a material substance, its matter and form and qualities? In Ockham's language these have "subjective" being. Initially he recognized a mode of unreal, mind-dependent being, called "objective" because its whole being is to be an object of thought.[229] Examples are the divine ideas, the object of an intuition of a nonexistent, and fictions (*ficta*) like the notion of a goat-stag or chimera. Later Ockham abandoned the idea of an objective

---

Ockham, according to which "only such individuals for which it is possible (at least by the divine power) to exist separately from other individual things are really distinct from one another and therefore can properly be said to exist." But for Ockham there are no other individuals than those that can exist separately, and they can exist separately precisely because of their nature as individuals. Ockham's basic intuition would seem to be the individual and not its separability.

228. *Ord.* 1.2.3 (*OTh* 2: 75.4–77.6); *Quodl.* 3.2 (*OTh* 9: 209.30–210.56). See below, pp. 197–199.

229. For subjective and objective being see below, p. 504.

being and substituted for it the notion of nothing (*nihil*). Then a divine idea and the object of an intuition of a nonexistent were conceived as a nothing (*unum nihil*). All these possible items, and even impossible ones, would seem to qualify as individuals.[230]

The emphasis on the individual in Ockhamism gives us a good point of comparison between it and its two chief scholastic rivals: Thomism and Scotism. The Ockhamist metaphysics reduces actual being to individual things (*res*), either real or of the mind's own making. Scotism is centered around the notion of the common nature. The focal point of Thomism is the act of existing (*esse*). Ockham's originality is shown in his choice of the individual as the capstone of his philosophy and theology.

7 Definition

Ockham's views on definition are consistent with his doctrine of universals. Realists such as Walter Burley defined definition as a phrase expressing the essence of a thing, understanding by "essence" something existing outside the mind.[231] We have seen Ockham oppose Burley's notion of essence, arguing that essences or quiddities are not extramental realities but only terms. As a consequence it is hardly surprising to see Ockham offer a non-realist account of definition.

---

230. On the testimony of Ockham's pupil, Adam of Wodeham, Ockham never referred to objectively existent particulars as *ficta*. This term is said to be universal in its signification and predication. For Wodeham's text see Marilyn Adams, "Ockham's Nominalism and Unreal Entities," *Philosophical Review* 86 (1977): 144–176, at p. 151 n24. Adams herself claims that Ockham refused to apply the objective-existence theory to thoughts and awarenesses of particulars (ibid., p. 176). It should be noted, however, that in *Quodl.* 4.35 (*OTh* 9: 473), when arguing against the fictum theory, he implies their singularity and even speaks of "individual *ficta.*" For Ockham's description of possibles as so many nothings see Arthur McGrade, "Plenty of Nothing: Ockham's Commitment to Real Possibles," *Franciscan Studies* 45 (1985): 145–156. Note, however, that Ockham does not admit any "real possibles." Whatever is real is a positive thing (*res*).

231. "[D]iffinitio est oratio indicans quidditatem rei" ("Walter Burley's Text, *De Diffinitione*," ed. Herman Shapiro and Frederick Scott, *Mediaeval Studies* 27 [1965]: 337–340, at p. 339). See above, pp. 64–65.

Definition and description are different from other terms, Ockham says, in that they do not apply to one item alone but to several taken together. This can be illlustrated by the two basic kinds of definition: real and nominal. These can be defined respectively as a definition expressing what a thing is (*quid rei*) and a definition expressing what a name is (*quid nominis*). In the strict sense a definition *quid rei* is a brief phrase denoting the whole essence of a thing, without mentioning anything extrinsic to the thing defined.[232] Sometimes the phrase contains inflected cases expressing the essential parts of a thing, as when a person is defined as "a substance composed of a body and an intellectual soul." This is called a natural definition because it states essentii parts of a human being. At other times the definition contains nothing in an inflected case but directly expresses the genus and difference or differences of the item defined, as in the definition of a person as "a rational animal" or "a living, sensory, rational substance." This is a metaphysical definition of the person. Some would add a third, logical, definition, but Ockham regards this as rather foolish, for the logician does not treat of human beings, nor does he have to define them; the logician's task is to teach others how to do this. It is just as inane to speak of a natural and metaphysical person. There is a natural and metaphysical consideration of the person, but it is the same person who is under scrutiny in the two cases.[233]

A nominal definition is defined as a phrase stating explicitly what is implied in a term; more simply it tells us the meaning of the

232. "Aliter accipitur hoc nomen 'definitio' stricte, et sic est sermo compendiosus, exprimens totam naturam rei, nec aliquid extrinsecum rei definitae declarans" (*Sum. log.* 1.26 [*OPh* 1: 85.18–20]). "[D]efinitio proprie dicta [quid rei] est oratio longa composita ex genere proprio et differentiis essentialibus significantibus partes essentiales definiti" (*Quodl.* 5.19 [*OTh* 9: 554.13–15]).

233. *Sum. log.* 1.26 (*OPh* 1: 85.21–87.79). In his logic written against Ockham, Pseudo-Richard of Campsall defends a realist doctrine of definition, adding that the logician can define man as a term predicated essentially of many men different in number. He also defends the notions of a logical, natural, and metaphysical man; see *Logica Campsale Anglicj* 24 (ed. Synan 2: 166–174).

term.[234] If someone wants to tell another what the concrete term
"white" (*album*) means, he can say that it means "something with
whiteness." This kind of definition properly applies to connotative
and relative terms, which signify one thing directly and another thing
obliquely, as in the above example of the definition of "white." Other
examples are "hot," "father," and "son." The nominal definition of
"father" is "a man having a son," denoting a man and connoting his
son. On the contrary, a definition *quid rei* applies only to absolute
names signifying composites of matter and form, such as "man," or
"lion," or a spiritual substance like "angel."[235] Another difference
between a definition *quid rei* and a definition *quid nominis* is that the
first applies only to possible things whereas the second also applies to
those impossible such as "vacuum," "nonbeing," and "chimera." There
is nothing real corresponding to these names, but only phrases having
the same meaning as the names.

Can something real be defined, and if so, what is this reality?
As we have seen earlier in the chapter, Ockham does not believe
there are real essences or natures in things that could be the object
of definitions. The only reality that could be defined is an extramental individual. Thus the definition of man as a living, sensory,
rational substance does not have for its object an essence in man,
but only all individual human beings. In other words, what is
defined is exactly the same as what is signified by the term defined.
The only other object of a definition is a term convertible with
the definition, and of which the definition can be predicated. In
this case what is defined is a concept or word, for they alone can
be predicated.

Besides real and nominal definitions there is a definition "by
addition" (*per additamentum*). This is formed from several terms,
one denoting the thing defined and the others something not

---

234. "Definitio autem exprimens quid nominis est oratio explicite declarans quid per unam dictionem importatur" (*Sum. log.* 1.26 [*OPh* 1: 88.113–
114]); cf. *Quodl.* 5.19 (*OTh* 9: 554.16–17).
235. *Quodl.* 5.19 (*OTh* 9: 554.22–555.48).

belonging to its essence. As an example, Ockham gives the nominal definition of the soul as the act of a physical, organized body, implying that the term "soul" signifies the soul and the body as something added and nonessential to it.

Unlike a definition, a description in the broad sense is a brief phrase containing accidental features of what is described but nothing essential to it. An example is the description of a person as "a biped, having two hands." A descriptive definition combines both substantial and accidental features of the thing described; for example, the description of a person as "a rational animal, walking upright and having broad nails."[236]

8 Propositions

Up to the present we have been examining Ockham's doctrine of terms in all its complexity. It is time to turn to his views on propositions, which are made up of terms and express a complete thought with its truth or falsity. Terms have meaning by themselves, but they are destined to be parts of propositions and it is only then that they enter fully into human discourse.

In general a proposition can be defined as a composite discourse (*oratio*) without essential unity but an aggregate made up of a subject, predicate, and a copula as it were uniting the subject to the predicate.[237] By the subject of a proposition is meant the part of the proposition preceding the copula, of which something is predicated. The predicate is the part following the copula, and the copula is the verb connecting the predicate with the sub-

---

236. *Sum. log.* 1.27–28 (*OPh* 1: 89–91).
237. "Intelligendum quod propositio est quoddam compositum non tamquam per se unum sed tamquam aggregatum ex subiecto et praedicato et copula quae quasi unit subiectum cum praedicato" (*Expos. in Periherm.* 1.2 (*OPh* 2: 389. 17–19). For the logic of propositions see Adams, *William Ockham* 1: 383–435; Alfred Freddoso's introduction to *Ockham's Theory of Propositions: Part II of the 'Summa logicae,'* trans. Freddoso and Henry Schuurman (Notre Dame, IN, 1980), pp. 1–76; Gabriel Nuchelmans, "The Semantics of Propositions," in *Cambridge History of Later Medieval Philosophy*, ed. Kretzmann et al., pp. 197–210.

ject.[238] From the point of view of its purpose, the proposition is a discourse signifying a truth or falsity.[239]

As we have already seen that terms are either spoken, written, or conceived, it will come as no surprise to find that propositions are also divided into oral, written, and mental. Oral propositions are composed of spoken terms, written propositions of written terms, and mental propositions of concepts. All are composed of signs and not precisely of things (*res*), as Walter Burley thought.[240] The Pseudo-Campsall, who was a realist like Burley, proposed that there is a real proposition (*propositio in re*) to which oral and mental propositions must be in agreement in order to be true. The real proposition remains unknown in itself and reveals itself only in the equivalent oral proposition.[241]

Nothing could be further from Ockham's mind than such a realist understanding of propositions. If we accept the theory that a concept is an act of knowing (the "intellectio" theory that Ockham seems to have ultimately favored), a mental proposition is composed of several acts of understanding and in no way composed of things: if we affirm or deny that Socrates is Plato, the proposition is not composed of the two men but of our thoughts about them. Another possibility is that the proposition is *one* act of understanding equivalent to the distinct understandings of Socrates, Plato and the copula. If the proposition is negative it would include the notion of "negation." In the hypothesis that the mental proposition is one mental act virtually containing all its parts, it is not properly composite or complex but a single act of understanding. When the mind reflects on the act which is the mental propo-

238. *Sum. log.* 1.30–31 (*OPh* 1: 92–94).

239. *Quodl.* 3.13 (*OTh* 9: 251.10–11). A proposition is also an enunciation (*enunciatio*), though they have different nominal definitions. An enunciation is a group of terms comprising a verb and a noun or its equivalent and expressing a truth or error. On enunciations see *Expos. in Periherm.* 1.4 (*OPh* 2: 391–396).

240. *Expos. in Periherm.* 1.prooem. (*OPh* 2: 354.68); for Burley see the editor's note *OPh* 2: 354 n3.

241. Pseudo-Richard of Campsall, *Logica Campsale Anglicj* 13.11 (ed. Synan 2: 117).

sition, there are simultaneously two mental acts: one is the proposition and the other is the awareness of the proposition.[242]

Another possible interpretation of the proposition is based on the theory that an intention or concept is not an act of knowing existing subjectively in the mind but a mental construct called a *fictum* or *idola*. A proposition could be formed of such constructs just as it can be composed of acts of understanding, and like them it could be known reflexively by the mind. However, it seems to Ockham that a proposition is more suitably and economically taken to be a composite of acts of understanding or one single such act than to think of it as composed of *idolae* or *ficta*.[243]

Both the act of forming a proposition and the act of knowing it are acts of apprehension or knowledge. The act of assenting to, or dissenting from a proposition must not be confused with either of these. Assent or dissent (or by another word, judgment) is clearly a distinct act, for it is possible to form a proposition and know it without giving one's assent or dissent to it, in which case it is a neutral proposition.[244]

There are many kinds and divisions of propositions, the most basic division being that between single and compound propositions (which Ockham, following earlier medieval logicians, calls categorical and hypothetical). A categorical or single proposition has a subject, predicate, and copula uniting the two, and it does

242. *Expos. in Periherm.* 1.prooem. (*OPh* 2: 355–358).
243. Ibid. (*OPh* 2: 359–361). For the two meanings of a concept and Ockham's final preference for the "intellectio" theory see below, pp. 504–510.
244. *Quodl.* 5.6 (*OTh* 9: 500–508). Ockham here uses the word "assent" in two senses. The first has for its object an external thing, as when the mind affirms that something exists or does not exist, or that it is good or white; the second is an assent to a proposition by which the mind adheres to it as true (see ibid. 3.8 (*OTh* 9: 233.12–234.38). The notion of judgment also has two corresponding meanings. The first is not distinct from intuitive or incomplex knowledge but is included in it. It consists in affirming that something is or is not, of that it has or has not a certain quality. This is not a judgment properly speaking but it is equivalent to a judgment. The second has a proposition for its object, affirming, denying or doubting its truth. For this distinction see *Sent.* 1.prol.1 (*OTh* 1: 16.12–17.2, 70.69.22–70.2).

not include several such propositions. A compound or hypothetical proposition, on the contrary, is composed of several categorical propositions. According to the common opinion there are five kinds of hypothetical propositions: copulative, disjunctive, conditional, causal, and temporal. A copulative proposition is made up of several propositions, which may be either categorical or hypothetical, joined by the conjunction "and." An example is "Socrates runs and Plato disputes." A disjunctive proposition is composed of several propositions by means of the conjunction "or." A conditional proposition is make up of several propositions by means of the conjunction "if," as in the example "If man runs, animal runs." A causal proposition is likewise composed of several propositions by means of the conjunction "because," as in the example "Because man runs, man moves." A temporal proposition is made up of several propositions by means of some temporal adverb, as in the example "When Socrates runs, Plato disputes."[245] Propositions are also divided into universal and individual, affirmative and negative, definite and indefinite, past, present, and future.

Still another division of propositions is into assertoric (*de inesse*) and modal (*de modo vel modalis*). In the present tense a proposition is *de inesse* when it states that something is or is not, or is or is not such and such.[246] A proposition is called modal when it contains a modal term, such as "necessary," "contingent," "possible," or "impossible." To these four classic modes Ockham adds many others, such as "true," "false," "known," "unknown," "spoken," "written," "mental," and so on. For example: "That man runs is contingent," "That man is an animal is necessary." An assertoric proposition is defined simply as one that does not contain a mode, as in the example "Every man is an animal."

---

245. *Sum. log.* 2.1 (*OPh* 1: 241.2–242.32).

246. In the proposition "Socrates exists," "exists" is predicated of "Socrates" *secundum adiacens*, without anything following it. In the proposition "Man is an animal," "animal" is predicated *tertium adiacens*, following the verb "exists"; see *Expos. in Periherm.* 2.1–2 (*OPh* 2: 429–430).

The addition of a mode in a proposition makes the proposition modal only if the mode is predicable of the whole proposition, or if a modal word is joined to the verb. An example of the first case is: "Every man is an animal is necessary"; an example of the second is: "Every man is necessarily an animal." Both propositions are modal, but not in the same way. The first is modal with the addition of the predicate "is necessary," and it is called modal *cum dicto*, its *dictum* being "That every man is an animal." The second proposition is modal because of the adverb "necessarily" modifying the verb, without an added predicate, and it is called modal *sine dicto*.[247]

When a modal proposition *cum dicto* is taken in a composite sense (*in sensu compositionis*), it denotes that the mode is predicated of the whole proposition. For example, the proposition "What is white is black is possible" in the composite sense denotes that the mode "possible" is verified of the whole proposition "What is white is black." When the same proposition is taken in a divided sense (*in sensu divisionis*), it is equivalent to the proposition "What is white is possibly black," and it denotes that the predicate "black" is verified of the subject "white" by means of the verb "is" modified by the adverb "possibly." In short, the proposition means "What is white can be black." The importance of this distinction is clear, for it entails that a modal proposition can be false in the composite sense but true in the divided sense. "What is white is black is possible" is false because it is impossible for white to be black. But "What is white can be black" is true, for it is possible for something white to become black.[248] We shall have occasion in a later chapter to return to the distinction between propositions understood *in sensu compositionis* and *in sensu divisionis*.

After considering modal propositions, Ockham treats of exponible propositions. These appear to be simple or categorical, but they are really equivalent to conjunctive or disjunctive compound

247. *Sum. log.* 2.1 and 2.9 (*OPh* 1: 242.44–243.62 and 1: 273.3–25).
248. Ibid. 2.9 and 3–1.20 (*OPh* 1: 273.3–274.38 and 1: 411.14–412.29); *Expos. in Periherm.* 1.6 (*OPh* 2: 417.16–38). On this subject see Moody, *Logic of William of Ockham*, pp. 198–199; Leff, *William of Ockham*, pp. 257–258.

propositions, as their analysis reveals. This can be illustrated by a proposition in which an infinite term like "non-man" is predicated of something; for example, "A donkey is a non-man." At first sight this appears to be a negative proposition, but in fact it is affirmative: it does not mean that a donkey is not a man, but that a donkey is something and a donkey is not a man. Hence an analysis shows it to be covertly a conjunctive proposition made up of two categorical propositions. Similarly "An angel is immaterial" is equivalent to "An angel is something and an angel does not have matter."[249]

Propositions containing terms of figments of the mind, such as "chimera" or "goatstag," to which nothing corresponds in the real world, are also exponible in several propositions. Thus "A chimera is a non-being" is expounded in the propositions "A chimera is something" and "that is a non-being." This shows that it is false to say "A chimera is a non-being" because a chimera is not something. It is true, however, to say "A chimera is not a man," for if the terms are taken with personal supposition, there is no individual for which the subject and predicate stand. Is it true to say, "A chimera is an impossible being"? No, for this implies that a chimera is a being, and that is false. Ockham insists that the logic of these propositions does not require a world of impossible beings as there is a world of beings. (To this it can be added that neither is there a world of possible beings: Ockham insists that "Every being is actual" is a necessary proposition.)[250] Is it true at least to say "A chimera is a chimera"? At first sight this seems to be true because it is a tautology, and nothing is truer than such a proposition. But Ockham demurs: if the terms are taken meaningfully and with personal supposition the proposition is strictly speaking false. Why? because it falsely implies that there is something for which the subject and predicate term "chimera" stands. Terms like "chimera" and "goatstag" are meaningful and they can have simple or material supposition when used in propo-

---

249. *Sum. log.* 2.12 (*OPh* 1: 283).
250. Ibid. 3–1.31 (*OPh* 1: 442.83).

sitions, but they cannot have personal supposition because they do not stand for what they signify.[251]

Ockham treats at length of the conditions of truth required of the many kinds of propositions he has described.[252] By way of illustration, we shall consider a few of the simpler cases. The truth of a singular assertoric (*de inesse*) proposition, such as "Socrates is a man" or "Socrates is an animal," does not require that the predicate and the subject are really the same, nor that the predicate really exists in the subject or is united to it. Neither do these propositions denote that Socrates has humanity or animality, nor that they are in Socrates and belong to his essence or quidditative concept. For the truth of the proposition it suffices that the subject and predicate terms stand for the same individual. This does not mean that the proposition is tautological: that the same thing is predicated of itself. Although the subject and predicate stand for the same thing, the terms themselves are not the same. In the proposition "Socrates is this man," the same thing is not predicated of itself. The subject and predicate stand for the same individual, but the terms of the proposition are different.[253]

Truth and falsity are ascribed to propositions, but they are not something added to them, such as mental relations to reality. Truth and falsity are relative concepts signifying a proposition, not in itself and absolutely, but as connoting the agreement or lack of agreement between what exists in reality and what is signified by the proposition.[254] Ockham seems to have avoided the classic

---

251. Ibid. 2.14 (*OPh* 1: 286–288).

252. *Sum. log.* 2.2–20 (*OPh* 1: 249–317). See Freddoso, introduction to *Ockham's Theory of Propositions*, trans. Freddoso and Schuurman, pp. 1–76; Adams, *William of Ockham* 1: 383–435.

253. *Sum. log.* 2.3 (*OPh* 1: 257.79–88).

254. "Ad aliud dico quod veritas et falsitas propositionis non dicunt parvos respectus rationis, sed sunt conceptus relativi significantes ipsas propositiones, non absolute, sed veritas, sive iste conceptus 'veritas', ultra propositionem quam significat, connotat quod ita sit in re sicut importatur per propositionem; et 'falsitas' importat quod non sit ita in re sicut importatur per propositionem" (*Quodl.* 6.29 [*OTh* 9: 697.88–97]). "Ad veritatem propositionis

definition of truth as the correspondence of mind and reality (*adae-quatio rei et intellectus*), perhaps because of its association with philosophies that posit an isomorphism of knowledge and reality.

Returning to the question of the requirements for the truth of propositions, what suffices for the truth of past and future individual propositions like "Socrates was white" and "Paul will be coming?" The first proposition is true if "Socrates is white" was true at some past time; the second is true if "Paul is coming" will be true some time in the future. The appeal to truth requirements in these cases is not directly to the requirement of the truth of a present tense proposition – that the subject and predicate stand for the same thing – but it presupposes it.[255] It should be noted that the truth of these propositions does not commit Ockham to the thesis that there are past or future entities. In the proposition "Socrates was white," "Socrates" is not said to stand for a past individual. The proposition is not said to be true now if "Socrates" stands for a past individual that "white" also stands for. Rather, the proposition is true if "Socrates is white" was once true, that is, if the terms "Socrates" and "white" once stood for the same individual in the present tense proposition "Socrates is white."[256]

What are the truth conditions of modal propositions? A modal proposition *cum dicto* such as "It is necessary that God exists," is not necessary because it is always true, but because it is true and it cannot be false. The mental, spoken or written proposition may not be true for it may not exist, and if it does not it is not true.

---

affirmativae non requiritur semper identitas praedicati cum subiecto, sed semper requiritur identitas rei significatae per subiectum et praedicatum, et hoc sufficit ad eius veritatem" (*Quodl.* 6.5 [*OTh* 9: 603.106–110]).

255. *Sum. log.* 2.7 (*OPh* 1: 269–272). "Ockham explicates the truth conditions of past-tense propositions in terms of the past truth of present-tense propositions rather than directly in terms of the supposition of subjects and predicates in past-tense propositions" (Freddoso, introduction to *Ockham's Theory of Propositions*, p. 37).

256. On this subject see Freddoso, ibid., pp. 37–38. Adams (*William Ockham* 1: 400–416) discusses the pros and cons of this subject.

But if it does exist it is true and cannot be false. Thus the mental proposition "God exists" is necessary, not because it is always true, for if no one thought the proposition it would not be true. But if anyone formed the proposition in his or her mind, it would be true. Similarly, if the proposition is spoken it is necessary, and nevertheless it is not always true, because after it has been spoken it no longer exists and therefore cannot be either true or false.[257]

As we have seen, a modal proposition *sine dicto* is equivalent to a proposition *cum dico* in the divided sense. But these propositions are not convertible; indeed one can be false and the other true and vice versa. Thus, in Aristotelianism the following proposition is true in the composed sense, "That every man is an animal is necessary," meaning that "Every man is an animal" is a necessary proposition. And yet in the divided sense it is false to say, "Every man is necessarily an animal" because it is contingent on God's will that men exist, and if he ceased to create them it would no longer be true that they are animals.[258]

In his *Quodlibeta* Ockham takes up the question touched upon above, whether a spoken proposition can be true. At first sight it seems that it cannot, because it does not exist as a whole but successively, part after part. In short, it is not a permanent but a successive reality. Hence it is not true at the beginning, when for

257. *Sum. log.* 2.9 (*OPh* 1: 275.72–79). "[S]i nullus intellectus esset, adhuc homo non esset lapis, et tamen haec non esset vera tunc 'homo non est lapis', quia nulla propositio esset tunc" (*Quaest. in Phys.* 115 [*OPh* 6: 708.83–85]).

258. *Sum. log.* 2.10 (*OPh* 1: 276.2–24). Ockham says that he is following "the way of Aristotle" (*secundum viam Aristotelis*), but in fact Aristotle had no doubt that man is necessarily an animal (*Anal. Prior.* 1.15, 34b 16–17). Ockham acknowledges this when he says later that it is contrary to Aristotle's words to say that a merely affirmative, categorical proposition in the present tense about creatures are not necessary but contingent; see ibid. 3–2.5 (*OPh* 1: 512.26–513.45). It was the intention of Aristotle that the proposition "Man is an animal" is necessary because in his view some individual man always exists. But according to the truth of faith the proposition is contingent because human existence depends on the will of God. Of course, Aristotle might take the proposition as conditional: "If man exists, he is an animal," and then it would be true; see *Quaest. in Phys.* 116 (*OPh* 6: 712.85–98).

example the speaker says "man," for the listener does not know what will follow. For the same reason neither is it true in the middle. At the end the spoken proposition is finished, but then it no longer exists and consequently it cannot be true.

Examining the difference and relation between mental and spoken propositions, Ockham shows how a spoken proposition can be true. A mental proposition is a permanent reality, and thus it can exist wholly at the beginning of a spoken proposition; and it can be true then and likewise in the middle and at the end of that proposition. A spoken proposition, on the other hand, is successive, and hence it can only be true at the end, when it does not actually exist but did exist. When the spoken words are finished, listeners who know their meaning can retain them in their memory, so that their minds can conceive the meaning of the proposition and know that it is in conformity with reality. Then for the first time the spoken proposition is true for them.

CHAPTER 2

Philosophy and Theology

THE FOREGOING DISCUSSION OF some of Ockham's logical and metaphysical notions has prepared the ground for the remaining chapters of this book. We now turn to his relation to Aristotle, to philosophy as a science, its methods and divisions, and to exploring the possiblity of theology as a science.

1 Aristotle and the Faith

For Ockham, as for all his contemporaries, Aristotle was The Philosopher. Dante voiced the common opinion at the time when he called Aristotle "the master of those who know."[1] In the Prologue to his commentary on Aristotle's *Physics,* Ockham praises the Greek philosopher as the most learned among the sages of antiquity, who "with the eyes of a lynx, as it were ... explored the deep secrets of nature and revealed to posterity the hidden truths of natural philosophy."[2] Nevertheless Ockham's commitment to Aristotelianism was not unqualified. His only purpose in commenting on Aristotle's works, he says, is to investigate his probable opinions, without vouching for the truth of everything he taught. With God's help, he continues, Aristotle has made many great discoveries, but he insists that the Philosopher was only human and has mixed the truth with errors, which should not be imputed to Ockham himself, especially if they are contrary to the Catholic faith.[3]

1. Dante, *Inferno* 4.131.
2. "Inter alios autem philosophorum peritissimus Aristoteles non parvae nec contemnendae doctrinae praeclarus apparuit, qui quasi lynceis oculis secretiora naturae rimatus philosophiae naturalis abscondita posteris revelavit" (*Expos. in Phys.* prol. [*OPh* 4: 3.7–10]).
3. Ibid. (*OPh* 4: 3.11–4.32).

With this word of caution, Ockham proceeds to set forth what he believes Aristotle held, or should have held, given his principles. He does not consider Aristotle infallible: far from saying the last word in philosophy, he must be corrected in the light of the Christian faith, and in any case his doctrines are not to be taken as the absolute truth but only as opinions. Ockham is equally modest about his interpretation of Aristotle, denying that it is the only possible one. Any author, except the author of sacred scripture, he says, admits of different and even opposed interpretations; but he defends his own as most compatible with the literal meaning of Aristotle's words and, more generally, with his mind and unexpressed intention.

In line with this program, Ockham wrote long commentaries on Aristotle's writings in logic and physics, and he seems to have intended others on the *Metaphysics* and *Nicomachean Ethics*, but unfortunately it seems that he did not write them.[4] He also commented on Porphyry's treatise on the predicables. The doctrine in these commentaries is no doubt an Aristotelianism, but freely interpreted in the light of Ockham's conceptualist views in logic, physics, and metaphysics. Far from wanting to return to a pure Aristotelianism[5] (whatever that might be), he gives us a new version of Aristotle, profoundly different from those of his fellow scholastics.

In Ockham's works other than commentaries – the lengthy *Summa logicae* and theological writings – for the most part we find the same basic philosophy, but modified whenever necessary to bring it into harmony with the orthodox teaching of the Church and "the saints," especially Augustine. Ockham did not want to

---

4. See *Sum. log.* 3–3.24 (*OPh* 1: 685 n3), 3–3.6 (*OPh* 1: 610.302 n10), 3–3.7 (*OPh* 1: 615.141).

5. Ernest A. Moody (*The Logic of William of Ockham* [New York, 1935], pp. 10–11) thought that in logic Ockham wanted to return to authentic Aristotelianism, which he believed had been corrupted by Neoplatonic, Islamic, and Augustinian ideas. On this question see Gordon Leff, *William of Ockham* (Manchester, 1975), pp. 178–179.

deviate from these authorities, and it is generally agreed that in fact his theology contains nothing heretical. When he weighed the probable opinions of Aristotle against the truth of the Christian faith, the faith always won out. If he found Aristotelianism wanting and unable to function as an aid to his theology, he did not hesitate to contradict it and devise original philosophical arguments in support of the faith.

Thus we find that, after showing in philosophy the high improbability of a relative reality (*res relativa*) and contending that all things are absolutes, he argues that in theology it is truer, if not easier, to hold with the Christian tradition that the divine Persons are distinguished from each other as relative realities.[6] In his Christology he concedes that the union of the human and divine natures in the one Person of Christ is a real relation really distinct from the terms of the relation and inhering in the human nature.[7] Having argued persuasively in philosophy against the validity of the formal distinction, he makes use of it, interpreted in his own non-Scotist manner, in explaining the distinction between the divine nature and the Trinity of Persons. In his new understanding of this distinction, it is said to be real (*ex natura rei*), but not based in the Scotist manner on different formalities or realities in things. Lacking this foundation, it is unclear how the formal distinction can be justified.[8] In his theology of the Incarnation he is careful to avoid the heresy of Nestorianism, which taught that there are two persons as well as two natures in Christ. He defends the orthodox position that Christ is one Person with two natures, divine and human, the human nature being assumed into the unity of the divine Person. This, he says, is "the truth of the theologians," but he does not think it is according to the mind of Aristotle, because in his view a person is identical with his or her individual humanity. And if this were true, by assuming a human nature Christ would also assume a human person, and there would be two per-

6. *Ord.* 1.26.1 (*OTh* 4: 156.22–157.25).
7. *Rep.* 3.1 (*OTh* 6: 9.1–8).
8. See above, pp. 74–77.

sons in Christ. As we have seen, Ockham avoids this impasse by distinguishing between the descriptions of person and individual nature – a distinction, however, that remains in the order of language and not in the order of reality.[9]

On these and other similar occasions Ockham behaves as a *theologus fidelis* and not as a *philosophus paganus* like Aristotle. In his role as a theologian Ockham cultivates philosophy as an aid to theology; and although this does not require that philosophy and theology prove the same truth with the same degree of understanding, it does demand that they communicate with the same language, each interpreting it in its own way. For example, the theologian, relying on faith, proves that God is a Trinity of Persons, and that God is good or wise, using the term "God" in the theological sense of a being better than anything else ("aliquid melius omnibus aliis a se"). The philosopher, using human reason, can only prove the existence of God with the humbler concept of the first cause, or some other notion that can be reached by natural reason. By the same means, and with the same limitations, the philosopher can predicate wisdom and goodness of God. For his part, the theologian, using his own method, can prove the same truths about God.[10] This shows that even though philosophy and theology (understood as collections of mental habits and propositions)[11] are autonomous disciplines, each with its own method and principles, they are not closed to each other, but they can communicate and share language and proofs. Moreover, such communication and sharing is vital to the role of philosophy as an aid to theology.

The question remains: how successful was Ockham the philosopher in his dialogue with theology? The fathers of the Church and the great theologians of the Middle Ages – Anselm, Bonaventure, Thomas Aquinas, and Duns Scotus, to mention the most eminent – each in his own way brought reason to bear upon faith

---

9. See above, pp. 38–40.

10. *Quodl.* 5.1 (*OTh* 9: 475–480). For the relationship between theology and metaphysics see *Ord.* 1.prol.1 (*OTh* 1: 7.4–15.3).

11. On science in this collective sense see below, pp. 142–144.

and achieved a close bond between them. Not that their reason was able to penetrate the depth of the Christian mysteries, but it was in harmony with them and threw light upon them. The same is not always true of Ockham's efforts to develop a philosophy that would be a fruitful *ancilla theologiae*. His philosophizing in behalf of the faith in the above cases remains on the level of language, without an intimate connection with "the truths of the theologian." This hardly counts against Ockham's philosophy for the non-Christian, but it does for the Christian for whom the concordance of faith and reason is indispensable.

2 Method[12]

Experience and Induction

Ockham learned from Aristotle that all science and art comes to us through experience.[13] Ockham explains this process as follows. After perceiving things with our senses, we can form images of them with our imagination and understand them with our intellect. In this way we can have evident knowledge of contingent propositions. Thus, after feeling heat, the intellect knows that it is hot, and it also knows that when something else is brought close to it, it too becomes hot. So we know with evidence the proposition "This hot thing heats." We can then generalize this and know that every hot thing heats. The generalization is warranted because we know that something belonging to one individual can also belong to another similar to it in the same species. After all, there is no greater reason why one heat is more heat-giving than another. But we can form a universal proposition on the basis of one individual only when it belongs to an ultimate species (*species specialissima*), such as the human species. If the proposition concerns something in a broader species or a genus, a knowledge of many individuals is required; and indeed even when the subject of a uni-

12. See Armand Maurer, "Method in Ockham's Nominalism," *The Monist* 61 (1978): 426–443, repr. in *Being and Knowing* (Toronto, 1990), pp. 401–421.

13. Aristotle, *Metaph.* 1.1, 981a1. See Ockham, *Sum. log.* 3–2.10 (*OPh* 1: 522–524).

versal proposition is an ultimate species we often have to know many individuals in order to have an evident knowledge of the proposition. It is not easy to know that a certain kind of herb cures a particular disease without experiencing many instances of the cure. A principle of this sort, drawn from experience, can always be questioned; it does not have the certitude of one that is self-evident. Ockham notes, with Averroes, that the facility with which a universal principle is drawn from particular experiences depends not only on the nature of the principle but also on the skill of the scientist. Some scientists are more competent than others in drawing universal principles from fewer individual instances.[14]

The advancing from experience of individuals to the formation of universal principles and conclusions is called induction.[15] Ockham regards this as a kind of argument or "consequence," for it leads us from something better known to something less known.[16] In his description of the process he takes issue with philosophers like Duns Scotus who justify it by the presence in individuals of the same species of a form or common nature. According to Scotus, "Even though a person does not experience every single individual, but only a great many, nor does he experience them at all times, but only frequently, still the expert knows infallibly that it is always this way and holds for all instances. He knows this in virtue of the proposition reposing in his soul: 'Whatever occurs in a great many instances by a cause that is not free, is the natural effect of that cause.'"[17] In short, the nature or form

---

14. *Sum. log.* 3-2.10 (*OPh* 1: 522–524), 3-3.31–36 (*OPh* 1: 707–721); *Expos. in Phys.* 2.12 (*OPh* 4: 380.54–382.2; see citation of Averroes, p. 380.54–62); *Ord.* 1.prol.2 (*OTh* 1: 90.10–95.8).

15. Following Aristotle, Ockham defines induction as "a passage from individuals to universals (inductio est a singularibus ad universale progressio)" (*Sum. log.* 3-3.31 [*OPh* 1: 707.4]). See Aristotle, *Top.* 1.12, 105a13–14; *Anal. Post.* 2.19, 99b15–100b17.

16. *Sum. log.* 3-3.31 (*OPh* 1: 707.2–3); see also *Expos. in Phys.* 2.12 (*OPh* 4: 380.63–65).

17. Scotus, *Ord.* 1.3.1.4 (Vatican ed. 3: 141), trans. Allan B. Wolter, in *Philosophical Writings: A Selection* (Indianapolis, 1987), p. 109 (modified).

common to individuals in a species is a natural cause that, unless impeded, produces the same effects. Since Ockham does not accept natures common to individuals, he justifies inductive reasoning, not by forms or natures in things, but by individuals themselves as like each other and therefore contained in the same species or genus.

Demonstration

Once in possession of universal principles, it is possible to deduce new propositions from them by the various types of syllogistic reasoning described by Aristotle in his *Prior Analytics* and *Topics*. The best type, and the ideal one for science, is demonstration. This is defined as "a syllogism productive of knowledge."[18] Clarifying this definition, Ockham distinguishes between three meanings of the term "knowledge." In one sense it is the evident apprehension of either a necessary or contintent truth. Second, it is the apprehension of a truth that cannot be false. This excludes contingent truths and retains only those that are necessary. In a third sense knowledge is the evident apprehension of a necessary truth through the evident apprehension of two necessary truths arranged in proper syllogistic form. In this strict sense knowledge or science (*scientia*) is the conclusion of a demonstrative syllogism.[19]

Besides demonstration in the strict sense, Ockham admits other arguments as demonstrative in a broad sense of the term, as long as they lead from something better known to something less known. They may not have the ideal form of syllogistic reasoning in which a strict demonstration is couched, but they can be called demonstrative as long as they lend support for the truth of a conclusion.[20]

---

18. *Sum. log.* 3–2.1 (*OPh* 1: 505.12–13); Aristotle, *Anal. Post.* 1.2, 71b 17–18. See Damascene Webering, *Theory of Demonstration According to William Ockham* (St. Bonaventure, NY, 1953).

19. *Sum. log.* 3–2.1 (*OPh* 1: 506.22–39).

20. *Expos. in Phys.* 2.12 (*OPh* 4: 380.63–65); *Sum. log.* 3–2 (*OPh* 1: 560. 88–100); *Elemen. log.* 7.1 (*OPh* 7: 187.6–13). The *Elementarium* is of doubtful authenticity, but its thought is generally held to be faithful to Ockham's. See the editor's introduction *OPh* 7: 7*–11*.

The conclusion of a strict demonstration is a universal truth made known through other universal truths called premises. But this is not the only way we can come to know general propositions. Some are self-evident to everyone, so that the mind immediately assents to them when it knows the meaning of their terms. Examples are the principles of noncontradiction and the excluded middle, which are presupposed by all the sciences. There are other self-evident principles assumed by the special sciences, such as physics or mathematics. An example in physics is, "Something is movable," and in mathematics, "If equals are subtracted from equals, the results are equal." Self-evident propositions are not premises in a demonstration but are necessary prerequisites in all demonstrations. Ockham calls them maxims, assumptions, or *dignitates*.[21]

Demonstrations make known either the fact that something is or the reason why it is. The former is called a demonstration *quia* or *a posteriori*, the latter a demonstration *propter quid* or *a priori*. It is called *a posteriori* because it proceeds from effect to cause and *a priori* because it proceeds from cause to effect. An example of *a posteriori* reasoning suitable for beginners is the following: If someone sees that the moon is eclipsed and does not know that the earth is in fact between the moon and the sun, he may reason: "When the moon is eclipsed, the earth is between the moon and the sun; the moon is now eclipsed; therefore the earth is now between them." An example of *a priori* reasoning is the following: If someone does not know that the moon is now eclipsed but knows the course and movement of the planets, he may reason: "When the moon is in such and such a position it will be eclipsed; the moon is now in this position; therefore the moon is now eclipsed." The first syllogism tells us that the eclipse has taken place but not why it did; the second syllogism gives the reason for it.[22]

21. *Sum. log.* 3–2.4 (*OPh* 1: 509.6–510.10).
22. Ibid. 3–2.17 (*OPh* 1: 533); see Aristotle, *Anal. Post.* 1.13, 78a22–79a16.

Because of the requirement of necessary propositions for scientific reasoning, Ockham finds another conflict between Aristotelianism and the Christian faith. According to Aristotle demonstration concerns what is necessary, eternal, and incorruptible. Since in his philosophy the world and its various species of things meet these conditions, there can be scientific knowledge of them. But the Christian believes that only God is eternal, necessary, and incorruptible. Creatures, on the contrary, exist by the will of God, and consequently their existence is not necessary and he can annihilate them. Hence every proposition about them that is affirmative, categorical, and about the present, is contingent. Lacking necessity, it cannot function as the premise or conclusion of a scientific demonstration. Consider the proposition "Man is a rational animal." At first sight this seems to be a clear example of a necessary proposition, but Ockham claims it is contingent, for if no man existed it would be false. And yet he contends that there can be science of contingent things, because necessary propositions can be formed about them in the negative, hypothetical or possible mode. For example, it is absolutely necessary that if man exists he is an animal, and that every man can laugh.[23]

It has been said that this situation arises because of the Christian doctrine of creation;[24] but it is truer to say that it stems from a notion of the contingency of creation which Ockham shared with many predecessors, including Henry of Harclay and Scotus. Aquinas' notion of the contingency of the world was quite different from theirs. Though granting that the world owes its existence to the free will of God, he insists that from the viewpoint of its formal principles it contains absolute necessities. Thus God did not have to create an animal composed of contrary parts, but, once created, it is absolutely necessary that it die. Indeed, Aquinas thought that spiritual beings, like angels and human souls, and the universe as a whole, exist with absolute necessity, once God has freely created them. Though

---

23. Ibid. 3–2.5 (*OPh* 1: 512–514).

24. Marilyn M. Adams, *William Ockham* (Notre Dame, IN, 1987), 1: 452.

he has the power to annihilate them, he has so created them that they have no natural tendency to go out of existence, and his will is immutable.[25] As a consequence of the formal necessities in nature, Aquinas can accept without revision this aspect of Aristotle's doctrine of science.

Dialectic and the Razor [26]

Besides demonstration and induction, Ockham, like all medieval philosophers, appeals to dialectical or topical reasoning to reach universal conclusions. The classical source of dialectic is Aristotle's *Topics*. Boethius translated the treatise in the sixth century and wrote his own *De topicis differentiis*, which introduced new elements into the art of dialectic.[27] Principally through the works of Boethius and Cicero's *Topica* dialectic became a subject of interest in the tenth century, and new developments in the art continued through the Middle Ages well into the fourteenth century. From the Aristotelian view of dialectic as a method of finding arguments in disputation based on commonly accepted opinions, it tended to become a theory of consequences, especially in connection with conditional sentences and hypothetical syllogisms. Moreover, there was a growing tendency to consider dialectical arguments to be not only probable but necessary, thus blurring the

25. Aquinas, *In Sent.* 1.8.3.2 (ed. Mandonnet–Moos 1: 212–215); *SCG* 2.55; *De pot.* 5.3. For a further discussion of this doctrine see Armand Maurer, "Henry of Harclay's Questions on Immortality," *Mediaeval Studies* 19 (1957): 79–107, repr. in *Being and Knowing*, pp. 229–271.

26. This section is taken substantially from my article, "Ockham's Razor and Dialectical Reasoning," *Mediaeval Studies* 58 (1996): 49–65.

27. Boethius' translation of the *Topics* can be found in the *Aristoteles Latinus* (ed. Minio-Paluello pp. 1–179). See Boethius' *De topicis differentiis* (PL 64: 1174–1216), trans. Eleonore Stump, as *Boethius's "De topicis differentiis,"* with notes and essays (Ithaca, NY, 1978). Boethius also commented on Cicero's *Topics: In Topica Ciceronis Commentariorum libri sex* (PL 64: 1039–1174), trans. Stump, as *Boethius's "In Ciceronis Topica,"* with notes and introduction (Ithaca, NY, 1988). See also Eleonore Stump, "Boethius's Works on the *Topics*," *Vivarium* 12 (1974): 77–93.

distinction between dialectic and demonstration.[28] We shall see presently how Ockham contributed to this development.

There are two accounts of dialectic in the works of Ockham: one in his commentary on Aristotle's *De sophisticis elenchis*, the other in his major and last work in logic, the *Summa logicae*.[29] The commentary divides dialectic in the traditional medieval manner into *dialectica utens* and *dialectica docens*. Medieval logicians defined *dialectica docens* as the part of logic that investigates and teaches the method of dialectical argumentation. As such, it is a special discipline using the demonstrative method. *Dialectica utens* was not regarded as a particular discipline but the common use of logical notions and axioms (*communia*) in all the sciences. Arguments based on these notions and principles may be mingled with those proper to any of the sciences, such as metaphysics, but the conclusions of dialectical arguments of this sort were generally regarded as probable opinions.[30]

Ockham is in this tradition when he writes that *dialectica utens* is not one science like *dialectica docens*, metaphysics, or geometry, but the use all the sciences can make of common notions and principles (*communia*). He specifies that this is the meaning of dialectic in Aristotle's *De sophisticis elenchis* – the work on which he is commenting.[31] In the broad sense, *dialectica utens* is any argu-

---

28. See N.J. Green-Pedersen, *The Tradition of the Topics in the Middle Ages: The Commentaries on Aristotle's and Boethius' "Topics"* (Vienna, 1984), pp. 304–307; Eleonore Stump, *Dialectic and Its Place in the Development of Medieval Logic* (Ithaca, NY, 1989), p. 158, and "Topics: Their Development and Absorption into Consequences," in *The Cambridge History of Later Medieval Philosophy*, ed. Norman Kretzmann et al. (Cambridge, 1982), pp. 273–299; Otto Bird, "Topic and Consequence in Ockham's Logic," *Notre Dame Journal of Formal Logic* 2 (1961): 65–78.

29. The *Summa logicae* is dated about 1323, the commentary on the *De sophisticis elenchis* a little earlier. See the editor's introduction *OPh* 1: 56*.

30. See Aquinas, *In Metaph.* 4.4 (ed. Cathala-Spiazzi nn. 573–576). For Albert the Great's notion of dialectic, see William A. Wallace, "Albert the Great's Inventive Logic: His Exposition of the *Topics* of Aristotle," *American Catholic Philosophical Quarterly* 70 (1996): 11–39.

31. "Notandum quod Philosophus in proposito loquitur de dialectica utente communibus ad probandum conclusiones speciales, et non loquitur de

ment that sets out to prove something, but not demonstratively. This includes not only dialectical arguments in the strict sense but also those that are tentative, contentious, and sophistic. Taken strictly, dialectic "proceeds to prove a true conclusion from true and probable [premises]: not from those that are self-evident or adequately known from experience, but from those that are known from authority or in some other plausible way."[32]

Continuing his description of *dialectica utens*, Ockham explains that it takes for granted first principles, such as the principles of the excluded middle and noncontradiction; it neither proves them nor questions them as though they were doubtful. Ockham's final point is that the dialectician sometimes makes use of necessary and evident propositions – even those that are self-evident – but his syllogism always contains a nonevident premise, implying that if the syllogism did not, it would not be dialectical but demonstrative.[33]

This description of dialectic conforms quite well to the traditional notion of dialectical reasoning. It is clearly distinquished from demonstration and induction, for its premises are not evident or adequately drawn from experience. Rather, their truth would seem to be in the order of probability, resting on authority or

---

dialectica docente, quia ista est ita determinati generis sicut aliae scientiae; nam ita considerat syllogismum dialecticum et alia pertinentia ad eum sicut geometria considerat magnitudinem et alia ad ipsam pertinentia. Secundo notandum quod dialectica utens, de qua loquitur Philosophus, non est una in tali unitate quali geometria vel metaphysica vel dialectica docens est una; et ideo a nullo philosopho in nullo tractatu est tradita; sicut nullus facit nec tradit syllogismos concludentes diversas conclusiones specialium scientiarum ex communibus, sed aliquando tales syllogismi in geometria permiscentur, et aliqui in metaphysica, et aliqui in aliis scientiis, a diversis tradentibus eas" (*Expos. Elench.* 1.18 [*OPh* 3: 118.31–43]).

32. "Large accipitur [dialectica utens communibus] pro quolibet procedente ad aliquid probandum non demonstrative; et sic comprehendit sophisticam et tentativam. ... Stricte accipiendo dialecticam, procedit solum ex veris et probabilibus, non tamen per se notis nec sufficienter notis per experientiam, sed ex notis per auctoritatem vel aliam viam probabilem, ad probandum conclusionem veram" (ibid. [*OPh* 3: 118.45–51]).

33. Ibid. (*OPh* 3: 118.54–119.62).

known by some other, unspecified, plausible means. Later in the commentary, however, we are surprised to find that a probable proposition agreed upon by the majority or the wise can be a *necessary* truth. Indeed, this is said to be the strict meaning of the term "probable." In a wide sense a probable proposition only appears to be true to many or the wise; if it is false, they are not truly wise. Since Ockham specifies that in the *Topics* Aristotle uses the term "probable" in the strict sense, we are led to believe that the premises of a dialectical syllogism can be both probable and necessary.[34] This unusual conjunction of probability and necessity – which historians of medieval logic find hard to understand or explain[35] – is confirmed by Ockham's explicit statement in the *Summa logicae*.

In the *Summa* Ockham begins his treatment of the dialectical or topical syllogism in the traditional way, by contrasting it with the demonstrative syllogism. The latter is said to give us knowledge of a conclusion from evidently known premises, whereas the former begins with probable opinions (*probabilia*). As for the meaning of "probable" in this context, Ockham cites Aristotle's *Topics*: "And those [opinions] are probable that seem [to be true] to all or to the majority or to the wisest."[36] This corresponds to the broad sense of "probable" in the commentary on the *De sophisticis elenchis*.

34. "Notandum est hic quod 'probabile' dupliciter accipitur, scilicet stricte et large. Stricte sumendo 'probabile' est aliquod necessarium cui plures vel sapientes assentiunt, quod nec est principium demonstrationis nec conclusio. Et sic non loquitur Philosophus hic de probabili, sed sic loquitur in libro *Topicorum* (1.1, 100b21–23); et sic numquam possunt praemissae esse probabiles et conclusio improbabilis. Large 'probabile' dicitur quod multis apparet esse verum vel sapientibus, sive sit verum sive falsum; si tamen sit falsum illi qui assentiunt in illo non sunt sapientes" (ibid. 2.18 [*OPh* 3: 315.32–40]).

35. See Green-Pedersen, *Tradition of the Topics*, p. 305; Stump, "Topics: Their Development and Absorption into Consequences," p. 295.

36. "Syllogismus demonstrativus est ille in quo ex propositionibus necessariis evidenter notis potest adquiri prima notitia conclusionis. Syllogismus topicus est syllogismus ex probabilibus. Et sunt 'probabilia quae videntur vel omnibus vel pluribus vel sapientibus, et de his quae videntur vel omnibus vel pluribus vel maxime sapientibus'" (*Sum. log.* 3–1.1 [*OPh* 1: 359.14–19]). See Aristotle, *Top.* 1.1, 100b21–23; trans. Boethius (ed. Minio-Paluello pp. 5–6).

In Boethius' version of the *Topics*, the Latin *probabilia* translates Aristotle's *endoxa*, which has the meaning of "generally accepted opinions."[37] Commenting on the meaning of *probabilia*, Ockham says that they should be understood as true and even as necessary (*vera et necessaria*). They are not self-evident (*per se nota*), or the premises or conclusions of a demonstration, nor are they known with evidence by experience. Nevertheless, because of their truth (*propter sui veritatem*) they are accepted as such by everyone or by the majority, especially by philosophers. This rules out propositions that are contingent or false, premises or conclusionss of demonstration, and the articles of the Christian faith, which appear to be false to everyone or to the majority or to the wisest. Clarifying this surprising statement of a Christian theologian, Ockham explains that here "the wise" means "wise men of the world" (*sapientes mundi*), that is philosophers, who strictly limit themselves to what can be known by natural reason.[38]

37. For the meaning of *endoxa* see G.E.L. Owen, "Tithenai ta phainomena," in *Aristote et les problèmes de méthode: Communications présentées au Symposium Aristotelicum*, ed. Suzanne Mansion (Louvain, 1961), pp. 83–103, repr. in his *Logic, Science, and Dialectic: Collected Papers in Greek Philosophy*, ed. Martha Nussbaum (Ithaca, NY, 1986), pp. 239–251. On Aristotle's notion of dialectic see W.A. de Pater, *Les Topiques d'Aristote et la dialectique platonicienne* (Fribourg, 1965); *Aristotle on Dialectic: The Topics: Proceedings of the Third Symposium Aristotelicum*, ed. G.E.L. Owen (Oxford, 1968); Yves Pelletier, *La dialectique aristotélicienne: Les principes clés des "Topiques"* (Montreal, 1991); Robert Bolton, "The Problem of Dialectical Reasoning (Συλλογισμός) in Aristotle," in *Logic, Dialectic, and Science in Aristotle*, ed. Bolton and Robin Smith, special issue of *Ancient Philosophy* 14 (1994): 99–132.

38. *Sum. log.* 3–1.1 (*OPh* 1: 360.20–34). Essentially the same notion of dialectic is found in two treatises of doubtful authenticity: *Tractatus minor* 4.4 and *Elementarium logicae* 7.15 (*OPh* 7: 28.15–25 and 205–6). For the possible authenticity of these works see the editor's introduction *OPh* 7: 7*–11*.

The description of philosophers as the wise men of the world recalls Boethius of Dacia's similar statement in his *De aeternitate mundi*, in *Opera: Opuscula*, ed. N.J. Green-Pedersen (Copenhagen, 1976), p. 365; trans. John F. Wippel, in *On the Supreme Good; On the Eternity of the World; On Dreams* (Toronto, 1987), p. 66. Stephen Tempier, the bishop of Paris, condemned the

Turning to the topical syllogism, whose premises are the *probabilia* he has just described, Ockham insists that it is not faulty in either its matter or form. So we should not think that topical reasoning always gives rise to doubt or fear of being wrong. In fact, it often causes a firm, undoubted belief, for we sometimes cling to probable views just as strongly and confidently as we do to those for which we have evidence.[39]

In the language of the commentary on the *De sophisticis elenchis* this is a description of useful dialectic in the strict sense, while leaving room for dialectical arguments in the broad sense that fail to meet its standard. The accounts of dialectic in the commentary and *Summa logicae* differ in two respects. In the commentary the premises and conclusions of a dialectical syllogism are said to be true and probable; in the *Summa* they are said to be true and necessary. This can be explained, however, if we take the term "probable" in the commentary in its strict meaning of "necessary." Another difference between the two accounts of dialectic is that in the *Summa* topical maxims seem to be true in themselves and not just on the authority of the philosophers: it is because they are true that they are seen to be true by everyone or the majority. In the commentary, however, their truth rests on the external authority and judgment of the wise. This, incidentally, was a traditional *locus* for dialectical arguments, appealing to the maxim, "What seems true to everyone or to the majority or to the wise should not be gainsaid."[40]

Clearly, Ockham's description of dialectic in the *Summa*, and probably in the commentary, radically alters the Aristotelian notion of dialectic. It is no longer restricted to the domain of probable reasoning and opinion but extends to reasoning that, in

---

proposition that philosophers are the *only* wise men of this world, but neither Boethius nor Ockham include the word *only* in their descriptions; see *Chartularium universitatis parisiensis* (ed. Denifle–Chatelain 1: 552, n. 154).

39. *Sum. log.* 3–1.1 (*OPh* 1: 360.35–42).

40. Boethius, *De topicis differentiis* 2 (trans. Stump p. 54; modified).

its own way (but different from that of demonstration, since it is not evident knowledge), involves both truth and necessity. The novelty of Ockham's notion of dialectic stands out when compared with the traditional Aristotelian view of his contemporary John Buridan, who held that "a dialectical argument does not lead to real knowledge of the conclusion, but merely persuades the other part or induces him to take a certain opinion (*persuasio, opinio*).[41]

Whether an argument is dialectical in the strict or wide sense, Ockham makes it clear that it always begins with probable premises (*probabilia*). He also explains that in this context *probabile* does not always mean probable in the sense of doubtful. He has told us that a dialectical argument in the strict sense is *ex probabilibus*, understood as propositions that are true and necessary, and assumed to be such by everyone or by the majority, especially by the wise. *Probabile* here should not be taken in our sense of "likely" or "probable" but in its etymological meaning of what is provable, or what is worthy of approval, or readily believable.[42]

Besides *probabilia*, the term *necessaria* in Ockham's description of dialectical reasoning raises a problem. How can a proposition that is probable also be necessary? Unfortunately, Ockham does

---

41. See Green-Pedersen, *Tradition of the Topics*, p. 305. The author points out, however, that as early as the end of the eleventh century the plausibility (*probabilitas*) of dialectical arguments was losing its importance; these arguments were thought to be necessary as well as plausible (ibid., pp. 161–162).

42. For the medieval meaning of *probabile* see the important article of Thomas Deman, "*Probabilis*," *Revue des sciences philosophiques et théologiques* 22 (1933): 260–290. Deman (p. 263 n3) cites Peter Olivi: "Quod Deum esse est per se notum et ratione necessaria probabile seu probatum et fide creditum" (Olivi, *De Deo cognoscendo* 3, in *Quaestiones in secundum librum Sententiarum* [ed. Jansen 3: 525]). Stump suggests the translation "readily believable"; see her *Boethius's "De topicis differentiis,"* p. 18 n14. Ockham also uses the terms "probable" and "more probable" in our meaning of "likely" and "more likely." For example, arguing against the widespread opinion that an impressed likeness is required for human knowledge, he says the opposite opinion is more likely (*probabilior*); see *Rep.* 2.12–13 (*OTh* 5: 256.5–9).

not answer the question, but perhaps an examination of his notion of necessity will help us to see what his answer would be. In general, he says, necessity implies that what a proposition signifies is really so and cannot be otherwise.[43] But there are two ways in which a proposition can be necessary: absolutely or conditionally (*ex suppositione*). A proposition is absolutely necessary when it would be contradictory for its opposite to be true; for example "God exists" and "Humans are capable of laughter." Other propositions are necessary only on some condition, as it is necessary that Peter will be saved if he is predestined.[44]

When Ockham says that the premises of dialectical arguments can be necessary, does he mean absolutely or conditionally? As he does not explicitly tell us, we must search for the answer in the hints he has given us. These premises cannot have the absolute necessity of first principles, such as the principle of noncontradiction, which is known with evidence through a knowledge of its terms and whose opposite is contradictory. This principle is so necessary that not even God could make it to be otherwise.[45] But there are other rules and laws, such as the laws of physics and moral commands, that have only conditional or hypothetical necessity, for they are necessary only on condition that God wills them to be so.[46] They do not come under God's absolute power (*potentia absoluta*) but under his ordered power (*potentia ordinata*).[47] Since dialectical maxims or principles are not true in virtue of their

43. "'Necessitas' importat quod ita sit in re sicut importatur per propositionem, et quod non potest aliter esse" (*Quodl.* 6.29 [*OTh* 9: 697.93–95]).

44. Ibid. 6.2 (*OTh* 9: 590.13–24). In his *Sum. log.* Ockham clarifies that the proposition "Every man can laugh" is necessary if "man" is taken as possibly existing. If taken as actually existing the proposition is contingent, for man's actual existence is contingent: only God is a necessary being; see *Sum. log.* 3–2.5 (*OPh* 1: 512.26–513.57).

45. God's omnipotence does not extend to contradictories. See *Quodl.* 3.1 (*OTh* 9: 204.114–122); *Ord.* 1.20.un. (*OTh* 4: 36.4–10).

46. Regarding moral laws see *Rep.* 2.15 (*OTh* 5.352–353). See also below, pp. 528–538.

47. For the meaning of these terms see below, pp. 254–265.

terms (that is, they do not have the evidence of first principles), their necessity would seem to be conditional rather than absolute. The principle of the razor (to be examined below) is a case in point. It holds good, Ockham asserts, in the world of natural and created voluntary causes, but God is not bound by it; he does many things by more means which he could do by fewer, and yet this is not done uselessly, because it is God's will.[48] Thus the razor is valid only on condition that God has willed it to be so for our world. The truth and necessity of dialectical propositions are also conditional on the authority and wisdom of the philosophers.[49]

However this might be, it is obvious that Ockham did not intend to confuse dialectic with strict demonstration. He has told us that a demonstrative syllogism causes knowledge from necessary and evident premises, whereas a dialectical syllogism causes belief from premises that are nonevident and probable. In traditional language a dialectical argument is not demonstrative but persuasive. Ockham uses this language when he says that arguments based on maxims such as "Whatever belongs to a lower nature should not be withheld without necessity from a higher nature" are persuasions rather than proofs that are demonstrative and necessarily convincing.[50] He calls some arguments of Aristotle "not absolutely demonstrataive but probable persuasions that induce belief."[51] The expression "to induce belief" (*facere fidem*), which is a classical

48. *Ord.* 1.14.2 (*OTh* 3: 432.16–21).

49. If the razor is a true principle, it is difficult to say in what its truth consists. According to Ockham, a proposition stating a fact is true if it signifies things to be as they are in reality. See *Expos. in Praedicamen.* 9 (*OPh* 2: 201.30), *Quodl.* 6.29 (*OTh* 9: 697.88–93). He does not seem to have considered the truth of practical propositions that tell us what we ought to do or not do. For Ockham's notion of truth see Adams, *William Ockham* 2: 1401 (sv), and "Ockham on Truth," *Medioevo* 15 (1989): 143–172.

50. *Ord.* 1.1.3 (*OTh* 1: 417.9–15).

51. *Expos. in Phys.* 2.11 (*OPh* 4: 359.8–9); cf. ibid. 2.12 (*OPh* 4: 374.55–57). See also *Brevis sum. Phys.* 2.1, 2.4, and 4.1 (*OPh* 6: 27.67–69, 36.24–37, and 56.9–12).

equivalent of "to persuade" (*persuadere*),[52] also appears in his description of the topical syllogism in the *Summa logicae*. We are told there that this kind of syllogism "does not always give rise to doubt or fear of being wrong, but it often induces a strong, undoubted faith (*facit firmam fidem, sine omni dubitatione*)."[53] This makes it clear that, for Ockham, topical or dialectical reasoning is not strictly demonstrative but only persuasive. Though we may be firmly attached to it and highly approve of it, we should not expect it to yield certain knowledge but at best a well-founded belief.

Ockham makes little use of induction and demonstrative reasoning in his philosophy. His preferred method is dialectic. His pervasive use of this style of argument leaves its signature on his whole philosophy. A good example of his use of dialectic is his reasoning on the basis of the principle of parsimony, usually called "Ockham's razor." He expresses the principle in several ways, usually in the traditional medieval forms: "It is useless to do with more what can be done with fewer" ("*Frustra fit per plura quod potest fieri per pauciora*"), and "A plurality should not be assumed without necessity" ("*Pluralitas non est ponenda sine necessitate*"). The axiom was in common use from the thirteenth century, when it was gleaned from Aristotle's logic and physics.[54]

52. *Totius latinitatis lexicon*, ed. Egidio Forcellini (Prati, 1839–1845), 3: 510.

53. *Sum. log.* 3–1.1 (*OPh* 1: 360.35–42).

54. Aristotle, *Anal. Post.* 1.25, 86a33; *Phys.* 1.4, 188a17 and 8.6, 259a8. Jan P. Beckmann lists forty-seven books and articles on the razor in his *Ockham-Bibliographie 1900–1990* (Hamburg, 1992), index on p. 162. See Philotheus Boehner, introduction to Ockham, *Philosophical Writings*, rev. Stephen F. Brown (1957; Indianpolis/Cambridge, 1990), pp. xx–xxi; C.K. Brampton, "Nominalism and the Law of Parsimony," *The Modern Schoolman* 41 (1963–1964): 273–281; Roger Ariew, "Did Ockham Use His Razor?" *Franciscan Studies* 37 (1977): 5–17; Adams, *William Ockham* 1: 156–161; Maurer, "Method in Ockham's Nominalism," pp. 426–443, and "Ockham's Razor and Chatton's Anti-Razor," *Mediaeval Studies* 46 (1984): 463–475, repr. *Being and Knowing*, pp. 403–421 and 431–443; John Boler, "Ockham's Cleaver," *Franciscan Studies* 45 (1985): 119–144; Jan P. Beckmann, "Ontologisches Prinzip

Ockham gives us little information about the status and justification of the principle. He did not take it to be self-evident, like the principles of noncontradition and excluded middle, nor did he think it can be proved by prior principles or induced from experience. If we examine his use of the razor, it becomes quite clear that in his view it is one of the *probabilia* or generally accepted axioms or commonplaces used in topical or dialectical arguments. He seems to regard it as a reasonable principle, justified by the fact that it is accepted by everyone, at least by the majority and the wise, that is, by philosophers. As we shall see, he uses it as a premise in a nondemonstrative, persuasive argument, indicating that it is one of the topical *probabilia* he has just described. Does it measure up to a principle in *dialectica utens* in the strong sense of the term, that is, with its own truth and (conditional) necessity? Ockham does not explicitly say so, but he does not reduce the razor to a mere opinion that may or may not be true. He uses it extensively and with confidence, recommending it highly as "a principle that ought not to be denied."[55]

The dialectical status of the razor is clear enough in the following persuasive argument that the matter of earthly and heavenly bodies is of the same kind:

> A plurality should never be assumed without necessity, as has often been said. Now there is no apparent reason for thinking that the matter here and there is of different kinds, because whatever can be accounted for by different

---

oder methodologische Maxime? Ockham und der Ökonomiegedanke einst und jetzt," in *Die Gegenwart Ockhams*, ed. Wilhelm Vossenkuhl and Rolf Schönberger (Weinheim, 1990), pp. 191–207. Beckmann (p. 203 n1) provides early modern formulae of the razor: G.W. Leibniz (1670): "entia non esse multiplicanda praeter necessitatem"; Libertus Fromondus (1587–1654): "novacula Occami et Nominalium"; E.B. de Condillac (1746): "le rasoir des nominaux"; and W. Hamilton (1852): "Law of Parsimony."

55. See below, note 57. Ockham's phrase echoes Boethius' description of a maximal proposition: "quod omnibus vel pluribus vel sapientibus hominibus videtur, ei contradici non oportere" (*De topicis differentiis* 2 [PL 64: 1190C]).

kinds of matter can be accounted for equally well or better by matter of the same kind.[56]

He also argues with persuasion that in the eucharist quality, like substance, can be quantified without a distinct, added accident of quantity.

It is useless to do with more what can be done with fewer. This is a principle that ought not to be denied; for a plurality ought not to be assumed unless we can be assured of it by reason, experience, or the authority of someone who cannot be deceived or fall into error. Now, from the fact that substance, and also quality, can be quantified without such a quantity distinct from substance and quality, we cannot be assured by reason or experience that there is another quantity of this sort. Neither do we find this stated by any author who cannot err, for we do not find that God has revealed it. Hence it is not necessary to assume quantity of this sort, and so it is useless to posit it."[57]

56. "Sic igitur videtur mihi quod in caelo sit materia eiusdem rationis cum istis inferioribus. Et hoc, quia pluralitas nunquam est ponenda sine necessitate, sicut saepe dictum est. Nunc autem non apparet necessitas ponendi materiam alterius rationis hic et ibi, quia omnia quae possunt salvari per diversitatem materiae secundum rationem possunt aeque bene vel melius salvari secundum identitatem rationis" (*Rep.* 2.18 [*OTh* 5: 404.4–10.])

57. "Quod primo persuadetur sic: frustra fit per plura quod potest fieri per pauciora. Hoc enim est principium quod negari non debet, quia nulla pluralitas est ponenda nisi per rationem vel per experientiam vel per auctoritatem illius qui non potest falli, nec errare, potest convinci. Sed ex quo substantia potest esse quanta et similiter qualitas potest esse quanta sine tali quantitate distincta a substantia et qualitate, nec per rationem nec per experientiam potest convinci quod sit talis quantitas alia. Nec hoc invenitur expressum ab aliquo auctore qui non potest errare, quia non invenitur a Deo fuisse revelatum; igitur non est necesse ponere talem quantitatem, et ita frustra poneretur" (*Tract. de corp. Christi* 29 [*OTh* 10: 157.9–158.19; slightly modified]). Ockham uses the same argument in the *Tractatus de quantitate*, but without calling it persuasive. He says that it is clear by induction that whatever can be accounted for by a quantity added to substance can be accounted for without it; see *Tract. de quant.* 3 (*OTh* 10: 58.100–107).

Ockham uses the razor as Aristotle did when arguing against Anaxagoras' assuming infinite bodies to explain the generation of things. When Aristotle says, "It is better to assume a smaller and finite number of principles, as Empedocles did," Ockham remarks:

> Here the Philosopher infers that it is better to assume finite principles, as Empedocles did when he assumed six principles, namely, four elements, strife, and friendship, than to assume infinite principles, as Anaxagoras did. This is because everything that can be explained by an infinite number can equally well be explained by a finite number; and a plurality should never be posited without necessity. Hence a finite number, and not an infinity, should be posited.[58]

These and other arguments in Ockham's works employ the razor as their operative principle leading to a conclusion in dialectical reasoning. When neither side of a disputed question can be strictly demonstrated and reasons can be given for both, the razor tips the scale in favor of the simpler solution. Ockham quotes with

---

58. "Hic Philosophus infert quod melius est ponere principia finita sicut fecit Empedocles qui posuit sex principia, scilicet quattuor elementa et litem et amicitiam, quam ponere infinita principia sicut posuit Anaxagoras, et hoc quia aeque possunt omnia salvari per finita sicut per infinita, et pluralitas numquam est ponenda sine necessitate. Ideo sunt ponenda finita, non infinita" (*Expos. in Phys.* 1.11 [*OPh* 4: 118.2–7]). See Aristotle, *Phys.* 1.4, 188a17–18; *De caelo* 3.4, 302b27–31.

Ockham says that Aristotle assumes (*supponit*) the principle (ibid. 3.10 (*OPh* 4: 525.15–20). But Aristotle does not assume it without giving reasons. One should prefer, he says, a proof deriving from fewer postulates or hypotheses, for "where they are fewer knowledge will be more speedily acquired, and that is a desideratum" (*Anal. Post.* 1.25, 86a33–36). Again, "We ought, however, to suppose that there is one [prime mover] rather than many, and a finite rather than an infinite number. When the consequences of either assumption are the same, we should always assume that things are finite rather than infinite in number, since in things constituted by nature that which is finite and that which is better ought, if possible, to be present rather than the reverse" (*Phys.* 8.6, 259a8–12; trans. Hardie and Gaye).

approval the saying of Duns Scotus: "Every plurality is reduced to unity or to the smallest possible number."[59]

The importance of the razor in Ockhamism is attested by the fact that Ockham's anonymous follower who wrote the *Tractatus de principiis theologiae* between 1328 and 1350 could draw eighty-one of his conclusions from it.[60]

Ockham does not call the razor a maxim – a term he seldom uses but one that was commonly employed by Boethius and earlier medieval logicians for a dialectical or topical proposition. Indeed the razor does not appear in the traditional lists of these maxims.[61] Rather, Ockham calls the razor a principle (*principium*); but it seems to fit the Aristotelian-Boethian description of a dialectical maxim, accepted by everyone or by the majority, especially by the wise. Another apt term for the razor is Boethius' "common conception of the mind" (*communis animi conceptio*), denoting a statement accepted by everyone or at least by the learned as soon as it is heard.[62] This was the term given to the razor by Peter of Candia, who died as Pope Alexander V in 1410.[63]

The razor is a rule prescribing that a plurality of items should not be affirmed without necessity, but by itself it does not tell us what counts as necessary. Ockham leaves us in no doubt about his own criteria. A plurality should not be affirmed, he says, unless we

59. "Omnis pluralitas reducitur ad unitatem vel ad paucitatem tantam ad quantam reduci potest" (Scotus, *Ord.* 1.2.2.1–4 (Vatican ed. 2: 305.14–15), cited by Ockham, *Ord.* 1.7.2 (*OTh* 3: 134.3–5). See Henry of Ghent, *Quodl.* 6.1 (*Opera omnia* 10: 2.43–52).

60. *Tract. de prin. theol.*, principia 2 (*OPh* 7: 607–639). For the author and date of the treatise see the editor's introduction *OPh* 7: 26*.

61. See the lists of maxims of Boethius and Peter of Spain in Green-Pedersen, *Tradition of the Topics*, pp. 46–57. Lists of traditional maxims are also found in Stump, *Dialectic and Its Place in the Development of Medieval Logic*. Ockham's list of maxims are rules for consequences not having syllogistic form. See *Sum. log.* 3-3.1–38 (*OPh* 1: 587–731).

62. Boethius, *De hebdomadibus* (PL 64: 1311B).

63. Peter of Candia, *In Sent.* 1.6.2 (Vatican City, BAV, MS Vat. lat. 1081, f. 131rb). I am indebted to Gedeon Gál for this reference.

are convinced of its necessity by reason, experience, or an infallible authority such as the scriptures or tradition.[64] In theology he appeals to the authority of the Church in conjunction with the razor when he cautions that we should not grant more miracles than the authority of scripture and the Church fathers allow.[65] In philosophy reason and experience dictate the limits to what must be assumed in order to verify a proposition. The razor is a general rule enjoining parsimony in this regard; but since it was accepted by almost all the schoolmen,[66] even by Ockham's opponents, by itself it clearly could not lead to his personal positions. For these, we must look not only to the razor but also to his views on what is reasonable or can be induced from experience.

It has been said that in Ockham's usage the razor has to do with concepts and propositions and not with realities; that it is a methodological tool and not an ontological principle.[67] It is true that the razor is expressly a methodological rule directing the affirmation and denial of propositions, but when they have to do with the real world the rule is not unrelated to that world. The method of any philosophy is an essential factor in determining its contents. If this is true, the razor has an ontological as well as a methodo-

---

64. *Tract. de corp. Christi* 29 (*OTh* 10: 157.9–158.16); *Ord.* 1.30.1 (*OTh* 4: 290.1–3); *Rep.* 3.9 and 4.3–5 (*OTh* 6: 281.6–17 and *OTh* 7: 51.24–52.8).

65. *Ord.* 26.1 (*OTh* 4: 157.20–25). Peter Aureol makes the same point regarding miracles (*Commentaria in Sent.* 4.12.3 [Rome ed. 2: 120a]).

66. A contemporary, John of Reading, criticized the razor as being of little use, enabling Ockham to prove few conclusions: "Unde ista propositione concessa paucas conclusiones posset ipse [Ockham] tenere, quia paucas isto modo probat" ("Quaestio Ioannis de Reading de necessitate specierum intelligibilium. Defensio doctrinae Scoti," ed. G. Gál, *Franciscan Studies* 29 [1969]: 142).

67. See Ariew, "Did Ockham Use His Razor?," pp. 5–17, and "Ockham's Razor: A Historical and Philosophical Analysis of Ockham's Principle of Parsimony" (PhD dissertaton, University of Illinois, 1976). According to Gordon Leff, Ockham made "extensive use of the Razor "to excise unnecessary concepts" (*William of Ockham*, p. 35 n141). Beckmann contends that the principle of economy is not an ontological but methodological maxim ("Ontologisches Prinzip oder methodologische Maxime?," p. 202).

logical bearing. It should be noted that Ockham does not restrict the principle to extramental realities; he also applies it to concepts, as when he contends that there need not be distinct concepts corresponding to all words, such as participles and pronouns.[68] But as we proceed, I hope it will be evident that he thought the principle implies something about the reality of the world and not just about how we know it or talk about it. It is in the spirit of the razor, for example, that he eliminates entities dear to Duns Scotus and his followers, especially what Ockham calls "small entities" (*res parvae*), such as relations, motion, and action. The thrust of the razor, for both Scotus and Ockham, is toward unity and simplicity in both concepts and reality.[69]

In defense of the reality of the "small entities" eliminated by Ockham, Walter Chatton, a contemporary critic of Ockham, devised his own counter-principle or anti-razor: "My rule," he declared, is that "if three things are not enough to verify an affirmative proposition about things, a fourth must be added, and so on."[70] He thought Ockham was too parsimonious in estimating what entities should be posited in order to verify propositions such as, "A is the efficient cause of B." In Ockham's view there is no need of a third reality, namely a real relation of causality. As we have seen, he considers the two absolute realities of cause and effect to be sufficient.[71] Chatton replied that a third, relative reality, is needed. For consider the proposition, "A produces B." Because God is omnipotent, he can produce A and B by himself; then the same two absolute realities exist but God and the two things by themselves cannot verify the proposition, for now it is

68. *Sum. log.* 1.3 (*OPh* 1: 11.13–26).

69. See above, note 59.

70. Walter Chatton, *Reportatio* 1, d. 30, q. 1, a. 4 (Paris, BNF, MS lat. 15887, f. 63rb); *Lectura* 1, d. 3, q. 1, a. 1 (Florence, Bibl. Naz., MS Conv. soppr. C. 5, 357, f. 82ra). See Maurer, "Ockham's Razor and Chatton's Anti-Razor," pp. 463–475 (repr. *Being and Knowing*, pp. 431–443). The anti-razor is also found in Chatton's *Reportatio et Lectura super Sententias*, prol.2.1 (ed. Wey p. 85.252–268).

71. See above, p. 51.

not A but God who produces B. In order to verify the proposition, a third reality – a real relation of causality – is needed.[72]

In his dispute with Chatton, Ockham does not reject the anti-razor out of hand, for he agrees with Chatton that all the items needed to verify a proposition must be affirmed. But he calls the anti-razor false "unless it is better understood," and again, "false as it is generally understood." The misunderstanding he refers to is the use of the razor in conjunction with the divine omnipotence. As we have seen, Chatton argues that if God miraculously made A and B exist, they could not verify the proposition "A produces B" and therefore a third relative reality of causality is required. But Ockham retorts that if God works a miracle, the addition of a hundred things would not be enough to verify the proposition "A produces B." Why not? Because now the proposition is false: not A but God produces B. In the ordinary course of nature, and excluding miracles, two things are sufficient to verify the proposition.[73] This shows that Ockham intended the razor to be used in philosophy along with the dictates of reason and experience and not with God's extraordinary workings.

The principle of parsimony has continued to be generally accepted in Western philosophy and science to our own day. Chatton's counter-principle was adopted by several of his contemporaries, and since then other efforts have been made to mitigate the austerity of the razor.[74] The anti-razor had the positive result

72. This generalizes Chatton's arguments in *Reportatio* 1, d. 30, q. 1, a. 4, cited in note 70. Ockham reports one of them in *Quodl.* 6.12 (*OTh* 9: 629.8–13).

73. *Quodl.* 6.12 (*OTh* 9: 632–633); cf. ibid. 1.5 (9: 32–34). For references to Chatton see the editor's notes *OTh* 9: 31 n8 and 629 n1.

74. Like Chatton, his contemporary pseudo-Richard of Campsall adopted the anti-razor: "quandocunque aliqua proposicio affirmativa verificatur pro rebus, si vna res non sufficiat ad verificandum talem proposicionem, oportet ponere duas, et si due non sufficiant, tres, et sic in infinitum" (Pseudo-Richard of Campsall, *Logica Campsale Anglicj* 41.19 (ed. Synan 2: 237). The anti-razor is also found in an anonymous Franciscan logic: *Anonymi auctoris franciscani Logica 'Ad rudium'* 59, ed. L.M. de Rijk (Nijmegen, 1981), p. 38 (I am indebted to Paul Vincent Spade for this reference). For modern versions of the anti-razor see Maurer, "Ockham's Razor and Chatton's Anti-Razor," pp. 465–466 (repr. *Being and Knowing*, pp. 433–434).

that Ockham began to reword the razor in terms of the verification of a proposition. In his *Quodlibeta* (a relatively late work), he sometimes uses the more precise philosophical formula: "When a proposition is verified of things, if three or two things suffice for its truth it is not necessary to assume a fourth."[75]

If the razor has the status of a dialectical principle in Ockham's philosophy and theology and in this capacity plays a significant role in them, it is important to know how much weight he gives to it and to his positions based explicitly or implicitly on it. Is the razor only a commonplace or expert opinion whose opposite might equally well be true, or is it a true and even a (conditionally) necessary axiom? Are the conclusions based on it plausible and not necessarily convincing, or do they call for our firm and unquestioning assent?

There are no sure answers to these questions in the works of Ockham. We can be certain that he regarded the razor as a principle, not in demonstrative but in dialectical reasoning, and as such it plays a significant though subordinate role in shaping his views on reality and the mind. It is also probable that the razor should be interpreted in the light of the notion of dialectical reasoning set forth in the two mature logical works of Ockham: the commentary on Aristotle's *De sophisticis elenchis* and the *Summa logicae*. The razor would then be not only a probable opinion but a true and (conditionally) necessary principle. Moreover, it would be true not only on the authority of the philosophers but in itself as a reasonable guide for thought. As for the conclusions flowing from it, they would not be doubtful but highly believable.

75. "[Q]uando propositio verificatur pro rebus, si tres res vel duae sufficiunt ad veritatem illius propositionis, quarta res superfluit" (*Quodl.* 7.1 [*OTh* 9: 704.17–19]). Is the later formulation of the razor an improvement over the older ones? John Boler believes that it was not meant to be, but it was used by Ockham because he was disputing with Chatton ("Ockham's Cleaver," p. 144 n68). That may be true. It is certainly true, as Boler says, that the later formula in terms of verification introduces "a new and special topic" in the razor. But it has the same function as the earlier formulas, so that Ockham can subtitute it for them and with more precise philosophical language.

The Principle of Noncontradiction
Besides the principle of parsimony Ockham employs the principle of noncontradiction as a powerful means of establishing his positions and rebutting those of his opponents. The nature of these two principles should be carefully distinguished. As we have seen, the razor is not a self-evident principle nor is it evident through experience or demonstration; rather, it is accepted as a maxim approved by everyone or almost everyone, especially by the wise. The principle of noncontradiction, on the contrary, is a primary self-evident proposition (*per se nota*), in the sense that it is known simply by knowing its terms.[76] It does not serve as the premise of a demonstration but it is the necessary prerequisite for all demonstrations.

We have seen how Ockham resorts to the notion of contradiction, and especially to the primary contradiction between being and nonbeing, to prove a distinction between things. Contradiction, in fact, is the best way to prove a distinction between things. If it can be said that A is and B is not, we can conclude that A is not B. Again, we can argue that this thing is A, that thing is not A, therefore this thing is not that thing. If we deny the validity of these syllogisms and claim that absolutely one and the same predicate can be truly affirmed and denied of the same thing, it would be impossible to show that there is any distinction between things. What is more, Ockham does not allow Duns Scotus to qualify contradiction with the syncategorematic mode 'formally,' so that one can argue: If A is formally A, and B is not formally A, then A and B are really identical but formally nonidentical. For Ockham, all contradiction is equal and proves a real distinction between things.[77]

In the dispute over the formal distinction Ockham takes it for granted that logical contradiction can be applied to things as well as to concepts. Ockham's world, which contains nothing but

76. On primary indemonstrable first principles see *Sum. log.* 3–2.4 and 3–2.13 (*OPh* 1: 509–511 and 1: 527–530); *Ord.* 1.prol.2 (*OTh* 1: 81–82).

77. See above, pp. 74–75. For Ockham's use of the principle of noncontradiction see Maurer, "Method in Ockham's Nominalism," pp. 431–436 (repr. in *Being and Knowing*, pp. 411–417).

individual things (*res*), each of which *is* itself and *is not* another, is perfectly attuned to the logical principle of noncontradiction.

The rule of contradictories is so absolute for Ockham that not even God is exempt from it. God is absolutely powerful and free, but he cannot do or make anything whose doing or making includes an evident contradiction. "I believe in God, the Father almighty" is the first article of the Apostles' Creed, and by this Ockham means that "everything that does not include a clear contradiction is to be attributed to the divine power." From this he derives the proposition: "Whatever God produces by means of secondary causes he can immediately produce and conserve without them."[78] However, this cannot be demonstrated by reason; only a persuasive argument can be given that God has infinite power, but this is not sufficient to demonstrate the divine omnipotence.[79]

The Principle of Omnipotence

In Chapter 5 we shall have occasion to treat of omnipotence as a divine attribute. Ockham also uses the divine omnipotence as one of his most potent principles in settling philosophical as well as theological questions. As we shall see, he employs this principle to establish the possibility of an intuition of something that does not exist.[80] To prove that a point is not an absolute reality, really distinct from a line or surface, he first offers arguments from philosophy and then from theology. One of the theological arguments appeals to the absolute power of God: If a point were a distinct reality, God could cause it to exist without a line or surface.[81] The metaphysical question of the real distinction between essence

---

78. *Quodl.* 6.6 (*OTh* 9: 604.13–605.20); *Quodl.* 4.22 (*OTh* 404.14–17); *Ord.* 1.prol.1 (*OTh* 1: 35.8–10). See *Enchiridion Symbolorum*, ed. H. Denzinger, A. Schönmetzer, 36th ed. (Freiburg-im-Br., 1976), p. 21 n12.

79. Natural reason cannot prove that God wills things other than himself, that he has power to cause anything, and consequently that his will is always fulfilled; see *Ord.* 1.46.2 (*OTh* 4: 679–680).

80. See below, pp. 480–487.

81. *Tract. de quant.* 1 (*OTh* 10: 5–45); for theological arguments see ibid. (10: 17–26).

and existence in creatures is settled by invoking the divine omnipotence: If they were really distinct they would be two realities
(*res*) and consequently God, being omnipotent, could produce one
without the other.[82] So widespread is Ockham's use of the principle of the divine omnipotence that the anonymous Ockhamist
who wrote the *De principiis theologiae* was able to derive one hundred and sixty-nine of Ockham's theological and philosophical conclusions from it. Indeed, the author aims to show that Ockham's
whole doctrine turns around this article of faith and the philosophical principle of the razor. He further wishes to show that his
master had no intention whatsoever to restrict the conclusions flowing from the principle of the divine omnipotence to theology and
those flowing from the principle of the razor to philosophy. As the
editors of the *De principiis* sum up the situation, in both theological
and philosophical discussions Ockham indifferently has recourse to
one of the principles at one time and to the other at another time.[83]
As a consequence the abundant use of the two principles puts its signature on both Ockham's theology and philosophy.

The reader will no doubt be surprised to find Ockham using the
revealed doctrine of the divine omnipotence as a premise from which
to draw philosophical conclusions. Is he not mixing faith with reason
and theology with philosophy? And yet he has no intention of confusing them. On the contrary, he distinguishes philosophy as a work
of human reason from theology as a discipline based on faith leading
to eternal salvation. Indeed, he does not countenance the inclusion of
faith in science or philosophy in the strict sense of the term.[84]

In order to appreciate Ockham's thinking in this regard it
must be pointed out that he was the heir of two traditions. On the

82. See above, p. 61.
83. "Nullo tamen modo tentavit [compilator] monstrare quod ex uno
conclusiones theologicae ex alio vero conclusiones philosophicae fluxerunt.
Fuisset enim tentamen prorus vanum. Ockham enim de hac re minime cura-
vit, sed in discussionibus, sive philosophicis sive theologicis, indifferenter
nunc ad unum nunc ad aliud recurrit" (editor's introduction, *Tract. de prin.
theol.* [*OPh* 7: 27*]).
84. See below, p. 136.

one hand he inherited the thirteenth-century distinctions between faith and reason, and between philosophy and theology developed by scholastic theologians confronting Aristotelianism and other non-Christian philosophies. On the other hand he embraced the Augustinian and Anselmian ideal of the theologian as a Christian sage, seeking to understand the truths of faith, and philosophizing under the influence of the light of faith. This was the ideal of the theologians of the thirteenth century, notably Bonaventure, Aquinas, and Duns Scotus. Their philosophies were Christian in the sense that, while keeping the two orders of reason and faith formally distinct, they looked to Christian revelation as an indispensable aid to reason.[85] Scholastic theologians, however, did not always use revelation in the same way as an aid to philosophy. Bonaventure gave a significant role to religious piety and the glorification of God in assessing the efficacy of free will and knowledge, and of created causes in general; the causal efficacy of creatures was minimized out of piety and for the enhancement of God's glory.[86] Others, such as Aquinas, thought that the use of theological arguments in behalf of philosophical propositions was inimical to the rationality of philosophy. Though philosophizing under the guiding light of faith, Aquinas did not draw philosophical conclusions from revealed premises, but only from premises that are self-evident or known from experience.[87]

Against this background, perhaps we can understand Ockham's use of the revealed truth of the divine omnipotence in a theological argument in support of a philosophical proposition. He had

---

85. This is Etienne Gilson's description of Christian philosophy in *The Spirit of Mediaeval Philosophy* (New York, 1936), p. 37.

86. See Etienne Gilson, *The Philosophy of St. Bonaventure*, trans. Illtyd Trethowan and Frank J. Sheed (1938; Paterson, NJ, 1965), pp. 431–432; *The Unity of Philosophical Experience* (New York, 1941), pp. 49–56. A different view of Bonaventure the philosopher can be found in John F. Quinn, *The Historical Constitution of St. Bonaventure's Philosophy* (Toronto, 1973).

87. Etienne Gilson, *The Christian Philosophy of St. Thomas Aquinas*, trans. L.K. Shook (New York, 1956), pp. 18–21.

no intention of confusing faith and reason or theology and philosophy. He makes it clear that an argument with the divine omnipotence as one of its premises is theological. But as a theologian he felt justified in bringing theological arguments to bear upon philosophical issues, at least when human reason failed to demonstrate them. Because in his view the mind seldom rises to a strict demonstration of philosophical tenets, he looked for other resources to confirm his philosophical conclusions. In this situation he turned to the principle of the divine omnipotence and to the razor to provide probable and persuasive arguments in their behalf.

Ockham saw this as one of the important ways in which philosophy and theology can communicate with each other. Theology uses philosophical arguments in its effort to understand the Faith. Why should not philosophy turn to theology and use theological arguments when they are helpful? Of course, no aid is needed if philosophy has strictly demonstrated its conclusion; but when the conclusion is only probable, a theological proof may lend it support.

This communication between theology and philosophy is possible because, as we shall presently see,[88] Ockham does not conceive the two disciplines as strictly differentiated, in the Thomist manner, by formal objects. Neither does he believe, with Aquinas and Henry of Ghent, that each is a single mental habit (*habitus*), but an orderly collection of habits disposing one to infer conclusions and to refute those of his opponent. Corresponding to each conclusion or argument there is an individual habit, so that a science is composed of a vast number of habits with their respective conclusions, organized and unified into a logical whole. Moreover, because the cognitive habits of a science have only the unity of a collection, Ockham sees no problem in the same habit being integrated into several sciences, such as metaphysics and theology. And if this is so, it is reasonable that cognitive habits and propositions belonging to philosophy should be taken over and used by the theologian as an aid to the understanding of faith,

88. See below, pp. 140–144.

and that in turn habits and propositions belonging to theology should be incorporated into philosophy when they prove useful to it. This would appear to justify his frequent use in philosophy of theological arguments based on the divine omnipotence.

3 Science

The Nature of Science

Ockham uses the term *scientia* in a broad sense to cover not only demonstrated scientific conclusions but also other types of knowledge and even belief. In general it is "the certain knowledge of any truth." This includes truths known only by faith. We may not have seen Rome, yet we know on the witness of others that it is a large city. We also know who our father and mother are even though this is not evident to us. As long as we adhere to a statement without any doubt and it is true, we can be said to know it. In a more restricted sense of the term, *scientia* is the evident knowledge of some contingent fact known by experience; for example, that a particular wall is white. More limited still, *scientia* is the evident knowledge of necessary truths, whether they are principles or conclusions drawn from them. In the strictest sense *scientia* is the evident knowledge of a necessary truth that can be caused by the evident knowledge of necessary premises used in syllogistic discourse. In short, it is the necessary conclusion of a demonstration. It is in this latter sense that Aristotle uses the word "science" as distinct from intuition (*intellectus*: the knowledge of principles) and wisdom (*sapientia*: knowledge of the highest causes).[89] But science is not restricted to scientifically demonstrated conclusions; it embraces the whole knowledge involved in the demonstration.[90]

89. Aristotle, *Eth. Nic.* 6.3, 1139b16–17.
90. *Expos. in Phys.* prol. (*OPh* 4: 5.27–6.52); *Ord.* 1.prol.2 (*OTh* 1: 87.20–89.4). For three meanings of "to know" (*scire*) see *Sum. Log.* 3–2.1 (*OPh* 1: 506.22–39); cf. Aristotle, *Anal. Post.* 1.2, 71b18–22. For Ockham's view of science see Robert Guelluy, *Philosophie et théologie chez Guillaume d'Ockham* (Louvain and Paris, 1947).

Science in the strict sense, then, excludes opinion, belief and conjecture (*suspicio*), for they are not evident knowledge. It also excludes knowledge of contingent truths and first principles: the former because they lack necessity, the latter because they cannot be known by syllogistic reasoning but only by self-evidence or experience. Ockham says that necessary conclusions of science *can be* caused by the evident knowledge of necessary premises because he does not exclude experience as another way they can be known.[91]

The Division of the Sciences

Science, understood in this strong sense, and including wisdom as the peak of science (that is, metaphysics), is synonymous with philosophy. This was the language of Aristotle and it was adopted by Ockham. Like Aristotle, too, he divides theoretical philosophy into three main kinds: natural philosophy or physics, mathematics, and metaphysics. Moral philosophy or ethics is practical philosophy. Logic is both a science in its own right and an instrument of the sciences. Grammar, rhetoric, and logic (the Trivium), and the mechanical arts, are called practical sciences, but these are arts rather than sciences in the strict sense.[92]

Some sciences fall between physics and mathematics, such as optics (*perspectiva*), music, and astronomy (*astrologia*). These sciences "which are in between mathematics and physics (*mediae inter mathematicam et physicam*)" use mathematics in order to draw conclusions about the physical properties of things. Ockham refers in this connection to Aristotle's remarks about medicine using mathematics to understand why circular wounds heal more slowly. The physical property of a wound being cured more slowly if it is circular is explained by a principle of geometry. Medicine can do this because it is in part subalternated to geometry. Similarly, the intermediate sciences of optics, music, and astronomy are in part sub-

---

91. *Ord.* 1.prol.2 (*OTh* 1: 88.2–13). For experience as the source of the knowledge of necessary conclusions see ibid. (*OTh* 1: 90–93).
92. *Sum. phil. nat.* praeam. (*OPh* 6: 149.298–314).

alternated to both physics and mathematics, and consequently they can use mathematical principles to account for the physical properties of things. Because these sciences use mathematics in order to draw conclusions about physical properties, they are more like physics than mathematics.

In his account of the mathematical-physical sciences Ockham is indebted to Aristotle and Averroes, and also, it seems, to Aquinas. Ockham's significant quotation from Averroes: "The practitioner of optics considers lines in a way in between (*media*) the two considerations of geometry and physics,"[93] points to Averroes as the source of the term *media* used by the medieval schoolmen in their description of mathematical physics as *scientia media*.[94]

Ockham's recognition and acceptance of mathematical-physical sciences should not go unnoticed. It is usually thought that Ockham was aloof from, and out of touch with, the contemporary mathematical approach to physics at Oxford through the efforts of Thomas Bradwardine and others *calculatores*. It has been said that Ockham separated mathematics and physics, with the consequence that he was not in harmony with "the development of mathematical physics – the single most important development in fourteenth-century science."[95] It is true that Ockham's approach to physics was empirical rather than mathematical; indeed, his conception of motion as a term rather than as a reality hardly lends itself to mathematical inquiry. He did not experiment with the motion and

93. The foregoing account is based on *Expos. in Phys.* 2.3 (*OPh* 4: 266–267). Ockham quotes Averroes' statement: "Aspectivus autem considerat de lineis in dispositione media inter illas duas considerationes; non enim considerat de linea secundum quod est linea simpliciter ut geometer, neque secundum quod est linea ignea, aut aerea ut naturalis, sed secundum quod est visualis: istud enim est quasi medium inter naturale et mathematicum" (Averroes, *In Phys.* 2, com. 20 [Junta ed. 4: f. 55vab]).

94. For Aquinas' doctrine of *scientia media* see *Expositio super librum Boethii De Trinitate* 5.3, ad 5.6.7, ed. Bruno Decker (Leiden, 1955), pp. 188–189; *Expos. in Phys.* 2, lect. 3, nn. 336, 338; *ST* 2–2.9.2, ad 3.

95. William J. Courtenay, *Schools and Scholars in Fourteenth-Century England* (Princeton, NJ, 1987), p. 209.

velocity of bodies and devise mathematical formulae to express them; but he knew and approved of the theory behind the mathematical study of nature. Moreover, in so doing he remained in the Franciscan tradition dating back to Robert Grosseteste, the first teacher of the Franciscans at Oxford. In his work on optics Grosseteste insisted on the necessity of applying mathematics to physics, and his Franciscan disciple Roger Bacon likewise declared that without mathematics nothing can be known about nature.[96]

The three main kinds of theoretical philosophy are examined at length in Ockham's *Expositio in libros Physicorum*. We shall limit our inquiry to a few aspects of his doctrine of the sciences that are a consequence of his conceptualism.

Philosophy is called a science of reality (*scientia realis*), in contrast to logic, which is a rational science (*scientia rationalis*). The distinction between them is not that philosophy treats of extramental things themselves and logic treats of mental constructs like concepts and propositions. "Every science," Ockham writes, "whether it be real or rational, is concerned only with propositions as with objects known, for only propositions are known."[97] In this context, "known" is to be understood as "scientifically known." There can be intuitive knowledge of individuals through the senses and intellect, but, as Aristotle said, scientific knowledge is only of universals. In Ockham's words, "science is not of individuals but of universals standing for indivi-

---

96. For the views of Grosseteste and Bacon see A.C. Crombie, *Medieval and Early Modern Science*, 2 vols. (New York, 1959), 2: 18–24. For Ockham and the Oxford calculators see James A. Weisheipl, "The Interpretation of Aristotle's Physics and the Science of Motion," in *Cambridge History of Later Medieval Philosophy*, ed. Kretzmann et al., pp. 530–536, and *The Development of Physical Theory in the Middle Ages* (1960; Ann Arbor, MI, 1971), pp. 72–87; Edith D. Sylla, "The Oxford Calculators," in *Cambrige History*, ed. Kretzmann et al., pp. 540–563.

97. "[E]st sciendum quod scientia quaelibet sive sit realis sive rationalis est tantum de propositionibus tamquam de illis quae sciuntur, quia solae propositiones sciuntur" (*Ord.* 1.2.4 [*OTh* 2: 134.7–9]). But note the qualification: "... dico quod scientia realis non est semper de rebus tamquam de illis quae immediate sciuntur sed de aliis pro rebus tantum supponentibus" (ibid. [*OTh* 2: 134.3–6]).

duals themselves."[98] Thus, properly speaking, natural philosophy does not treat of generable and corruptible things, natural substances, or movable things for concepts, not things, are the subjects and predicates of the conclusions known in natural science. Strictly speaking, natural science concerns mental concepts signifying things and standing for them in propositions. Only metaphorically and improperly can natural science be said to treat of corruptible and movable things themselves.[99]

The question of the immediate object of scientific knowledge was warmly debated in Ockham's day. His Franciscan confrere Walter Chatton opted for the realistic position that science is directly founded on the reality signified by the terms of its propositions, namely subjects and predicates. Its immediate object is not (as Ockham claimed) the propositions demonstated by science. Ockham's follower, Adam of Wodeham, tried to find a *via media* between these two opinions. In his view, the object of science is neither the conclusions of scientific demonstrations nor external reality itself, but the adequate signification or meaning of the conclusions thus demonstrated. Adam's suggestion was not popular in the Middle Ages, but it assumes some importance in the modern philosophy of meaning.[100]

The mathematical sciences are also *scientiae reales*, for they treat of properties of bodies like surfaces, lines, and points; but unlike the natural sciences they do not consider them as accidents of natural bodies. When mathematicians define their object, they abstract from the motion and change that accompany it in the real world. Thus mathematics is a science distinct from physics, but

98. *Expos. in Phys.* prol. (*OPh* 4: 11.22–24). See Aristotle, *Anal. Post.* 1.4–5, 73b26–74a13.

99. Ibid. (*OPh* 4: 11.15–26).

100. For Wodeham's views see Gedeon Gál, "Adam of Wodeham's Question on the *Complexe Significabile* as the Immediate Object of Scientific Knowledge," *Franciscan Studies* 37 (1977): 66–102. The notion of *complexe significabile* was studied by Hubert Élie, *Le complexe significabile* (Paris, 1936); though, as Gál has shown, he has attributed it to Gregory of Rimini, not to Adam of Wodeham.

each in its own way treats of the same things. But does not mathematics demonstrate the relations between its subjects, as geometry shows the equality of the sides of a triangle, and has it not been proved that relations are not realities distinct from related things? So it would seem that the subjects of mathematics are not realities. In reply, Ockham concedes that mathematical properties are relative or relations, but in his view this does not destroy mathematics as a *scientia realis*. For a science to be "real," it is not required that the terms of its propositions are real but only that they stand for (*supponant*) realities. A relative term does not stand for a real relation but for related things. Mathematical properties, like those of all the human sciences, are only intentions or concepts in the mind, but they stand for real things, and consequently the mathematical sciences are counted among *scientiae reales*.[101]

Like physics and mathematics, metaphysics is a science of reality, but because it treats of being absolutely (*ens simpliciter*), which includes both extramental and mental being, its concepts are both first and second intentions. In contrast, concepts of physics and mathematics are only first intentions, while those of logic are only second intentions.[102]

In the debate over the subject of metaphysics: is it being, as Avicenna said, or God and the separate substances, as Averroes said? Ockham chooses both sides. He sees no reason why both being and God cannot function as subjects of metaphysics. In his view a science is so loosely organized that it can have several subjects. But more about this later.[103]

Do the sciences differ by their formal objects and by the different ways they consider their subjects? This is how Aquinas and his pupil

101. *Ord.* 1.30.1 (*OTh* 4: 318.17–319.2). On the difference between mathematics and physics see *Expos. in Phys.* 2.3 (*OPh* 4: 256–267).

102. *Sum. Log.* 3–2.22 (*OPh* 1: 543.34–47). For the meaning of first and second intentions see above, pp. 22–23. For a brief account of Ockham's metaphysics see Philotheus Boehner, "The Metaphysics of William Ockham," *The Review of Metaphysics* 1 (1947–1948): 59–86, repr. in his *Collected Articles on Ockham*, ed. E.M. Buytaert (St. Bonaventure, NY, 1958), pp. 373–399.

103. *Expos. in Phys.* 1.18 (*OPh* 4: 208). Scotus chose the side of Avicenna.

Giles of Rome distinguished between the sciences. According to Giles of Rome (whom Ockham cites without naming), we can discern in things "something material and something formal." The same things, taken as it were materially, can be apprehended under different formal aspects (*rationes*) and with different methods, giving rise to different sciences. Everything known in a science is apprehended under a special formal aspect (*ratio*), as natural philosophy considers the sun and moon under the aspect of mobile bodies. Mathematics is a different science because it views the same objects under a different aspect, namely quantity.[104] Aquinas had already distinguished between the sciences on the basis of their various formal objects and the different ways they apprehend reality.[105]

In Ockham's view, the Thomist account of the distinction between the sciences is unsatisfactory because it presupposes that within one and the same thing there are many distinct *rationes*, or intelligible aspects, which can be the basis of different sciences. For example, natural philosophy can apprehend something under the *ratio* of its mobility; mathematics can apprehend the same thing under the *ratio* of its quantity; and metaphysics can apprehend it under the *ratio* of its being. Moreover, the Thomists were of the opinion that many things can share the same nature of movement, quantity, and being, so that even though the things are materially different, they can fall within the various sciences because of their formal possession of the same nature.

We have already seen Ockham's opposition to the notion that individuals can share the same nature, and that one and the same individual is the locus of several diverse *rationes*, one of which can be known in abstraction from another. To him, a *ratio* is a concept, which can signify and stand for things but which does not exist in them; it exists only in the mind.[106]

---

104. Giles of Rome, *Commentaria in octo libros Physicorum Aristotelis* 2.3, dub. 1 (Venice, 1502; repr. Frankfurt, 1968), f. 30vb. See Ockham, *Expos. in Phys.* 2.3 (*OPh* 4: 261).

105. Aquinas, *Expositio super librum Boethii De Trinitate* 5.1-4 (ed. Decker pp. 161-200); *ST* 1-2.54.2.

106. See below, p. 197.

The Subject, Object, and Unity of a Science

As a consequence Ockham devised his own conception of the subject and object of a science, its unity, and its distinction from other sciences. He defines the object of a science as the whole proposition known in the science and its subject as the subject term of the proposition.[107] Since a science is made up of many propositions, each of which may have its own subject, a science cannot be said to have just one primary subject which gives unity to the science. A total science is composed of many parts with many subjects. For example, metaphysics draws conclusions about being but also about God, so that both being and God function as subjects of metaphysics.[108]

Each science, then, is a collection of many propositions and mental dispositions (*habitus*) to know or to demonstrate them. A science is not a single *habitus* of the mind, as Aquinas and Henry of Ghent believed. Its unity is that of an collection, "in the same sense that a city, a nation or an army, which includes men and horses and other necessities, or a kingdom, a university, or the world, is said to be one."[109] Of course, these are not pure aggre-

107. *Expos. in Phys.* prol. (*OPh* 4: 9.87–91). Walter Chatton, as a realist, criticized Ockham's notion that the subject of a science is the subject-term or concept of a scientific conclusion. He argued in part that one can come to a conclusion in science without being aware of the subject-term of the conclusion. We become aware of this term or concept only by an act of reflection. Hence the subject of the conclusion is not the subject of the science but the reality signified by it: "Igitur subiectum conclusionis non est subiectum scientiae, sed res significata per illud" (Chatton, *Reportatio et Lectura*, prol.5.2 [ed. Wey, p. 286.44–50]). The whole prologue 5.2 treats of various notions of the subject of theology.

108. Being is the primary subject of metaphysics from the viewpoint of predication; God is the primary subject from the viewpont of perfection. Natural substance is the primary subject of natural philosophy regarding predication, man or the heavenly bodies regarding perfection; see *Expos. in Phys.* prol. (*OPh* 4: 10.115–120).

109. Ibid. (*OPh* 4: 7.26–29). Ockham criticizes Aquinas and Henry of Ghent for claiming that a science is a single intellectual habit (*habitus*) whose unity is based on the science's having one formal object or one formal mode of knowing; see *Ord.* 1.prol.8 (*OTh* 1: 208–225). Walter Chatton argued against Ockham and Peter Aureol for teaching that the unity of theology, like that of any science, is

gates: they have a unity of order, and so too does a science. The propositions of a science, such as physics, mathematics, or metaphysics, have a logical relation to each other which gives the science its unity. For example, the science may demonstrate of the same subject many properties which are logically related as superior and inferior. Thus geometry demonstrates of the subject "figure" the attributes of magnitude and its logical inferiors "circle" and "triangle." The unity of a science may also be found in its subjects, as in the science of animals the properties of animal in general are demonstrated not only of animal but also of the different genera and species of animal. Lastly, the unifying order of a science may consist in both its subjects and predicates, as, for example, the properties of animal are predicated of animal, and the properties of the various species of animal contained under the genus are predicated of these species. Because the terms of a science have a logical relation of this sort, it is called one science.[110]

Consequently a science does not have numerical unity but the unity of a organized collection of cognitive items: primarily habits of knowing (which are qualities of the mind), but secondarily propositions (mental, spoken, or written) which are the objects of these habits. These habits and propositions do not by nature belong to the whole science. An item of knowledge may be integrated into a whole science, but it does not by nature belong to that science to the exclusion of other sciences. Thus the truth that

---

not based on one mental *habitus*; see *Reportatio et Lectura*, prol.5.3 (ed Wey, pp. 297–311). For Aureol's doctrine of the unity of science see Paul Vincent Spade, "The Unity of a Science according to Peter Auriol," *Franciscan Studies* 32 (1972): 203–217. For discussions of Ockham's doctrine of the unity of a science see Armand Maurer, "Ockham's Conception of the Unity of Science," *Mediaeval Studies* 20 (1958): 98–112; and "The Unity of a Science: St. Thomas and the Nominalists," *St. Thomas Aquinas 1274–1974: Commemorative Studies*, ed. A Maurer (Toronto, 1974), 2: 269–291, repr. Maurer, *Being and Knowing*, pp. 71–93.

110. *Ord.* 1.prol.8 (*OTh* 1: 219.14–220.6). In ibid. 9 (*OTh* 1: 255.13–22), Ockham lists among the kinds of order the subjects of a science may have the order of perfection, one being more excellent than another; also the order of totality, one being a whole and another an essential or integral part.

God is one, or the habit of demonstrating it, is neither theological nor metaphysical in itself. It does not in itself belong to theology or metaphysics, any more than a man of himself is part of a nation or an army. Just as he can be included in either or both, so a truth can be integrated into one science or many.[111]

It was usual in the late Middle Ages to distinguish between the mode of abstraction proper to each of the theoretical sciences, as Aquinas does in his commentary on the *De Trinitate* of Boethius. For Aquinas, each of the sciences grasps its formal object by a special mental act in which it leaves out of consideration other intelligible features united to that object, as mathematics apprehends the quantity of bodies apart from their qualities and motions.[112] Ockham takes up the theme of abstraction in the sciences, but in terms of his own notion of a science. Abstraction in a science occurs, he says, "when one attribute is predicated of a subject and another attribute is not predicated of the same subject, or vice versa." In short, abstraction is simply knowing one proposition and not another. For example, mathematicians abstract when they entertain propositions such as "Every body is long, wide, and deep," but leave out of consideration propositions such as "Every body is movable." Thus mathematics differs from physics by abstracting from motion. Echoing Aquinas, Ockham says that all the sciences abstract the universal from the individual; but for him this is not the abstraction of a nature from the individuals in which it exists, but rather the mind's producing a universal concept that signifies and stands for the individual.[113]

---

111. *Ord.* 1.prol.1 (*OTh* 1: 13.14–14.5).

112. Aquinas, *Expositio super librum Boethii De Trinitate* 5.2–4 (ed. Decker, pp. 173–200).

113. *Expos. in Phys.* 2.3 (*OPh* 4: 264.164–265.194). The first meaning of abstraction is the mind's understanding one thing (*res*) without understanding another thing to which it is joined. This notion of abstraction has to do with individuals, not with intelligible natures or forms or the act of existing (*esse*). Ockham says that this abstraction is found even in the senses, for a sense can perceive one sensible thing without perceiving another; see ibid. (*OPh* 4: 264.153–163).

Theoretical and Practical Science

The distinction between theoretical and practical knowledge or science was warmly debated in Ockham's day. All the participants in the discussion agreed with Aristotle's dictum, that "the end of theoretical knowledge is truth, while that of practical knowledge is action,"[114] but they could not agree on its interpretation. To Henry of Ghent, Aristotle's meaning is clear enough: he is saying that theoretical and practical sciences are distinguished by their ends. Now the end can be either the end of the science or the end of the scientist. The end of the science is that to which the science itself is directed; the end of the scientist is that to which the scientist directs science. Now the basis of the distinction between theoretical and practical science is not the end intended by the scientist, but rather the principal end to which the science by its very nature is directed. In the case of theoretical science the end is truth; in the case of practical science it is something made or done (*opus*).[115]

The fallacy in Henry's reasoning, according to Ockham, is to suppose that science, taken just in itself and by its nature, has some end or final cause. He reminds his reader that a final cause is something intended by an agent, so that the end or purpose of science cannot be different from the end intended by the scientist. The end of every action is an intended end. There is no difference between the end of an agent, or the end he intends to achieve, and the end of his action or of the form he produces. This is clear from the fact that science really and essentially comes into existence only because of the end or purpose of the scientist. He may learn science in order to earn money or for some other reason, but without some such intention there would absolutely be no science.[116]

---

114. Aristotle, *Metaph.* 2.1, 993b20–21; *De anima* 3.10, 433a14–17.

115. Henry of Ghent, *Summa* 36.4 (*Opera omnia* 28: 107, 115–116); see Ockham, *Ord.* 1.prol.11 (*OTh* 1: 303.2–304.13). For practical and speculative science see also Ockham, *Sum. phil. nat.* praeam. (*OPh* 6: 147–152).

116. *Ord.* 1.prol.11 (*OTh* 1: 304.15–306.5).

An end may be either something one wants to acquire by taking some action, as walkers walk for the sake of their health; or the end may be an object loved for its own sake, as the acquiring of health is for the sake of the well-being of the walker. Applying this distinction to science, it can be said that the end of science, properly speaking, may be either an object acquired by the pursuit of science, such as wealth, or it may be the achievement of the scientist's own personal excellence loved for his own sake. Either end can motivate a person to learn and acquire science, so that it can be said that the end of the scientist and of science are absolutely the same. Science does not have an end or final cause of itself; its end is the end intended by the scientist.

What, then, is the meaning of the common adage that theoretical knowledge is for the sake of truth and practical knowledge is for the sake of some action or work? It does not mean that these knowledges have specific ends of themselves apart from the intentions of the knower. As was said above, the end or final cause of knowledge is strictly that which moves a person to acquire it. But the person's motive may not be correct; he may freely pursue knowledge for inappropriate ends. If he follows right reason, his intention in acquiring practical knowledge will be the doing or making of something, and his intention in acquiring theoretical knowledge will be simply to know.

Not only may these two kinds of knowledge have different final causes, as defined above, but they are by themselves formally and intrinsically distinct as qualities of the mind. They are not distinct by their subjects, for the two kinds of knowledge can sometimes have the same subject. An instance is the earth, which has many properties that do not come under our power, such as its roundness, dryness, and gravity. If they can be demonstrated of the earth, all the conclusions about them are purely theoretical and belong to natural science. But the earth has other properties that do come under our power, such as its capacity to be cultivated, and conclusions about such matters belong to the practical science of agriculture.

Theoretical and practical knowledge, however, are not so distinct that practical conclusions cannot be deduced from theoretical principles. Thus, from the purely theoretical truth that the earth is hard many practical conclusions follow. Though writers commonly speak of purely theoretical principles, they are in fact virtually practical: no principle is so purely theoretical that it does not have some bearing on our action or practice (*praxis*).[117] Thus mathematics is useful in the mechanical arts, and practical science is subalternated to theoretical science; for example, music to arithmetic. This would not be so if practical conclusions could not be reduced to theoretical principles.

If theoretical and practical knowledge are not distinguished by their ends (except in the sense explained above) or by their subjects, what is the difference between them? Ockham claims they are distinguished by their conclusions, which, as we have seen, are the objects of science. If the conclusion contains something we can do or make (*operabile*), the knowledge if practical; if not, it is theoretical. Again, practical knowledge directs action and practice, so it always concerns something doable. Of course theoretical knowledge can also treat of our actions and works, not in order to direct or accomplish them but in order to understand them. Thus Aristotle's treatise on the soul (*De anima*) comes under theoretical science, though for the most part it concerns things we do. On the other hand, logic, rhetoric, and grammar do not come under theoretical but practical knowledge, because they direct the mind's activities over which we have control through the mediation of the will. These sciences are not practical in the sense that they dictate that

117. For Ockham, the acts of intellect and will and external actions under the control of the will are most properly called *praxis*. But even acts of the sensory or lower powers are in a sense *praxis* insofar as they are directed to a further end; see *Ord.* 1.prol.10 (*OTh* 1: 294.16–296.8). Ockham opposes the view of Robert Cowton, that *praxis* is restricted to external acts and acts of powers below the intellect and will, and Scotus' opinion that it is the act of the will in conformity with right reason and thus excludes acts of the intellect; see ibid. (*OTh* 1: 277.5–285.21). Walter Chatton criticized Ockham's notion of *praxis* in his *Reportatio et Lectura*, prol.6.2 (ed. Wey, pp. 330–332).

something should or should not be done or made; they simply show how it should be done or made. Thus the art of architecture shows how to construct a building, but it does not say whether or when it should be made. This is left to the art of prudence.[118] We shall see later the role of moral science in directing human acts.[119]

4 Theology

The translation into Latin of the major works of Aristotle in the twelfth and thirteenth centuries brought about a veritable revolution in theology in Western Europe. Now the full range of his philosophy was available as an instrument for advancing the understanding of the Faith. Theology was even organized and structured on the lines of an Aristotelian science, resulting in what is known as scholastic theology.[120]

Is Theology a Science?

Ockham has an important place in this theological movement, both carrying on the scholastic tradition begun in the twelfth century and turning it in new directions in the fourteenth.

Following Duns Scotus, Ockham distinguishes between theology in itself and theology as it actually exists in us. Theology in the first sense is evident knowledge, the evidence being provided by its object. This is the sort of theological knowledge God has of himself and of everything else and the blessed have in heaven. Our theology lacks this evidence and is based in the final analysis on the authority of scripture, the pronouncements of the Church and the Church fathers. In short, the truths of our theology rest on faith and not on the evidence of its object.[121]

Ockham distinguishes between two meanings of theology as we actually know and possess it. In a narrow sense it is the knowledge

118. *Ord.* 1.prol.11 (*OTh* 1: 310.16–317.5).
119. See below, pp. 517–520.
120. See Yves M.-J. Congar, *A History of Theology*, trans. and ed. Hunter Guthrie (Garden City, NY, 1968), pp. 85–143; M.-D. Chenu, *La théologie comme science au XIIIe siècle*, 3rd ed. (Paris, 1957).
121. *Ord.* 1.prol.12 (*OTh* 1: 340.11–342.11).

of everything that is necessary to attain eternal life. This does not extend to everything but only to what is essential for reaching beatitude. It does not call for study and research into particular topics, as practiced by theologians in the universities; it is difficult enough to know what is needed to save one's soul! In a broader sense theology extends to everything of a theological nature, whether or not it is necessary for salvation. We can recognize this as the kind of theological investigation undertaken by the schoolmen, including Ockham himself. This investigation does not extend to all propositions (*complexa*), for many are not theological. For example, mathematical propositions like "Every triangle has three angles" are not theological and do not come within the ambit of theology, unless some theological property is predicated of them. But theology can extend to all concepts (*incomplexa*) and the things for which they stand, because it can prove theological properties of every one of them, such as that they are creatable, subject to annihilation, separable from every other absolute thing, producible by God without any secondary cause. Only theology takes into account these and other theological properties of all things, as metaphysics is the only science that takes into account all the properties of being.[122]

The importance of Ockham's description of theology for our present study should not be overlooked. Ockham insists that the study of theology in a way includes everything, but without absorbing all the other sciences or philosophy. We shall see in the next section that Ockham criticizes Aquinas' notion of the object of theology as "the divinely revealable" (*divinitus revelabile*) for its implication that all the conclusions of all the sciences belong to theology, because these propositions *can be* objects of revelation. Ockham is here insisting that the propositions of the other sciences are not theological but mathematical, logical, ethical, metaphysical, and so on. In other words, there are sciences distinct from theology with their own propositions and conclusions. Philosophy, in particular, has a status of its own, and it is not contained within theology.

---

122. Ibid. 1.prol.9 (*OTh* 1: 273.9–274.24).

To the question whether theology is a science in the proper sense of the word, Ockham answers with a distinction. No doubt God has the power to grant us an evident knowledge of theological truths that would be a science in the strict sense, (and perhaps he does grant to some an evident knowledge of certain theological truths), but in fact theology as it is usually practiced (*de communi lege*) is not strictly a science. This is because most theological truths are held on faith and not known with evidence. Since science properly so-called is evident knowledge, our theology is not properly speaking a science.

Ockham upholds this position against the views of many of his predecessors, including Henry of Ghent and Thomas Aquinas, both of whom contended that theology is indeed a science. Henry of Ghent maintained that both the principles and conclusions of theology are known by a special supernatural light between the light of faith and the light of heavenly glory.[123] Aquinas granted that the principles of theology are a matter of faith and not of reason, but he pointed out that there are also some natural sciences that use principles held on faith in a higher science. For example, optics takes principles from geometry and music from arithmetic. On the model of these sciences Aquinas conceived theology as a science subalternated to the knowledge of God and the blessed. They know with evidence the principles that the theologian believes because they have been revealed to him, and from which he can reason to conclusions.[124]

Ockham's main objection to these conceptions of theology as a science is that they introduce faith into science, which, as we have seen, has no place in it. Science, strictly speaking, is evident knowledge, not opinion or belief. Both principles and conclusions must be known with evidence if science is to measure up to its

---

123. Henry of Ghent, *Quodl.* 12.2 (*Opera omnia* 16: 14–27); see Ockham, *Ord.* 1.prol.7 (*OTh* 1: 187.3–14).

124. *ST* 1.1.2. Ockham interprets Aquinas to mean that the conclusions of theology constitute an acquired science while the principles are a matter of belief. Aquinas does not make this distinction, saying only that theology, thus subalternated to the divine knowledge, is a science; see Ockham, ibid. (*OTh* 1: 184.7–20).

ideal. This rules out theology as a science in the proper sense of the term. No doubt there are subalternated sciences, like optics, but their conclusions are not known with evidence unless they are known through experience or through premises known with evidence. "It means nothing," Ockham remarks, "to say that I know some conclusions because you know the principles in which I believe because you tell them to me. In the same way it is childish to say that I know the conclusions of theology because God knows the principles in which I believe because he reveals them."[125] Ockham places himself in the camp of Duns Scotus, who rejected the notion of our present theology as a subalternated science and called it a science only in a very broad sense of the term.[126]

The Unity of Theology

Like sciences in the strict sense, theology does not have the unity of a single mental habit (*habitus*). Rather, it is a complex of habits, including the infused habit of faith, an acquired habit of faith, and many scientific habits that the theologian uses to elucidate his beliefs and to dispute with non-believers. Its unity is a unity of order.[127] Ockham rejects Aquinas' view that theology, like other sciences, has one formal object which gives it its unity. According to Aquinas, theology treats of what has been divinely

---

125. Ockham, *Ord.* 1.prol.7 (*OTh* 1: 199.15–18).

126. Duns Scotus, *Ord.* prol.4.1–2 (Vatican ed. 1: 141, n. 208); 3.24.un. (Vivès ed. 15: 44, n. 13). Ockham criticizes Scotus' doctrine of the subject of theology in *Ord.* 1.prol.9 (*OTh* 1: 227–240). For Scotus' notion of theology see Etienne Gilson, *Jean Duns Scot* (Paris, 1952), pp. 47 (theology in itself), 50–53, 90, 118, 193, 357–58 (our theology); Congar, *A History of Theology*, pp. 129–130; Stephen D. Dumont, "Theology as a Science and Duns Scotus's Distinction between Intuitive and Abstractive Cognition," *Speculum* 64 (1989): 579–599. For Robert Holcot's views on theology as a science see Joseph T. Muckle, "Utrum theologia sit scientia: A Quodlibet Question of Robert Holcot, O.P.," *Mediaeval Studies* 20 (1958): 127–153.

127. *Ord.* 1.prol.8 (*OTh* 1: 220.7–20). Theology, in the sense of the supernatural infused habit of faith, is one in number; but with acquired faith (necessary for belief in the particular articles of the creed), and evident habits of knowledge, it has only the unity of an ordered whole: see *Ord.* 3.9 (*OTh* 6: 289–314).

revealed (*divinitus revelata*), so that everything revealed shares in the one formal object of this science. But, as we have seen, Ockham finds the notion of a formal object, as distinct from a material object, incomprehensible.[128] When Aquinas further claims that the formal object of theology is not only what has actually been revealed but also what can be revealed (*divinitus revelabile*), Ockham protests that, if this were so, "every conclusion in geometry would belong to theology, because every [conclusion] of this sort is divinely revealable." In short, theology would be the only science, embracing the conclusions of all the sciences.[129]

Aquinas avoids this unacceptable consequence because in his view each science has its own formal object, which for theology is divine revelation. Theology includes doctrines of the other sciences insofar as they are revealable and assist the theologian to understand the contents of faith. But this does not preclude the autonomy of the other sciences, each of which has its own formal object.

According to Ockham, Aquinas compounds his mistake by adding that God is the subject of theology. How can theology treat of all things under the aspect of God (*sub ratione Dei*), who is its subject, and also under the aspect of revelation, which is its object? Ockham writes: "Being divinely revealable is not the formal object of theology, ... because according to him (that is, Aquinas) God, under the aspect of deity, is the subject of theology."[130] But Aquinas saw no contradiction in his descriptions of the object and subject of

---

128. See above, p. 141.

129. *Ord.* 1.prol.8 (*OTh* 1: 208–211). See Aquinas, *ST* 1.1.3. Ockham reports Aquinas' shift in terminology from *divinitus revelata* to *divinitus revelabilia.* For Aquinas' notion of *revelabilia* see Gilson, *Christian Philosophy of St. Thomas Aquinas*, trans. Shook, pp. 10–15. It is hardly conceivable that Ockham should have been so knowledgeable about Thomism here and elsewhere if, as William Courtenay says, "Thomism was all but extinct at Oxford when Ockham was a student of theology" (*Schools and Scholars in Fourteenth-Century England*, p. 217). For a general comparison of the doctrines of Ockham and Aquinas see Marino Damiata, "Ockham e San Tommaso d'Aquino," *Studi francescani* 91 (1994): 21–88.

130. *Ord.* 1.prol.8 (*OTh* 1: 210.25–211.3); see Aquinas, *ST* 1.1.7.

theology. As he used the term, the subject of a science is the end or goal of the whole science, which in the case of theology is God. "The divinely revealable" is the object of theology considered as a mental *habitus*, with its unique formal perspective or light by which the theologian views both God and creatures.[131] This distinction was meaningless to Ockham because of his divergent notions of the object and subject of a science.

Theology as both Theoretical and Practical

Is theology a theoretical or practical science? Late medieval theologians gave different answers to the question. Some held that theology is purely theoretical, others that it is purely practical. Among the former were Henry of Ghent, Robert Cowton, and William of Alnwick. While not denying that for the most part theology can be called practical because it treats of human actions and affairs, they thought that absolutely speaking it should be called speculative wisdom because it concerns itself with eternal things, to which the things of time are directed. Although moral science theorizes about the truth, its aim is to bring about some good, and accordingly it is called practical. Theology, for its part, devotes all its efforts to speculation, and hence it should be said to be purely speculative. Alnwick defended this view by contending that, beyond speculation, theology extends to the love of God uniting our will to him. But the act of love is not *praxis*, or practical activity; rather, it is in the speculative order, like the love of God in heaven. Hence theology is also purely speculative and not practical.[132]

---

131. For Aquinas' notion of the subject of a science see *Expositio libri Posteriorum* 1.28.41 (Leonine ed. 1.2: 305). For the subject of theology see Gerald F. Van Ackeren, *Sacra Doctrina: The Subject of the First Question of the Summa Theologica of St. Thomas Aquinas* (Rome, 1952), p. 108. For the notion of theology as *sacra doctrina* see Etienne Gilson, *Elements of Christian Philosophy* (Garden City, NY, 1960), pp. 22–42; James A. Weisheipl, "The Meaning of *Sacra Doctrina* in *Summa Theologiae* 1, q. 1," *The Thomist* 38 (1974): 49–80.

132. *Ord.* 1.prol.12 (*OTh* 1: 325.8–328.7); for references to Henry of Ghent, Cowton, and Alnwick see *OTh* 1: 325 nn1–2. Stephen Brown has

Other theologians considered theology to be a purely practical science. Among their number were Peter Aureol and Duns Scotus. According to Scotus the primary object of theology is the final goal of the human race, which is the love of God. Since the principles derived from this final end are practical, both the principles and conclusions of theology are practical. Scotus is here following the Franciscan tradition as exemplified by Bonaventure, who viewed the main purpose of theology as making the human race good.[133]

Both these groups of theologians were convinced that theology is one science; more precisely it is one stable disposition or quality (*habitus*) of the mind, enabling it to engage in correct reasoning in order to achieve its end of either speculation or practice. We have already seen Ockham abandon this view of science in favor of a pluralism of mental habits. A science, in his view, is not a single *habitus* of the mind but it contains a great number, one corresponding to each conclusion reached in the science. The unity of the science consists in the order among these conclusions and among their respective mental habits.[134] It is not surprising, then, to find Ockham denying that theology is one knowledge or science. Rather, it contains many really distinct knowledges, some of which are purely practical and others speculative. The knowledge that God created the world, or that he is triune, can only be theoretical or speculative. On the other hand, the truth that God ought to be loved with one's whole heart, or that we ought to pray, is clearly practical. Hence one part of theology is practical,

---

edited the Questions of Robert Cowton and William of Alnwick on whether theology is a speculative or practical science ("Sources for Ockham's Prologue to the *Sentences* – Part II," *Franciscan Studies* 5 [1967]: 39–107).

133. *Ord.* 1.prol.12 (*OTh* 1: 333.8–335.6); for references to Aureol and Scotus see *OTh* 1: 333 n1 and 334 n2. For Bonaventure, the *habitus* of theology is both speculative and practical. It is the *habitus* of wisdom, containing both knowledge and love. It is for the sake of contemplation, and its principal end is to make humans good. See Quinn, *Historical Constitution of St. Bonaventure's Philosophy*, p. 683.

134. See above, pp. 142–144.

because it concerns our works and actions; in short, everything within our power to do or make. Another part is speculative, for it does not concern these matters.[135]

Ockham's view of theology as divided into two parts, speculative and practical, was opposed by his Franciscan confrere Walter Chatton. Chatton preferred the common opinion that the theologian has only one *habitus*, which is both speculative and in its own way practical. As the theologian comes to more conclusions, Chatton says, he does not acquire more theological habits; rather, the many conclusions he forms of the same subject coalesce into one conclusion. Accordingly he can acquire one habit corresponding to every conclusion he comes to about God. This habit is no doubt speculative; but in a way it is also primarily practical, because in God's intention it is directed to action. As is said in 2 Timothy 3:16–17: "All scripture is inspired by God and profitable for teaching, for reproof, for correction, and for the training in righteousness, that the man of God may be complete, equipped for every good work."[136]

135. "Dico igitur quod aliqua pars theologiae est practica, quia est de operibus nostris, accipiendo opera nostra pro omnibus quae sunt in potestate nostra, sive sint operationes sive operata; et aliqua est speculativa, quia non est de talibus" (*Ord.* 1.prol.12 [*OTh* 1: 338.15–18]). Ockham is here preparing the way for the modern division of theology into dogmatic and moral.

136. Chatton, *Reportatio et Lectura*, prol.7.4 (ed. Wey pp. 386.12–387.38). See Luciano Cova, "L'unità della scienza theologica nella polemica di Walter Chatton con Guglielmo d'Ockham," *Franciscan Studies* 45 (1985): 189–230. Aquinas (whom Ockham does not mention in this regard) also held the common view that theology is one science, extending to both speculative and practical issues, "just as by the same science God knows both himself and his works." However, theology is more speculative than practical, because it is more concerned with divine things than human acts (*ST* 1.1.4).

PART II

God

CHAPTER 3

The Existence of God

I T MIGHT SEEM OUT of place to treat of the existence and attributes of God at this point in an empirical philosophy such as Ockham's. It can be justified, however, from an heuristic point of view. At crucial moments in his physics, noetic, and ethics, he presupposes the existence of God and especially the attribute of omnipotence. It is therefore helpful to explore his views about God before launching into these areas of his philosophy.

1 Is the Existence of God Self-Evident?

Before offering proofs of God's existence medieval schoolmen usually asked whether his existence might be self-evident, in which case proofs would be unnecessary. Ockham follows this common practice, beginning his treatment of the existence of God by asking whether his existence is known *per se* or naturally, or whether it stands in need of proof.[1] But before answering the question he clarifies what he means by a proposition that is self-evident or known *per se*, using as a foil to his own opinion the opposed view of Duns Scotus.

Ockham reports that according to the Subtle Doctor a proposition known *per se* is one whose truth is evident solely through its terms and not through the truth of another proposition. The terms of the proposition alone suffice for an evident knowledge of it. It is important to notice that Scotus defines a proposition known *per se* considered just in itself, abstracting from whether anyone knows it *per se*. In other words, a proposition is not known *per se* because some mind knows it *per se* but because such is its very nature. As

---

1. *Ord.* 1.3.4 (*OTh* 2: 432–442).

a consequence Scotus refuses to distinguish between a proposition known *per se* and one knowable *per se*. For the same reason he rejects Thomas Aquinas' distinction between a proposition known *per se* in itself and one known *per se* to us. Whether or not we perceive the evidence of the truth of a *per se* known proposition does not alter its nature; it remains a *per se* known proposition even to us, though we may be ignorant of its terms.[2]

Scotus here defines a proposition known *per se* as he defines an essence or nature just in itself, abstracting from the existential conditions of the proposition, such as whether or not a mind actually knows the terms in which it is expressed. It is the nature of the terms of a proposition that makes it known *per se*. Scotus forcefully asserts: "[A] proposition is said to be known *per se* because by the nature of its terms it can have the evident truth contained in the terms, whatever the mind that conceives them may be. But if some mind does not conceive the terms, nor consequently the proposition, it is nonetheless known *per se*, taken just in itself; and it is thus that we speak of a proposition known *per se*."[3]

Accordingly Scotus would have us look to the nature of the terms of a proposition to determine whether or not it is a proposition known *per se*. Now the terms may be either names expressing the concept of an essence confusedly or indistinctly conceived, or a definition expressing the concept of an essence distinctly conceived. In other words, the terms may be either "the thing defined" or "the definition," for example "man" or "rational animal." In Scotus' view not all propositions that are necessary and in the first mode of *per se* predication are known *per se* but only those that include the definition of the subject. Thus, "Man is an animal" is not known *per se*, but only "A rational animal is an animal." In the latter case "animal" appears in both the subject and predicate

---

2. Scotus, *Ord.* 1.2.1.1–2 (Vatican ed. 2: 131–136, nn. 15–23). See Aquinas, *ST* 1.2.1.

3. Scotus, *Ord.* ibid. (Vatican ed. 2: 136, n. 22).

of the proposition, so that the inclusion of the predicate in the subject is self-evident.[4]

We are now in a position to understand Scotus' answer to the question: Is the proposition "God exists" known *per se?* He replies that it is if we mean by "God" "this divine essence," that is, the individual essence of God. The proposition is then known *per se* because it is evidently true in virtue of its terms, which give the evidence for its truth to anyone who perfectly understands them, such as God himself or the blessed in heaven, who enjoy an intuition of the divine essence, for existence belongs to nothing more perfectly than to that essence. Existence is not a predicate outside the notion of the subject but is contained in it, so that the proposition is immediately evident solely through its terms. In fact, however, we do not enjoy an intuition of the divine essence in this life, so that we do not know it as "this divine essence." Since existence belongs to God primarily as "this essence," we do not have direct access to the evidence of the truth of the proposition "God exists." We can form concepts of God proper to him, such as "necessary being," "infinite being," and "the highest good," but existence is not included in any of these concepts. So the propositions: "Infinite being exists" or "The highest good exists" are not *per se* known but must be proven to be true. Their evidence is not directly contained in their terms, but rather through the truth of other propositions by which they are demonstrated.[5]

Ockham grants some validity to Scotus' position when rightly understood, but he has two objections to it. First, Ockham protests that Scotus is wrong in thinking that something can be *per se* known regarding a definition but not regarding the thing defined. Thus it is impossible that "Every rational animal is capable of laughter" is *per se* known but not "Every man is capable of laugh-

---

4. Scotus, ibid. (Vatican ed. 2: 134–135, nn. 19–21). See Ockham, *Ord.* 1.3.4 (*OTh* 2: 432.13–433.5). For the first mode of predication *per se* see Aristotle, *Anal. Post.* 1.4, 73a34–37.

5. Scotus, ibid. (Vatican ed. 2: 137–140, nn. 25–27). See Ockham, *Ord.* ibid. (*OTh* 2: 433–434).

ter." His reason is that we can never know that a predicate belongs *per se* to a composite subject (for example, "rational animal") unless we know *per se* that its parts are united. He feels on sure ground here because Scotus himself concedes that "Nothing is *per se* known regarding a concept that is not absolutely simple unless it is *per se* known that the parts of that concept are united." Scotus' point is that "infinite" and "being" are not *per se* known to be united, and hence it is not self-evident that existence belong to the composite subject "infinite being"; in short, that infinite being exists.[6]

Ockham extends Scotus' rule to all composite concepts or definitions, contending that it is never *per se* known that the parts of a definition are united. An examination of the two kinds of definition bear this out. A definition in the proper sense joins a genus to a specific difference, as the definition of man unites "animal" to "rational." These concepts signify really distinct parts of the defined subject. Thus "animal" signifies all individual animals, while also signifying (though improperly) their matter or sensory soul. "Rational" signifies man's rational soul. Now matter, the sensory soul, and the rational soul are really distinct parts of man, and we cannot know *per se* that they are really united. Another type of definition, by addition (*per additamentum*) adds an accidental note to the subject defined, for example the definition of the soul as the actuality of the body. In this kind of definition, as in the previous type, it is not known *per se* that the parts of the definition are united, for we cannot know *per se* that an accident is related to something extrinsic to it. Indeed, the union of any parts that can enter into a definition is not necessary but contingent, and hence not *per se* known; for example, the union of matter and form, subject and accident, the integral parts of a whole, and the dependence of an effect on a cause. Being contingent, their union cannot be known simply by knowing the parts but only by experiencing their conjunction.[7]

6. Scotus, *Ord.* 1.2.1.1–2 (Vatican ed. 2: 140–141, n. 29).
7. Ockham, *Ord.* 1.3.4 (*OTh* 2: 435.10–436.8). For the distinction between a "real" definition (*quid rei*) and one by an addition outside the essence of the thing (*per additamentum*), see above, pp. 91–93.

Is it possible that the actual union of the parts of a definition be contingent but not their potential union? Not at all according to Ockham, for when we define man we say he is a rational animal, not that he can be a rational animal. But even if the definition expressed only a potential union of its parts, the union would still not be known *per se* or solely through these parts. Knowing matter and form, we could still doubt if form can be joined to matter. Knowing intuitively a subject and an accident, and never having seen them together, we could doubt the possibility of their being united.[8]

These remarkable statements of Ockham are a logical consequence of his elimination from reality of essences in some way distinct from individuals. For Scotus, a definition such as "rational animal" expresses the essence of humanity, with its own reality and real less-than-numerical unity.[9] In Ockham's account, to the contrary, a definition does not signify the human essence, but rather all individual humans or the concept of humanity.[10] From this, Ockham draws the logical conclusion that the union of the parts of a definition is not necessary but contingent and consequently not known *per se*.

The second difficulty Ockham finds with Scotus' doctrine of the perseity of the proposition "God exists" is that it seems to imply a distinction between the divine existence and essence. Ockham says "seems" because he is aware that Scotus explicitly taught the identity of essence and existence in God.[11] But why then does Scotus say that in the proposition "God exists" the predicate "existence" belongs to God prior to, and more perfectly than, any other predicate, such as "goodness" or "wisdom"? This is just not true, Ockham urges, "for if there is no distinction between the

8. Ibid. (*OTh* 2: 436.9–21).
9. See above, pp. 69–71.
10. *Sum. log.* 1.29 (*OPh* 1: 91); *Quodl.* 5.20 (*OTh* 9: 557.8–558.19).
11. For the Scotist doctrine of the identity of God's essence and existence see Etienne Gilson, *Jean Duns Scot* (Paris, 1952), p. 149 and n2, and *Being and Some Philosophers*, 2nd ed. (Toronto, 1952), pp. 92–93.

divine essence and the goodness or wisdom that is really the divine essence, much more, or equally, is there no distinction between the divine essence and existence that is really the divine essence itself."[12]

Ockham was not alone in suggesting that Scotism implies a distinction between essence and existence in God. Though Scotus himself taught that existence belongs to the concept of the divine essence, some of his followers considered existence to be an intrinsic mode outside the concept of God's essence.[13] This was a betrayal of Scotus' philosophy, but it was a consequence of the Scotist notion of essence (derived from Avicenna) as solely *what* something is, to the exclusion of any of its determinations, including its existence. As Gilson says in this context, "If essence is just what it is, then it cannot be its own existence."[14] Ockham seems to be aware of the obscurity in Scotus' doctrine of the divine essence and existence leading to its development in later Scotism.

After voicing his difficulties with Scotus' notion of a *per se* known proposition, Ockham proposes his own. According to Scotus, all that is required to know the truth of this type of proposition is the knowledge of its terms. But Ockham protests that this is not enough; there is also needed the formation of the proposition from the terms, and this is possible only by an act of the will. Hence the will is needed as the efficient cause of a *per se* known proposition – at least as its indirect or mediate cause (*causa mediata*). After the will has brought together the terms of the proposition, knowledge of the terms is the immediate cause of knowing the truth of the proposition.[15] The Scotists, for their part,

12. *Ord.* 1.3.4 (*OTh* 2: 437.9-13).

13. This was the teaching of the Scotists Francis of Meyronnes (*fl* 1323) and Antonio Trombetta (*ca* 1468). See Gilson, *Being and Some Philosophers*, pp. 94-96. See also Armand Maurer and Alfred Caird, "The Role of Infinity in the Thought of Francis of Meyronnes," *Mediaeval Studies* 33 (1971): 201-227, repr. *Being and Knowing* (Toronto, 1990), pp. 333-359.

14. *Being and Some Philosophers*, p. 95.

15. *Ord.* 1.3.4 (*OTh* 2: 438.12-19). A *causa mediata* is called the cause of a cause, because it causes an effect, and that effect causes a second effect, so that if

denied the role of the will in the assent to an evident truth. Thus John of Bassolis (d. 1347) thought that the command of the will has nothing to do with the assent: the mind makes the assent by virtue of the object and the mind's natural power.[16]

Sometimes the incomplex knowledge of terms and their formation in a proposition suffice for the evident knowledge of the proposition, and yet the proposition is not *per se* known. This is the case with a contingent proposition; for example, "Socrates is white." In order to know the truth of a contingent proposition there is required the intuitive knowledge of its terms and the things signified by them. Thus, anyone who intuitively sees Socrates and whiteness existing in him, can evidently know that Socrates is white. If he only knows Socrates and his whiteness abstractively (that is, in abstraction from their existence, by imagining them in their absence), he cannot have an evident knowledge that Socrates is white. Hence a contingent proposition, whose terms are known intuitively, does not qualify as *per se* known. Ockham implies that only necessary propositions meet this requirement.[17]

After these general considerations concerning propositions known *per se*, Ockham answers the question: Is the proposition "God exists" among them? He begins by distinguishing between the terms of this proposition which we have and those which the blessed in heaven have. It is clear that our concepts of God and existence do not yield the evidence of his existence, for we can

---

the first effect remains it can cause the second effect without the prior cause. Thus the father of Socrates is the indirect cause of Socrates' son; see *Expos. in Phys.* 2.5 (*OPh* 4: 283.19–284.33).

16. John of Bassolis, *In Sent.* 1.prol.1 (Paris ed. f. 3ra), cited anonymously by Ockham, *Ord.* 1.prol.1 (*OTh* 1: 20.22, with the editor's note 20 n1).

17. *Ord.* 1.3.4 (*OTh* 2: 438.12–439.9). See *Ord.* 1.prol.1 (*OTh* 1: 6.15–7.3). For the meaning of intuitive and abstractive knowledge, see below, pp. 473–478. A proposition is contingent which is neither necessary nor impossible; see *Sum. log.* 2.27 (*OPh* 1: 334.5–6). A proposition is not said to be necessary because it is always true but because, if someone forms it, it is true and cannot be false. If no one states or conceives the proposition, it cannot said to be true. An example of a necessary proposition is "God exists"; see ibid. 2.9 (*OPh* 1: 275.72–79).

doubt his existence, and there can be no doubt about the truth of a *per se* known proposition. For their part, the blessed in heaven can form two propositions that God exists, both of which are known *per se*. The first results from their intuitive knowledge of the divine essence. Seeing that essence, the blessed can predicate the divine existence of it. Since these are identical, the blessed predicate the same thing of itself (*essentia de essentia*). A predication of this sort is evidently known to be true and the mind necessarily assents to it. The second proposition of God's existence the blessed can form is also a consequence of their vision of the divine essence, but in this case they predicate the abstract term "existence" of the divine essence. The result is a *per se* known proposition, for no one seeing the divine essence can doubt its existence, even though it is known abstractively.[18]

In the present life, however, neither of these *per se* known propositions that God exists is within our power, for we do not enjoy an intuition of the divine essence. Our proposition joins together two different terms, "God" and "exists." In doing this we do not predicate the same thing of itself, as Aquinas thought, because the predicate "exists" is not the deity itself, nor is it a term predicable of it alone, but it is a term common to God and creatures. Neither is it a part of the subject term "God" or intrinsic to it. This is in accord with Ockham's general rule that a common term is never of the essence of the term of which it is predicated, nor is it essentially included in its quidditative concept; but, if the predication is essential or *in quid*, the predicate is said essentially of the subject, for it expresses the essence of the subject or the thing signified by it. This rule depends on Ockham's fundamental doctrine that what we predicate are only terms and not something in some way existing in reality. It follows that for Ockham the term that is predicated is not part of the thing of which it is

---

18. *Ord.* 1.3.4 (*OTh* 2: 440.3–22). Ockham claims that the blessed can also demonstrate God's existence through propositions formed as a consequence of their abstractive knowledge of him; see ibid. (*OTh* 2: 441.8–10).

predicated nor of its essence, and yet it is predicated of it essentially or *in quid*.[19]

Consequently in the proposition "God exists" the term "exists" is not part of the term "God" nor is it intrinsic to its quidditative concept. However, it is predicated essentially or *in quid* of God because it signifies his essence.[20] But since the proposition can be doubted, it is not like those propositions that are immediately evident through a knowledge of their terms. In short, it is not known *per se*. And if this is the case, the truth of the proposition "God exists" must be established by demonstrating it from more evident premises. It is to this problem that we shall now turn.

2 Proof of the Existence of God

In his *Ordinatio* Ockham does not devote a special *Quaestio* to the possibility of proving God's existence; but when he asks whether there is only one God, he gives his views on proving both God's existence and oneness.[21] In later works, the *Quodlibeta* and *Quaestiones* on Aristotle's *Physics*, he returns to the topic of God's existence, adding important clarifications to his doctrine but not changing it in any essentials.[22]

The *Ordinatio* begins with an abbreviated presentation of Scotus' proof of the existence of God as the first efficient cause, omitting the proofs of his existence as the final cause and transcendent being. Ockham also passes over the apogee of the Scotist ascent to God: the proof of his infinity. So closely are Ockham's views tied in with those of Scotus, that we should begin, as Ockham does, with a summary account of Scotus' doctrine.[23]

---

19. *Ord.* 1.2.7 (*OTh* 2: 255.20–256.20); Aquinas, *ST* 1.2.1.

20. Ibid. 1.3.4 (*OTh* 2: 441.21–442.7).

21. Ibid. 1.2.10 (*OTh* 2: 337–357).

22. *Quodl.* 1.1 (*OTh* 9: 1–11); *Quaest. in Phys.* 132–136 (*OPh* 6: 753–769).

23. *Ord.* 1.2.10 (*OTh* 2: 338–340), quotes *verbatim* from Scotus, *Ord.* 1.2.1.1–2 (Vatican ed. 2: 151–159, nn. 43–53). Scotus' similar proof of the existence of God in his *Reportata Parisiensia* is edited and translated in William A. Frank and Allan B. Wolter, *Duns Scotus, Metaphysician* (West Lafayette, IN, 1995), pp. 40–107. The

Scotus begins his proof with the proposition "Some being is producible," which he takes as an evident truth because we observe that some beings actually are produced. Now if some being is producible, it must be producible either by itself, by nothing or by something else. It is not producible by itself, for nothing can bring itself into existence; nor by nothing, since nothing cannot produce anything. It must, then, be producible by something else, which can be called A. Now A is either the absolutely primary being (and then Scotus has proved what he intends), or it is not absolutely primary, and then it is producible by another being, which we can call B. B is then either the absolutely primary being, or it is producible by still another being. This process will either go to infinity or it will finally halt at a being that is absolutely first. But an infinite regress in efficient causes is impossible, and therefore there must be an absolutely primary being or God.

The main difficulty with this proof concerns the impossibility of an infinite regress in causes. Did not philosophers like Aristotle show that the series of generations extends to infinity, and so there must be an infinite regress in causes?[24] Scotus replies that the infinite series of causes Aristotle had in mind was one in which the causes are related to each other accidentally and not essentially. An infinity of causes in an accidental order is possible but not one in an essential order.

Clarifying these statements, Scotus first explains the difference between an essential cause (*causa per se*) and an accidental cause (*causa per accidens*). The former causes an effect through its own nature, as fire produces heat; the latter produces an effect through something accidental to it, as a white body may be said *per accidens*

---

final version of the proof is in Scotus' *De primo principio*. For Scotus' proof see Gilson, *Jean Duns Scot*, pp. 131–143; Wolter, "Duns Scotus and the Existence and Nature of God," *Proceedings of the American Catholic Philosophical Association* 28 (1954): 94–121, repr. *The Philosophical Theology of John Duns Scotus*, ed. Marilyn M. Adams (Ithaca, NY, 1990), pp. 254–277.

24. Aristotle, *De generatione et corruptione* 2.11, 338b5–19.

to cause heat. Causes are said to be arranged in an essential or accidental order because of three different relations they have to each other in the production of an effect:

(1) In an essentially related series of causes a second cause depends on the primary cause for its causality, whereas in an accidentally related series the second cause does not depend on the primary cause for its causality but only for its existence or something else. An example of an accidentally arranged series of causes is a number of human generations, one human begetting another, who in turns begets still another. In the act of begetting, the second parent does not depend on his father for his causality but only for his existence. An example of an essentially arranged series of causes is a primary and instrumental cause, such as a writer and his pen. The pen depends on the writer both for its power to cause the writing and for its actual causing it.

(2) In a series of causes essentially related, their causality is not of the same nature or order. The causality of the primary cause is superior to, and more perfect, than that of the second cause.

(3) All causes essentially related must be simultaneously present in order to produce the effect, but this is not the case with causes accidentally related.

After these clarifications, Scotus shows the impossibility of an infinite series of essentially related causes, and also the impossibility of an infinite series of causes accidentally related unless there is a finite series of essentially related causes.

(1) Consider the sum total of effects produced by a series of essentially related causes. That totality has been caused, and not by a cause that is a member of that totality, because it would be its own cause. The whole aggregate of those dependent beings is dependent, and not on one member of the aggregate. Hence the aggregate depends on a cause transcending it, and this is the absolutely primary being.

(2) If there were an infinite series of essentially related causes, there would be an actual infinity of existing causes, for we have seen that causes so arranged must be simultaneously present to produce their effect.

(3) As Aristotle explains, something is prior because it is closer to the beginning.[25] But if there is no beginning there is nothing essentially prior. Hence there must be an absolutely prior being.

(4) It was shown above that a higher cause has a more perfect causality. It follows that an infinitely higher cause is infinitely more perfect, and so its causality will be infinitely perfect. Consequently it will not cause anything through the power of some other cause.

(5) A productive cause does not necessarily have some imperfection. Consequently there can be a perfect causal power that does not depend on any prior cause.

Unfortunately Ockham's citation of Scotus' proof of the existence of an absolutely primary being ends at this point, omitting its crucial completion. Up to now, Scotus has only shown the *possibility* of a primary cause or God, for he began with the obvious proposition that some being is *producible*. He has yet to prove the *actual existence* of a primary cause or God. This he does by showing that if this being is possible, it must actually exist, for otherwise it would be impossible. He makes this move from the possible to the actual order of being by arguing that the possibility of the absolutely primary being cannot be realized by something else; otherwise something would be prior to it and it would not be the absolutely primary being. Hence it must have its possibility from itself, and it can do this only if it actually exists. In short, the only conceivable reason why the primary cause is possible is that it exists.[26]

Ockham not only truncates the Scotist proof of God's existence as the absolutely primary efficient cause, but he mentions only in passing that Scotus offers similar arguments that there exists an absolutely primary final cause and transcendent being, and that the threefold primacy of efficiency, finality, and transcendence coincide in the one divine being.[27]

25. *Metaph.* 5.11, 1018b9–11.

26. Scotus, *Ord.* 1.2.1.1–2 (Vatican ed. 2: 164–165, n. 58).

27. *Ord.* 1.2.10 (*OTh* 2: 340.14–16). See Scotus, *Ord.* 1.2.1.1–2 (Vatican ed. 2: 165–173, nn. 60–73).

Ockham strikes at the heart of the Scotist proof of God's existence by denying its basic distinction between an essential and accidental cause. Scotus defined an essential cause as one that causes through its own nature, whereas an accidental cause causes through something accidental to that nature. For example, a hot body heats *per se* whereas a white body heats *per accidens*. But Ockham protests that if the same body is both hot and white, it is just as true to say a white body heats *per se* as it is to say a hot body heats *per se*, for in this case the terms "white body" and "hot body" stand for precisely the same thing. Of course, it does not follow formally that if "The hot thing heats" is a *per se* proposition, so also is the proposition "The white thing heats." Nor does Ockham think Scotus thought otherwise, "because of his expertise in logic."[28]

This leads Ockham to redefine the distinction between a cause *per se* and a cause *per accidens*. The latter is one that produces its effect not through its whole self but through one of its parts. The former produces its effect through itself and not through something else really distinct from it. In line with these definitions, we must say that fire heats *per accidens* because the substance of fire heats through the quality of heat. If fire were annihilated by God and the quality of heat conserved by him (a real possibility since God is omnipotent), the quality would nonetheless heat without the substance of fire. Similarly it is true to say that humans reason *per accidens*, because they reason through a part of themselves, that is, through their intellectual souls. If the soul is separated from the body, it can still reason and will. In general, therefore, "an action that first of all belongs to a part is said to belong to the whole *per accidens* because it belongs to it through something else."[29]

We are here encountering another important consequence of Ockham's banishing natures or essences from things. For schoolmen like Aquinas and Scotus, who thought that individual things

---

28. Ockham, ibid. (*OTh* 2: 344.18–20).

29. "[A]ctio quae primo convenit parti, dicitur convenire toti per accidens, quia convenit sibi per aliud" (ibid. [*OTh* 2: 345.7–9]).

are endowed with natures, an individual causes an effect *per se* when it acts in accordance with its nature. Thus Aquinas writes: "One thing is the cause of another essentially (*per se*) if it produces its effect by reason of the power of its nature or form." It produces an effect accidentally (*per accidens*) if it causes it indirectly, by removing an obstacle to the production.[30] For Ockham, however, there are no natures or essences in things through which they might cause effects. Hence his definitions of causes *per se* and *per accidens* are not in terms of nature or form but of a whole and its parts, which, it will be recalled, are only contingently united in the composite whole.

It should come as no surprise that Ockham, having redefined causes *per se* and *per accidens*, rejects Scotus' distinction between series of causes related *per se* and *per accidens*. Scotus contended that in a series of essentially related causes the secondary cause depends on the first cause for its causality, whereas this is not the case in accidentally related causes. Ockham asks what is meant by "depends on the first cause for its causality"? Does it mean that the secondary cause cannot produce its effect without the first cause? No, for just as in many instances the secondary cause cannot produce its effect without the first cause, so the first cause often needs the secondary cause for its causality. For example, many efficient causes in the sublunar world need the sun in order to produce their effects, but neither can the sun act as a cause without these secondary agents. Does it mean that a secondary cause depends on the first cause for its existence? No, because this is the case with causes related accidentally in a series. If this is all that is meant, all causes in a series would be related *per accidens*. Does it mean that a secondary cause receives an active power or some other influence from the first cause? If so, the influence can only be local motion or some substantial or accidental form. But it often happens that when a secondary cause acts it does not receive local motion or any absolute form from the first cause.[31]

---

30. *ST* 1–2.85.5.
31. *Ord.* 1.2.10 (*OTh* 2: 347.8–348.11).

Do causes that are related *per se* have different natures and belong to different orders because the superior cause is more perfect, as Scotus contends? But if "superior" means prior in perfection, this begs the issue, for you are only saying that what is more perfect is more perfect. If "superior" means more universal, it is simply not the case that the more universal cause is always more perfect than the less universal cause. As Scotus admits, the more universal cause is sometimes less perfect. For example, the inanimate heavenly bodies are less perfect than living things, and yet they are the universal causes of the generation of living things on earth.[32]

Must all the causes in a *per se* arranged series be present simultaneously in order to produce the effect? Ockham points out that even Scotus grants an exception to this rule. In medieval physics the heavenly bodies and particular agents on earth usually concur in the generation of living things, but when they are produced by spontaneous generation the heavenly bodies act without the concurrence of particular agents.[33]

There are, then, serious reasons to doubt the distinction between series of causes related *per se* and *per accidens*. Despite this, in his *Ordinatio* Ockham concedes that the Scotist proof of the existence of a first efficient cause carries some weight. It is, he says, adequate (*sufficiens*). Moreover, it is the proof advanced by almost all philosophers, including Aristotle and Averroes.[34]

Later, in his *Quaestiones in libros Physicorum*, arguing against both Scotus and his follower Walter Chatton, Ockham is less optimistic about the adequacy of the Scotist proof for the existence of God by way of productive causality. Now he contends that by way of production, distinct from conservation, there is no adequate proof of the existence of a first efficient cause, or God.[35]

---

32. Ibid. (*OTh* 2: 349.1–14).
33. Ibid. (*OTh* 2: 350.4–10); Scotus, *Ord.* 1.2.1–4 (Vatican ed. 2: 322–328, nn. 327–337).
34. Ibid. (*OTh* 2: 354.17–18; for references to Aristotle and Averroes see the editor's note 354 n8).
35. *Quaest. in Phys.* 135 (*OPh* 6: 762–767).

However, Ockham believes the proof can be made adequate and more evident if it is based on the conservation of things rather than on their production. His reason is that it is difficult to prove that there cannot be an infinite series of causes of the same nature, each of which can exist without the other, as the philosophers held that there has been an infinite number of humans, each begetting an offspring. Moreover, it is difficult to prove that one human cannot be the total productive cause of another. If these two statements are true, it would be hard to prove the impossibility of an infinite series of causes, unless there were a being that always remains and on which the whole infinite series depends.[36]

Ockham here casts doubt on the mainspring of Scotus' proof of the existence of a first efficient cause. Scotus did not deny the possibility of an infinite series of efficient causes related *per accidens*, but he contended that this would be impossible unless there were a finite series of efficient causes related *per se*. In other words, even if the world were eternal and there were not a first human, as Aristotle taught,[37] the infinite series of causes and effects would depend on a being outside the series. In short, the temporally infinite world would be dependent and created.

Ockham, on the contrary, sees no reason why such an infinite world would not be self-sufficient, at least if it is viewed from the perspective of productive efficient causes. An infinite series of humans, begetting and begotten, is possible, each of which is the total cause of the next in the series – a total cause being one that can produce its effect in the absence of every other cause.[38]

36. *Ord.* 1.2.10 (*OTh* 2: 355.3–11); *Quaest. in Phys.* 135 (*OPh* 6: 765.78–87).
37. Aristotle, *De generatione et corruptione* 2.10, 336a23–337a33.
38. "Nec illud est verum quod dicit Ioannes [sc. Scotum], quod causa totalis est illa qua posita ponitur effectus, et qua non posita non potest poni. Quia, sicut alias dictum est, idem effectus potest habere duas causas totales; et si una destruatur, nihilominus potest causari per aliam. Sed sicut dictum est, causa totalis est illa qua posita, omni alio circumscripto, potest poni effectus" (*Ord.* 2.3–4 [*OTh* 5: 64.1–6]). A total cause is also called an adequate and precise cause; see *Quodl.* 1.1 (*OTh* 9: 8.171–177). On Ockham's variation in describing a total cause see Rega Wood, "Ockham on Essentially-Ordered Causes:

Ockham replies to the Scotists that human reason cannot adequately prove the impossibility of an infinite series of productive efficient causes related either *per accidens* or *per se*. In both cases the whole series of causes is caused, but not by one member of the series or by something outside of it. Rather, one part of the total series is caused by another part and another by another part, and so on to infinity. So it does not follow that one thing produces the whole series or that a thing produces itself.[39]

Consequently, as Scotus and his follower, Walter Chatton, formulated the proof of the existence of God as the first productive efficient cause, it is open to serious objections. Having first thought the proof to be adequate (*sufficiens*), he later denies this and contends that the only adequate proof is based on the necessity of a first conserving cause – a move, incidentally, that was also made by Descartes.[40] The argument for the existence of God is then reformulated as follows:

Whatever is produced by something is really conserved by something as long as it really exists. Ockham considers this to be evident. It was the common view of the schoolmen that everything in the universe is contingent, and therefore it would lose its existence unless it were conserved in being as long as it exists. God alone is a necessary being, requiring neither a productive nor conserving cause.[41] An example of a conserving cause, taken from Aristotelian physics, is the sun. A man begets a son, but the offspring must be conserved by the universal causality of the sun and not by the father.[42] Both productive and conserving causes are

---

Logic Misapplied," in *Die Gegenwart Ockhams*, ed. Wilhelm Vossenkuhl and Rolf Schönberger (Weinheim, 1990), pp. 25–50, at pp. 38–39. Wood shows that Ockham "effectively refuted only a caricature of Scotus' position" (p. 41).

39. *Quaest. in Phys.* 136 (*OPh* 6: 769.47–59).

40. Descartes, *Meditationes de prima philosophia* 3, ed. Adam-Tannery (Paris, 1904), 7: 40.

41. *Sum. log.* 3-2.5 (*OPh* 1: 512.27–30). Besides God, there are of course necessary propositions (ibid. 30–34).

42. *Ord.* 2.8 (*OTh* 5: 157.13–14).

efficient causes, but only the latter must always be present to its effect. Now the conserving cause is either produced by something else or it is not. If it is not, it is the primary efficient cause. But if the conserving cause is produced by something else, it is also conserved by something else. Now there cannot be an infinite series of conserving causes, because this would entail an actual infinity of existing things, which Aristotle has shown reasonably enough to be impossible.[43] We must conclude, then, that there is a primary conserving cause and hence a primary efficient cause.[44]

What value does Ockham give to this proof? Having reformulated Scotus' proof in terms of conserving causes, he believes it is more evident that there is a first efficient cause. "[F]rom efficiency," he concludes, "insofar as it means that a thing receives existence immediately after non-existence, it cannot be proved that a first efficient being exists. But from efficiency, insofar as it means that a thing continues in existence, it can indeed be proved (*bene potest probari*) through conservation that this being exists."[45] However, the proof does not appear to be a strict demonstration, which requires true and necessary premises.[46] In Ockham's proof the premise stating the impossibility of an actual infinity of beings is said to be reasonable enough (*satis rationabilis*), which leaves the conclusion short of certainty and necessity. Indeed, elsewhere Ockham concedes the possibility of an actual infinity of human souls and revolutions of the heavenly bodies.[47]

43. Aristotle, *Metaph.* 2.2, 994a1–b31.

44. *Ord.* 1.2.10 (*OTh* 2: 355.12–356.12); *Quaest. in Phys.* 136 (*OPh* 6: 767.10–769.64).

45. "Ad argumentum principale dico quod per efficientiam, secundum quod dicit rem immediate accipere esse post non-esse, non potest probari primum efficiens esse, sed per efficientiam secundum quod dicit rem continuari in esse bene potest probari hoc esse per conservationem" (*Quaest. in Phys.* 136 [*OPh* 6: 769.60–64]).

46. For the meanings of demonstration see above, pp. 109–112.

47. *Quaest. variae* 3 (*OTh* 8: 68.164–172). Anneliese Maier, "Diskussionen über das aktuell Unendliche in der ersten Hälfte des 14 Jahrhunderts," *Divus Thomas* (Freiburg) 25 (1947): 147–166, at p. 166.

The probative force of the argument, accordingly, does not measure up to a strict demonstration of the existence of God. While having some weight, and even amounting to an adequate proof, it contains premises that are not strictly necessary.

Even granting the value of the proof, does it conclude to the existence of a primary efficient cause that is recognizably the Christian God? In the next section of this chapter, when considering the possibility of proving that God is one, we shall see that it does not. The same conclusion is reached if we examine several quodlibetal questions on the capacity of natural reason to prove that God is the efficient cause of anything. Ockham there denies that natural reason can prove that God is the immediate efficient cause of all things. His reason is that no adequate proof can be given that other causes, such as the heavenly bodies, are not the sufficient cause of many effects, and so it would be useless to posit another immediate efficient cause for them. What is more, natural reason cannot prove that God is the efficient cause of any effect, for there is no adequate proof that there are other effects than generable and corruptible things. Now their sufficient causes are natural bodies in the sublunar world and the heavenly bodies; and there is no adequate proof that the heavenly bodies have an efficient cause.[48]

Neither can it be proved that God is the mediate or remote cause of any effect, because then it would be possible to prove that he is the immediate cause of some other effect. This is because a mediate or remote cause is said to produce an effect by causing the cause of that effect, as a grandfather may be said to cause his grandson by begetting his own son. So the remote cause must have

---

48. *Quodl.* 2.1 (*OTh* 9: 107–111). It cannot be proved that God acts contingently and freely in causing his effects, or that he causes all things immediately and by himself alone; see *Ord.* 1.42. q. u. (*OTh* 4: 617.5–618.20). Neither can it be proved demonstratively that God is the efficient or moving cause of anything, or that he acts contingently – indeed, that he acts at all. Contingency can be explained by the created will, which is a partial cause, along with God, of many effects; see *Quodl.* 2.2 (*OTh* 9: 116.101–110, 112.18–20).

its own immediate effect in order to be called the remote cause of a later effect. And if human reason cannot prove that God is either the immediate or mediate cause of any effect, neither can it prove that he is the total or partial cause of any effect. A total cause is one that can produce its effect in the absence of every other cause; a partial cause is insufficient by itself to produce the effect. We can reasonably be persuaded, however, that God is the efficient or moving cause of some effect, for otherwise his existence would be useless, but this does not amount to a demonstration of the fact.[49]

If this is true, there can be no strict demonstration that there is one primary efficient or moving cause of the world. There may be many such causes, and these, Ockham suggests, may be simply the heavenly bodies. He feels he is on sure grounds in attributing efficient causality to them, for we experience their effects in the sublunar world.[50]

Just as there is no strict demonstration that God effectively causes anything, so none can be given that he is the final cause (*finis*) of things, in the sense that they strive after or tend toward him. This is beyond proving by self-evident principles or by experience. True, natural agents act uniformly and without knowing what they are doing, but this is no proof that they strive after God by their actions. "An agent of this sort," Ockham contends, "acts to produce its effect whether or not God is intended." Natural bodies do not move because they desire the good of the universe or its ruler. A heavy body moves upward, not for the good of the ruler of the universe, but simply to fill a vacuum. Moreover, there can be two final ends of one and the same effect. If someone goes to a tavern to drink and eat, both of these purposes can be the sufficient final cause of his going; even if he does not go to eat, he

49. *Quodl.* 2.1 (*OTh* 9: 108.22–109.45).

50. Ibid. (*OTh* 9: 111.99–103). In the created world the fact that one thing is an efficient cause of another cannot be demonstrated but is known only by experience, that is, through the fact that at the presence of the cause the effect follows and at its absence it does not; see *Rep.* 2. 12–13 (*OTh* 5: 268.10–269.15). For the notion of an efficient cause see below, pp. 400–412.

would still go to drink. And even if there cannot be two ultimate ends of the same effect, there can be two ultimate ends of different effects. So it cannot be demonstrated that the universe is directed to one principle on which it depends. As regards beings that act freely, like the heavenly Intelligences, Ockham thinks no demonstration can be given that God is the final end of their actions. An Intelligence acting freely can set up or determine its own ends.[51]

Accordingly we cannot demonstrate the existence of God as either the efficient productive cause or the final cause of the universe. However, we can give an adequate proof of his existence as its primary conserving cause. The question remains whether this cause is the one God of Christianity or possibly the many gods of paganism.

3 Proof That There is Only One God

Before answering the question, Ockham gives two descriptions of the term "God." In one sense it means "a being more excellent and better than anything else"; in another "that than which nothing is better or more perfect."[52] As the editor of Ockham's *Quodlibeta* notes, his likely source for these descriptions of God was William of Ware, a Franciscan who taught at Paris about 1293. William called these positive and negative notions of God. In the positive sense God is described as the best and most perfect of all beings, and hence as the unique God of Christianity. In the negative sense nothing can be said to be more perfect than God, but this is compatible with there being many gods. Several gods can have the nature of deity most perfectly, no one more perfectly a god than another, and nothing more perfect than any of them.[53] August-

---

51. *Quodl.* 4.2 (*OTh* 9: 302–309). Aristotle means that inanimate things act for an end in the sense that, following the ordinary course of nature and without an impediment, their actions have definite results as though they were foreseen and willed by an agent. Thus there is finality in inanimate things even if no will directs or moves them; see *Sum. phil. nat.* 2.6 (*OPh* 6: 227–230), *Expos. in Phys.* 2.12 (*OPh* 4: 378–382).

52. *Quodl.* 1.1 (*OTh* 9: 1.17–2.20).

53. William of Ware, *In 1 Sent.* 15, ed. P. Muscat, "Quaestio inedita De unitate Dei," *Antonianum* 2 (1927): 335–350, at p. 346. William of Ware uses

ine saw clearly that the conception of God as "a nature than which nothing more excellent or more exalted exists" is applicable not only to the Christian God but also to the many gods of paganism.[54]

Can we prove that there is only one God in either of these two meanings of the term? Ockham denies that we can demonstrate that there is only one God in the first, for we cannot even know with evidence that such a God exists. With this meaning the proposition "God exists" is not self-evident, for many doubt it; nor can it be known from self-evident propositions, for every argument advanced to prove it presupposes something doubtful or derived from faith; nor is it known from experience, as is all too clear. Neither can an evident proof be given that God is one in the second sense of the term "God"; as we have seen, in this sense there can be several gods. Accordingly Ockham believes that the oneness of God is not a matter of rational demonstration but of Christian faith.[55]

Ockham is here taking issue again with Duns Scotus, who taught that the oneness of God is rationally demonstrable as a corollary of his doctrine of God's absolute primary in being and infinity, both of which he regarded as rationally demonstrated.[56] Ockham, for his

---

the example of two white things that are both most white, no one whiter than the other. Before Ockham, he denied that it can be demonstrated that God is one.

54. Augustine, *De doctrina christiana* 1.7.7 (CCL 32: 10). This is the source of Anselm's description of God as "that than which none greater can be conceived" ["aliquid quo nihil maius cogitari possit"] (Anselm, *Proslogion* 2 [*Opera omnia* 2: 227]).

55. *Quodl.* 1.1 (*OTh* 9: 2-3). Ockham offers a proof that there is only one God which he attributes to Scotus, but he does not consider it an adequate demonstration but only a probable argument; see *Ord.* 1.2.10 (*OTh* 2: 356.14-357.9).

56. Scotus, *Ord.* 1.2.1 (Vatican ed. 2: 151-159, nn. 43-53), cited by Ockham, *Ord.* 1.2.10 (*OTh* 2: 338-342). For the Scotist proofs that there is only one God see Gilson, *Jean Duns Scot*, pp. 171-177. Gilson writes: "Il est donc hors de doute que l'auteur de l'*Opus Oxoniense* tienne l'unicité de Dieu pour une vérité rationnellement démontrable" (ibid., p. 176). Léon Baudry analyzes Ockham's criticism of these proofs, in "Guillaume d'Occam, critique des preuves scotistes de l'unicité de Dieu," *Archives d'histoire doctrinale et littéraire du moyen âge* 20 (1953): 99-112.

part, sees no rational justification for asserting either the absolute primacy or the infinity of God. He agrees with Scotus that a plurality of infinite beings is a contradiction, for a being that is absolutely infinite cannot be exceeded. Now, if there were several infinite beings, taken together they would contain more perfection than any one of them. Hence no one of them would be infinite. The difficulty with this proof is that it presupposes the intensive infinity of God, which natural reason cannot demonstrate.[57]

Ockham also rebuts Scotus' arguments for the oneness of God based on the infinity of the divine mind and will. No demonstration is possible that the divine mind is infinite or that, supposing it is, that it has a perfect knowledge of anything. Neither can it be demonstrated that God loves anything perfectly, for this presupposes God's infinite will, which is only a matter of faith. Indeed, many philosophers held that God neither knows nor wills anything besides himself.[58]

Scotus also contended that there can only be one necessary being, namely God. But Ockham sees no compelling reason why there cannot be several necessary beings, no one of which would depend on the other. Philosophers like Aristotle and Averroes seem to have thought that the Intelligences were necessary beings. In this case they would be using "necessary being" as a univocal term, applicable to all of them in exactly the same sense. These necessary beings would not share a common nature and be distinct from each other by individual differences, as Scotus thought, but they would differ from each other just by themselves.[59]

Ockham also criticizes other Scotist proofs that there is only one God. Scotus argued that there cannot be two most eminent beings in the universe nor consequently .two primary efficient causes, because, as Aristotle says, species are like numbers, which cannot belong to the same rank or order. Much less can there be

57. *Quodl.* 1.1 (*OTh* 9: 10.203–207).
58. Ibid. (*OTh* 9: 6.131–8.162).
59. Ibid. (*OTh* 9: 10.209–11.228); *Ord.* 1.2.10 (*OTh* 2: 350.16–351.18).

two primary or most eminent beings. To this, Ockham retorts that it has not been adequately proved that species are like numbers and that one is always more perfect than another.[60] Scotus also thought that, because there is only one universe, it must have only one primary efficient cause and one ultimate final cause or end. In Aristotle's words, it can have only one ruler.

Ockham does not dismiss these arguments out of hand, but he thinks a stubborn opponent could raise objections that would be difficult to answer. It might be objected, for example, that other universes are possible; and even if only one exists it does not follow that there is only one God. Ockham has shown that the same effect can have several total causes, so that many gods are possible without introducing disorder in the universe. Accordingly the oneness of God is not demonstrable by reason but held only on faith.[61]

Throughout his criticism of Scotus' doctrine of the existence and oneness of God, Ockham remains faithful to his basic philosophical notions, which are radically different from those of the Subtle Doctor. The two theologians do not differ in what they believe about the Christian God, but they diverge on what human reason left to its own resources can prove about him. Ockham finds only "adequate reasons" for affirming his existence – reasons that fall short of strict demonstration. Philosophy assures us of an ultimate ground of the universe: a primary conserving cause or causes, but these might be the heavenly bodies whose causality we experience in our world. Scotus can go further in his rational pursuit of the Christian God because he makes use of a different philosophy, according to which there is real community among beings along with individuality. Ockham fragments the universe

---

60. *Ord.* 1.2.10 (*OTh* 2: 341.14-19 and 354.4-7); Aristotle, *Metaph.* 8.3, 1043b32-34.

61. Ibid. (*OTh* 2: 341.14-342.16 and 354.4-14); *Quodl.* 1.1 (*OTh* 9: 3.57-59). Cf. Aristotle, *Metaph.* 12.8, 1074a32-38; *De caelo* 1.8, 276a19-272a12. On the possibility of many worlds, see below, pp. 326-338.

into myriad individuals, from which all real community has been eliminated. This leads him to an empirical notion of causality, according to which a cause shares nothing with its effect (except perhaps some of its matter), their bond being simply the recognized presence of effect to cause. As Léon Baudry perceptively remarks, Scotism and Ockhamism are not just two doctrines but two different styles of thinking.[62]

62. Baudry, "Guillaume d'Occam, critique des preuves scotistes," p. 110. For the notion of cause see below, pp. 400–412

Philotheus Boehner believed that Ockham proves the existence of the Christian God, because even though he does not prove the concept of that God as including his oneness, the pre-Christian concept that he does prove can only stand for the Christian God. "Was Ockham beweist, ist die Existenz der christlichen Gottes, weil der vor-christliche Begriff Gottes im Sinne von II nur für den christlichen Gott supponiert; nicht bewiesen ist aber der Begriff des christlichen Gottes, der die Einzigkeit Gottes einschliesst" ("Zu Ockhams Beweis der Existenz Gottes," *Franziskanische Studien* 32 [1950]: 50–69; repr. in his *Collected Articles on Ockham*, ed. E.M. Buytaert [St. Bonaventure, NY, 1958], pp. 399–420). But only as a Christian, not as a philosopher, can Ockham know that the concept of God he has reached by human reason stands for the Christian God. The concept of God is not strictly Christian unless it contains the note of oneness. Neither is it evident that the concept of Primary Mover stands for the same reality as the Trinity; see *Quodl.* 2.3 (*OTh* 9: 122.115–130). For a further criticism of Boehner's view in this matter see Baudry, "Les rapports de la raison et de la foi selon Guillaume d'Occam," *Archives d'histoire doctrinale et littéraire du moyen âge* 29 (1962): 88–89.

4

The Divine Attributes

I N BOTH THE SCRIPTURES and the works of theologians and philosophers we find many names of God; for example, they call him one, wise, good, true, and beautiful. The fathers of the Church reflected on the meaning of the divine names, and medieval theologians debated at length how the names are related to God: whether they are predicated of him univocally, equivocally or analogously, and how there can there be many divine names if God is really one and simple in his essence. In answering these questions medieval theologians brought into play their philosophical notions of being, knowledge, and language; and if their answers were profoundly different, it was because they did not see eye to eye on fundamental metaphysical and epistemological issues.

The possibility of theology as a "discourse about God" *(theologos)* is here at stake, and so it was usual for medieval theologians to devote a section of their theological works to a tract on the divine names or attributes. Ockham was no exception. His most complete treatment of the subject is in Book One of his commentary on the *Sentences* of Peter Lombard (*Ordinatio*), distinction 2, questions 1–2. These questions begin the tract on the unity of the divine essence, prior to the tract on the Trinity. So clearly did Ockham realize the importance of philosophy in treating of the divine attributes that he made a radical innovation in his commentary on the *Sentences*. He inserted in his treatise on the divine unity the long series of questions on universals (4–8) that we examined in Chapter 1. How could he resolve the problem of the divine attributes without carefully investigating the nature of a universal concept and its relations to reality, the mind, and language? He also probes more systematically than his predecessors the nature and kinds of distinction, in order to pinpoint the exact kind of distinction between God and his attributes and between the attributes themselves. Thus the treatise on the divine unity in his commentary on the *Sentences* is one of the richest mines for discovering his basic philosophical themes.

In the late Middle Ages there were two main positions on the status of the divine attributes. Scotus held that they are distinct from the divine essence and from each other by a formal distinction or non-identity *ex parte rei*. Others, including Thomas Aquinas, Godfrey of Fontaines, and Henry of Ghent, contended that the distinction between them is not found on the side of reality but is made by the mind. After critically examining each of these doctrines and finding them wanting, Ockham offers his own solution of the problem.

1 The Doctrine of Scotus and Alnwick

The first of Ockham's two questions on the divine attributes is precisely formulated to engage the Scotist position: "Is there as great an identity of the divine essence – in every sense of real identity – with the perfections attributed to it, and of these perfections among themselves, as there is of the divine essence with the divine essence?"[1] In other words, granted that the divine essence is identical with itself, in every sense of identical in reality (*ex natura rei*), is there as great a real identity between the divine essence and the perfections we attribute to it, and between the perfections themselves? For example, is God's goodness in every sense really identical with his essence and with his wisdom?

Ockham knew that Scotus and his follower, William of Alnwick, gave a negative answer to this question. Quoting from Scotus, he shows that according to the Subtle Doctor the distinction between the divine essence and the perfections attributed to it is not only made by the mind (*differentia rationis*), as though

---

1. "Utrum sit tanta identitas divinae essentiae et omnis modus identitatis ex natura rei ad perfectiones attributales et ipsarum perfectionum attributalium inter se, qualis est divinae essentiae ad divinam essentiam" (*Ord.* 1.2.1 [*OTh* 2: 3.12–15]).

the mind simply considers the same formal object in different ways, nor is the distinction only between formal objects in the mind. Rather, the distinction is present in reality before the mind sets to work: wisdom and goodness, for example, exist in reality (*in re et ex natura rei*), and one is formally not the other in the real world. We know that one of these is formally not the other because they have different definitions, and in Scotus' view a definition signifies not only a concept (*ratio*) produced by the mind but the quiddity of a thing. Consequently, if the definition of one quiddity or essence does not include the definition of another, they are formally distinct *ex parte rei*. It follows as a corollary that the truth of the proposition "Wisdom is not formally goodness" is not caused by the mind's bringing the terms "wisdom" and "goodness" together, but by the mind's finding them in the object, and by bringing them together the mind forms a true proposition.[2]

The formal non-identity Scotus invokes to explain the distinction between the divine attributes does not have to do with their grade of existence, which is infinity, but only with their status as formalities or essences, one of which does not enter into the definition of the other. Taken precisely in itself, each attribute is formally non-identical with each other and with the divine essence; but each is actually infinite in existence. God's wisdom is infinite, and so too are his goodness and love. On the level of essence the attributes are formally irreducible to each other; but they are really one in their infinite existence. The grade of infinity gives the attributes and the divine essence real identity without suppressing their formal distinction.[3]

---

2. *Ord.* 1.2.1 (*OTh* 2: 4.15–5.27); Ockham quotes from Scotus, *Ord.* 1.8.1.4 (Vatican ed. 4: 260–262, 264, 267, nn. 191–194).

3. Scotus, *Ord.* 1.8.1.4 (Vatican ed. 4: 272–273, n. 215). Gilson (*Jean Duns Scotus* [Paris, 1952], pp. 251–252) points out that here infinity plays a role in Scotism similar to that played by *esse* in Thomism. According to Aquinas the most perfect concept of God is *Ipsum esse* or the pure act of existing; for Scotus it is infinite being (*ens infinitum*). In Thomism the pure act of being embraces *eminenter* and with perfect unity all the divine perfections; in Scotism infinite being assures the real identity of all the divine attributes.

William of Alnwick, called an "independent Scotist," supported his master's position against the objections of the contemporary Franciscan Richard of Conington. William contended that the divine intellect and will cannot be formally the same, for if they were they would have the same essential properties, whereas in fact they do not. If we speak of the reality of God in itself, abstracting from all connotations and relations to other things, we must say that God really (*ex natura rei*) knows through his intellect and not through his will, and he wills through his will and not through his intellect. If he willed through his intellect he would not will freely, because the intellect, unlike the will, is not self-determining. Moreover, the divine intellect knows evil but the divine will does not will it. Hence these powers cannot be formally the same.[4]

2 Ockham's Criticism of the Doctrine of Scotus and Alnwick

The main thrust of Ockham's criticism of the Scotist doctrine of the divine attributes is against the general notion of a formal distinction or non-identity. We have already examined his reasons for rejecting this kind of distinction when we treated of his doctrine of universals. We saw that in Ockham's view there are no essences existing in individuals and formally distinct from them; universals are nothing but words or concepts signifying and standing for individuals.[5] Now Ockham argues that there are no divine perfections formally distinct from the divine essence and from each other: there is only the one divine reality and many words and concepts which signify and stand for it when we think and speak about it.

Ockham offers an argument that he feels is equally effective in disproving the formal distinction wherever the Scotists use it.[6] If

---

4. See *OTh* 2: 13.10–14.6, quoting William of Alnwick, *Quodl.* 2 (ed. Ledoux p. 217).

5. See above, pp. 68–77.

6. In a marginal note in one manuscript the argument is attributed to Henry Costesey, O.F.M., who taught at the Franciscan convent at Cambridge about 1325. On this point and in general on Ockham's relation to the Scotist formal distinction see Hester G. Gelber, "Logic and the Trinity: A Clash of Values in Scholastic Thought, 1300–1335" (PhD dissertation, University of Wisconsin,

there is a distinction between several items, contradictory propositions can be verified of them. Indeed, the Scotists themselves concede that contradiction is the best criterion to prove a distinction
between things. Now there are only three possible items of which
contradictories can be verified: things (*res*), concepts (*rationes, entia
rationis*), and things and concepts. So there can be only three kinds
of distinction or non-identity: a real distinction between things, a
mental distinction between concepts, and an unnamed distinction
between a thing and a concept. No room is left for the Scotist
formal distinction *a parte rei* between essences or quiddities.

Ockham's proof that there are only three kinds of items about
which contradictories can be verified takes the form of a *reductio ad
absurdum*. If the Scotist contends that contradictory statements can
also be verified of essences that are formally distinct but really
identical, for example wisdom and goodness in God, Ockham retorts
that then he could claim that whenever contradictory statements are
verified of two items in the real world they are formally distinct and
really identical. If someone asserted that a man is rational and an ass
is not rational and consequently they are really distinct, it would be
just as plausible to say they are formally distinct. Thus, if we admit
the validity of the formal distinction we are left with no way of proving a real distinction between any two things.[7]

Applying this argument to the distinction between the divine essence and its attributes, Ockham concludes that "The divine wisdom
is the same as the divine essence in every way in which the divine
essence is the same as the divine essence, and this is equally true of
the divine goodness and justice: between them there is absolutely no
distinction *ex natura rei* or even non-identity."[8] In other words, there

---

1974), pp. 172–185; Rolf Schönberger, "Realität und Differenz: Ockhams Kritik
an der *distinctio formalis*," in *Die Gegenwart Ockhams*, ed. Wilhelm Vossenkuhl
and Rolf Schönberger (Weinheim, 1990), pp. 97–122.

    7. *Ord.* 1.2.1 and 1.2.11 (*OTh* 2: 14.8–17.7 and 373.11–14). See above, p. 75.

    8. "Ideo propter istam rationem dico quod sapientia divina omnibus
modis est eadem essentiae divinae quibus essentia divina est eadem essentiae
divinae, et sic de bonitate divina et iustitia; nec est ibi penitus aliqua distinctio ex natura rei vel etiam non-identitas" (*Ord.* 1.2.1 [*OTh* 2: 17.9–12]).

is no distinction in reality between what is designated by the concepts "divine essence" and "divine goodness," or by "divine goodness" and "divine justice." When these terms are used with personal supposition, that is, as standing for and signifying that for which they stand, they designate the same divine reality and not, as Scotus and Alnwick thought, different realities or formalities in God.

If this is true, we can say that God knows with his will and wills with his intellect, if "will" and "intellect" are taken in their absolute sense as signifying God himself. For a Scotist like Alnwick this language is improper, for the terms designate distinct realities in God. Ockham grants that his language is unusual, but justifies it on the ground that all language is conventional and is subject to change. Once it is conceded that "whatever belongs to the reality that is the divine intellect belongs to the reality that is the divine will, and vice versa," there is no reason why we cannot say God knows through his will and wills through his intellect.[9]

As we saw in Chapter 1, words are not natural but conventional signs, so they can be changed at will. Of course the ordinary use of words must be respected if we want to communicate with others. Grammatical forms are devised for words, such as the plural "men" and the singular "man," so that now we cannot say "Man is men." But if the word "men" signified precisely what the word "man" signified, and it did not differ in its grammatical form, we could establish a new linguistic convention and quite properly say "Man is men."[10]

---

9. "Dico quod circumscribendo omnia connotata ita quod per ista nomina 'intellectus,' 'voluntas,' 'intelligere,' 'velle,' nihil connotetur, sed praecise significetur hoc nomine 'intellectus' illa res quae est formaliter intellectus, et hoc nomine 'voluntas' praecise illa res absoluta quae est formaliter voluntas, et sic de aliis nominibus, et non plus, hac institutione nova vocabuli facta ita erit haec vera 'actus dicendi est actus voluntatis,' et 'Deus intelligit per voluntatem' sicut haec 'intelligit per intellectum' quia tunc termini de novo instituuntur ad significandum, et ideo non est mirum si illa propositio sit vera quae prius erat falsa" (ibid. [*OTh* 2: 46.6–15]).

10. Ibid. (*OTh* 2: 46.16–47.2). In fact, according to Ockham, the terms "man" and "men," when taken absolutely, precisely signify the same reality, namely all individual men. "Man" does not designate human nature in some way distinct from individual men.

To the Scotist this diverts attention away from reality to the way we talk about it. He insists that he wants to talk about things and not about words. In rejoinder Ockham points out that we cannot speak about things without using words or concepts or other signs. As these signs differ in their signification or connotation, our response to propositions must also differ in the manner described above.[11]

Why do fathers of the Church, like Augustine and current masters, say that God knows through his intellect and not through his will? It is because they use the terms "divine intellect" and "divine will" to connote different realities with a definite grammatical and logical mode, so that something can belong to the intellect that does not belong to the will. When they speak of the divine intellect they mean the divine essence as eliciting the act of generating the Son, and when they speak of the divine will they mean that same essence as eliciting the act of breathing forth the Holy Spirit. Understood in the context of the Trinity, we can distinguish between the divine intellect and will and say that the Son is produced by way of intellect and the Holy Spirit by way of will. But the terms "intellect" and "will" can be taken in their precise and absolute meaning, apart from all connotations, and then they designate the same divine reality; they have strictly the same meaning and they can be used interchangeably in sentences.[12]

A similar reply can be made to the claim that if there is no distinction in reality between God's intellect and will it would be correct to say that he not only knows evil but wills it. The statement "God wills evil" entails that he does something he ought not to do. This implies that he is a creature, for only creatures can do

---

11. "Si dicas: nolo loqui de vocibus sed tantum de rebus, dico quod quamvis velis loqui tantum de rebus, tamen hoc non est possibile nisi mediantibus vocibus vel conceptibus vel aliis signis; et ideo secundum quod illa signa, quaecumque fuerint, aliter significant et connotant vel non connotant, aliter ad propositiones est respondendum modo praedicto" (*Ord.* 1.2.1 [*OTh* 2: 47.3–8]). Ockham seems to be disputing here with William of Alnwick. We would not wish for a stronger statement of the importance of language in Ockhamism. Ockham expresses a similar notion in *Expos. in Phys.* prol. and 1.15 (*OPh* 4: 11.36–12.45 and 152.77–83).

12. *Ord.* 1.2.2 (*OTh* 2: 44.22–45.22).

what they ought not to do. The statement "God knows evil" simply implies that he causes or permits creatures to do something they ought not to do. So the two statements "God knows evil" and "God wills evil" differ because of their different connotations and not because of any non-identity of intellect and will in God. Indeed, if the terms "knowing" and "willing" are not taken connotatively but as precisely signifying the absolute divine reality, it would be just as true to say that God wills evil as it is to say that he knows it.

The same point can be illustrated by an analysis of the statements "God beatifies Peter" and "God does not damn Peter." These do not imply a formal distinction in God between a beatifying and a damning power. The first statement means that God gives Peter eternal life; the second that he does not punish Peter eternally. The truth of these statements does not depend on a distinction on God's part but only on a non-identity or variation on the side of creatures, for by absolutely the same power God gives Peter eternal life and does not meet out to him eternal punishment. A similar analysis can be given to the assertions "God wills A" and "God knows A." The former implies the existence of A, the latter does not. So too, the propositions "God can create A" and "God does not create A" do not point to any distinction in God but to one in the order of creatures.[13]

Thus all attempts to find in reality a formal non-identity between God and his attributes, and between the attributes themselves, fail. There remains the possibility that the distinction between them is made by the mind itself. In that case, how are we to understand this mental or conceptual distinction? This is the question to which Ockham now turns.

3 Partisans of the Distinction of Reason
Ockham tells us that everyone who rejected a distinction *ex natura rei* between the divine essence and its attributes held that the perfections attributed to that essence are really the same as that

---

13. Ibid. (*OTh* 2: 47.9–49.11).

essence and distinct from it only in concept (*sola ratione*). The editors of Ockham's *Ordinatio* identify some of these masters as Godfrey of Fontaines, Henry of Ghent, Thomas Aquinas, Richard of Middleton, and Thomas of Sutton.[14] Ockham gives most of his attention to the positions of Godfrey of Fontaines and Henry of Ghent, as illustrating two different ways of using the distinction of reason (*distinctio rationis*) to reconcile the plurality of the divine attributes with the simplicity of the divine essence.

In the opinion of Godfrey of Fontaines, the perfections attributable to God are really the divine essence itself; they are distinct from that essence and from each other only in concept (*ratio*). Godfrey lays down three conditions for this type of distinction. (1) There must be a something serving as the foundation of the various concepts the mind forms; otherwise there is no point in the mind making the distinction. (2) The diversity of *rationes* does not belong to the thing as it really exists but only as it comes within our knowledge. (3) In order that our knowledge of the one thing give rise to several concepts of it, we must relate it to several other realities, for if we know it just in itself we can have only one concept of it. Now, in the present case what is known is the divine essence. This essence is conceived in different ways (for example, as eternal, living, wise, powerful, and so on) by relating it to really distinct perfections in creatures. The divine essence contains all pure perfections, which imply no limitation, in a higher manner than they exist in creatures (*eminenter*), so that it can serve as a foundation for the various concepts we form of it. The difference between the divine attributes is thus virtually contained in the divine essence, but this difference can be made actual only by the act of the mind as it relates the divine essence to the really distinct perfections in creatures.[15]

14. *Ord.* 1.2.2 (*OTh* 2: 50 n1, 53 n1).

15. Ibid. (*OTh* 2: 50.17–51.18); Godfrey of Fontaines, *Quodl.* 7.1, in *Les Quodlibet cinq, six et sept*, ed. M. de Wulf and J. Hoffmans (Louvain, 1914), pp. 264–278. See John F. Wippel, *The Metaphysical Thought of Godfrey of Fontaines* (Washington, DC, 1981), pp. 115–123.

Why must the mind relate the divine essence to multiple created perfections in order to make a conceptual distinction between the divine attributes? This is necessary, according to Godfrey, because in himself God is absolutely one. Hence, if we think of him just in himself, as strictly one, he must be conceived through absolutely one concept. We can think of him as having many perfections only by relating him to a number of perfections outside himself.[16]

In adopting this position Godfrey opposed Henry of Ghent, who held that the distinction of reason between the divine attributes does not require relating the divine essence to really distinct perfections in creatures. Godfrey complained that Henry failed to see the difference between the distinction of reason involved in the divine attributes and in the divine ideas. The distinction of reason between the divine ideas implies a relation to the creatures of which they are the ideas. For example, the divine idea of "stone" is a *ratio idealis* in the mind of God, distinct in *ratio* from him and from other divine ideas. This idea is necessarily related to a creature, for it is the idea *of a stone*, and it exists in God only because there is something (actually or potentially) in the created world corresponding to it. But the divine attributes are not like divine ideas; they are predicated of God absolutely, not in relation to creatures. Thus we say that God is good or wise in himself, and not because there is goodness or wisdom in his creatures. God knows his essence directly and without reference to creatures when he views himself as having many attributes.[17]

Henry of Ghent was one of the first schoolmen to treat explicitly and in detail the nature and kinds of distinction.[18] In his view, there are three main kinds: a real distinction, an intentional distinction, and a distinction of reason. A real distinction (*distinctio*

16. *Ord.* 1.2.2 (*OTh* 2: 51.19–52.3). See Godfrey of Fontaines, ibid. (ed. de Wulf–Hoffmans 3: 272).

17. For Ockham's treatment of Henry's opinion on the divine attributes see *Ord.* 1.2.2 (*OTh* 2: 53.13–54.7).

18. See Henry of Ghent, *Quodl.* 5.1 (Paris ed. f. 150v–154r). For an excellent account of Henry's doctrine see Jean Paulus, *Henri de Gand: Essai sur les tendances de sa métaphysique* (Paris, 1938), pp. 199–257.

secundum rem) is present between several things, one of which can exist without the other. By a thing (*res*) he means anything that is not a figment of the mind or a mental construct (*ens secundum animam*), or a relation. Things include not only individuals, like this man, but also absolute essences or natures, like humanity. The real distinction between individuals is in the order of physics, that of essences in the order of metaphysics.

Henry's "intentional" distinction (*distinctio intentionalis*) is his most personal contribution to the subject.[19] He describes this as present between several concepts or objects of concepts which can be thought apart from each other, though they are based on the same nature or essence. In the presence of one reality the mind can express its nature in two or more concepts whose contents are not identical. The resultant "intentional" distinction is on the conceptual level, though it is not in the order of logic but of metaphysics, for it is the business of the metaphysician to study essences and to distinguish in them intelligible notes that are conceivable apart from each other. For example, there is an intentional distinction between "animal" and "rational," "this man" and "humanity," the soul and its powers, an absolute reality and its real relations. The "intentional" plurality of intelligible notes of which Henry speaks is present within the essence or reality itself; it is not made by the mind but exists before the mind begins to act. However, it is only potentially in reality and it must be made actual by the mind.

Unlike the first two distinctions, the distinction of reason (*distinctio rationis*), is not based on a diversity in reality but on an act of the mind. Henry's example is a definition and the thing defined; for example, "rational animal" and "man." These are the same in reality and intention (*re et intentione*), but two different ways of conceiving the same thing.

This is the kind of distinction Henry places between God's essence and his attributes. They cannot be really or intentionally dis-

---

19. "Intentional," in this context, does not have the meaning of "deliberate" but "conceptual." An *intentio* is a concept, or more precisely the meaning of a concept, understanding meaning as objectively in reality.

tinct, for this would imply a real diversity in God, and he is absolutely one and simple in his essence. The divine attributes are nothing but different conceptual expressions of one and the same divine reality, enabling us to conceive that reality more perfectly and distinctly. To the question: what is the basis for their difference in meaning? Henry replies that it is not the relation of God to different created perfections, as Godfrey of Fontaines claimed, but various conceptual relations within God himself. All the divine attributes include in their meaning the divine essence (for otherwise they would have no object), but they also include this essence under different relations conceived within it (otherwise they would be synonyms). These relations are not real, like the divine Persons, but relations of reason or rational relations (*relationes secundum rationem, sive rationales*). Even God conceives his essence under different relations of this sort. By his simple intelligence he first knows his essence as such. Then, scrutinizing his essence thus conceived, he knows it as an object known and as a knower. And because in knowing himself he is pleased with himself, he knows his essence as an object willed and as exercising volition. Of course God conceives all this at once by simple intuition, unlike our knowledge of God, which is piecemeal and in time. As we progress in our knowledge of God we bring the relations of reason we conceive in him from potency to act. Thus the plurality of the divine perfections, as we conceive them, directly stems from the discursive procedures of our mind and not from the divine essence itself. Their multiplicity, and even the order of their succession, have a certain foundation in God's essence, not in itself but as we conceive it. They are present there as regards their origin (*originaliter*), though the mind's analysis brings them forth in their perfect actuality (*completive*).[20]

---

20. For the doctrine of Henry of Ghent see Paulus, *Henri de Gand*, p. 246. According to Henry the order of the concepts attributed to God is not arbitrary: one precedes the other and must be formed before it. The concept of being comes first, followed by truth (which adds to being the relation of knowledge), then goodness, which presupposes the notion of truth. Scotus also insists that the divine attributes are ordered as prior and posterior. See below, p. 203.

Before Godfrey and Henry, Aquinas in his own way taught that divine attributes that are pure perfections, like wisdom and goodness, are really identical with God and with each other. They differ, however, in meaning (*ratio*), "not only on the side of the one who reasons but also from the nature of the reality [of God] itself."[21] In other words, they are not really distinct, but neither does their distinction depend solely on an act of our mind. The distinction between the attributes originates in that act but it has an immediate foundation in God himself. In a sense even the plurality of the attributes has its basis in him, namely in his fullness of perfection, which is the pure act of existing (*ipsum esse*).[22] As usual, when Aquinas takes up a metaphysical theme the ground shifts from essence to being, understood as the act of existing (*esse*).

Aquinas does not mean that the attributes, as concepts, exist in God, for that would contradict his unity and simplicity. As concepts, they exist only in our mind. Concepts, however, have meanings (*rationes*), and these can be said to be present in things insofar as there is something in them corresponding to the mind's concepts. In the present case, the fullness of the divine perfection, which is subsistent being (*esse*), is the ground of the truth of all the perfections we attribute to him.[23]

Firmly grounded in the divine being, divine names like "goodness" and "wisdom" are ascribed to God absolutely, without any connotation of created perfections. Otherwise, we could not say that God is wise or good for all eternity, even if no creatures existed. However, negative divine names, like "infinite" and "immutable" connote a relation of God to creatures, for they deny to God limitations of creatures. Relative names, such as "lord," "king" or "creator," are also connotative. But this is not the case

---

21. *In Sent.* 1.2.1.3, sol. (ed. Mandonnet–Moos 1: 66); *ST* 1.13.4.

22. *In Sent.* 1.2.1.3 (ed. Mandonnet–Moos 1: 70). As *ipsum esse per se subsistens*, God contains in a superior way the perfections of all things (*ST* 1.4.2).

23. Ibid. (ed. Mandonnet–Moos 1: 66–72). In this context *ratio* does not signify the reality of the concept but its meaning (*intentio*). Like the logical term "definition," it is a term of second imposition or intention.

with pure perfections, such as "goodness" and "wisdom." We know the difference between these perfections through our acquaintance with creatures, but once in possession of the concepts we attribute them to God in himself and not in relation of creatures.

4 Ockham's Criticism of the Partisans of the Distinction of Reason

Ockham rejects all the above interpretations of the distinction of reason as applied to the divine attributes. His criticism of his predecessors leads him to define precisely his own conception of this kind of distinction. The importance of this conception in his philosophy and theology can hardly be exaggerated. As Robert Guelluy says, "The whole nominalism of Ockham is contained in the way he treats of the problem of distinction,"[24] and this is nowhere more evident than in his notion of a distinction of reason.

The key to the understanding of this kind of distinction is the meaning of *ratio*. As Ockham uses the term, it means either human reason or a being produced by reason (*ens rationis*). A being of this sort exists in the mind and not in extramental reality. He variously calls it a concept, definition, "intention," or mental name corresponding to a spoken or written name. A distinction of reason, then, is one between *entia rationis*, as a real distinction is one between real beings.[25] Again, properly speaking, a distinction in *ratio* exists between terms or names which have different definitions or descriptions.[26] Hence identity and distinction in

---

24. "Tout le nominalisme d'Ockham est contenu dans sa façon de traiter le problème de la distinction" (Robert Guelluy, *Philosophie et théologie chez Guillaume d' Ockham* [Louvain and Paris, 1947], p. 333). As Paulus says (*Henri de Gand*, p. 249) one of the main innovations of the nominalists was their refusal to see *distinctiones rationis* elsewhere than between concepts. On the problem of distinction see Marilyn M. Adams, "Ockham on Identity and Distinction," *Franciscan Studies* 36 (1976): 5–74.

25. *Ord.* 1.2.3 (*OTh* 2: 78.4–12).

26. "[Distinctio rationis] est distinctio nominum, quia rationes et definitiones sunt nominum; tum quia quaelibet ratio quae convenit uni nomini, et alteri; igitur res significata per nomina non distinguitur per tales rationes"

ratio have to do with names and concepts, as real identity and distinction have to do with real entities. "Nothing real," Ockham writes, "can be distinguished from, or be the same as, something real according to reason (*ratione*); so that just as a distinction of reason and identity of reason are related to beings of reason, so a real difference and real identity are related to real beings."[27]

In support of this, Ockham appeals to the ordinary use of language. If a thing differed from itself or from something else in concept (*ratio*), this would be either because the mind formed different concepts of the thing or things, or because the mind conceived one and the same thing in different ways. No doubt the mind can form different concepts of the same thing, but on this account we would never say that the thing differed from itself in concept, but that one concept is different from another. Neither would we say that the composite of one thing and its concept differs conceptually from the composite of another thing and its concept. Suppose something caused really distinct qualities in the same subject, for example whiteness and sweetness in milk. We would not say that the milk is different from itself because of the different qualities in it, but that whiteness is really different from sweetness, and that the composite of milk and whiteness is really different from the composite of milk and sweetness. Again, if a thing is conceived in different ways, we would not say that the

---

(*Quodl.* 1.3 [*OTh* 9: 20.19–23]). "Tertio sciendum quod 'distingui ratione' dupliciter accipitur: uno modo proprie, secundum quod competit diversis quae habent diversas descriptiones. Isto modo nomina diversa distinguuntur ratione quando habent diversas definitiones" (ibid. 3.2 [*OTh* 9: 209.30–34]).

27. "[N]ihil reale potest distingui nec esse idem ratione cum aliquo reali, ita quod sicut distinctio rationis et identitas rationis se habent ad entia rationis, ita differentia realis et identitas realis se habent ad entia realia, et hoc forte non excludendo distinctionem formalem et identitatem ubi debet poni" (*Ord.* 1.2.3 [*OTh* 2: 75.5–9]). "[N]ihil reale est idem sibi ipsi vel alteri rei secundum rationem, quia nihil est dictu quod homo et asinus sunt idem secundum rationem et non realiter, vel quod homo et homo sunt idem secundum rationem; igitur eodem modo nihil reale est distinctum secundum rationem ab aliquo reali" (*Ord.* 1.2.2 [*OTh* 2: 65.7–11]).

thing is distinguished from itself in reality or in concept, but that the ways of conceiving it are different. The different ways of conceiving an object do not presuppose a difference within it, any more than do the different ways of seeing and hearing it. In other words, nothing can be distinguished from itself through mental acts that bear upon it; there is only a distinction between the mental acts and their products, such as concepts.[28]

This undercuts the distinction of reason with a foundation in one and the same thing as proposed by Henry of Ghent and Thomas Aquinas. Each in his own way defended the absolute oneness and simplicity of the divine essence, but they thought that it contains a foundation for the many attributes we ascribe to it. That foundation, for Henry, is a multitude of conceptual relations within God. But Ockham retorts that this cannot be true, for the wisdom and goodness of creatures are absolute perfections without any relations, and so too are the wisdom and goodness that are really God himself.[29] Aquinas thought the foundation for the attributes is God's absolute perfection, which so transcends our puny mind that we cannot fully grasp it in one concept. Ockham understands Aquinas to mean that the mind cannot fully comprehend the divine essence but must know it bit by bit (*particulatim*). This strikes Ockham as indefensible, for God's essence does not have parts that can be grasped one by one. We know it totally or not at all. Moreover, we cannot know it under one real aspect that is God himself and not under another. In fact, what we precisely grasp are certain terms that are predicable of the divine essence – terms that are neither severally nor really the divine essence itself; we know that essence so to speak through them, while it remains unknown in itself.[30]

More to Ockham's liking is the position of Godfrey of Fontaines, that the divine essence is strictly one both in reality and in *ratio*, but we can conceive it in many attributes by relating it to

28. *Ord.* 1.2.3 (*OTh* 2: 75.12–78.3).
29. Ibid. 1.2.2 (*OTh* 2: 61.5–8).
30. Ibid. (*OTh* 2: 67.9–18).

different perfections in creatures. If the attributes signified only the divine essence, they would have exactly the same meaning; in short, they would be synonyms. But they differ in meaning because they connote different created perfections. Thus the distinction between the divine attributes or names of God depends on a real distinction – not in God, to be sure, but in creatures. Ockham agrees with Godfrey, then, that "all the attributes either connote some really distinct things or are common to really distinct things."[31] Godfrey went wrong, however, in thinking that essential attributes like "wise" and "good" signify God in relation to creaturely wisdom and goodness. In fact, they apply to God absolutely and not in relation to creatures. They are not names like "creator," which denotes God as relative to creatures. God is not wise because he is the cause of created wisdom, nor because he contains created wisdom in a transcendent way; he is simply wise, and indeed wisdom itself.[32]

We are now in a position to understand Ockham's answer to the question: Are the perfections that we attribute to God (*perfectiones attributales*) the divine essence itself? His reply depends on the meaning of *perfectio attributalis*. If it means the divine reality itself there is only one such perfection, namely the reality of God, which is indistinct both in reality and in concept (*re et ratione*). Strictly speaking, we should not say that a *perfectio attributalis* is *in* God, for it is identical with him. However, if the term *perfectio attributalis* means a concept or name that can be truly predicated of God, there are many such attributes. Some are absolute and affirmative names of God, like "knowing" and "willing"; some connote other things, like "predestinating" and "creating"; some are negative, like "incorruptible" and "immortal." All these names signify God and stand for him in our statements about him, but they are not really identical with him. They are not, strictly

---

31. "Et ideo concedo quod omnia attributa vel connotant aliqua distincta realiter vel sunt communia aliquibus distinctis realiter" (*Ord.* 1.2.2 [*OTh* 2: 70.18–20]).

32. Ibid. (*OTh* 2: 72.11–14).

speaking, perfections at all, but only concepts produced by an act of the mind as signs of the divine essence.[33]

In defining the nature of the divine attributes and in reconciling their multiplicity with the unity of the divine essence, Ockham resorts to his doctrine of universals and individuals described in Chapter 1. We saw that every reality (*res*) is an individual whose unity is so absolute that it cannot be the foundation of several concepts. By itself, it does not offer the mind a basis for conceiving it in various ways. We may think of it in different general terms, as we think of Socrates as a man or an animal, but universals are only names or concepts signifying individuals in their actual or possible likenesses to each other. There is nothing in Socrates himself that would prompt us to give him different general names or to conceive him by different universal concepts. For this, a real diversity, either actual or possible, is necessary.

These conclusions apply equally to the divine essence. Though the divine Persons differ formally from the divine essence, they are really one in being or essence. In short, there is only one God. If we could conceive his essence in itself, we would have only one concept of it, but this concept is reserved to the next life. Here and now we conceive it in many universal concepts and give it many general names, but there is nothing in God's essence itself corresponding to these different concepts and names or that offers a basis for them. Their diversity comes from the different created perfections they connote or to which they are otherwise related.

---

33. Ibid. (*OTh* 2: 61.14–62.22). Ockham here refers to concepts as *ficta* or purely "beings of reason," having no reality but only "objective" being in the mind. Later, in the *Quodlibeta*, he speaks of the divine names as concepts having the real being of mental qualities. The names are then both really and mentally distinct; see *Quodl.* 3.2 (*OTh* 9: 209.30–210.36). This opinion is already presented, but not as his own in *Ord.* 1.2.2 (*OTh* 2: 66.3–18). For the two opinions on the nature of a concept see below, pp. 504–510. Ockham adds the historical note that, when writing about God, the saints of old, such as Augustine and Anselm, did not use the word "attribute" but "name" (he could have added Dionysius the pseudo-Areopagite). In fact, the term "attribute" is Aristotelian. Ockham uses both this term and also "name"; see *Quodl.* ibid. (*OTh* 9: 208.9–209.27).

To Duns Scotus this amounts to saying that the divine attributes really have the same meaning, so that we know God as well under one as we do under all. If there is no distinction between the attributes on the side of God, it is a wasted effort for theologians to fill so many folios, demonstrating one attribute from another.[34] But Ockham retorts that the names we give to God are not synonyms but differ in meaning owing to their relations to really distinct created perfections. So we know God more perfectly under many concepts than we do under one.[35]

Scotists, however, cannot accept this, for if Ockham is correct the concepts of the divine attributes have the same meaning when signifying precisely God himself. In short, they are synonyms. In their view Ockham's understanding of the oneness of God (or of any reality) renders him unintelligible; for, as the Platonists have shown, what is purely one escapes discursive knowledge, and without discourse theology is impossible.[36]

The Scotist raises still another objection to Ockham's view of the oneness or simplicity of God: it renders theology as a strict, *propter quid* science impossible, not only as theologians now practice it, but also in the more perfect way we could have it through the divine power.[37] The Aristotelian notion of a science requires that it have a primary subject whose attributes are demonstrated

34. Scotus, *Ord*. 1.8.1.4 (Vatican ed. 4: 267, n. 204), cited by Ockham, *Ord*. 1.2.1 (*OTh* 2: 7.3–11). Scotus' argument is directed against the doctrine of Henry of Ghent, but Ockham sees it as also an objection to his own.

35. "Et quando dicitur quod tunc 'aeque perfecte cognosceretur Deus cognoscendo ipsum sub uno attributo sicut sub ratione omnium attributorum', dico quod consequentia non valet, quia – secundum ipsos [i.e. Scotistas] etiam – Deus non potest cognosci a nobis nisi sub aliquo conceptu, et tamen perfectius cognoscitur quando cognoscitur sub pluribus quam sub uno" (*Ord*. 1.2.1 [*OTh* 2: 33.20–34.3]).

36. See Anton C. Pegis, "The Dilemma of Being and Unity," *Essays in Thomism*, ed. R.E. Brennan (New York, 1942), pp. 151–183.

37. For the evident, abstractive kind of theology that God can cause in the wayfarer (*viator*), but which is beyond his or her present capacity, see above, p. 150.

of it. Moreover, in Scotus' view the attributes have an essential order among themselves as prior or posterior with respect to the subject. It is owing to this order that the theologian can demonstrate one attribute from another. Now, theology is a strict science whose primary subject is the divine essence or deity.[38] The natures (*rationes*) of the attributes demonstrated of this essence are distinct from it and from each other either by a distinction of reason or, as Scotus holds, by a formal distinction *a parte rei*. In either case the distinction is not one solely made by the mind but it has a basis in the deity itself. What is more, there is an essential order among the natures of the attributes, allowing one to be demonstrated from another – an order that is not purely mental but is present in God himself.

How is the theologian to know what this order is? Scotus replies with his "famous proposition" (*propositio famosa*) – to use the expression of his follower Walter Chatton: "Whatever the real order would be among things were they really distinct, that is their order according to reason where they are distinct by reason."[39] In other words, if we want to know the essential order of the natures of the divine attributes (which are distinct by reason, and even more radically by a formal distinction), we should look to the order these same natures have in creatures where they are really distinct. Thus we will know that the divine mind and its acts (which are distinct conceptually or formally) have the essential order of prior and posterior, for that is their order in creatures, where they are really distinct. The isomorphism of the essential

---

38. Scotus, *Rep. Paris.* prol.1 (Vivès ed. 22: 6a–7b, nn. 1–3).

39. "Minor probatur, qualis ordo realis esset inter aliqua, si essent distincta realiter, talis est ordo illorum secundum rationem, ubi sunt distincta secundum rationem" (Scotus, *Rep. Paris.* prol.1 [Vivès ed. 22: 28a and 29b, nn. 39 and 43]; *Quodl.* 7 [Vivès ed. 25: 287a, n. 5]). Chatton defends "the famous proposition" against Ockham in his *Reportatio et Lectura super Sententias*, prol.3.2 (ed. Wey, pp. 183–188). For an excellent study of this proposition see Stephen D. Dumont, "The *Propositio Famosa Scoti*: Duns Scotus and Ockham on the Possibility of a Science of Theology," *Dialogue* 31 (1992): 415–429.

order of features in God and creatures is justified by the Scotist doctrine of common natures. As we saw in Chapter 1, Scotus conceived a nature or essence as having a reality or formality that can be defined in itself, and which is the same whether it is present in reality or in thought. Moreover, common natures have an absolute order among themselves independently of whether they are found in thought or reality. And if this is true, we can be sure of an absolute order among the divine attributes sufficient to ground a *propter quid* science of theology.

Ockham's rejection of common natures removes the possibility of an absolute order among the divine attributes. The attributes in his view are nothing but names or concepts which signify and stand for God. These have their own order, which need not be similar to the order of real things. There is no absolute order of natures common to concepts and realities. Consequently Scotus' "famous proposition" is wrong, because "the order in things and in their corresponding concepts is not always similar." For example, man and whiteness are related as subject and accident, but this is not the relation between their corresponding concepts.[40]

An important consequence of Ockham's dismissal of the Scotist correlation of the order of the divine attributes with features in God is his denial that theology can be a science in the strict sense of the term. It cannot be a science as theologians now practice it, or even in the more perfect way we could have it through the divine power. Ockham's repudiation of theology as a proper science was not without its effect. As has been said, "Indeed, after Ockham, many theologians would cease treating the question of whether theology was a science as a topic at all."[41]

---

40. "Similiter ista propositio adhuc est falsa intelligendo eam sic quod 'qualem ordinem haberent aliqua si essent distincta realiter, talem ordinem habent rationes vel conceptus correspondentes illis rebus si essent, qui tamen conceptus non sunt una res'; quia non est semper consimilis ordo in rebus et in conceptibus correspondentibus" (*Ord.* 1.prol.2 [*OTh* 1: 121.7–12]).

41. Dumont, "The *Propositio Famosa Scoti*," p. 424.

CHAPTER 5

The Divine Knowledge, Will, and Power

IN THE PREVIOUS CHAPTER we have considered the divine attributes in general in relation to the divine essence. We shall continue by examining in some detail the three most significant attributes of God: knowledge, will, and power.

1 Divine Knowledge

Does God Know?[1]

Ockham had no intention of flouting the traditional doctrine of "the saints and philosophers" (that is, the fathers of the Church and non-Chistian philosophers like Aristotle, Avicenna, and Averroes), that God truly knows and understands, but he insists that God's knowledge is not the same as our own. We can use the univocal term "knowledge" of both, but the meaning is different. Our knowledge in the strict sense (*scientia*) is the result of a demonstration, by which a proposition is deduced from premises that are true and necessary. Demonstration produces in the mind a stable disposition (*habitus*) inclining us to acts of knowing. But the divine knowledge answers neither of these descriptions. God does not know by demonstrating conclusions, nor does he acquire mental dispositions to know them. Indeed, we should not say that he *has* knowledge or that knowledge is *in* him, but that he *is* his knowledge, for it is identical with his essence. In him, knowledge and essence are not distinct by a distinction made by the mind, as Aquinas thought, nor by a formal distinction, as Scotus maintained.[2]

---

1. The following three sections are taken substantially from Armand Maurer, "The Role of Divine Ideas in the Theology of William of Ockham," *Studies Honoring Ignatius Charles Brady, Friar Minor*, ed. Romano S. Almagno and Conrad L. Harkins (St. Bonaventure, NY, 1976), pp. 357–377, repr. *Being and Knowing* (Toronto, 1990), pp. 363–381.

2. For God and his attributes see above, pp. 184–204.

With his penchant for finding an order among intelligible features even in something that is really one and self-identical, Scotus contends that in a sense God's knowledge is not absolutely identical with his essence. Rather, there is an essential order between the nature (*ratio*) of his essence and that of his knowledge, the essence being absolutely first and the divine attribute of knowledge coming after as a sort of property or accident of the essence. In defence of this position Scotus appeals to his "famous proposition" (*propositio famosa*), which we have already met when treating of Scotus' doctrine of the divine attributes: "Whatever the real order would be among things if they were really distinct, they have a similar order according to reason where they are distinct by reason."[3] Applying the principle to the present topic, Scotus argues that if God's knowledge and intellect were really distinct, his intellect would be closer and more intimate to his essence than his knowledge, for knowledge is gained through the intellect. Following his principle, the same order must be present between God's essence, intellect, and knowledge, even though they are only distinct according to reason. Consequently the divine knowledge is not absolutely identical with the divine essence.[4]

There is perhaps nothing in the Scotist philosophy more repugnant to Ockham than its isomorphism of mind and reality. As we have seen, Ockham strongly insists that a mental or formal distinction or order can have no counterpart in a reality that is truly one. The mind makes distinctions and orders among its concepts, but we should not expect to find a parallel in the real world. So Scotus' principle must be rejected wherever it is applied. In a creature that is really one and the same there can be no imaginable order, either real or mental. Certainly if the divine essence were really distinct from the divine essence there would be an order between them, but how can there be an order between an essence

3. "Quaecumque enim ordinem realem haberent aliqua distincta realiter, similem ordinem secundum rationem habent, ubi essent distincta ratione" (Scotus, *Rep. Paris.* prol.1 [Vivès ed. 22: 29b, n. 43]). See above, p. 203 n39.

4. Scotus, *Quodl.* 6 (Vivès ed. 25: 264, n. 20); *Rep. Paris.* prol.1 (Vivès ed. 22: 29–30, n. 43).

and itself? Now the divine essence, intellect, and knowledge are really God, and so there can be no order whatsoever between them. We can put an order between the names, but it would not always correspond to the order of the realities, were they really distinct. In fact the order of these names, and even of the corresponding concepts, is irrelevant here, for they are not really the same nor are they in God.[5]

Here, as elsewhere, Ockham finds language leading one astray. We say "God is intellectual" or "God is an intellectual substance," and the form of our language makes it appear that "intellectual" is a property or specific difference added to God's essence. But the intent of the first proposition is that God *is* an intellect and of the second that God is a substance that *is* an intellect. In other words, these are essential or *in quid*, not *in quale*, predications. So it is with all statements about God, such as "God is a substance, living, wise, knowing, willing, etc." They mean that he is a substance that is intellect, life, wisdom, knowledge, will, and so on. Too much weight should not be given to grammatical constructions, Ockham protests. They are usually based on some convenience or necessity; but no other reason can be given why one is allowed and another forbidden except that those who use them want it this way.[6]

Can it be proved that God is a knower? Aquinas thought it is possible on the ground that he is immaterial. According to Aquinas a knower is different from a non-knower because a non-knower has only its own form, whereas a knower can also have the forms of other things by receiving their *species* or likenesses. Thus a non-knower is by nature more limited and restricted than a knower. Now the limitation of a form comes from matter. So it is clear that something is cognitive because it is immaterial, and because God is immaterial in the highest degree he has the highest place in knowledge.[7]

5. *Ord.* 1.35.1 (*OTh* 4: 429.9–15; 431.21–432.12).

6. Ibid. (*OTh* 4: 429.17–431.20). For other examples of Ockham's awareness that the conventionalities of language can lead to errors in philosophy see Armand Maurer, "Method in Ockham's Nominalism," *The Monist* 61 (1978): 426–443, repr. *Being and Knowing*, pp. 403–421.

7. Ibid. (*OTh* 4: 425.4–11); cf. Aquinas, *ST* 1.14.1.

Though Ockham agrees with this conclusion, if correctly understood, he finds the argument unconvincing. It is simply untrue that only knowers are receptive of the forms of others things. Aquinas himself admits that the medium between the knower and its object receives the likenesses of things. He would reply that the medium receives likenesses materially, whereas a knower receives them immaterially, following the principle that what is received in something is received according to the mode of the recipient.[8] But then he should have argued from the immateriality of the knower to the immaterial mode of its reception of likenesses, rather than from the reception of species to the immateriality of the knower. In any case, Ockham undercuts Aquinas' line of reasoning later by showing that likenesses (*species*) are not necessary to account for our knowledge of things.[9] It is clearly untrue that immateriality is the reason for something's being a knower. There are many immaterial accidents (for example, spiritual qualities, such as divine grace) that do not know, and God could create a pure immaterial form – like the pure forms of the celestial spheres envisaged by Averroes – that are not receptive of other forms and consequently are not knowers.[10]

Ockham can find no general reason why something is capable of knowing; it depends on the nature of a thing whether or not it is able to know.[11] In God's case, since he is uncaused, no cause

8. Aquinas, *ST* 1.75.5.

9. *Ord.* 1.35.1 (*OTh* 4: 425.13–426.12); *Rep.* 2.12–13 (*OTh* 5: 268–276).

10. *Ord.* 1.35.1 (*OTh* 4: 427.4–14); Averroes, *De substantia orbis* 1 (Junta ed. 9: f. 5va).

11. "Nec potest aliqua ratio generalis dari quare aliquid est cognitivum, sed ex natura rei habet quod sit cognitivum vel quod non sit cognitivum" (*Ord.* 1.35.1 [*OTh* 4: 427.11–14]). Marilyn Adams understands the first part of this sentence to mean that "the properties of being able or being unable to know are not, in general, logically guaranteed by other properties but are primitive and sui generis" (*William Ockham* [Notre Dame, IN, 1987], 2: 1020). Robert Pasnau (*Theories of Cognition in the Later Middle Ages* [Cambridge, 1997], pp. 60–62) thinks this makes cognition too mysterious for Ockham. He argues that Ockham is suggesting that there is not only one way of being cognitive; there are divine, angelic, and human ways of knowing. Moreover, when Ockham says that being

or reason can be given why he knows and understands; no strict *a priori* or *propter quid* demonstration can be given for the fact. However, Ockham offers an *a priori* argument in the broadest sense that runs as follows: "God is the supreme being; consequently he is understanding and knowing." By an *a priori* proof in this instance he means a formal inference from one true and necessary proposition to another, when the converse is not a formal inference. Thus it follows formally that if God is the supreme being he is understanding and knowing, but not that if God is knowing and understanding he is the supreme being. The proof is not a strict demonstration, for this would require an evident knowledge that the premise "God is the supreme being" is true and necessary, and this, as we have seen, is beyond us in the present life.[12]

The Object of God's Knowledge

Granted that God is a knower, what exactly does he know? Let us begin with the question: what is the first object of his knowledge?

As is often the case, Ockham begins by confronting the doctrine of his illustrious Franciscan predecessor, Duns Scotus. Scotus thought that the first and adequate object of God's knowledge is his own essence: first, both in origin and perfection; adequate, because it alone satisfies his infinite mind. His knowledge of all other things somehow originates in the vision of his essence and falls away from the perfection of that vision.

---

cognitive or noncognitive results from a thing's nature, he does not mean that no account at all can be given except "the brute fact itself." A list can be drawn up of what it means to be a knower; for example, seeing, feeling, imagining, etc., and cognition can be reduced to them, and Ockham sometimes analyses various aspects of cognition. However, Ockham would hardly consider these "a general reason" (like Aquinas' "immateriality") why some things can know and other cannot. Cognition is indeed *that* mysterious for Ockham.

12. *Ord.* 1.35.1 (*OTh* 4: 428.3-19). For our inability to know with evidence that God is the highest being see above, pp. 179–180. Ockham's argument is an enthymeme, leaving unexpressed the minor premise "But the supreme being is understanding and knowing." For his notion of an *a priori* demonstration see above, p. 110.

In a remarkable passage – conveniently quoted by Ockham – Scotus conceived of "moments" (*instantia*) in God's knowledge: not temporal moments to be sure, for he does not dwell in time, but so to speak natural stages of that knowledge. In the first stage God knows his own essence just in itself. In the second he produces all possible creatures within his mind, giving them intelligible being there and knowing them. In the third stage the divine mind relates its understanding to these intelligible objects and causes a mental relation between them. In the fourth the divine mind reflects on this relation and knows it. Thus Scotus would have everything virtually contained in God's essence and in his knowledge of that essence. They flow, so to speak (but not properly), from the divine essence.[13]

There is much in this doctrine that is unintelligible to Ockham. He is willing to grant that God first knows himself, if "first" means prior in perfection, but not if it means first in origin. God does not know things in a certain order, according as they somehow flow from his essence. There are no moments in his knowledge; he knows himself and creatures in one unique and indistinct act. When several things are known in the same act, one is not known before the other.[14]

Ockham also takes exception to Scotus' description of the divine essence as the primary adequate object of God's knowledge. This is correct, he says, if adequate means perfect, but not if it has the logical sense, described by Aristotle, of a prior object of which essential attributes are demonstrated; for example, as a triangle is logically prior to its property of having three angles. In the logical sense of adequation, the primary object of God's knowledge is not God, but rather the notion of being, which is univocally predicable of both God and creatures.[15]

---

13. Scotus, *Ord.* 1.35.un. (Vatican ed. 6: 254–256, nn. 24–26), cited by Ockham, *Ord.* 1.35.4 (*OTh* 4: 467.21–468.12). For an analysis of this text see Etienne Gilson, *Jean Duns Scot* (Paris, 1952), pp. 282–306.

14. Ockham, *Ord.* 1.35.3 (*OTh* 4: 447.18–456.19; 468.14–470.9).

15. Ibid. (*OTh* 4: 450.15–451.8; 462.8–19). See Aristotle, *Anal. Post.* 1.4, 73b31–74a3.

Does God know distinctly all other things, or does he know only himself? Averroes thought he could prove that God knows only himself, using, among other arguments, Aristotle's judgment that it would be demeaning for God, the most perfect being, to know things of lesser value than himself.[16] But this is not convincing to Ockham. It is not the nature of knowledge, he insists, to be more or less perfect than, or equal to, its object. So there can be perfect knowledge of a lowly or unworthy object. Would knowing other things imply that God depends on them? Not at all, according to Ockham; it is not essential for knowledge to be caused by or to be dependent on an object. Sometimes our knowledge is not caused by an object, Ockham says – alluding no doubt to the possibility of an intuition of something that does not exist.[17] Averroes is also mistaken in saying that what is understood is the perfection of the one understanding. We can know a stone, but the stone does not perfect us. God understands himself, but properly speaking he is not the perfection of himself; he is in every way identical with himself. When knowing is caused by an object, the object is the perfection of the knower, not formally or properly speaking, but effectively. However, when knowledge is not caused, as in God, then the object understood is either identical with the act of knowing or it is something he can create.[18]

Turning to his immediate predecessors, Ockham finds weaknesses in Aquinas' reasoning that perfect knowledge of something entails the knower's perfect knowledge of its power and consequently of the full range of that power. From this it would follow that, since God knows himself completely, he must know everything to which his power extends, and consequently he knows everything perfectly.[19] Ockham does not believe this can be ade-

16. Averroes, *In Metaph.* 12, com. 51 (Junta ed. 8: f. 336v–r); see Aristotle, *Metaph.* 12.9, 1074b29–35.

17. *Ord.* 1.35.2 (*OTh* 4: 440.18–441.11). For the doctrine of intuitive knowledge of a nonexistent object see below, pp. 479–490.

18. Ibid. (*OTh* 4: 442.9–20).

19. *ST* 1.14.5.

quately proven. In fact, a cause can be completely known without knowing any of its effects. It is basic to Ockham's notion of causality that a simple knowledge of one thing cannot adequately lead to a simple knowledge of another thing. Another weakness in Aquinas' argument is its assumption that God is the cause of all things, which has not been sufficiently proven.[20]

Ockham records several arguments of Duns Scotus proving that God knows all creatures distinctly, but in Ockham's view most are only probable; one is invalid. All of them have unproven presuppositions; for example, that the first efficient cause is the absolutely first being, and that the first efficient cause produces its effects knowingly and contingently. But these propositions go beyond the competence of natural reason and the arguments based on them fail to convince philosophers.[21]

Ockham concludes that human reason cannot demonstrate that God's knowledge is limited to himself and that he does not know creatures distinctly. But neither can it be proved by reason that God knows everything besides himself. Only by faith are we assured of it. Ockham's concern is the limitation of human reason to prove this truth. No satisfactory proof can be given that God is the efficient productive cause of all things, or that in any case a cause knows any of its immediate effects. Ockham grants, however, that a probable argument can be given that God knows something other than himself. He has shown that God is probably the cause of some effects, and from this it would seem to follow that he does know some of them. But he does not consider this argument to be conclusive or strong enough to silence a stubborn adversary.[22]

Divine Ideas

Granted the certainty, at least by faith, that God has a distinct knowledge of all details of his creation, does this entail his having

20. *Ord.* 1.35.2 (*OTh* 4: 436.7–437.9). For Ockham's views on the possibility of proving that God is the efficient cause of all things see below, pp. 303–304.

21. Ibid. (*OTh* 4: 437.11–440.10).

22. Ibid. (*OTh* 4: 440.12–442.7).

the ideas of creatures in his intellect? This is the next question Ockham raises. It was the common teaching of medieval theologians that God does possess the ideas of creatures, though they were far from agreeing on their exact status or their relation to the divine mind. Most of them, Ockham reports, thought that the divine ideas are really identical with the divine essence and differ from it only through a distinction made by the mind (*distinctio rationis*).[23] This was the teaching of most thirteenth-century masters of theology, including Albert the Great, Bonaventure, and Aquinas.[24] As a representative of this opinion Ockham chooses Henry of Ghent – a theologian closer to his own time.

According to Henry of Ghent, Ockham reports, God knows creatures both as really identical with himself and as distinct from himself. The first and essential object of God's knowledge is his own essence; this most perfect object alone befits the divine knowledge. In this first act of knowing, God knows his essence in itself or absolutely. In a second act, by knowing his essence he knows all possible creatures, for he sees that his essence can be imitated in many different ways. Thus the divine essence is the means whereby God knows things other than himself. His essence is the means of knowing (*ratio cognoscendi*) creatures, and as such it is the divine idea of creatures. The divine ideas are not the divine essence understood just in itself or absolutely but as having a relation of imitability to other things. More precisely, the divine ideas are the relations of imitability of the divine essence to possible creatures.

23. *Ord.* 1.35.5 (*OTh* 4: 480.1–3).

24. Albert the Great, *Commentarii in Sententiaurm* 1.35E.9 (*Opera omnia* 26: 192–195); Bonaventure, *In Sent.* 1.35.un.3 (*Opera omnia* 1: 608); Aquinas, *ST* 1.15.2. Henry of Harclay also says that it is the more common opinion that a divine idea is the divine essence with a relation of imitability to creatures (Armand Maurer, "Henry of Harclay's Questions on the Divine Ideas," *Mediaeval Studies* 23 [1961]: 163–193, at p. 178). For Aquinas' doctrine of the divine ideas see L.B. Geiger, "Les idées divines dans l'oeuvre de S. Thomas," in *St. Thomas Aquinas 1274–1974: Commemorative Studies*, ed. Armand Maurer (Toronto, 1974), 2: 175–209. For Bonaventure see J.F. Quinn, *The Historical Constitution of St. Bonaventure's Philosophy* (Toronto, 1973), pp. 492–497, 506–509.

They are really identical with that essence and differ from it only as distinct ways the divine mind conceives itself.[25]

This is as far as Ockham goes in reproducing Henry's doctrine of the divine ideas. He does not tell the reader – perhaps because it did not suit his purpose – that Henry, under the influence of Avicenna, conceived the divine ideas in still another way. The Islamic philosopher taught Henry to think of these ideas as so many possible essences produced in the divine mind by God's knowledge of himself as imitable by creatures.[26] In this view the divine ideas are not precisely the divine essence or relations of imitability of that essence, but rather a world of possible essences constituted by God's knowledge of himself. This was a departure from the usual thirteenth-century conception of the divine ideas and one that was to influence Duns Scotus and Ockham himself. Henry of Ghent was turning speculation about the divine ideas in the direction of creatures rather than the divine essence. He was proposing that the divine ideas are *objects* of the divine knowledge, and that these objects constitute a world of possible creatures: an infinite pool of possibles from which God chooses some to be created. As we shall see, it was along these lines, though with profound differences, that both Scotus and Ockham tried to solve the problem of divine ideas.

The basic mistake of the common view of the divine ideas, in Ockham's opinion, is to identify them with the divine essence. Every attempt to explain them in these terms runs into insuperable difficulties. If they are really the divine essence, they are either precisely that essence, or relations of imitability of that essence, or a combination of the two. No theologian claims that they are the

25. *Ord*. 1.35.5 (*OTh* 4: 480.5–19); Henry of Ghent, *Quodl*. 9. 2 (*Opera omnia* 13: 26–29). For Henry's doctrine see Jean Paulus, *Henri de Gand: Essai sur les tendances de sa métaphysique* (Paris, 1938), pp. 87–103.

26. "Modus tamen theologorum magis consuetus est appellare ideas ipsas rationes imitabilitatis ... . Sed positionem idearum secundum quod essentiae rerum appellantur ideae quoad naturas essentiarum secundum quod essentiae sunt, optime exponit Avicenna in sua Metaphysica" (Henry of Ghent, *Quodl*. 9. 2 [*Opera omnia* 13: 37]). See Avicenna, *Liber de philosophia prima* 8.7 (ed. Van Riet 2: 423–433).

divine essence considered just in itself, for then there would be only one divine idea, as there is only one divine essence. All agree that there are many divine ideas, and it was to explain this fact that theologians introduced the notion of relations of imitability into the doctrine of the divine ideas. Though the divine essence is one, it can be imitated or participated in many different ways by creatures, and these constitute the multiplicity of divine ideas.

Ockham turns the full force of his dialectic against this notion of the divine ideas. What, he asks, is the nature of the relations of imitability of the divine essence to creatures? They cannot be real relations, for it is agreed that the only real relations in God are the divine Persons. There is also consensus that God is not really related to creatures, though creatures are really related to God. Consequently we must suppose that the divine ideas are relations of reason (*relationes rationis*), but then they cannot be identical with an *ens reale* like the divine essence. The remaining alternative is that the divine idea is a composite of the divine essence and a conceptual relation of imitability. But this is also impossible, because on this supposition the divine ideas could not be described as the divine essence, for a composite is not identical with any of its components. For example, a composite of matter and form is not identical with either the form or the matter.[27]

Though Ockham does not explicitly appeal to his so-called razor in this issue, the principle of economy of thought is clearly operative in his rejection of relations of imitability as an explanation of the divine knowledge of creatures. They are indeed superfluous. A created artist does not need them in order to produce his works of art; why should the divine artist need them? Ockham also believes it degrading for God to need these relations. Since he is self-sufficient and independent, his own essence should suffice for his knowledge of everything. No other entities or relations should be needed. In any case, Ockham contends, relations of imitability cannot account for God's knowledge of creatures, for they

27. *Ord.* 1.35.5 (*OTh* 4: 481.2–482.6).

either precede or follow it. If they precede it, they could not be the result of God's knowledge, as Henry of Ghent claimed. If they follow it, they could not be God's means of knowing creatures.[28]

What, then, are the divine ideas? Ockham's reply begins, characteristically, with an analysis of the term "idea." It is a connotative or relative term, for it does not precisely signify one thing but rather one thing along with something else. Like all connotative terms it has only a nominal quiddity (*quid nominis*), not a real quiddity (*quid rei*). Hence it can be defined only nominally, as "something known by a productive intellectual principle, to which that principle looks and is thereby able to bring something into real being."[29] Augustine's description of the divine ideas happily confirms all the elements of this definition. "Where should these ideas be thought to reside," Augustine wrote, "except in the mind of the creator? He did not look to anything located outside himself in order to create, in accordance with it, what he created." If this is true, the ideas are objects known by the divine mind, which, as an intellectual, productive principle, gazes upon them in order to give real existence to creatures. Augustine also specifies that the ideas are within, not outside, the divine mind.[30]

To the weight of Augustine's authority Ockham adds that of the Roman philosopher Seneca. After enumerating Aristotle's four causes, Seneca described a fifth, which he says was introduced by Plato. This fifth cause, in Seneca's words, is "the pattern which he himself (i.e. Plato) calls an 'idea'; for it is this that the artist gazed upon when he created the work which he had decided to carry out. Now it makes no difference whether he has his pattern outside himself, that he may direct his glance to it, or within himself, conceived and placed there by himself." The main point, Ockham

28. *Ord.* 1.35.5 (*OTh* 4: 483.8–485.9).

29. "[I]dea est aliquid cognitum a principio effectivo intellectuali ad quod ipsum activum aspiciens potest aliquid in esse reali producere" (ibid. [*OTh* 4: 486.2–4]).

30. Ibid. (*OTh* 4: 485.11–486.18); Augustine, *De diversis quaestionibus octoginta tribus* 46.2 (CCL 44A: 72.53–57).

agrees, is that ideas are exemplars or patterns that a knower can look at in order to produce something real.[31]

These classic descriptions of an idea, Ockham continues, fit neither the divine essence nor relations of imitability, but rather creatures themselves. All theologians agree that there are many divine ideas. To cite but one, Augustine claims that God created human beings through one idea and horses through another.[32] But the divine essence is one and incapable of being many. Of course the theologians would concede this, but they would add that the divine essence can be identical with distinct ideas through its different relations to creatures. On this supposition there are many ideas in God, differing not in reality but only conceptually. But Ockham has already dismissed as unintelligible the notion of a divine idea as a conceptual relation that is identical with the reality of God.

Thus every attempt to identify the divine ideas with the divine essence fails. And if they are not that essence, what else can they be except creatures? In fact, if we examine the above description of an idea, we see that it perfectly fits creatures. An idea is something an artist or maker looks at and uses as a model for his work of art. What else but the creature does God know or look at so that he can create it intelligently? Knowing his own essence is not enough; unless he knows what he is about to create, that is the creature, he works in ignorance and unintelligently, which is but another way of saying that he works without ideas.

Ideas are posited in God on analogy of ideas in an artist. Now, all the artist has to know in order to produce his work of art is something similar to what he intends to made. This is his exemplar or idea. So too, God has foreknowledge of the creatures he can create, and these creatures as preconceived by him are his

31. Seneca, *Ad Lucilium epistulae morales* 65, trans. R.M. Gummere (Cambridge, MA, and London, 1917–1934), 1: 449.

32. Augustine, *De diversis quaestionibus octoginta tribus* 46 (CCL 44A: 72.50–52), cited by Ockham, *Ord.* 1.35.5 (*OTh* 4: 487.7–8).

ideas.[33] Plato was wrong in conceiving the ideas as realities, each really distinct from the other, as Aristotle interpreted his doctrine, but Plato was right in his belief that these exemplars are not God but objects at which he looked when he produced the world. Augustine shared the Platonic view that the idea of man is man, that is, man's essence, or universal man. So, if the theologian is searching for the most suitable description of the divine ideas, he will say that they are creatures themselves.

These observations of Ockham give us a better notion of what he conceived an idea or exemplar to be. It may be something real, used as a model for making something similar, as a house may serve as the model for building another house; the architect, knowing the first house, uses it as an exemplar for making another like it. Or the architect may simply draw up the plan of a house and then use it to construct the same house. In this case the house is the idea of itself. As for the term "divine idea," it signifies both directly (*in recto*) and indirectly (*in obliquo*) the creature itself, conceived by God as something creatable, though indirectly it also signifies the same creature produced in reality and the divine knowledge or knower. So the term can be applied to the creature, but not properly to God or to his knowledge, for neither is an idea or exemplar.

In Ockham's language the divine ideas are not means by which God knows creatures, or likenesses representing creatures to the divine mind; neither are they beings produced by the divine mind within itself (*entia rationis*).[34] God may be said to know "through" them, but this does not mean that they move the divine mind, or are identical with it, or are objects located between the divine mind and other things known by God. The ideas are simply the things themselves God knows to be other than himself and creatable by him. He may be said to known "through" them in the sense that they are objects of the divine act of knowing. The preposition "through" is used in a similar way when we say that

---

33. "Igitur cum Deus ipsammet creaturam producibilem praecognoscat, ipsamet vere erit idea" (Ockham, *Ord.* 1.35.5 [*OTh* 4: 489.15–16]).

34. Ibid. (*OTh* 4: 490.5–492.6).

in heaven we shall see God "through" his essence, meaning that we shall see the divine essence itself.[35]

If the divine ideas are not identical with the divine essence, why does Augustine describe them as eternal, immortal, and unchangeable? Are not these terms applicable to God alone? Ockham does not grant that the divine ideas can properly be called eternal; only God is eternal in the strict sense of a being that truly, really, and actually exists for all eternity. The divine ideas are said to be eternal only in the sense that God knows them eternally and immutably.[36] In Ockham's words, they are not eternal "subjectively," that is, as really existing eternally in God, but only "objectively," that is, as eternal objects of his knowledge.[37] If they existed eternally in the divine mind as in a subject, their multiplicity would compromise the absolute oneness and simplicity of God; their eternal objectivity to the divine mind does not.

In the Question devoted to the divine ideas in his commentary on the *Sentences*, Ockham does not enlighten his reader further concerning the status of the divine ideas. We are given to understand that, though creatures, they are not things or realities really existing in God; they are nothing but objects known by him. But what precisely are they if not things? Ockham throws more light on this crucial point a little later, when inquiring if the perfections of creatures are in God. There he explains that the statement, "All things are in God" is equivalent to "All things are known by God," or "All things are creatable by God." To many of his predecessors and contemporaries, such as Henry of Ghent, Duns Scotus, and Henry of Harclay, the presence of creatures to the divine mind as possible objects of creation entailed their production in that mind in a special mode of being called *esse intelligibile, esse cognitum,* or *esse diminutum.* But Ockham protests that these theologians have let their imagination run wild. Creatures are eternally known by

35. Ibid. (*OTh* 4: 493.22–494.9).
36. Ibid. (*OTh* 4: 498.3–499.8); Augustine, *De diversis quaestionibus octoginta tribus* 46 (CCL 44A: 72.57–73.62).
37. *Ord.* 1.35.5 (*OTh* 4: 497.15–498.2).

God, but as objects of his eternal knowledge they have no positive entity (*entitas positiva*). Ockham implies that they are not things at all but no-thing (*nihil*).[38] In another context, he calls all possible objects of creation (*creabilia*) – which are the divine ideas – pure nothing (*purum nihil*).[39] When defending the possibility of an intuition of a nonexistent object, he likens the intuition to God's eternal vision of possible creatures to a vision of *nihil*.[40]

If the divine ideas are not things (*res*) with subjective existence (*esse subiectivum*), are they beings with at least objective existence (*esse obiectivum*), like the images (*ficta*) an artist composes in his mind as models of what he intends to make, or unreal beings like chimeras or goatstags? As we shall see when discussing human knowledge, something with subjective being is a reality, existing either in the mind or outside the mind. Things with objective being are not real: their whole being is their being known (*eorum esse est eorum cognosci*).[41] When Ockham claims in his *Ordinatio* that the divine ideas do not exist in the divine mind subjectively,

---

38. *Ord.* 1.36.un (*OTh* 4: 550.8–554.16); *Sum. log.* 3–4.6 (*OPh* 1: 780.243–262). Cf. Henry of Ghent, *Quodl.* 9.2 (*Opera omnia* 13: 28–31); Duns Scotus, *Ord.* 1.35.un. (Vatican ed. 6: 258, n. 32). For Henry of Harclay see Armand Maurer, "Henry of Harclay's Questions on the Divine Ideas." Though at the start Henry followed Scotus, in a later Question on the divine ideas Harclay adopts the common view that they are the divine essence with relations of imitability regarding creatures. For Scotus, the production of the divine ideas in God is not a creation, for their *esse intelligibile* is not a real being. Scotus places the being of the divine ideas between real being and a simple being of reason (*ens rationis*). William of Alnwick, opposed Scotus on this point, denying that the divine ideas are produced by God in *esse intelligibile*, on the ground that this would amount to an eternal creation of the ideas. See William of Alnwick, *De esse intelligibili* 5 (ed. Ledoux p. 124). Ockham treats of Alnwick's doctrine in *Ord.* 1.3.un. (*OTh* 4: 524.12–532.20).

39. "[C]um omnia creabilia sint purum nihil ... ." *Rep.* 4.9 (*OTh* 7: 178.11). The context is not the divine ideas but the power of a created agent to annihilate separately existing accidents; see *Rep.* 2.12–13 (*OTh* 5: 259.11–12).

40. "Unde Deus ab aeterno vidit omnes res factibiles, et tamen tunc nihil fuerunt" (*Quodl.* 6.6 [*OTh* 9: 607.67–68]).

41. *Ord.* 1.2.8 (*OTh* 2: 271.14–273.22). See below, p. 504.

that is, as realities, but only objectively, as objects known, he implies that they do indeed have objective existence there, but he does not explicitly say so. And in a later work, in which he no longer defends the theory of *ficta* with only objective existence, he denies that the divine ideas have this mode of being. In his *Quodlibeta* – written after the *Ordinatio* – he contends that if the objects of God's knowledge other than himself were *ficta*, from all eternity there would be a system of as many *ficta* as there can be different intelligible beings, endowed with so great a necessity that God could not destroy them, which is clearly false.[42] Again, Ockham dismisses the *fictum* theory, with its notion of objective existence as being superfluous. He sees no need to posit "another world of objective beings," which neither are nor can be real things. In short, what is not a thing (*res*) is entirely nothing.[43]

Ockham is here following his argument to its logical conclusion, paradoxical as it may be. How can a divine idea be nothing and still be an object of God's knowledge? An analysis of the term "nothing" will help to clarify this question. "Nothing" has two meanings according to Ockham. It can be a syncategorematic term, and then it is a universal negative sign predicable of all its logical inferiors. Thus we say "Nothing is running," meaning "John is not running," "Paul is not running," and so on. "Nothing" can also be used as a categorematic term for something that is said to be "a nothing" (*unum nihil*). It can then have two meanings: (1) That which does not really exist or have any real being. In this sense an angel from eternity was "a nothing," because the angel did not really exist for all eternity. (2) That which neither has nor can have real being because it is contradictory for it to exist in reality. In this meaning a chimera is "a nothing," but not a human being, for it is contradictory that a chimera really exist but not that a

---

42. "Praeterea eadem ratione Deus intelligendo alia, intelligeret talia ficta; et ita ab aeterno erat coordinatio tot entium fictorum quot possunt esse diversae res intelligibiles, quae fuerunt ita necesse esse, quod Deus non potuit ea destruere, quod videtur falsum" (*Quodl.* 4.35 [*OTh* 9: 473.92–96]).

43. Ibid. 3.4 (*OTh* 9: 218.97–219.100).

human being exist. The being of creatures, as an object of the divine mind, from eternity was a nothing in the first categorematic sense but not in the second. In other words, creatures did not really exist for all eternity; but it was not contradictory for them, eternally known by God, to exist in reality, provided that God chose to create them.[44]

Ockham does not expressly say that a divine idea is "a nothing" in the above first sense, but he implies this by his statement that a creature, known from all eternity by God as something creatable, is *unum nihil*, for a divine idea is precisely something creatable and therefore a possibly real being. Since his ideas have no reality – divine or created – but are only possible beings, and basically "nothings," they impose no restrictions on him. He does not need to look at any reality outside himself in order to create the world, as the Platonists thought. Nor is he dependent on ideas. All that is required is the knowledge of the ideas, and this knowledge is identical with God himself. Hence from the fact that he is God, God knows everything.[45]

Ockham was not the first to make the important distinction between several meanings of the word "nothing." Henry of Ghent had already described two senses of the term: a pure nothing (*purum nihil*) that is both impossible and unknowable, and a "nothing" in actuality that is possible and knowable.[46] The Franciscan Matthew of Aquasparta also distinguished between two kinds of non-being or nothing: one absolute and the other relative. Absolute non-being is nothing in itself or in its cause, in potentiality or actuality. It was nothing in the past, nor will it be in the future. It is not now, nor can it ever be. According to Matthew, non-being in this absolute sense cannot be the object of knowledge, for the intellect is naturally directed to knowing being. However, it can know what is non-being in a relative sense (*secundum quid*), for this is not completely nothing. It is not actually anything,

44. *Ord.* 1.36.un. (*OTh* 4: 547.6–20).
45. *Ord.* 1.35.5 (*OTh* 4: 506.7–24).
46. Henry of Ghent, *Quodl.* 3.9 (Paris ed. f. 61v).

but it can be something. It is nothing in itself, but it has being in its efficient or exemplar cause. This kind of non-being, Matthew writes, "is intelligible and it can be an object of the mind."[47]

A prime example of a non-being in Matthew's relative sense is a pure essence or quiddity, such as man or circle. An essence of this sort is not absolutely nothing; it is a definite something or object of thought. Of itself it does not actually exist, but it is possible for it to exist if God creates it. In short, it is something possible or creatable. As such, it is not something insignificant in Matthew's estimation; it is in fact a necessary, immutable, and eternal truth. Does not Augustine say there is nothing so eternal as the essence of a circle?[48]

Matthew of Aquasparta's reference to Augustine alerts us to the Augustinian Neoplatonism inspiring this notion of eternal essences. According to Augustine the divine ideas are immutable and eternal forms or likenesses (*species*) contained in the divine mind as archetypes of creation.[49] In the thirteenth century the Augustinian doctrine was blended with Avicenna's notion of the divine ideas as possible beings or essences that God actualized in creation. Matthew was but one of several theologians who shaped this amalgam of Augustine and Avicenna; others were Henry of Ghent and Duns Scotus. Central to their doctrines was the notions of a creatable essence as an immutable "something" in the order of essence that offered to the mind – both divine and human – a stable and eternal object of thought. Since an essence of this sort does not exist of itself but is only possible, awaiting the creative act of God in order to exist in reality, it can be described as relatively non-being or nothing.

47. Matthew of Aquasparta, *Quaestiones de cognitione* 1 (Quaracchi ed. p. 209). See Anton C. Pegis, "Matthew of Aquasparta and the Cognition of Non-Being," in *Scholastica ratione historico-critico instauranda* (Rome, 1951), pp. 461–480, at p. 464.

48. Matthew of Aquasparta, ibid. (Quarrachi ed. p. 214); cf. Augustine, *De immortalitate animae* 4.6 (PL 32: 1024).

49. Augustine, *De diversis quaestionibus octoginta tribus* 46.1-2 (PL 40: 29–30).

There is no place in Ockham's philosophy for the notion of essence as conceived by these theologians. In his view there are no essences, in their sense of the term, in the real world or in the mind, either human or divine.

Ockham's criticism of his predecessors' doctrines of essences and universals was bound to have repercussions on his notion of the divine ideas. It is significant that he does not grant that, strictly speaking, there are universal or general ideas in the mind of God. He insists that God has distinct ideas of both actual and possible creatures; but because creatures are individual, his ideas are primarily and precisely individual and not specific or generic. As we have seen, an idea is an exemplar to which God looks in order to create something; but only individuals are creatable. It follows that the divine ideas are precisely of individuals and not of universals. There are distinct ideas of matter and form and all the essential and integral parts of individuals, but not of genera or differentia or other universals, for these cannot exist in reality. Neither are there distinct ideas of negations, privations, evil, sin, or anything else that is not a positive reality distinct from other realities.[50]

Though God does not primarily or precisely have universal ideas, his knowledge extends to both the individual and the universal. After all, his knowledge is not inferior to that of an artist or craftsman, who has both a particular and general idea of what he intends to make. But God has no need of universal ideas in order to create the world. His knowledge is infinitely greater than that of any creature, and through his ideas of individuals he has a distinct and particular knowledge of everything he actually creates or can create, and this includes a knowledge of universals.[51]

A second important consequence of Ockham's critique of current notions of essence is his new conception of the divine ideas as nothing (*nihil*). The nothing described by Henry of Ghent and Matthew of Aquasparta as an object of the intellect is a *something*

---

50. *Ord.* 1.35.5 (*OTh* 4: 492.13–493.21). Note, ibid., that since God can create an infinite number of things there is an infinity of divine ideas.

51. Ibid. (*OTh* 4: 505.19–506.6).

in the order of essence; it is a pure essence that of itself is not something actual but only potential with respect to existence. As Anton Pegis has shown, Ockham revolutionized the notion of nothing by emptying it of the "somethingness" of essence, leaving nothing but the pure possibility of an individual's existence.[52] The nothing that is the idea of a creature in the divine mind is a pure possibility of being – a possibility that is defined as an absence of contradiction. The *nihil* of possibility is "a remnant of the metaphysical destruction of pure essences" in Ockham's philosophy.

Ockham's reduction of the divine ideas to the status of nothing was even more radical than that of Scotus. Scotus did not agree with Henry of Ghent that creatures, as eternal objects of the divine mind, possess the being of an essence (*esse essentiae*), for in Scotus' view this is a type of real being. If prior to creation creatures had this kind of reality, they would not be created from nothing, and as eternal objects of God he would depend on them for his knowledge. Hence Scotus insisted that a creature, known by God for eternity, is not something but nothing: *lapis ab aeterno intellectus non est aliquid, sed nihil.*[53] But he thought this consistent with the creature's possessing a "diminished" being (*esse diminutum*) or "intelligible being" (*esse intelligibile*) in the divine mind. As eternally known by God, they have objective being (*esse obiectivum*). As we have seen, in his maturity Ockham denied even this minimal being to the divine ideas. They are objects of the divine mind, but their objectivity gives them no positive status as beings. In short, they are pure nothings.

52. See Pegis, "Matthew of Aquasparta and the Cognition of Non-Being," pp. 479–480.

53. "Nec etiam videtur mihi quod ibi sit relatio aliqua propter aliquam dependentiam intellectionis divinae ad lapidem intellectum, ut patet, quia tunc non esset mensura ejus; nec etiam propter aliquam dependentiam e converso in lapide respectu intellectionis, quia lapis ab aeterno intellectus non est aliquid, sed nihil; igitur ejus nulla est dependentia, ut habet esse objective, et cognitum in Deo" (Scotus, *Rep. Paris.* 1.36.2 [Vivès ed. 22: 443, n. 29]). Scotus' point is that there is no dependence of the divine knowledge on the object God knows for eternity to be a possible creature, nor is there any dependence of the object on the divine knowledge.

This is indeed a bold solution of the age-old problem of the divine ideas, but it is in perfect harmony with the principles and spirit of Ockhamism. No theologian in the Middle Ages was more concerned than Ockham to uphold the autonomy and liberty of God against all philosophical threats to these divine prerogatives. Ockham saw one of these dangers in the Platonic notion of ideas as models of creation that have some kind of being of their own. Whether these ideas are in the divine mind or outside of it, God would depend on them, and he would cease to be the absolutely free creator in whom Christians believe. In fact, according to Ockham, God needs nothing but himself in order to know both himself and all possible creatures:

> It can be said that God himself, or the divine essence, is a single intuitive cognition as much of himself as of all things creatable and uncreatable – [a cognition] so perfect and so clear that it is also evident cognition of all things past, future, and present.[54]

Strictly speaking, in order to create the universe God does not depend on anything but himself. He does not need ideas but only knowledge of ideas, and this is identical with himself. Ockham writes:

> In order to act, God has no need of anything whatsoever besides himself. So God does not need ideas in order to act, nor are ideas themselves required, properly speaking, so that God can act. All that is required is knowledge of the ideas themselves, and this in every way is God himself. From the fact that God is God, God knows everything.[55]

---

54. "Potest tamen dici quod ipse Deus, vel divina essentia, est una cognitio intuitiva, tam sui ipsius quam omnium aliorum factibilium et infactibilium, tam perfecta et tam clara quod ipsa etiam est notitia evidens omnium praeteritorum, futurorum et praesentium" (*Ord.* 1.38.un [*OTh* 4: 585.1–5]); trans. Marilyn M. Adams and Norman Kretzmann, in *Predestination, God's Foreknowledge, and Future Contingents* (New York, 1969), p. 90.

55. "[D]icendum quod Deus nullo alio indiget quia nihil requirit ad hoc quod agat. Et ideo Deus non indiget ideis ad hoc quod agat, nec ipsae ideae requiruntur proprie loquendo ad hoc quod Deus agat, sed tantum requiritur cognitio ipsarum idearum quae est ipse Deus omni modo. Et ex hoc ipso quod Deus est Deus, Deus cognoscit omnia" (*Ord.* 1.35.5 [*OTh* 4: 506.17–23]).

This is an echo of Scotus' words:

> Much indeed has been said about the [divine] ideas, but even if it were never said, indeed, were the ideas never mentioned, no less will be known of your perfection. This is clear, because your essence is the perfect ground for knowing each and every thing that can be known to the extent that it can be known. He who wishes may call this an *idea*, but here I do not care to dwell further upon this Greek and Platonic word.[56]

But Ockham had to take the divine ideas more seriously than Scotus, because unlike Scotus he did not believe the divine essence is the exemplar of creatures. They have their own exemplars in the divine mind, and these are nothing but creatures themselves as eternal objects of God's knowledge.

The significance of Ockham's novel doctrine of divine ideas should not go unnoticed. His problem was the reconciliation of the need for divine ideas with the divine autonomy, and he solved it by reducing the ideas to the status of "nothing." Because they are stripped of all positive being, the ideas can still be objects of God's knowledge and yet pose no threat to his self-sufficiency. Even if God were said to depend on them, he would still depend on nothing.

The question remains why Ockham felt he had to identify the divine ideas with creatures rather than with the divine essence, as most of his immediate predecessors had done. As we have seen, Ockham believed that because of its absolute oneness and simplicity, the divine essence could not offer to the divine mind the multiplicity of objects needed for the creation of the world. If Augustine was right – and what medieval theologian would say he was not? – God created a man through one idea and a horse through another. So there must be many ideas in God's mind, and this plurality cannot be identified with the one divine essence. The reason for Ockham's rejection of the Thomist and Scotist notions

---

56. Scotus, *A Treatise on God as First Principle*, trans. with commentary by Allan B. Wolter (1966; rev. ed., Chicago, 1983), p. 146, n. 4.85.

of the ideas is that, in his view, they failed to account for the plurality of the ideas as objects of the divine knowledge. If the ideas are really identical with the divine essence, and this essence is absolutely one, it presents to God but a single object of knowledge. Ockham required ideas that are other than the creator of the world and different from each other. Without this otherness and consequent plurality, the world could not be known and created by God.

It would take us too far afield to show how Aquinas was able to reconcile the oneness of God's essence with the multiplicity of his ideas through his conception of God as *Ipsum Esse*,[57] or how Scotus could do this with his notion of God as Infinite Being.[58] Ockham's metaphysics did not follow either of these paths. In his later writings being is always a thing (*res*), and what is not a being is no-thing (*nihil*). Since the divine ideas cannot be things, for the reasons that have been given, Ockham drew the inevitable conclusion that they are so many "nothings."[59] This satisfies the requirement of a plurality of ideas, while ensuring the independence and freedom of God.

God's Knowledge of the Contingent Future

A special problem relating to the divine knowledge concerns future contingent events: Does God foresee all of them, both those that happen necessarily and those that happen by chance or by free choice? The question is of particular interest to the theologian as it relates to predestination: Does God foreknow and predestine that a person will be saved or damned? Ockham wrote a treatise

---

57. *ST* 1.15.2. See Etienne Gilson, *The Christian Philosophy of St. Thomas Aquinas*, trans. L.K. Shook (New York, 1956), pp. 124–127; and *Christian Philosophy*, trans. Armand Maurer (Toronto, 1993), pp. 103–109.

58. See Gilson, *Jean Duns Scot* (Paris, 1952), pp. 279–306.

59. Among the "nothings" that God knows are not only objects that do not exist or are only possible existents, but also some that do not and cannot really exist, like chimeras and goatstags. Arguing in behalf of the theory that our concepts are acts of understanding, Ockham contends that when we imagine nonreal objects like chimeras or construct castles in our imagination, we elicit an act of knowing to which nothing corresponds in reality, and that is why they are called *ficta*; see *Expos. in Periherm.* 1.prooem. (*OPh* 2: 366–367).

on the subject,[60] and he takes up the question of God's foreknowledge of future contingents, including events, objects, and effects, in his *Ordinatio*, commentary on Aristotle's *De interpretatione* (*Perihermenias*), *Quodlibeta*, and *Summa logicae*.[61]

The question is raised in the *Ordinatio* as follows: Does God have a definite and necessary knowledge of all future contingents? Two arguments are given for the negative side of the debate: (1) A future contingent event (for example, that Socrates will sit) is not definitely true. So it cannot be definitely true for God any more than it can be for us. But only what is definitely true can be definitely known. It follows that God cannot have definite knowledge of a future contingent event. (2) Neither does God have a necessary knowledge of such an event, for if he did the proposition concerning that event would necessarily be true and not contingent, and the event itself would not be contingent.[62]

The notion that it is not definitely true that a future contingent event will occur comes from Aristotle's *De interpretatione*. While treating of disjunctive propositions about the contingent future, he argues that in such cases one part of the disjunction must be true and the other false, but we cannot say definitely which is true or false. For example, a naval battle must either take place tomorrow or not, but since it is not necessary that it will take place tomorrow it is not definitely true or false that it will. Prop-

---

60. *Tractatus de praedestinatione et de praescientia Dei respectu futurorum contingentium*, ed. Philotheus Boehner (*OPh* 2); trans. Adams and Kretzmann, in *Predestination, God's Foreknowledge, and Future Contingents* (parallel passages from Ockham's other works, except the *Quodlibeta*, are translated in the appendices). I have used this translation with slight modifications. On the subject of God's knowledge of future contingents see Calvin G. Normore, "Divine Omniscience, Omnipotence, and Future Contingents: An Overview," in *Divine Omniscience and Omnipotence in Medieval Philosophy: Islamic, Jewish, and Christian Perspectives*, ed. Tamar Rudavsky (Dordrecht, 1985), pp. 3–22.

61. *Ord.* 1.38.un. (*OTh* 4: 572–588); *Expos. in Periherm.* 1.6 (*OPh* 2: 414–424); *Sum. log.* 3–3.32 (*OPh* 1: 710–714).

62. *Ord.* 1.38.un. (*OTh* 4: 572–573).

ositions relating to the present and past must be either definitely true or false, but not those about the contingent future. To hold otherwise would be to say that everything happens of necessity and thus to deny that there is chance and contingency in the world.[63]

Aristotle did not apply his doctrine to the divine knowledge, but its implications for theology were of great interest to medieval schoolmen. Aristotle was not concerned about God's possible fore-knowledge of the future, for his God did not know or care about the world. For the Christian, however, scripture makes it clear that "all things are open and laid bare to [God's] eyes" (Heb. 4:13). The Christian believes that God knows everything, and "knows" can only mean "definite knowledge." His knowledge of the contin-gent future must also be necessary, Ockham contends, for he has only one knowledge, the same for what is necessary or contingent. Since his knowledge of necessary matters is necessary, his knowl-edge of future contingents must also be necessary.[64]

Thus Ockham draws sharp lines between Aristotelianism and the Christian faith on God's knowledge of future contingents. Their opposition is clearly stated in his *Summa logicae*. Aristotle, Ockham reports, holds that in a disjunctive proposition about the present one part is true and the other false, but this is not the case when the disjunction concerns the contingent future. According to the truth of faith, however, God knows all future contingents; for example, he knew from eternity that the Blessed Virgin should be saved and he never knew that she should be damned.[65] The same opposition between Aristotelianism and Christianity is found in the commentary on the *Perihermenias*. It was Aristotle's intention, Ockham says, that neither side of contradictory propositions about the contingent future is true or false, just as it is not determined that a future event itself will happen or not happen. So Aristotle would claim that God does not know one side of the contradiction to be true any more than the other. Indeed, God knows neither

---

63. Aristotle, *De interpretatione* 9, 18a28–19b4.
64. *Ord.* 1.38.un. (*OTh* 4: 573.4–12).
65. *Sum. log.* 3–3.32 (*OPh* 1: 710.63–69).

alternative, for neither is true, and only what is true can be known. Opposed to Aristotle's opinion is the truth itself and the teaching of the theologians, that God has a definite knowledge of one side of the contradiction. Ockham adds that it is up to the theologian to explain how this can be.[66]

Before examining what light Ockham the theologian might throw on this subject, we should note that he does not oppose the Aristotelian doctrine on purely logical or philosophical grounds, but leaves the impression that Aristotle has done the best a philosopher could. Moreover, he believes that he has correctly interpreted Aristotle's intention, but he is not sure about it. Neither does he think that Aristotle's conclusion has been demonstrated. According to his contemporary Peter Aureol, "The opinion of the Philosopher is a conclusion wholly demonstrated, so that no individual proposition can be formed about a future contingent about which it can be granted that it is true and its opposite false or vice versa, but each is neither true nor false."[67] Thus Aureol was a partisan of a three-value logic: in his view there are propositions that are true, others that are false, and still others that are neither true nor false but neutral with regard to truth or falsity.

Ockham the theologian does not grant this; enlightened by faith, he believes that God knows with certainty and evidence everything that will happen in the future, with the consequence that he knows all propositions about the contingent future to be either true or false. Since faith teaches the truth, there cannot be propositions about the future that are neither true nor false. In short, a three-value logic is impossible for the theologian. But Ockham's position as a logician and philosopher is not the same. Aristotle's argument is sound, he says, when it is a matter of events depending on the will, but not when it is a question of

66. *Expos. in Periherm.* 1.6 (*OPh* 2: 421.2–422.16).
67. "Sententia philosophi est penitus conclusio demonstrata, ita quod nulla propositio singularis formari potest de futuro contingenti, de qua concedi possit, quod sit vera, et ejus opposita falsa, vel e converso; sed quaelibet est nec vera, nec falsa" (Aureol, *Commentaria in Sent.* 1.38.3 [Rome ed. 1: 883bD]).

those that occur naturally, as that the sun will rise.[68] This does not mean that the argument is demonstrative or even true, but only that it is the best pure reason can do. As Ockham says, the light of faith can alert us to the fact that certain arguments that are apparently conclusive are not so in reality.[69]

Accordingly we should look to the theologian and not to the philosopher for an explanation of how God can have a determinate knowledge of future contingents. But if we turn to Ockham's theological writings for this explanation we are doomed to disappointment. He reports several attempts by theologians to explain the matter, but none is acceptable to him. In the end he confesses his inability to give a clear account of how God can have a certain and evident knowledge of the contingent future.[70]

Ockham gives little attention to the Thomist doctrine, that God knows with certainty all future contingents because the whole temporal sequence of events, with all its details, is present to his eternal knowledge.[71] Scotus objected that Aquinas' position was too intellectualist. It explained how God could have a speculative knowledge of all *possible* future contingents but not of their actual existence. In order that future contingents be present to God's eternity in their actual existence, his will must come into play and choose certain ones to be created or as already created. Only on this condition does God have a certain knowledge of all future contingents, not only as possible but as actually existing. What is

68. *Ord.* 1.38.un. (*OTh* 4: 584.11–15).

69. See *Quodl.* 2.3 (*OTh* 9: 119.56–120.63).

70. "Ista tamen ratione non obstante, tenendum est quod Deus evidenter cognoscit omnia futura contingentia. Sed modum exprimere nescio" (*Ord.* 1.38.un. [*OTh* 4: 584.20–585.1]).

71. *ST* 1.14.13; *SCG* 1.67; *De ver.* 2.12. This was also Boethius' solution of the problem in his *Consolation of Philosophy* 5 (CCL 67: 107–127), and Anselm's in his *De concordia praescientiae et praedestinationis et gratiae Dei cum libero arbitrio* (*Opera omnia* 2: 245–288). Ockham alludes briefly to this solution (*Ord.* 1.38.un. [*OTh* 4: 585.15–16]), but he denies that God knows all future contingent events because they are present to him, or because they are known through the divine ideas.

more, the reason for this knowledge cannot be the presence of its objects to the eternal mind of God, for the only object of his mind is his own essence: whatever he knows, he knows in that essence and not as caused by anything else. Aquinas places the contingency of future events in their secondary causes, while insisting on the necessity of their first cause, which is the divine knowledge.[72] But if this were so, Scotus rejoins, God would necessarily produce the whole series of causes and their effects. Necessity would reign in the world and there would be no place for contingency and free will. For an effect to be contingent, it must stem not from a necessary but a contingent cause. Hence, in order to account for the evident contingency in the world, the first cause, or God, must immediately cause things contingently "as Catholics hold."[73]

Ockham appears to be convinced by Scotus' criticism of the Thomist doctrine; while mentioning it in passing, he feels no need to repeat Scotus' refutation of it. He also briefly alludes to what appears to be the Bonaventurian solution of the problem of the divine knowledge of future contingents: that they are known in the eternal ideas of God.[74] But this too he passes over quickly, as though Scotus' rejection of it were definitive.

The only theological opinion on God's knowledge of the contingent future that Ockham considers at length and argues against is that of Duns Scotus. The reader has the impression that Ockham regarded this alone as worthy of serious consideration in his day.

According to Scotus, there is no doubt of the existence of contingent events, though he did not think this could be demonstrated *a priori* by natural reason. Only *a posteriori* arguments can be given; for example, that if everything happened by necessity we

72. *ST* 1.14.13, ad 1.
73. Scotus, *Ord.* 1.39.un. (Vivès ed. 10: 626a, n. 14). Distinction 39 was added by a follower of Scotus but it is consistent with his thought. It is printed as Appendix A in the Vatican edition, 6: 415–416.
74. Ockham seems to refer to the Thomist and Bonaventurian doctrines in *Ord.* 1.13.un. (*OTh* 4: 585.15–17). For Bonaventure's doctrine see Etienne Gilson, *The Philosophy of St. Bonaventure*, trans. Illtyd Trethowan and Frank J. Sheed (1938; Paterson, NJ, 1965), p. 142.

would have to deny responsibility for our acts, the need for deliberation, and punishment of bad acts. But how can we account for contingency in the world? Only by supposing the existence of a God who, as the first cause, acts directly and contingently in the world with perfect causality, as Catholics maintain. As for the root of contingency in God, it cannot be his understanding but only his will, for the divine knowledge is purely natural and necessary, but the divine will is free and open to an infinity of effects. The only necessary object of his will is his own essence; to everything else his will is related contingently, so that at the moment it wills one thing it could will its opposite. The human will is also free with regard to willing opposite effects, but besides this it has the power to will and not to will in a series of successive acts. In short, we can change our will from one moment to another. This freedom implies temporal succession and change, which are alien to God. But there is a kind of human freedom that is not so obvious as the power to change one's will at different times. At the very moment that it elicits a particular act of willing it does so contingently and not necessarily; it could have elicited the opposite act. Similarly, in the instant that God wills that a contingent event will occur in the future it could will the opposite.

We are now in a position to see the Scotist answer to the question: How does the divine intellect know with certainty that such and such a contingent event will definitely occur? Scotus distinguishes between several "instants of nature" (*instantiae naturae*) in the divine acts – instants having no temporal succession but only a natural priority and posteriority. In a first "instant of nature" the divine will decides that a certain contingent event will take place. In a second "instant" the divine intellect, seeing that determination of the divine will, knows infallibly that the event will take place. Another way of putting it is that the divine mind holds before itself the terms of a contingent proposition, or the proposition itself. In itself the proposition is "neutral" with regard to truth or falsity. It is neither true nor false until the divine will chooses the conjunction of the terms of the proposition and realizes them in creation; whereupon the proposition becomes true. Thus it is through the determination of the divine will, choosing one of the alternatives of a disjunctive proposition concerning the contingent future, that the divine mind knows the truth about that event.[75]

Ockham's criticism of the Scotist doctrine strikes at several of its essential points. He does not dispute Scotus' contention that the human will is free either to will or not to will, and to will something or its opposite, at successive moments of time. This is what Scotus called the evident freedom of the will. Ockham does object, however, to Scotus' notion of another nonevident capacity of the will to will opposites at the same moment in time. Ockham describes this freedom of the will as follows:

> Scotus maintains that in the created will there is a double capacity for opposites. The one is evident and is a capacity for opposite objects or for opposite acts in succession, so that [a created will] can will something at time A and not will it or will against it at time B. The other is a nonevident capacity, which is for opposites without succession. For it is imagined [by Scotus] that at one and the same instant of time there is more than one instant of nature. And in that case, if there were now a created will that only remained through one instant and at that time willed some object contingently, that will itself, as naturally prior to that volition, has a capacity for the opposite act at the same instant of duration at which that

---

75. *Ord.* 1.38.un. (*OTh* 4: 573–578); *Tractatus de praedestinatione et de praescientia divina* 3 (*OPh* 2: 533.10–22), trans. Adams and Kretzmann, pp. 71–72. Ockham relates the Scotist doctrine with quotations from Scotus' *Ord.* 1.38.2.39.1–5 (Vatican ed. 6: 416–428). For Ockham's criticism of the notion of "instants of nature" see *Expos. Praedicamen.* 18 (*OPh* 2, 327.81–328.115). Ockham opposes Scotus' doctrine in *Ord.* 2.1.1 (Vatican ed. 7: 15–22, nn. 27–37). For the historical background of the notions of "instants of nature" and "synchronic contingency" see Stephen D. Dumont, "Time, Contradiction and Freedom of the Will in the Late Thirteenth Century," *Documenti e studi sulla tradizione filosofica medievale* 3 (1992): 561–597; "The Origin of Scotus's Theory of Synchronic Contingency," *The Modern Schoolman* 72 (1995): 149–167.

[willed] act is posited, so that, as naturally prior, it can will against that [willed act] at that instant. And so this capacity is called nonevident, for it is a capacity for opposite acts at one and the same instant of time without any succession.[76]

In Ockham's view the nonevident freedom presupposes a capacity of the will that cannot be actualized by any power, not even by the divine omnipotence, and an unrealizable capacity is no real capacity at all. The reason it cannot be actualized is that, if it were, the will would will an object at a given moment and not will it at the same moment, with the result that contradictory propositions would be true at the same time, namely "The will wills this object" and "The will does not will this object."[77]

What is at stake in this disagreement between Ockham and Scotus is the validity of the notion of an "instant of nature," and more profoundly the concept of nature itself. Scotus avoids contradiction by distinguishing instants of time from instants of nature. He agrees that the will cannot will two opposites at the same time or that they can be realized at the same time, but he contends that at the same moment of time there are several moments of nature, at one of which the will can will one opposite and at a subsequent moment the other. The notion of instants of nature, one of which is naturally (but not temporally) prior to another, is consistent with the Scotist idea of nature as a reality or formality in itself, formally distinct from individual things. Scotus often resorts to the notion of instants or moments that succeed each other naturally but not temporally; for example, in his analysis of the divine act of understanding as naturally prior to an act of will, and in his account of the divine knowledge and the genesis of its ideas.[78] But once Ockham rejected the Scotist notion of nature with a real-

---

76. *Tract. de praedes.* 3 (*OPh* 2: 533.10–22), trans. Adams and Kretzmann, pp. 71–72.

77. Ibid. (*OPh* 2: 533.24–534.30). See *Ord.* 1.38.un. (*OTh* 4: 578.7–15).

78. Scotus, *Rep. Paris.* 1.17.3 (Vivès ed. 22: 213, n. 3), trans. Adams and Kretzmann, pp. 47–48.

ity of its own, and instead proposed that nothing is real but individual things, he was bound to rule out all instants of nature and retain only instants of time. "I do not agree with Scotus," Ockham writes, "as regards that nonevident capacity in the will, for he is mistaken in all those 'instants of nature'."[79] If there are no instants of nature in the acts of the divine will, Ockham writes:

> [I]t is inconsistent to say that the divine will, as naturally prior [to its act], posits its effect in reality at time A in such a way that it can *not* posit it in reality at the same instant. For there are no such instants of nature as he [Scotus] imagines, nor is there in the first instant of nature such an indifference as regards positing and not positing. Rather, if at some instant it posits its effect in reality, it is impossible by means of any capacity whatever that both the instant occurs and [the effect] does not occur at that instant, just as it is impossible by means of any capacity whatever that contradictories are true at one and the same time.[80]

Even if God has certain knowledge of future events through the determination of his will, this would hold only regarding events flowing from natural causes and not from a created will. The choice of a created will is free, and hence it is not a necessary consequence of the determination of the divine will. So the determination of this will alone does not account for God's knowing that an event, depending on a created will, will occur. Could his certain knowledge of this occurrence be explained by his seeing the determination of the human will? Hardly, for once our will is made up it can always change. Hence, if God sees the will choose one of two opposites, he cannot be certain of this choice, for the human will is free and can always choose the other alternative.[81]

---

79. *Tract. de praedes.* 3 (*OPh* 2: 535.77–82). See *Ord.* 1.9.3 (*OTh* 3: 294.25–297.25).
80. *Ord.* 1.38.un. (*OTh* 4: 581.9–17), trans. Adams and Kretzmann, p. 87.
81. Ibid. (*OTh* 4: 583.5–11).

For these reasons Ockham rejects the Scotist explanation of how God knows with evidence and certainty all future contingents. This leaves him with no satisfactory theological account of the mystery of the divine knowledge of the contingent future. Aristotle and the other philosophers are of no help to the Christian in this matter, and he must resort to revelation and the authority of the Church fathers.

> Although this conclusion, he writes, cannot be proved *a priori* by means of the natural reason available to us, nevertheless it can be proved by means of the authorities of the Bible and the saints, which are sufficiently well known.[82]

Ockham's suggests, however, that the issue can be clarified by an analogy of the divine knowledge with human intuitive knowledge:

> Despite [the impossibility of expressing it clearly], the following way [of knowing future contingents] can be ascribed [to God]. Just as the [human] intellect, on the basis of one and the same intuitive cognition of certain simple things, can have evident knowledge of contradictory contingent propositions, such as "A exists," "A does not exist," in the same way it can be granted that the divine essence is intuitive knowledge that is so perfect, so clear, that it is evident cognition of all things past and future, so that it knows which part of a contradiction [involving such things] is true and which part false.[83]

On this analogy, God has (or rather is) intuitive knowledge of all future contingents, as a human being has intuitive knowledge of things. On the basis of this intuition, a person can make an evident judgment that a thing either exists or does not exist. Similarly God enjoys such a clear and evident intuition of everything that he knows determinately the truth or falsity of all propositions concerning the contingent future.

---

82. *Ord.* 1.38.un. (*OTh* 4: 585.21–24), trans. Adams and Kretzmann, p. 90.
83. *Tract. de praedes.* 1 (*OPh* 2: 518.280–287), trans. Adams and Kretzmann, p. 50.

2 Divine Will and Freedom

We have seen that there is no distinction between essence, intellect, and will in God himself, or even in our concepts of them, if the concepts signify precisely the divine reality. In this case the terms "intellect" and "will" are synonyms, and it is correct to say that God knows through his will and wills through his intellect, for the two terms refer to exactly the same reality. Only if the terms are used connotatively, designating creatures in different ways, do they cease to be synonyms. Thus, if we say God knows A, this does not imply that A exists, for it may only be a possible and not an actually existing being. But if we say God wills A, we imply that it actually exists. Again, we can say God knows through his intellect and not through his will, if we mean that he knows more than he wills, or that he knows but does not will evil, that is, makes or allows a creature to do what it ought not to do. But this connotative use of language about God should not blind us to its absolute meaning when it designates the divine reality just in itself and not in relation to creatures. Speaking absolutely or precisely, "God knows through his intellect and through that reality which is formally and really [his] will."[84]

This is consistent with Ockham's rejection of Scotus' formal distinction *a parte rei* between the divine intellect and will. To the Scotist, the formal nonidentity between them forbids us to say that God knows through his will or wills through his intellect if we are talking about the divine reality itself. William of Alnwick, a follower of Scotus, wrote that if we leave aside all connotations and speak precisely of the divine reality itself, we must say that God knows through his intellect and not through his will.[85] But to Ockham this is only a matter of language and not of the reality we are talking about. We usually say that God knows through his intellect and wills through his will because we use connotative

---

84. *Ord.* 1.2.1 (*OTh* 2: 45.18-20). See above, p. 189.
85. William of Alnwick, *Quodlibet* 2 (ed. Ledoux p. 217), cited by Ockham, *Ord.* 1.2.1 (*OTh* 2: 46.1-5).

language; but if we use the terms "intellect" and "will," or "knowing" and "willing" to signify precisely the divine reality, leaving aside connotations, there is no reason why we cannot change our language and say "God knows through his will" just as we now say "God knows through his intellect." After all, we make up our language as we wish; for example, our grammar distinguishes between the singular and plural, so that we say "Man is man" and not "Man is men." But this does not prevent us from making up a new language and saying "Man is men."[86]

To Ockham's opponent in this discussion (who appears to be William of Alnwick), this turns the philosopher away from reality to language. When he objects: "I do not want to talk about words but only about things," Ockham expresses his firm conviction of the essential role of language in philosophy:

> Though you only want to talk about things, you can only do it with words or concepts or other signs. And so it is only as these signs – whatever they might be – have different significations or connotations, or no connotations, that we must give different replies, in the aforesaid manner, to the [above] propositions.[87]

The opponent might equally object to Ockham's linguistic explanation of necessity and freedom or contingency in the acts of the divine will. According to Ockham, the term "divine willing," just like "divine will," has both an absolute and connotative meaning. Taken absolutely, it refers to an action of God as it is really identical with his essence. Action, power, and essence in this case are one and the same. The action of willing is then subject to the same necessity as the divine essence and will, for they are identical. But when the divine willing is taken connotatively, it designates the willing of the existence of a creature, or the willing to reward a creature, or to give something else to it. The term then does not signify precisely the divine will but connotes the real existence of a creature. "Willing" is then identical with

---

86. *Ord.* 1.2.1 (*OTh* 2: 46.6–47.2).
87. For the Latin text see above, p. 190 n11.

creating or conserving something in its real existence. In this latter sense, willing is not subject to necessity; it is an action within the divine power either to exercise or not. In short, it is contingent, just like its effect. Ockham calls the divine act of willing, so conceived, a divine doing (*praxis divina*), because it lies within God's power to do it or not. The creature itself can also be called a "divine doing" (*quaedam praxis divina*) because it is a freely produced effect of the divine will.[88]

Further light is thrown on the divine will and its action of willing by the traditional distinction between God's will of what is well-pleasing to him (*voluntas beneplaciti*) and his will as manifested by signs (*voluntas signi*). The latter are not the divine will itself but different revelations of it that are figuratively applied to it. There are five of these signs: prohibition, command, counsel, fulfillment, and permission. Thus, when scripture says God wills, the meaning is: "God commands it." When it says that something is contrary to God's will, this means that it is against his command or prohibition, and so on.[89]

God's *voluntas beneplaciti* is twofold: antecedent and consequent. Saying he has an antecedent will does not mean that he has a will like ours, preceding the act of willing, and another will subsequent to the act by which he takes delight in the act. We use many words to denote what is really one in God. His antecedent will is equivalent to his giving someone natural or antecedent conditions by which he can carry out a project with which God is willing to cooperate, if the creature is willing and there is no command or counsel against it. For example, God antecedently wills everyone to be saved, giving them all the help they need for salvation, along with commands and counsels to help them persevere to the end. He will never command them to do the contrary, and he will be prepared to cooperate with them, allowing them freely to work for their salvation. Creatures, however, may freely

---

88. *Ord.* 1.35.6 (*OTh* 4: 516.1–24).

89. These distinctions are found in Peter Lombard's *Sententiae* 1.45.5–7 (Grottaferrata ed. 1: 309–312).

act contrary to the antecedent divine will, as they are free to disobey his commands, counsels, and prohibitions.

The case is different with God's consequent will, which is omnipotent and unobstructable; by it God wills something efficaciously and thus brings it to pass.[90] In this sense God willed to create the universe. In the same sense he predestines some to eternal life and others to eternal punishment, but not without foreknowledge of their freely performed good or evil actions. "Eternal life," Ockham writes, "is conferred on an adult only because of a meritorious deed," and "no one is condemned to eternal punishment – that is, bodily punishment – unless he deserves it."[91]

It was customary for medieval theologians to distinguish between the divine intellect and will in connection with the production within God of the second and third Persons of the Trinity. It has been traditional since the patristic period to maintain that the Son issues from the divine intellect as the *Verbum* or wisdom of the Father, while the Holy Spirit issues from the divine will as the love between Father and Son.[92]

Scotus was able to give a reasonable account of the orthodox Christian doctrine because of his formal distinction between the divine essence, intellect, and will. The intellect is a productive principle in God acting naturally (*per modum naturae*) and not freely, its product being the divine *Verbum*. The divine will, in contrast, does not act naturally but freely (*libere*). Being an infinite and perfect will, there issues from it a love proportionate to its infinite perfection: the divine Person known as the Holy Spirit. Just as the created will is the source of a love adequate for the loving of its object, so the divine will is the source of a love

90. *Ord.* 1.46.1 (*OTh* 4: 674.7–13).

91. Ibid. 1.40.un. (*OTh* 4: 593.24–594.8). While the reprobate are always condemned to eternal punishment because of their perseverance in evil to the end of their lives, the just are sometimes given eternal life simply because God wills it, as in the case of the Blessed Virgin; see *Ord.* 1.41.un. (*OTh* 4: 606.11–20).

92. See Augustine, *De Trinitate* 15, 16–19 (CCL 50A: 500–514).

proportionate to the loving of its infinite object, namely the divine essence. Since the divine intellect and will are the only productive principles in God, there can be only two productions in God and only two Persons produced: the *Verbum* and the Holy Spirit.[93]

Ockham acknowledges the traditional doctrine that the will is the principle of the spiration of the Holy Spirit. This is clear, he says, from the writings of the fathers of the Church, who identify the Holy Spirit with love and charity. But he does not think it is sufficiently proven that the will is the productive principle of the Holy Spirit. In God there is no distinction between essence, intellect, and will. If they were formally distinct, as Scotus held, it would be reasonable to say that the will alone is the source of the Holy Spirit and that the intellect alone is the source of the *Verbum*, but in fact there is no distinction between these alleged sources. Hence there is only one productive principle in God – the divine reality itself. So it cannot be evidently known that there are several productions in God, nor that there are only two, for it cannot be evidently demonstrated that one productive principle is incapable of more products than two. Only by faith do we hold that in God there are only two Persons produced (the Son and the Holy Spirit) and one unproduced (the Father). In short, the Trinity of Persons is solely a matter of faith and not of reason.[94]

Can it be said that the Holy Spirit issues from the divine will freely? While answering this question, Ockham takes the opportunity to clarify the meaning of the term "freedom." Scotus used the term so broadly that it was not opposed to necessity. Thus he held that the Holy Spirit proceeds from the divine will freely and yet necessarily. In this context "freely" is not opposed to "necessarily" but to "naturally." According to Scotus the *Verbum* proceeds from the divine intellect naturally (*per modum naturae*) and not freely, while the Holy Spirit proceeds freely (*per modum voluntatis*), but necessarily. Thus

93. Scotus, *Ord.* 1.10.un. (Vatican ed. 4: 341–342, nn. 8–9), cited by Ockham in *Ord.* 1.10.1 (*OTh* 3: 318–320).

94. *Ord.* 1.10.1 (*OTh* 3: 326–328); ibid. 1.9.1 (*OTh* 3: 275.11–15).

Scotus sees necessity as consistent with freedom regarding the same object (*necessitas stat cum libertate respectu eiusdem*).[95]

Ockham shows no liking for this use of the term "freedom." When we say something is done freely, we mean that it is done spontaneously or voluntarily, not that it is done necessarily. All theologians agree that the Holy Spirit is produced necessarily and in some way through the divine will, or at least that its production in some way pertains to the will. But they do not mean that the Holy Spirit is produced freely, any more than that the Father produces the Son or the Holy Spirit spontaneously (*sponte*). Rather, they seem to use the word "free" in the sense of "contingent" or "indifferent," and with this meaning freedom is not consistent with necessity regarding the same object. If something is not produced contingently, it cannot be said to be produced freely. Since everyone denies that the Holy Spirit is produced contingently, they should grant that he is not produced freely.[96]

Although Ockham is willing to accept current meanings of freedom, he prefers to describe it as the power of producing different things contingently and indifferently, and of either producing or not producing the same thing, without being determined by anything outside that power.[97] Taken in this sense, God necessarily and eternally wills himself, while willing everything besides himself freely and contingently.[98] Indeed, the freedom and continency of God's act of creation is the ultimate source of all freedom and contingency in the universe. However, this is a truth of faith and not of rational demonstration. Only the following persuasive argument can be advanced to prove it. If there is a cause that cannot be prevented from acting, and it equally envisages a number of things, and even an infinite number, and then produces one of them and not another at a given moment, it

---

95. Ockham, *Ord.* 1.10.2 (*OTh* 3: 331.12–13), citing Scotus, *Quodl.* 16 (Vivès ed. 20: 193–194, n. 8).
96. *Ord.* 1.10.2 (*OTh* 3: 340.12–341.17).
97. *Quodl.* 1.16 (*OTh* 9: 87.12–15).
98. Ibid. 6.2 (*OTh* 9: 590.32–33).

is a contingent and free cause. There seems to be no other reason why the cause produces one thing rather than another except that it is free to do so. Now God is precisely a cause of this sort regarding everything producible from eternity; and so he seems to create them freely and contingently.[99]

3 Divine Power

The Christian confesses his faith in the omnipotence of God every time he recites the Apostles' Creed: "I believe in God, the Father almighty." The meaning of his belief, however, is far from clear. He reads in scripture: "all things are possible with God" (Mt 19:26), but if he has an inquiring mind, a host of questions are bound to occur to him: Is it indeed true that God can do anything, even what is contradictory? Can he make a square circle or a stone too heavy for him to lift? Can he make something both exist and not exist at the same time? Can he sin or do what is evil? Can he make himself not exist? In short, what is the meaning of "all things" in the scriptural verse? The meaning of possibility might also puzzle the Christian. How is he to define what is possible or impossible? Is the primary reason for something's being possible or impossible in God or in the thing in question? If the Christian is a philosopher, he might wonder whether the omnipotence of God is only a matter of faith or also demonstrable by natural reason or philosophy.

Aristotle and the Divine Power

The notion that God has infinite power was not unknown to philosophers. Aristotle and his commentator Averroes ascribed infinite force to the Primary Mover of the heavenly bodies, for it moves them over an infinite time. As Averroes says, however, this is only an infinite motive power, not an infinite perfection of the Prime Mover itself. The Prime Mover is a form, and forms are finite in themselves. Citing Aristotle and Averroes in this connection, Ockham sums up their doctrine by saying that in their view the

---

99. *Rep.* 2.3–4 (*OTh* 5: 55.16–56.5).

Primary Mover is infinite "extensively," that is, in its moving force and duration, but not "intensively" or as an intrinsic perfection.[100] Scotus thought otherwise, contending that the arguments of Aristotle and Averroes lead to the conclusion that, because the Primary Mover moves with an infinite motion, it must have an intensive infinite power, for no intrinsically finite power can move in an infinite time.[101] But Ockham rejects this interpretation of the philosophers, pointing out that they simply wanted to prove that the Primary Mover is not a power in a body and consequently divisible into parts. As an immaterial form, it can be finite in its being but infinite in its motive force.[102]

In Ockham's opinion, Scotus' many efforts to prove that God is a power intrinsically infinite misrepresent the doctrine of Aristotle and Averroes and, what is more, they fail as demonstrations. They rest on the supposition that there is a proportion between the Primary Mover, or God, and the bodies he moves: because he moves the heavenly bodies in an infinite time, he himself must be an infinite being. But there is no possible proportion between God and anything finite.[103]

At best, a persuasive argument can be given to prove that God has infinite power in himself and not just as a mover. Over and above every species God has made, he can make another even more perfect. Now Aristotle has shown that no finite power is capable of this, for it reaches a limit or maximum. Hence God has infinite power "intensively" or in himself. Only by faith, however, can we be certain of this conclusion.[104]

The Range of Divine Omnipotence

Is there any restriction on what God can do, given his infinite divine power? In general, he can do anything that does not include

---

100. *Quodl.* 7.16 (*OTh* 9: 762–766).
101. Scotus, *Ord.* 1.2.1.1–2 (Vatican ed. 2: 189–190, nn. 111–112).
102. *Quodl.* 7.17 (*OTh* 9: 766–774).
103. Ibid. 7.18 (*OTh* 9: 778.104–135).
104. Ibid. (*OTh* 9: 774.14–18); Aristotle, *De caelo* 1.11, 281a10–11.

an evident contradiction.[105] This rules out the possibility that he can make contraries belong to the same subject at the same time, or make contradictories be true in an instant, so that a body is moved from one place to another instantaneously.[106] Another qualification to be made is that in the statement "God can do or make (*facere*) anything not involving a contradiction," "anything" does not include God himself. He does not involve a contradiction, and yet he cannot produce himself. It must be said that he can make everything makable (*factibile*) that does not include a contradiction, and this excludes God.[107]

Is God omnipotent if he can do or make everything doable or makable, but only by using secondary causes? Avicenna, among other philosophers, maintained that the Primary Being, being one, immediately produces only one effect and through it all other beings. Acting alone, God could not produce everything producible. But in Ockham's view this is not what Christians mean by the divine omnipotence. They agree that God can act through secondary causes, but they believe that he does not need them. Their belief is expressed in the famous proposition of the theologians, "Whatever God produces by means of secondary causes, he can immediately produce and conserve without them."[108] Absolutely speaking, then, God does not need creatures in order to produce his effects.

105. *Quodl.* 6.6 (*OTh* 9: 604.13–16).

106. *Rep.* 4.10–11 (*OTh* 7: 204.14–15); *Quodl.* 4.10 (*OTh* 9: 346.38–48).

107. *Ord.* 1.20.un. (*OTh* 4: 36.4–10); *Quodl.* 6.1 (*OTh* 9: 586.24–26). At the beginning of the treatise *De principiis theologiae*, the anonymous Ockhamist author clarifies the meaning of the principle of the divine omnipotence: "I do not say that God can make or do (*facere*) everything that does not include a contradiction, for then he could make himself, for he does not include a contradiction. But he can make everything whose making does not include a contradiction; that is to say, everything about which a contradiction does not follow from the proposition "'It is made'" (*De principiis theologiae* [*OPh* 7: 507.4–8]).

108. "Praeterea in illo articulo fundatur illa propositio famosa theologorum 'quidquid Deus producit mediantibus causis secundis, potest immediate sine illis producere et conservare'" (*Quodl.* 6.6 [*OTh* 9: 604.18–20]). See Scotus, *Lectura* 1.42.un. (Vatican ed. 17: 524); *Ord.* 1.42.un. (Vatican ed. 6: 342–343, n. 8); *Quodl.* 7.15 (Vivès ed. 25: 297–298); Peter Olivi, *Quaestiones in secundum librum Sententiarum* 28 (ed. Jansen 1: 494–495).

Does the divine omnipotence extend to sinning or doing what is evil, perhaps even to dying? All of these are possible, and so they would seem to come within the divine power. Various attempts have been made to solve these knotty problems. Aquinas argued that God cannot sin or do anything evil because this would be contrary to his omnipotence. Sinning is a defective action and omnipotence implies perfect active power.[109] Ockham takes a different approach, calling upon the resources of logic. If someone argues: "God cannot sin or die; now these are possible; therefore he cannot do everything possible," Ockham denies the validity of the conclusion, for the argument commits the logical fallacy of "figure of speech." In the major premise ("God cannot sin or die") the terms are taken in the absolute sense of certain actions or omissions, whereas in the minor premise ("now these are possible") the terms are taken connotatively, that is to say, the term "sin" means not only something that is done or omitted, but it also connotes that it is contrary to what one has an obligation to do or omit. With this connotation it cannot be said that God can sin, for there is nothing he is obliged to do or omit. Similarly, the term "die" means not only the destruction of something, but it connotes the destruction which is called "dying." This meaning of the term does not apply to God, for, "Although he can somehow destroy the thing that dies, nevertheless he himself cannot die."[110]

Implicit in Ockham's opinion regarding God's ability to sin is the notion that actions in themselves are not morally good or bad, but they become good or bad when commanded or forbidden by a lawgiver. One has the obligation to obey the law: to act contrary to it is to sin or do evil. As the supreme lawgiver, however, God is not under an obligation to obey commands, and hence he cannot sin or do evil.[111]

109. *ST* 1.25.3, resp. and ad 1, 2.
110. *Ord.* 1.42.un. (*OTh* 4: 621.15–622.8). For fallacies of figure of speech see Ockham, *Sum. log.* 3–4.10 (*OPh* 1: 791–818).
111. For Ockham's views on whether God can will or do evil see below, p. 533.

Does God's omnipotence extend to undoing the past? Can he make what has happened in the past not to have happened? This is impossible, in Aquinas' opinion, because it is clearly contradictory, and nothing contradictory falls under God's omnipotence. It is contradictory to say that Socrates sits and does not sit, and so also that he sat and did not sit. Hence past events are irrevocably past, and not even God can undo them. Aquinas finds confirmation of this in Aristotle's saying: "For this alone is lacking even to God, to make undone things that have once been done."[112]

Not all medieval thinkers agreed with this opinion. Some of Ockham's contemporaries and successors extended the divine omnipotence to the undoing of the past, notably John of Mirecourt, Gregory of Rimini, and Peter of Ailly.[113] In their view God alone is necessary, and everything created, including past events, is contingent. As such, these events could be done away with or changed at God's will. It would then be true that they never happened or happened differently.

On this subject Ockham aligned himself with the common opinion of philosophers and theologians, who taught that God cannot make what is past not to be past, so that after an event has occurred it is afterward always true that it occurred.[114] Commenting on Aristotle's saying quoted above, Ockham understands it to mean that "if the proposition 'this thing is' – something or other having been indicated – is true now, then 'this thing was' will be true forever after, nor can God in his absolute power bring it about that this proposition be false."[115] Ockham's reason is not that of Aquinas – that it would be contradictory for the past to cease to be past – but

112. *ST* 1.25.4. Aristotle, *Eth. Nic.* 6.2, 1139b10 (Oxford trans.).

113. William J. Courtenay, "John of Mirecourt and Gregory of Rimini on Whether God Can Undo the Past," *Recherches de théologie ancienne et médiévale* 39 (1972): 224–256; 40 (1973): 147–174; Leonard A. Kennedy, *Peter of Ailly and the Harvest of Fourteenth-Century Philosophy* (Lewiston, NY, 1986).

114. *Ord.* 1.38.un. (*OTh* 4: 578.20–579.2).

115. *Tract. de praedes.* 1 (*OPh* 2: 507.18–23), trans. Adams and Kretzmann, p. 36; *Sum. log.* 1.59 (*OPh* 1: 189.33–46); *Ord.* 1.30 2 (*OTh* 4: 323.6–324.13).

rather that a true proposition about the past is necessary and cannot be otherwise. This is explained as follows: Propositions about a future event are contingent, because even though God wills for all eternity that it will happen, he can (owing to his freedom) still will that it not happen as long as the event has not taken place. After the event has occurred, however, propositions about it are necessary, and consequently they are always true. However, the necessity of propositions about the past is not essential (*per se*), like the necessity of the proposition "Humans are capable of laughter," but accidental (*per accidens*), "because it was contingent that they would be necessary, and they were not always necessary."[116] In other words, the necessity of a proposition about a past occurrence is not absolute, because it depends on the truth of the corresponding contingent proposition about its occurrence in the present.

The Basis of Possibility

The notions of possibility and impossibility often arise in discussions of the divine omnipotence but their meanings are not immediately clear. Ockham distinguishes between several equivocal senses of the term "possible." First, it means what actually is. For example, when someone actually walks, it can be said that it is possible for him to walk. In general, anything actual is said to be possible. This meaning of possible is equivalent to "necessary." Second, something is said to be possible, not because it actually is but because it will be and can actually be. This is equivalent to what is neither necessary nor impossible. Third, something is said to be possible because it is not impossible. This is equivalent to the first and second senses of "possible."[117] Another distinction in

---

116. *Ord.* 1.prol.6 (*OTh* 1: 178.4–7). Elsewhere Ockham claims that propositions about the past are not necessary but contingent, just like corresponding propositions about the present; but in the context he is referring to propositions like "Peter was predestined." This is because propositions having to do with predestination and reprobation "are equivalently about the future even when they are verbally (*vocaliter*) about the present or about the past" (trans. Adams and Kretzmann, p. 38, with n14).

117. *Expos. in Periherm.* 2.7 (*OPh* 2: 482–483); *Sum. log.* 2.25 (*OPh* 1: 330–332).

the meaning of "possible" is between what is in fact possible, that is, what can be, given the order of the world freely established by God; and what is absolutely possible, that is, what is not contradictory. This depends on the distinction – to be explained in the following section – between the ordained or conditioned power of God (*potentia ordinata*) and his absolute power (*potentia absoluta*).

With these meanings of "possible" in mind, let us turn to the problem of the ground of possibility and impossibility. Does it reside primarily in God or in things? In other words, is something possible or impossible first of all because God can or cannot do it, or because the thing can or cannot be done? Ockham reports the conflicting opinions of Henry of Ghent and Duns Scotus on the subject, criticizes both, and then proposes his own answer to the question.

In Henry's first treatment of the question he maintains that God's capacity to do what is possible comes before (not in time but nature) the possible's capacity to be done, but the capacity of what is impossible to be done comes before God's incapacity to do it. This is because the term "capacity" signifies a relation between God and creatures, and when it indicates a perfection it applies to God before creatures. Since the ability to do the possible is an active, absolute perfection, it applies to God before the creature's passive capacity to receive the action applies to it. But the impossible's incapacity to be done is not a perfection, and hence it pertains to creatures before God's incapacity to do it pertains to him.[118]

Ockham does not have far to look to find an argument against this position: Henry himself provides one in his second treatment of the question, written several years later. Ockham writes:

> Against this view we can use [Henry's] own counterargument. For he claims elsewhere that we don't say, "It is impossible for God to do something because it is impossible for the thing in question to be done." Rather we assert the reverse, viz., "It is impossible for God to do this, therefore it is impossible for

---

118. Henry of Ghent, *Quodl.* 6.3 (*Opera omnia* 10: 42–51). Henry's argument is summarized and criticized by both Scotus (*Lectura* 1. 43.7 [Vatican ed. 17: 530–531, nn. 4–9]), and Ockham (*Ord.* 1.43.2 [*OTh* 4: 641–645]).

this to be done." Similarly, one argues affirmatively that "Because it is possible for God to do this, therefore it is possible for this to be done" and not the reverse, viz., "It is possible for this to be done, therefore God can do it." This argument clearly gives God's power as regards creatures priority over the creature's recipient capacity as regards God, and by implication it also gives God's inability to do the impossible priority over the impossible's inability to be done by God.[119]

Historians have often taken the conclusion of this argument as an expression of Ockham's own position: that God's power to do the possible, and his lack of power to do the impossible, take precedence over the possible's capacity to be done and the impossible's incapacity to be done.[120] But this is not at all Ockham's considered view of the matter. He cites Henry's second position against his first only as a dialectical ploy. In fact, Ockham dismisses both of Henry's answers to the question. Presenting his own opinion, he points out that correlative terms, such as "ability to act" and "capacity to be acted upon," are by nature simultaneous. "Because they are such and each entails the other, one is no more the cause of the other than vice versa." It is no more "the case that the son has a father because the father has a son than it is that the father has a son because the son has a father." Thus, "to be able to make" and "to be able to be made" are simultaneous by nature: one does not come before the other. Similarly,

> I say that the inability to do the impossible is not something that God has prior to the impossible's inability to be done by God. Neither is the impossible's inability to be made by God prior to God's inability to do the impossible. And in the same fashion I say of the affirmative form: the ability to do the possible or to

119. *Ord.* 1.43.2 (*OTh* 4: 642.21–643.3); Ockham, "On Possibility and God [*Ord.* 1.43]," trans. Allan B. Wolter in *Medieval Philosophy: From St. Augustine to Nicholas of Cusa*, ed John F. Wippel and Allan B. Wolter (New York and London, 1969), pp. 447–454, at p. 448. For Henry of Ghent's counterargument see his *Quodl.* 8.3 (Paris ed. f. 304v).

120. This is pointed out by Allan B. Wolter, "Ockham and the Textbooks," in *Franziskanische Studien* 32 (1950): 70–96.

create a creature is not something God has prior to the creature's ability to be made by God but they are simultaneous by nature in the same way that "to be able to make" and "to be able to be made" are simultaneous by nature, according to the Philosopher; that is to say, "Something can make" does not come before "Something can be made," neither is the reverse true.[121]

Before Ockham, Duns Scotus rejected Henry of Ghent's opinion, but for another reason. In Scotus' view the primary reason something is impossible is not to be found in God but in the thing itself, which is simply impossible because it is contradictory that it should occur. Scotus envisaged a twofold production of creatures. In a first "moment of nature" (*instans naturae*) the divine mind produces them within itself in intelligible being; in a second "moment" they have possible being in themselves; that is, they can actually be created outside the divine mind. Similarly, God produces each of the possible elements which make up something impossible, say a square circle. Because they are incompatible by their very nature, their combination is strictly impossible. Hence the primary reason why something is impossible is not found in God but in the thing itself.[122]

We have already encountered Scotus' notion of "moments of nature" and Ockham's rejection of it.[123] To him, it is meaningless to speak of the divine mind producing within itself a creature with a kind of intelligible being prior to its being possible. Why would it not be possible at the very first "moment of nature"? The very idea of a thing's receiving some kind of existence by God's knowing it (or, for that matter, by our knowing it), appears superfluous to Ockham. All that the thing acquires by God's knowing it is a new name by extrinsic denomination; that is, it is said to be "known" in reference to God.[124]

---

121. *Ord.* 1.43.2 (*OTh* 4: 649.1–11); Ockham, "On Possibility and God," trans. Wolter, pp. 452–453.

122. Scotus, *Ord.* 1.43.un. (Vatican ed. 6: 359–360, n. 16), cited by Ockham, ibid. (*OTh* 4: 645.9–646.6).

123. See above, p. 210.

124. *Ord.* 1.43.2 (*OTh* 4: 646.8–17).

There is no need, then, to suppose that possibility is a kind of being, or property of a being, really inhering in a creature. We should not say that possible being *belongs* to a creature, but that the creature *is possible*, not because of anything pertaining to it, but because it can exist in the real world. And just as "to be able to make something" belongs to God of himself and not from anything else, so "to be possible" does not belong to a creature from God, but from itself.[125]

Implied in this resolution of the question is the rule of parsimony, which enjoins that one should not do with more what can be done with fewer. Ockham sees no compelling reason to posit a distinct "possible being" in order to explain possibility. Nothing is needed but things, which are possible of themselves either because they actually exist or can exist in reality.

Divine Absolute and Ordered Power

This distinction was formulated in the thirteenth century in the wake of the dispute in the previous century over God's power and freedom in creation. Peter Abelard was of the opinion that God can only do what in fact he has done; he could not have created the world differently nor at another time than he actually did.[126] Contradicting Abelard, Peter Lombard protested that God is not restricted to doing what he has done; he has the power to will and to do other things than those he now wills or has ever willed.[127]

125. "Nec est proprius modus loquendi dicere quod esse possibile convenit creaturae, sed magis proprie debet dici quod creatura est possibilis, non propter aliquid quod sibi conveniat sed quia potest esse in rerum natura" (*Ord.* 1.43.2 [*OTh* 4: 650.3–6]).

126. Abelard, *Theologia christiana* 5 (CCL 12: 358–372, nn. 29–58); *Theologia "Scholarium"* 3 (PL 178: 1093D–1101A, n. 5). This is one of Abelard's propositions condemned in 1140 or 1141 by the Council of Sens, recanted in his *Apologia seu fidei confessio* (PL 178: 107).

127. Lombard, *Sententiae* 1.42–44 (Grottaferrata ed. 1.2: 294–306). For the notion of God's omnipotence in the twelfth century see Ivan Boh, "Divine Omnipotence in the Early *Sentences*," in *Divine Omniscience and Omnipotence in Medieval Philosophy*, ed. Rudavsky, pp. 185–211. For the history of the notion in the later Middle Ages see William J. Courtenay, "The Dialectic of Omnipotence in the High and Late Middle Ages," in ibid., pp. 243–269, "Covenant and Causality in Pierre d'Ailly," *Speculum* 46 (1971): 94–119,

The belief in God's omnipotence and his freedom in creation led theologians to distinguish between God's ordered and absolute powers. According to Aquinas, what God can do in the universe, following out the commands of his will and directed by his wisdom, is ascribed to his ordered power. He can do other things, absolutely speaking, which he does not wish to do, nor has he foreseen or foreordained that he would do. These fall within his absolute power, which is his power considered just in itself and unrelated to his will and wisdom.[128]

Does this mean that once God has established the order of the universe he is unable to change that order or act contrary to it? Aquinas anwers with a distinction. If we consider the order as depending on God as its first cause, he cannot act contrary to it, for that would be opposed to what he foreknows and wills. But if we regard the order of creation from the perspective of secondary causes, then, if God wishes, he can act contrary to the established order. Thus he can do by himself what he normally does through secondary causes, or bring about effects, such as miracles, beyond the power of secondary causes.[129] Being omnipotent, he can do anything that does not imply a contradiction: he can, for instance, annihilate the heavens, create another world, or restore sight to the blind.[130] But if he acts in this way, he does not exercise his

---

"Nominalism and Late Medieval Religion," *The Pursuit of Holiness in Late Medieval and Renaissance Religion*, ed. Charles Trinkaus and Heiko A. Oberman (Leiden, 1978), pp. 37–43, and *Capacity and Volition: A History of the Distinction of Absolute and Ordained Power* (Bergamo, 1990); Heiko A. Oberman, *The Harvest of Medieval Theology: Gabriel Biel and Late Medieval Nominalism* (Cambridge, MA, 1963), pp. 30–56; Gedeon Gál, "Petrus de Trabibus on the Absolute and Ordained Power of God," *Studies Honoring Ignatius Charles Brady*, ed. Romagna and Harkins, pp. 283–292; Klaus Bannach, *Die Lehre von der doppelten Macht Gottes bei Wilhelm von Ockham* (Wiesbaden, 1975); Adams, *William Ockham* 2: 1151–1231.

128. *ST* 1.25.5, resp. and ad 1; *De pot.* 1.5; *In Sent.* 1.42.2.2 (ed. Mandonnet–Moos 1: 991–992).

129. *ST* 1.105.6.

130. *In Sent.* 1.42.2.3 (ed. Mandonnet–Moos 1: 991–992). Aquinas holds that God can create a better world but not many; see above, p. 333.

power alone, or *potentia absoluta*, for he foresees and wills these effects. Since they are part of his master plan for creation, he produces them in an orderly fashion, or *ordinate*.

Scotus defines God's absolute power as the ability to do everything that does not involve a contradiction.[131] However, he gives a new turn to the meaning of this power, as distinct from God's ordered power, when he expresses it in legal terms. Ordered and absolute power are now distinguished as the ability to act according to right law or to act outside of it or contrary to it. This is likened to the jurists' distinction between the ability to act *de facto* (that is, with respect to absolute power) or *de jure* (that is, with respect to power according to the law).[132] As the supreme lawgiver, God has laid down certain laws for his creation, and when he acts according to them he acts according to his ordered power. But he can do many things that are not in agreement with these laws but opposed to them, and these he does according to his absolute power.[133] When he acts *per potentiam absolutam*, does he act illegally or disorderly? Not at all, for, being free, he can lay down another law and then he acts orderly according to this law. Scotus offers the following example:

> [God] established that no one should be glorified unless he first receives grace. When his action is ordered according to this law, he acts according to his ordered power. And he cannot act otherwise except by ordaining and establishing another law – which he can do, since he contingently willed that every sinner should be damned. Thus, by doing the contrary [that is, by glorifying a person without his first receiving grace] he

131. Scotus, *Ord.* 2.7.un. (Vivès ed. 12: 394, n. 18).

132. Ibid. 1.44.un. (Vatican ed. 6: 363, n. 3), cited in Adams, *William Ockham* 2: 1190 n106. Jurists to whom Scotus refers are Gregory IX and Hostiensis. For references see Courtenay, "The Dialectic of Omnipotence," p. 267 n43.

133. Scotus, ibid. (Vatican ed. 6: 366, n. 8); see Adams, *William Ockham* 2: 1193 n111.

establishes another law, according to which he acts in an orderly fashion.[134]

Thus God can act with both his ordered and absolute power: in the former case when he acts in conformity with the law he has established, in the latter case when he acts contrary to that law and in accord with a newly established law. In both cases he acts in an orderly way because he acts in conformity with law.

Scotus here introduces juridical and temporal factors in God's actions through his ordered and absolute power. Being omnipotent, he can from time to time change the laws he makes; and even though the laws are opposed to each other, he still acts in an orderly way because he acts according to his will. Scotus gives the example of a king who is so free that he can make a law and then change it: by his absolute power he can act outside the law, because he can change it and establish another.[135]

Ockham's distinction between God's absolute and ordered power continues in the tradition of his predecessors but with important modifications. In one of his fullest statements of the subject he begins by dispelling the illusion that there are really two powers in God. He insists that God has only one power in his dealings with creatures, and this is identical with God himself. The distinction between *potentia absoluta/ordinata* is not in God himself but in our ways of considering his power: considered in itself and absolutely it is called *absoluta*; considered in relation to the divine will and wisdom it is called *ordinata*. Another misunderstanding is to think that God can do some things in an orderly manner and others absolutely and without order. This too is wrong, for God never does anything in a disorderly way. The correct meaning of the distinction, Ockham continues, is that God can do something in accord with the laws he has ordained and instituted, and beyond this he can do everything that it is not contradictory to do,

---

134. Scotus, *Lectura* 1.44.un. (Vatican ed. 17: 535–537, n. 4), trans. Adams, in her *William Ockham* 2: 1195.

135. Scotus, ibid. (Vatican ed. 17: 535).

whether he has decided to do it or not. There are many things he could do but does not want to do; and these fall under his absolute power. The power of the pope can serve as an example: there are things the pope cannot do according to the laws he has instituted, but absolutely speaking he has the power to do them.[136]

What Ockham is saying seems clear enough. God has many possibilities of acting in the world, some of which he has established in law by his will and wisdom, and these come under his ordered power. There are other things that are possible, absolutely speaking, because they involve no contradiction, but they remain unwilled and unchosen, and these come under his absolute power.

Ockham expresses the same doctrine somewhat differently in his *Opus nonaginta dierum*, which dates from his post-Avignon period. He writes:

> Thus, to say that God can do some things through his absolute power that he cannot do through his ordered power, if rightly understood, is only to say that God can do some things that he has not in the least ordained that he will do; which, however, if he did them, he would do them through his ordered power.[137]

---

136. "Circa primum dico quod quaedam potest Deus facere de potentia ordinata et aliqua de potentia absoluta. Haec distinctio non est sic intelligenda quod in Deo sint realiter duae potentiae quarum una sit ordinata et alia absoluta, quia unica potentia est in Deo ad extra, quae omni modo est ipse Deus. Nec sic est intelligenda quod aliqua potest Deus ordinate facere, et aliqua potest absolute et non ordinate, quia Deus nihil potest facere inordinate. Sed est sic intelligenda quod 'posse aliquid' quandoque accipitur secundum leges ordinatas et institutas a Deo, et illa dicitur Deus posse facere de potentia ordinata. Aliter accipitur 'posse' pro posse facere omne illud quod non includit contradictionem fieri, sive Deus ordinaverit se hoc facturum sive non, quia multa potest Deus facere quae non vult facere, secundum Magistrum Sententiarum, lib.1, d.43; et illa dicitur Deus posse de potentia absoluta. Sicut Papa aliqua non potest secundum iura statuta ab eo, quae tamen absolute potest" (*Quodl.* 6.1 [*OTh* 9: 585.14–30]).

137. "Et ita dicere quod Deus potest aliqua de potentia absoluta, quae non potest de potentia ordinata, non est aliud, secundum intellectum recte intelligentium, quam dicere quod Deus aliqua potest, quae tamen minime ordinavit se facturum; quae tamen si faceret, de potentia ordinata faceret ipsa; quia si faceret

In this laconic statement Ockham takes the proposition "God can do some things through his absolute power" in two senses: (1) God can do some things absolutely and by sheer power, without foreseeing or willing them; (2) God can do some things by his absolute power with the condition that he wills and foreordains them. In the first sense it is impossible for God to do anything by his absolute power, because it is contradictory for him to act by power alone, without knowing and willing what he does. In the second sense it is possible for God to do some things by his absolute power, supposing that he has so ordained from eternity, and these he does through his ordered power.

This will be clarified if we recall the distinction made in Chapter 1 between propositions taken in the composite sense (*in sensu compositionis*) and in the divided sense (*in sensu divisionis*).[138] In the composite sense it is impossible for God to do something by his absolute power, for, being unwilled and unordained it would be contradictory, as it is contradictory for white to be black. In the divided sense, however, God can do something by his absolute power, provided that he has willed to do it, as it is possible for what is white to be black. Neverthless, if God did it, he would do it with his ordered power ("tamen si faceret, de potentia ordinata faceret ipsa").[139]

It is in the divided sense of a proposition that God can work miracles. As we shall see, God can do them *per potentiam absolu-*

---

ea, ordinaret se facturum ipsa" (*Opus nonag. dierum* 95 [*OP* 2: 726]). "Ita haec est impossibilis: 'Aliquid fit a Deo, et non de potentia ordinata'; haec tamen habet unum sensum verum: 'Aliquid potest fieri a Deo, quod non fiet de potentia ordinata'; et tamen, si fieret, de potentia ordinata fieret" (ibid. [*OP* 727–728]). In the *Opus* the distinction is said to be only verbal; see *OP* 2: 725).

"[A]d recte intelligendum distinctionem de potentia Dei absoluta et ordinata, non intendunt quod in Deo sint diversae potentiae, quarum una est absoluta et alia ordinata, per quarum unam potest Deus aliqua, quae non potest per aliam. Sed intendunt solummodo quod Deus posset aliqua, quae non ordinavit se facturum; quemadmodum posset aliqua facere, quae non praevidit se facturum, quia non est ea facturus; quae tamen, si faceret, et praeordinasset praescivisset se facturum" (*Tractatus contra Benedictum* 3.3 [*OP* 3: 233–234]).

138. See above, p. 97.
139. I owe this explanation to Gedeon Gál.

tam, but because they are foreknown and foreordained, he actually does them with his ordered power. However, there are some things that God can do by his absolute power that he will never do by his ordered power. Having made a covenant with his people, God will not break it by doing what is absolutely possible but contrary to his decrees. Ockham gives as an example God's power to damn someone who is predestined for eternal life. Absolutely speaking, this is possible *in sensu divisionis*, as it is possible for something white to be black. However, it is not possible that a predestined person *be* damned, for this contradicts revealed doctrine, and consequently it cannot be done by the divine ordinary power, for it would be contradictory, like something white *being* black.[140] As we shall see, the case of miracles is different. Far from being contrary to Christian doctrine, God performs them in support of it. By God's absolute power *in sensu divisionis* he *can* work miracles contrary to the laws of nature, and since they are foreknown and willed he actually performs them with his ordered power.

140. "Rationes vero, per quas probare conatur quod praemissa distinctio de potentia Dei absoluta et ordinata non est approbanda, facile dissolvuntur. Prima enim ex falso intellectu procedit, quasi haec esset possibilis secundum sic distinguentes: 'Deus aliquid facit de potentia absoluta, quod non facit de potentia ordinata'. Haec enim de inesse secundum eos est impossibilis et contradictionem includit; quia eo ipso quod Deus aliquid faceret, ipse faceret illud de potentia ordinata. Haec tamen de possibili: 'Deus potest aliquid facere de potentia absoluta quod nunquam faciet de potentia ordinata', in sensu divisionis accepta, vera est: quemadmodum ista de possibili: 'Ille qui est praedestinatus potest dampnari' vera est in sensu divisionis; et tamen ista de inesse: 'Praedestinatus dampnatur', est impossibilis et contradictionem includit" (*Opus nonag. dierum* [*OP* 2: 727]). For the example of the propositions: 'Album potest esse nigrum', and 'Album est nigrum', see *OP* 2: 729.

According to William Courtenay, the nominalists understood that God made two covenants with the world: one with the world in general, made at creation and guaranteed by promises made to Adam and Noah, committing God to sustain the universe and its laws; the other with God's chosen people, committing God to uphold the revealed laws of salvation. See William J. Courtenay, "Covenant and Causality in Pierre d'Ailly," and *Covenant and Causality in Medieval Thought* (London, 1984).

Ockham proves the distinction between the divine absolute and ordered power by citing Jesus' words in Jn 3:5: "Unless one is born of water and the Spirit, he cannot enter the kingdom of God." According to Christian law now in force, salvation is possible only through baptism. There was a time, however, when salvation was possible without baptism, as in Jewish law children who died before the use of reason could be saved by circumcision. This is still possible, absolutely speaking, Ockham continues, for it involves no contradiction; but it is not possible according to the present law. It was the law and not God's power that changed in the Jewish and Christian dispensations. But that power must be viewed under different aspects: as absolute when seen in abstraction from any law, and as ordered when seen in conjunction with a given law. What is absolutely possible is the same throughout the change in law, but not what is possible according to the law.

The distinction between God's absolute and ordered power is illustrated by Ockham's reply to the question whether we can be saved by God's simply accepting us for eternal life, or whether we need a created supernatural grace by which we are disposed for this life. With the distinction of the divine power in hand, Ockham has no difficulty in answering the question. By God's absolute power a person can be saved without a created gift of grace. We can be sure of this because whatever God can do by means of secondary causes he can do by himself. Now, if created grace disposes a person for eternal life, it will be a secondary cause of this effect. Hence God can give eternal life to someone without it. Furthermore, an agent that is not restricted to a definite course of action can bring about an effect in different ways. Since God is an agent of this sort, he can grant eternal life to someone without a created grace, simply as a reward for doing a good deed. In fact, even this is not required, for absolutely speaking God's gifts need not be a reward for merit. It was not as a reward for anything Paul did that he was caught up to heaven and saw the divine essence (2 Cor 12:1–4). Surely, then, God can give eternal life without presupposing a created grace in the soul. A person can be loving in the sight of God without such a grace, simply because he accepts that person. The case is quite different from the standpoint of God's ordered power. According to the laws now in effect, we could not be saved, nor could we even perform a meritorious act, without created grace residing in the soul, as scripture and the fathers of the Church testify.[141]

In the process against Ockham at Avignon his doctrine of grace was censured as Pelagian,[142] but Ockham protested that it has no taint of the Pelagian error. Pelagius claimed that de facto grace is not needed to gain eternal life; the acts we perform with our purely natural powers are meritorious *ex condigno* for eternal life. Ockham, on the contrary, holds that in fact created grace is necessary for our acts to be meritorious according to the present law. He stresses, however, the freedom of God and the contingency of his laws for salvation. God is not compelled to give salvation as a reward for merit, and accepting a person without merit or created grace is not contradictory, and consequently this is possible by the divine absolute power.[143] In the present dispensation created grace disposes a person for eternal life and it is thus a secondary cause of this gift. But God can always do by himself what he usually does through secondary causes. Consequently he can dispense with grace and merit and grant eternal life to some-

---

141. *Quodl.* 6.1 (*OTh* 9: 587.42–588.78). The last reference is to Paul 1 Cor. 13, and the words of Augustine: "Caritatem voco motum animi ad fruendum Deum" (*De doctrina christiana* 10.16 [PL 34: 72]) and "Nec more nec vita poterit nos separare a caritate Christi. Caritas Dei, inquit, his dicta est virtus quae animi nostri rectissima affectio est, quae conjungit nos Deo" (*De moribus ecclesiae catholicae* 11.19 [PL 32: 1319]). Luther interpreted Augustine and Peter Lombard to mean that God unites us to himself by the act of love, but the virtue or *habitus* of love is nothing but the Holy Spirit. He rejected the notion of love or charity as a created virtue or *habitus* – a term borrowed from Aristotle, "the loathsome philosopher." See Paul Vignaux, *Luther, commentateur des Sentences* (Paris, 1935), pp. 39–44.

142. J. Koch, "Neue Aktenstücke zu dem gegen Wilhelm Ockham in Avignon geführten Prozess," *Recherches de théologie ancienne et médiévale* 7 (1935): 353–380, at pp. 375–380.

143. *Quodl.* 6.1 (*OTh* 9: 588.81–85); *Ord.* 1.17.1 (*OTh* 3: 454.18–456.4).

one without them. Nevertheless God has ordained that this will never happen.[144]

This assures us that, although God has the absolute power to do anything not involving a contradiction, he cannot actually do anything with this power alone. God does not act with sheer power but also with wisdom and goodness. What he does issues from him with the marks of all his attributes. His power is said to be absolute because it is not limited to the ability to do just what he has done, or to act according to the laws he has instituted for our present world. Other courses of action are open to him, other laws can be established, other worlds can be created, as long as they involve no contradiction. In short – to use the apposite words of Gedeon Gál – God's range of possibilities is much larger than the range of facts.[145] He remains absolutely powerful, whether he has decided to do something or not, "for God can do many things he does not wish to do." However, if he has decreed that he will follow a certain course of action, it is not due to his power alone, but to his wisdom and will, and then he acts according to his ordered power.

Like Scotus, Ockham takes into account the temporal dimension of the divine plan for the world, which allows for changes in its laws from one time to another and for exceptions to them. Ockham does not portray God as a capricious monarch: his world is ruled by physical and moral laws which give it order and rationality, but they are contingent on his freely establishing them. The

---

144. *Quodl.* 6.1 (*OTh* 9: 587.42–589.90); *Ord.* 1.17.1 (*OTh* 3: 452.2–456.4). Ockham opposes the opinion of Peter Aureol, who held that in order for the soul to be pleasing and acceptable to God it must be informed by a created quality; without such a form it cannot be pleasing to God *de potentia absoluta* (Peter Aureol, *Commentaria in Sent.* 1.17.2 [Rome ed. 1: 408b–410b]). Ockham cites Aureol at *Ord.* 1.17.1 (*OTh* 3: 441.2–445.11) and replies to his doctrine (*OTh* 3: 445.13–451.26). See Paul Vignaux, *Justification et prédestination au XIVe siècle: Duns Scot, Pierre d'Auriole, Guillaume d'Occam, Grégoire de Rimini* (Paris, 1934), pp. 97–140. Oberman (*Harvest of Medieval Theology*, pp. 160–184) discusses the problem of *habitus* and *acceptatio*, especially in the doctrine of Gabriel Biel.

145. "Petrus de Trabibus on the Absolute and Ordained Power of God," p. 289.

laws are necessary, though their necessity is not absolute but contingent on the divine will. Since God is omnipotent, he could have decreed them to be otherwise; and even in his chosen plan for the world he allows for changes in the law and miraculous suspensions of it. There was a change from the Jewish to the Christian law of salvation, and God has also made exceptions to the laws for good and merciful purposes. An eminent example is the eucharist, in which "the whole Christ is present in the whole host and totally in every part." A Christian, Ockham says, should not deny that God can do this through his absolute power (*per potentiam suam absolutam*). There is nothing surprising about this, for it is not contradictory; and the divine power, which infinitely exceeds the power of creatures, is not restricted to the way natural causes act. In fact, by his absolute power God can change the whole order of natural causes, and it is clear that he has often acted contrary to them. Among other miracles he has made a virgin conceive without a man, two bodies coexist, the dead rise to life, and accidents subsist without a substance.[146] Though God *can* work these and other miracles by his absolute power *in sensu divisionis*, he does not actually work them unless he wills to do so, and then they are done by his ordered power, for God does nothing *inordinate*.[147]

146. "Non enim iuxta modum causarum naturalium divinam potentiam artare debemus, cum divina potestas virtutem omnium creatorum excedat in infinitum; nec ad negandum aliquid posse fieri virtute divina experimenta sufficiunt, cum totum ordinem causarum naturalium possit Deus immutare. Et contra cursum communem causarum naturalium constat eum multa fecisse. Quis enim experiebatur umquam virginem naturaliter sine viro concipere, duo corpora simul exsistere, mortuos ad vitam resurgere, accidentia sine subiecto subsistere, et alia innumera, quae tamen constat divinitus esse facta? ... non ergo debet christianus negare quin Deus per potentiam suam absolutam possit facere aliquam substantiam coexistere alicui corporeo ita quod tota coexsistat toti illi corporeo et cuilibet parti eius ... ." (*Tract. de corp. Christi* 7 [*OTh* 10: 103.22–45; 13: 115.4–116.38]; *Quaest. variae* 6.9 [*OTh* 8: 268.372–381]).

147. As Courtenay says, miracles do not prove that God acts with his absolute power; these are divinely ordained acts, and consequently when God actually does them they come within his ordained power, though they are deviations from the normal course of events. "Ockham," he continues, "never

Ockham's doctrine of the divine absolute and ordered power can by summarized as follows:

(1) In God there is really only one power. We can consider this power in two different ways: as absolute or in itself, abstracting from God's decrees for his creation, or as ordered or determined in his eternal decrees.

(2) God never does anything by his absolute power, for it would be unwilled and unordained.

(3) Whatever God actually does, he does by his ordered power, that is, by his power as regulated by his knowledge and will.

(4) When Ockham says that God can do something by his absolute power (*per potentiam absolutam*) and the proposition is taken *in sensu divisionis*, that is, supposing that God so ordained it from eternity, he can do it with his ordered power. This is not contradictory, as neither it is contradictory that something white can be black. But God can do nothing by his absolute power *in sensu compositionis*. This would be contradictory, like saying that white is black.

(5) What God does by his ordered power he usually does according to the laws he has instituted, but these can change because they are not absolutely but contingently necessary. An example is the law of salvation, revealed in scripture, from the Jewish to the Christian dispensation. But since this has been willed and foreseen by God, it comes within his ordered power.

(6) By his absolute power *in sensu divisionis* God can cause miracles contrary to the laws of nature as long as they involve no contradiction. And by his ordered power he actually works the miracles he has foreordained, as recorded in scripture and the lives of the saints.

---

confuses *potentia absoluta* speculation with the possibility of divine intervention, which he considered a separate issue" ("The Dialectic of Omnipotence," p. 255; and "Covenant and Causality in Pierre d'Ailly," p. 95 n4). However, in the texts cited above in n146, the possibility of divine intervention in the case of miracles is said to be *per potentiam absolutam*. Consequently speculation about the possibility of divine intervention in miracles is inevitably tied up with the divine absolute power.

CHAPTER 6

How We Know God

HAVING SEEN THAT WE have some knowledge of God, however limited, we would like to know what sort of knowledge this may be and to what extent and under what other conditions we can know him.

Ockham distinguishes between two basic types of knowledge, intuitive and abstractive. We shall treat of these kinds of knowledge in detail in Chapter 10.[1] For the present it is enough to say that intuitive knowledge, or intuition, is that knowledge by which we can know with evidence whether a thing exists or does not exist. Abstractive knowledge, as opposed to intuitive, abstracts from existence or nonexistence. Thus, if we see Socrates and his whiteness and can judge with evidence that he is white, our knowledge is intuitive. But our awareness of an image in the imagination is abstractive, for on its basis we cannot judge with evidence whether the imagined thing really exists or not.[2]

As a Christian, Ockham believed that the blessed in heaven enjoy a face to face vision of God. In his language this is intuitive and beatific knowledge. Immediately following upon the intuition of God in his existence, the blessed have an abstractive knowledge of him in a simple concept proper to him and to him alone. This concept gives the blessed a distinct knowledge of the essence of God.

In the present life we cannot have an intuitive knowledge of God, but Ockham believes that God can give us an abstractive knowledge of himself in a simple and proper concept. This concept

1. See below, pp. 473–478.
2. *Ord.* 1.prol.1 (*OTh* 1: 30.12–33.12). Ockham here shows that in another sense abstractive knowledge has for its object a universal abstracted from individuals.

of God is beyond our natural powers, but he does not lack the power to make it available to us through his absolute power (*de potentia Dei absoluta*). Because the intuitive and proper abstractive knowledge of himself are extrinsic to each other, God can give us the latter without the former.[3] Ockham's concern at this point is not whether anyone on earth actually has such an abstractive knowledge of God, but rather with something that is possible owing to the omnipotence of God. Moreover, it enables him to define more precisely the normal type of conceptual knowledge we have of God. Up to the present he can clarify that it is neither an intuition of God nor an abstractive knowledge through a simple concept proper to him. What kind of knowledge of God, then, do we actually have in the present life?

1 Is God the First Object of Our Intellect?

In answer to this question, Ockham begins by ruling out the doctrine of Henry of Ghent, that God is the first object of our knowledge.[4] According to Henry we can derive two kinds of knowledge of God from creatures. The first is an immediate and natural knowledge of the divine essence through the primary concept of being; the second is a rational and deductive knowledge of that essence.[5] Ockham argues against the validity of the first type of knowledge, contending that our first cognition of things does not include a knowledge of the divine essence.

An important issue is at stake in this confrontation of Henry and Ockham. What indeed is the starting point of human knowledge? Ockham insists that it starts with something individual and definite, then passes on to the general or universal and the indefinite. For Henry the process of knowing is just the reverse: it goes from the indefinite to the definite. When we see an object coming from a distance, we know it to be a body before knowing it to be

3. Ibid. (*OTh* 1: 48.2–49.8).
4. Ibid. 1.3.1 (*OTh* 2: 381–393).
5. Henry of Ghent, *Summa* 24.7 (Paris ed. 1: f.144F), cited by Ockham, ibid. (*OTh* 2: 381.2–9).

an animal, an animal before a man, and a man before this individual man. The process of intellectual knowledge follows a similar pattern. The intellect first knows something as a being before knowing it as this being or as a substance, as good before this definite good. This indicates that the more indefinite an intelligible object is, the more primary it is in intellectual cognition.

The indetermination that Henry here alludes to is not that of a universal that is predicable of, and exists in many individuals, which he calls "privative indetermination." It is rather the "negative indetermination" of our awareness that something is not this or that. The primary object of our intellect is indeterminate in this negative sense. When we conceive objects such as being or goodness, we are aware of an absolute perfection, no doubt vague and general, unrestricted to this or that being or good, and including every being or good, even the subsistent being and goodness of God. Accordingly in the first moment of our knowledge, we cannot conceive being or good without including in our conception, at least indistinctly, the being and goodness of God. Moreover, we cannot know the being or goodness of creatures except by knowing the divine being and goodness. To quote Henry: "Just as this [particular] good cannot be known except through the absolute good and being, neither can participated goodness and being be known except through non-participated goodness and being, as St. Augustine says in his *De Trinitate*."[6]

Henry does not mean that we can distinguish the being of God from that of creatures in the primary data of our intellect. At the outset both are known together in our primary notion of being. Only at the end of our intellectual search for God will we enjoy a clear vision of the divine essence. Yet at the inception of our intellectual life we have a vague and general awareness of that essence, and only through this primary cognition can we know anything else. Hence, just as God is the beginning and end of the natural being of all things, so he is the beginning and end of our knowledge of them.

---

6. *Summa* 24.8 (Paris ed 1: f. 145vP). Augustine, *De Trinitate* 8.3 (CCL 50: 271–274).

Ockham relates Henry's doctrine at length, using it as a foil for his own. To Ockham, the phrase "first object of the intellect" has several meanings. In one sense it means the first thing we know in the genesis of our knowledge (*primitas generationis*). This is the object of our first act of understanding. In a second sense it can refer to the adequate object of our intellect (*primitas adaequationis*). This is the term predicable of every conceivable object of cognition; in short, the most universal of all terms, namely being. Thirdly, it can mean the most perfect intelligible object (*primitas perfectionis*).

Now God is the primary object of our knowledge only in the third sense. In the present life he cannot be the object of our first cognitive act, for if he were we would know him either in himself, that is, in his individual divine nature, and then we could not deny his existence; or we would know him in a concept, and this presupposes an intuitive knowledge of him, which is reserved for the next life. Neither is God the primary object of our knowledge as a term predicated of all intelligible objects. So the only sense in which he can be said to be the first object known is as the most perfect being; but this knowledge does not come at the start of our cognitive life.[7]

Henry of Ghent's main mistake, in Ockham's view, was to think that the mind progresses from an indeterminate to a determinate object, whereas in fact it begins with something definite and determinate, namely an individual thing. Ockham argues that the immediate object of our mind is either some reality outside the mind or a conceptual being (*ens rationis*) within the mind. If the first object known is an extramental reality and it is not a creature, it must be the divine nature itself. In that case we would have a particular cognition of the divine nature, which Henry of Ghent does not allow. The other possibility is that the object immediately terminating our act of understanding is a concept. But can God be known in that concept, so that he is the first object we know? Hardly. For a concept is either an entity having only objective

7. *Ord.* 1.3.1 (*OTh* 2: 388.21–389.22).

being in the mind or some other mental construct, and such an entity or construct does not precede every act of the mind, which it must do to qualify as the mind's first object. Hence no concept, or anything known through a concept, can be the first object of our mind.[8]

Henry also made the mistake of thinking that our original, imperfect knowledge of God can be the means of our imperfect knowledge of creatures. But if this were so, the incomplex knowledge of one reality (God) would be the cause of our first incomplex knowledge of another reality (creatures). Now this is impossible, for we gain our first simple and incomplex knowledge of anything by experiencing it directly and intuitively.[9]

2 Can We Know the Essence of God?

Granted that the divine essence is not the first object we know, can we be said to know it at all? According to Henry of Ghent there are two ways of knowing the essence or *quid est* of anything: distinctly and in particular, and indistinctly and in general. We cannot know God in the first way, for this would be a perfect knowledge of him, and this is beyond any creature. We can only know the divine nature in the second way through the substantial properties or attributes it shares with creatures. Through concepts of these general attributes, like being and goodness, which are analogous to God and creatures, we can come to know the essence or *quid est* of God. Henry describes two stages in this knowledge. First, we know the particular goodness of a material substance and abstract from it the notion of goodness pure and simple, leaving out of account whether it is this or that goodness but retaining the note of created goodness. Second, by a further abstraction we conceive absolute or self-subsisting goodness, which belongs to the creator alone. Similar abstractions can be performed with all the other attributes common to God and creatures. The first of these

---

8. *Ord.* 1.3.1 (*OTh* 2: 384.4–19).
9. Ibid. (*OTh* 2: 387.1–3); *Ord.* 1.prol.9 (*OTh* 1: 241–244).

two stages involves the formation of concepts analogous to God and creatures. These concepts – which Henry calls "first intentions," that is, concepts of reality and not logical notions – are formed by the mind's producing two different concepts, one of the goodness of the creature and the other of the divine goodness, and then, because of their great likeness, joining them together in one confused concept. Through these analogous concepts the mind achieves a quidditative knowledge of the divine nature; but it approaches even closer to God when it passes to the second stage and conceives him, not in analogy with creatures but in his own subsistent goodness.[10]

We shall have occasion later to examine Ockham's criticism of Henry's doctrine of knowing God through analogous concepts.[11] For the moment we shall concentrate on Ockham's own views on how we know things. First, we can know something directly and just in itself, as when we see a fire. Second, we can know something, not in itself but in a concept proper to it and verifiable of it. Now, when we know something in itself, we know at once that it is (*quia est*) and what it is (*quid est*), for we cannot know it unless we know its essence or some part of its essence in itself. But when something is not known in itself, we know that it is before knowing what it is. For example, in a lunar eclipse we first know that something has come between the sun and moon and only later what this is.[12]

Now, as far as God is concerned, we cannot know his essence in itself, or anything intrinsic to him, or anything that is really God himself, in such a way that nothing else accompanies our knowledge of him. A cognition of the divine reality just in itself would be an intuition of that reality, and, as we have seen, this surpasses our natural powers.

10. Henry of Ghent, *Summa* 24.6 (Paris ed. 1: ff. 142rP–143rZ). Ockham cites Henry's views on further ways of knowing God, culminating in the knowledge of him as the first and most simple being whose essence is entirely one with his existence (*Ord.* 1.3.2 [*OTh* 2: 394.8–396.4]).

11. See below, p. 283.

12. *Ord.* 1.3.2 (*OTh* 2: 401.15–402.16). Ockham adds that we do not know the essence of fire in itself but only the essence and existence of one of its accidents, such as heat; see ibid. (*OTh* 2: 402.4–11).

Lacking this intimate knowledge of God's essence, we can still know it in a concept proper to him alone, though this concept is not simple but composed of elements abstracted from creatures. Thus, we can know him through the simple concepts of being and goodness, each of which is common to God and creatures. In order to form a concept proper to him, we have to form a complex concept by joining together incomplex concepts, conceiving him as a being identical with goodness, wisdom, love, justice, and so on.

God is also knowable in a simple connotative or negative concept that is proper to him. We can know that there is an absolutely primary being, a creative being, a first cause or primary act and an immaterial being. These are incomplex concepts of God, but they are connotative or negative. Like all concepts of this sort they signify one thing primarily and another secondarily, or one thing directly and another indirectly.[13]

What does it mean to say that we know God in a concept? If God is entirely external to a concept, by knowing the concept how can we say we know God? It would seem that only by extrinsic denomination could anything known of a concept be said of God; and if this is so, can anything at all be said or known of him? Ockham meets this objection by frankly granting that what is said of a concept of God is applied to him only by extrinsic denomination. The immediate object of our knowledge is not God but our concepts of him. But we can say we know God in, or by means of, a concept because the concept is proper to him and stands for him. Being unable to know God in himself, we use a concept proper to him, attributing to it whatever can be ascribed to God, not for the concept's sake but for God's.[14]

---

13. *Ord.* 1.3.2 (*OTh* 2: 405.5–13); cf. ibid. 1.2.9 (*OTh* 2: 315.3–11).

14. *Ord.* 1.3.2 (*OTh* 2: 405.15–19, 408.20–409.10). For other examples of extrinsic denomination see *Quodl.* 1.20, 2.15 (*OTh* 9: 106.155, 181.67). Ockham's doctrine was censured by the Avignon commission: see J. Koch, "Neue Aktenstücke zu dem gegen Wilhelm Ockham in Avignon geführten Prozess," *Recherches de théologie ancienne et médiévale* 8 (1936): 168–197, at pp. 172–176, and 196.12–16.

Ockham here presupposes that a concept is a mental construct (*fictum*) with "objective being," distinct from the act of knowing. In an addition to his *Ordinatio* he insists that even if the concept were a real quality of the mind and identical with the act of knowing (an opinion he seems to have adopted in later works), we would still not know God in himself. On this supposition God would be the direct object of the act of knowing, but we would not know him in himself, because our knowledge would be general and include other beings as well. Ockham leaves unexplained, however, how God could be the immediate object of our act of knowing and yet be known only in a general way.[15]

In contending that in this life we cannot know the divine essence in itself, Ockham is opposing Scotists like William of Alnwick. William argued that through univocal concepts we can arrive at a knowledge of God in himself and not just in a concept. Moreover, we can know the divine essence in its individuality, as differing from other essences, for it is possible to demonstrate the unity, oneness, and infinite power of God, which distinguish him from every other being. To this, Ockham retorts that we do not know any divine perfection in itself. What we know directly are certain concepts that we use in propositions about God. If the concept is identical with the act of knowing, we know him only in a general way.[16]

Ockham's reply to the Scotists shows how wide a gulf he places between concepts and reality in comparison with them. Ever concerned to keep terms distinct from the realities for which they stand, he insists that the demonstration of a divine attribute should not be taken as demonstrating the divine perfection itself but only the concept of that perfection. If we say we demonstrate the unity and absolute perfection of God, the proposition is absolutely false if its terms have personal supposition (that is, if they stand for and signify God himself), for we do not know these divine perfections in themselves. The proposition is true only if the terms have simple supposition (that is, if they stand for concepts in the mind),

15. *Ord.* 1.3.2 (*OTh* 2: 410.4–9).
16. Ibid. (*OTh* 2: 406.9–19, 413.8–15); for Alnwick see *OTh* 2: 406 n1.

because we demonstrate the concepts of the divine attributes of another concept, namely the concept of God. We know the concepts in themselves, (and through them God and other beings), but not God himself, though the concepts stand for him.[17]

But surely we know that existence is contained in the divine essence, for it belongs *per se* to the notion of God. If we do not know his essence and existence, how can we know they are united in him? Ockham replies that we do not know the existence of God any more than we know his essence. We know the propositions "God exists" and "God is an essence," and this entails a knowledge of the terms of the proposition, but not of the reality they stand for.[18]

We can say that we know what God is (*quid Deus est*) or that we know him quidditatively, but we do not mean that we grasp the real essence of God or any part of it in itself; we only know him in a quidditative concept. The *quid est* of God escapes us; only the *quid nominis* is accessible to us.[19]

3 Can We Have Many Quidditative Concepts of God?

Granted that we can predicate quidditative concepts of God, that is, terms that are predicable of him *in quid*, how many concepts of this sort are there? Scotus contended that there is only one, namely essence or being. In his view other concepts of God, such as wisdom, are not quidditative but denominative, in which case the concept directly signifies a perfection and at the same time connotes the subject possessing it. Scotus' reason for his position is that, if there is something common to many beings, and if it is predicated of one denominatively, it must be predicated of all in the same way. Now wisdom is common to God and creatures, and it is predicated of creatures denominatively. So it must be predicated of God in the same way.[20]

17. *Ord.* 1.3.2 (*OTh* 2: 413.16–414.4).
18. Ibid. (*OTh* 2: 415.7–15). In his *ST* 1.3.4, ad 2, Aquinas also holds that when we affirm "God exists" we do not know his existence itself, but rather the truth of the proposition.
19. Ibid. (*OTh* 2: 415.16–20).
20. Scotus, *Ord.* 1.3.1.1–2 (Vatican ed. 3: 16–17, n. 25); *Rep. Paris.* prol.1 (Vivès ed. 22: 32, n. 50). See Ockham, *Ord.* 1.3.3 (*OTh* 2: 418.19–419.6). A

Ockham argues, to the contrary, that there are many quidditative concepts of God, not only "being" but also "wisdom," "truth," and "goodness." All of these transcendental terms stand for the deity itself when they are predicated of it, and they do not denote a subject different from the perfections they directly signify. Thus the concept "wisdom" expresses, on the part of God, precisely what the concept "being" does, and it does not differ in its grammatical or logical mode. Hence it is a quidditative concept just like "being."[21]

When considering the divine attributes, we saw that these concepts of God do not have the same meaning, for if they did they could be predicated of each other: we could say, for example, "Wisdom is goodness." But this is impossible, because each of these concepts has its own intelligible meaning (*ratio*). If these quidditative concepts had exactly the same meaning, they would blend into one simple, proper concept of God, which would be the abstractive concept of him enjoyed by the blessed in heaven.[22]

Is there one quidditative concept of God that is more simple and perfect than the others? Scotus was of the opinion that the concept of infinite being answers this description. It is simpler than the concept of God as a good or true being, because infinity is not an attribute or property (*passio*) of being, like truth or goodness, but an intrinsic mode of being. When we conceive God as infinite being, we do not form a notion composed of a subject along with a property, but a notion of a subject with a certain grade of perfection, namely infinity. Similarly, when we think of intense whiteness, our concept is not an accidental composite like "visible whiteness," which is made up of the subject "whiteness" and the property "visible"; "intense" simply expresses the intrinsic grade of whiteness. Hence the simplicity of the concept "infinite being."[23]

---

concept that precisely expresses the quiddity of a thing and nothing else is quidditative (*Ord.* 1.prol.2 [*OTh* 1: 104.6–7]).

21. *Ord.* 1.3.3 (*OTh* 2: 419.18–420.21).

22. Ibid. See also *Quodl.* 5.7 (*OTh* 9: 506.57–61).

23. Scotus, *Ord.* 1.3.1.1–2 (Vatican ed. 3: 40–41, nn. 58–59). See Ockham, *Ord.* 1.3.3 (*OTh* 2: 421.13–23).

In Ockham's view, however, the concept of infinite being cannot be our most perfect concept of God, for it is a negative concept, adding to the notion of being the negative note of infinity. The positive concepts of God as the highest being (*ens summum*), or the highest good (*ens summum bonum*) are more perfect. Scotus claimed that the notion of infinite being is more perfect because it is simpler, but in fact a concept composed of a positive and a negative note is no more simple than one composed of two positive ones. Moreover, contrary to Scotus, Ockham considers infinity to be an attribute or property of being, just like truth or goodness. This is clear, because infinity is not attributed to God in the first mode of essential (*per se*) predication (that is, as part of his essence), but in the second mode as a property of the essence. Hence the concept of infinite being applies to God at a latter stage than quidditative concepts.[24]

Ockham does not specify which is the most perfect quidditative concept of God, but he offers a principle by which to evaluate concepts of God. As far as it is proper to speak of degrees of perfection among concepts, a less general concept is more perfect than a more general one. Following this rule, the concept of God that is common to him and to the highest perfection, and less general or equally general than the least general concept, is formally the most perfect concept of God. Perhaps he has in mind concepts such as "the highest being" or "the highest good." Among all non-quidditative concepts of God, the concept of infinite being is the most perfect, for it most clearly expresses God's supreme perfection.[25]

Thus Ockham agrees with Scotus that the concept of infinite being, while negative in form, signifies the divine perfection. But

24. *Ord.* 1.3.3 (*OTh* 2: 422.11–423.10). Something belonging to the essence of the subject is predicated of it essentially (*per se*) in the first mode; for example, "Man is an animal." A property is predicated in the second mode of *per se* predication; for example, "Man is capable of laughing" (*Sum. log.* 2.29 [*OPh* 1: 342.45–50]); see Aristotle, *Anal. Post.* 1.4, 73a34–73b1.

25. *Ord.* 1.3.3 (*OTh* 2: 423.15–424.13). Though the term "infinite" is negative, Ockham says it is predicated affirmatively of God (*Quodl.* 5.7 [*OTh* 9: 508.108–112]).

unlike Scotus, he does not regard infinity as a positive mode of the divine being, expressed negatively by the concept of infinity. "Infinite being," as Ockham sees it, is simply one concept among others that we can form of God, and it comes after all quidditative concepts of him. Like other notions of God, it stands for and signifies the divine being without yielding any knowledge of that being in itself. This is one of the most profound disagreements between Ockham and Scotus.[26]

4 Are There Univocal Concepts of God and Creatures?

Our knowing God depends upon our being able to abstract universal notions from creatures which we then apply to him. It is in these concepts that we gain some knowledge of the divine essence. They enable us to know that essence not only in general concepts but also in concepts applicable to him alone. These "proper" concepts are complex notions, like "the highest good," "infinite being," and "pure act," which are composed of simple concepts common to God and creatures.[27]

In Ockham's day there was a lively debate whether concepts common to God and creatures were analogous or univocal. The two sides of the debate, as Ockham sees it, are represented by Henry of Ghent, who opted for analogous concepts of God and creatures,[28] and Duns Scotus, who defended the necessity of uni-

26. For Scotus' notion of infinity see Etienne Gilson, *Jean Duns Scot* (Paris, 1952), pp. 191–192.

27. *Quodl.* 5.7 (*OTh* 9: 503–508). Chatton defended Scotus' position against Ockham's in his *Reportatio et Lectura super Sententias*, prol.3.1 (ed. Wey pp. 145–182). Chatton's question has been studied by Luciano Cova, *Walter Catton: Commento alle Sentenze; Prologo - Questione Terza* (Rome, 1973), pp. 11–51.

28. Henry of Ghent, *Summa* 21.2 (Paris ed. 1: ff. 123E–125A). For Henry's notion of the analogous concept of being as opposed by Scotus see Stephen F. Brown, "Avicenna and the Unity of the Concept of Being: The Interpretations of Henry of Ghent, Duns Scotus, Gerard of Bologna and Peter Aureoli," *Franciscan Studies* 25 (1965): 117–150; Jean Paulus, *Henri de Gand: Essai sur les tendances de sa métaphysique* (Paris, 1938), pp. 52–66. For Henry of Ghent in relation to Scotus, Alnwick, and other contemporaries,

vocal concepts.[29] Like Scotus before him, Ockham chooses
Henry of Ghent as the main defender of analogy as a means of
knowing God. Incidentally, neither Scotus nor Ockham comes to
grips with Thomas Aquinas' doctrine of analogy, which above all
is a doctrine of a *judgment* of analogy or proportion rather than an
analogous *concept*. The Thomist judgment of analogy, moreover,
is focused, not upon essence, as in the mind of Henry, but upon
being, understood as the act of existing *(esse)*.[30]

Both Henry of Ghent and Duns Scotus raised the question
whether any *concepts* are univocal to God and creatures. To Ockham, this is not exactly the correct way to put the question. We
should rather ask whether any *universal* is univocal to them. The
difference between these two statements of the question is not
without significance, for according to Ockham univocity is not

---

with excellent bibliographies, see Stephen D. Dumont, "The Univocity of the
Concept of Being in the Fourteenth Century: John Duns Scotus and William
of Alnwick," *Mediaeval Studies* 49 (1987): 1–75.

29. Scotus, *Ord.* (Vatican ed. 3: 18–38, n. 26–55). See Timotheus Barth,
"Being, Univocity, and Analogy according to Duns Scotus," in *John Duns Scotus,
1265–1965*, ed. John K. Ryan and Bernadine M. Bonansea (Washington, DC,
1965), pp. 210–262; Ludger Honnefelder, *Ens inquantum ens: Der Begriff des
Seienden als solchen als Gegenstand der Metaphysik nach der Lehre des Johannes Duns
Scotus* (Münster, 1979), pp. 268–313; Allan B. Wolter, *The Transcendentals and
Their Function in the Metaphysics of Duns Scotus* (St. Bonaventure, NY, 1946);
Cyril L. Shircel, *The Univocity of the Concept of Being in the Philosophy of John
Duns Scotus* (Washington, DC, 1942); Gilson, *Jean Duns Scot*, pp. 100–115, 223–
234; Dumont "The Univocity of the Concept of Being." As Dumont shows, Aln-
wick defends the general position of Scotus, but he departs from him on several
fundamental points.

30. Contrasting the doctrines of Scotus and Aquinas, Gilson sees the
former as based on concepts common to God and creatures, whereas the
latter is primarily based on a judgment of analogy: see Gilson, *Jean Duns Scot*,
p. 101; and *The Christian Philosophy of St. Thomas Aquinas*, trans. L.K. Shook
(New York, 1956), pp. 103–110, 360–361. Since judgments are expressed in
concepts, however, the Thomist can speak of an analogous concept. See also
Gilson's *Being and Some Philosophers*, 2nd. ed. (Toronto, 1952), pp. 221–223.
For Ockham's doctrine of univocal concepts see Matthew C. Menges, *The
Concept of Univocity regarding the Predication of God and Creatures according
to William Ockham* (St. Bonaventure, NY, 1952).

properly a property of concepts but of words. This is because "univocal" is opposed to "equivocal," and since equivocity applies to words and not to concepts, the same is true of univocity. Thus it is meaningless to ask whether being is a concept univocal to God and creatures; rather, we should ask whether one concept is predicated essentially (*in quid*) of them. Having made this precision, however, Ockham concedes that the term "univocal" can be applied improperly to concepts, and he is willing to argue the question in the language of his contemporaries.[31]

A spoken or written word is equivocal when it is used to stand for several different concepts. It is equivocal by chance (*a casu*) if it stands for one as if it did not stand for any other. An example is the name "Socrates" given by chance to several men. Other words are equivocal by design (*a consilio*) when the word is first given to some thing or things and it stands for one concept, but afterward it is given to something else because that thing bears a likeness to the first thing signified. Thus "man" was first used to signify all rational animals but later it was given to signify the picture of a man.

A univocal word, in the proper sense, stands for one concept that can signify several things equally primarily. An example is the word "man," which stands for the one concept "man," which in turn signifies in the same way all rational animals.

It should be noted that the division of terms into equivocal and univocal is not between terms considered in themselves, for the same word can be both equivocal and univocal depending on how it is used. All concepts, on the contrary, are univocal in themselves; that is, each has only one meaning and it can signify equally primarily many individuals.

A univocal concept is universal, for it is predicable of many subjects, unlike a "proper" concept that is predicable of only one. Can a single concept be formed that is proper to just one individual? Ockham replies by distinguishing between two opinions

---

31. *Ord.* 1.2.9 (*OTh* 2: 306.18-307.9); *Sum. log.* 1.13 (*OPh* 1: 44-47). Aristotle distinguishes between *things* named equivocally, univocally, or derivatively (or denominatively) in *Categories* 1, 1a1-15.

about the nature of a concept. If a concept is thought to be a mental construct (*fictum*) with only "objective" being, or an entity produced by the act of knowing and hence subsequent to that act, it cannot signify just one individual. Ockham's reason is that this concept would be abstracted from some thing, and it would equally represent every other thing very similar to it; and every creature can have something very closely resembling it, if not in fact, at least as a possibility owing to God's infinite power. But if the concept is nothing but the act of understanding (the opinion Ockham seems to have finally adopted), there can be a concept proper to one individual.[32]

A univocal concept is also different from a denominative concept. The latter signifies one thing directly and something else obliquely. The same distinction obtains between univocal and denominative spoken or written words. For example, in the proposition "God is the cause of things," the term "God" stands for the divine reality, but obliquely it connotes creatures. As we shall see, this rules out the possibility of an analogous concept or predication, for every analogy involves a connotative term or terms, unlike a univocal term, which is strictly one in meaning.[33]

In short, a univocal concept is common or universal, not proper; and it is absolute, not connotative or denominative. All univocal concepts, however, are not univocal in the same way or in the same degree. They can, in fact, be univocal in three different ways. (1) A univocal concept may be common to several things having a perfect likeness in all essentials, without any unlikeness either in substantial or accidental features. Only the concept of an ultimate species (*species specialissima*) like "man" is univocal in this perfect way. Individuals in a species of this sort most closely resemble each other and they are of the same nature (*ratio*). (2) In a second way a univocal concept may be common to several things that are neither entirely similar nor dissimilar; in some respects they are alike and in others they are unlike, either in intrinsic or extrinsic features. This is the way a generic con-

32. *Ord.* 1.2.9 (*OTh* 2: 307.13–308.8). For opinions about the nature of a concept see below, pp. 496–510.

33. Ibid. (*OTh* 2: 308.9–309.18).

cept, like "animal," is univocal to man and ass. These have a lesser degree of likeness than things in a *species specialissima*; yet the generic concept predicable of them is one concept and it is predicated of them quidditatively (*in quid*). (3) In a third way a univocal concept may be common to several things having no likeness to each other, either as to substantial or accidental features. This is the way concepts are univocal to God and creatures. There is absolutely nothing in them, either intrinsic or extrinsic, that is of the same nature (*ratio*).[34]

The third mode of univocity is the one that concerns us at present, for Ockham claims that this is the way univocal concepts and words are applied to God and creatures. It bristles with difficulties, for if there is nothing of the same nature (*ratio*) in God and creatures, nor any substantial or accidental likeness between them, what justifies our applying univocal terms to them? We shall return shortly to this thorny problem.

Ockham uses the term "analogy" out of respect for "the saints," that is, the fathers of the Church, but he himself shows little liking for it. Indeed, strictly speaking he does not need the term, for he does not think there is an analogical predication of terms distinct from equivocal, univocal, and denominative predication in the broad sense of the word.[35] Thus he reduces the following cases of analogy either to univocity or equivocity by design:

(1) In the proportionality, "As a color is similar to a color, so a figure is similar to a figure," the term "similar" is purely equivocal by design.[36]

(2) In the proportionality, "As man is related to animal, so whiteness is related to color," the relation of likeness of man to animal is univocally the same as that of whiteness to color, that is to say, the relation of species to genus.[37]

---

34. *Rep.* 3.10 (*OTh* 6: 335.18–337.17); *Ord.* 1.2.9 (*OTh* 2: 310.21–311.24). In the latter passage a concept or word is said to be univocal when it is predicable of several subjects which are really one thing, as when "relation" is predicated of the Persons of the Trinity.

35. *Ord.* 1.2.9 (*OTh* 2: 326.13–17); *Rep.* 3.10 (*OTh* 6: 319–320).

36. *Ord.* 1.2.9 (*OTh* 2: 328.16–22, 329.8–20).

37. *Rep.* 3.10 (*OTh* 6: 338.16–339.4).

(3) When a term primarily signifying one thing is attributed to others because of a relation they have to that thing, the term predicated of them is equivocal by design. For example, "healthy," which is primarily said of living beings, is transferred to diet by equivocity by design.[38]

(4) When a term is transferred from that which it originally signified to something else because of a likeness it bears to the original, the name is equivocal by design. For example, the term "man" transferred to the picture of a man.[39]

This shows that for Ockham the term "analogy" is not univocal, that is, it is not strictly one concept but includes several different concepts. Some analogies are deliberate equivocities and others are univocities. In the latter case they admit of degrees. Some analogies are perfect univocities, as in the second instance mentioned above. Others have the most tenuous univocity, as in the case of concepts predicable of God and creatures. Here the concept is one and not several. It does not have the perfect univocity of the concept of a species, nor the less perfect univocity of a concept of a genus. It is nevertheless one univocal concept at the lowest level of univocity. Being so imperfectly univocal, it can be said to be situated between pure univocity and equivocity. But this does not exclude it from the rank of univocal concepts; it is simply the least univocal of all. Quidditative concepts predicated of God and creatures fall into this category. Thus the concept of being is said to be predicated neither purely univocally nor purely equivocally but in an intermediate way: *ens non dicitur pure univoce nec pure aequivoce, sed medio modo.*[40] This does not mean that the concept of being is not univocal, but only that it does not have the perfect univocity of a species nor the less perfect univocity of a genus.

Ockham's coolness toward the notion of analogy is probably due in large measure to Henry of Ghent's use of the term.[41]

38. *Ord.* 1.2.9 (*OTh* 2: 328.2–15).

39. Ibid. (*OTh* 2: 327.23–328.2).

40. *Rep.* 3.10 (*OTh* 6: 339.5–6). Aristotle, *Metaph.* 4.2, 1003a33–35.

41. For Henry of Ghent's notion of analogy see his *Summa* 24.6 (Paris ed. 1: ff. 142P–143Z); Paulus, *Henri de Gand*, pp. 52–66.

Like Scotus, Ockham does not believe the human mind can form analogous concepts in the way Henry describes. As we have seen, Henry understood an analogous concept to be composed of several concepts which, being very similar to each other, are conceived as one concept. For instance, although the concepts of divine and created goodness are different, they are so close to each other that the mind conceives them together as one analogous concept.[42] Ockham retorts that this implies that we have a distinct concept of the divine goodness, and hence that we know the divine perfection in itself and in particular, which is contrary to Henry's own teaching.[43] Moreover, the concepts of created and uncreated goodness are not like each other; in fact they are very dissimilar and removed from each other.[44] For these and other reasons Ockham rejects Henry's claim that we can know God through analogous concepts. He agrees with Scotus that in the present life we need univocal concepts in order to know God.

Ockham's relations to Scotus on this subject are complex. While siding with him in the general conclusion that there are univocal concepts of God and creatures, and accepting some of his reasons for this, Ockham finds others inconclusive or poorly stated. He also rejects Scotus' contention that the univocal concept of being does not extend to the ultimate differences and properties of being.[45] More importantly, Ockham's notion of a univocal concept, such as the concept of being, radically differs from that of Scotus owing to Ockham's new doctrine of a concept and its relation to reality.

For Ockham as for Scotus, the most persuasive argument in favor of univocal concepts of God and creatures is simply that without them we could have no conceptual knowledge of God, which is contrary to the general opinion. Since analogous concepts cannot account for this knowledge, there must be univocal

42. *Ord.* 1.3.2 (*OTh* 2: 395.9–14).
43. Ibid. (*OTh* 2: 397.15–20).
44. Ibid. (*OTh* 2: 401.7–13).
45. Ibid. 1.2.9 (*OTh* 2: 318.20–322.22).

ones.[46] One of Ockham's arguments for the univocity of the concept of being, also drawn from Duns Scotus, rests on the fact that, if there are three propositions about the same subject, two of which are doubtful but the other certain, the predicates of these propositions are different. Consider, for example, the propositions: "Socrates is a man," "Socrates is an animal," and "Socrates is a being." If Socrates is seen at a distance, the first two propositions can be doubted while the third is certain. This shows that the concept of being is different from, and indeed more general than, the concepts of "man" and "animal." It can be predicated of anything whatsoever in exactly the same sense. In short, it is univocal. And the same is true of the word "being."[47]

Ockham specifies that the univocal concepts predicable of both God and creatures are not concrete but abstract. Thus "wise," taken just in itself and abstractly, is predicated essentially (*in quid*) of both divine and created wisdom. But wisdom can also be taken concretely, that is, with a particular nominal definition, and then it cannot be applied univocally to God and creatures. For example, when we say concretely that a creature is wise, "wise" is understood with the nominal description "having the accidental quality of wisdom." Clearly, wisdom in this sense cannot be predicated of God. In the concrete, he is said to be wise using another description of wisdom, namely, "being wisdom itself" – which can hardly be said of creatures. Anselm made this distinction when he said that God is wise, but creatures have wisdom. Thus, when concepts are taken concretely, they are applied to God and creatures equivocally.[48]

46. *Rep.* 3.10 (*OTh* 6: 340.17–341.19); *Quodl.* 5.14 (*OTh* 9: 536–538). For Scotus, too, this is the decisive reason for the necessity of univocal concepts of God and creatures.

47. *Quodl.* 5.14 (*OTh* 9: 536.10–537.34); *Sum. log.* 1.38 (*OPh* 1: 106.2–107.32). Scotus, *Ord.* 1.3.1.3 (Vatican ed. 3: 92, n. 149).

48. *Quodl.* 2.4 (*OTh* 9: 123–128); *Ord.* 1.3.3 (*OTh* 2: 430.20–431.10); see Anselm, *Monologion* 16 (*Opera omnia* 1: 30). Walter Chatton argues at great length against Ockham's position in *Quodl.* 2.4, contending that the proposition "God is wise, or wisdom" is not in the first but second mode of essential (*per se*) predication. Moreover, "God is wisdom" means that God and wisdom

At first sight the univocity of the concept of being goes counter to Aristotle's doctrine that being is an equivocal term. According to Aristotle, when "being" is predicated of the ten categories it has different meanings: primarily substance and secondarily quantity, quality, and the other categories because of their relation to substance. "Being" is like the term "healthy," which is properly attributed to living beings, but it is extended to food and urine because they are related to the health of animals.[49]

But Ockham contends that Aristotle's equivocal use of the term "being" is compatible with his own univocal meaning of the term. Ockham has shown that there is a univocal concept of being predicable of every reality (*res*). Among the categories, this includes only substances and qualities, for, as we have seen, these alone are real entities.[50] When the other eight categories are called "beings," the term is extended to them because of their relation to substance.[51] When being is attributed to substance, nothing else is connoted by the term; but when it is attributed to quantity, substance is connoted. If we say "something quantified is a being," we mean nothing else than that some substance is extended in space. If we say "the relation of likeness is a being," we mean that two substances are like each other. Similarly, the other categories are concepts connoting a relation to substance. Since these concepts are different, the term "being" that is predicated of them is not univocal but

---

are identical in reality (Chatton, *Reportatio et Lectura*, prol.3.1 [ed. Wey pp. 181–182]). Ockham replies to Chatton's arguments in *Quodl.* 2.4 (*OTh* 9: 125–128).

49. Aristotle, *Metaph.* 5.2, 1003a33–b11; 7.4, 1030a27–1030b4.

50. See above, pp. 33–34, 42–43.

51. The fact that Ockham includes qualities among "absolute realities" raises a difficulty for him as an Aristotelian. For Aristotle, "being" is predicated of the categories relative to substance, not to quality. But if quality, like substance, is an absolute entity, the other categories could also be called beings relative to quality. To this objection Ockham gives several answers, none of which is very convincing; for example, that Aristotle mentions substance and not quality because it is better known that the other categories are related to substance than to quality (*Ord.* 1.2.9 [*OTh* 2: 334.8–21]).

equivocal; for an equivocal term is defined as one that stands not for just one concept but for several. A univocal term, on the contrary, stands for just one concept. Accordingly, the term "being" that is equivocal when predicated of the ten categories is not the concept but the word "being." While there is a univocal concept of being predicable of all realities, there is also an equivocal use of the word "being" when it is ascribed to the different categories.[52]

According to Scotus, every metaphysical inquiry about God presupposes univocal concepts of God and creatures. In this inquiry we first center our attention on some formal nature (*ratio*), such as wisdom. Then we take from it the imperfection it has in creatures and, while retaining that formal nature and ascribing to it the absolutely highest perfection, we attribute it to God. For example, we consider the formal nature of wisdom, intelligence, or will just in itself, and finding that it contains no imperfection or limitation, we abstract from it the imperfections accompanying it in creatures and ascribe it to God in the most perfect possible mode.[53]

Ockham does not reject Scotus' method of arriving at univocal concepts of God, but he fears that Scotus understood it incorrectly. It is absolutely false, he says, to think that a formal nature (*ratio*) found in creatures – whether or not anything is abstracted

52. *Ord.* 1.2.9 (*OTh* 2: 333.17–334.7); *Quodl.* 5.14 (*OTh* 9: 537.36–41). Etienne Gilson interprets Ockham to mean that "being" is univocal when predicated of all individual beings, but that it is equivocal when predicated of them with signification (*significative*), for they are "irreducibly distinct singular beings" (*A History of Christian Philosophy in the Middle Ages* [New York, 1955], pp. 496, 788 nn22–23). He bases this interpretation on a variant reading of a sentence in Ockham's *Summa logicae*, but this reading is rejected in the critical edition, 1.38 (*OPh* 1: 107.35). Parallel passages corroborate the reading of the critical edition (*Expos. in Praedicab.* 2 [*OPh* 2: 44.83–95]; *Quodl.* 5.14 [*OTh* 9: 537.36–41]). Ockham's point in these passages is that the term "being" is equivocal when predicated of concepts such as "man" and "animal," taken not as realities in themselves but as signifying individual beings. This does not prevent the concept and word "being" from signifying all individual realities univocally; see Menges, *Concept of the Univocity of Being*, pp. 164–166.

53. Scotus, *Ord.* 1.3.1.1–2 (Vatican ed. 3: 26–27, n. 39), cited by Ockham, *Ord.* 1.2.9 (*OTh* 2: 295.7–19).

from it – can be ascribed to God as though it exists in him. Ockham insists that nothing really existing in a creature, no matter how abstracted from it, can be attributed to God. He points out that Scotus himself claimed that nothing real is univocal to God and creatures; they have only a concept in common, and this exists neither in God nor in creatures.[54]

Ockham alerts us here to the basic opposition between himself and Duns Scotus and his followers on the nature of univocal concepts. The Scotists would form univocal concepts by abstracting the formal natures (*rationes*) of things, leaving aside their differences. Being, for example, would be abstracted from all its modes, ultimately even from the primary modes of finiteness and infinity, and considered only as being: *ens inquantum ens*.[55] The result is the univocal concept of being. A similar abstraction enables us to form univocal concepts of transcendentals such as truth, wisdom, and goodness. The *rationes* of these perfections are present in creatures with the mode of finiteness; they are also present in God with the mode of infinity. Abstracting from these different modes, we can form univocal concepts of these perfections and ascribe them to both God and creatures. Scotus insists that what is common is the univocal concept and not a reality, for being and the other transcendentals exist in them with different modes, which place them infinitely apart in reality. Thus Scotus says, "God and creatures are not fundamentally different (*primo diversa*) in concepts, but they are fundamentally different in reality, because they agree in no reality."[56]

Ockham agrees with this basic tenet of Duns Scotus, but he does not accept Scotus' claim that the univocal concepts of being

54. *Ord.* 1.2.9 (*OTh* 2: 300.1–13). "Deus et creatura non sunt primo diversa in conceptibus; sunt tamen primo diversa in realitate, quia in nulla realitate conveniunt" (Scotus, *Ord.* 1.8.1.3 [Vatican ed. 4: 190, n. 82]).

55. Scotus, *Metaph.* 4.1 (Vivès ed. 7: 147, n. 5). See Honnefelder, *Ens inquantum ens*, pp. 268–313. Gilson shows the background of Scotus' doctrine of the univocity of the concept of being in the metaphysics of Avicenna (*Jean Duns Scot*, pp. 84–94).

56. See above, note 54.

and the other transcendentals are based on formal *rationes* existing in both creatures and God. As we saw in Chapter 1, in Ockham's view a *ratio* is nothing but a concept, and concepts are not in the things which they signify. If this is true, we cannot say, with Scotus, that through univocal concepts we know something of the essence of God *in itself*, but that we know it only *in a concept*. A univocal concept is not of the essence of the things of which it is predicated, nor does it really posit anything in them.[57]

If univocal concepts are not based on formal *rationes* in things, have they any real foundation at all? In particular, is there any basis in God and creatures for the concepts we ascribe to them in common? The basis in reality for general concepts, in Ockham's view, is individual beings in their likenesses to each other. But he has denied that God and creatures are alike in any substantial or accidental respect. Lacking the perfect likeness of things in the same species and the imperfect likeness (along with unlikeness) of things in the same genus, God and creatures would seem to be totally unlike each other. Indeed, Ockham insists that nothing in them is of the same *ratio*, which can only mean that they differ in concept or definition.[58] We would expect him to conclude that terms predicated of God and creatures are not univocal but equivocal. At the extreme limit of unlikeness, God and the created world would seem to have neither a real essence nor a concept in common.

And yet Ockham, like Scotus, refuses to accept this conclusion, for it rules out any possibility of knowing God. Ockham contends that even though God and creatures have nothing real in common, at least we can conceive them in common concepts. We can abstract from creatures a concept of wisdom that is common

---

57. "[D]ico quod nullum univocum est de essentia suorum univocatorum, nec ponit aliquid in eis realiter" (*Ord.* 1.2.9 [*OTh* 2: 312.2–3]).

58. "Tertio modo accipitur univocum pro conceptu communi multis non habentibus aliquam similitudinem nec quantum ad substantialia nec quantum ad accidentalia. Isto modo quilibet conceptus conveniens Deo et creaturae est eis univocus, quia in Deo et creatura nihil penitus, nec intrinsecum nec extrinsecum, est eiusdem rationis" (*Rep.* 3.10 [*OTh* 6: 337.12–17]).

to both creatures and God, and through this concept we can know that God is wise.[59] Univocal concepts of this sort are not strictly univocal like the concept of the species "man." Individuals in an ultimate species resemble each other very closely, both as regards their substance and their accidents. Granted that God and creatures do not resemble each other in this way, are they at all alike, so as to justify the attribution of univocal concepts to them?

Ockham suggests an answer to this question when he takes up the traditional theme of creatures as vestiges of the Trinity and man as its very image.[60] A vestige and an image are alike, he says, because they are means by which we come to know that of which they are the vestige and image. They differ in that a vestige is caused by that of which it is the vestige, whereas an image is produced by something other than that of which it is the image. An example of a vestige is the footprint of an ox, which is caused by the ox; an example of an image is a statue of Hercules, which is carved by a sculptor. In order to know that something is a vestige or image, we must have previously known what they represent and keep it in our memory. Thus we would not know that the mark on the ground is a vestige of an ox unless we previously had some knowledge of an ox, nor would we know that the statue of Hercules is his image unless we were acquainted with Hercules himself or some likeness of him. Our habitual knowledge of an ox or of Hercules is therefore a partial cause of the vestige or image making us remember its original and recognizing the vestige or image for what it is.

Under these conditions can we say that all creatures are vestiges of the Trinity? Augustine thought that they are, and what is more, that rational creatures are its very image.[61] Ockham had too much respect for Augustine to deny this, but he interprets it in his own way, in conformity with his own philosophical views.

59. *Rep.* 3.10 (*OTh* 6: 344.5–345.5). For references to Scotus, see notes to these pages.
60. *Ord.* 1.3.9–10 (*OTh* 2: 543–568).
61. Augustine, *De Trinitate* 6.10 (CCL 50: 242–243).

He has said that a vestige never leads us to know something unless we are already familiar with the thing. Thus, a footprint of an ox leads us to know an ox only if we are previously acquainted with one; then the footprint represents an ox and causes us to remember it. But this is not the case with the Trinity, for we do not know it prior to our knowing creatures, and consequently creatures could not make us remember it. Nevertheless Ockham finds reasons for calling all creatures vestiges of the Trinity, thus saving the Augustinian thesis.[62] We can abstract from creatures a univocal notion of beauty that is common to both creatures and God. Encountering a beautiful creature, then, we recall the divine beauty: the creature leads us to remember the beauty of God so that it is truly his vestige. Though beauty is an attribute of the divine essence and not of one Person, it is traditionally "appropriated" to the second Person of the Trinity, and consequently the beauty of creatures can be said to be a vestige of the Trinity. Another reason for calling creatures vestiges of God is that just as a work of art is a vestige of the artist who made it, so creatures are vestiges of their creator, leading us to the knowledge that he caused them.[63]

Irrational creatures share with God many univocal concepts, such as being, strength, beauty, goodness, truth, causative power, and perfection. In these respects they resemble God. But the rational creature, or man, is most like him, for he also shares with God, in their proper sense, the concepts of knowing, willing, mercy, justice, wisdom, and many other perfections. Knowing a

62. "Ad aliud patet quod vestigium nunquam ducit in notitiam illius cuius est nisi praesupposita notitia habituali ipsius, et ideo trinitas personarum, cum non praecognoscatur creaturae, quamvis creatura non duceret in notitiam Trinitatis de facto, adhuc posset dici vestigium Trinitatis" (*Ord.* 1.3.9 [*OTh* 2: 551.21–25]).

63. Ibid. (*OTh* 2: 549.3–21). For the appropriation of the term "beauty" to the Son see Aquinas, *ST* 1.39.8, citing Hilary of Poitiers, *De Trinitate* 6.10 (PL 42: 931). Since the divine beauty is not known prior to the beauty of creatures, the latter could hardly make us remember it. Perhaps Ockham uses the Augustinian language of remembrance, as God's continual presence in the soul, to which the soul can turn at will.

rational creature, we are led to remember God, and so in a way he can be called his image.[64]

Ockham's treatment of creatures as vestiges and images of God reveals that he does not rule out every kind of likeness between them. They do not have the likeness of things in a *species specialissima*, nor the lesser likeness of things in a genus. In fact, there is nothing either essential or accidental in a creature that is perfectly like anything really in God. This is the only reason, Ockham believes, that "the saints and authors" (*sancti et auctores*) have denied any univocity regarding God and creatures.[65] They are correct, he continues, if they mean univocity in the strict sense, which applies to terms in the categories. But he insists that beyond the categories, and all genera and species, there are univocal "transcendent" concepts, like "being," that are predicable of both God and creatures.[66]

---

64. *Ord.* 1.3.10 (*OTh* 2: 555.12–556.13). Man is imperfectly and as it were radically the image of God through the substance of his soul; he is perfectly the image of God with the added acts of knowing and willing. As Augustine says, through these acts he is *capax Dei*, and God's image (ibid. [*OTh* 2: 557.4–558.2). According to Augustine (*De Trinitate* 14.8 [CCL 50A: 435–436, n. 11]) man is the image of the Trinity through his mind, knowledge, and love; also, and more clearly, through his memory, intelligence, and will. It was the general opinion, Ockham says, that these refer to powers of the soul, but in his view these powers are not really different from the substance of the soul or from each other (*OTh* 2: 554.6–555.10).

65. *Ord.* 1.2.9 (*OTh* 2: 317.1–6). "Saints" are the fathers of the Church; "authors" are writers whose works have the weight of authority, like Aristotle, Avicenna, and Averroes. See M.-D. Chenu, "*Authentica* et *magistralia*: Deux lieux théologiques aux XII-XIII siècles," *Divus Thomas* (Piacenza) 28 (1925): 257–285.

66. Ockham uses the term *conceptus transcendens* of being in *Quodl.* 7.13 (*OTh* 9: 752.74–75). God also has in common with creatures a transcendent concept of substance; see ibid. (*OTh* 9: 750.35–39). As an individual through itself differs from another individual in number, and through its same self is like (*convenit*) another individual in species, so in reality God in a way is completely like creatures through the same divine reality by which he is completely different from them. Because of their likeness common concepts can be abstracted from them: "per idem Deus totaliter convenit aliquo modo ex natura rei cum creatura, et ex natura rei per idem totaliter distinguitur a creatura" (*Ord.* 1.2.9 [*OTh* 2: 319.9–17]).

With his Christian predecessors and contemporaries, Ockham faced the awesome problem of how we can know an infinitely transcendent God. All agreed that some knowledge of God is possible, for did not St. Paul write that the invisible God is clearly seen through his visible creation (Rom 1:20)? Like Scotus, Ockham holds that we can know God, however precariously, through univocal concepts abstracted from creatures, but he thoroughly revises the Scotist doctrine. Scotus convinced him that the way to God by analogy, as proposed by Henry of Ghent, was unintelligible and incoherent. There remained the possibility of knowing God through univocal concepts. Scotus chose this way to God, contending that we can form concepts common to God and creatures, though they have nothing real in common. The latter provision was intended to safeguard the absolute transcendence of God to all creation. To Ockham this was eminently reasonable, but he thought that Scotus compromised the doctrine by adding that God and creatures have in common a formal intelligible character (*ratio formalis*) that is the basis of our univocal concepts of them. Ockham thought this objective foundation of univocal concepts superfluous, arguing that they can be adequately explained by the individual realities of God and creatures in their resemblance to each other, just as univocal specific and generic concepts of creatures need no other foundation than individual things in their mutual likenesses. In this way Ockham "saves" the problem of the predication of univocal concepts of God and creatures, but his difficulty in accounting for a likeness between them leads one to surmise that his solution is more verbal rather than real.

PART III

Creatures

7

Creation

THE APOSTLES' CREED CLOSELY links the omnipotence of God with his creation of the world. The Christian confesses: "I believe in God, the Father almighty, creator of heaven and earth." Thus, enlightened by faith, he is assured at once that God exists, that he is omnipotent, and that he is the creator of the universe. But the theologian who is also a philosopher will not be content to believe this article of faith; he will want to probe into it and try to answer the many questions spontaneously arising from it. What does it mean to create? What is included in the object of creation? Could God create an eternal world? Is creation a work of God alone, or can creatures also create? Does the creation of our world exhaust the divine power, or can God create other and better worlds than our own? By the fourteenth century these were old questions for theologians; Ockham addressed them in his own way, consistent with his fundamental philosophical principles.

1 God's Causal Relation to the World

Before taking up the problem of creation let us ask if, in any sense, God is the efficient cause of the world. Ockham's early work, the commentary on the *Sentences*, contends that God's efficient causation of the world is not only the teaching of faith but also of philosophers such as Aristotle. Following Avicenna and Duns Scotus, he thought it was the mind of Aristotle that God is the efficient cause of everything, but not in the same way. He necessarily produces the first celestial Intelligence and by means of it the other Intelligences in serial fashion. He is the remote and partial cause of things in the sublunar world by acting in concert with the

Intelligences, which produce that world out of love and desire for God. Thus God is both the partial efficient cause and final cause of our world.[1]

As Henry of Ghent interpreted Aristotle, God can be the efficient cause of the sublunar world, where things come to be and pass away, but hardly of the celestial Intelligences, which are eternal and necessary beings. One of Henry's most telling arguments for this is based on Aristotle's definition of an efficient cause as "the source of the beginning of motion." Since God could not bring the immaterial Intelligences into being by moving or changing matter but only by producing their total reality, Aristotle could not have intended him to be their efficient cause.[2]

Ockham meets Henry's objection with the claim that Aristotle distinguished between two meanings of efficient cause. In one sense it draws a form from the potentiality of matter, and consequently it is the source of the beginning of motion. This description of an efficient cause holds good only for a natural and created efficient cause. In another sense an efficient cause is "that at whose existence there follows the existence of something else." In this second meaning of the term God can be the efficient cause of the Intelligences.[3]

---

1. At *Rep.* 2.5 (*OTh* 5: 81.15–82.6, 84.2–16) Ockham is following Avicenna's and Scotus' interpretation of Aristotle: see Avicenna, *Liber de philosophia prima* 9.4 (ed. Van Riet 2: 476–488); Scotus, *Rep. Paris.* 2.1.3 (Vivès ed. 22: 532–536, nn. 5–9).

2. Ockham, *Rep.* 2.5 (*OTh* 5: 82.8–83.70). See Henry of Ghent, *Quodl.* 8.9 (Paris ed. ff. 314–320); Aristotle, *Phys.* 2.3, 194b29–32, *Metaph.* 5.2, 1013a29–32.

3. "Ad aliud dico quod Philosophus aliquando accipit causam pro eo quod extrahit formam de potentia subiectiva, et sic nihil causatur nisi quod extrahitur etc. Aliquando accipit causam pro eo ad cuius esse sequitur aliud esse. Et sic potest aliquid causari licet non extrahatur etc. Et sic est in proposito" (*Rep.* 2.5 [*OTh* 5: 85.22–86.3]). When treating of sacraments as the cause of grace, Ockham cites the second kind of efficient cause: "... causa est ad cuius esse sequitur aliud" (*Rep.* 4.1 [*OTh* 7: 3.5–7]), attributing it to Aristotle (*Metaph.* 5.2, 1013a29–32). But here Aristotle describes an efficient cause in the first sense, that is, as the source of the beginning of motion.

Ockham's editors give no reference to Aristotle's works for the second kind of efficient cause, but they found it *verbatim* in an anonymous "Collection of philosophical opinions of Aristotle and other outstanding men,"[4] written probably in the fourteenth century. The anonymous author ascribes the second notion of cause to Aristotle's *Physics*, book 2, but more correctly to the *Liber de causis*. The unknown author of this Neoplatonic work, based on Proclus's *Elements of Theology*, often writes of a cause not as "the source of the beginning of motion," as Aristotle does in his *Physics*, but as "that at whose existence there follows the existence of something else."[5] Attributing this notion of efficient cause to Aristotle, Ockham in his *Reportatio* thought it was Aristotle's intention that God is the immediate and total cause of all the Intelligences and the mediate or indirect efficient cause of the sublunar world.[6]

Writing in his own name in the same work, Ockham offers proofs – persuasive, if not demonstrative – that God is the immediate and free efficient cause of everything. He is not in fact the total cause of everything, for secondary causes are partial causes of some effects. But it is within his power to withhold the causality of secondary causes and produce everything by himself.[7]

---

4. It is entitled, in brief, *Sententiae ex Aristotele collectae* and ascribed to the Venerable Bede! Its fuller title is *Venerabilis Bedae Sententiae, sive axiomata philosophica ex Aristotele et aliis praestantibus collecta* (PL 90: 966–1054). The description of cause in question is: "Causa est, ad cujus esse sequitur aliud (II *Phys.*, *et per auctorem causarum in de Causis*). Intelligitur de causa totali et sufficienti, quia posito tali causa, etiam statim sequitur effectus, sed sic non est de causa partiali. Nisi velis dicere: Causa est, ad cujus esse sequitur aliud pro natura istius esse." For the notion of a total and adequate cause see Duns Scotus, *Ord.* prol.1.1.un. (Vatican ed. 1: 36, n. 59); see also Ockham, *Rep.* 2.3:4 (*OTh* 5: 63.19–64.6).

5. *Liber de causis* 1.3.5 (ed. Pattin pp. 134–135); see also 5.49, 50, 52 (ed. Pattin, p. 145).

6. *Rep.* 2.5 (*OTh* 5: 87.2–5).

7. Ibid. (*OTh* 5: 62.21–63.25). A total cause is "that which, when posited, abstracting from everything else, the effect can be posited" ("...causa totalis est illa qua posita, omni alio circumscripto, potest poni effectus") (*OTh* 5: 64.5–6). Ockham's doctrine of causality will be further examined below, pp. 400–412.

In his *Quodlibeta*, written after the *Sentences*, Ockham changed his mind about Aristotle's views on God's causal relation to the world. He now holds, with Averroes, that according to Aristotle, God is not the immediate efficient cause of the separated substances or Intelligences, and through them the remote cause of the sublunar world. Rather, it was Aristotle's intention that "the primary being is the final, but not the efficient cause of other things, because he [i.e. Aristotle] holds that the heavenly bodies, with other lower causes, produce these lower beings."[8] The interpretation of Aristotle's notion of cause in the *Sentences* has given way in the *Quodlibeta* to the Averroist notion that God causes the world only as an object of desire or love.

The *Quodlibeta* also strictly limits the ability of human reason to prove convincingly anything about God's causal relation to the world. The Christian believes that God is the immediate efficient and final cause of the world, and he can argue persuasively in behalf of his belief, but he cannot demonstrate it. Natural reason cannot prove that God is the efficient cause of any effect. No adequate proof is forthcoming that there are other effects than those that come to be and pass away, and we know from experience that their efficient causes are the natural bodies in the sublunar world and heavenly bodies like the sun. What is more, there is no adequate proof that the heavenly bodies or the Intelligences themselves have an efficient cause. Only persuasive arguments can be offered that God is the efficient cause of any effect: it can be argued, for example, that if he produced nothing, his existence would be useless. Neither can it be proved convincingly that God is the final cause of any effect. These are matters known with certainty only by faith.[9]

8. "Ad ultimum dico quod intentio Philosophi fuit quod primum ens sit causa finalis aliorum sed non efficiens, quia posuit quod corpora caelestia cum aliis causis inferioribus producunt ista inferiora" (*Quodl.* 4.2 [*OTh* 9: 309.212–215]). According to Averroes the Intelligences exercise final and formal, but not properly efficient, causality in the sublunar world; see Averroes, *In De caelo* 4, com. 1 (Junta ed. 5: f. 234).

9. See *Quodl.* 2.1 and 4.2 (*OTh* 9: 107–111 and 301–309). In the latter *Quodlibet*, Ockham says it is evident from experience that God can be the

Can human reason prove that God produced the world freely and contingently, that is, without constraint or necessity to act?[10] On this point Ockham's interpretation of the philosophers does not waver. It was their mind, he says, that God is not a free or contingent cause of the world, but rather that he produced it naturally. Even though the world issued from God acting through his intellect and will, he caused it by natural necessity (*per necessitatem naturae*). Moreover, Ockham does not think that human reason can conclusively disprove this. All the arguments of Thomas Aquinas and Duns Scotus to the contrary he rejects as inconclusive.

In his *De potentia* Aquinas gives four reasons for holding "that God brought creatures into being not by natural necessity but by the free choice of his will." The first argument is based on the premise that the universe as a whole is directed to an end; otherwise everything in it would happen by chance. Hence God had some end in view in the production of creatures. Could he have produced them acting through his nature and not through his will? No, for a natural agent does not determine the end for which it acts; rather, it must be directed to an end predetermined by an intelligent and voluntary agent, which in the case of the universe can only be God. So God directs the universe to its end through his will, and consequently he produced it through his will and not by natural necessity.

Aquinas' second proof also stresses the difference between a natural and voluntary agent. A natural agent is limited to produce one effect equal to itself, unless there is some defect in its active power or in the recipient of the effect. Now, far from being

---

final cause of things we freely do, as when we do or make something for the honor of God (*OTh* 9: 303.67–71).

10. An agent acts contingently in two senses: First, it can simply produce an effect or not. In this sense anything that produces an effect acts contingently, for God can prevent it from producing it. Second, it produces an effect and, without any change on its part or on the part of anything else, it has within its power not to produce it, so that of its nature it is determined to neither course of action. Freedom is the opposite of necessity, negated in the second sense of contingency; see *Ord.* 1.1.6 [*OTh* 1: 501.2–24]).

defective, the divine power is infinite. Only one 'effect' proceeds from it naturally, namely the Son, who is equal to the Father. Hence creatures, being unequal to the divine power, proceed from the divine will.

The third argument of Aquinas is based on the fact that an effect preexists in its cause according to the mode of being of the cause. Since God is an intellect, creatures must preexist in him as in an intellect. But what exists in an intellect can be produced only by means of the will. Consequently creatures proceed from God through his will.

The fourth argument also presupposes that God is an intelligent agent. His actions must be understood as immanent operations, like understanding and willing, not as transient actions, such as heating or moving. Aquinas' reason for denying that God's actions can be transient is their identity with the divine essence, which always remains within God and does not proceed outside of him. Hence everything God creates outside himself is created by the divine knowledge and will. All these arguments lead to the same conclusion, in Aquinas' view: "Therefore we must say that every creature proceeded from God through his will and not by necessity of his nature."[11]

After faithfully reproducing the arguments of Aquinas, Ockham hastens to add that all of them are inconclusive. They prove that God produced creatures by his will, but they do not establish that his act of willing was free and contingent. God may produce creatures through his will, as a voluntary agent, and yet produce them naturally and necessarily. Does not Aquinas himself admit

---

11. *De pot.* 3.15. His *ST* 1.19.4 contains only the first three arguments. In reply to the fourth argument, Ockham insists that the creation of the world is not an immanent but transient action, for it produces creatures outside of him. "Just as the production of creatures does not imply anything except God and the creatures produced, which would not exist except at the presence of God, so the production of fire implies nothing but the fire that produces, along with its absolute [qualities], and the fire produced, which would not exist except for the presence of that fire" (*Ord.* 1.43.1 [*OTh* 4: 629.12–16]).

that the will acts both naturally and freely? Thus he says that the will wills the end naturally and the means to the end freely and contingently.[12] Hence the fact that God acts through his will does not mean that he does not act by necessity of nature. This is confirmed by Aristotle, who held that the first cause acts through intellect and will and nevertheless by natural necessity. And does not Aquinas himself teach that the Holy Spirit proceeds from the Father through the divine will and yet naturally and necessarily? There is no contradiction, then, in God's producing creatures through his will and yet by natural necessity.[13]

Ockham's criticism of the first argument of Aquinas pinpoints the weakness he finds in all of them. Aquinas assumes that the end for which one acts can be willed necessarily while the means to that end are willed freely. Thus God necessarily wills himself as the goal of his creatures, while willing them freely as ordained to that goal. But Ockham finds this explanation wanting, "because it has not been sufficiently proven that the divine will wills contingently what is ordained to an end, and yet this is in special need of proof."[14]

In Ockham's view, then, Aquinas has failed to prove beyond any doubt that God acted freely and contingently in producing the universe. For a cause to act in this way, nothing can impede its

---

12. *ST* 1.19.3; 1.60.2. God wills his own goodness necessarily and our will necessarily wills happiness. However, the means to these ends are willed freely unless the end cannot be achieved without them.

13. *Ord.* 1.43.1 (*OTh* 4: 625.8–626.7).

14. Ibid. (*OTh* 4: 626.13–19). Elsewhere Aquinas gave this proof, but Ockham does not seem to be aware of it. In any case he does not allude to it here. Aquinas' proof rests on the fact that the divine goodness is the only natural and principal object (*principale volitum*) of the divine will. As such, it alone is proportionate to the divine will, and consequently it is willed necessarily. The human will also necessarily wills its natural and proportionate end, which is happiness; but it chooses particular goods (which are means to happiness) freely. Since the good of creatures is not proportionate to the divine will, it does not necessitate that will but is willed freely and contingently (*De pot.* 1.5; *ST* 1.19.3; *De ver.* 23.4; *SCG* 1.81). On God's freedom in creation see Anton C. Pegis, "Necessity and Liberty: An Historical Note on St. Thomas Aquinas," *The New Scholasticism* 15 (1941): 18–45.

action and, after equally considering several options, it chooses one and not the other.[15] But for an unbeliever this is not the way God is related to the universe. He would say that God does not immediately and equally consider everything producible, but that he necessarily produces the first Intelligence, and by its means produces another, or that the first Intelligence itself produces another one. Only if it could be demonstrated by natural reason that God created the universe with a beginning in time (*de novo*), freely choosing one creature in preference to another possible one, could it be proved that he acted contingently; but no adequate proof of this is possible.[16]

If contingency in God's actions cannot be proven in the Thomist way, by considering the nature of the divine will, can it be done on the basis of the contingency of creatures? This was the method of Duns Scotus. The fact that contingent events occur in nature is proof to him that the first cause acts contingently. If the first cause produced its effect necessarily, this effect, acting as a secondary cause, would in turn produce a necessary effect, and so on for the whole series of causes. So the whole chain of primary and secondary causes would act necessarily, with the result that nothing would happen contingently. Since secondary causes exercise their causality only through the power of the first cause, the fact that they do cause contingently is proof of the contingency of the first cause. The same conclusion can be drawn from the existence of evil in the world. A necessary cause, Scotus contends, produces its effect in the recipient to the greatest possible extent. Now the effect of the first cause is goodness and perfection. Hence, if the first cause acted necessarily, it would produce the greatest possible amount of goodness in things, and there would be no evil in them. Moreover, the existence of secondary causes itself argues against the necessary causality of the first cause. An agent acting necessarily acts to the limit of its power (*causa necessario agens agit*

15. See above, note 10.
16. *Rep.* 2.5 (*OTh* 5: 84.2–16).

secundum ultimum potentiae suae). Consequently, if the first cause acts necessarily, it will produce everything it can produce. Now it can produce everything producible. Therefore, in the event that the first cause acts necessarily, there would be no secondary causes.[17]

In a note appended to these arguments Scotus concedes that they would not convince the philosophers (*non valent contra philosophos*). Ockham readily agrees that they are inconclusive from the philosophical point of view. It cannot be evidently proved that, because something occurs contingently, the first cause acts contingently. The philosophers would reply that the contingency of the effect must result from the contingency of the action of some creature, such as the act of the created will. The will is a contingent cause, according to the philosophers, and however much other causes may act naturally, when it concurs with them the resultant effect is contingent. The fact that the will is moved or conserved by a necessary first cause does not necessitate its act; it may be left free to act or not to act.[18]

The concurrence of the will can also account for evil in the world. We need not suppose that the first cause is the immediate and total cause of everything, and hence that evil should be imputed to it. The created will has a role in many effects, and evil may reside in it and not in the divine will. In general, to prove that secondary causes have no part in causation, we would have to demonstrate by natural reason, against the philosophers, that God, acting by himself, can cause everything producible, or that he immediately concurs in its production. But neither of these propositions can be proved.[19] By proof in this connection Ockham means a strict demonstration or sufficient proof, which would dispel all doubt and settle the matter philosophically. He grants that persuasive arguments can be given that God is the immediate

17. *Ord.* 1.43.1 (*OTh* 4: 629.23–631.21). For the references to Scotus see the editors' notes *OTh* 4: 629–631.
18. Ibid. (*OTh* 4: 631.23–632.8).
19. Ibid. (*OTh* 4: 635.24–636.8).

cause of all things, and that he is their free and contingent cause, but these do not amount to a demonstration.[20] Human reason cannot disprove the opposite thesis of the philosophers, namely, that God, as the first cause, stands in necessary relation to his effects, and that these effects flow from him in hierarchical order. From the standpoint of human reason, the world of the philosophers (which is represented by Aristotle, Avicenna, and Averroes) is entirely plausible.

To Ockham the Christian theologian, however, this is not the truth of the matter. For this we must turn to the faith, which teaches that God is the free and contingent cause of the world, producing it without intermediaries and in its total reality. In short, he is its creator.

2 God as Creator of the World

The first matter to be settled is the meaning of the term "creation." Ockham finds it used in several senses, one of which is purely equivocal. Thus, in canon law it means raising someone to a dignity, as the pope is said to "create" cardinals! In philosophy and theology, however, it has four meanings. (1) In a broad sense creation simply means the production or making of something, as Averroes says that the agent intellect creates its intelligible objects by making them exist within the mind.[21] (2) In the strict sense it means the production of something from nothing or from some-

---

20. *Rep.* 2.3-4 (*OTh* 5: 55.16-56.5). God is the first and immediate cause of all things, even those produced by secondary causes. By an immediate cause Ockham means one at whose presence the effect can exist and at whose absence it cannot. In fact, every cause is immediate; a remote cause is not properly speaking a cause. What does not exist cannot cause something to exist; Adam cannot be said to be my cause. Thus, if God acts along with a secondary cause, both are immediate causes of the effect. "This is proved," Ockham asserts, "by Jn 1:3: 'All things were made through him'" (ibid. [*OTh* 5: 60.20-61.11]). In *Quodl.* 3.4 (*OTh* 9: 215.12-16), however, Ockham asserts that Abraham can be called the father and cause of Jacob because he is the father of his father; see *Expos. in Phys.* 2.5 (*OPh* 4: 283.19-33).

21. Averroes, *In De anima* 3, com. 5 (ed. Crawford p. 390.109-110).

thing that is itself drawn from nothing by an agent, as Augustine speaks of crops being created.[22] (3) In a still stricter sense creation means the production of something that before was nothing by an agent that can produce it outside of a subject. Ockham is here alluding to the creation of the accidents of the eucharist without their underlying substance. (4) In its strictest meaning creation is the production by God alone of something that before was nothing, without his cooperating with an agent that necessarily requires matter on which to act. This excludes the creation of something by God which at the same time is caused by a natural agent. For example, the same fire that is caused naturally in matter is also created by God as the first cause of every event in nature, but this is not creation in its most proper sense.[23]

With these meanings of creation in mind, can we say that every effect is created by God? In the first and second senses the answer is yes, for God either creates the effect or at least he creates the material out of which it is formed by creatures. In the third sense a composite effect produced by a creature is not said to be created by God, but he may be said to create simple effects, such as forms, especially if, by the divine power, they can exist apart from the subjects in which they inhere. This is the case with the accidents in the eucharist: God can create them without the substance in which they naturally exist. In the fourth and strictest sense neither a composite being nor a simple form produced by a creature can be said to be created by God.[24]

What, then, is creation in the proper sense of the term? For something to be created there are two requirements. First, before creation it must be purely nothing (*purum nihil*); that is to say, no

22. Augustine, *De symbolo* 5, n. 13 (PL 40: 635).
23. *Quodl.* 2.8 (*OTh* 9: 146.29–147.58). When God acts along with a secondary cause, both he and the secondary cause are immediate causes of the whole effect, but de facto he is not its total cause. However, because he is omnipotent, he can produce the effect without the secondary cause, and consequently he can be its total cause; see *Rep.* 2. 3–4 (*OTh* 5: 63.19–25).
24. *Quodl.* 2.8 (*OTh* 9: 147.44–148.69).

one of its parts must pre-exist. Second, it must be produced by an agent which, in order to act, presupposes no subject or part of a subject on which to act. Thus creation can be defined as "the production of a thing from absolutely nothing, so that nothing intrinsic and essential to it pre-exists."[25] This rules out any subject prior to creation either in time or nature. The addition of "in nature" can be clarified by an example. Suppose God in an instant created the whole body of air, and the sun in an instant illuminated it. The sun cannot be said to create the illumination, for it presupposes the existence of air, if not in time at least in nature.[26] Similarly, if there were something naturally prior to God's action, that action could not be called creation. Creation is literally a production from nothing, the word "from" simply indicating an order between nothing and something, which is the same as saying that before something is created it was nothing.[27]

Hence everything produced (*omnis effectus*) is in some sense of the word created. It is either brought into being from nothing by God alone, or it is fashioned or generated by a creature from material created from nothing. In the latter case the effect is not created in the strictest sense of the word.[28]

Because God creates the whole being of a creature from nothing, it totally depends on him, so that he must conserve it in existence as long as it endures. There is no real difference between his act of creation and conservation. These terms signify the same thing in reality and differ only in their connotations. Creation connotes that in the moment preceding the existence of the creature it does not exist; conservation connotes that there is no interruption in the duration of the creature. Thus the whole positive

---

25. "[C]reatio est simpliciter de nihilo, ita quod nihil intrinsecum et essentiale rei praecedat" (*Ord.* 1.2.4 [*OTh* 2: 116.17–18]).

26. *Quodl.* 2.9 (*OTh* 9: 150.8–15).

27. *Rep.* 2.3–4 (*OTh* 5: 66.19–67.3).

28. Even figments of the mind, like chimeras, lies, and impossible things, are creatable by God, for they are real beings, understood as terms in propositions, not with personal but with material or simple supposition; see *Quodl.* 2.8 (*OTh* 9: 148.80–82, 149.89–97).

content of the two notions is identical; they differ only in their negative connotations. Only when a creature makes something from the materials of creation does the act of production really differ from that of conservation.[29]

It was customary for medieval schoolmen to distinguish between creation as an action of God (*creatio actio*) and creation as the reception of this action in the creature (*creatio passio*). Ockham adopts this language from his predecessors, but it takes on a new meaning in his theology because of his nominalist conception of relation. Whether creation is thought of in an active or passive sense, it is a relative notion, and its precise meaning will depend on the philosopher's conception of relation. By Ockham's day a number of divergent notions of relation had emerged, all of which he rejected, and along with them their implied notions of creation.[30]

It was generally agreed that creation as a divine action sets up a mutual relation between God and creatures, but it was thought that their relations are not the same: the relation of creatures to God is real whereas that of God to creatures is only mental (*respectus rationis*). Whenever there are two mutually related beings and one depends on the other but not vice versa, the independent being is not related to the dependent being in reality but only by the mind. Now this is the case with God and creatures: he does not depend on them, though they depend on him. Consequently creation as a divine action expresses only a mental relation.[31]

This was the opinion of Scotus, Henry of Ghent, and Aquinas. According to Aquinas "Creation in the active sense means the divine action, which is God's essence with a relation to the creature. But in God, relation to the creature is not a real but only a mental relation (*secundum rationem tantum*), whereas the relation of the creature to God is a real relation."[32]

---

29. *Rep.* 2.8 (*OTh* 5: 158.17–159.12); *Quodl.* 7.1 (*OTh* 9: 706.72–78).
30. For the notion of relation see above, pp. 47–53.
31. *Rep.* 2.1 (*OTh* 5: 4.15–20).
32. *ST* 1.45.3, ad 1; cf. 1.13.7. As Ockham's editor indicates (*OTh* 5: 4 n1) Henry of Ghent and Duns Scotus held the same view.

Ockham's criticism of this doctrine is radical, for it strikes at the root of its implied notion of relation. In his view, creation cannot express *any* relation, real or mental, for the simple reason that there are no such relations. As we have seen in Chapter 1, he did not believe that relations are beings or things existing along with absolute things and accounting for their relatedness. They are nothing but words or concepts signifying absolute things. Hence Ockham's terse conclusion: "Creation as an action does not signify a mental or real relation."[33]

Why cannot creation signify a mental relation between God and creatures? Simply because there cannot be relations of this sort. If there were, they would have either subjective or objective being.[34] The first is impossible, because then they would be realities and therefore real relations. The second is also impossible, for if there were such mental relations they would most certainly exist between a subject and predicate in a proposition. But it is unnecessary to assume such relations between parts of a proposition. The whole proposition – subject, copula, and predicate – can be understood without adding mental relations with objective being between them. Neither do the logical concepts of genus and species (assuming they have objective being in the mind), involve any mental relation.[35]

Ockham is not always so severe in his rejection of a mental relation (*relatio rationis*). Sometimes he accepts the notion in deference to the common opinion, though he does not regard it as very philosophical, nor does he recall seeing it in the works of Aristotle. Conforming to the language of his time, he distinguishes between a mental and real relation as follows. A relation is said to be mental (*rationis*) when that of which one speaks is not what the relative term denotes except through a mental act. For example, there are no subjects or predicates without an act of the mind; a

---

33. "Ideo dico quod creatio actio non dicit respectum rationis, nec respectum realem" (*Rep.* 2.1 [*OTh* 5: 8.13–14]).

34. For the meaning of subjective and objective being see below, p. 504.

35. *Rep.* 2.1 (*OTh* 5: 6.19–7.8).

word has meaning only because it has been given it by a mental act; a coin has value only because of the will of a community. In contrast, a relation is real when that of which one speaks is what the relative term denotes without the mind having anything to do with it. For instance, two white things are like each other, whether or not the mind relates them to each other. "Likeness," then, is called a real relation.[36]

Even if we grant the validity of the notion of a mental relation, we cannot say that creation expresses a relation of this sort between God and creatures. If it did, God could not be called a creator unless there were a mind present to conceive God in this way. The term "creating" would have meaning only through the intervention of a mind; but even if *per impossibile* there were no mind, God would truly be a creator.

If creation does not imply a mental relation between God and creatures, does it imply a real relation between them? This is equally impossible, if by a real relation is meant a reality either really or formally distinct from God. If the relation signified by creation were really distinct from God, the act of creating would add a new reality to the divine essence, and that essence would be really changed by the new relation. If the relation were only formally distinct from the divine essence, it would be present in that essence from all eternity, just like all the divine attributes, so that God would eternally create and creatures would eternally exist.[37]

Ockham often criticized his predecessors for needlessly multiplying entities corresponding to our words. Because absolute words signify absolute entities, they thought that relative words must signify relative entities, and so they endowed relations with a kind of entity of their own. This led them to conceive creation as implying a relative entity – either real or mental; and having given the relation a being, they conceived it as somehow existing in the related subject. They asked: Does creation reside in the divine essence

---

36. *Ord.* 1.30.5 (*OTh* 4: 385.16–386.20).
37. *Rep.* 2.1 (*OTh* 5: 8.13–9.6).

or in the creature? They replied that it exists in the former actively and in the latter passively. But this was asking the wrong question. They should rather have inquired: What does the name or concept "creation" signify? To this, Ockham replies that, taken as an act of God, it signifies principally the divine essence and secondarily or connotatively the existence of creatures. Besides this, it implies the creature's essence as caused by God.[38]

Consequently, terms like "creating," "governing," "conserving" do not imply a mental relation between God and creatures. A relation of this sort is brought about by the mind's relating one thing to another or to itself. But it is not owing to our mind that God is the creator, governor, and conserver of the world; he is really and truly all of these, as the sun really warms the earth. The created mind has nothing to do with the fact that God is a creator: he can really create a stone, whether there is a human mind or not. So God's independence of the world does not preclude his being really related to it as its cause. In this sense it can be said that creation expresses a real relation – not that the relation is a reality, but that it conjointly denotes two absolute realities: primarily God and secondarily and connotatively the creature. In this respect creation is like the relation of likeness. This is a real relation, not because it is a reality distinct from the things related, but because it implies real things which are like each other without the mind having anything to do with it.[39]

We are now in a position to understand what is meant by creation in both its active and passive senses. Taken as an action, it is identical with the divine reality; taken as a reception (*passio*), it is nothing else than the creature directly proceeding from God and immediately depending on him and relating to him.[40]

An appeal to the principle of parsimony shows that it is unnecessary to conceive creation and conservation as relations added to

38. *Rep.* 2.1 (*OTh* 5: 9.7–10.18).

39. *Ord.* 1.30.5 (*OTh* 4: 382–385).

40. Ockham treats at length of creation in its receptive or passive sense in *Rep.* 2.2 (*OTh* 5: 27–49).

the absolute realities of God and creatures. The principle, as formulated in Ockham's later works, states, "When a proposition is verified of things, if two or three things suffice for the truth of the proposition, a fourth is superfluous." Now the propositions "A stone is created" and "A stone is conserved" are the sort that are verified of things. In order to verify the first, all that is needed is God, a stone, and the first instant in which it is created; once these are granted, "A stone is created" must be true. Similarly, in order to verify the proposition "A stone is conserved," all that is required is God, a stone, and an instant after the instant of creation. Consequently there is no need to posit creation and conservation as relations over and above God and creatures.[41]

3 Can Creatures Create?

Up to this point, Ockham has not queried whether anyone except God could properly speaking be a creator. All the passages in his works we have examined take it for granted that in the strictest sense creation is an act of God alone. This was the common view of medieval theologians and he did not disagree with them. However, he did not think one could demonstrate the impossibility of a creature's having the power of creating; only persuasive arguments can be offered to disprove the thesis of philosophers such as Avicenna, that not only the First Cause but also the celestial Intelligences share in the creative power. Ockham offers several proofs that creatures cannot create as total or partial natural causes, or even as voluntary causes; but perhaps his most telling argument is his observation that, as far as we can have experience in this matter, we never see a creature produce anything *ex puro nihilo* but out of some material: there must always be something present to receive the action of a created efficient cause.[42]

---

41. *Quodl.* 7.1 (*OTh* 9: 704.17–27).
42. Ibid. 2.9 (*OTh* 9: 150.16–151.29); *Rep.* 2.6 (*OTh* 5: 91.9–92.7). The question whether it is contradictory for creatures to create is treated at greater length in two appendices of *OTh* 5: 449–475.

After examining the opinions of Giles of Rome, Aquinas, and Scotus on this topic, Ockham finds himself in agreement with their negative views on the capacity of a creature to create, though he is often critical of their reasons for them.

Aquinas attracts his attention because he seems to contradict himself on the subject. In Aquinas' writings (*scripta*) on the *Sentences* of Peter Lombard (an early work dating from his period as bachelor of the *Sentences*: 1252–1256), he thought there was some basis for Lombard's opinion, that God cannot share with creatures his primacy in causality, but through the power of the first cause working in them they could produce something without preexisting matter. In this way philosophers like Avicenna have held that the celestial Intelligences can create other Intelligences and primary matter, though Aquinas adds that this is heretical.[43] In later works, however, Aquinas changed his mind and declared without qualification that creation is an act of God alone: it could not be shared with creatures acting either as proper or instrumental causes.[44]

Ockham heartily agrees with the later view of Aquinas, but he thinks Aquinas' reasons for it are either weak or wrongheaded. Thus, when Aquinas contends that God alone can create because he alone can produce being (*esse*), Ockham retorts that this is simply not the case: every productive creature produces some being.[45] Clearly, there is no meeting of minds here between Aquinas and Ockham on the meaning of being (*esse*). In Aquinas' view, being is the most universal of all effects, and so it must be the proper effect of the first and most universal cause, namely

---

43. Aquinas says that Peter Lombard's opinion that the power of creation has not actually been shared with creatures but it could have been seems to have some basis: "videtur habere aliquid cui innitatur" (*In Sent.* 2.1.1.3 [ed. Mandonnet–Moos 2: 22]). The Parma edition reads: "videtur mihi secundum aliquid vera esse." See Peter Lombard, *Sententiae* 4.5.3 (Grottaferrata ed. 4: 267.13–17).

44. *De pot.* 3.4; *ST* 1.45.5.

45. *Rep.* 2.6, Appendix (*OTh* 5: 454); *ST* ibid.

God. The proper effect of secondary and less universal causes is not being purely and simply but this or that being, or being of such and such a kind. So a creature does produce some being, but not being absolutely, which is the kind of production called creation.[46] But this reasoning is meaningless unless one takes into account the Thomistic notion of being (*esse*) as the act of existing (*actus essendi*), the supreme perfection of things, and hence the proper effect of God – a doctrine that does not come within Ockham's purview.[47] Neither can he accept Aquinas' distinction between a universal and a particular effect. In his view, a universal, such as being, is nothing but a word or concept; every effect is a particular being.

Aquinas also contended that a creature cannot create because it does not have the infinite power needed to bridge the gap between pure nonbeing and being involved in creation. Creation is the production of something from nothing, and only God is able to span this infinite distance.[48] Later schoolmen were not unanimous in accepting this as a sound argument against the philosophers' claim that a creature can create. Duns Scotus, for one, protested that the creature's power to create cannot be denied on the ground that it would have to bridge an infinite distance between nonbeing and being. For even though, from God's standpoint, the distance between God and creatures is infinite, from the creature's perspective the distance is finite; and this is also true of the distance from the creature to the nonbeing from which it is created. In fact, from this viewpoint the distance is finite, determined by the being of the creature. Consequently, on this score one cannot prove the creature's incapacity to create.[49]

---

46. *ST* ibid.
47. *De pot.* 7.2, ad 9.
48. *ST* 1.45.5, ad 3.
49. Scotus, *Ord.* 4.1.1 (Vivès ed. 16: 37, n. 11); *Rep. Paris.* 4.1.1 (Vivès ed. 23: 537–538, n. 10). See Etienne Gilson, *Jean Duns Scot* (Paris, 1952), pp. 348–351.

Ockham agrees with Scotus that Aquinas' argument is invalid, but for another reason. If the argument were sound, Ockham says, we would have to conclude that a creature can do nothing at all. His reason is that, when a form is produced by a natural agent, the distance between the *terminus a quo* and the *terminus ad quem* is just as great as if the form were immediately created by God, for in both cases the *terminus a quo* is pure nothing. This is clear, for when a natural agent produces a form in matter, the *terminus a quo* of the production is not matter, or the form opposed to the form to be introduced into the matter, or some part of the form to be introduced. Rather, it is simply the negation of that form, and this is pure nothing (*purum nihil*). At first sight it might seem that the *terminus a quo* is not purely nothing but the composite of matter and the nonbeing of the form to be produced, but on reflection it will be seen that the opposition involved in the generation of a form in matter is precisely between the negation of the form in matter and the positive presence of the form after the production has taken place. In short, the opposition is between nonbeing and being, and the distance is similarly between pure nothing and being.[50]

4 Can God Create an Eternal World?

Another fact about creation that, in Ockham's view, cannot be rationally demonstrated but is held on faith is that the world had a beginning in time. The Christian is certain of the fact, for according to Genesis 1:1, "In the beginning God created the heavens and the earth." "In the beginning" was usually understood in a temporal sense.[51] But granted the fact of the temporal origin of the world, can it be demonstrated that an eternal world is

50. *Rep.* 2.6 (*OTh* 5: 94.11–12). Ockham here refers to ibid. 3–4 (*OTh* 5: 78.3–17).

51. Other interpretations have been given. Thus, for Augustine, "in the beginning" (*in principio*) does not mean the beginning of time but, symbolically, the principle of all things, namely the Word. See Etienne Gilson, *The Christian Philosophy of Saint Augustine*, trans. L.E.M. Lynch (New York, 1960), p. 197.

impossible? According to Ockham, neither side of the question can be adequately proven: not the negative side, that it would be impossible for God to create an eternal world, because this is not clearly contradictory; nor the positive side, that God could have made an eternal world, for the arguments in favor of this thesis are not so conclusive that they cannot be refuted.[52]

The possibility of an eternal world was a subject warmly debated in the thirteenth and fourteenth centuries. Aristotle's arguments that the world could not have had a beginning in time presented philosophers and theologians with a serious challenge to the Christian notion of creation.[53] Their replies were varied and nuanced. Siger of Brabant and Boethius of Dacia, philosophers in the Faculty of Arts at Paris in the thirteenth century, were sympathetic to Aristotle's position on the eternity of the world, though they did not consider it to be true; the truth regarding creation they reserved to Christian revelation.[54] The philosophers were strongly opposed by some theologians, notably Bonaventure and Henry of Ghent, who contended that the notion of an eternal created world is contradictory; indeed, that reason can prove that the world was created with a temporal beginning, just as scripture reveals.[55] Aquinas was of another mind. In his view, reason can-

---

52. *Quodl.* 2.5 (*OTh* 9: 128.7-10); *Quaest. variae* 3: 'Utrum mundus potuit fuisse ab aeterno per potentiam divinam' (*OTh* 8: 59-97). This disputed question begins: "I say that both sides can be held and neither can be adequately disproved" (ibid. 59.4-5). The question was printed in the Lyons edition of Ockham's *Sentences* in 1495 (*Rep.* 2.8), but it is a separate *Quaestio disputata*, reported by Ockham's disciple Adam of Wodeham (*OTh* 8: intro. 12*-13*). See Norman Kretzmann, "Ockham and the Creation of the Beginningless World," *Franciscan Studies* 45 (1985): 1-31.

53. Aristotle argues for the eternity of motion in *Phys.* 8.1-2.

54. For the position of Siger see Fernand Van Steenberghen, *Maître Siger de Brabant* (Louvain, 1977), pp. 230-257, 309-311. For Boethius of Dacia see *On the Supreme Good, On the Eternity of the World, On Dreams*, trans. John F. Wippel (Toronto, 1987), and Van Steenberghen, *La philosophie au XIIIe siècle* (Louvain, 1966), pp. 404-410.

55. See Etienne Gilson, *The Philosophy of St. Bonaventure*, trans. Illtyd Trethowan and Frank J. Sheed (1938; Paterson, NY, 1965), pp. 171-178; John

not demonstrate either the eternity or noneternity of the world. Nevertheless, the eternity of the world is not impossible, and the arguments to the contrary can be resolved. We believe on faith alone that the world had a beginning in time.[56]

Ockham takes up the question of the possibility of an eternal world in both Disputed and Quodlibetal Questions. His position is the same in both: the mind cannot satisfactorily settle the issue whether or not it lies within the divine power to create an eternal world.[57] Like Godfrey of Fontaines before him, he contends that both sides of the dispute can be held as probably true but not as demonstrable by human reason.[58] Ockham leaves no doubt, however, where his own preference lies. Taking the stand that there is probably no contradiction in the notion of an eternal world, he marshals the most persuasive arguments against it and then answers them in turn.

(1) If the world has always existed, there has been an infinite number of revolutions of the heavenly spheres, so that an infinity has actually been traversed to the present day. But it is impossible to pass through an infinity.[59]

F. Quinn, *The Historical Constitution of St. Bonaventure's Philosophy* (Toronto, 1973), pp. 591–603. For the doctrine of Henry of Ghent see Raymond Macken, "La temporalité radicale de la créature selon Henri de Gand," *Recherches de théologie ancienne et médiévale* 38 (1971): 211–272.

56. *ST* 1.46.1–3; *De aeternitate mundi* (Leonine ed. 43: 85–89); Etienne Gilson, *The Christian Philosophy of St. Thomas Aquinas*, pp. 147–152; Oliva Blanchette, *The Perfection of the Universe according to Aquinas* (University Park, PA, 1992), pp. 221–228; John F. Wippel, "Did Thomas Aquinas Defend the Possibility of an Eternal Created World? The *De aeternitate mundi* Revisited," *The Journal of the History of Philosophy* 19 (1981): 21–37; repr. as "Thomas Aquinas on the Possibility of Eternal Creation," in his *Metaphysical Themes in Thomas Aquinas* (Washington, DC, 1984), pp. 191–214.

57. *Quodl.* 2.5 (*OTh* 9: 128.7–10); *Quaest. variae* 3 (*OTh* 8: 59.4–5).

58. For Godfrey of Fontaines see Wippel, *The Metaphysical Thought of Godfrey of Fontaines* (Washington, DC, 1981), pp. 159–169.

59. *Quodl.* 2.5 (*OTh* 9: 129.15–20); *Quaest. variae* 3 (*OTh* 8: 60.10–15).

Ockham does not regard this argument as cogent. In the Disputed Question he simply replies that it is not contradictory for the heavens to have revolved an infinite number of times. The Quodlibet distinguishes between a past and future infinity. In the hypothesis of an eternal world one can say that an infinite number of revolutions of the heavens have occurred and that an infinity has been passed through (*pertransita*); but it cannot be said that in the future an infinite number will be passed through (*pertranseunda*, because this number has no end.[60]

(2) On the supposition of an eternal world there would be an infinite number of actually existing beings. Suppose that each day in the past God created one human being or intellectual soul. Then Aristotle and Averroes would be right: there was no first human being. On this hypothesis there would now be an infinite number of actually existing human souls, because they are immortal. Moreover, all these souls would be actually infinite in perfection – a hardly appropriate consequence, for God's perfection alone is actually infinite.[61]

Ockham offers several answers to this objection. First, he sees no reason for denying the possibility of an actually existing infinity of things. Why cannot there be an actual infinity of souls and concepts? This is a surprising concession, for later in his *Quodlibeta* he claims that it would be contradictory for God to create a simultaneously existing infinity of things.[62] Again, in his *Quaestiones in libros Physicorum* he contends that there cannot be an infinity of simultaneously existing conserving causes, because "then there would be an actually existing infinite multitude, which is impossible."[63] Ockham's vacillation on this subject reflects the uncertainty among the medieval schoolmen regarding the possibility of an actually existing infinity of beings. Most denied this

---

60. *Quodl.* 2.5 (*OTh* 9: 130.48–50); *Quaest. variae* 3 (*OTh* 8: 68.164–167).
61. *Quodl.* 2.5 (*OTh* 9: 129.22–23); *Quaest. variae* 3 (*OTh* 8: 60.16–25).
62. *Quodl.* 3.1 (*OTh* 9: 204.114–122).
63. *Quaest. in Phys.* 136 (*OPh* 6: 768.20–27).

possibility; but some, including Aquinas, had no difficulty in accepting it.[64]

Even granted the impossibility of an actually existing infinity of things, Ockham continues, we would not have to deny the eternity of the world. It is true to say: each day God could have produced one soul, but it does not follow that he produced an infinite number, for he may have begun to produce them on a certain past day. It is false to say in the composite sense (*in sensu compositionis*): each day God produced one soul, because then he would have created an infinite number. But the proposition is true in the divided sense (*in sensu divisionis*), because this does not imply that he actually created a soul each day. Similarly the proposition: Both sides of a contradiction can be true, is false *in sensu compositionis*, for this implies that both sides are true at the same time; but it is true *in sensu divisionis*, which does not carry this implication.

There is no objection to an infinity of souls on the ground that they would constitute an infinite perfection, for unlike the divine infinity it would not be a single entity with infinite perfection.[65]

(3) On the supposition of an eternal world there would be many infinities, one greater than another. For example, there would be more infinite revolutions of the moon than of the sun, for the moon revolves more often than the sun. But whatever can be exceeded is not infinite.[66]

Ockham points out in reply that the word "more" is used in equivocal senses. In one sense one group of things is said to be more than another when there are as many in one as in the other and still more in a definite number. In this sense one infinite num-

---

64. For Ockham's views on the possibility of an actual infinity of simultaneously existing things see Adams, *William Ockham* (Notre Dame, IN, 1987), 1: 162–167. Thomas Aquinas saw no reason to deny this possibility: see his *De aeternitate mundi* (Leonine ed. 43: 89.306–308).

65. *Quodl.* 2.5 (*OTh* 9: 131.52–71); *Quaest. variae* 3 (*OTh* 8: 60.16–61.25).

66. *Quodl.* 2.5 (*OTh* 9: 129.25–26); *Quaest. variae* 3 (*OTh* 8: 61.26–31).

ber is not more than another, because neither exceeds the other by a definite number. In another sense a group of things is said to be more than another because there are as many in the first group as in the second and more besides, but not more in a definite number. The term "exceeds" has the same equivocal meanings. Now it is in the second sense, not the first, that one infinity is said to be more than, or to exceed, another.[67]

(4) All infinities are equal. But if there were many infinities (say, infinite revolutions of the moon and sun), one would be part of another and hence not equal to it, for a part is not equal to a whole.[68]

Ockham removes this difficulty by elucidating the equivocal meaning of the term "equal." Something is said to be equal to another in two senses. First, it means that one of two things called equal contains everything the other contains and no more. In this sense it cannot be said that one infinity is always equal to another; indeed, sometimes one is greater than another, for it often happens that there is as much in one as in the other and even more. This would be the case with infinite revolutions of the moon and sun. Second, one thing is said to be equal to another when the first has a definite quantity and the other has the same quantity and no more. In this sense one infinity cannot be said to be equal to another, for they do not have definite quantities. Consequently, if the term "equal" is used in the first sense, when equality does not imply definite quantities, infinities can be equal, but they can also be unequal: one can be greater than another. Thus, contrary to the premise of the opposing argument, all infinities need not be equal.[69]

(5) If the world were created from eternity, God would have created it necessarily, because everything eternal is necessary.[70]

Ockham retorts that only if God created the world from eternity did he necessarily create it from eternity. This is because the

67. *Quodl.* 2.5 (*OTh* 9: 131.73–79); *Quaest. variae* 3 (*OTh* 8: 61.26–31).
68. *Quodl.* 2.5 (*OTh* 9: 129.28–29).
69. Ibid. (*OTh* 9: 132.81–96).
70. Ibid. (*OTh* 9: 130.31–32).

proposition "The world existed from eternity" would be necessary; it would be true and never can be false. Nevertheless, it could have been false, just as true propositions about the past are necessary, and yet they could have been false.[71]

In the *Disputed Question* Ockham gives great attention to the following argument for the noneternity of the world. Consider today's revolution of the heavenly bodies and then ask: Is some revolution infinitely distant from it or not? If not, the sum total of revolutions is not infinite, for finite revolutions added together make up a finite, not an infinite, number. Similarly one permanent finite continuum added to another adds up to something finite. But if some revolution is infinitely distant from today's revolution, consider the revolution immediately following that revolution infinitely distant from today's and then ask: Is it infinitely distant from today's or not? If not, neither will the preceding one be infinitely distant from today's, for there is only a finite distance between them. If it is infinitely distant from today's revolution, the one immediately following it will also be infinitely distant, and so too will the one immediately preceding it. Following this process up to yesterday's revolution, we will have to conclude that it is infinitely distant from today's – which is clearly false. We are obliged to conclude, then, that no revolution is infinitely distant from today's, and hence that the world cannot be eternal.[72]

This argument stirs Ockham to a lengthy response in which he supports the possibility that there never was a first revolution of the heavenly spheres, and that the total number of these revolutions could be infinite. He sets out by defending the proposition, "No revolution is infinitely distant from today's revolution." That is to say, we cannot point to one revolution and say, "This one or that one is infinitely distant"; and if this is true, the universal proposition is also true: "No revolution is infinitely distant from today's." This follows from the general rule: "If something is true

71. *Quodl.* 2.5 (*OTh* 9: 132.98–102). I am omitting argument 6 and its reply.
72. *Quaest. variae* 3 (*OTh* 8: 61.32–51).

of each individual in a class, it is generally true of the class" (*Haec est universalis cuius quaelibet singularis est vera*).

An opponent can raise the following argument against this conclusion: From any revolution you choose, another is infinitely distant from it. Therefore some revolution is infinitely distant from any given revolution. But Ockham finds a fallacy of speech (*fallacia dictionis*) in the argument, because there is a change in the supposition of terms from the premise to the conclusion.[73] In the proposition "From any revolution you choose another is infinitely distant" the predicate term "other revolution" has only confused supposition; that it is say, it does not stand for any one definite revolution. Hence, from it a logical descent to this or that determinate revolution is impossible. But in the conclusion, "Therefore some revolution is infinitely distant from any given revolution," the subject term "some revolution" stands determinately for this or that one. Here a logical descent is possible, so that we can say: "Therefore *this* revolution is infinitely distant from any given revolution."

Similarly, in the first proposition the subject term "revolution" has confused and distributed supposition, because of the universal sign "any" that is added to it. Hence a logical descent is possible to definite revolutions. But the subject term in the conclusion has only confused supposition, and consequently no logical descent is possible to this or that definite revolution. So the argument commits a fallacy of speech, involving as it does a change in the supposition of terms from premise to conclusion.

Should we grant, accordingly, the truth of this proposition: "Some revolution is infinitely distant from today's"? At first Ockham absolutely denies this, for "revolution" in the subject stands determinately for this or that revolution. Hence it is absolutely false, for neither this nor that revolution is infinitely distant from today's. But the following proposition should absolutely be conceded: "From today's revolution another is infinitely

---

73. For this kind of fallacy see *Sum. log.* 3–4.10 (*OPh* 1: 799.209–230).

distant," for "revolution" in the predicate has only confused supposition, and consequently it does not stand determinately for any
one definite revolution.

On second thought, however, Ockham is inclined to deny
both propositions: "Some revolution is infinitely distant from
today's," and "From today's revolution another is infinitely distant." The first should be denied because a common term used as
a predicate never stands confusedly unless there is placed a
universal term, or some term, with the subject to indicate that the
subject has confused and distributed supposition. The correct
proposition would then be: "Some revolution is distant to infinity
from every revolution." The second proposition should also be
denied, namely: "From today's revolution another is distant to
infinity." The correct proposition is: "From every revolution there
is distant some one to infinity."[74]

Ockham is preoccupied with the correct wording of these propositions in order to avoid any indication that, if you take your stand
at today's revolution of the heavenly spheres, any definite revolution
can be said to be infinitely distant from it. In an eternal world, *some*
revolution is infinitely distant, but not definitely this or that one.
This undercuts the opponent's argument, which is based on the premise that, on the hypothesis of an eternal world, we can single out a
particular event in the past as infinitely distant from the present day.

Ockham pays special attention to Henry of Ghent's attempt
to prove the noneternity of the world, for he considers his arguments in this behalf more cogent than those given above. Henry
insisted that creation means something different to the Christian
and the philosopher. To believers, God produces creatures from
nothing, so that nonbeing precedes their being. Philosophers like
Avicenna would agree with this, but to them the precedence of the
nonbeing of the world to its being is not real but only natural or
conceptual, so that the world is not *really* made from nothing. The
Christian doctrine is quite different: it tells us that the creature of

74. *Quaest. variae* 3 (*OTh* 8: 69.183–74.266).

itself or of its nature is nothing. It is not produced by God as a ray of light issues from the sun, which, if it were eternal, would eternally give existence to the ray. The sun would make the ray exist (*factum esse*), but it would not make it come into existence (*fieri esse*); that is, it would not effect the change from one contradictory (nonbeing) to the other contradictory (being). Neither is creation like the production of the Son by the Father in the Trinity. The Father makes the Son to be (*esse*), but he does not make him come into being (*fieri*). Creation, on the contrary, implies a transition from nonbeing to being: a real coming into being of something from nothing.

According to Henry of Ghent, then, the nonbeing of a creature really precedes its being in duration and not just in the way we think about them: the creature really is nothing before it is a being. Hence there must be a certain "extent" (*mensura*) prior to its being, when the creature really is nothing – not just in the sense that God can create it, but that it really has no being. Since creation is precisely God's making the creature to be *after* its nothingness, it cannot be eternal. If the creature existed eternally, God could make it *to be* but not *to become* from nothing, which is the Christian notion of creation.[75]

Ockham finds Henry's views on creation mistaken on two counts. First, Henry claims that a creature by nature is nonbeing and that its nonbeing really precedes its being. Now this is clearly false, for no power can give being to something whose nature is nonbeing, for this would be contrary to its very nature – something not even God can do. It is sometimes said that a creature of itself is nonbeing, but this positive statement is intended as equivalent to the negative statement: By its nature a creature is not a being, nor does it have being from itself but from God. So we need not think that two opposites – nonbeing and being – really

---

75. Ibid. (*OTh* 8: 64.82–67.141). See Henry of Ghent, *Quodl.* 1.7–8 (*Opera omnia* 5: 36–37).

belong to a creature in the order of duration, as two positive opposite properties can belong to it, though not at the same time.[76]

Scotus already criticized Henry of Ghent's notion of creation on the same grounds. Following the Subtle Doctor, Ockham strikes at the heart of Henry of Ghent's doctrine, with its implication that nonbeing has a kind of positive status attaching to a creature in reality, prior in duration to its acquiring being from God. For Ockham, nonbeing is nothing but the negation of being; and in the hypothesis of an eternal world it would never be characterized by nonbeing but only by the being eternally created by God.[77]

The second mistake Ockham finds in the position of Henry of Ghent is his distinction between the creation and conservation of the world. Henry was of the opinion that if the world existed from eternity, we would have to say that it was never created in the Christian sense of the term, because this implies nonbeing immediately preceding the being of the creature; but in an eternal world nonbeing would not really precede being. The coming to be (*fieri*) of the creature would not be in any way different from its having been made (*factum esse*); in fact, its being created (*suum creari*) would be its being conserved (*suum conservari*).

Ockham points out an equivocation in Henry's use of the term "creation." In one sense it means the total production of something by an efficient cause; and in this meaning the world would have been created even if it were eternal; indeed, even you are now created by God. In this sense creation does not differ from conservation, because the creature is created as long as it is conserved. In another sense creation means the thing produced, connoting that the nonbeing of that thing really precedes it. This is how Christians speak of creation. There is reason for them to distinguish

---

76. *Quaest. variae* 3 (*OTh* 8: 82.402–417).

77. Ibid. (*OTh* 8: 83.417–445). Cf. Scotus, *Ord.* 2.1.3 (Vatican ed. 7: 84–85, nn. 166–167). Scotus here treats of the possibility of creation from eternity. Henry of Ghent is one of his main objects of criticism. Against Aristotle, Avicenna, and Averroes, he proves the possibility of the creation of the world in time: that it actually has a temporal beginning is a matter of faith.

between creation and conservation, and between the becoming (*fi-eri*) of the creature and its being made (*factum esse*).

Henry of Ghent also argued that an eternal world would be necessary and not contingent, as Christians hold. According to Aristotle, "That which is must needs be when it is."[78] So for the time in which a thing is, it has no potentiality to nonbeing either on its part or on the part of its efficient cause; otherwise contradictories would be true at the same time. Hence an eternally actual world would be necessary, for everything in it would be necessary as it actually exists.

But to Ockham this misconstrues the meaning of Aristotle's famous dictum. What Aristotle meant was that this proposition is necessary: "Everything that is, is when it is." So too this proposition is necessary: "Everything that was, was when it was," and "Everything that will be, will be when it will be." Only in the case of God is it true to say, "When God is, he must be," for he alone is a necessary being. Because Socrates is a contingent being, it is false to say: "When Socrates is, he must be." For the truth of a temporal proposition about creatures both parts of it must be true at the same time. Thus the temporal proposition: "When, or while, Socrates is, he must be" is false, because it is false to say "Socrates must be." Ockham's reading of Aristotle's dictum astutely shifts necessity from the creature to the proposition about it, thus saving the contingency of all created beings and reserving necessary being for God alone.[79]

Like Duns Scotus, Ockham was concerned to maintain the contingency of the created world. Even if it has not been created in time but from eternity – an option that remained open to God – its eternal being would not have been necessary but contingent, since it would have had its origin in God's free decision to create what he wished. Lacking a knowledge of the divine omnipotence

78. Aristotle, *De interpretatione* 9, 19a23.
79. *Quaest. variae* 3 (*OTh* 8: 88.528–539); *Expos. in Phys.* 1.6 (*OPh* 2: 420.26–49).

and freedom, philosophers like Avicenna believed that God created the world naturally and necessarily, with the consequence that the world itself exists necessarily and eternally. Probable arguments can be given to show that the world could have been eternal or had a temporal beginning; none of them, however, are strictly demonstrative. Through God's revelation of his free will in creation we can be assured that the world in fact was created from nothing freely and with a beginning in time.

5 Can God Create a Better World?[80]

While commenting on the *Sentences* of Peter Lombard, Ockham reached the point where the Lombard treats of the power and omnipotence of God. The Lombard takes the orthodox Christian stand that God is all-powerful, and in this connection he criticizes theologians such as Abelard, who in his view restricted the power of God by denying that he can create things he has not created or make them better than he has made them. Of course, God could not beget a Son better than the one he did, as Augustine correctly points out, but this is because the Son is equal to the Father. But when it is a question of creatures, who are not equal to God or consubstantial with him, he can make others better than those he has created, and he can make those he has created better than they now are.[81]

On the occasion of these remarks of Peter Lombard it was usual for his medieval commentators to discuss problems concerning God's power to create, the range of his creative power, his freedom to create or not create, and the possibility of his making

80. This section has been taken from my article, "Ockham on the Possibility of a Better World," *Mediaeval Studies* 38 (1976): 291–312; repr. *Being and Knowing* (Toronto, 1990), pp. 383–402.

81. Peter Lombard, *Sententiae* 1.44.1 (Grottaferrata ed. 1: 304). The Lombard refers to certain *scrutatores* who claimed that God cannot make something better than he has made it, for if he could and did not he would be envious and not supremely good. The editor notes (p. 303) this as a reference to Abelard. See Abelard, *Theologia christiana* 5 (PL 178: 1326B–1327B); *Theologia "scholarium"* 3.5 (PL 178: 1093D–1094C). Abelard (ibid.) refers to Augustine, *De diversis quaestionibus octoginta tribus* 50 (CCL 44A: 77).

something that he has not made nor will make. Ockham follows this tradition when he raises several questions à propos of the divine power, among them: Can God make a world better than the one he has made?[82]

Before answering this question, Ockham clarifies the meaning of the terms "world" and "better." A world can be understood in two senses: (1) as the total aggregate of all creatures, whether substances or accidents, or (2) as a whole composed of a multitude of things contained under one body and the body containing them. In the second sense "world" can be taken precisely for its substantial parts or indifferently for everything contained in it. Ockham specifies that in the present discussion he is using the term "world" to mean "precisely one universe composed as it were of parts that are substances, not as including accidents with substance."[83]

Ockham's second description of this world is close to that of Richard of Middleton, which runs as follows: "I call the universe the collection of creatures contained within one surface – which is contained by no other surface within the universe – including also the surface that contains these creatures."[84] Richard of Middleton's specification that the surface of the sphere containing the universe is not itself contained within the surface of another sphere

82. *Ord.* 1.44.un. (*OTh* 4: 650–661). Ockham previously raised the question: "Can God make something he has not made nor will make?" (ibid. 43.1 [*OTh* 4: 622–640]).

83. "Sed in ista quaestione accipiendus est mundus praecise pro uno universo quasi composito ex partibus quae sunt substantiae, et non secundum quod includit accidentia cum substantia" (*Ord.* 1.44.un. [*OTh* 4: 651.14–17]). This description fits in well with Ockham's doctrine of a collective whole. A world has the same kind of unity as a science, city, nation, army, kingdom, or university. They are not one in the strict or proper sense, which applies only to individuals, since they have only a collective unity: see *Expos. in Phys.* prol. (*OPh* 4: 7.23–29); *Quodl.* 7.8 (*OTh* 9: 728.56–66); *Ord.* 1.24.1 (*OTh* 4: 76.17–77.17).

84. "Respondeo, vocando universum universitatem creaturarum infra unam superficiem contentarum, quae a nulla alia superficie continetur infra illam universitatem, comprehendendo etiam superficiem continentem" (Richard of Middleton, *Super quatros libros Sententiarum* 1.44.4 [Brescia, 1591; repr. Frankfurt, 1963], 1: 392).

rules out the hypothesis that our universe might be incased in another; that beyond the outermost sphere that limits our world there might be another world contained in another sphere far distant from that which encircles our own. The hypothesis of several worlds, one included in another like layers of an onion, was raised and rejected by William of Auvergne on the ground that the outermost sphere of the second world, enveloping and containing the heavens of that world, would also contain the outermost sphere of our world, and thus it would constitute but one world. The supposed two worlds would be contiguous, one enveloped in the other, with no void separating them, for Aristotle has proved convincingly that there is no void in nature.[85]

Against this background, Ockham's second definition of a world as "a whole composed of a multitude of things contained under one body and the body containing them" becomes clearer. The containing body is the outermost sphere of the universe that envelops and contains the heavens and the earth. Properly speaking, the parts included in the universe are its substances, not its accidental properties. There are qualities in the universe really distinct from substances, but these accidents are not contained in the universe as principal parts but as modifications of substances.

What is meant by asking whether God can create a "better" world? One thing can be better than another essentially or accidentally. A world essentially or substantially better than the present one would be different from it not only in number but in species; that is, it would contain individuals of more perfect species than those in our present world. A world accidentally better would contain individuals of the same species as ours but with an increased goodness.[86]

Having clarified the terms of the question, Ockham proceeds to answer it. He holds as possible that God can produce another world substantially or essentially better than ours. He sees no

85. William of Auvergne, *De universo*, primae partis principalis, pars 1, c. 13 (Paris, 1674), 1: 607.

86. *Ord.* 1.44.un. (*OTh* 4: 651.18–652.2).

compelling reason why God cannot create substances more perfect in species than any he has created, and this to infinity. Can he not increase the perfection of a quality, such as grace, without limit? Why can he not increase the goodness of individuals to the point where they constitute a new and better species? Even if one maintains that there is a limit to the perfection of a creature, so that there is a most perfect creatable substance, it can still be held as probably true that God can create another world distinct in species from our own, and hence substantially better than it.

To confirm this, Ockham appeals to both Augustine and Peter Lombard. According to Augustine, God could have made a human being who could neither sin nor will to sin, and if he did there can be no doubt that the person would be better than we are. Ockham, for his part, contends that the person would not only be better but belong to a different and higher human species. The individuals in our human species are able to sin and will to sin. This he considers to be a defining property of our species, belonging formally to all its members. If there are individuals who cannot sin, they must belong to an ultimate species (*infima species*) different from our own. It follows that if God created such individuals, the world in which they lived would belong to a different and better species than our own.[87]

An objection that readily occurs to a Christian is that Christ could not sin, and yet he belonged to the same human *infima species* as we who can sin. Ockham replies that Christ's incapacity to sin was due to the fact that he possessed the divine nature. Sin is incompatible with the divine Word; it is not incompatible with the human nature united to the Word. If Christ's human nature were separated from the Word, it could sin.[88]

Ockham's hypothesis of a human nature specifically different from our own runs counter to the usual notion of man as an ultimate species. How can there be a human species different from the

87. Ibid. (*OTh* 4: 652.3–653.4).
88. Ibid. (*OTh* 4: 653.5–9).

one we know? Ockham hopes to show the possibility by clarifying the meaning of the term "man." In one sense it means a composite of a body and an intellectual nature. Taken in this broad sense, man does not constitute a *species specialissima* or *infima species*. In this meaning of the term there could be a man who is by nature incapable of sinning, but he would not belong to the same species as the man who can sin. In another sense "man" means a composite of a body and an intellectual soul *such as we have*. Thus understood, man is an *infima species*, and this human species would not contain the hypothetical man who is incapable of sinning.[89]

It is at least probable, then, that God could create another world better than the present one and specifically different from it. This better world would contain things of different species, and a greater number of species, than our world. God could also create a better world that is only numerically different from ours. Nothing prevents him from creating an infinite number of individuals of the same species and nature as those presently existing; nor is he restricted to creating them within the confines of our world. He could produce them outside of it and form another world from them, just as he has formed our world from the things he has created.[90]

The hypothesis of a plurality of worlds was not new in Ockham's day; it was debated throughout the thirteenth century in the wake of the translation of Aristotle's works into Latin. The scholastics could then read his arguments that there can be only one world. If there were a number of worlds, Aristotle reasoned, they would contain elements of the same nature as ours; otherwise they would be worlds in name only. They would be equivocally the same as our world. Now, each of the four elements has its proper place. For example, earth is at the center and fire at the circumference of our world. When they are removed from these places they naturally tend to return to them: earth naturally moves downward to the center and fire upward to the circumference. On

89. *Ord.* 1.44.un. (*OTh* 4: 653.10–654.8).
90. Ibid. (*OTh* 4: 655.5–12).

the supposition of a plurality of worlds, the particles of earth in the worlds outside our own would naturally move to our center, and their fire would move to our circumference. If they naturally moved away from the center and circumference of our world, they would act contrary to their nature. Hence there cannot be many worlds.[91]

The possibility remains that there are many worlds, each with its own center and circumference. On this hypothesis, the earth in each of them would always move to the center and fire to the circumference, but to numerically different centers and circumferences. Individual particles of the same species would then naturally move to the same place in species but not in number. But Aristotle rejected this possibility on the ground that there would be no reason why, in our own world, different particles of earth would move to numerically different centers – which is contrary to the evidence of the senses. So there can be only one center to which all particles of earth naturally move, and only one circumference to which all particles of fire naturally move. It follows that there can be only one world.[92]

Aristotle also reasoned that there cannot be many worlds because our own heaven contains all the available material, with none left over for other worlds. The form or nature expressed by the word "world" could be realized in many particular worlds, as the form of circle can exist in many particular bronze or gold circles. But he ruled out this possibility because the world of our experience exhausts all matter. The case would be the same if one human being were created containing all flesh and bones; there would be none left for other humans.[93]

In the first half of the thirteenth century there were Christian thinkers who did not find these arguments convincing. Better informed than Aristotle through revelation, they believed that God created the world from nothing, and that his infinite creative power has not been exhausted by the production of a single world.

91. *Ord.* 1.44.un. (*OTh* 4: 655.19–656.11); cf. Aristotle, *De caelo* 1.8, 276a18–b22.
92. Ibid. (*OTh* 4: 656.12–18); cf. Aristotle, ibid. 277a1–13.
93. Ibid. (*OTh* 4: 656.19–21); cf. Aristotle, ibid. 277b26–278b9.

Writing about 1230, Michael Scot reported: "There are some who pretend that God, being omnipotent, had the power and is still able to create, over and above this world, another world, or several other worlds, or even an infinity of worlds, composing these worlds either of elements of the same species or nature as those that form this one, or from different elements." Michael Scot himself did not share this opinion. While acknowledging that God is all-powerful, he was too good an Aristotelian to think that in fact there could be many worlds. "God can do this," he wrote, "but nature cannot bear it, as Aristotle says in *De caelo et mundo*, book 1, chapter 3 [8]. It follows from the very nature of the world, from its proximate and essential causes, that a plurality of worlds is impossible. Nevertheless, God could do this if he wanted."[94] In other words, we must distinguish between the power of God taken absolutely and his power relative to the subject of his operation. Absolutely speaking, he can do many things that can never be realized because nature is not amenable to them. This is the case with the creation of plural worlds.

Michael Scot's ingenious method of harmonizing Aristotle and the Christian faith was followed by others in the thirteenth century. William of Auvergne never doubted the omnipotence of God and yet, like Aristotle, he could not conceive of a plurality of universes. He pointed out that the word "universe" itself contains the notion of oneness: a *universitas* is "a multitude gathered into a unity" (*in unum versa multitudo*). A "universe" of colors is the union of all colors under one genus. Similarly, there is a universe of beings all united by their sharing in the nature of being. Outside this universe there can be nothing. The oneness of the universe is also proved by the oneness of its divine source.[95]

---

94. Michael Scot, *Super auctore Spherae* (Venice, 1518), f. 105b. See Pierre Duhem, *Études sur Léonard de Vinci* (Paris, 1906–1913), 2: 73–74, and 57–96, 408–423 for the history of the problem of plural worlds.

95. William of Auvergne, *De universo*, primae partis principalis, pars 1, c. 11 (Paris ed. 1: 605C).

In a similar vein, Aquinas argued that the universe is one by its very nature. It has a unity that consists in the order of all its parts to each other and to its creator. Since the universe has one order, all creatures belong to one universe.[96] The appeal to the omnipotence of God did not shake Thomas' conviction of the oneness of the universe, for God did not create it with sheer power but with wisdom, and wisdom demands that everything have one order and be directed to one end. Aquinas was also sympathetic to Aristotle's argument that the present universe exhausts all the available material, and that the elements, no matter how widely dispersed, naturally tend to one place.[97] Of course, God could make the present universe better by creating many other species or by ameliorating all its parts. If this added to the universe's essential goodness, the result would be a different universe essentially and specifically better than ours; but in any case there would be but one universe.[98]

To the Franciscan Richard of Middleton this conceded too much to Aristotelianism and failed to give proper weight to the divine omnipotence. God could have produced another universe besides the present one, and he has the power to do so if he wishes. Nothing prevents this on his part, for he can do everything that is not contradictory, and there is no contradiction in there being many worlds. No finite universe exhausts the infinite creative power of God. Neither does anything on the side of the universe stand in the way of a plurality. Matter does not, for it has been created out of nothing; it was not created from a preexistent stuff that would limit the scope of the divine action. Moreover, there is no receptacle, such as space, that receives the whole universe and makes it one. Neither do the special natures of the

96. *ST* 1.47.3.

97. Ibid. ad 3. See *Commentaria in librum De caelo et mundo* 1.19 (Leonine ed. 3: 78).

98. *In Sent.* 1.44.1.2 (ed. Mandonnet–Moos 1: 1019). God has the power to create things he has not actually created (*De pot.* 1.5; *ST* 1.25.5). Any world God created would be the best in relation to his goodness and wisdom; in short, there is no best of all possible worlds (*De pot.* 1.5 ad 15). See Blanchette, *Perfection of the Universe*, pp. 218–221.

four elements prevent a plurality of worlds. God could create other worlds with elements of the same nature as ours. In these worlds earth would naturally move to the center and rest there, just as it does in our world. In the hypothesis of many worlds, each with its own center, earth would naturally tend to be at rest in whichever center it was located, and it would not naturally tend to move to the center of another world.[99]

Richard of Middleton felt he was on sure ground, for in 1277 Stephen Tempier, the Bishop of Paris (and also a master of theology, as Richard pointedly adds), condemned the proposition that God could not produce many worlds.[100] And this is not all God could do. If he has infinite power, he could give the outermost sphere of the heavens, which according to the Aristotelians has only circular movement, a lateral one as well. He could also create a universe which, though not actually infinite or infinitely divided, could be expanded or divided beyond any given limit. Writing in an age whose cosmology was shaped by Aristotle, this Franciscan theologian was raising the possibility of viewing the universe differently from Aristotle and his commentators.

Ockham's speculation about the possibility of other worlds shows the same effort to free Christian thought from the shackles of Aristotelianism. Like Richard of Middleton, he does not consider Aristotle's arguments for the oneness of the world demonstrative. Elements of the same species need not move to numerically the same place; there could be several worlds, each with its own center and circumference to which the elements would naturally tend if displaced from them. Ockham argues for this possibility not only a priori, like Richard of Middleton, but also from experience. If two fires were lighted in different places on the earth, say in Oxford and Paris, they would naturally move upward to the circumference of the heavens, but not to numerically the same place.

99. Richard of Middleton, *Super quatuor libros Sententiarum* 1.44.4 (Brescia ed. 1: 392).

100. Tempier condemned the proposition: "Quod prima causa non posset plures mundos facere" (*Chartularium universitatis parisiensis* [ed. Denifle–Chatelain 1: 543, n. 473]).

Only if the fire in Oxford were moved to the same spot as the fire in Paris, will it move to the same place as the fire in Paris. Similarly, if the earth of another world were placed in ours, it would by its nature tend to the center of our world; but within the heavens of another world the earth would naturally tend to rest at its center. The reason why particles of earth in the two worlds would move to numerically different centers is not only that these particles are different in number, but also that they are in different situations in their respective heavens. The case is similar to the two fires that would move to different places on the circumference of our universe because of their different situations in this universe.[101]

It is true that the outermost sphere or circumference of our world is one continuous body and hence one in number; but it does not follow that two fires in different places on earth tend upward to numerically the same place. In fact, they move to numerically different parts of the circumference. By the same token, different particles of earth within the confines of distinct worlds could move to different centers.[102]

But if a particle of earth in another world naturally moves to the center of that world, would it not naturally move away from the center of our world? If it moved to the center of our world, its motion would be violent and not natural, which is clearly false, because in our experience earth moves naturally to the center of our world. Ockham grants that, on the hypothesis of another world, earth moving toward its center would naturally move away from the center of our world, but he insists that this behavior of the earth would not be *per se* but *per accidens*, owing to the situation of the particle of earth within the boundary of its own world. If placed between the center and circumference of the world, fire naturally tends upward to the circumference, but it moves away from the opposite side of the circumference. It recedes from the opposite side *per accidens*, owing to its situation in the world. If the same fire were located between the center and *that* part of the circumference, it would naturally move upward to it.

---

101. *Ord.* 1.44.un. (*OTh* 4: 657.2–658.5).
102. Ibid. (*OTh* 4: 658.6–659.15).

Thus not only the nature of the elements but also their situation in a world must be taken into account when explaining their motion. A particle of earth can naturally move downward to the center of one world and *per accidens*, owing to its position in that world, move away from the center of another world.[103]

Accordingly the nature of the elements and their natural movements place no barrier to a plurality of worlds. Neither does the limited amount of matter available for their production. Granted that the present world exhausts all the matter God has created, it does not contain all he can create. An omnipotent God is not restricted to produce a certain amount of matter; he can always create more, both celestial and terrestrial, and from it form other worlds like, or better than, our own.[104]

Can God create other worlds essentially better than ours without limit, or would he finally reach a best of all possible worlds? Ockham does not presume to settle this question but is content to remark that the answer depends on whether or not there is a limit to the degree of perfection God can give to individuals in other species. Those who say there is no limit would conclude that there is no best possible world; those who affirm a limit would conclude the opposite. However this may be, there is no doubt that God can create a world essentially and accidentally more perfect than the present one.[105]

Ockham's treatment of the possibility of a better world is a good illustration of his complex relationship to Aristotelianism. He has no quarrel with Aristotle as far as the actual constitution of the world is concerned. He does not suggest that the world is different from Aristotle's, or that in fact there are other worlds besides the one described by him. What interests Ockham is not so much the scientific question of the actual structure of the world as the theological issue of what worlds are possible, given the absolute power of God. Lacking the Christian faith, Aristotle was ignorant of the

103. *Ord.* 1.44.un. (*OTh* 4: 658.10–18, 659.16–660.7).
104. Ibid. (*OTh* 4: 660.8–11).
105. Ibid. (*OTh* 4: 660.12–661.7).

divine freedom and omnipotence. He did not realize that the present world is governed by God's *potentia ordinata*, but that there are other and better worlds that come under his *potentia absoluta*.[106] Hence he took the limitations of the present world to be those of all possible worlds. He also failed to see that his arguments for the oneness of the world are not demonstrative but only probable, leaving open the possibility of other worlds better than our own.

The question remains why Ockham, unlike other Christian theologians, did not consider the Aristotelian arguments for the oneness of the world truly demonstrative. As we have seen, Michael Scot believed as firmly as Ockham that God has the power to create other worlds, but he denied the possibility of plural worlds because "nature cannot bear it." A plurality of worlds is impossible, in his view, not because of any limitation on the side of God but because of the nature of the world.

This suggests that Ockham's conception of nature was not Aristotelian; and this indeed is the case. For Aristotle, each of the four elements has a form or nature in virtue of which it naturally moves to its proper place when removed from it. Having the same nature, particular instances of each element must naturally have the same movement. As Aristotle says, "The particular instances of each form must necessarily have for their goal a place numerically one."[107] From this he deduced the oneness of the world. Its oneness follows strictly from the oneness of the forms or natures with which the elements are endowed. For Ockham, on the contrary, bodies share no forms or natures. All particles of earth or fire have been created very similar to each other, and hence their movements are also very similar; but this is not because they have the same form or nature. With the removal of natures or essences from individuals, the force of the Aristotelian argument for the oneness of the world is lost. There is no longer a strict necessity for bodies to move to one place or that there be but one world. Ockham

---

106. For the meaning of these terms see above, pp. 257–265.
107. Aristotle, *De caelo* 1.8, 276b32.

introduces the notion of the "situation" (*conditio*) of the elements, thereby profoundly modifying the Aristotelian conception of their natural movement. Because they are differently situated in their respective worlds, heavy and light bodies move naturally up and down, but not to the same center or circumference. Even within the same world a light body, owing to its different situation, will naturally move upward to one place in the heavens and away from the opposite side of the heavens. We are here in the presence of a new, non-Aristotelian, conception of nature, which is the philosophical basis of Ockham's doctrine of the possibility of plural worlds. If more and better worlds are possible for him, it is because the Ockhamist nature, unlike the Aristotelian, can bear it.

From a theological perspective, Ockham's guiding principle is the freedom and omnipotence of God. Above all else, he wished to vindicate these attributes of the Christian God against the necessitarianism of the Greek and Islamic philosophers. Relying solely on natural reason, they concluded that God is not a free but necessary cause of the world, that his immediate causation does not extend to all its details, and that he is limited to producing the present world. Ockham did not think natural reason can demonstrate these philosophical tenets, but neither did he think it can prove their contrary. In his view, philosophy can at best offer persuasive arguments for the freedom of God as a creator. Lacking a truly demonstrative proof of the divine freedom, Ockham's faith alone assured him that God can produce things he has not made or will not make, and that he can create many worlds and better ones than our own.

The medieval musings about the possibility of a plurality of worlds through the divine omnipotence is a good example of how the theological imagination can have a bearing on philosophical and scientific speculations. Ockham's thoughts on the subject would not be lost to history. It has been shown that there is an historical bond between them and Leibniz' conjectures of possible worlds in the seventeenth century.[108]

---

108. See Amos Funkenstein, *Theology and the Scientific Imagination from the Middle Ages to the Seventeenth Century* (Princeton, NJ, 1986), pp. 117–201.

CHAPTER 8

Angels

A T FIRST SIGHT IT might seem that angels are not an appropriate subject for a book devoted to Ockham's philosophy. These celestial beings play a large role in the Christian and Jewish scriptures, and indeed their equivalent can be found in many religions and cultures, but it is questionable whether natural reason can prove they exist. Thomas Aquinas thought their existence is reasonable, for without them the universe would lack perfection. The order of the universe requires that between God who is infinite spirit and human beings who are a composite of matter and spirit, there be a realm of created spiritual beings.[1] Separate substances, as the angels were sometimes called in the Middle Ages, occupy an essential position in the universe and it would be incomplete without them.

Quite apart from faith, then, speculation about angels to some extent has a place in philosophy. Indeed, for philosophical reasons both ancient and medieval thinkers required the existence of immaterial or separate substances. Aristotle postulated them as necessary for the structure of the world, and he arrived at a certain number of them to explain the movements of the spheres and generation and corruption in the sublunar world. Both Avicenna and Averroes followed Aristotle in this regard, passing on the Aristotelian and Neoplatonic speculations about the separate substances to Christian medieval theologians and philosophers.

Like the fathers of the Church, the medieval masters found the angels a fascinating object of study, and with the recovery of

---

1. *ST* 1.50.1; *De spiritualibus creaturis* 5 (ed. Keeler pp. 61–71). See Oliva Blanchette, *The Perfection of the Universe according to Aquinas* (University Park, PA, 1992), pp. 27–28, 169–170, 275–280.

the works of Aristotle in the twelfth and thirteenth centuries they had new philosophical resources for understanding them. They were confronted with a host of new questions. Granted that angels exist, what is their nature or essence? Is their existence really distinct from their essence? Do they all belong to the same genus and species? How precisely do they differ in species from humans? How are they related to matter, time, and duration? Do they exist in place, and, if so, do they move from one place to another? What does it mean for them to know and will? How do they communicate with each other, with God, and with us? These and other philosophical questions about the angels aroused the curiosity of the schoolmen, and they brought to their solutions their personal philosophical views.

1 The Nature of Angels

Ockham does not offer a rational demonstration or even a persuasive proof of the existence of angels. He takes their existence as a matter of faith, and then inquires into their nature and activities. He describes angels as created spiritual beings, situated between God and humans and sharing in the properties of both. Like God, they are spiritual, intellectual substances, and absolutely simple or incomposite in their essence. In these respects they also resemble the human intellectual soul, which is a simple intellectual substance without homogeneous parts.[2] Angels differ from human souls in species, however, because they are movers and not forms of bodies. Angels can thoroughly penetrate and occupy bodies, so that they are totally present in each of their parts, as was the case of the angel Raphael who appeared to Tobias in a body. Intellectual souls are also totally present to all the parts of the bodies they animate, but unlike angels they are not movers of bodies but their substantial forms,

---

2. *Tract. de quant.* 3 (*OTh* 10: 52.11–15). Angels are *simpliciter simplex*, for their substance has no intrinsic composition, such as the composition of matter and substantial form; see *Ord.* 1.8.1 (*OTh* 3: 175.18–176.2). However, they are composed of substance and accident.

giving to human beings their specific human perfection. There can be no doubt, then, that angels are really distinct from human beings.[3]

Being completely immaterial and simple in essence, angels are not composed of matter and form.[4] This was also the view of Thomas Aquinas and Duns Scotus, though some works attributed to Scotus have been cited in favor of a possible hylomorphic composition of the angel.[5] To the early Franciscans, Alexander of Hales and Bonaventure, God alone is an absolutely simple being; the essences of both angels and human souls are composed of a spiritual form and spiritual matter. This composition was deemed necessary in order to explain change in human souls and angels. If they were pure forms, it was thought, they would be purely actual, like God, without any potentiality to change or annihilation.[6]

Aquinas avoided this conclusion by conceiving the essence of an angel as potential to its act of existing (*esse*). Though in his view the substance of an angel, unlike that of a corporeal being, is not composed of form and matter (and hence it does not have the potentiality of matter), it is not completely actual. It has the more fundamental composition of essence and existence, the former being potential to the latter. Hence angels, unlike God, are not

3. *Ord.* 1.2.2 (*OTh* 3: 368.12-19). In the book of Tobias 5-12 the angel moved a body, but he was not its form. The composite of angel and assumed body was said to eat, drink, walk, understand and judge. Ockham concludes that in a sense it can be said that, even if the intellectual soul were only the mover of the body and not its form (which is possible according to experience and human reason), we could still say that the body understands through the intellectual soul. This is because a thing can be given a name because of its instrument, as a man is called a rower because of the oars he uses. If the intellectual soul were only the instrument of the body, the body could be said to know because of the conjoined soul. See *Quodl.* 1.10; 4.15 (*OTh* 9: 63.22-37, 65.88-97; 9: 372.28-50).

4. See above, note 2.

5. For Aquinas see *ST* 1.50.2; *De spiritualibus creaturis* 1 (ed. Keeler pp. 1-19); for Scotus see Gilson, *Jean Duns Scot* (Paris, 1952), p. 392 and n1.

6. Alexander of Hales, *Summa* 2.1.2.un.2 (Quaracchi ed. 2: 136, n. 106); Bonaventure, *Sent.* 2.3.1.1.1 (*Opera omnia* 2: 91). See John F. Quinn, *The Historical Constitution of St. Bonaventure's Philosophy* (Toronto, 1973), pp. 143-145.

purely actual substances but contain a basic potentiality, which accounts for their capacity to change and to be annihilated.[7]

We have already seen Ockham's general criticism of the real distinction between essence and existence in creatures.[8] In one of his *Quodlibeta* he applies this criticism to the case of the angels, contending that the existence of an angel is nothing else than its essence. If its existence were something other than its essence, it would either be an accident of the essence or a substance added to the essence, both of which are impossible. Existence is not among the nine accidents described by Aristotle; neither is it a substance, for it is not matter or form or the composite of the two. In short, it does not fit into any of the categories recognized by Aristotle and his commentator Averroes. Perhaps the existence of angels is their relation of dependence on God? If it were, it would be nothing real, for there are no real relations distinct from the things related.[9] In any case an angel depends less on a relation of this sort than an effect on a cause, an accident on a subject, or form on matter, and God can produce all the former without the latter. Being omnipotent, he could also create an angel without a relation of dependence on him. Since he can always produce something prior by nature without something posterior, he could produce the angel's essence without existence! The conclusion is evident: there is no real distinction between the angel's essence and existence; indeed, these terms have entirely the same meaning.[10]

Because angels and intellectual souls are absolutely simple or incomposite substances, they admit of no intrinsic or essential distinctions, but only those that are extrinsic and accidental.[11]

---

7. *ST* 1.50.2, Resp. and ad 3; *SCG* 2. 52–54.
8. See above, pp. 60–61.
9. For Ockham's doctrine of relation see above, pp. 47–53.
10. *Quodl.* 11.7 (*OTh* 9: 141–145).
11. "Ad argumentum principale patet quod [nec] in anima nec in creatura rationali pure spirituali est distinctio realis intrinseca et essentialis; est tamen ibi distinctio extrinseca et accidentalis" (*Ord.* 1.3.10 [*OTh* 2: 568.12–15]). When completing the *Ordinatio*, Ockham added *pure spirituali* to make it clear that he meant angels and not humans.

The substance of an angel is really distinct from its acts of know-ing and loving, but these are accidents (more specifically, qualities) of its substance. Hence they do not introduce any distinction with-in the angel's essence or substance. As for the angel's powers, such as knowing, willing, remembering, these are really identical with the angelic substance and with each other. An intellectual soul is likewise impervious to any intrinsic or essential distinction. Distinc-tions apply to it, however, in its extrinsic and accidental relations to the body it animates and to its manifold activities.

We have seen that according to Ockham every reality (*res*) is an individual, one in number and undivided in itself. Intellectual souls and angels are the most perfect created individuals. Each is absolutely simple or incomposite (*simpliciter simplex*) in its essence or substance. As such, there is no place in it for an intrinsic or essential distinction. The only distinction it allows is one that is extrinsic and accidental to its substance, such as that between its substance and the matter it can move or its accidental qualities. By this criterion the substance of an angel is more simple than that of an intellectual soul, for the soul is the substantial form of a body, whereas an angel is a substance independent of matter. Thus, even though both soul and angel are like God in their simplicity, the angel is more simple than the soul and consequently closer to him.

Owing to their simplicity angels do not have a proper defini-tion. Every definition in the strict sense presupposes parts in the thing defined. If the definition is quidditative, expressing what a thing is (*quid est*), the thing is composed of essential parts. An example is the definition of man as "a substance composed of a body and intellectual soul," in which "body" and "intellectual soul" express man's essential parts. The definition of man as "a rational animal" also expresses these parts but in a different way. If the definition is nominal, indicating the meaning of a name (*quid nominis*), parts are also implied; for example, the nominal definition of "white" (*album*) as "something having whiteness."

Unlike creatures composed of matter and form, angels do not belong to a genus divided by positive essential differences, as the genus "animal" is divided by the essential differences "sensitive" and "rational." Angels or Intelligences, however, do admit of a definition expressing their genus along with a negative difference; for instance, an angel can by defined as "an immaterial substance." Neither do angels have a strict nominal definition. This is because nominal definitions properly apply to connotative and relative terms like "white" and "father," and not to an absolute term like "angel." But we can give nominal descriptions of angels, such as "an intellectual and incorruptible substance," or "a simple substance, not composed of anything."[12]

In these descriptions substance is given as the genus of angels. It is problematic, however, whether absolutely simple beings like God and angels can be in a genus. It is also a good question whether angels are in the same species, or whether each angel is a species of its own. Ockham gives the views of Aquinas and Scotus on these subjects, finds them wanting, then offers his own opinions as more reasonable than those of his predecessors.

According to Aquinas anything properly in a genus cannot be absolutely simple or incomplex but must be composed of really distinct principles, one of which is related to the other as potency to act. Thus material things can be in a genus because they are composed of matter and form, matter being potential to form, which is an actual principle. The genus of a material thing is derived from its matter and its specific difference from its form.[13] For example, in the species "man" the genus "animal" is taken from his sensitive nature, understood concretely, for anything is called an animal that has a nature capable of sensation. The specific difference "rational" is taken from his intellectual nature, for what is rational has a nature capable of reasoning. Moreover, these two natures are not on the same footing: the

---

12. *Quodl.* 5.19; *Ord.* 1.8.3 (*OTh* 9: 554.22–48; 3: 207.10–214.18). For the notion of definition see above, pp. 90–93.

13. *ST* 1.50.2.ad 1, cited by Ockham, *Ord.* 1.8.1 (*OTh* 3: 159.3–14). Aquinas often relates genus to matter and difference to form: see *De ente et essentia* 2 (Leonine ed. 43: 372); *In Metaph.* 5.22 (ed. Cathala–Spiazzi, n. 1123).

intellectual nature, on which man's difference is based, is related to the sensitive nature, on which his genus is based, as act to potency. Hence, in the last analysis it is owing to the real distinction of matter and form in material things, related as potency to act, that they are in one genus.[14]

Since angels are purely spiritual creatures, Aquinas cannot appeal to the distinction of matter and form to explain how they can be in a genus. Like all creatures, however, the essence of an angel is really distinct from his existence (*esse*), the essence being related to the existence as potency to act. This distinction enables all creatures – including angels – to be in a genus, for they can all share in the essence of the genus while differing in their existence. Thus man and horse are in the same genus of animal, but human existence is not the same as equine existence. So too, all angels can share in the generic essence of angel, while each angel has his own existence.[15]

Ockham does not disagree with Aquinas' conclusion that angels are in a genus, but he finds his arguments supporting it worthless. Aquinas argues that, although an angel is not composed of matter and form, it can still be in a genus because it is composed of essence and existence. But Ockham, here as elsewhere, disputes the validity of a real distinction of essence and existence. If an angel is composed of essence and existence, Ockham asks in what genus is his existence? It must be either in the genus of substance or accident. If it is in the genus of accident, a substance would differ *as a substance* by reason of an accident, which is clearly false. If existence were in the genus of substance, it would either be a species or individual or reducible to them, which Aquinas himself denies. In opposition to Thomas, Ockham argues as usual that the only real distinction in a substance composed of

14. *ST* 1.3.5, cited by Ockham, *Ord.* 1.8.1 (*OTh* 3: 157.3–11).

15. *ST* ibid. Angels are not mentioned in the argument, which aims at proving that God is not in a genus. Elsewhere Aquinas uses the distinction between essence and existence to explain how separate substances, or angels, can have a genus, species, and difference (*De ente et essentia* 5 [Leonine ed. 43: 378.44–379.84]).

several principles is the distinction between matter and form:

> Whenever something substantially one (*per se unum*) is composed of principles of different natures, one of them is form and the other matter. Hence if essence and existence (*esse*) are really distinct in an angel, the essence must truly be act and existence potency or vice versa. Consequently one will truly be matter and the other form.[16]

Reading these lines we are aware how far Ockham was from grasping Aquinas' notion of the real distinction between essence and *esse* in all created beings. Like so many of his contemporaries, Ockham accepted the Aristotelian distinction between matter and form (now conceived in a non-Aristotelian manner as two *things*) but not the Thomist distinction between essence and *esse* as two principles within a created being.

Besides disagreeing with Aquinas on this metaphysical topic, Ockham finds him contradicting himself in explaining how angels can be in a genus. Quoting from the *Summa theologiae*, he shows that Aquinas conceived of form and matter in material things as distinct, each having its own function: form determines a thing to have a special degree of being (for example, canine or human); matter, which is other than form, is that which is determined to this degree. The thing's genus is taken from matter and its specific difference from form. But this is not the case with immaterial beings like angels, who are not composed of matter and form. In them, that which determines and that which is determined are

16. "Tunc arguo: quandocumque aliquid per se unum componitur ex aliquibus principiis alterius et alterius rationis, unum illorum est forma et aliud materia. Igitur si essentia et esse in angelo distinguuntur realiter, oportet quod essentia sit vere actus et esse potentia vel e converso. Et per consequens unum erit vere materia et aliud forma" (*Ord.* 1.8.1 [*OTh* 3: 160.21–161.2]). In his polemic against Aquinas, Ockham argues that if two angels differed in their specific essences they would also differ in the specific existences, for "a distinct essence has a distinct *esse*, and a distinct essence corresponds to a distinct *esse*." He notes that Augustine says that the word *esse* comes from *essentia* ("ab essentia dicitur esse"); hence angels proportionately agree and differ in their essences and existences: see ibid. (*OTh* 3: 164.17–165.3); Augustine, *De Trinitate* 7.4 (CCL 50: 260.146–147, n. 9).

identical. Consequently their genus and specific difference are not taken from two different items (*secundum aliud et aliud*) but from one and the same reality. This is possible because we can conceive the reality in different ways: either vaguely and indeterminately, and then we conceive it as being in a genus, or definitely and determinately, and then we conceive it as a specific difference.[17]

This shows that according to Aquinas there are not two really distinct factors or principles in an angel corresponding to its genus and specific difference. Notwithstanding their absolute simplicity, angels can be in a genus when the mind conceives them vaguely or indeterminately.[18] But Aquinas seems to contradict himself when he said above that in the species "man" the genus "animal" is based on his sensitive nature and his specific difference "rational" on his intellectual nature, and what is more, that the sensitive nature is potential to the intellectual nature. This seems to imply a real distinction between these natures, which Aquinas does not admit. In his view, a human person has only one substantial nature with one substantial form, namely the rational soul.[19]

In behalf of Aquinas, it must be pointed out that the contradiction Ockham finds in his two accounts of genus is not one of doctrine but of mode of expression. When Aquinas says that the genus "animal" is derived from man's sensitive nature, he adds that this is taking sensitive nature concretely (*per modum concretionis*) – a qualification Ockham fails to take into account. In Thomistic language, to understand something concretely, as opposed to abstractly, is to take it in union with something else.[20] In the pre-

---

17. *ST* 1.50.2, ad 1, cited by Ockham, *Ord.* 1.8.1 (*OTh* 3: 159.3–14).

18. *Ord.* 1.8.1 (*OTh* 3: 158.21–159.2, 159.15–17); see Aquinas, *ST* 1.13.12.

19. Ibid. (*OTh* 3: 162.22–163.4). Ockham probably refers to *ST* 1.76.4, 76.6. ad 1.

20. "Sed unitio et concretio est diversorum in unum reductorum" (*ST* 1.60.3, obj. 2). Concretion (*concretio*) is more than simple unity; it is a union that makes something to be one absolutely (*simpliciter*): see Aquinas, *In Sent.* 3.27.1.1. ad 5 (ed. Mandonnet–Moos 3: 858). It is "a union where the elements exist together as one and exercise one act of being" (Robert W. Schmidt, *The Domain of Logic according to Saint Thomas Aquinas* [The Hague, 1966], p. 211).

sent case, Aquinas takes man's sensitive nature as united to his intellectual nature, with which it is really identical. As he explains elsewhere, the human person has only one substantial form – the intellectual soul – which virtually contains the sensitive soul.[21] The passage in question, then, does not mean that the sensitive and intellectual natures in the human person are really distinct, or that they are really related as potency to act. Their relation cannot be real but only conceptual, that is, the relation between the concepts of the genus and specific difference.[22]

If this interpretation is correct, Aquinas was consistent in holding that an angel's genus and specific difference are not taken from really distinct factors or principles in the angels, but from different ways that the mind considers their simple and incomplex essence. Considering it indeterminately, the mind forms the generic notion of an angel, such as "intellectual substance"; considering it determinately, it forms the notion of the angelic specific difference (which in fact is unknown). Consequently the distinction between the angel's genus and specific difference does not rest on a real distinction in the angel's essence but on a distinction made by the mind (*distinctio rationis*).[23]

This conclusion is tenable because Aquinas believed that the mind can know a simple reality or being in different ways or from different perspectives and thus form different concepts of it. In short, he accepted a distinction of reason with a foundation in reality. But this goes counter to one of Ockham's most cherished

21. *ST* 1.76.4, 1.76.6 ad 1.

22. Ockham comments that it is meaningless to speak of potency and act as related logically (*Ord.* 1.8.1 [*OTh* 3: 163.5–16]). In the same place he recognizes that for Aquinas the human sensory and intellectual natures are not really distinct. He insists, however, that this is implied by Aquinas' saying they are related as potency to act, so that he contradicts himself.

23. According to Aquinas, angels are like one another in being spiritual substances, but they differ in their degree of perfection, some having more act and less potentiality than others, and hence being closer to God, who is pure act. "Their genus, then, is derived from what follows upon their immateriality, as for example intellectuality, or something of this sort. Their difference, which in fact is unknown to us, is derived from what follows upon their degree of perfection" (*De ente et essentia* 5 [Leonine ed. 43: 379]).

principles: a distinction in simple concepts (*rationes*) can have no foundation in one and the same thing.[24] We have seen that in his view the different absolute concepts predicable of God have exactly the same meaning unless they are related to really distinct perfections of creatures.[25] Similarly, the distinction between the concepts of a thing's genus and specific difference cannot be based on the thing itself, but on the thing's really distinct parts.

Can the genus and difference be based on two formally distinct realities in the species, as Duns Scotus thought? The Subtle Doctor held that in every species there are two realities, from one of which the genus is taken and from the other the difference. In his words, quoted by Ockham, "the genus is taken from a reality that in itself is potential to the reality from which the difference is taken."[26] This is in accord with Scotus' doctrine of the formal distinction of several realities within one thing (*res*) – a doctrine we have already seen disputed by Ockham.[27] It is absolutely false, he contends, to say the genus is taken from one reality in a thing and the difference from another, for some individuals [for example, angels] are absolutely simple, and consequently they do not include two realities of this sort (*aliquod individuum est simpliciter simplex, igitur non includit tales duas realitates*). *A fortiori* species do not include two different realities of this kind.[28]

If a thing's specific or essential difference is not taken from an intrinsic reality formally distinct from the genus, as Scotus believed, what is its origin? One thing can be accidentally different from another, for example by its color. But if it is essentially different, the thing must be composite in its essence. This is the case with everything composed of matter and form. The genus is

24. See above, p. 89. "Ideo dico quod nulla res nec a se ipsa nec a quacumque alia potest distingui vel esse eadem secundum rationem" (*Ord.* 1.2.3 [*OTh* 2: 75.9–11]).

25. See above pp. 199–200.

26. Scotus, *Ord.* 1.8.1.3 (Vatican ed. 4: 200, n. 103), cited by Ockham, *Ord.* 1.8.1 (*OTh* 3: 166.23–167.1).

27. See above, pp. 73–77.

28. *Ord.* 1.8.1 (*OTh* 3: 169.14–22).

not taken from either of these but from the whole human essence or reality: *genus importat totam rem*. Thus if one asks "What is a man?," it can be replied simply and essentially, "Man is an animal." Man's essential difference "rational," however, is taken from a part of him, namely his intellectual soul. To say that man is rational is not to say what he is (*quid est*) but of what sort he is (*qualis est homo*). Thus, the species or definition of man, "rational animal," contains two parts: the genus "animal" signifying the whole reality of man and the specific difference "rational" denoting a part of him, namely his rationality or rational soul.[29] This necessity of parts to account for the distinction of genus and difference is in accord with Ockham's basic notion that if there is a distinction in concepts, it is owing to some distinction in reality.[30]

Turning to angels, Ockham describes them as absolutely simple beings in the genus of substance; but because of their absolute simplicity they cannot have positive specific differences which would denote a part of their reality. Their differences are negative or privative; they are called, for example, immaterial substances, or substances lacking the composition of matter and form. As a consequence, they do not have a proper definition in terms of genus and specific difference, though they can be defined by an accidental difference, for instance by the office with which God has entrusted them.[31]

Are all angels in one species, or does each angel constitute a species of its own? This question was warmly debated by thirteenth-century theologians without arriving at any consensus.

---

29. *Ord.* 1.8.4 (*OTh* 3: 221–228). It was not Aristotle's intention that the genus is taken from matter any more than from form, but that it expresses the whole reality of the individual. Rather, he meant that the genus and difference combine to make up a definition convertible with the species, and that the definition expresses explicitly what the species does implicitly. See *Expos. in Praedicab.* 3 (*OPh* 2: 74.116–131); cf. ibid. 1 (*OPh* 2: 22.72–100).

30. "Consequentia patet, quia ex quo conceptus est quasi similitudo rei, non potest esse distinctio in conceptibus nisi propter aliquam distinctionem a parte rei" (*Ord.* 1.8.3 [*OTh* 3: 204.13–16]).

31. Ibid. (*OTh* 3: 208.21–210.2, 213.15–214.10); *Expos. in Praedicab.* 3 (*OPh* 2: 69.19–31).

Bonaventure argued that angels are not exempt from the composition of matter and form, though their matter is spiritual rather than corporeal. Since they have matter of a sort in their constitution, it can account for the individualization of the form, with the consequence that angels can be many in number but one in species.[32] Aquinas was of another opinion. Contending that angels are not constituted of matter and form but are pure created forms, he concluded that they cannot be individuated by matter. Hence there cannot be several angels in the same species, but each angel constitutes as it were a species of its own.[33]

Scotus approached the question with his own conception of the cause of individuation. In his view a common nature or essence is rendered individual, not by matter but by the added reality of a "thisness" (*haecceitas*) which renders the nature "this" individual in the species.[34] Like all other essences, (with the exception of the divine essence, which is communicable to the divine Persons while being one in number) that of an angel is not individual of itself but communicable to many individuals. This is the case even with the human soul which, like an angel, is a pure form, but unlike an angel has a natural inclination to inform and animate a body. As pure forms, human souls and angels are indeterminate and common essences which can always be rendered individual by a principle of individuation (that is, an *haecceitas*). In the doctrine of Scotus, the angelic nature can be multiplied in individual angels, just like all other creaturely natures or essences.[35] In support of his thesis Scotus invoked the authority of Stephen Tempier, Bishop

---

32. Bonaventure, *In Sent.* 2.9.un.1 (*Opera omnia* 2: 242–243). See Gilson, *The Philosophy of St, Bonaventure*, trans. Illtyd Trethowan and Frank J. Sheed (1938; Paterson, NJ, 1965), pp. 226–229. For the meaning of spiritual matter and composition in angels see Quinn, *Historical Constitution of St. Bonaventure's Philosophy*, pp. 143–159.

33. *ST* 1.50.4; *De ente et essentia* 4 (Vatican ed. 43: 376.83–88); *SCG* 2.95; *De spiritualibus creaturis* 8 (ed. Keeler pp. 87–101).

34. See above, pp. 69–70.

35. Scotus, *Ord.* 2.3.1.7 (Vatican ed. 7: 500–505, nn. 227–237); *Quodl.* 2 (Vivès ed. 25: 61–62, nn. 3–4).

of Paris, who condemned 219 propositions, among which are the
following: that because the Intelligences (or angels) do not have
matter, God could not make many in the same species; that God
cannot multiply individuals in one species without matter; that
forms can only be divided according to the division of matter.[36]

In this lively controversy, with its religious overtones, Ockham
agrees with Aquinas that angels are not composed of matter and form,
but he parts company with him on the question whether angels can
be in the same species. He reserves his sharpest criticism for Aquinas'
statement that because angels are not composed of matter and form
it is impossible for two angels to be in one species. No Christian, he
protests, should deny that God can divide the heavens into two
halves, as a creature can divide a stone or piece of wood. One half
can then be separated from the other and they will be two individuals
in the same species. If anyone claims, then, that God cannot make
two individual heavenly bodies or angels in the same species, he talks
like a pagan and not a Christian.[37] This comment is in the spirit of
Scotus, who already criticized Aquinas' doctrine as contrary to the
propositions condemned in 1277.[38]

Though Ockham, like Scotus, thought there are many angels
in one species, he understood it in his own way. For Scotus, all
angels share the common nature of angel and are individuated by

36. Scotus, *Quodl.* 2 (Vivès ed. 25: 61, n. 4), trans. Felix Alluntis and
Alan B. Wolter, in *God and Creatures* (Princeton, NJ, 1975), pp. 33–34. The
three propositions condemned in 1277 are found in *Chartularium universitatis
parisiensis* (ed. Denifle–Chatelain 1: 548, n. 81, 549, n. 96, 554, n. 191). For
the position of Godfrey of Fontaines and others in this heated debate see
Wippel, *The Metaphysical Thought of Godfrey of Fontaines* (Washington, DC, 1981),
pp. 364–369.

37. "[N]ullus christianus debet negare quin Deus possit caelum dividere
in duas medietates, ex quo est quantum et divisibile, sicut agens creatum
potest dividere lapidem vel lignum. Et per consequens una medietas potest
separari ab alia, et sic erunt duo individua eiusdem speciei. Unde ponere quod
Deus non potest facere duo individua in eadem specie in corporibus caelesti-
bus vel angelis est potius dictum pagani quam christiani" (*Rep.* 2.18 [*OTh* 5:
398.21–399.2]). See also *Sum. log.* 1.22 (*OPh* 1: 73.67–70).

38. See Gilson, *Jean Duns Scot*, p. 397 n3.

their individual differences or *haecceitates*. For Ockham, there is no angelic nature or essence common to all angels; there is only the term "angel" predicable *in quid* of all individual angels and standing for them in a proposition. An individual angel is individual of itself and essentially different from every other angel.

2 The Duration of Angels

Theologians in the high Middle Ages recognized three kinds of duration: eternity, aeviternity (*aevum*), and time, the first being proper to God, the second to angels, and the third to material things. There was little agreement, however, on the meaning of this distinction. Ockham was sharply critical of his predecessors' views on the subject, especially their notions of the duration of angels. More generally, he reinterpreted the concept of duration in all its modes – even eternity – in terms of time.

To the question: What is duration? Ockham replies: "The duration of a thing is not something added to the thing that endures. Enduring is nothing but existing while time exists."[39] Bonaventure contended that the duration of an angel is not the angel itself but a succession in the angel's states without a change or alteration in its essence; lacking a succession of states, the angel's duration would be the same as God's. But Ockham sees no grounds for this opinion; and besides, he implies that it posits entities beyond necessity. If duration were something distinct from the thing that endures and formally inhering in it, it would be a substance or accident or relation, all of which are impossible. Angels, of course, are related to God as their creator, but the relation cannot vary without some variation in the angel's essence, and this would involve a change and novelty in the angel and not a mere succession of states.[40]

---

39. "Ad hoc dico quod duratio rei non est aliqua res adveniens illi rei quae durat, sed durare non est nisi exsistere dum tempus exsistit, et duratio perpetua non est nisi exsistentia rei perpetua, hoc est semper dum tempus durat" (*Sum. phil. nat.* 4.13 [*OPh* 6: 382.76–79]).

40. *Rep.* 2.8 (*OTh* 5: 153.5–155.3). See Bonaventure, *In Sent.* 2.2.1.1.3 (*Opera omnia* 2: 62).

When we speak of the duration of an angel, we are talking of nothing but permanent things and the angel's essence. This is proved by the fact that at the first moment of the angel's creation God does not have to add any other positive thing, either absolute or relative, except for the angel's relation to God (if such a relation be granted), which is permanent. God can likewise perpetually conserve the same angel in existence without causing any new reality. Since he cannot conserve the angel without duration, it follows that duration denotes nothing positive over and above the angel's essence.

Up to now Ockham has been talking about an angel's duration in the absolute sense, and from that viewpoint he has shown that its duration is identical with its essence. But duration can also be understood connotatively, and then it implies, over and above the angel's essence, the succession with which the angel can coexist. Though the principal meaning of duration is the angel's essence, its whole meaning is contained in its connotation of succession.

What proof can be given for this statement? Ockham offers the following: If contradictory terms can be verified of something, there must be some distinction involved. Now these contradictory statements are successively verified of an angel: "The angel is conserved" and "The angel is not conserved." This is proved by the fact that in the first moment in which the angel is created it is not properly speaking conserved, for immediately after that moment it can be annihilated, and then it never was conserved. Thus in the first moment it is not said to be conserved, but later it is said to be conserved. Hence there must be something different from the angel by reason of which these contradictories are verified. This is nothing but some succession, which is not in the angel but somewhere else; and because the angel coexists with it its duration is greater or less according as the succession is greater or less. So the extent of one angel's duration is greater than another's because it coexists with a more extended succession. For example, one endures for a thousand years, another for ten years, because the first coexists with a thousand years' movement of the heavenly spheres while the second coexists with only ten years'.

Suppose there were no heavenly bodies or temporal succession. Would an angel still endure? Yes, because an angel's duration does not necessarily connote an actual succession; a potential succession suffices. If there actually were no temporal things or succession, an angel would still endure, and one angel would still endure longer than another because it coexists with a potential longer succession. In short, "The angel's duration connotes some succession, either actual or potential."[41]

Does this not eliminate the distinction between the duration of angels, which is aeviternity, and the eternity of God? Just as angels can coexist with a greater or lesser or infinite succession, so also can God, and so God's eternal duration would be nothing but his coexistence with an infinite succession.[42] One reply to this objection is that angels cannot be said to endure unless there were an actual or possible temporal succession; but even without this succession God or his eternity could still exist. Another possible answer is that the duration of angels is not simultaneously complete (*tota simul*), because it connotes a succession whose parts are not all together at the same time. This of course is also true of the duration of God. But an angel's duration, unlike God's, is not necessary, for an angel does not necessarily exist; and the angel can coexist with one part of a succession and not with another, whereas God so coexists with one part of a succession that he cannot not coexist with another part. In this sense, then, the duration of God can be called *tota simul*.

Ockham had no liking for the common expression that God is measured by eternity, angels by aeviternity, and mutable things by time.[43] Aristotle defined a measure as that by which a thing or its quantity is known, and it was his mind that time is the only measure of the quantity or extent of any duration.[44] Strictly speaking, then, we cannot say that God is measured by eternity, because he is

41. *Rep.* 2.8 (*OTh* 5: 155.5–156.15).
42. Ibid. (*OTh* 5: 156.17–157.2).
43. See, for example, Aquinas, *ST* 1.10.4–5.
44. Aristotle, *Metaph.* 10.1, 1052b20, cited in *Rep.* 2.9 (*OTh* 5: 164.10–11).

absolutely immeasurable, not even by his own essence, for a measure and what is measured must be really distinct. We can say God is measured by eternity only in the sense that we measure his duration by the whole extent of time, both actual and potential. In other words, he necessarily coexists with every part of time. Angels are also measured by time and not by aeviternity (*aevum*) – an expression Ockham sometimes dismisses as meaningless: "aevum nihil est."[45]

We would not wish for a better summary of Ockham's doctrine of duration than the one made by the anonymous Ockhamist who wrote the *De principiis theologiae*:

> In accord with the aforesaid, he [Ockham] held as a consequence that aeviternity (*aevum et aeviternitas*) is not other than the aeviternal being (*aevo et aeviterno*), nor is the duration of anything other than the thing itself. But duration, aeviternity, and eternity, and all measures of duration, are terms that signify the enduring aeviternal or eternal being by connoting motion or time and succession, either actual or potential. Hence, just as a human being is called a centenarian because he has lived for a hundred years and coexists with them, so an angel is called aeviternal because he does not coexist with the whole time possible to have been in the past. But God is said to be eternal because he cannot not coexist with time existing, or possible to have been, or possible to be in the future. So if time had no beginning in the past nor would it end in the future, God would still coexist with the whole of past time and he will coexist with all future time.[46]

45. *Rep.* 2.11 (*OTh* 5: 236.18–237.16); *Sum. phil. nat.* 4.14 (*OPh* 6: 384–386); *Quaest. in Phys.* 54 (*OPh* 6: 540–543).

46. "Secundum praedicta ponit [scil. Ockham] consequenter quod aevum et aeviternitas non sunt alia ab aevo et aeviterno, nec duratio cuiuscumque rei est alia res ab ipsa. Sed duratio, aevum et aeternitas, et omnes mensurae durationum, sunt quidam termini qui important rem durantem aeviternam vel aeternam et connotando motum sive tempus et successionem, vel actualem vel possibilem.

Unde sicut homo dicitur centenarius qui vixit per centum annos et coexsistit eis, ita angelus dicitur aeviternus quia non coexsistit toti tempori possibili fuisse in praeterito, sed quia coexsistit toti tempori futuro et possibili fore. Deus autem

Ockham's conception of the duration of an angel – like the duration of God and bodies – as a term signifying the enduring reality while connoting time and motion as their measure, is in the line of his constant effort to reduce supposed entities to names or terms. Even when he does not explicitly invoke the razor, it is generally implicit in his thought. His approach to the present subject reveals his tendency to empiricism: the term "duration" has meaning not simply as denoting an enduring reality, but as connoting the observable succession of time and movement that measures its duration. Aquinas and Scotus, being of a more metaphysical cast of mind than Ockham, viewed duration as a mode of existing. Eternity, aeviternity, and time were conceived as the modes of being respectively of God, angels, and material things. Time was the measure of the latter, but not of the substance or essence of God and angels. Their duration was measured by nothing external to them but by themselves. Aquinas, with Ockham, thought that angels' acts of knowing and willing, involving succession, are measured by time, but unlike Ockham he contended that as regards their natural being (*esse naturale*) they are measured by aeviternity.[47] Scotus, for his part, was of the opinion that angels are measured by aeviternity both in their being and actions.[48]

3 Angels in Place and Motion

Scripture gives us many examples of angels being in places and moving from one place to another. We have seen Ockham refer to the angel Raphael, who appeared to Tobias, journeyed with him from place to place, spoke, and restored his father's sight (Tob 3:16–12:16). Since an angel is a purely spiritual substance and essentially unassociated with matter, how is it possible to conceive the

---

dicitur aeternus, quia non potest non coexsistere cuicumque tempori exsistenti, vel possibili fuisse, vel possibili fore. Unde si tempus non fuisset in praeterito inceptum, nec esse terminandum in futuro, adhuc Deus toti tempori praeterito coexstitisset et futuro coexstiturus esset" (*De prin. theol.* 119 [*OPh* 7: 578–579]).

47. *ST* 1.10.5, ad 1.
48. Scotus, *Rep. Paris.* 2.2 (Vivès ed. 22: 575–576, n. 4).

localization and movement of angels? In order to throw some light on the meaning of these scriptural episodes, theologians turned to the philosophers' notions of place and motion.

It was usual at the time to distinguish between two ways of being in place: circumscriptively and definitively. We shall treat of this subject at greater length in the next chapter. For the moment it will be enough to say that something is in place circumscriptively when the whole thing is in the whole place and a part of it is in a part of the place. A thing is in a place definitively when the whole thing is in the whole place and not outside of it, and the whole thing is in every part of the place. This is how Christ is definitively in the eucharist: his whole body coexists with the whole place of the consecrated host, and the whole coexists with each part of that place. Similarly, the intellectual soul is in the whole body and in every part, though it is not there as in a place but as the body's substantial form.[49]

Now, angels through their substance cannot be present in a place circumscriptively, for they are spiritual beings and hence without parts. However, they can be in a place definitively through their substance. The angel's whole substance can be in the whole place (for example a body), and as a whole it can be in every part of that place. The substance of the angel is not only present to the place as God is present to it, but unlike God angels are somehow also surrounded and contained by the place, so that they exist in that place and not outside of it. In short, angels can be substantially in a place, but their existence is restricted to the place, so that unlike God they are not present everywhere. There is also a limitation to the way an angel's substance is present to

---

49. "Circa secundum articulum dico quod esse in loco dupliciter accipitur: circumscriptive, et definitive. Circumscriptive est aliquid in loco, cuius pars est in parte loci, et totum in toto loco. Definitive autem est, quando totum est in toto loco et non extra, et totum est in qualibet parte illius loci; quo modo corpus Christi est in loco definitive in Eucharistia, quia totum eius corpus coexistit toti loco speciei consecratae, et totum coexistit cuilibet parti illius loci" (*Quodl.* 1.4 [*OTh* 9: 25.47–54]). See also *Quodl.* 4.21 (*OTh* 9: 400.14–19).

every part of its containing body: if a part of the body were divided, the angel would not be present to still another intervening part. As a finite spirit, an angel cannot be present to the infinity of possible parts into which a body can be divided.[50]

In adopting this position Ockham takes sides in a lively current debate. Are angels in a place through their substance or only by the application of their power or action to a place? Aquinas chose the latter as the more reasonable opinion. In his view a spiritual being cannot properly be said to be contained in a place, since it lacks dimensive quantity. But it has "virtual" quantity or power, and by applying it to a certain place it may equivocally be said to be there. As God is intimately present in all things because he acts upon them, so angels can be said to be in a particular place because they apply their power to it and have some effect upon it.[51] Scotus was of another opinion, contending that angels must be present in a place by their essence prior (by a priority of nature) to their being able to act there. As God is present everywhere by his immensity, by a priority of nature, to his being there as a cause, so angels (whose power is finite and further removed from things than the divine power) must be present in a place by their essence or substance prior to their acting in it.[52]

Ockham follows Scotus' notion that an angel must be in a place by its substance, but unlike the Subtle Doctor or Aquinas he does not mention the angel's acting in that place. Some action on the part of the angel seems to be indicated, however, by Ockham's example of the sun or a candle illuminating a whole place all at once and not part by part. This illustrates how an angel as a whole is present in a place and wholly in every part.[53]

Is there a minimum size of the place in which an angel can be present? Ockham thinks there is not; for any given place is divisible into parts, and an angel can exist in one part of the place and then in

50. *Quodl.* 1.4 (*OTh* 9: 26.56–73).
51. *ST* 1.8.1; 1.52.1; *In Sent.* 1.37.3.1 (ed. Mandonnet–Moos 1: 868–872).
52. Scotus, *Rep. Paris.* 2.2 (Vivès ed. 22: 575, n. 3).
53. *Quodl.* 1.4 (*OTh* 9: 27.88–98).

a part of that part, and so on *in infinitum*. Can several angels occupy the same place? This would be impossible if angels were circumscriptively in place, but not if they were localized definitively. We have seen that by the divine power two bodies can occupy the same place. Is it not much more likely that two angels can be definitively in the same place?[54] The Pseudo-Campsall, a contemporary of Ockham, saw no reason why many spirits could not occupy the same place. Scripture tells us that a legion of devils was present in one demoniac (Mk 5:9), and if a legion, why not an infinity of infinities?[55] This gives us a medieval answer to the nonmedieval question: How many angels can dance on the point of a pin?

Granted that angels by their substances can occupy places, can they move from place to place? Ockham defines local motion as the successive coexistence in different places, without intermediate rest, of something in place. This gives us the answer to our question. It has been shown that an angel can continually exist in place, and it is clear from scripture that an angel can successively coexist in different places without resting in between. We have the word of Isaiah (6:6): "Then flew one of the seraphim to me," indicating that an angel is capable of local motion.[56]

It is easy to find a philosophical objection to this. According to Aristotle, "[W]henever a thing is in motion, part of it is at the starting-point while part is at the goal to which it is changing."[57] Since angels are indivisible spirits without parts, they do not seem to be capable of moving. To this, Ockham replies that Aristotle wrote about the only kind of mobile things he knew: bodies cir-

---

54. *Quodl.* 1.4 (*OTh* 9: 28.105–114).
55. "[S]ecundo potest sic describi: quantitas continua est illud per quod repugnat vni rei esse in eodem loco naturaliter cum altera. Ista descripcio statim patet, tamen, quia infinita – non quanta – possunt esse in eodem loco, sicut patet quia legio fuit in vno demoniaco et, qua racione legio, eadem racione infinities infinita" (Pseudo-Richard of Campsall, *Logica Campsale Anglicj* 41.05 (ed. Synan 2: 233). I am grateful to Edward Synan for drawing my attention to this passage.
56. *Quodl.* 1.5 (*OTh* 9: 29.6–30).
57. Aristotle, *Phys.* 5.6, 230b32–33 and 6.4, 234b15–17.

cumscribed in place. The truth of the Christian faith teaches that there are other beings definitively in place that can move, such as angels.[58] The very notion of motion is here at stake. For the Philosopher, motion is primarily the property of a body; it is "The fulfillment of what exists potentially, insofar as it exists potentially."[59] But this is not so for the theologian, whose definition of local motion is not limited to bodies in potency to fulfillment, but extends to pure forms such as angels. As we have seen, Ockham defines local motion as "the successive coexistence of something in place in different places without resting in between." Now this definition is verified of angels, for they are in place and they can be successively present in different places without an intermediary rest. Of course, this requires that angels first move in the intervening space before reaching their goal; they would not properly be said to move if they first occupied one place and then another, without passing through the medium.[60] However, if angels existed in a void, with nothing between their starting point and goal, they could move in the void. Ockham thinks at least God can bring this about, adding, "I do not know if this would be possible naturally."[61]

4 Angelic Knowledge

God knows everything simply by viewing his essence, and humans acquire their knowledge through a direct perception or intuition

---

58. *Quodl.* 1.5. (*OTh* 9: 34.121-125). "Nam secundum Sanctos et Doctores authenticos - et satis est de intentione Scripturae canonicae - angelus est in loco et transfertur de uno loco ad alium, quantumcumque non sit quantus sed indivisibilis, carens omnibus partibus natis distare localiter" (*Tract. de corp. Christi* 26 [*OTh* 10: 148.66-70]).

59. Aristotle, *Phys.* 3.1, 201a10.

60. *Quodl.* 1.5 (*OTh* 9: 35.139-140).

61. For Ockham, a void can be said to exist in the sense that "between two bodies there is no positive medium, between which there was a positive medium or could be a positive medium, without the local motion of those bodies." An angel can exist in a void and move through it, just like a body, at least by the divine power (*Quodl.* 1.8 [*OTh* 9: 48.67-102]).

of things. The question remains: how do angels know? Do they take their knowledge from things, either spiritual or corporeal, or do they know everything besides themselves through innate species infused in them by God?[62]

The latter solution was proposed by Aquinas, who argued at length that angels, as pure spirits, are too lofty in the scale of beings to receive any perfection from material things. As celestial bodies do not receive any perfection or form from lower bodies, neither do angels receive a perfection, such as knowledge, from less perfect, material things. Human souls can receive knowledge from bodies and by means of bodies because they are the substantial forms of bodies. But this is impossible for spiritual beings like angels. For their knowledge of material things – indeed, for all their natural knowledge – they depend on species created with them at the first moment of their existence. For these and other reasons Aquinas concludes that angelic knowledge, unlike human knowledge, does not originate in material things but in a divine illumination in which angels receive species or ideas from God. Through these innate species angels have such perfect natural knowledge from the first moment of their creation that, unlike us, they do not have to reason from the known to the unknown; they simply see all that can be known in the ideas God has given them.[63]

In Ockham's view, however, the Thomist position on the natural knowledge of angels fails to explain how they can know things themselves and not just their species or likenesses. As we shall see in Chapter 10, Ockham raises the same objection to the notion that human knowledge is mediated by sensible and intelligi-

---

62. In this context the term "species" (*species*) means a likeness caused by a thing and, coming before knowledge, represents the thing to the knower. Though the term was widely used in this sense, Ockham rejects it in explaining both human and angelic knowledge. He accepts the term in the sense of a cognitive habit or act by which a thing is known. This, he says, is Aristotle's meaning of the term when he says (*De anima* 3.8, 431b29–432a1) that the stone is not in the mind but the species of the stone (*Expos. in Praedicab.* 2.1 [*OPh* 2: 31.14–22]).

63. *ST* 1.55.2, 58.3, cited by Ockham, *Rep.* 2.14 (*OTh* 5: 311.12–313.8).

ble species by which a thing is known. He finds no reason to posit species between the knower and the intuitive knowledge of the known object in order to explain how we know it. Furthermore, species would stand in the way of knowing things themselves.[64] In order to justify a realist doctrine of knowledge in both the human and angelic orders, Ockham rejects species as means by which humans and angels know things.

Ockham's strategy is to show that the angelic natural intuitive knowledge depends on an existing thing – and not on a species – as its cause. Every effect, he contends, depends on its essential causes and by their closeness and disposition. Now the natural intuitive knowledge of angels depends essentially on the thing known, for angels cannot have natural intuitive knowledge without the existence of the known thing. And the known thing is not a state (*dispositio*) of the angelic mind, nor is it a species by which angelic minds are assimilated to things, thus causing their minds to know them. It follows that the cause of angelic natural intuitive knowledge is the thing itself; more precisely, it is not the material, formal, or final cause of angelic knowledge, but its efficient cause.[65]

Ockham further dismantles the Thomist epistemology of the angels by denying that higher angels know by means of fewer and less universal species than lower ones. Aquinas reasoned that this should be so, because God knows everything through his one essence, and consequently angels closest to him and possessed of a keener intelligence should use fewer means of knowing than lower angels. Aquinas illustrates his point with the example of persons who cannot grasp a truth unless it is explained to them at great length, while others with better minds can grasp it more quickly and simply.[66]

64. For Ockham's criticism of sensible and intelligible species see below, pp. 501–503.

65. *Rep.* 2.14 (*OTh* 5: 314.3–11).

66. *ST* 1.55.3, cited by Ockham, *Rep.* 2.12–13 (*OTh* 5: 255.8–18). Ockham remarks that Scotus agreed with Aquinas (but for different reasons) that both human and angelic intellects gain their knowledge through species impressed on them. But Scotus did not accept the idea that a higher angel knows through

On Ockham's account, however, the fact of one angel's being closer to God is no reason to believe that it requires fewer means of knowing than another more remote from him. It simply indicates that the closer angel has a more powerful mind. It is true that a boy requires a more lengthy explanation of a truth than an old man, but this is because the man has a greater store of knowledge than the boy; or perhaps one person is naturally better endowed than another.[67]

Following the intuitive knowledge of things, angels, like humans, have another type of natural knowledge called abstractive. Later, in Chapter 10, we shall treat at length of the difference between these kinds of knowledge. For the moment it will be enough to say that natural intuitive knowledge – as distinct from supernatural intuition – must have for its object an actually existing thing. All that is needed for this knowledge is the presence of the thing known and the angelic or human intellect, without anything else coming between them, such as a species of the object or a habit (*habitus*) of knowing it. In virtue of natural intuitive knowledge angels and humans can judge with evidence that the thing known actually exists. Abstractive knowledge immediately follows upon the intuition of a thing, and it can remain even after the object is no longer present or has been destroyed. In the latter case, all that is required to judge that the thing once existed is the mind and its habit of knowing the object. It cannot be proved by natural reason, however, that angels have the habitual knowledge or *habitus* that we do, and which is required for abstractive knowledge; but we experience this habit in ourselves, and so it is reasonable to suppose it is also found in angels.[68]

As for Aquinas' claim that angels do not reason but know everything intuitively, Ockham counters that they do not know

fewer and less universal species than a lower one: see ibid. (*OTh* 5: 256.2–4, 297.12–298.6); cf. Scotus, *Ord.* 1.3.3.1 (Vatican ed. 3: 201–244).

67. *Rep.* 2.12–13 (*OTh* 5: 297.12–298.1).

68. Ibid. (*OTh* 5: 276.13–277.19). Ockham treats at length the difference between intuitive and abstractive knowledge (ibid. [*OTh* 5: 256–267]). See below, pp. 473–478.

everything in the beginning. They know principles, and through them they can gain further knowledge by reasoning to conclusions just as we do. If they did not reason, their knowledge of a premise would entail their knowing the infinite conclusions following from it. But it seems that angels can be ignorant of something and later come to know it. In short, they do not know everything, but they progress in knowledge just as we do.[69]

Ockham is not impressed by Aquinas' arguments that angels know things through species infused in them by God and not by things themselves. In one of his arguments Aquinas contends that angels, being spiritual beings, cannot be acted on by bodies and receive knowledge from them. In this respect they are unlike human souls, which, as forms of bodies, can receive knowledge from bodies and by means of them. But Ockham counters that it is just as possible for a body to act on a spiritual being as a partial cause of its knowledge as it is for a body to cause something in a soul joined to a body. The reason a body acts on the soul in the acquiring of knowledge is not precisely because it is united to the body, but because by itself the soul cannot acquire all the perfection it can have by means of the body. Now, it is for the same reason that bodies act on an angel: the angel can have some perfection through bodies that it cannot have without them.[70]

The assertion that a body can act on a spirit flies in the face of Augustine, who expressly denied this possibility. But Ockham interprets Augustine liberally to mean that a body cannot act on a spirit as a primary and principal agent, though it can as a secondary agent. True, a body cannot destroy the very substance of a spiritual being by acting on it, but as a partial cause a body can have an accidental effect on it. This should be obvious to Christians, for they believe that the fire of hell or purgatory acts on the soul and makes it suffer.[71]

69. *Rep.* 2.14 (*OTh* 5: 315.12–22).

70. Ibid. (*OTh* 5: 331.3–12); see Aquinas *ST* 1.55.2.

71. *Rep.* 2.14 (*OTh* 5: 326.17–24); see Augustine, *De Genesi ad litteram* 12.16 (CSEL 28.1: 402).

Another potent objection to Ockham's claim that bodies directly act on angelic minds, so that angels receive knowledge from them, is that in every natural action the agent and patient must be together and touch each other. But an angel cannot touch something else by contacting it in place or in essence. The first is impossible because angels do not naturally exist in place; so too is the second, because this contact would be a penetration of the essence of a thing, which is reserved to God alone.

Ockham, for his part, sees no impossibility in the known thing's being present to angels by penetration (*per illapsum*), if this means that there is no distance between them. He adds, however, that this is not necessary in order to explain angelic knowledge, for something in a distant place can be the partial cause of an angel's knowledge, and so too one angel can cause the knowledge of another angel at a distance. But if presence by penetration (*per illapsum*) means not only absence of distance but also dependence and conservation, then an angel is not present to the thing known in this way. In any case, essential contact is not required, but only local or virtual contact. An angel can have local contact with the thing it knows, because (as we have seen) the angel can be in place by its substance and occupy a place next to the thing it knows. An angel can also have virtual contact with the known object when it is only a slight distance from it and can know it intuitively. This kind of contact is impossible, however, if there is a great distance between them and the angel cannot know the thing intuitively.[72]

The reader cannot fail to be struck by the similarity between Ockham's accounts of angelic and human knowledge. He himself draws attention to it in his summary of six conclusions regarding the knowledge of angels, all of which equally apply to human knowledge. First, angels can have intuitive knowledge of both material and immaterial things, the things themselves being partial causes of that knowledge. Second, following upon intuitive knowledge, angels can have abstractive knowledge of things. If that

72. *Rep.* 2.14 (*OTh* 5: 323.17–324.13).

knowledge remains after the intuition of a thing ceases, the habit of knowing it is the partial cause of the abstractive cognition. Third, like humans, angels can abstract from individual things a knowledge of universals. Fourth, from intuitive and abstractive cognition angels can have a knowledge of contingent propositions, and either assent to, or dissent from them. Neither an angel nor a human intellect can have an evident knowledge of, or give an evident assent to a contingent proposition unless its terms exist and they are grasped intuitively. The existence of the terms and their intuitive knowledge are required for an affirmative judgment such as "The wall is white." By abstractive knowledge they can only judge that something was, not that it is. In order to have an evident knowledge of a negative contingent proposition, for example "The wall is not white," an intuitive cognition of the terms and the nonexistence of the thing suffice. Ockham adds that he is talking about knowledge in the natural order and not what is possible by the divine power. Fifth, angels can acquire from things the knowledge of necessary propositions whose terms are grasped intuitively. Sixth, an angel can reason and thus acquire the knowledge of contingent propositions; for example, seeing someone laugh, an angel can conclude that the person is in a joyful mood. Ockham points out that it is the common opinion of the masters that it is only by reasoning from exterior signs to interior acts that a bad angel can know the hidden secrets of hearts. So there is no doubt that angels, like humans, can reason. Indeed, in his *Quodlibeta* Ockham explicitly states that they not only can reason but must reason.[73]

This makes it possible for angels to err in their natural knowledge. They may reason from exterior signs to the existence of corresponding interior acts in a person, as in the above example, but there is no contradiction in the signs being present without the interior acts. Since God can do anything that is not contradictory,

---

73. *Quodl.* 1.7 (*OTh* 9: 44.76). Walter Chatton, on the contrary, held that, although angels can reason, they need not do so (ibid., with editor's note 44 n10).

he could produce the signs without the interior acts they signify, leading the angel to a false conclusion in this regard. By reasoning, angels can also gain a knowledge of necessary conclusions from premises. Of course they cannot know the infinite conclusions following from any one premise, but by reasoning they can arrive one by one at previously unknown conclusions.[74]

Aquinas denied this parity between human and angelic knowledge. In his view angels are unique beings with their own specific mode of knowing, which is simple insight (*intellectio*). This absolves them from the more complicated human way of knowing by judgment and reasoning.[75] It is significant that Duns Scotus conceived of intelligence as such to be a univocal perfection possessed in common by men and angels. Though unequal in substantial perfection, he thought they share univocally in the common nature of *intellectualitas*. There is no specific difference between human and angelic intelligence, understood as such. Scotus saw no reason why angels cannot reason to gain new knowledge, as humans grasp principles by simple insight.[76] Ockham had no liking for Scotist common natures, but Scotism had a definite influence on Ockham's conviction of the close resemblance of human and angelic intelligences. Indeed, we have Ockham's own word that with respect to their mode of knowing the intellectual powers of angels and humans have the same nature.[77]

5 The Speech of Angels

Angels can receive some information from sensible things, but their main source of knowledge is the spiritual world in which they dwell. They can have an intuitive knowledge of themselves,

74. *Rep.* 2.14 (*OTh* 5: 316.2–321.9).
75. *ST* 1.58.3–4.
76. Scotus, *Ord.* 2.1.6 (Vatican ed. 7: 155–157, nn. 319–322).
77. "Confirmatur, quia quando potentiae aliquae sunt eiusdem rationis, quidquid est obiectum naturale unius potentiae, est vel esse potest obiectum naturale alterius. Sed potentiae intellectivae angelorum [sunt eiusdem rationis] inter se, et intellectiva nostra quantum ad modum cognoscendi est eiusdem rationis cum intellectiva angelorum" (*Rep.* 2.16 [*OTh* 5: 377.5–10]).

their fellow angels, human souls, and even (by the divine power) God. These spiritual beings communicate with each other with a mental language that far surpasses in enlightenment and power our own halting material means of transmitting knowledge.[78]

We have already seen that Ockham, following the Aristotelian and Boethian tradition, distinguishes between three kinds of human language (*oratio*): written, spoken, and mental.[79] Mental language, existing only in the mind, is composed of mental words (*verba*), which may be either terms or propositions formed from them. In a famous passage of his *De Trinitate* Augustine described a mental word as "the thought (*cogitatio*) formed about something we know, which we say in our heart, and which is neither Greek nor Latin nor any other tongue."[80]

Since angels are spiritual creatures, they do not communicate by means of oral or written language (except when occupying a human body), but they have mental language in common with us. The notion that angels speak is implied in the words of Paul: "If I speak in the tongues of men and of angels ..." (1 Cor 13:1). Meditating on these words, theologians have tried to understand the reality underlying the obvious metaphor of angelic speech, bringing to bear upon it their basic philosophical ideas. Ockham follows a long tradition when he inquires what it might mean for angels to speak and hear mentally. His reply is couched in the analogy of bodily and mental language. As oral speech is the uttering of spoken words so that someone else might hear them bodily and grasp their meaning, so mental speech is having a mental word so that someone else might hear it mentally and understand what it means. A mental word is nothing but a thought someone actually entertains. Speaking mentally, then, is

---

78. On the speech of the angels see *Quaest. variae* 6 (*OTh* 8: 195–206).

79. See above, pp. 14–15.

80. "Formata quippe cogitatio ab ea re quam scimus verbum est quod in corde dicimus, quod nec Graecum est nec Latinum nec linguae alicuius alterius" (Augustine, *De Trinitate* 15.10 [CCL 50A: 486, n. 19], quoted by Ockham, *Quodl.* 1.6 [*OTh* 9: 37.25–29]).

nothing but actually thinking so that the thinker or someone else might know what the thought means. Hearing mentally is nothing but seeing the actual thought of another angel or human, as hearing vocally is simply the perception of spoken words.[81]

It sounds strange to equate hearing with seeing in mental communication. In us, these are two kinds of perception belonging to two different bodily organs. But, as Augustine says, "Hearing and sight are two things apart from each other in the bodily senses; but in the soul seeing and hearing are not different. And thus, even though outward speech is not seen but heard, interior utterances, that is thoughts, are seen by God, in the words of the Evangelist: 'Since Jesus saw their thoughts'."[82]

The following passage summarizes Ockham's explanation of angelic communication of thoughts and their objects:

> [I] say that, since mental speaking is nothing but actually thinking, and one angel can actually think so that another angel might hear or see his thought, and thus as through a natural sign in some way understand the object of that thought, and the other angel can see that thought (which is hearing it mentally, as has been shown), it follows that one angel can speak to another and the other can hear him. Consequently an angel, in speaking to another angel, does nothing but cause the thought of something in itself, which thought, as an object, causes effectively the thought of that thought in the angel who hears, and thus as a result it causes in some way the thought of the object of the first thought in the angel who hears.[83]

---

81. *Quodl.* 1.6 (*OTh* 9: 36.14–24).

82. Augustine, *De Trinitate* 15.10 (CCL 50A: 485, n. 18), cited by Ockham, ibid. (*OTh* 9: 37.25–43).

83. "Circa secundum articulum dico quod cum loqui mentaliter non sit nisi cogitare actualiter, et angelus potest cogitare actualiter ut alius audiat sive videat suam cogitationem ac per hoc tamquam per signum naturale aliquo modo intelligat obiectum illius cogitationis; et illam cogitationem potest alius videre, quod est mentaliter audire sicut ostensum est; sequitur quod unus angelus potest alteri loqui, et alius potest audire. Ex quo sequitur quod angelus

This gives angels a direct access to each other's thoughts and desires. Simply because angels have thoughts and wishes, they are open to the intuitive gaze of other angels, contrary to the common opinion that this privilege is reserved to God alone. In Thomism (which represents the common opinion for Ockham), an angel cannot intuit the individual thoughts and desires of another angel or a human being simply because they are there to be seen, but only when the angel or human being who speaks *wills* that they be seen. Their thoughts and desires depend on their will, for they think and desire as they will. Now God alone, as the principal object and final end of the will, can penetrate its inner sanctum and know the secret thoughts and desires of angels and humans. Lacking this intimacy, "the secrets of the heart" can be known only by observing their effects. For example, a person can sometimes surmise what another is thinking about from his or her actions and even from facial expressions. A doctor diagnoses an illness by observing exterior signs. Angels and demons are keener in interpreting these signs. Angels can also know each other's thoughts by seeing the more or less universal intelligible species God has created in their intellects. But this is only a general knowledge, and it does not extend to the particular uses angels make of these species when they actually think.[84]

It was inevitable that Ockham would reject Aquinas' doctrine, for in his view neither human nor angelic knowledge is mediated by sensible and intelligible species. We have seen him criticize the notion that God infuses intelligible species in the angelic mind at the moment of its creation. Furthermore, Ockham argues that if one angel sees a species or concept in the mind of another angel and thus knows its object, the angel would know it only as a universal and not as a particular. The angel would not see individual thoughts and

---

loquendo alteri nihil facit nisi causat cogitationem in se de aliquo, quae cogitatio tamquam obiectum causat effective cogitationem illius cogitationis in angelo audiente; et sic ex consequente causat aliquo modo in angelo audiente cogitationem obiecti primae cogitationis" (*Quodl.* 1.6 [*OTh* 9: 37.45–56]).

84. *ST* 1.57.4, resp. and ad 2; Ockham, *Rep.* 2.16 (*OTh* 5: 359.7–360.18).

affections and their objects but only universals; for example, the angel would see that I am thinking of animal but not this particular animal.

Bringing his own notion of intuitive knowledge to bear on the problem, Ockham counters that angels have an intuitive power that enables them to see thoughts and their objects not just as universals but also as particulars. He adds that even you (that is, Aquinas) hold that one angel sees the thought and affection of another angel intuitively, and hence in its individuality and not just as a universal. But, as the editors of Ockham's *Reportatio* point out, Aquinas means this to be true only of thoughts and affections that an angel directs to another angel and wills that the other angel see. Angels, according to Aquinas, can speak to themselves and thus conceive a word (*verbum*) within their mind. They can then will that their inner word be revealed to the mind of another angel. This is what is meant by angelic speech: the deliberate manifestation of the mental concept of one angel to another.[85]

This is different from Ockham's notion of mental speech cited above: "[M]ental speaking is nothing but actually thinking."[86] But this definition of mental speech is open to the objection that it does not allow for one angel's speaking to another angel without speaking to every angel, and even to all human minds separated from bodies. If an angel actually has a thought, it seems that *ipso facto* it is spoken to every mind receptive of it.

Ockham meets this difficulty head on, granting that "naturally speaking, an angel cannot speak to one angel without speaking to another, if other things are equal; for example, if they are at an equal distance and are equally attentive and not impeded in some way."[87] A person speaking to a group cannot determine that certain members hear what is said and others not; the spoken word is available to everyone. So too the mental word or thought of an angel is naturally accessible to all angels and it cannot be concealed from them.

85. *ST* 1.107.1, resp. and ad 3, cited by Ockham, *Rep.* 2.16 (*OPh* 5: 360.13–18; see the editor's note 360 n2).

86. See above, p. 370.

87. *Quodl.* 1.6 (*OTh* 9: 39.74–77).

The consequence of this conception of angelic mental language is frightening. Since it can be assumed that every angel has at least one thought, and perhaps many, and the number of angels is traditionally high, the mental confusion in the angelic world would be as great as the vocal disorder in a proportionately large human crowd where everyone speaks at once. To avoid this muddle, Ockham proposes a second notion of mental speech which takes into account the will of the speaker and not just the natural sequence of cause and effect between a thought and its apprehension. Angels, like humans, can will that their thoughts be accessible to one listener and not to another, so that they can hide their thoughts from one angel and reveal them to another. An angel can also will not to hear what another says. There should be no fear of cacophony in the angelic world, for in fact God often does not allow one angel to see the thoughts of another angel or even of a human person. God must act along with angels to communicate their thoughts and with listeners to perceive them, and he can always withhold his cooperation.[88]

In his *Celestial Hierarchy* Dionysius the pseudo-Areopagite classified angels as higher and lower, depending on their likeness and closeness to God. Superior angels receive illuminations from God which they in turn pass on to lower angels.[89] If this is true, a higher angel can certainly speak to a lower one; but the question remains whether inferior angels can speak to their superiors. Ockham replies with his distinction between two meanings of mental speech. If it only means eliciting a thought open to another mind, angels in lower and higher orders or hierarchies are equally able to speak to each other. The same is true if mental speech means speaking with the desire that one listener hear and not an-

---

88. Ibid. (*OTh* 9: 39.89–98). But in the *Reportatio*, which predates the *Quodlibeta*, Ockham states that it is not in an angel's power to reveal or hide something, because the angel acts only as an object, and hence that object is accessible to any intellect. Whether the object is revealed or hidden depends on God's coacting or not with the angel's act (*Rep.* 2.16 [*OTh* 5: 366.12–16, 371.7–14]).

89. Dionysius, *De caelestia hierarchia* (PG 3: 119–370).

other. Lower angels can speak to higher ones when they want to be illuminated by them, and they can likewise want higher angels to see their thoughts. However, God reveals many thoughts to higher angels that are not disclosed to lower ones, unless the higher angels pass them on to the lower angels.[90]

Can an angel directly cause thoughts in the human mind as it can in another angelic mind? Ockham denies this possibility, as long as the human mind is in a body. In its present state the mind knows only what has been previously in the senses. This limits it *de facto* to knowing sensible things and its interior acts and concepts. These suffice to account for all our knowledge without the intervention of angels. However, both good and bad angels can indirectly act on the mind by manipulating sensible things and presenting them to the exterior or interior senses. For example, demons can cause illusions in the senses and make them appear to be real. Good angels can also act indirectly on the mind, for example by presenting objects to the interior senses or altering the proportion of one's humors and spirits.[91]

Ockham is concerned with the language of angels only insofar as it is a means of communicating concepts and propositions, along with a knowledge of their objects. Scripture gives a much wider role to angelic speech: angels are said not only to utter statements, but also to shout with joy, praise, give advice and commands, question, and pray. But these forms of language are not of interest to the logician, who centers his attention on propositions, where truth and falsity are found. Ockham recognizes other types of language, such as praying, but he regards them as belonging to rhetoric or poetry rather than logic.[92] Limiting the speech of angels to conceptual and propositional language, Ockham, in the spirit of his contemporaries, approaches his subject primarily as a logician and not as a philosopher interested in the full range of language.

---

90. *Quodl.* 1.6 (*OTh* 9: 41.122–133).
91. *Rep.* 2.16 (*OTh* 5: 370.13–371.2).
92. *Expos. in Periherm.* 1.4 (*OPh* 2: 391.13–20).

CHAPTER **9**

The Universe

O CKHAM'S PHILOSOPHICAL INTERESTS LAY chiefly in the areas of logic and natural philosophy or physics. In logic he wrote commentaries on works of Aristotle and Porphyry and his own monumental *Summa logicae*, which had a lasting influence on English philosophy. In natural philosophy he commented literally and at length on Aristotle's *Physics*, wrote two summaries of natural philosophy, a long series of questions on the *Physics*,[1] besides occasional disputed questions and a treatise on topics in natural philosophy.[2] Numerous discussions of topics in natural philosophy are also contained in his theological writings.

1 Natural Philosophy

As was customary at the time, Ockham uses the terms "physics," "natural philosophy," and "natural science" as synonyms. Like all

---

1. See *Expositio in libros Physicorum Aristotelis* (*OPh* 4–5). In the Prologue Ockham states his intention to investigate Aristotle's opinions in physics without giving his own views as a Catholic (*OPh* 4: 4.24–32). See also *Brevis summa libri Physicorum, Summula philosophiae naturalis* (*OPh* 6). In the proem to the *Summula* Ockham cautions the reader that he writes as a commentator on Aristotle, repudiating anything he says contrary to his Catholic faith (*Summ. phil. nat.* prooem. [*OPh* 6: 137]). The editor, Stephen Brown, defends the authenticity of both works: see *OPh* 6: 10*–13*; 25*–27*. C.K. Brampton denied the authenticity of the *Summula* in "Ockham and His Authorship of the *Summulae Physicorum*," *Isis* 55 (1964): 418–426; James A. Weisheipl ("Ockham and some Mertonians," *Mediaeval Studies* 30 [1968]: 163–213, at pp. 172–173), also expressed doubts in this matter. Finally, see also Ockham, *Quaestiones in libros Physicorum Aristotelis* (*OPh* 6).

2. For example, Ockham wrote a Question on the possibility of an eternal world in *Quaest. variae* (*OTh* 8), and a treatise *De quantitate* in connection with the eucharist (*OTh* 10). For a general study of Ockham's physics see André Goddu, *The Physics of William of Ockham* (Leiden/Cologne, 1984).

his contemporaries he did not distinguish between the science and philosophy of nature; indeed, they continued to be identified well into modern times. In the seventeenth century Newton called his great work in physics *The Mathematical Principles of Natural Philosophy*. It was only in the last century that the non-philosophical character of modern physics began to be recognized. There is little agreement, however, on its relation to the philosophy of nature.[3]

In Ockham's day Thomas Bradwardine and his fellow *calculatores* of the Merton School at Oxford were revolutionizing physics by using mathematics in the study of moving bodies. It has been said that they were among the first to use algebraic functions to describe motion.[4] Bradwardine's goal, though unrealized, was not unlike that of modern physics: "to embrace all motions, terrestrial and celestial, and all variations of velocity, in a single mathematical formula."[5] The Mertonians and other fourteenth-century physicists accelerated and refined the efforts of Robert Grosseteste and Roger Bacon in the previous century to use mathematics in the study of natural phenomena.[6]

Ockham must have been aware of this important development in physics taking place at his own University of Oxford and also on the continent, but he had no part in it. In the Aristotelian tradition he emphasized the necessity of experience in natural

3. See Jacques Maritain, *Philosophy of Nature*, trans. Imelda Byrne (New York, 1951) and "The Conflict of Methods at the End of the Middle Ages," *The Thomist* 3 (1941): 527–538; Yves Simon, *The Great Dialogue of Nature and Space* (Albany, NY, 1970); James A. Weisheipl, *The Development of Physical Theory in the Middle Ages* (1960; Ann Arbor, 1971), and "Medieval Natural Philosophy and Modern Science," in his *Nature and Motion in the Middle Ages*, ed. W.E. Carroll (Washington, DC, 1985), pp. 261–276.

4. Alistair C. Crombie, *Medieval and Early Modern Science* (Garden City, NY, 1959), 2: 56. For the history of medieval science at Oxford, Paris, and Padua see William A. Wallace, *Causality and Scientific Explanation* 1: *Medieval and Early Classical Science* (Ann Arbor, 1972).

5. Weisheipl, *Development of Physical Theory*, p. 81.

6. In the spirit of Grosseteste, Roger Bacon insisted that one cannot know anything of this world without knowing mathematics; see *The Opus Majus of Roger Bacon* 4.1.2, trans. R.B. Burke (Philadelphia, 1928), 1: 117.

science,[7] and he made a place in his classification of the sciences for a mathematical study of nature. Like Thomas Aquinas, among others, he recognized an "intermediate science" (*scientia media*), situated between physics and mathematics, and studying nature by means of mathematics.[8] He came to physics, however, not as a scientist using the methods of observation, experimentation, and mathematical analysis, but as a philosopher and even a theologian. He brought about his own revolution in Aristotelian physics by applying to the study of nature his basic logical and philosophical principles, particularly his notion of reality as radically individual and the rule of parsimony, to which should be added the Christian belief in the omnipotence of God.

In order to be *a* science, physics obviously has to have some sort of unity. In Ockham's view, its unity, like that of all the other sciences, is not strictly numerical but collective. In a broad sense it may be said to be one in number, as we may call a house or kingdom numerically one; but more properly it has the unity of a collection or ordered whole. We saw in Chapter 2 that the collective unity of a science is first of all that of a number of associated mental abilities (*habitus*) to think and to reason about a given subject, and secondarily the unity of the conclusions reached in a science.[9] Physics has this kind of collective unity. It has many parts, but all of them "have a definite relation among themselves, such as they do not have with logic or moral philosophy or any other science, and hence they are called one science."[10]

The parts of natural philosophy and their respective subjects can be gathered from the division of Aristotle's works on natural science. First of all there is his *Physics*, whose general subject is

7. "Anyone who wanted to acquire natural science without experience would attempt the impossible, for one cannot acquire natural science without experience, though one can acquire belief in the things of nature without experience by believing the reports of others"; see *Expos. in Phys.* 1.3 (*OPh* 4: 46.108–112).

8. See above, p. 136.

9. See above, p. 142–143.

10. *Sum. phil. nat.* praeam. (*OPh* 6.140.70–74).

natural being (*ens naturale*) or natural substance (*substantia natur-alis*), embracing both the simple and composite beings in the universe. Following Aristotle's *Physics*, Ockham defines nature, in contrast to the products of art or the results of chance or fortune, as having an inner essential (*per se*) principle of motion and rest.[11] From the point of view of predication or the generality of the subject-terms of the propositions of natural philosophy, nature is the primary subject of Aristotle's *Physics*. Specific natural beings are the subjects of Aristotle's other physical treatises; for example, the soul in the *De anima*, the heavens in the *De caelo*, animals in *De partibus animalium*, and *Historia animalium*, and so on. These works contain the primary subject of natural philosophy from the point of view of the perfection of the realities of which it treats. Ockham declines to say, however, whether its most perfect natural subject is the human person or the heavenly bodies or something else.[12]

In short, though natural philosophy treats of many subjects, some of which are more general and some more excellent than others, it is not a mere aggregate or collection of mental *habitus* or propositions. It has a kind of unity from the fact that there is an order among them – an order described above as not real but logical.[13]

Corresponding to the logical unity of natural philosophy, the natural world itself has the real unity of an ordered whole. Its unity is not numerical but that of a collection, like a city, army or university.[14] To account for the order and unity of the universe is it necessary to posit a special relation or bond (*ligamen*) connecting all its parts to each other, as Simplicius (6th c. AD) ima-

---

11. For the notion of nature see *Expos. in Phys.* 2.1 (*OPh* 4: 213–241); *Brevis sum. Phys.* 2.1 (*OPh* 6: 25–28). See Aristotle, *Phys.* 2.1, 192b8–24.

12. "Sed primum subiectum primitate totalitatis nullum est, quia nullum subiectum cuiuscumque conclusionis significat aliqua vel aliquid quae vel quod includat tamquam partes omnia considerata in ista scientia, nisi forte dicas quod mundus sit tale totum" (*Sum. phil. nat.* praeam. [*OPh* 6: 141.103–106]). For the notion of science in general and in particular natural science see *Expos. in Phys.* prol. (*OPh* 4: 4–14).

13. See above, pp. 142–144.

14. *Expos. in Phys.* prol. (*OPh* 4: 7.18–29).

gined? Not at all, according to Ockham. All that is required is the absolute things of which the universe is composed and which are related by themselves to each other.[15] In the sublunar world the four elements of earth, air, water, and fire are arranged in proper order; above them are the heavenly bodies and spheres and their movers, which are immaterial or "separated" substances. Natural philosophy treats of all these: principally sensible substances composed of matter and form and subject to generation, corruption, and motion; secondarily the separate or immaterial substances moving the heavenly spheres.[16]

Ockham hastens to add that natural philosophy, properly speaking, does not treat of individual natural and movable things, but rather of universal concepts and propositions formed about them. As we have seen, science is not about particular things but about universal terms standing for and signifying them. If we say that natural science is about corruptible and mobile things, we are speaking metaphorically and improperly; what we mean is that it treats of terms that take their place in discourse. This does not put physics in the same order as logic, as though it only concerned concepts and propositions and not reality itself. The concepts in the two disciplines do not have the same substitutive value: concepts in physics stand for realities, whereas logical concepts stand for themselves. In technical language, explained above in Chapter 1, the terms of physics, as a science of reality (*scientia realis*), have personal supposition whereas the terms of logic have simple supposition.[17]

Because natural science is properly about propositions and not about things, it can be said to be about what is necessary and not contingent. Some of the realities studied in natural science are in fact contingent and corruptible, like bodies in the sublunar world; others are necessary, like the heavenly bodies. But all the conclu-

15. *Quodl.* 7.8 (*OTh* 9: 728.56–66. The notion of a *ligamen* is also found in Walter Chatton; for references to Chatton and Simplicius see *OTh* 9: 729 n9.

16. *Expos. in Phys.* prol. (*OPh* 4: 10.3–8).

17. Ibid. (*OPh* 4: 11.9–12.54); Aristotle, *Anal. Post.* 1.4–5, 73b26–74a13; see also above, pp. 26–30. For the object of science see above, p. 142.

sions reached in natural science, and indeed in any science, are necessary, eternal, and incorruptible. Even though the things signified by the terms of the conclusions of the science are purely contingent and corruptible, nevertheless necessary propositions can be formed about them, at least when they are expressed in the mode of possibility. Thus "Every body moves" is a contingent proposition; "Every body can move" is a necessary proposition.[18]

Philosophers search for the causes of things; and so it is incumbent on them to look for the causes of natural science. Aristotle recognized matter and form as causes intrinsic to things, and efficient and final causes as extrinsic to them. Which of these are causes of science? The answer depends on the nature of science. For Ockham, the first and most basic meaning of science is a stable mental ability or disposition (*habitus*) to reason to a certain conclusion. In itself each scientific habit is a single quality produced in the mind by numerous mental acts in accord with the scientific method. Some of these individual scientific habits naturally come together to make up a total science, as in the case of natural science. Now, in the first meaning of science (as a single mental habit) its causes are not matter and form, for these causes only apply to a composite reality and not to something that is *per se* incomposite. The mental quality that is a part of science is an accidental form of the human mind, and so it does not *have* a form, and for the same reason it does not have matter. In sum, as a simple reality (*res simplex*) science does not have matter and form as its causes. In the second meaning of science (as a collection or aggregate of mental habits) its intrinsic causes are not matter and form, for it is not composed of them but of many mental habits in the category of quality.

Strictly speaking, then, science has only efficient and final causes. Ockham reports several opinions of what its efficient cause might be. Some say the efficient cause of science is the mind; others that it is the object of science; others that it is the incomplex knowledge of terms, or a combination of these opinions, or

18. *Sum. phil. nat.* praeam. (*OPh* 6: 144.164–188).

something else. He does not discuss the matter further in his *Summula philosophiae naturalis*, but its excellent editor helps us to identify the authors of these opinions and Ockham's own position. Peter Olivi held that the mind is the efficient cause of science; Godfrey of Fontaines that the efficient cause is not the mind but the object of science. Ockham himself seems to have opted for the incomplex terms of science.[19] In his *Ordinatio* he says that evident knowledge is the knowledge of a complex truth or proposition that is adequately caused immediately or mediately by the incomplex knowledge of its terms.[20] It seems to be Ockham's mind that a self-evident proposition is known immediately by the knowledge of its terms; a scientific proposition is evident mediately, through the terms of the premises of which it is the conclusion. As for the final cause of natural philosophy, it is what is intended by the one learning and acquiring it.[21]

Less strictly, natural philosophy, and indeed any science, may be said to have four causes. Its material cause is the reality of which it treats, always remembering that (by the absolute power of God) there can be propositions about nonexistent things in this science. Its formal cause is its method of procedure. Its efficient cause is primarily the one who teaches the science. Lastly, its final cause is the right purpose the student should have in learning the science, though (Ockham adds with a touch of irony) sometimes students in their perversity or necessity study it for other reasons.[22]

Another question: Is physics a theoretical or practical science? It is wholly or for the most part theoretical, for it is entirely or mainly concerned with things we do not make, such as the earth,

---

19. See the editor's note to at *OPh* 6: 146 n12.

20. "[D]ico quod notitia evidens est cognitio alicuius veri complexi, ex notitia terminorum incomplexa immediate vel mediate nata sufficienter causari" (*Ord.* 1.prol.1 [*OTh* 1: 5.18–21]).

21. *Sum. phil. nat.* praeam. (*OPh* 6: 145–146). The editor cites Peter Olivi and Henry of Ghent as holding the first opinion, and Godfrey of Fontaines as holding the second, and Ockham the third: see *OPh* 6: 146 nn12–14.

22. Ibid. (*OPh* 6: 146.224–237).

heavens, animals and other bodies. The practical sciences treat of things we can make or do. Examples are the sciences of grammar, logic, and rhetoric, to which should be added the mechanical arts. They are practical in the sense of teaching or showing how something should be made. In still another sense a science is practical if it directs one to do or omit something, like prudence and moral philosophy. Natural science can be said to be practical in part because our acts of knowledge come within our power and we sometimes control our sensations. These acts are truly our work and hence they can be called praxis. Scientific knowledge enables us to elicit these acts more quickly, easily, and better, and consequently from this perspective it can be called practical.[23]

We have been told that the formal cause of physics is its method of procedure. In the beginning of his *Physics* Aristotle describes the method of physics as an inquiry into the causes and principles of natural things. The scientist should begin with what is most knowable and obvious to us, namely generalities, and proceed by analysis to discover the particular principles, conditions or elements of things. Thus physics proceeds from the general to the particular – "general" including even what is first indistinctly known through sense perception, for "a child begins by calling all men 'father' and all women 'mother', but later on distinguishes each of them."[24]

In his *Summary of Natural Philosophy* Ockham clearly has this passage of Aristotle in mind when he treats of "the method of proceeding, considering, and demonstrating" in physics. However, he uses it to describe, not the method of scientific inquiry, but of *teaching* physics, which after all is the purpose of his *Summary*. He mentions, incidentally, that physics, like the other sciences, offers *propter quid* demonstrations, that is, proofs that assign causes to

---

23. *Sum. phil. nat.* praeam. (*OPh* 6: 147.239–149.314). For the various meanings of praxis see *Ord.* 1.prol.10 (*OTh* 1: 285–302). In the first and broadest sense praxis is the activity of any virtue, whether it is free or natural. In this sense it is equivalent to energy. In the strictest sense it is activity elicited in conformity with the dictate of reason and the will's choice.

24. Aristotle, *Phys.* 1.1, 184b12–14.

things, but his main interest in this work is the order of teaching physics. That order requires the teacher to begin with what is better and more easily known to the students. He should proceed from effects to causes and from the more to the less general, that is to say, from propositions having more general terms to ones with less general terms. For instance, in teaching the nature of animals he should begin with the general notion of animal and explain its properties, before treating of kinds of animals like horses and lions. After all, some people may know a horse but not a lion and vice versa, but everyone will know the meaning of animal.

Ockham has here identified Aristotle's method of inquiry with the method of teaching or learning. Both begin with the general or universal and advance to the particular. But Ockham adds that what everyone knows first is the individual; no one can know the universal before the individual, though the individual can be known confusedly before it is known distinctly. It is understandable that children at first call all men fathers, for they only have sense knowledge, and that only imperfectly. Later they distinguish with their senses one individual from another. Their first concepts are accordingly general rather than distinct and proper. Following this order, Ockham proposes to teach physics starting with the general properties and conditions of natural things and then going on to specific topics.[25]

2 Matter and Form

Carrying out this program, the first point to be made is that natural things that come into being and cease to be must be composed of two principles or causes, which Aristotle called matter and form. Ockham proves this *a posteriori*, beginning with observable effects and proceeding to a knowledge of their causes. We see that bodies like animals, plants, fire and air are naturally generated and destroyed. Now nothing is generated from nothing but from something, and this must be within the generated thing. If it were

---

25. *Sum. phil. nat.* praeam. (*OPh* 6: 152–153).

outside of it, the thing would be generated from nothing. Since it is in fact generated from something, the 'something' in question must be a part or subject of the generated thing. The presupposed 'something' cannot be what is generated, for in that case nothing new would be generated. That in fact something new comes into being shows that there is another part of the generated thing accounting for its novelty. Hence the generated thing must have two parts: one presupposed to the thing's generation called matter, and the other which is not presupposed but is new, called form.[26]

We can know from experience that nothing comes into being unless something is presupposed to its generation, for we never see a thing begin to be without some previous thing being destroyed, as earth and wood are destroyed when fire is generated. True, something can come to be in another thing without the other thing being destroyed, as the sun illumines the air while the air remains, and sensation occurs in the eyes and nothing is destroyed. But in these cases a subject is clearly presupposed to the effect, and so it is not generated from nothing.[27]

These are examples of generation in the strict sense of the term. When fire is generated from wood a new substance comes into existence; matter receives a substantial form that before did not exist. When air is illumined or a substance is whitened, a quality begins to exist that before did not exist. In this strict sense generation occurs only in the categories of substance and quality. In a broad sense, however, we can speak of generation in all the categories. Whenever a change takes place in something, as when it acquires a new place or shape, it can be said that something is generated. But no new reality is added to the subject of the generation; it only acquires a new name. This is the case with artificial things. A workman or artist (*artifex*) does not produce an entirely new reality or add something new to his materials, such as an artificial form. All he does is to remove parts from a natural substance, as

26. *Sum. phil. nat.* 1.1 (*OPh* 6: 155.5–156.37).
27. Ibid. (*OPh* 6: 157.54–64).

when he carves a statue from stone, or change the position and arrangement of his materials, as when he builds a house.[28]

For a true generation there must be two distinct realities: matter and form. They are mutual causes and essential principles of a natural thing both in its coming to be and in its being. To these Aristotle adds a third principle called "privation."[29] "Privation" is not a positive term, designating something really different from matter, form, and the composite of the two. It is a negative term, signifying that in generation the matter was previously without (or "deprived of") the form that it has now acquired. If the term has any positive meaning it is equivalent to form and matter. It can designate the form to be expelled when another form is introduced into matter. Blackness, for example, is the privation of the contrary quality of whiteness and vice versa. Again, the substantial form of fire is the privation of the substantial form of air and vice versa. Privation can also designate matter as the subject of generation, for matter is first without ("deprived of") a certain form and afterward it possesses it.

Aristotle's and his commentator Averroes' description of generation raises a difficulty at this point. They sometimes say, "A man becomes musical," and again, "From being unmusical he becomes musical." The latter expression: "Musicus fit ex non musico" might lead one to think that the musician becomes musical from acquiring some thing that is the privation of musical. The correct interpretation, according to Ockham, is that the privation 'nonmusical' is not a thing distinct from the man who lacks musical talent; it is only a name standing for the subject of generation.

Strictly speaking, then, it is incorrect to say that generation takes place 'from the opposite' (*ex opposito*); for example, the musical from the nonmusical. The opposite is a privation, and privation is not a reality distinct from the subject of the generation

---

28. Ibid. 1.16 (*OPh* 6: 197.2–199.46); *Expos. in Phys.* 1.15 (*OPh* 4: 150.2–151.47).

29. Aristotle, *Phys.* 1.7, 190b23–191a4.

but only a mental concept or word, and nothing real can be generated from them, but only from a reality.[30]

To Walter Burley, a contemporary of Ockham and staunch realist, Aristotle was not only referring to a concept or word when he wrote that generation takes place "from the opposite." The difference between the subject of generation and the opposite from which the generation takes place was intended to be real and not only mental or verbal. This is clear, according to Burley, because the subject and its opposite (for example, man and nonmusical) have different definitions, and hence they have different essences and different entities. Consequently, when Aristotle spoke of form, subject, and privation as three principles of generation, he was referring not only to three names but also to three realities.[31]

In replying to Burley, Ockham reiterates his conviction – so crucial to his philosophical program – that in physics and the other sciences of reality Aristotle often mixes propositions whose terms stand for concepts or words with those whose terms stand for realities. In other words, physics and other sciences of the real world contain not only propositions whose terms have personal supposition, but also many whose terms have simple and material supposition. This brings logic and even grammar right into the heart of physics. Physics is an investigation of the real world, but sometimes its study is mediated by logic and grammar. This is justified because "the truths of many propositions of this sort [that is,

---

30. *Expos. in Phys.* 1.15 (*OPh* 4: 151.48–152.76). See Aristotle, *Phys.* 1.7, 190 a26; Averroes, *In Phys.* 1, com. 61 (Junta ed. 4: f. 36v–37r).

31. "Cum Philosophus posuit differentiam inter subiectum et oppositum secundum vocem, ponit inter ea differentiam quae est secundum rem ... . Illa sunt diversa quae habent diversas diffinitiones; sed obiectum (leg. subiectum) and oppositum habent diversas diffinitiones; ergo. Maior patet, quia illa quae habent diversas diffinitiones habent diversas quiditates, et per consequens diversas entitates. Sed omnia talia sunt diversa. Minor apparet, quia homo et immusicum habent diffinitiones diversas, quia alia est diffinitio hominis et alia est diffinitio immusicum" (Walter Burley, *In Physicam Aristotelis expositio et quaestiones* 1 [Venice, 1501; repr. Hildesheim/New York, 1972], f. 27rb–va). See Ockham, *Expos. in Phys.* 1.15 (*OPh* 4: 152.68–78 and n9); *Sum. phil. nat.* 1.5 (*OPh* 6: 166.45–47).

of logic or grammar] are caused by reality (*ex natura rei*), and from the knowledge of propositions of this sort we can come to know reality." In short, logic and grammar can be significant aids to the study of reality. In the present case, the truth of all the Aristotelian propositions concerning generation arises from the fact that the same subject first lacks a certain form or has a contrary form, and afterward it has the previously absent form. Now this generation can be expressed in various ways. We can say, "From being a man he becomes musical," the terms of the proposition having personal supposition because they stand for the realities they signify. Or we can say, "From not being musical he becomes musical," where the term "not being musical" expresses the privation of musicality and hence stands for a concept or word. Or we can say, "From being a nonmusical man he becomes musical," where once again the privative term "nonmusical man" stands for a concept or word and hence has simple or material supposition.[32]

This example is found in Ockham's *Expositio in libros Physicorum*. He makes the same point with another example in his *Summula philosophiae naturalis*. Once again he asserts that even though Aristotle acts as a philosopher of the real in natural philosophy and other sciences, he frequently uses logical propositions in which names are predicated of names standing for names, in short with simple supposition. To Ockham this is legitimate, for the propositions are convertible with propositions in which all the terms are taken with signification and hence with personal supposition. Thus "Animal is predicated of man" is convertible with "Man is an animal," and "White is predicated of body" is convertible with "The body is white." These propositions are also convertible: "'Principle' is predicated of subject, privation, and form," and "The subject is a principle, privation is a principle, and form is a principle." Ockham concludes:

> And therefore because logic is a presupposition for every science of reality, it is not inappropriate in a science of reality for The

32. *Expos. in Phys.* 1.15 (*OPh* 4: 152.79–89).

Philosopher to use a logical term and a proposition convertible with one or more propositions in which all the terms are taken with signification. And this is so in the present case.[33]

Contrary to Burley, then, Ockham finds that among the three principles required for natural generation, two of them (matter and form) are real, while the third (privation) is only a concept or word. This was unacceptable to the realist Burley, for whom physics is a study of the real world and not of words and concepts. Since privation is a necessary principle in the generation of real things and is defined differently from matter and form, he assumes that, like matter and form, it has the status of a real essence or entity. For Ockham, on the contrary, there is no need to think of privation as a reality but only as a name. It has its own definition, but this is no assurance that it has its own reality. Nor is privation's status as a name incompatible with physics as a science of reality. In Ockham's nominalist view of physics, its direct object is not reality itself but propositions composed of names standing for reality. In this schema there is plenty of room for privation as a name.

Having shown that matter and form are the two substantial (*per se*) principles of generation and the generated thing, Ockham describes each of them in turn. Matter is defined as "a thing (*res*) actually existing in the real world, capable of receiving all substantial forms, but having no one of them necessarily and always existing in it."[34] This is *materia prima*, the first and strict sense of the term "matter." In a second sense matter is a composite of form and matter, capable of receiving new names and the real accident of quality. Primary matter should not be imagined as some-

---

33. *Sum. phil. nat.* 1.5 (*OPh* 6: 167.59–63).

34. "Circa quam est sciendum, quod materia est quaedam res actualiter exsistens in rerum natura, quae est in potentia ad omnes formas substantiales, nullam habens necessario et semper sibi inexsistentem" (ibid. 1.9 [*OPh* 6: 179.5–8]). For Ockham's notion of matter see James A. Weisheipl, "The Concept of Matter in Fourteenth Century Science," in *The Concept of Matter*, ed. Ernan McMullin (Notre Dame, IN, 1963), pp. 328–334; and Allan B. Wolter, "The Ockhamist Critique," ibid., pp. 144–166.

thing purely potential; rather, it is actual of itself with its own proper being (*esse suum proprium*); and yet by itself it does not have a determinate actual being; this it receives from form. Lacking the determination of form, matter cannot exist by itself, but only in conjunction with form. The two partial beings of matter and form unite to constitute the total being of a thing. Things composed of matter and form come into being and pass away, but primary matter, as the subject of successive forms, cannot be generated or destroyed; in short, it is the permanent subject of substantial change.

Primary matter receives in succession different substantial forms, and it is one in number in each of the resultant composite individuals. Their matters are numerically different in the individuals, but they are entirely of the same nature (*omnino eiusdem rationis*); and if brought together they can constitute a matter one in number, as two waters separated from each other can unite and constitute a water numerically one.[35]

We saw in Chapter 1 that quantity is not really different from matter; it is only a term denoting matter as extended and having parts distant in place from each other.[36] In other words, matter is not extended by some reality added to it but simply by itself. Matter is never without some quantity and dimensions, but its exact amount or extent depends on the form it receives.[37] Of itself quantity has an indeterminate quantity and dimension, to use Averroes' expression.[38] Numerically the same matter can have

---

35. *Sum. phil. nat.* 1.9 and 1.12 (*OPh* 6: 179–181 and 188–191); *Expos. in Phys.* 1.16 (*OPh* 4: 175.2–182.87). Matter is actually and truly a substance in potency to substantial form, but it is not a *hoc aliquid*, that is, a subsistent reality capable of existing of itself without form (*Expos. in Phys.* 2.1 [*OPh* 4: 238.26–30]). It cannot be proved by demonstration that primary matter is a nature (ibid. 2.2. [*OPh* 4: 244.21–25]).

36. See above, pp. 40–41.

37. Though this is true naturally, through the divine power the body of Christ in the eucharist has quantity but it is not quantitative, that is, it does not have parts outside parts, or length, breadth or width (*Quodl.* 7.19 [*OTh* 9: 780–782]; *Tract. de corp. Christi* 42 [*OTh* 10: 226–234]).

38. Averroes, *In Phys.* 1, com. 36 (Junta ed. 4: f. 24r).

different extensions depending on its form. Under the form of fire it is less extended than under the form of air, and less extended under the form of water than under the form of earth. It might be asked why matter has a greater quantity under one form and less quantity under another. The reason is that the natural agent inducing substantial form in matter first suitably disposes matter by condensing or rarefying it. And even when the form has been introduced into matter, the agent in a twinkling rarefies or condenses the matter along with the form to the exact quantity suitable to that form. Rarefaction and condensation are nothing but moving the parts of matter closer to, or more distant from, each other.[39]

Though primary matter is an actually existing reality and is really distinct from the substantial form it receives, it cannot be perceived by the senses or known in itself in a simple concept proper to itself. How then do we know this hidden factor in all material substances subject to substantial change? We know it in relation to substantial form which it receives, and by analogy with the subject of accidental change. We observe that there is an entity underlying the different accidental qualities a body receives or can receive in turn; for example a man who is now white and afterward tan. Copper is the matter of the statue carved from it, and wood the matter of the bed. By analogy we can reason to the existence of an entity that is the subject matter underlying the substantial forms that in turn inform it or can inform it. This subject, which is an entity in itself, undetermined by any one specific substantial form, but able to receive all of them, is primary matter.[40] Similarly, we do not know substantial form in a simple concept but only in a complex concept in relation to matter:

> Just as we know matter only by knowing that matter is related to substantial form, as man to whiteness, so we know substan-

39. *Sum. phil. nat.* 1.13 (*OPh* 6: 191–194); *Expos. in Phys.* 1.15 (*OPh* 4: 160.85–108). For the notions of rarefaction and condensation see Adams, *William Ockham* (Notre Dame, IN, 1987), 1: 178–186.

40. *Sum. phil. nat.* 1.9, 1.14 (*OPh* 6: 180.37–44, 194–195); *Expos. in Phys.* 1.16 (*OPh* 4: 176.4–177.57).

tial form only by knowing that just as whiteness is related to man by informing him and making with him an accidental composite, so substantial form is related to matter by informing it and making it a substantial (*per se*) composite.[41]

Clearly, Ockham's notion of primary matter owes much to Duns Scotus. Before Ockham, the Subtle Doctor contended that matter is the receptacle of forms and hence it must be something real; if it were nothing it could not receive them.[42] Scotus concludes: "Matter has a certain positive being (*entitatem*) outside the mind and its cause, and it is through this reality that it can receive substantial forms, which are purely and simply acts."[43] He appeals to Aristotle that matter is a nature: "the immediate material substratum of things which have in themselves a principle of motion or change."[44] He also quotes Augustine's statement in his *Confessions*: "You made heaven and earth, these two, one close to you, the other close to nothing (*prope nihil*)."[45] If earth, understood as matter, is close to nothing, it must be something. And if it is something, it has its own being (*esse*) and does not receive it from its form.[46] Scotus here opposes the position of Aquinas, that primary matter does not have its own being distinct from form: taken in itself it is not an actually existing being (*ens aliquid actu existens*) but a pure potentiality to receive form and to

41. "Unde sicut non intelligimus materiam nisi intelligendo quod materia se habet ad formam substantialem sicut homo ad albedinem, ita non intelligimus formam substantialem nisi intelligendo quod sicut se habet albedo ad hominem informando ipsum et faciendo cum ipso unum compositum per accidens, ita forma substantialis se habet ad materiam informando eam et faciendo unum compositum per se" (*Expos. in Phys.* 1.16 [*OPh* 4: 177.45–51]).

42. Scotus, *Ord.* 2.12.1 (Vivès ed. 12: 556, n. 10).

43. Scotus, ibid. (Vivès ed. 12: 505a, n. 13).

44. Aristotle, *Phys.* 2.1, 193a28–31.

45. "Tu eras et aliud nihil, unde fecisti caelum et terram, duo quaedam, unum prope te, alterum prope nihil, unum, quo superior tu esses, alterum quo inferius nihil esset" (Augustine, *Confessiones* 12.7.7 [CCL 27: 220.13–16], cited by Scotus, *Ord.* 2.12.2 [Vivès ed. 12: 578a, n. 6]).

46. Scotus, *Ord.* 2.12.1 (Vivès ed. 12: 560–561, n. 14).

exist.[47] It is form that gives being to matter (*forma dat esse materiae*).[48] For Scotus and Ockham, to the contrary, matter has its own being and does not receive it from form.

Turning to the notion of form, Ockham distinguishes between a wide sense of the term, which embraces the substantial and accidental forms of composite beings and the separated substances or angels. In the strict sense a form is one part of a composite substance, the other part being the matter it informs. A substantial form of this sort is a reality (*res*) that (with the exception of the human soul) cannot exist by itself but only in the composite. Matter always exists, while form begins to exist in matter (*de novo*) with the generation of the composite and ceases to exist with its destruction.[49] Matter is a reality (*res*) really distinct from form, which itself is another reality. Thus the composite is made up of the two realities of matter and form, which nevertheless is a substantial unit (*per se unum*).[50]

Besides the substantial form and matter of a natural substance, the schoolmen of the late Middle Ages generally agreed on the need of a third principle called "the form of the whole" (*forma totius*), which they identified with the whole nature or essence of the substance. They contrasted the *forma totius* with the substance's substantial form, which they called "the form of the part" (*forma partis*), since it is only part of the essence of the substance. For Aquinas, the *forma totius* of a material substance is the whole nature or essence of a species, including both its substantial form and matter. An example is humanity. The *forma partis* is the formal

47. "Materia enim dicitur substantia non quasi ens aliquid actu existens in se considerata, sed quasi in potentia, ut sit aliquid actu, haec dicitur esse hoc aliquid" (Aquinas, *In Metaph.* 8.1 [ed. Cathala–Spiazzi n. 1687]).

48. Aquinas, *De principiis naturae* 1 (Vatican ed. 43: 39b).

49. *Sum. phil. nat.* 1.15 (*OPh* 6: 195–197).

50. "Primo modo dico quod materia est una res realiter distincta a forma et faciens per se unum cum ea, et similiter forma" (*Brevis sum. Phys.* 1.3 (*OPh* 6: 22.99–100). "Sed tamen sunt [materia et forma] duae res distinctae realiter, quamvis materia non possit denudari ab omni forma ita ut sit sine forma, et distinguuntur ratione et definitione, quia scilicet habent distinctas rationes in anima quae est declarativa essentiae unius et non alterius, et ex hoc ipso sunt distinctae res" (*Expos. in Phys.* 2.2 (*OPh* 4: 248.93–97).

part of the essence of a material being, uniting with matter to make up the complete essence; for example, the soul of a living being.[51] This was also the position of Giles of Rome, a pupil of Aquinas,[52] and Duns Scotus. According to the Subtle Doctor, the *forma totius* is not another form perfecting both the matter and form of a substance, but the essence or quiddity of the whole substance.[53]

Not surprisingly, Ockham would have nothing to do with the notion of *forma totius* as the whole essence or quiddity of a material substance, in some way distinct from its individual form or *forma partis*. We have already seen his sharp criticism of any attempt to differentiate in reality between an individual (for example, Socrates) and his essence (humanity).[54] The same criticism is valid when it is a question of an individual form and the essence of the whole individual composed of form and matter. If there were any doubt in Ockham's mind about the provenance and meaning of the notion of *forma totius*, Scotus would have dispelled it by describing "the form of the whole" "as the whole individual itself precisely considered in the way expressed by Avicenna when he says *Equinitas est tantum equinitas*."[55] We have

51. *In Metaph.* 7.9 (ed. Cathala-Spiazzi n. 1469). At n. 1467 Aquinas criticizes Averroes' identifying in reality the *forma totius* and the *forma partis* of a material substance; for example, the humanity of man with his soul, as though his whole essence is in his soul. See also *De ente et essentia* 2 (Leonine ed. 43: 370.10–25), and Armand Maurer, "Form and Essence in the Philosophy of St. Thomas," *Mediaeval Studies* 13 (1951): 165–176, repr. in *Being and Knowing* (Toronto, 1990), pp. 3–18.

52. Giles of Rome, *Theoremata de esse et essentia*, ed. Edgar Hocedez (Louvain, 1930), pp. 39–46.

53. "Ideo dico quod ultra formam quae perficit materiam ultimate, quae dicitur forma partis, non est necesse ponere aliquam formam quasi perficientem tam materiam quam formam. ... Si tamen intelligatur formam totius non aliquid constituens totum, sed ipsa natura tota, ut quiditas, hoc modo concedi bene potest quod forma totius sit alia a forma partis et quod natura vel quiditas posset dici forma, patet ex Philosopho, 5 *Metaph.*, com. de causa [5.2, 1013a27–29]" (Scotus, *Ord.* 3.2.2 [Vivès ed. 14: 141–142, n. 9]).

54. See above, pp. 71–72.

55. "Et hoc modo totum est ens formaliter forma totius, sicut album dicitur album albedine, non quidem quod forma totius sit quasi causa ipsius

seen above Ockham's dismissal of Avicenna's notion of essences understood as in some way on the side of reality. In Ockham's view, abstract essences like "horseness" are only concepts or words. There is simply no room in his world of radically individual things for essences as conceived by Avicenna.

Some defenders of the notion of *forma totius* found a more distant background for it in Aristotle. According to the Stagirite, if there is a whole like the syllable BA, which does not have the unity of a mere heap or aggregate, it is something other than its two elements B and A. This "something other" makes the syllable to be what it is; in short, it is its cause or formal nature.[56] Citing this passage of Aristotle, Ockham presents their argument as follows: There must be something in the whole BA over and above its parts, because if B and A are separated they both remain, but the syllable BA does not. Hence BA is something over and above B and A. This is understood to be the *forma totius* or essence of the composite.[57]

To Ockham this misconstrues Aristotle's position. He did not mean that a whole, like a syllable, is anything else than its parts joined and united at one point in time. If the whole had a form or entity besides its parts, it would be either simple or complex. It could not be simple, because then it would be matter or form, and the whole would have two partial substantial forms totally distinct from each other, and no one of these forms would be the form of the matter rather than the other. If the third entity were complex, it would be another composite of matter and form, which would

---

totius cum materia et forma partiali, causans quasi totum, sed est ipsum totum praecise consideratum secundum illum modum quo loquitur Avicenna, 5 *Metaph.*: *Equinitas est tantum equinitas*" (Scotus, ibid.); see Avicenna, *Liber de philosophia prima* 5.1 (ed. Van Riet 2: 228.33).

56. Aristotle, *Metaph.* 7.17, 1041b12–33.

57. *Sum. phil. nat.* 1.19 (*OPh* 6: 205.8–12). To the best of my knowledge, the author or authors of this interpretation of Aristotle have not yet been identified. Giles of Rome or Walter Burley have been suggested, but neither seems to be correct. Léon Baudry opts for Giles of Rome, but his doctrine of *forma totius* is Thomistic; see Baudry, *Lexique philosophique de Guillaume d'Ockham* (Paris, 1958), p. 97, with bibliography in n1.

be superfluous. As usual, Ockham's conclusion is on the side of simplicity: "[C]onsequently there is nothing besides matter and form except the composite, which is nothing else than the parts joined together."[58] This is the case with a man-made or artificial composite like a syllable; but it is also true of a natural composite that is substantially one (*per se unum*) like a human person. The whole is nothing but its parts conjoined and existing together. When its matter and form come together at the same time and in one place, the form necessarily informs matter, so that both form and matter, each in its own way (to be explained below),[59] are causes of the composite. No third principle or cause, like an essence or *forma totius*, is needed to explain a composite entity.[60]

The Matter of the Heavenly Bodies

Aristotle's universe was a vast but finite sphere, whose center was the spherical earth and whose circumference was the sphere of the fixed stars. Surrounding the earth were the other three elements arranged in order: water, air, and fire. Beyond them were the crystalline spheres, eternally circling the earth and each carrying with it one of the heavenly bodies, respectively the moon, Mercury, Venus, the sun, Mars, Jupiter, and Saturn. The matter of the universe beyond the four terrestrial elements was different in nature: it was a fifth essence or quintessence (*quinta essentia*), as it was later called. Unlike the matter of the four elements, the crystalline matter of the heavens could not undergo generation or destruction; its only change was uniform circular motion.[61]

With some later important additions and modifications, this was basically the universe known to Ockham. It was generally

58. "[I]gitur praeter materiam et formam nihil est nisi quoddam compositum quod non est aliud a partibus simul iunctis" (*Sum. phil. nat.* 1.19 [*OPh* 6: 206.27–29]).

59. See below, pp. 398–399.

60. *Sum. phil. nat.* 1.19 (*OPh* 6: 206.30–207.76).

61. See Crombie, *Medieval and Early Modern Science* 1: 75–76; see plate 1 facing p. 136.

agreed at the time that, beginning with the sphere of the moon, celestial matter was of a different kind from that of the four earthly elements. However, there were some indications of dissent from the common opinion. In the eleventh century Avicenna and Avicebron (Ibn Gabirol) thought that the earth and heavens shared a common corporeal foundation. Aquinas disagreed with them, arguing on the basis of the difference between the acts and movements of earthly and heavenly bodies that they do not share a common potentiality or matter. However, since there is a proportion between their acts and potencies (earthly bodies being potential to substantial and accidental change, celestial bodies potential to only local motion), he suggested that by analogy they have the same matter.[62]

Ockham's position is different from those of his predecessors. He begins by insisting on the materiality of the heavenly bodies. Both the saints and doctors of the church, like Augustine, assert that in the beginning God created matter, and from this matter he formed both the heavenly and earthly bodies. Thus from the start we have the assurance of the Christian religion that there is matter in the heavenly bodies. Ockham felt it was necessary to underline this important fact, for, according to Aristotle and his commentator Averroes the heavens are completely immaterial. In their view, the heavens have no matter subject to generation and destruction but only to change in place, and the matter underlying the quantity and other accidents in the heavens is in fact substantial form.[63]

In Ockham's opinion, not only do the heavenly bodies have matter, but their matter is entirely the same in kind as that of earthly bodies. He concedes his inability to demonstrate the fact, but he does not believe his opponents can demonstrate the oppo-

---

62. Aquinas refers to the opinion of these philosophers in *In Sent.* 2.12.1.1 (ed. Mandonnet–Moos 2: 303–304); *ST* 1.66.2.

63. *Rep.* 2.18 (*OTh* 5: 399.15–400.11). See Augustine, *De Genesi contra Manichaeos* 1.5–6 (PL 34: 177–178); Bonaventure, *In Sent.* 2.12.2.1 (*Opera omnia* 2: 302–303). Ockham reads Aristotle through the eyes of Averroes, *In Metaph.* 12, com. 10 (Junta ed. 8: f. 296v–297r).

site. Once the weakness of their arguments has been exposed, he hopes to persuade them to accept his own position. They argue that celestial and earthly matter must be different in nature because of the excellence of the celestial form. But they overlook the fact that this form is inferior to the human intellectual soul, which informs the same kind of matter as other sublunar forms. They also argue that heavenly matter, unlike earthly matter, is incorruptible, and consequently it must have a different nature. But primary matter is also incorruptible, as is also the intellectual soul; yet these two come together to form a composite that is corruptible. So incorruptibility by itself does not prevent the heavens from having matter of the same kind as earthly bodies. Moreover, the heavens are not absolutely incorruptible, for the omnipotent God can destroy them. Nor is there any contradiction in his introducing new forms into celestial matter. A thought-experiment persuades us that even a creature can do this. Suppose God introduces the form of fire into the matter of the heavens. If water is then poured on the fire, and if water has a greater active force than fire, the form of fire would be destroyed and the form of water would take its place. We can conclude that celestial matter is receptive of many forms through the agency of creatures.

The principle of the omnipotence of God is central to Ockham's vision of a universe whose matter is uniformly the same. The principle of the razor also supports this view. "As we have often said," Ockham writes, "a plurality should never be assumed without necessity. Now there is no clear necessity of assuming matter of a different nature here [below] and there [above], because everything that can be explained by a difference in nature of matter can equally well or better be explained by an identity in nature."[64]

---

64. "Sic igitur videtur mihi quod in caelo sit materia eiusdem rationis cum istis inferioribus. Et hoc, quia pluralitas nunquam est ponenda sine necessitate, sicut saepe dictum est. Nunc autem non apparet necessitas ponendi materiam alterius rationis hic et ibi, quia omnia quae possunt salvari per diversitatem materiae secundum rationem possunt aeque bene vel melius salvari secundum identitatem rationis" (*Rep.* ibid. [*OTh* 5: 404.4–10]).

The Christian belief in the divine omnipotence persuades Ockham that God could animate the heavenly bodies with an intellectual soul, but he does not think that in our universe these bodies are living creatures. The Intelligences move but do not inform or animate them. In this opinion he believes he has the support of Aristotle and also the fathers of the Church. The law of parsimony, enjoining one not to assume a plurality unnecessarily, adds weight to this conclusion, for there is no apparent reason to think the heavens are animated.[65]

3 The Causality of Natural Things
Material and Formal Causality

In the Aristotelian tradition, Ockham distinguishes between four kinds of causes: material, formal, efficient, and final. The first two are intrinsic to a thing, the latter two are extrinsic. We shall consider these types of causes in turn.

We saw above that matter and form are really distinct entities, the former being passive to, and receptive of the latter, which is actual. From the union of the two arises a composite entity. Thus material and formal causality present little difficulty. A material cause is simply the thing that is changed by an agent introducing a form into it: its causality is its passivity or receptivity of form. A formal cause is the form introduced into matter and inhering in it. Its causality is its informing matter or giving being formally to

---

65. *Rep.* 2.18 (*OTh* 5: 404.13–405.3). Modern historians dispute whether Aristotle intended the unmoved mover of the outermost sphere to be also its animating form. For a discussion of the subject see Joseph Owens, *The Doctrine of Being in the Aristotelian Metaphysics: A Study in the Greek Background of Mediaeval Thought*, 3rd ed. (Toronto, 1978), p. 438 n10. For Ockham, the Intelligences or unmoved movers are not the forms or souls of the heavenly spheres but only their extrinsic movers. The substantial form of the heavens is not an active but passive principle. In Ockham's interpretation of Aristotle and Averroes, the heavens are not composed of matter and form but are pure form. The Christian faith, however, teaches that the heavens are composed of matter and form. Ockham's editors cite Augustine, Basil, and Damascene as teaching that the heavens are not living (*Rep.* ibid. [*OTh* 5: 404 n2]). On this whole subject see *Quaest. in Phys.* 123 (*OPh* 6: 730.10–731.44).

the composite.[66] The form may be either substantial or accidental. If substantial, it informs matter and unites with it to make up a substantial (*per se*) unit. If accidental, it informs a subject and makes up with it an accidental (*per accidens*) unit. Thus, when a man becomes white, the result is a composite with an accidental unity which is neither man nor whiteness but at once man and whiteness. In a less proper sense we can speak of matter and form and their causality even though the form received by matter is not really distinct from it. For example, we can say that figure is the form of the statue and its formal cause, though figure or shape is not something really distinct from the bronze but only a new arrangement of its parts. The same is true of all works of art or human industry. They bring about a definite change in matter, but not through a really distinct form. In still another sense an exemplar or paradigm can be called a cause; but it is only a mental concept and not, as Plato thought, a reality.[67]

The novelty of Ockham's notion of a form should not be overlooked; it brings us close to the heart of his conceptualism. In his view, form and matter are two really distinct individual realities, the former actual and the latter potential. The form is not the formal cause of matter but of the composite of the two. As an individual, the form of any particular substance can have absolutely nothing in common with the form of any other substance. However, they can be similar to each other, and because of their similarity they can cause individuals that are alike and hence conceptualizable in universal notions. In this perspective the form does not endow the individual with a nature or essence in any way distinct from the individual. Rather, individuals are distinct not only in number but in essence.[68]

---

66. *Quodl.* 4.1 (*OTh* 9: 293.15–17). "Sed causatio causae materialis est materiare sive esse materiam compositi vel aliquid tale. Et causatio causae formalis est dare esse formaliter composito vel aliquid huiusmodi" (*Quaest. variae* 4 (*OTh* 8: 107.184–187).

67. *Sum. phil. nat.* 2.1–2 (*OPh* 4: 213–217); *Expos. in Phys.* 2.5. (*OPh* 6: 278–283); *Brevis sum. Phys.* 2.2 (*OPh* 6: 28.1–19).

68. See above, pp. 88–89.

This notion of form is radically different from that of Thomas Aquinas or Duns Scotus. Aquinas does not hesitate to speak of form as universal in itself, in the sense of an intelligible principle that can be shared by many individuals in the same species. In each individual, however, the form is individualized by matter and quantity, but basically by the individual's unique act of existing or *esse*.[69] According to Scotus, the form of a material thing confers on it an essence that is of itself common to many individuals, but contracted or limited to the individual by an added positive entity called an individual difference or *haecceitas*.[70] What stands between Ockham's notion of form and that of Aquinas and Scotus is the centerpiece of his metaphysics: the notion of an individual that is one of itself and incommunicable in essence with any other. A form is an individual that unites with matter (which is another individual), to constitute a composite reality; but the form does not give to the composite an essence or nature, distinct in some way from the composite individual and communicable to other individuals in the same species.

Efficient Causality

Ockham begins his treatment of efficient causality in his *Summula philosophiae naturalis* with the reminder that Aristotle always calls an efficient cause "that from which movement first begins (*unde principium motus*)."[71] This forewarns us that here Ockham intends

---

69. "Dicendum quod universale dupliciter potest considerari. Uno modo, secundum quod natura universalis consideratur simul cum intentione universalitatis. ... Alio modo potest considerari quantum ad ipsam naturam, scilicet animalitatis vel humanitatis, prout invenitur in particularibus" (*ST* 1.85.3.ad 1). "Forma autem vel est ipsa natura rei, sicut in simplicibus, vel est constituens ipsam rei naturam, in his scilicet quae sunt composita ex materia et forma" (*ST* 3.13.1). For Aquinas' notion of the individuation of form by existence (*esse*) see Joseph Owens, "Thomas Aquinas," in *Individuation in Scholasticism: The Later Middle Ages and the Counter-Reformation (1150–1650)*, ed. Jorge J.E. Gracia (Albany, NY, 1994), pp. 173–194.

70. See above, pp. 69–71; and Allan B. Wolter, "John Duns Scotus," in *Individuation in Scholasticism*, ed. Gracia, pp. 271–298.

71. *Sum. phil. nat.* 2.3 (*OPh* 6: 217.2–5); Aristotle, *Phys.* 2.3, 194b29–32; *Metaph.* 5.2, 1013a29–32. At *Expos. in Phys.* 2.5.4 (*OPh* 4: 283.2–4), he completes Aristotle's definition: the efficient cause is the beginning of both motion and rest.

to discuss efficient causality as an Aristotelian. In this perspective, an efficient cause is anything that initiates motion. Motion (*motus*), as we shall see, is not limited to local movement but includes change in quality (alteration) and change in quantity (augmentation or diminution).[72] In a broad sense there is also change in substance (generation and corruption), but this is not change properly speaking, for it is not successive or extended but instantaneous.[73]

An efficient cause in the strict sense is one that causes a newly existing form in a subject, as when fire produces fire and the sun heats wood. In the former case a new substantial form comes into being and in the latter a new accidental form. Broadly speaking, an efficient cause makes something to be different than it was before, either by producing a new substantial or accidental form, or by joining or separating preexisting parts, as in making a house, or in some other similar way. In the widest sense, an efficient cause is any mover, even if it only changes a thing's shape or place. Thus the Prime Mover is said to be the efficient cause of the movement of the heavens, though motion adds no new reality to them.

In other words, an efficient cause "is that at whose real existence something has a new different being completely distinct from that cause." Ockham adds that if this description is denied, there is no longer any way of persuading someone or knowing that one thing causes another. Why do we say, for example, that fire is the cause of heat? Because we see that when fire is applied to wood heat follows in the wood, and unless fire is applied the wood is not heated.[74]

---

72. *Motus* in the strict sense is limited to the three categories of quantity, quality and place; see *Brevis sum. Phys.* 5.2 (*OPh* 6: 87–91).

73. *Sum. phil. nat.* 3.2 (*OPh* 6: 249.3–9).

74. "Sic autem accipiendo causam efficientem, sciendum est quod causa efficiens est illa ad cuius exsistentiam realem habet aliquid aliud esse de novo totaliter distinctum ab illa causa. Si enim ista descriptio destruatur, perit omnis via persuadendi et cognoscendi aliquid est causam efficientem alterius. Propter hoc enim quod videmus quod igne approximato ligno sequitur calor in ligno, et nisi ignis esset approximatus ligno non esset calor in ligno, ideo dicimus quod ignis est causa caloris; et similiter est de aliis" (*Sum. phil. nat.* 2.3 [*OPh* 6: 218.26–33]).

In the above description of an efficient cause Ockham conflates two meanings of the term that in his *Reportatio* he keeps carefully distinct. He has told us above that Aristotle always uses the term in the sense of "that from which movement first begins (*unde principium motus*)." We have seen, however, that in Ockham's treatment of God's efficient causation of the world and creation, he claims that besides this kind of efficient cause Aristotle recognized another "at whose existence there follows the existence of something else." In this meaning, an efficient cause does not only extract a form from the potentiality of matter but causes the very existence of its effect. Taken in this sense, God can be the efficient cause and creator of the world.[75] What is this second meaning of an efficient cause but the one described above as "that at whose real existence something has a new different being completely distinct from that cause"? But in the *Summula philosophiae naturalis* Ockham, curiously enough, seems to identify it with an efficient cause that initiates motion.

In fact, the two meanings of an efficient cause come from two different philosophical traditions. Ockham is correct in saying that Aristotle always described an efficient cause as that from which motion first begins. The notion of an efficient cause as the giver of existence to something else following upon the cause is Neoplatonic. The medieval schoolmen encountered this notion in the *Liber de causis*, which is based on Proclus' *Elements of Theology*,[76] but especially in the *Metaphysics* of Avicenna and Algazel's summary of it. Besides an agent cause that initiates movement, Avicenna defines another as "the cause that gives to the thing being (*esse*) distinct from its own." Avicenna adds that this is the agent investigated by the "divine philosophers," that is, metaphysicians, and not the agent of natural philosophers, which is only the principle of movement. "The divine philosophers," he writes, "do not understand by an agent only the starting point of motion, as natural philosophers do, but rather the origin of existence (*prin-*

---

75. See above, pp. 296–297.
76. *Liber de causis* 1 (ed. Pattin pp. 134–138).

cipium essendi) and its giver (*et datorem eius*), like the creator of the world."[77] In this spirit, Albert the Great defines a cause in general as something after which another being follows and to which it gives being. An efficient cause is either a moving cause or a giver of being after non-being. Peter of Auvergne, a disciple of Aquinas, neatly formulated the two kinds of efficient cause respectively as *unde principium motus* and *unde principium esse*.[78]

Seen in the light of the history of efficient causality, Ockham's doctrine becomes more understandable and its originality is enhanced. An heir to both the Aristotelian and Neoplatonic notions of cause, he felt free to use their languages, but his own conception of an efficient cause is determined by his personal philosophical principles.

Ockham often employs Aristotelian language in describing an efficient cause: it is said to be the source of movement, whether it is itself moved in the process of bringing about its effect or remains immobile and separated from the motion it causes. In the latter case it is the simple being and pure act known to the metaphysician.[79] This distinction was known to Aristotle, but he did not rise to the Christian conception of the pure act who creates the total being of his effects and conserves them in being. He knew that an efficient cause gives its effects being, in the sense of

77. "Agens vero est causa rei quae acquirit rei esse discretum a seipso ... divini philosophi non intelligunt per agentem principium motionis tantum, sicut intelligunt naturales, sed principium essendi et datorem eius, sicut creator mundi; causa vero agens naturalis non acquirit esse rei nisi motionem aliquam ex modis motionum; igitur acquirens esse naturalibus est principium motus" (Avicenna, *Liber de philosophia prima* 6.1 [ed. Van Riet 2: 291.14–292.24]). See also Etienne Gilson, *A History of Christian Philosophy in the Middle Ages* (New York, 1955), pp. 210–211; "Avicenne et les origines de la notion de cause efficiente," in *Atti del XII Congresso internazionale di filosofia* (Florence, 1958–1961), 9: 121–130.

78. William B. Dunphy, "St. Albert and the Five Causes," *Archives d'histoire doctrinale et littéraire du moyen âge* 41 (1966): 7–21. According to Albert it was Plato and his followers who distinguished a first efficient cause from a first moving cause. On this subject see Etienne Gilson, "Notes pour l'histoire de la cause efficiente," the same journal 37 [1962]: 7–31.

79. *Brevis sum. Phys.* 2.6 (*OPh* 6: 38.70–39.89)

form, but only through motion and not through creation and conservation. As an agent cause and creator, God does not necessarily produce form in matter but he can create form absolutely.[80]

Whether the efficient cause is the source of motion or being, the effect follows upon the cause (*Causa est illud ad cuius esse sequitur aliud*) – a pseudo-Aristotelian definition of cause often used by Ockham to describe an efficient cause.[81] He makes it clear that this is not a succession in time but nature: cause and effect are simultaneous and together (*simul*).[82] Hence a true cause must be immediate and not remote from its effect. The sequence of cause and effect can be either natural (*ex natura rei*) or the result of someone's willing it, as a meritorious act causes a reward only because God wills it.[83]

Reflecting the language of Aristotle, a cause is also said to be present to its effect.[84] The Stagirite called the presence of the pilot of a ship the cause of its safety, as his absence is the cause of its destruction.[85] Commenting on this statement, Ockham points out that absence cannot strictly be a cause: something must be actually existing to merit this name. Only *per accidens* and improperly can something's absence be called a cause.[86] But according

80. *Rep.* 2.3–4 (*OTh* 5: 76.6–23)
81. The definition of cause is found in the works of Pseudo-Bede, *Sententiae philosophicae ex Aristotele collectae* (PL 90: 982). In the thirteenth century it gained currency through its use by Peter of Spain, *Summulae logicales* 5.19, ed. L.M. de Rijk (Assen, 1972), p. 67.6.
82. *Ord.* 1.3.6 (*OTh* 2: 490.23–491.1); *Rep.* 2.3–4 (*OTh* 5: 61.1–11).
83. "Quia causa, cum sit illud ad cuius esse sequitur aliud, dupliciter potest accipi. Uno modo quando ex natura rei ad praesentiam et esse unius sequitur naturaliter esse alterius. Alio modo quando ad esse unius sequitur esse alterius ex sola voluntate alterius. Et isto modo dicimus quod actus meritorius dicitur causa respectu praemii ex sola voluntate divina" (*Rep.* 4.1 [*OTh* 7: 12.14–20]).
84. "Unde, proprie loquendo, quaelibet causa proprie dicta ad cuius praesentiam potest poni effectus et ipsa non-praesente non potest poni, potest dici causa immediata. Et ex hoc sequitur quod causa remota non est causa, quia ad eius praesentiam non sequitur effectus" (*Rep.* 2.3–4 [*OTh* 5: 61.1–5]).
85. Aristotle, *Phys.* 2.3. 195a12–14.
86. *Expos. in Phys.* 2.5 (*OPh* 4: 289.2–16). A cause *per accidens* is not really a cause. Ockham defines such a cause as "something which, when not posited, the effect is nevertheless posited" (*Rep.* 4.1 [*OTh* 7: 18.6–7]).

to Ockham, presence, along with causal sequence, enters into the very notion of efficient cause, at least when defined nominally as "that at whose being or presence something follows."[87]

In reality, however, there is more to efficient causality than is suggested by its nominal definition. A natural efficient cause must have an active power (*virtus*) to produce the effect, a power that is not really different from the cause itself. It belongs to the very nature of a natural cause that by its own power the effect can follow upon it.[88] Hence causality implies an active production (*productio activa*) that brings about a new effect.[89] However, Ockham makes it clear that for a cause to produce (*efficere*) an effect is "nothing else than that the effect exists at the presence of the thing."[90] The effect in turn depends on the cause.[91] Thus there is eminently an essential order and dependence between a cause and its effect.[92] The cause is not only a condition or occasion of the existence of the effect – a cause *sine qua non* –, as the opening of a window is necessary to let in the sun's light, or as certain signs are a condition, but not properly a cause of God's granting grace in the sacraments.[93] When considering final causality, we shall see that there is a necessary relation between cause and effect in causes acting by necessity of nature. There is a necessary con-

---

87. "[D]efinitio causae efficientis est esse illud ad cuius esse sive praesentiam sequitur aliud" (*Quodl.* 4.1 [*OTh* 9: 294.23–25]).

88. "Ad aliud de causa et effectu dico quod de ratione causae est quod possit virtute propria ad eam sequi effectus ex natura rei et naturaliter" (*Rep.* 4.1 [*OTh* 7: 17.14–16]).

89. *Quodl.* 6.12 (*OTh* 9: 629.19).

90. "[Q]uando effectus natus est naturaliter causari et esse ad praesentiam agentis, tunc efficere non est nisi effectum sic esse" (*Quodl.* 2.9 [*OTh* 9: 156.148–150]).

91. "[I]llud a quo dependet aliquid, ita quod sine illo nullo modo potest esse, est causa eius" (*Quodl.* 3.21 [*OTh* 9: 285.9–10]).

92. *Ord.* 1.prol.9 (*OTh* 1: 241.15–16).

93. *Sum. phil. nat.* 2.3 (*OPh* 6: 218.33–36); *Rep.* 4.1 (*OTh* 7: 12.13–18.17). Ockham here argues against Aquinas' view that the sacraments are instrumental causes of grace. According to Ockham, the sacraments exercise their power through the divine will.

nection between the particular cause and effect, "for every naturally producible effect by its very nature is determined to be produced by one efficient cause and not by another, just as it is determined to be produced in one matter and not in another." Thus a
particular act of knowing is definitely caused by one particular
object and not by another of the same species.[94] However, the
necessary connection between cause and effect is not absolute but
conditional, for God can suspend the action of the secondary cause
and produce the effect by himself.

Examining the relation (or better, the relations) implied in the
notions of cause and effect brings us to the heart of Ockham's doctrine of efficient cause. Is the relation of efficient causality a reality
distinct from the absolute things that are related; for example, the
relation of what is able to heat to what is able to be heated?[95]
We have seen that the term "relation" does not signify a reality
different from the things related.[96] It is only a name designating
both of the terms of the relation, which are themselves absolutes.
Thus the real relation of what can heat to what can be heated is
not a reality (*res*) distinct outside the mind from the absolute terms
of the relation. Duns Scotus imagined that a relation like causality
and paternity is a reality (a small thing: *res parva*) somehow existing between the cause and effect and binding them together.[97]
Though Scotus was mistaken in thus reifying a relation, it is a fact
that cause and effect are really related to each other: the sun really
heats wood, a sick soul really affects the health or sickness of the
body and vice versa; but they are related *by themselves* and not by
an added real relation.

Another misconception to be avoided is the belief that cause
and effect can share in the same form or essence. According to
Aquinas, a cause communicates in form with its effect, as in the

---

94. *Rep.* 2.12–13 (*OTh* 5: 287.16–289.7).
95. *Quodl.* 6.12–13 (*OTh* 9: 629–634).
96. See above, pp. 47–49.
97. *Quodl.* 6.12 (*OTh* 9: 631.51–56); *Ord.* 1.30.1 (*OTh* 4: 300.20–301.2).
Scotus, *Ord.* 2.1.4–5 (Vatican ed. 7: 105–108, 112, nn. 210–215, 226).

univocal causation of a human being begetting another human being. Both cause and effect share the same specific form and hence are very similar to each other.[98] Duns Scotus was of the same mind, defining a univocal agent as one that "introduces into the effect a form of the same nature (*ratio*) as that through which it acts." This is in contrast to an equivocal agent, which does not act through a form of the same nature as that of its effect.[99] As we have seen, in Ockham's world of radically individual beings there is no communication in form between any of them. Each is an essence of its own, sharing with no other an intelligible form or essence.[100] In his view, both a univocal and equivocal cause "give being (*esse*) or produce an effect," the former producing an effect that measures up to the power of the agent and is in the same species, the latter causing an effect less perfect than itself and of a different species.[101] Cause and effect can be more or less like each other, but their likenesses are not based on the sharing of form or essence.

It is important to realize that on the nature of efficient causality Ockham separated himself not only from his immediate predecessors but also from Aristotle and the whole Aristotelian tradition. Aristotle makes it clear that the efficient cause is the same in form (*eidos*) as the thing produced, as man begets a man, though the form is individualized in another subject.[102] In breaking this ontological bond between cause and effect, Ockham began a new concept of cause whose influence would be pervasive in modern empiricism.

It should also be remarked that when Ockham says that an efficient cause "gives *esse*" he immediately equates it with "producing an effect." He is not saying with Aquinas that the cause gives to an essence an act of existing really distinct from the essence, or even with Scotus that it gives to an essence a condition or mode

---

98. *ST* 1.4.3.

99. Scotus, *Ord.* 1.3.3.2 (Vatican ed. 3: 303–304, n. 543).

100. See above, pp. 88–89.

101. *Quaest. in Phys.* 140 (*OPh* 6: 777.26–39).

102. Aristotle, *Metaph.* 7.7, 1032a24–25; 7.8, 1034a4–8. See Owens, *Doctrine of Being*, pp. 358–359.

really identical with the essence. As we have seen, *esse* for Ockham is just another name for essence, being (*ens*), or thing (*res*).[103] Consequently, for him, the giving of *esse* means nothing but the production of a being or thing. It has been pointed out that Aristotle treated efficient causality from the viewpoint of form, unaware of the special problem of existence.[104] As noted above, thirteenth-century philosophers, under the influence of Avicenna, began an existential interpretation of efficient causality. With Ockham, among others, this view of causality faded from the intellectual scene.[105]

With the severing of an ontological link between cause and effect, how can we know that one thing is the cause of another? In a world of radically individual things, there may be an eminently essential order and dependence between them; and yet Ockham writes, foreshadowing Hume:

> The simple knowledge of one thing does not entail the simple knowledge of another. And this is also something that everyone experiences within himself: that however perfectly he may know a certain thing, he will never be able to come to know (with a simple and proper knowledge) another thing that he has never before perceived by sense or by intellect.[106]

103. See above, p. 59. For the meanings of *esse* in Thomism and Scotism see Etienne Gilson, *Being and Some Philosophers*, 2nd ed. (Toronto, 1952), pp. 84–89, 154–189. For Scotism see also Allan Wolter, "Is Existence for Scotus a Perfection, Predicate, or What?" in his *The Philosophical Theology of John Duns Scotus*, ed. Marilyn M. Adams (Ithaca, NY, 1990), pp. 278–284.

104. Writing on Aristotle, Joseph Owens says: "The agent has the form, and so is able to cause that form in another matter. All that has to be accounted for is the *same* form in a different matter. The one preoccupation seems to be the establishing of a basis for universal predication. The sensible form in the thing itself is sufficient to account for the formal sameness in all the individuals produced. No [Platonic] Ideas are needed. This seems to be Aristotle's one interest in the problem. Nothing prompts him to ask how *existence* can be given to the new individuals by their efficient cause" (*Doctrine of Being*, p. 359).

105. For the eclipse of the existential view of being after Aquinas see Gilson, *Being and Some Philosophers*.

106. "Quia, sicut prius argutum est, inter causam et effectum est ordo et dependentia maxime essentialis, et tamen ibi notitia incomplexa unius rei non

Ockham is here taking a determined stand against Scotus' conviction that the knowledge of one simple object of thought can be virtually contained in the knowledge of another, and consequently that the former can be known through the latter. For Scotus, this is required for the very existence of a deductive science like mathematics or theology. The primary subject of the science virtually contains knowledge of its attributes; for example, the notion of triangle virtually contains in itself all the truths pertaining to it, and the knowledge of God as infinite being necessarily implies his attributes of goodness and truth.[107] The basis for Scotus' thesis is his doctrine of the formal distinction between a subject and its necessary attributes. But once Ockham has dismissed the formal distinction in philosophy, he cannot maintain that the knowledge of a subject always virtually contains a knowledge of its attributes.

---

continet notitiam incomplexam alterius rei. Hoc etiam quilibet in se experitur quod quantumcumque perfecte cognoscat aliquam rem quod nunquam cogitabit cogitatione simplici et propria de alia re quam nunquam prius apprehendit nec per sensum nec per intellectum" (*Ord.* 1.prol.9 [*OTh* 1: 241.15–21]). For the meaning of a simple and proper knowledge see below, p. 492. The intuitive knowledge of one thing can never give us the intuitive knowledge of another; intuitions are as radically individual as realities themselves. The union of cause and effect is not known *per se* but by experience; see above, pp. 410–411.

"When we reason *a priori*," Hume writes, "and consider merely any object or cause, as it appears to the mind, independent of all observation, it never could suggest to us the notion of any distinct object, such as its effect" (David Hume, *An Inquiry Concerning Human Understanding* 4, 1, 27, ed. L.A. Selby-Bigge [La Salle, IL, 1963], p. 31). Ockham also prepares the way for Hume with his conviction that two individuals, like a cause and an effect, are distinct and separable, at least by the divine power. Again Hume writes: "The separation, therefore, of the idea of a cause from that of a beginning of existence, is plainly possible for the imagination; and consequently the actual separation of these objects is so far possible, that it implies no contradiction nor absurdity" (*Treatise of Human Nature* 1.3.3, ed. L.A. Selby-Bigge, 2nd ed. [Oxford, 1978], pp. 79–80). However similar the two doctrines are on this point, they differ radically on others. Hume, for example, would not agree with Ockham that an efficient cause has an active power to produce an effect, that it is really related to an effect, or that it is simultaneous with it, as pointed out by Adams, *William Ockham* 2: 741–758.

107. Scotus, *Rep. Par.* prol.2 (Vivès ed. 22: 35, n. 4).

These must be known previously by a distinct and proper knowledge. Hence his conclusion that the incomplex knowledge of one thing existing in reality is never the sufficient cause of the first incomplex knowledge of another thing.[108]

However, we are not without resources to know, and even to prove, that one thing is the efficient cause of another. This can be done by inductive reasoning, as we saw in Chapter 2.[109] After experiencing the cure of a sick person by a certain kind of herb, and removing all other causes of his recovery, we know with evidence that this herb caused his health. This particular experience can be generalized, so that we have evident knowledge that every herb of this sort cures fever. We know this in virtue of the principle that all individuals of the same kind have effects of the same kind in an equally disposed subject. We can also know a causal relation exists between two things by their likeness. Suppose someone saw a statue of Hercules and had no knowledge of the god. By seeing the statue he would not know Hercules any more than he would Achilles. But if knew Hercules beforehand and had an habitual knowledge of him, when he saw the statue he would remember Hercules and know that it was made in his likeness.[110] On the basis of habit we can also infer that on a particular occasion fire caused smoke, even if we did not see the fire. If at other times we saw smoke at the presence of fire and formed the habit of associating them as cause and effect, seeing the smoke without the fire we would remember the fire and know that this smoke was caused by fire.[111]

---

108. *Ord.* 1.prol.9 (*OTh* 1: 240.14-17). The subject does not always virtually contain its attributes because the attributes are often relative or connotative concepts and hence imply things not virtually contained in the subject; see ibid. (*OTh* 1: 244.22-245.2). On this subject see Gordon Leff, *William of Ockham* (Manchester, 1975), pp. 324-328.

109. See above, pp 107-109.

110. *Ord.* 1.prol.9 (*OTh* 1: 253.24-254.19). See above, p. 107.

111. *Quodl.* 1.6 (*OTh* 9: 40.108-115); *Quaest. variae* 6.1 (*OTh* 8: 199.107-114).

Although Ockham has confidence that these arguments give us evident knowledge of causal relations, he does not mean the hard evidence of demonstration, for he asserts:

[I]t cannot be demonstrated that any effect is produced by a secondary cause, because even though fire always follows when fire is brought close to combustible material, it is possible that the fire is not its cause. For God could have ordained that he alone caused combustion whenever fire is present to a patient close by, just as he has ordained with the Church that when certain words are spoken grace is caused in the soul. Thus, there is no effect by which it can be proved that someone is a human being, especially no effect that appears to us, because everything we see in the human being can be done by an incarnate angel; for instance, eating, drinking and the like. This is clear in the case of the angel with Tobias (Tob 12:19). It is no wonder, then, that it cannot be demonstrated that something is a cause.[112]

Consequently there can be no demonstration dispelling all doubt that A is the cause of B; for it is always possible for B to be caused by God alone without a secondary cause, or he may act through a different secondary cause from the apparent one, as when an angel and not a man spoke to Tobias. We know on the authority of scripture that an angel and not a human being talked to Tobias. But without a revelation or some other good reason for denying cau-

---

112. "Et ex hoc sequitur quod non potest demonstrari quod aliquis effectus producitur a causa secunda: quia licet semper ad approximationem ignis combustibili sequatur combustio, cum hoc tamen potest stare quod ignis non sit eius causa. Quia Deus potuit ordinasse quod semper ad praesentiam ignis passo approximato ipse solus causaret combustionem, sicut ordinavit cum Ecclesia quod ad prolationem certorum verborum causaretur gratia in anima. Unde per nullum effectum potest probari quod aliquis sit homo, maxime per nullum effectum qui apparet in nobis, quia omnia quae videmus in homine potest angelus incorporatus facere, sicut comedere, bibere etc. Patet de angelo Tobiae. Ideo non est mirabile si non possit demonstrari quod aliquid sit causa" (*Rep.* 2.3–4 [*OTh* 5: 72.21–75.9]).

sality to something, Ockham thinks we should accept the evidence of experience and reason and grant that the apparent cause of something is its real cause. He writes: "...that at whose existence something else follows ought to be assumed to be its cause unless it is evidently apparent that causality should be denied to it."[113]

Ockham's aim is to do justice to both the divine omnipotence and the evidence of experience and reason. He has no intention of denying the Christian belief in the omnipotence of God; neither does he wish to neglect the evident knowledge gained from experience and reasoning. Striking the right balance between the demands of faith and reason is one of Ockham's main preoccupations. His method of doing so in the present case will appear again, when we examine his doctrine of the possibility of an intuition of a nonexistent.[114]

Final Causality

A final cause is that for whose sake something is done or made. In general a cause always answers the question "why?" If you ask someone why he is walking and he replies "To be healthy," he is giving the end (*finis*) or final cause of his action.[115]

A final cause is unlike other causes in that it need not actually exist in order to be a cause. Matter, form, and agent must actually exist if they are to exercise their causality; all that is required of a final cause is that beforehand it be known, loved or desired by an agent.[116] It is usually said that the causality of a final cause is

---

113. "Quod probatur, quia illud ad cuius esse sequitur aliud, illud debet poni causa eius nisi evidenter appareat quod sit ab eo neganda causalitas" (*Rep.* 3.12 [*OTh* 6: 397.9–12]). Ockham here argues that acts are the efficient cause of a habit. The habit follows upon repeated acts and it cannot naturally exist without them. Hence the acts are its efficient cause.

114. See below, pp. 479–490.

115. *Expos. in Phys.* 2.5.5 (*OPh* 4: 284.2–9); *Sum. phil. nat.* 2.4 (*OPh* 6: 220.5–221.10). Aristotle, *Phys.* 2.3, 194b32–35. See Stephen F. Brown, "Ockham and Final Causality," in *Studies in Medieval Philosophy*, ed. John F. Wippel (Washington, DC, 1987), pp. 249–272.

116. *Quodl.* 4.1 (*OTh* 9: 294.28–39).

to move an efficient cause to act. But Ockham points out that the so-called "motion" of the final cause is nothing real but only metaphorical. It is simply the fact that something is desired or loved by an agent, stimulating it to act. Thus a final cause, in the proper sense, can be defined as "that which is truly loved and desired by an agent, because of which what is loved is brought into existence."[117]

Now there are two kinds of love: the love of desire (*amor concupiscentiae*) and the love of friendship (*amor amiticiae*). Corresponding to them are two kinds of final causes or ends, unequal in their nobility. The end may be something a person strives to acquire with the love of desire, as health is the end of walking. However, this is not the noblest and primary end for which the person strives. He walks for the sake of health, and he wants health for the sake of his life. For the sake of his health he is even willing to take a bitter medicine. But walking, health, and medicine are not only ends; they are also means to a further and final end, which is the person's life. The person loves himself with a love of friendship and sets up intermediate goals in order to achieve a final aim, which is nothing but himself and his own good. Beyond the good of his own person, he can love God for the sake of God himself with the greatest love of friendship and direct all his actions to him.[118]

---

117. "[D]efinitio causae finalis est esse amatum et desideratum efficaciter ab agente, propter quod amatum fit effectus" (*Quodl.* 4.1 [*OTh* 9: 294.22–23]). There is a twofold causality of the final cause: first, the causality by which it moves the agent to *will* to cause the effect; second, the causality of the end by which it *actually moves* the agent to act. The latter "motion" of the end is the end to be loved, because of which loved thing the agent causes the outward effect; see *Quaest. variae* 4 (*OTh* 8: 111.266–112.289) and *Sum. phil. nat.* 2.4 (*OPh* 6: 221.16–28).

118. *Ord.* 1.prol.11 (*OTh* 1: 306.7–22); *Quaest. variae* 4 (*OTh* 8: 104.125–106.151; 120.462–128.632). The latter reference is to a *Quaestio disputata*, printed in the Lyons edition of 1495 as *Sent.* 2.3. In this *Quaestio* (*OTh* 8: 103.91–92), Ockham says that "properly speaking, a final cause is that which an agent does for the sake of that which is loved with the love of friendship." He corrects this at 124.538–540, saying that "not every final cause is loved

Up to now Ockham has been using the terms "final cause" and "end" as synonyms. Both imply a knowing and loving agent that acts out of desire or love of something. There is another meaning of "end" that does not have the connotation of desire or love but only of limit or completion. In this sense we can speak of a point as the end of a line and form as the end of a change. Form can be called the "end" of matter, since matter is potential to receiving form, which limits the composite to be of a definite kind.[119]

If we use the term "end" to include this meaning, we can say with Aristotle that every agent acts for an end.[120] Clearly agents that act with purpose and will, such as human beings, act for an end and their actions have a final cause. But even animals act for an end, since they have sense knowledge, imagination, and desires, and they act in order to get what they want. However, they do not know or decide what their ends will be or pursue them freely. Rather, nature implants these ends in them. Nature does the same in birds and insects: when spiders weave webs and birds build nests they act for an end. This is not so evident in plants, but even in them we see nature acting for an end, though naturally and necessarily, without conscious purpose. Nature gives them leaves to guard and cover their fruit, and it sends their roots down and not up for nourishment. Extending this line of inductive reasoning, Ockham concludes that since we see nature acting for an end both in animals, birds, insects, and plants (and there is no greater reason for nature to act for an end in them than in nonliving things), it follows that nature everywhere acts for an end.[121]

---

with the love of friendship, but some with the love of friendship and some with the love of desire"; see editor's note *OTh* 8: 103 n15.

119. *Quaest. variae* 4 (*OTh* 8: 99.23–28); *Expos. in Phys.* 2.4 (*OPh* 4: 274.24–32).

120. Aristotle, *Phys.* 2.5, 196b21–22.

121. *Expos. in Phys.* 2.12 (*OPh* 4: 378.2–20). See Aristotle, *Phys.* 2.8, 199a9–30. An argument beginning with the phrase "there is no greater reason ..." ("non est major ratio ...") is equivalent to one based on the principle of parsimony. Both assume unity in nature and call for simplicity in its explanation.

It is important, however, to define correctly the sense in which nonliving things may be said to act for an end. If they are moved and directed by someone with knowledge and will, they act for an end, like an arrow shot from a bow with the intention of killing someone. The arrow hits the target, but the intention of killing is not properly in the arrow but in the archer. It is the archer and not the arrow who properly acts for an end. But even if nonliving things are not directed to an end by an agent with knowledge and will, they may be said to act for an end in a broad sense, because in the ordinary course of nature their actions result in uniform effects, just as though they were foreseen and willed by an agent. Fire, for example, unless impeded always produces fire. Thus in the wide sense of an end that terminates an action there is finality in nonliving things, even if they are not moved and directed by a knower, but they cannot properly be said to act for a final cause or purpose.[122]

The Christian faith teaches that everything in the world acts in view of God, their transcendent end. But as we have seen in Chapter 3, Ockham did not think natural reason can demonstrate this belief by evident principles or experience. In his view, the philosophers' contention that every particular nature desires the good of the whole universe and of its ruler more than it does its own, is meant to be only probable and not strictly demonstrated, for they cannot demonstrate that God is loved and desired by anything.[123]

In the philosophers' universe, however, everything acts for an end in some sense of the word. Some agents act with knowledge and purpose to attain their goals; others reach their ends acting by necessity of nature. In both cases chance or fortuitous events may

---

122. *Sum. phil. nat.* 2.6 (*OPh* 6: 228.25–230.3). In *Quodl.* 4.1 (*OTh* 9: 299.131–137), only agents that are free and capable of sinning or failing are said to have a final cause. This excludes agents that act by natural necessity from having a final cause in the strict sense.

123. "Ad aliud dico quod philosophi posuerunt illud tamquam probabile, sed non tamquam sufficienter demonstratum, quia non potest demonstrari quod [rector universi] sit amatus et desideratus ab aliquo" (*Quodl.* 4.2 [*OTh* 9: 306.129–131]).

occur. This is most obvious with agents acting for a purpose. Someone may go to the forum to make a purchase and encounter a debtor who pays him what he owes. He meets the debtor by chance (and also has a stroke of good fortune) if he did not intend to meet him there and if it rarely happens that he meets him in that place. However, the meeting is not fortuitous on the side of the debtor if he went to the forum to meet his creditor.[124] A chance event can also occur when a natural cause produces an effect through the intervention of a voluntary cause. If someone puts a cloth over a horse and the cloth falls from the horse browsing near a fire and burns, the burning of the cloth happens by chance. The immediate causes of the burning are the fire and horse, which are natural causes, but the accident would not have happened unless the rider freely put the cloth on the horse.[125]

For Ockham, chance events properly speaking always involve an agent acting freely. There can be rare occurrences resulting from causes acting necessarily, as when they concur to eclipse the sun or to produce rain and lightning during the dog days of summer. But only in a broad sense do these events happen by chance, for their causes act by necessity of nature.[126] A truly chance event is contingent and avoidable, and this presupposes an agent acting freely and not necessarily.[127] Now the only agent acting

124. *Sum. phil. nat.* 2.11 (*OPh* 6: 241.15–39).

125. *Quodl.* 1.17 (*OTh* 9: 91.35–92.54). For the difference between chance and fortune see *Quaest. in Phys.* 130 (*OPh* 6: 747–749). Here Ockham defines chance in the strict sense as an event that is found in natural things and not in voluntary matters, but always requiring either a mediate or immediate free cause. It is defined: "casus est causa agens propter determinatum finem ex cuius actione per accidens et in minori parte aliquid consequitur praeter intentum." Fortune is defined: "fortuna est causa agens sponte et libere propter determinatum finem, ex cuius actione per accidens et in minori parte aliquid consequitur praeter intentum." The only difference in the definitions is the addition of the phrase "sponte et libere" in the definition of fortune.

126. *Quodl.* 1.17 (*OTh* 9: 90.12–92.54).

127. *Sum. phil. nat.* 2.12 (*OPh* 6: 242.2–243.38). The notion of fortune is closely allied to the notion of chance. Fortune is a rare occurrence happening as the result of natural causes along with a free cause, or a free cause, over and

freely and contingently known to the philosopher is the human will. As Ockham states, "There is contingency in things because of the freedom of the created will."[128] As we saw in Chapter 5, there is no convincing proof that God acts contingently and introduces contingency in the world.[129] Thus from the perspective of human reason the world of nature is ruled by necessity; it contains fortuitous and contingent events owing to the human will.

4 Motion

Thus far we have been following Ockham's account of the principles and causes of natural things. He next treats of their properties or attributes, the first of which (or among the first), he says, is motion, for "every natural self-subsisting body is able to move."[130]

Motion and Nature

The study of motion has been central to physics from antiquity to modern times. Aristotle already pointed out that the meaning of nature (*physis*) depends on the notion of movement, for nature is a "principle of motion and change." Consequently if we do not know the meaning of motion the meaning of nature would also remain unknown. Ockham echoes these words of Aristotle when commenting on the *Physics*.[131]

Ockham recognizes a static concept of nature as a positive, absolute thing able to exist outside the mind.[132] The term here

---

above its intention. If someone digs into the ground and finds a treasure, this happens by chance and good fortune; see *Quodl.* 1.17 (*OTh* 9: 91.35–40).

128. *Quodl.* 2.2 (*OTh* 9: 116.101–102).

129. See above, pp. 244–245.

130. *Sum. phil. nat.* 3.1 (*OPh* 6: 247.7–8).

131. Aristotle, *Phys.* 3.1, 200b12–14. *Expos. in Phys.* 3.1 (*OPh* 4: 411.10–17. For the concepts of motion and nature in the Middle Ages see James A. Weisheipl, "The Concept of Nature," *The New Scholasticism* 28 (1954): 377–408, repr. in his *Nature and Motion in the Middle Ages*, pp. 1–23; Herman Shapiro, *Motion, Time and Place according to William Ockham* (St. Bonaventure, NY, 1957).

132. "Secundo dico quod per 'naturam' intelligo rem absolutam positivam natam esse extra animam" (*Rep.* 3.1 [*OTh* 6: 5.12–13]).

has the meaning of a real being as distinguished from a being of reason, which can only exist in the mind. Both substantial form and matter are natures, the former active and effective, and the latter passive or receptive. So too the composite is a nature.[133] As we saw in Chapter 1, there are no common natures, as Duns Scotus would have it. No two things have a nature in common, individuated in each particular. As an absolute reality, a nature is at the peak of singularity, being individual of itself and by essence. The sum total of all individuals in their order and relation to each other make up what we ordinarily call "nature" or the universe.

As we saw above, nature can also be described dynamically as a principle of movement or change. This brings us to the root of the meaning of the word "nature," which is derived from the Latin *natura*, from *nasci*, to be born. Similarly in Greek the word *physis* is probably derived from *phuein*, to bring forth or make grow. According to Aristotle, nature originally meant "the genesis of growing things," then "the inner part of a growing thing from which its growth first proceeds," finally "the source from which the primary movement in each natural object is present in it in virtue of its own essence."[134] Ockham accepts this dynamic notion of nature, listing among the items that move or are moved naturally all animals with all their parts, plants, simple bodies like earth, fire, air and water, and the celestial spheres. Excluded are everything acting with knowledge and purpose, events occurring by chance, and works of art.[135]

Kinds of Motion
Though all natural things can move or be moved with an inner spontaneity, their movement can be of different kinds. In a broad

133. *Expos. in Phys.* 2.1 (*OPh* 4: 237.2–238.44).
134. Aristotle, *Metaph.* 5.4, 1014b16–20.
135. *Expos. in Phys.* 2.1 (*OPh* 4: 214.28–51). All the spheres, except the outermost (i.e. the eighth) are naturally moved by both a conjoined and a separate mover; see *Brevis sum. Phys.* 8.3 (*OPh* 6: 128.36–45). What is natural is distinguished from what is done: (1) by art or will, (2) by custom or doctrine, (3) by violence, (4) supernaturally, (5) by accident; see *Rep.* 3.6 (*OTh* 6: 173.15–176.14).

sense change (*mutatio*) is either instantaneous or successive. This includes change in the four Aristotelian categories of substance, quantity, quality, and place. Motion does not strictly apply to the other categories. Substantial change takes place in an instant by a substance acquiring or losing its substantial form. These changes go by the names of generation and corruption. The other three changes take place with succession and are properly called movements (*motus*). In quantity there is increase and decrease; in quality alteration, for example, gaining or losing a quality like heat; in place locomotion, or the acquiring of one place in whole or in part and the losing of another place.[136]

The term "motion" (*motus*) is the strict sense applies to change in the three categories other than substance, for only in them do we find changes that are successive and take place in time. Ockham adds an important note at this point: there is no motion without a mover and agent, taking agent in a broad sense. So too there is always something movable and passive.[137] We shall return to these requirements for motion when we take up the questions of gravitational and projectile motion.

Definition of Motion

More difficult than classifying the kinds of motion is knowing what it is. To some, motion appears to be a *way* to something; for example, locomotion is imagined to be a way to reaching a new place, and alteration a way to acquiring a new quality. Motion would then have its own reality, really and totally distinct from the permanent being of the things from which motion begins and ends. Albert the Great described motion as a flowing form (*forma fluens*) or the flowing of a form (*fluxus formae*), and John of Jan-

---

136. *Sum. phil. nat.* 3.1 (*OPh* 6: 248.19–249.40). For the kinds of change (*mutatio*) see *Expos. in Phys.* 5.2 (*OPh* 5: 332–347). For the kinds of motion (*motus*) see ibid. 5.4 (*OPh* 5: 367–376). For Aristotle's restricting change to the four categories, see *Phys.* 3.1, 200b32–34. Ockham defends this limitation in *Expos. in Phys.* 5.3 (*OPh* 5: 347–367).

137. *Sum. phil. nat.* 3.2 (*OPh* 6: 249.6–250.1).

dun and William of Alnwick conceived it as the flowing of the parts of the form introduced into matter. Walter Burley and Walter Chatton also contended that motion is a reality (*res*) completely outside the essence of all permanent things and that no permanent thing is of the essence of motion.[138] In opposition to this way of conceiving motion, Ockham cites Aristotle to the effect that there is no such thing as motion over and above the things involved in motion, such as substance, quantity, quality or place. Motion and change do not refer to anything except these, "for there is nothing over and above them."[139]

Ockham argues at great length to prove that neither instantaneous change nor successive motion is an absolute reality, really distinct from permanent things. For our purpose several of his arguments will suffice to show his mind on the subject. When matter receives a substantial form in an instantaneous change, the first thing received in matter is the substantial form. Nothing prior to that form is immediately received in matter, nor is it necessary to assume that some thing must be destroyed after the substantial form. In short, the sudden substantial change can be accounted for by form and matter, without assuming any other positive thing. For the change to take place it is enough that matter now have some form that it did not previously have. All that is needed for this is matter, form, and the agent inducing form in matter. Over and above these permanent things, change itself is not required as another positive thing. Hence the term "sudden change" signifies nothing but the permanent things it involves, while connoting the negation immediately preceding or immediately following the form that is generated or destroyed. These negations are expressed when we say that the form acquired by the change now exists but did not exist before. When the form is destroyed we imply that it does not exist now but that it did exist immediately before. This posi-

---

138. *Expos. in Phys.* 3.2 (*OPh* 4: 421.12–15). For references to these philosophers see p. 421 n2. For the history of the nature of motion see Anneliese Maier, *Zwischen Philosophie und Mechanik* (Rome, 1958).

139. Ibid. 3.2 (*OPh* 4: 419.9–15); Aristotle, *Phys.* 3.1, 200b32–201a2.

tion is sustained by the principle of the razor, for permanent things suffice to verify the proposition "this changes with an instantaneous or sudden change." Hence it is unnecessary to posit another reality besides the permanent things mentioned.[140]

Must we assume that successive motion, like local motion, is a reality distinct from the permanent things it involves? Must we think of it as a kind of "flowing reality" between the thing from which it starts and the thing at which it ends? Walter Chatton's anti-razor would seem to support this view of local motion. It does not seem that permanent things alone can verify the proposition "the movable thing moves," for there can be permanent things without motion. Hence if they move, there must be a "flowing reality" over and above permanent realities. The problem Chatton poses for Ockham is how things can really change and move if every thing is permanent. Ockham retorts that the proposition "the movable thing moves" not only implies the existence of permanent things, such as the mobile thing and space, but also the fact that the mobile thing is first present in one part of space and then in another, and so on, without stopping at any one of them. Hence local motion can be explained without recourse to anything besides the permanent realities of the mobile thing and the parts of space.[141] It is nothing but "the successive coexistence, without intermediate rest, of something continually existing in place with different places."[142]

Alteration in the category of quality and increase in the category of quantity can likewise be explained without implying anything distinct from permanent things. Consider something that

140. *Quaest. in Phys.* 8 (*OPh* 6: 413.7–415.73). Ockham contends (ibid. q. 9) that neither is a relative reality needed to account for sudden change. There is no such relative reality; moreover, absolute realities (*res*) suffice to verify all propositions concerning sudden change.

141. Ibid. 13 (*OPh* 6: 425.4–429.132). See *Quodl.* 1.5 (*OTh* 9: 29.10–35.157).

142. "Circa primum dico quod motus localis est coexistentia successiva, sine quiete media, alicuius continue existentis in loco diversis locis" (*Quodl.* 1.5 [*OTh* 9: 29.10–12]).

becomes white. Is this alteration a reality distinct from permanent things? Ockham contends that it is not, if by "permanent things" is meant presently existing things. To account for the alteration of whitening all that needs to be assumed is that whiteness has parts which are successively and continually received by something without any interruption. Since the parts of whiteness are themselves permanent things, the alteration of whiteness does not call for any reality besides them. It may be called something permanent only improperly as the form acquired at the end of the change. It is not yet something permanent but it *will be* something permanent.[143]

Similarly changes like increase and decrease can be explained without assuming that they are permanent things. Increase in quantity means that in the changeable thing there is a greater and greater quantity, not simultaneously but successively and continually. The change implies parts of quantity, some of which exist in the present and others in the future. Thus understood, it is not a permanent thing, for no permanent thing has present and future parts.[144]

Can an appeal be made to self-evident principles or to experience to prove that motion and change imply something besides permanent things? Ockham denies this possibility. He believes he can answer all objections to the contrary, and he insists that we only experience permanent things (*nullam experientiam habemus nisi de rebus permanentibus*).[145]

If this is so, does motion really exist? To Walter Burley, the Ockhamist position implies that it does not, for motion is not conceived as a reality but as an abstract term. In reply Ockham distinguishes between two uses of "exists" in propositions. In one way we say something exists, and it is true without implying other propositions following upon it. An example is "man exists." In another way we say something exists, but the truth of the proposition requires the truth of at least one other proposition. Thus the proposition "the day exists" is true only if other propositions are true, such as "some time

---

143. *Quaest. in Phys.* 15 (*OPh* 6: 432.4–433.41); *Rep.* 2.7 (*OTh* 5: 103.2–20).
144. *Quaest. in Phys.* 16 (*OPh* 6: 434.9–435.36); *Rep.* 2.7 (*OTh* 5: 104.1–8).
145. *Quaest. in Phys.* 17 (*OPh* 6: 435.13–15).

exists," "some time was," and "some time will be." It is in the second sense that the proposition "motion exists" is true, for its truth requires the truth of the propositions clarifying it: "the movable thing now has something" (e.g. a place) and "previously it did not have it but something else," and "immediately afterward it will have it."[146]

Commenting on Aristotle's *Physics*, Ockham encountered the Philosopher's definition of motion as "the act (*entelecheia*) of something existing in potency insofar as it is in potency."[147] To Ockham this definition confirms his view that motion involves nothing but permanent things. In Ockham's interpretation, the definition simply means that when something moves it actually has something and actually lacks something else to which it is potential. Continuous motion means that "when something moves continually it actually has something or actually lacks something in potency to have or lose something else of the same genus." For example, in continuous motion in which something is acquired, something must actually have something (a certain quantity, quality, or place) and be in potency to something of the same genus that it lacks, but immediately afterward it will have it. In order to account for this there is no need to assume anything besides past, present, and future permanent things. Ockham adds that in a continuous motion the mobile thing does not acquire that to which it is moving or changing all at once but part by part. In the case of instantaneous motion, Aristotle's definition is equivalent to the proposition "what moves actually has something that it did not have before but could have." For instance, when matter acquires a new substantial form, the change is the act of this matter insofar as it is potential. In other words, this matter is now under a substantial form that it did not have before but could have had.[148]

---

146. Ibid. 36 (*OPh* 6: 491.3–47). For Walter Burley's criticism of Ockham's doctrine of motion see Maier, *Zwischen Philosophie und Mechanik*, pp. 46–57.

147. "[M]otus erit *entelecheia*, id est actus, alicuius exsistentis in potentia in quantum huiusmodi" (*Expos. in Phys.* 3.2 [*OPh* 4: 452.15–16]); cf. Aristotle, *Phys.* 3.1, 201a10–11.

148. *Expos. in Phys.* 3.3 (*OPh* 4: 453.26–454.61); *Sum. phil. nat.* 3.6 (*OPh* 6: 265.37–266.63).

Aquinas offers a different interpretation of the Aristotelian definition of motion or change based on the metaphysical notions of being,
its modes of act and potency, and participation. Motion, he says, is
the imperfect actuality of something existing in potency, not insofar
as it only exists in act but insofar as, already being in act, it has a
relation (or tends) to further actuality. Thus what moves is between
pure act and pure potency, being partly in act and partly in potency.
For example, when water is only potentially hot it is not yet changing, and when it is already hot the change has ended. But when it
participates in some heat, though imperfectly, it is then moving
toward being hot, gradually participating more fully in heat.[149]

Ockham has little liking for this metaphysical language of motion.
He does not dismiss the Aristotelian definition of motion as the act
of a being in potency insofar as it is in potency, but he thinks it can
be "saved" in another and better way by using his own basic principles. The chief of these is that everything real is individual, which
he has shown to be permanent and not flowing or successive. Motion,
then, is not a reality but a connotative concept, signifying one thing
while referring to another thing or things, or even to a negation (as
in the definition of local motion).[150] His nominal definitions of successive and instantaneous motion are, in fact, empirical descriptions
whose explication rests not upon metaphysics but upon logic and

---

149. Aquinas, *In Phys.* 3.2 (Leonine ed. 2: 105, n. 3). See Maier, *Zwischen
Philosophie und Mechanik*, pp. 31–35.

150. For motion as a connotative concept see *Quaest. in Phys.* 9 (*OPh* 6:
417.41–44. The principle of parsimony is always present to Ockham's mind
as he treats of motion. For example: "Ideo dicendum est quod motus non est
talis res distincta secundum se totam ab omni re permanente. Quia frustra fit
per plura quod potest fieri per pauciora, sed sine omni tali alia re possumus
salvare motum et omnia quae dicuntur de motu, ergo talis alia res frustra
ponitur. Quod autem sine tali alia re possimus salvare motum et omnia quae
dicuntur de motu, patet discurrendo per singulas partes motus. De motu autem locali patet. Ponendo enim quod corpus sit primo in uno loco et postea
in alio loco et sic procedendo sine omni quiete et sine omni re media vel alia
ab ipso corpore vel ipso agente quod movet, vere habemus motum localem;
ergo frustra ponitur talis alia res" (*Expos. in Phys.* 3.2 [*OPh* 4: 432.53–62]).

grammar. We have already seen him accomplish the daunting task of explaining the relatedness of things, all of which are absolute. We are now witnessing him perform the equally astonishing feat of accounting for the motion of things, all of which are permanent.

Gravitational and Projectile Motion

The majority of schoolmen in the thirteenth century accepted without question Aristotle's axiom, "Everything that is moved (or is in motion) must be moved by something else (*Omne quod movetur ab alio movetur*)."[151] To Aquinas this proposition is not self-evident but in need of proof. He agrees with Aristotle that the same thing cannot be in act and potency at the same time and in the same respect. Now everything that is moved is as such in potency, whereas that which moves is as such in act. Hence with respect to the same motion, nothing is both mover and moved. In short, nothing moves itself but must be moved by another.[152] To the objection that animals obviously move themselves, he replies that they owe their motion to an inner principle or the soul. In their case, one part (the soul) moves the other part (the body) or one part of the body moves another part.[153]

Serious problems also arise regarding gravitational and projectile movement. What moves a heavy body when it naturally moves downward? It appears to move itself as a whole, without one part moving another. But Aquinas ruled this out, for he did not believe that anything can move itself wholly or be the first principle of its

151. The first Latin *movetur*, translating the Greek *kinoumenon*, a middle passive participle, admits of both translations in English according to the context; see Anthony Kenny, *The Five Ways: Saint Thomas Aquinas' Proofs of God's Existence* (London, 1969), pp. 8–9. James A. Weisheipl contends that for Aristotle and Aquinas *movetur* should be translated by the passive "is moved": see Weisheipl, "The Principle *Omne quod movetur ab alio movetur* in Medieval Physics," *Isis* 56 (1965): 26–45, repr. in his *Nature and Motion in the Middle Ages*, pp. 75–97. Marilyn Adams (*William Ockham* 2: 828 n65) leaves the question open but seems to prefer the translation "in motion." Ockham often uses *movetur* in this sense.

152. *SCG* 1.13 (Leonine ed. 13: 31); Aristotle, *Phys.* 8.5, 257a35–257b13.

153. Aquinas, *In Phys.* 7.1 (Leonine ed. 2: 322, n. 2).

own motion. This would contradict the axiom that whatever is moved is moved by another. But a heavy body does have a cause of its downward motion according to Aristotle and Aquinas. It is moved essentially (*per se*) by the external producer or generator of the body; *per accidens* by anything removing an impediment to its natural, spontaneous motion.[154] Besides the external cause of gravitational motion, the heavy body has an internal formal principle (*principium formale*) of motion. This is its substantial form given to the body by its producer, who for a Christian is God. The internal principle is not a mover (*motor*), moving the heavy body downward as an efficient cause. The heavy body has only one *per se* or essential cause of its motion, namely the agent that produces it. The internal formal principle of its motion is not called an active but a passive principle of motion. Heaviness (*gravitas*) of earth is a passive principle by which earth is moved, not an active principle of its motion.[155] Consequently in gravitational motion a body does not move itself; it is moved by an extrinsic cause or mover, which is the producer of the heavy body. The same is true of the upward movement of a light body.

It has been shown that both Avicenna and Averroes thought that a heavy body has not only an extrinsic but also an intrinsic, conjoined mover, and that many modern historians have taken this to be the true doctrine of Aristotle. To Aquinas this is a misunderstanding of Aristotle. In Aquinas' view, Averroes was simply wrong when he claimed that for Aristotle the form of a heavy or light body is an active principle, in the sense of a mover of the body. The body has only one efficient cause or mover, and that is

154. Aquinas, *In Phys.* 8.8 (Leonine ed. 2: 392–393, n. 7).

155. "In corporibus vero gravibus et levibus est principium formale sui motus (sed huiusmodi principium formale non potest dici potentia activa, ad quam pertinet motus iste, sed comprehenditur sub potentia passiva: gravitas enim in terra non est principium ut moveat, sed magis ut moveatur): quia sicut alia accidentia consequuntur formam substantialem, ita et locus, et per consequens moveri ad locum: non tamen ita quod forma naturalis sit motor, sed motor est generans, quod dat talem formam, ad quam talis motus consequitur" (ibid. 2.1 [Leonine ed. 2: 56, n. 4]).

extrinsic to the body. Hence in gravitational motion the mover is not always present to the moving body. And yet the body cannot be said to move itself; rather, it is moved by its producer or generator. Gravitational motion is no exception to the rule, "Everything that is moved is moved by another."[156]

The rule also holds good regarding the motion of a projectile after losing contact with its thrower. Unlike the downward motion of a heavy body or the upward motion of a light body, the projectile's motion is not natural but violent: the body has no natural inclination to move to its place but it is compelled to go there by something else. Hence violent motion is obviously "from another." A theory called *antiperistasis*, attributed to Plato, would have the air or water pushed in front of the projectile, gathering in behind it and pushing it upward or forward. Aristotle adopted this explanation in principle, but he raises the difficulty that in this case the mover would only give motion to the air or water, leaving unexplained how it can continue to move the projectile after losing contact with the original source. In order to do this, Aristotle thought the thrower must not only move the air or water or other medium but also give it a motive power. When this power in the medium lessens through resistance, the projectile slows and its natural movement upward or downward takes over.[157]

Commenting on Aristotle's *Physics* and *De caelo*, Aquinas explains and defends the Philosopher's views on projectile motion. He dismisses the possibility of the projector's impressing a power directly upon the projectile because then violent motion, like

156. See Weisheipl, "The Principle *Omne quod movetur ab alio movetur*," and "The Specter of *Motor coniunctus* in Medieval Physics," *Studi sul XIV secolo in memoria di Anneliese Maier*, ed. A. Maierù and A. Paravicini Bagliani (Rome, 1981), pp. 81–104, repr. in his *Nature and Motion in the Middle Ages*, pp. 99–120. Weisheipl ("The Principle," pp. 79, 84) is critical of Anneliese Maier's view that every physical motion would require "a particular mover bound to it and generating it directly" ("'Ergebnisse' der spätscholastischen Naturphilosophie," *Scholastik* 35 [1960]: 161–187, at p. 170).

157. Aristotle, *Phys.* 8.10, 266b25–267a20. See Weisheipl, "Natural and Compulsory Movement," *The New Scholasticism* 29 (1955): 50–81, repr. in his *Nature and Motion*, pp. 25–48.

natural motion, would result from an intrinsic principle, which he takes to be contrary to the nature of violent motion.[158] In other works, however, Aquinas speaks of the transient power (vis, virtus) an archer impresses on an arrow, which he likens to the power a principal agent gives to its instrument. Though here he does not mention the role of a medium in projectile motion, neither does he exclude it.[159]

It was left to late medieval philosophers, under the influence of Philoponus and the Islamic thinkers, to propose that the projector immediately impresses a motive power or impetus on the projectile without the intermediary of air or water. Among them were Francis of Marchia and especially John Buridan, who showed by experiments that air plays no part in rotational or projectile motion. When a stone is thrown, Francis of Marchia says, all that is needed is "a power (virtus) left behind in the stone by the thrower."[160]

158. "Non est autem intelligendum quod virtus violenti motoris imprimat lapidi qui per violentiam movetur, aliquam virtutem per quam moveatur, sicut virtus generantis imprimit genito formam, quam consequitur motus naturalis: nam sic motus violentus esset a principio intrinseco, quod est contra rationem motus violenti" (Commentaria in librum De caelo et mundo 3.7 [Leonine ed. 3: 252, n. 6]).

159. De pot. 3.11, ad 5. For similar texts see SCG 3.24 (Leonine ed 14: 62); Quaestiones disputatae De anima 11, ad 2 (Leonine ed. 24.1: 102). On this subject see Weisheipl, "Natural and Compulsory Movement," p. 31; M.-D. Chenu, "Aux origines de la 'science moderne'," Recherches des sciences philosophiques et théologiques 29 (1940): 206–217.

160. See Anneliese Maier, Zwei Grundprobleme der scholastischen Naturphilosophie (Rome, 1951), pp. 174, 278–285; Weisheipl, Nature and Motion, pp. 31–32. In the sixth century AD, John Philoponus of Alexandria showed that the movement of air cannot explain projectile motion and proposed the impetus theory: "On the contrary," Philoponus argued, "it is necessary that a certain incorporeal motive power be given to the projectile through the act of throwing." See Weisheipl, Nature and Motion, p. 29. The Middle Ages knew Philoponus' theory through Simplicius (d. 549), a Greek commentator on Aristotle, but his account of it is not clear and it is questionable if it influenced medieval writers. The Islamic philosopher, Avicenna (d. 1037), took up the position of Philoponus, defining the power impressed on the projectile as a quality given to the projectile by the projector, as heat is given to water by fire. In a void this "borrowed power" would persist indefinitely. See Shlomo Pinès, "Les précurseurs musulmans de la théorie de l'impetus," Archeion (Argentina) 21 (1938): 294–300, at p. 298, repr. in his Studies in Arabic Versions of Greek Texts and in Mediaeval Studies

While the theory of the impetus gave a plausible account of projectile motion, it still assumed the axiom that whatever is moved (or moves) is moved by another. At the turn of the century Duns Scotus challenged the axiom itself. The axiom implies that the mover and the recipient of motion are always and necessarily two distinct things. But Scotus argues that this cannot be a genuine metaphysical principle, for it is contradicted by experience and it leads to evident absurdities.[161] We experience the fall of heavy bodies, and there is nothing to prevent their moving themselves. Is the cause of their downward motion the agent generating or producing them? Scotus replies that the producer can be its remote cause but hardly its actual cause, for the motion continues when the body is not in contact with its producer and even if the producer no longer exists. The producer can give the heavy body the power to move downward, but the body can keep this power when the producer is absent. It follows that the heavy body's active power to fall downward must be within the body itself as the efficient cause of its motion. In short, the body moves itself.[162]

This is contrary to Aristotle's clear position that only living things can move themselves, because they alone have souls which can move their bodies and heterogeneous parts, one of which can move another. Heavy and light bodies are inanimate and homogeneous and do not admit of two parts, one the mover, the other the moved.[163]

(Jerusalem and Leiden, 1986), pp. 409–417; Crombie, *Medieval and Early Modern Science* 2: 52–53. Marshall Clagett, *Science of Mechanics in the Middle Ages* (Madison, WI, 1959) reviews the controversy over Philoponus and the knowledge of his theory in the Middle Ages; Peter King, "Duns Scotus on the Reality of Self-Change," in *Self-Motion from Aristotle to Newton*, ed. Mary Louise Gill and James G. Lennox (Princeton, NJ, 1994), pp. 227–290.

161. Scotus, *Metaph.* 9.14 (Vivès ed. 7: 600, n. 23); *Ord.* 1.3.3.2 (Vatican ed. 3: 306–307, nn. 516–517). For Anneliese Maier Scotus marks a turning point in the history of the problem of gravity: see Maier *An der Grenze von Scholastik und Naturwissenschaft*, 2nd ed. (Rome, 1952), p. 164. For Scotus' opposition to the universally received axiom see Roy R. Effler, *John Duns Scotus and the Principle "Omne quod movetur ab alio movetur"* (St. Bonaventure, NY, 1962).

162. Scotus, *Ord.* 2.2.2.6 (Vatican ed. 7: 360–361, nn. 458–461); *Metaph.* 9.14 (Vivès ed. 7: 589, n. 10). See Effler, *John Duns Scotus*, pp. 108–110.

163. Aristotle, *Phys.* 8.4, 254b33–255a19.

Scotus agrees that heavy bodies cannot move themselves as living things do, but with his noted subtlety he finds a way in which they can be self-moving. This requires that he explain how a heavy body can move itself primarily, that is, as a whole and essentially, and not just in one of its parts. Now a property of a substance, like a person's ability to laugh, belongs to the person primarily and essentially. Moreover, the property flows from the substance, so that in a sense it is caused by the substance. The relation of the substance to its property is one of primary causal motion, though here motion is not to be taken as corporeal motion but analogous to it. On the model of the relation of a substance to its property, a heavy body, having received its primary power from its producer, can cause its own secondary power of moving locally, either downward if the body is heavy or upward if the body is light. In brief, it can be the efficient cause of its own motion.[164] Nor does this violate the principle that nothing can be in act and potency at the same time and in the same respect. Potency and act are here to be taken as modes of being and consequently as opposites. But taken as active and passive principles they can coexist in the same thing. Thus in the case of a heavy body moving downward the body's form is the active principle while its matter is the passive principle of the movement. The same thing is at once both active and passive respecting the same downward motion. This should not be surprising, for the will is both the efficient cause of an act of willing and it is also the passive principle or recipient of this act.[165] Roy R. Effler sums up Scotus' doctrine as follows:

> What then is the intrinsic principle of the free fall of a body? The Scotistic answer to this question is succinctly expressed in the words, *aliquid intrinsecum ipsi gravi*, or *ipsummet grave per*

164. See Effler, *John Duns Scotus*, pp. 56–62.
165. *Ord.* 2.3.2.1 (Vatican ed. 7: 543, n. 298); *Metaph.* 9.14 (Vivès ed. 7: 596–597, n. 17). See Effler, *John Duns Scotus*, pp. 76–80.

aliquid intrinsecum. By means of the gravity inherent in it, the heavy body itself is the active principle of free fall. The very substance of the heavy body with its property of gravity causes downward motion and at the same time receives the downward motion it causes.[166]

Scotus is here setting the stage for Ockham's position that not all things in motion are moved by something else; in short, that there are instances in which things move themselves, not just in the sense that one part moves another or that the whole moves through the movement of one of its parts, but that the whole thing moves itself essentially and primarily (*per se et primo*). Commenting on the *Physics*, Ockham agrees with Aristotle that if something is moved that does not have the source of motion within itself and is visibly seen to be moved by an external mover, clearly the moved object is moved by something else, as in the case of things moved violently; for example, when earth moves upward and a stone is dragged along. In these instances it is obvious that the mover is different from the object moved. Ockham adds, however, that it was not Aristotle's intention to deny absolutely that something can move itself, at least if the movement is instantaneous. A case in point is the human will, which causes its own volition and thus moves itself. If our act of willing were not in our own power but were naturally and adequately caused by something external, it would not be worthy of praise or blame. Consequently an act of this sort is in some way produced by the will. By itself the will causes the act and thus moves itself, taking "moves" at least in a broad sense, which includes spontaneous movement. But self-movement is not limited to the will; even bodies are able to move and change themselves. A heavy body is the efficient cause of its downward motion through its quality of heaviness, and heated water effectively and by itself renders itself

---

166. Effler, *John Duns Scotus*, p. 126. See Scotus, *Ord.* 2.2.2.6 (Vatican ed. 7: 359–360, nn. 457–458).

cold again by causing coldness in itself. Thus the will is not the only agent effectively causing its motion and properties.[167]

To Giles of Rome this was a misunderstanding of Aristotle. Giles insisted that Aristotle never thought that something can act on itself and be both the efficient and material cause of something in the same respect. Quite the contrary, they must be really distinct. Ockham, for his part, does not put too much weight on Aristotle's authority in this matter, for Aristotle, he says, never grants or denies that one and the same thing can be the efficient cause and subject of the same thing. Even if he denied it, Ockham places little value on a negative authoritative opinion.[168]

The important shift in meaning of the axiom, Whatever is moved (or moves) is moved by another, initiated by Duns Scotus, should not go unnoticed. In the thirteenth century it was generally taken to be a strict principle, admitting of no exceptions and prov-

---

167. *Expos. in Phys.* 7.1 (*OPh* 5: 595.21–596.29; 598.87–600.128). It is commonly said that a stone moves itself downward, its quality of heaviness (*gravitas*), which is not substantially one with the stone, being a partial cause of the movement. A living thing moves itself through its soul, which is one in substance with it (*Brevis sum. Phys.* 8.2 [*OPh* 6: 126.115–125]). However, in the case of bodies moving in the sublunar world, there is at least one stage when the motion comes from outside that body; see *Expos. in Phys.* 7.2 (*OPh* 5: 608.56–63). On this subject and Ockham's views in general on self-motion, see Calvin G. Normore, "Ockham, Self-Motion, and the Will," in *Self-Motion from Aristotle to Newton,* ed. Gill and Lennox, pp. 291–303.

168. "Nam grave movet se ipsum effective deorsum et similiter aqua calefacta per se ipsam effective redit ad frigiditatem causando in se ipsa frigiditatem, et voluntas movet se ipsam causando in se volitionem vel odium; et ita non solum idem specie sed etiam idem numero est subiectum alicuius effectus et efficiens eiusdem. Nec auctoritas ista Aristotelis multum debet movere, cum nec concedat nec neget idem posse esse subiectum et efficiens eiusdem, et locus ab auctoritate negative parum valet" (*Expos. in Phys.* 2.2 [*OPh* 4: 353.45–52]; cf ibid. 7.1 [*OPh* 5: 599.111–600.128]). Cf. Giles of Rome, *Commentaria in octo libros Physicorum Aristotelis* 2.12 ('Veniunt autem tres'), dub. 1 (Venice, 1502; repr. Frankfurt, 1968). The immediate active principles of moving elementary bodies are their qualities of heaviness and lightness. Often the substantial form of the elements is the remote active principle of these movements, for they are often the efficient principle of heaviness and lightness; see *Quaest. in Phys.* 124 (*OPh* 6: 732.18–35).

able through the metaphysical notions of act and potency. Ockham regards it as a proposition that needs to be verified by experience or authority. It is justified by the experience of seeing one thing move another, or one part of a thing moving another part or the whole thing. But when there is movement but no visible mover, as in the case of the natural movement of the four elements, we naturally conclude that they move themselves. The circular movement of the heavenly bodies around the earth raises a problem: do they move themselves or are they moved by something else? They appear to move themselves, but it is the common opinion, supported by the conjoined authority of the philosophers and theologians, that they are in fact moved by celestial Intelligences or angels. Since their movement is natural, they must have within themselves a principle of movement, which is their very substance. However, this is not an active but a passive principle of motion, and consequently it must be activated by external movers.[169]

We have seen several attempts to explain the motion of projectiles: the Aristotelian opinion that a projectile after leaving its thrower is moved by the adjacent air, and the theory of Philoponus that it is moved by a power or impetus left in it by the thrower. But in Ockham's view neither of these theories solves the very difficult problem of identifying the mover or efficient cause of projectile movement. Clearly, the thrower cannot adequately explain the motion of the projectile, for it can continue to move even after it leaves the thrower's hand. Neither can the mover be the adjacent air, for this is contrary to experience. If an archer shoots an arrow that is struck by an oncoming stone, and the air moves both the arrow and stone, the same air would simultan-

---

169. *Quaest. in Phys.* 123 (*OPh* 6: 730.10–20). Aristotle and Averroes thought that the heavens are pure form and that this functions as the passive principle of its local movements. The heavens also have an active role, as when the sun illuminates the moon. According to "the truth of faith" the heavens are composed of form and matter, for the fathers of the Church and masters of theology say that at the beginning God created matter from which the heavenly bodies were formed; see ibid. (*OPh* 6: 730.21–731.32) and *Rep.* 2.18 (*OTh* 5: 399.15–400.8).

eously move in two contrary directions, which is impossible. The other possibility is that the projectile is moved by a power given to it by its thrower. But this is also impossible, for when an agent and patient come together under the same conditions the same effect should follow. Now if my hand slowly approaches a body and touches it, the body will not move. But if my hand approaches and touches the same body as before but more quickly and vigorously, it will move. Since the hand does not impart a power of movement to the body in the first case, neither does it in the second. Does the local motion of the thrower cause a motive power in the projectile? That too is impossible, because local motion has no effect except to bring the agent close to the patient.[170]

Consequently neither of the above theories correctly identifies the moving or efficient principle of projectile motion. It is left to Ockham to propose his novel theory that the efficient principle of this motion is none other than the projectile itself; in short, that the projectile moves itself after leaving its first projector.

> I affirm, therefore, that in motion of this sort, after the movable object has separated from the first projector, the mover is the object moved in itself and not through an absolute or relative power in it, so that this mover and object moved are entirely indistinct.[171]

---

170. *Rep.* 3.4 (*OTh* 6: 142.13–144.4); *Rep.* 3.2 (*OTh* 6: 66.2–10). Ockham does not seem to recognize the difference in situations in the two cases of the hand approaching the object. Marilyn Adams asks, "might we not maintain that it is differences in *how* the hand is moving that accounts for its ability to move the rock in the one case and not in the other?" (*William Ockham* 2: 843).

Ockham explains the Aristotelian theory of the movement of the projectile by the adjacent air as understood by Averroes. The air is not one uniform mover but is easily divisible into many parts which move in different ways, some naturally and other violently and with different velocities. These different parts of air, moved by themselves, move the projectile; see *Expos. in Phys.* 7.3 (*OPh* 5: 626.146–159).

171. "Ideo dico quod ipsum motivum in tali motu post separationem mobilis a primo proiciente est ipsum motum secundum se, et non per aliquam virtutem absolutam in eo nec respectivam, ita quod hoc movens et motum est penitus

The motion of a projectile, then, is different from gravitational motion. As we have seen, a body naturally moves downward through its heaviness (*gravitas*), which is an accidental quality of the body really distinct from its substance.[172] In the unique case of projectile motion, the body does not move itself through an added quality but through its own substance.

This is a remarkable solution of the problem of projectile motion. Ockham seems to have been the first to propose it, but Duns Scotus cleared the way for it by denying the universal principle that everything that is moved (or moves) is moved by another. Ockham adds projectile motion to the other instances in which both Scotus and he acknowledged that even inanimate bodies can sometimes move themselves.

If this is the case with projectile motion, it would seem that there can be local motion without a cause. But does not local motion always require a cause? Is it not something newly brought about or effected and therefore caused? To Ockham, however, the question is wrongheaded, for it assumes that local motion is *something*, whereas it is only an abstract term signifying that a movable body is verifiably in different places at difference times without resting in between. The objection makes the fundamental mistake of assuming that there must be a reality corresponding to every abstract term. There is no such *thing* as local motion, about which we can ask whether or not it needs to be caused. For the same reason we should not think that local motion can cause anything. "It would be aston-

---

indistinctum" (*Rep.* 3.4 [*OTh* 6: 143.11–14]). Ockham uses the unusual construction – permitted in Latin – of a dual subject ("movens et motum") followed by a singular verb ("est") in order to emphasize that the two subjects stand for and signify entirely the same thing. Ockham's theory presupposes that one and the same thing can be both active and passive with respect to the same thing, but he does not find this contradictory: "dico quod idem potest esse activum et passivum respectu eiusdem, nec ista repugnant" (*Quodl.* 1.16 [*OTh* 9: 89.52–53]).

172. A stone moves itself through its heaviness (*gravitas*), which does not constitute a substantial unit (*per se unum*) with the stone. On the contrary, a living body moves itself through its soul as a partial cause, making up a substantial unity with the living body (*Brevis sum. Phys.* 8.2 [*OPh* 6: 126.119–125]).

ishing," Ockham says, "if my hand could cause a power in a stone by the fact that it touches the stone by local motion."[173]

Ockham is here insisting that, as an abstract term, local motion does not need a cause or that it itself can be a cause. But the term signifies and stands for all real things moving in space, and they do require either an external cause or a cause identical with themselves. As he says in the *Summula philosophiae naturalis*, there is no motion without a mover and agent, taking agent in the broad sense of causing either instantaneous or successive motion.[174] Thus whatever is moved is moved by something, either by another or – as in the case of a projectile after leaving its projector – by itself. By causing its own motion it is not causing a new reality but only its successive presence in different parts of space without remaining in any one of them. These parts of space, or places, are not "new" absolutely, but only in relation to the bodies that move through them. In Ockham's words, "Although each part of space that the movable thing passes through is new with respect to the movable thing passing through, insofar as the mobile object is passing through these parts now and did not earlier, nevertheless the part (of space) is not absolutely new."[175]

Some historians claim that Ockham's novel doctrine of projectile motion anticipated or at least opened the way to Newton's law of inertia, which revolutionized seventeenth century physics. According to the law, "Every body continues in its state of rest, or of uniform motion in a right line, unless it is compelled to change that state by forces impressed upon it."[176] Ockham is said to have taken the

---

173. *Rep.* 3.4 (*OTh* 6: 143.15–144.4).

174. "[M]otus non est sine movente et agente, large accipiendo agens" (*Sum. phil. nat.* 3.2 [*OPh* 6: 249.9–10]).

175. "Unde licet quaelibet pars spatii quam transit mobile sit nova respectu mobilis transeuntis, quatenus mobile nunc transit per illas partes et prius non, tamen nulla pars est nova simpliciter" (*Rep.* 3.4 [*OTh* 6: 143.20–144.2]). According to Descartes and Newton, on the contrary, "the change in spatial relationships in passing from a state of rest to a state of motion *was* a new effect" (Crombie, *Medieval and Early Modern Science* 2: 65).

176. "Corpus omne perseveraret in statu suo quiescendi vel movendi uniformiter in directum, nisi quatenus illud a viribus impressis cogitur statum

first step toward the law by his denial of the Aristotelian principle that whatever is moved (or moves) is moved by another. In his doctrine of projectile motion he is said to have envisioned the possibility of motion without any motive power, thus opening "the way to the principle of inertia and to the seventeenth-century definition of force as that which *alters* the state of rest or of uniform velocity."[177]

We have seen, however, that Ockham did not deny that projectile motion has a cause: its first projector is the initial efficient cause of its motion and afterward it is its own efficient cause of motion. "Efficient cause" in this context does not have the strict sense of a cause of a thing (*res*) that begins to exist for the first time and never existed before, but the very broad meaning of a mover that changes a thing's shape or only its place.[178] "An efficient cause," Ockham says, "is not always so-called because it produces a thing (*res*) that did not exist before, but because it makes a preexisting thing to be somewhere where it was not immediately before."[179]

If this is so, Ockham's notion of projectile motion does not anticipate Newton's law of inertia nor does it give a "first draft" of the law.[180] Rather, it belongs to a conceptual world quite different

---

suum mutare" (Isaac Newton, *Principia philosophiae naturalis*, 3rd ed., ed. Alexandre Koyré and I. Bernard Cohen, trans. Andrew Motte and Florian Cajori [Cambridge, MA, 1972], 1: 54).

177. Crombie, *Medieval and Early Modern Science* 2: 64–65. Weisheipl remarks: "Hence the term 'motion' designates no reality other than an individual body negatively described as not being at rest. From this Ockham concluded that the search for a 'cause of motion' is entirely superfluous, since motion is nothing over and above the individual physical body" (*Development of Physical Theory*, p. 68). The same view is expressed by Wallace in his *Causality and Scientific Explanation* 1: 55, 57. Pierre Duhem wrote that for Ockham local motion continues without any efficient cause and concluded that his position anticipated the law of inertia (*Le système du monde* [Paris, 1913–1935], 7: 196). I owe these references to Adams, *William Ockham* 2: 843 nn101–102; I concur with her interpretation of Ockham's doctrine on the present subject.

178. *Sum. phil. nat.* 2.3 (*OPh* 6: 217.6–218.20).

179. *Expos. in Phys.* 7.3 (*OPh* 5: 634.141–143).

180. Citing Duhem, among others, Léon Baudry thought that Ockham's position is "comme une première ébauche de la loi d'inertie" (*Lexique philosophique*

from that of the law. The law finds its proper place in science whereas Ockham's notion belongs to the philosophy of nature. Though the Ockhamist conception of motion breaks with Aristotle's principle that everything that is moved (or moves) is moved by another, it still retains basic Aristotelian features, such as efficient causality and the distinction between natural and violent motion. For Ockham, projectile motion is a kind of violent motion called *expulsio*, forcing the projectile to move contrary to its natural inclination downward. But the projectile retains that natural inclination as well, and so it will eventually fall to the ground. Hence its motion is said to be mixed, having a twofold source: the thrust from its initial external projector and its internal inclination to move downward.[181] There is no suggestion that a body in motion will continue indefinitely in a straight line, as Newton's law of inertia postulates. His conception of inertia abstracts from the notions of efficient causality and natural and violent motion. It contains the concept of force, but it is treated solely as a quantitative notion suited to a quantitative mechanics.[182] Under these circumstances the most that can be said for Ockham's contributing to the law is that he cleared the way for it by his denial that everything that is moved (or moves) must be moved

---

de Guillaume d'Ockham [Paris, 1958], p. 159). See also Baudry, "En lisant Jean le chanoine: Les rapports de Guillaume d'Ockham et de W. Burley," *Archives d'histoire doctrinale et littéraire du moyen âge* 9 (1934): 175–197, at p. 167.

181. *Sum. phil. nat.* 3.9 (*OPh* 6: 278.36–280.84). Aristotle describes the motion of "pushing off" and "throwing" as "more violent than the natural locomotion of the thing moved, which continues its course so long as it is controlled by the motion imparted to it" (*Phys.* 7.2, 243a19–243b2).

182. See Richard S. Westfall, *Force in Newton's Physics* (New York, 1971), pp. 323–423. J.E. McGuire contends that Newton's thought also moves on an ontological level. From this perspective, Newtonian matter is in itself an intrinsic source of activity in virtue of a *vis insita,* and natural motion is a species of self-motion. What is changed or moving has "both an active and passive principle (*vis insita* and *vis inertiae*)." See McGuire, "Natural Motion and Its Causes: Newton on the *vis insita* of Bodies," in *Self-Motion from Aristotle to Newton,* ed. Gill and Lennox, pp. 305–329, at p. 329. Consequently a projectile, being at once active and passive, moves itself. If true, this would bring Ockham's view of a projectile movement closer to Newton's.

by something else, and by his proposal that the projectile is self–moving after leaving its first projector.[183]

5 Time

The treatment of time follows immediately upon that of motion in all Ockham's works on physics. And this is to be expected, for in his view time is really identical with motion, with the added connotation of the mind as its measurer. Aristotle observed that time is not independent of movement and change, for we experience time and movement together. Even if we are in the dark and have no bodily feelings, if we are aware of a movement or change in the mind we are at once aware of a passage of time. Time, then, would seem to be either movement or something attendant upon movement. Since it is not movement it must be something accompanying it.[184]

Like many statements of Aristotle this is not easy to interpret. What does he mean when he says that time is not motion? Ockham takes it to mean that they do not have the same nominal definition nor are they convertible or synonymous terms, because time connotes the mind whereas motion does not. Nevertheless, the two terms stand for and signify exactly the same permanent things. It is true to say, then, that time is motion. Aristotle defined time as "the number of motion in respect to before and after," and Ockham accepts his definition.[185] But in order to emphasize that time is really motion, he himself describes time as the motion by which the mind knows how great another motion is. In other words it is the motion by which the mind measures motion.[186] More generally, it enables us to measure the extent of something's endurance, motion or rest.[187]

---

183. "The Ockhamist critique was no anticipation of an inertial principle, but it may have been a preparation of one" (Goddu, *The Physics of William of Ockham*, p. 203).

184. Aristotle, *Phys.* 4.11, 218b21–219a9; Ockham, *Expos. in Phys.* 4.20 (*OPh* 5: 212.2–15).

185. Aristotle, *Phys.* 4.11, 220a24; Ockham, *Rep.* 2.10 (*OTh* 5: 188.2–4).

186. *Quaest. in Phys.* 40 (*OPh* 6: 503.10–13).

187. "Est autem tempus mensura qua cognoscitur aliquid quantum durat, movetur vel quiescit" (*Sum. phil. nat.* 4.13 [*OPh* 6: 379.3–4]; *Rep.* 2.10 [*OTh* 5: 200–202]).

Some writers on time believe there is something mysterious and unknowable about it, but Ockham assures us that this is not so; it is known not only by the wise but by any reasonable person.[188] No one is so ignorant as to be unaware that time enables us to know that one thing remained or moved or endured longer than another or equally so; for example, that we were in a certain place for a longer or shorter time than someone else. We must be very well acquainted with time, Ockham continues, since it is the cause and occasion of our knowing so many things, as everyone can experience for himself. Time is thought to be mysterious because of the many enigmas occasioned by misconstruing statements of the philosophers. Misunderstanding the linguistic habits of the philosophers, these philosophizers have more difficulties with time than simple folk using only their experience and the meaning of the word. The same people have more trouble with motion, even though it is clear enough to our senses.[189]

With this revealing statement of his empirical and linguistic approaches to the nature of time – approaches that are constant in his philosophy – Ockham sets out to elucidate its meaning and to clear up the difficulties others have with it. It must be acknowledged, however, that he does not manage to remove all the mystery from time.

Suppose we want to know something's quantity. One way we can do it is by applying to the thing to be measured the quantity of something we do know. For example, if we want to know the length of a piece of cloth we can lay a ruler of a known length on it once or several times, and so we can be certain of the length of the cloth. After much experience we can tell the length of the cloth just by looking at it.

---

188. Ockham may have Galen in mind; see Averroes, *In Phys.* 4, com. 97–98 (Junta ed. 4: f. 177v–179r). More likely he is thinking of Augustine's well-known remark about time: "What then *is* time? If no one asks me, I know; if I want to explain it to a questioner, I do not know" (*Confessiones* 11.14 [CCL 27: 202.8–9]).

189. *Sum. phil. nat.* 4.3 (*OPh* 6; 350.21–351.37).

The cloth and its measure are permanent things, but a similar method can be used to measure successive items like motion. If we do not know the extent of something's motion, we can be certain of it through some other motion whose extent we do know. Thus the mind can apply the sun's known motion to another motion, and, considering that the other thing moved while the sun moved from one point to another, we shall know how long that thing moved. Sometimes it is clear that one body moves longer than another just by looking at them, though we cannot be as certain as when we use the first method. In the same way, with due proportion, we can know how long a thing is at rest, and that one thing is equally at rest as another, and that one thing endured or endures longer than another.

It should now be clear that we do not have to assume anything but a body in motion in order to be certain that a thing endures for a shorter or longer time, or that it is longer at rest or in motion. All we need to know is a body with uniform velocity; anything else is superfluous.[190]

In medieval physics the swiftest and most uniform motion is that of the outermost sphere of the heavens called the *primum mobile*. This is time in the strictest sense of the term, for if it were known it would be the ideal and most certain measure of all other motions, both celestial and terrestrial. Unfortunately it lies beyond our sight, and so we use the motions of the lower spheres of the sun and moon as guides to measure sublunar motions. Even these motions can be called time, for they can be used to measure other motions. An example is the movement of a clock which is known to be uniform and regular. A clock is made so that it will complete its circle when the sun has finished its daily round. Knowing the movement of the clock, we can then measure the movements of other things, even those of the heavenly bodies.[191] In a less strict sense

190. Ibid. 4.3 (*OPh* 6: 351.38–353.112).
191. Ibid. 4.7 (*OPh* 6: 357.2–358.7); *Quaest. in Phys.* 42–43 (*OPh* 6: 507–514).

imagined and conceived movements can also be called time. These exist only in the mind, but by means of them we can measure motions in the real world, somewhat as a geometer measures real quantities by imagined quantity. A person born blind can measure the movement of the sun and other bodies by imagined movement.[192]

This account of time proposes that it is a concept signifying the same permanent things signified by the concept of motion but in a different way, namely with the connotation of the mind as the measure of motion with respect to before and after. But if motion has a before and after it would seem to be nothing permanent but a continual flowing, and this would also be true of time. The parts of time are past, present, and future, of which only the present exists. The present is an instant, and this seems to be a flowing reality that never remains but continually changes into another instant. Hence both an instant of time, and time itself, appear to be entirely different from permanent things.

The notion of time and a moment of time as a flowing reality (*res fluens*) was held by Henry of Ghent and Duns Scotus just prior to Ockham,[193] but it did not fit into his conceptual framework. In his view every reality (*res*) is either a substance or a quality, and these are permanent things. Unlike them, the parts of time are simply nothing (*purum nihil*): neither the past nor the future exist, and neither does the present instant, for it does not remain. Hence time is not something distinct from permanent realities. Could time be a mental construction, with the mind making a whole out of the parts of time? Ockham rejects this notion of time – which

192. *Quaest. in Phys.* 44 (*OPh* 6: 515.8–23); *Rep.* 2.10 (*OTh* 5: 192.3–20). For this rather obscure notion of imaginary and conceptual time Ockham refers to Scotus, *Ord.* 2.2.1.2 (Vatican ed. 7: 208, nn. 116–117). If there were no celestial motions would there be any time at all? At the time of Joshua the sun stood still, but the battle raged on. These movements, and others like them, were measured by movements in the sublunar world or by imaginary movements; see *Quaest. in Phys.* 42 (*OPh* 6: 510.63–67); *Rep.* 2.10 (*OTh* 5: 225.24–226.9).

193. Henry of Ghent, *Quodl.* 3.11 (Paris ed. 1: f. 63–65); Scotus, *Quodl.* 12 (Vivès ed. 25: 480–481, n. 9).

Augustine favors in his *Confessions* – because simply by taking thought the mind could not produce something outside itself.[194]

With his penchant for simple solutions, Ockham attempts to explain time with only the notions of permanent things and the mind as the measurer of their motions. As we have seen, Aristotle's nominal definition of time is "the number of motion with respect to before and after." Now the term "number" has two meanings: either the plurality of things that is or can be numbered, say ten horses, or the abstract number "ten" by which we can count them. According to Aristotle time is number in the first and not in the second sense.[195] Ockham agrees with this distinction in the meaning of number, but he insists that time is not only number in the first but also in the second sense. It is the number by which we count things, and not just the things themselves. Moreover, we can count things not only by an act of the mind but also by a number of other things, as we can use pebbles or beans to count other things.[196] Ockham does not want us to forget that time is not just number, but any uniform motion by which, through an act of the mind, we can measure another motion.

In treating of the notions of before and after in Aristotle's definition of time, Ockham as usual appeals to experience and the rule of parsimony. We become aware of before and after, he says, by observing the movement of bodies over a continuous quantity with different places. The moving body is first is one place and afterward in another. The places are not really different from the quantity; we distinguish between them and between the places because the moving body passes over one before the other. Our perception of time comes about precisely when we distinguish movement with its before and after. We make this distinction by taking one part of the movement as before and another part as after, and another part as in between the before and after. There

194. *Rep.* 2.10 (*OTh* 5: 183–191).
195. Aristotle, *Phys.* 4.11, 219b5–10. See Ockham, *Expos. in Phys.* 4.21 (*OPh* 5: 225.2–8).
196. *Expos. in Phys.* 4.23 (*OPh* 5: 251.11–18).

must be an intermediary movement for the notion of time. Because an instantaneous motion (*mutatio*) has a before and an after but lacks an in-between motion, it does not occur in time. Thus in a substantial change there is a different substance before and after, but there is no movement between them, and therefore there is no time.

Neither the before nor the after of motion and time are real *things* distinct from the bodies in motion; rather, they are distinct only as we conceive or define them. Neither are the moments of time *things* really distinct from motion, with a being that quickly passes away, as Scotus imagined. It is the mind that divides motion into several moments. We are aware of two moments when we first say that this mobile body is now in place A, and later that it is now in place B. After we have said that this mobile body is now in place A, and before we can say that this mobile body is in place B, we can truly say that this mobile body is moving.

This makes it clear that, paradoxical as it may seem, time and moments of time, like motion itself, can be fully explained by permanent realities. No recourse to flowing being or reality is required.[197]

6 Place

When treating of the angels in Chapter 8 we saw that there are two ways of being in place: circumscriptively and definitively. Something is in a place circumscriptively when the whole thing is in the whole place and a part of it is in a part of the place. Something is in a place definitively when the whole thing is in the whole place and in every part of the place. Bodies are in a place in the first way; spiritual substances like angels and Christ in the eucharist are in a place in the second way. Our concern in this chapter is the circumscriptive mode of being in place. In his physical works Ockham devotes considerable attention to it and to the many problems it occasions.

197. *Expos. in Phys.* 4.21 (*OPh* 5: 222.26–224.70); Scotus, *Quodl.* 12 (Vivès ed. 25: 480, n. 9).

Ockham assures us that our experience of place, just like our experience of motion and time, can be completely accounted for by bodily substances and their accidents. There is no need, then, to think of place as having a reality of its own, distinct from that of bodies and their quantity. As Aristotle said, place is nothing but the boundary of a containing body at which it is in contact with the contained body.[198]

Clarifying this description of place, Ockham explains that since the containing and contained bodies are distinct, they are not continuous but contiguous. Moreover, the place of a body is primarily the contiguous boundary of the containing body that is equal to the body in place. We can say that something is in the heavens as in a place because it is in the air, and the air is in the heavens. But the thing in question is not in the air because it is in the whole air and coextensive with the whole air. Its proper and primary place is in that part of the air immediately touching it. It can be said to have its secondary place in the whole air, and beyond that, in the heavens. But it would not have its secondary common place unless it first had its own proper place. Its proper place is the body whose extremities or surface touch the body in place, and the extremities or surface of the body in place touch the containing body, so that every extremity touches some part of the containing body. An example would be a vase filled with water, without any opening in the vase, so that there would be no interior surface of the vase that did not touch the water.

The surface or boundary that marks and limits a body's place is not really different from the body surrounding the body in place. It follows that neither is place really different from the inner surface of the surrounding body. It would be superfluous and contrary to the principle of the razor to hold that they are different. All the attributes of place can be accounted for by the

---

198. "Locus est ultimum [corporis] continentis contigui immobile primum" (*Expos. in Phys.* 4.6 [*OPh* 5: 50.6–7]). Cf. Aristotle, *Phys.* 4.4, 212a5–6.

inner surface of the surrounding body: it can contain and locate a body just as well as if place were a distinct reality.[199]

Common folk sometimes think of place as the space between the sides of a body that can contain other bodies. They often see one body contained in another body change from place to place while the place remains the same. They observe, for example, that while a vase remains stationary, water is poured out of the vase and another body enters it. So it appears that place is the space between the sides of the container that remains the same, though the body in the space varies. If this is true, place is a sort of vacuum existing between the sides of the container, and some call this vacuum the three dimensions of length, width, and depth, apart from any natural body.

Ockham here refers to a common notion about place as an empty space that can be filled successively by different bodies, a vacuum or mathematical body of three dimensions that bodies can occupy for a time and then leave for other bodies to occupy. In his view, as in Aristotle's, there is no empty space of this sort. There are only bodies with their extended quantities, one playing the role of the container and the other the role of the contained. If place were an empty mathematical space we would have to conclude that there are an infinite number of places. Suppose that a quantity of air or water were in place in such a space. Each part of the air or water would also be in place in the whole space; and since there are an infinite number of parts of the air or water, there would be an infinity of places – a conclusion that neither Aristotle nor Ockham would admit.[200]

Aristotle thought that place is motionless. A boat moving on a river changes its place because it is carried along with the water to new places. But Aristotle preferred to call the moving water containing the boat a vessel rather than a place. The place of the

199. *Expos. in Phys.* 4.6 (*OPh* 5: 50–51); *Quaest. in Phys.* 72–75 (*OPh* 6: 597–607).

200. *Expos. in Phys.* 4.6 (*OPh* 5: 69–70); *Quaest. in Phys.* 74 (*OPh* 6: 602–604).

boat is the whole river, and as a whole the river is motionless, for it does not change its whole place.[201]

This is contrary to Ockham's conviction that everything in the lower world of generable and corruptible beings can be moved in place either *per se* or *per accidens*. The lower world contains substances composed of form and matter, and accidents inhering in substances. It is clear by induction that substances with their forms and matters are movable, and accidents must also be movable because they depend on substances. Since they are movable and provide the place of bodies, place itself must be movable. Ockham does not think Aristotle intended to deny this. When he said that place is immovable he meant an "immobility by equivalence." This means that several numerically distinct and movable places can equally well explain all the facts connected with place as a really immovable place. For instance, different bodies can succeed each other in the same place while the place remains the same, without presupposing that the place is absolutely immovable.[202]

Giles of Rome offered a different interpretation of Aristotle's notion of the immobility of place. He distinguished between place considered materially as the surface of the containing body and formally as the order of the universe. The latter consideration of place plays a key role in Giles' notion of place. Giles asks us to consider a boat anchored in a river with water flowing around and under it. The boat has a different relation to the parts of water, but it maintains the same relation to the whole river. For this reason the river is said to be its place, and its place is motionless from its relation to the whole river. This example helps us to see that place can be immovable because of the order of the universe. True, every part of the universe is movable and thus changes its place, but the universe as a whole does not substantially change its

---

201. Aristotle, *Phys.* 4.4, 212a13–18. Ockham reports Aristotle's doctrine in *Expos. in Phys.* 4.7 (*OPh* 5: 79.4–80.22).
202. *Expos. in Phys.* 4.7 (*OPh* 5: 85.3–26); *Quaest. in Phys.* 78 (*OPh* 6: 610.7–611.41).

place. Thus the higher region (or pole) of the universe is immovable because the orbit of the moon is always at the same distance to the universe's center. So too the lower region (or pole) of the universe is immovable owing to its unchanging distance to the same center. An everyday example will make this clear. Suppose you are at rest and the air or some other body surrounding you moves, do you remain in the same place? Materially speaking you do not, for you are now contiguous to a new container. Formally speaking, however, you are always in the same place, because you are always at the same distance to the center of the universe and its poles, both of which are immovable.[203]

Ockham has no quarrel with Giles' account of place taken materially, but he objects strongly to his view of place as formally the relation (ordo) or distance of a part of the universe to its center and poles. To begin with, that relation will be formally in the containing body and not in the body contained in place. This is clear, because if it were in the contained body it would follow that place would formally be in that body, which is contrary to Aristotle. And if the relation is located in the containing body, the relation would change with the change in that body. Since Giles thinks of relation as an accident of the bearer of the relation, the relation could not be immovable while the bearer of the relation moved.

A more telling argument against Giles' position is that he falsely imagines that the universe has immovable poles and a center. In fact, Ockham insists, there are no immobile poles in the heavens nor is there a fixed center of the earth. As we have seen, nothing in the universe, either in the heavens or on earth, is immovable.[204]

---

203. Ockham reports Giles' doctrine in his *Expos. in Phys.* 4.7 (*OPh* 5: 80.3–81.33). Aquinas, Giles' teacher, also explains the immobility of place through the immobility of the poles and center of the universe; see *De physico auditu* 4.6 (ed. Angeli-Pirotta n. 898).

204. *Expos. in Phys.* 4.7 (*OPh* 5: 81.3–83.8).

Leaving aside the question whether the universe has fixed poles and a center, Ockham still finds a way to justify Aristotle's thesis that place is immovable. Imagine a square body a hundred leagues from the higher parts of the heavens and the same distance from its lower parts, and at an equal distance from the right and left sides of the universe. As long as the heavens are motionless or move in a circle and not in a straight line, the square body will be motionless because of its fixed distance from all parts of the heavens. It can move in a circle if the heavens rotate, but it will keep its same distance from all parts of the heavens and in this respect it is motionless. Here, then, is another way to interpret "by equivalence" Aristotle's dictum that place is immovable.[205]

Does the last and eighth sphere surrounding and containing the universe occupy a place? This outermost sphere continually moves in a circle around everything in the universe, but it itself is not in a place because there is nothing containing it. The twelfth-century Spanish philosopher Avempace thought that the surface of this sphere could be considered its place, but this is incorrect because the surface is not something separable from the sphere and containing it as its place. His contemporary Averroes found another reason for saying that the outermost sphere can be thought of as in place, at least *per accidens*. Does it not circle the earth, which is by its very nature (*essentialiter*) at rest in the center of the universe, and does not this function serve, in a way, to give it a place or to locate it?

Ockham does not dispute Averroes' contention that the heavenly bodies move around the earth, which is at rest in the center of the universe. For Ockham, however, the location of the earth at the center of the universe is not essential but a fact that could be otherwise. He has insisted that there is nothing in the lower world that is immovable, and if this is true the earth itself is movable. But if it did move, the heavens would also move, and

---

205. *Quaest. in Phys.* 78 (*OPh* 6: 611.14–39).

then it would not move around something at rest. But it would keep the same relation to the earth and it would circle it as though it were at rest. "In this way," Ockham concludes, "we can solve the problem of how the heavens move around the earth at rest, and how it is in place *per accidens*."[206] As for the universe as a whole, it was the mind of Aristotle that it is not in a place, for there is nothing outside of it and containing it. In short, the universe is nowhere.[207]

Several centuries later Galileo found evidence that the world actually does move, and in a way Ockham would never have suspected. Ockham never doubted that the earth is at rest at the center of the universe encircled by the heavenly spheres, but he did not subscribe to the Aristotelian notion, expressed by Averroes, that this is of the very nature of the earth. For Ockham, it was a fact that could be otherwise owing to the divine omnipotence. When treating of the possibility of a better world we saw the gulf between the Aristotelian and Ockhamist conceptions of nature.[208] The present issue helps to confirm this judgment.

206. "Verumtamen sciendum est quod quamvis corpus caeleste moveatur circa terram quiescentem in medio mundi, tamen posito quod terra moveretur, nihilominus posset caelum moveri. Et tunc de facto non moveretur circa aliquod quiescens, nec propter hoc tunc diceretur moveri. Sed tunc moveretur, quia taliter se haberet quod si esset aliquod quiescens in medio, partes suae diversimode approximarentur continue partibus illius quiescentis. Et per istum modum potest salvari quomodo caelum movetur circa terram quiescentem, et quodmodo est in loco per accidens" (*Expos. in Phys.* 4.8 [*OPh* 5: 97. 116–123]). Ockham also treats of the movement of the eighth sphere in *Quaest. in Phys.* 80 (*OPh* 6: 614–616). For the reference to Averroes (who cites Avempace) see the editors' note *OPh* 5: 95 n5.

207. "Ex ista conclusione patet quod de intentione Philosophi est quod totus mundus non est in loco, quia non habet aliquid extra ipsum continens mundum, tamen multae partes mundi sunt in loco, scilicet omnes partes contentae ab aliis partibus, cuiusmodi sunt omnia elementa et omnia corpora mixta" (*Expos. in Phys.* [*OPh* 5: 95.33–37]).

208. See above, pp. 336–338.

The Human Person

L IKE SCOTUS, OCKHAM BELIEVED that the individual, and not an essence or common nature, is the ultimate perfection of reality. The human person stands as a central witness to this conviction.

1 The Metaphysical Structure of the Person

The centerpiece of Ockham's philosophy is the individual, under-stood as any thing (*res*) that is not many but one in number. This includes both substances and some accidents in the category of quality. Another name for substance is suppositum. More pre-cisely, a suppositum is a substance with the added connotation of being complete and incapable of uniting with something else to constitute one being. A person is an intellectual substance or, more exactly, a suppositum. Boethius gives a nominal definition of per-son as "an individual substance of a rational nature."[1] By indivi-dual substance he means individual suppositum, and by rational nature he means intellectual nature. This is brought out in Richard of St. Victor's definition of the person as "the incommunicable existence of an intellectual nature."[2] According to Ockham, the most perfect description of a person is "a complete intellectual na-ture that does not exist in another as in a subject, and it cannot

1. *Ord.* 1.23.un. (*OTh* 4: 62.5–16). Boethius, *De persona et duabus naturis* 3 (PL 64: 1343). For the meaning of the terms "substance" and "suppositum" see above, pp. 35–40.

2. Richard of St. Victor, *De Trinitate* 4.21–23 (PL 196: 944–946). Ock-ham's editors note that this definition was gathered from Richard's works by Scotus; see *OTh* 4: 62 nn1–2.

form a substantial unity with something else as its part."[3] Thus an intellectual soul does not measure up to the perfection of a suppositum, for by its nature it is destined to be a part of a human person. A suppositum enjoys a certain independence, wholeness, and unity of being, the higher forms of supposita like the human person possessing these qualities to a higher degree. It might be tempting to identify a human nature with a human suppositum, but the revealed doctrine of the Incarnation warns us that this would be a mistake. The human nature of Christ is not a suppositum or person when it is assumed by the divine Person, but it could be a suppositum or person if not assumed but existing on its own. This shows that one and the same human nature can be a suppositum when it is not assumed in existence by another person, but later it can cease to be a suppositum when it is thus assumed and supported in existence by another person.

Substances are either simple or composed of parts. Purely spiritual substances, like angels and intellectual souls, do not have substantial parts. Human persons, being partly spiritual and partly material, are composed of primary matter and several substantial forms: a corporeal form and sensory and intellectual souls. Since each of these is a substantial element in the person with its own distinct reality, it would seem that a human person is not one being. Thomas Aquinas, convinced of the substantial unity of the person, contended that a substantial composite can have only one being (*esse*) and consequently only one substantial form, for "a form gives being." Ockham, on the contrary, sees no difficulty in holding that the person contains several partial beings and hence several substantial forms, all of which make up the person's one total being (*unum esse totale*).[4]

3. "[D]ico quod persona est natura intellectualis completa quae nec sustentificatur ab alio, nec est nata facere per se unum cum alio sicut pars" (*Rep.* 3.1 [*OTh* 6: 4.21–5.1]).

4. "Quia unius compositi est tantum unum esse; sed homo est unum compositum; igitur hominis est tantum unum esse; igitur tantum una forma, quia forma dat esse. ... Ad principale dico quod hominis est tantum unum esse totale,

We are here in the presence of two radically different notions of the unity of the person. Ockham does not believe the person is one in the absolute sense of excluding a number of really distinct parts, each of which is a being or thing (*res*). Rather, the person is one in number in the broad and improper sense of being a totality of parts: not a mere collection of parts of the same nature, like the unity of an army, city or heap of sand, but the coming together of parts having different natures and yet constituting something substantially one (*unum per se*).[5]

Contrary to Ockham, Thomas Aquinas does not locate the *per se* unity of a person in the unique coming together of several distinct parts, such as a body and a soul, but in the one act of existing (*esse*) they possess in common. The person is one *per se* and not *per accidens*, because it is one substantial being possessing one act of existing (*esse*). The soul is not only the substantial form of the human being; it is a spiritual substance or *suppositum* in its own right, possessing its own act of existing, which accounts for the fact that, when separated from the body, it can continue to exist. But as the form of the body, the soul communicates to the body its own act of existing, so that they have one single act of existing. In short, they constitute one being. The body does not contribute anything to the existence of the soul, for that is already complete. But the soul does not have a complete essence; it is only a part of the human essence and needs the body for its completion. Thus the soul is in a sense a complete substance, for it has a complete act of existing (*esse*); but in another sense it is incomplete, because it is only part of the human essence or species. Thus in the metaphysics of Thomas Aquinas a person's substantial unity is funda-

---

sed plura sunt esse partialia" (*Quodl.* 2.10 [*OTh* 9: 156.4–6, 161.118–119]). The editor has identified the first position, opposed by Ockham, as that of Thomas Aquinas, *ST* 1.76.4, sed contra. For his doctrine of the unity of substantial form in the human person see ibid. 1.76.3–4. For commentaries on his doctrine of the unicity of the soul as the substantial form of the person see below, note 6.

5. For the meanings of the term "one" see *Ord.* 1.24.1 (*OTh* 4: 76.17–77.17); *Sum. log.* 1.39 (*OPh* 1: 109–111). See above, pp. 58, 142–143.

mentally that of *esse* – the perfection and actuality that is most inward and central in any being.[6] As we have seen, Ockham also speaks of the person's unity as substantial (*per se*), but in the much looser sense of a total being containing several beings or realities.

A corollary of Aquinas' doctrine is the oneness of the substantial form in the human person. Since in his view a substantial form confers substantial existence or being (*esse*) on a substance, one substance can have only one substantial form, which in the case of the human person is the intellectual soul. Any subsequent form received by the substance could only be an accidental form, like a quality, which does not give a substance its being but, for example, its being white.[7]

Ockham does not find this argument convincing. Taking a counter-argument from Aquinas' own *Summa theologiae*, he contends that in the person's embryonic development he is by nature first a living being and later human. So it would seem that the person is living and human through different forms.[8] Hence a person must have a sensory soul really distinct from an intellectual soul. Ockham concedes that he cannot prove this a priori, by self-evident propositions, but he thinks he can by experience. We can desire something sensually and at the same time refuse it intellectually. Now these acts cannot be rooted in the same subject, for they are naturally contrary to each other. Hence the person must have a sensory soul really distinct from an intellectual soul. We can reach the same conclusion by reflecting on the fact that we can

6. "Ad primum ergo dicendum quod licet anima habeat esse completum, non tamen sequitur quod corpus ei accidentaliter uniatur, tum quia illud idem esse quod est animae communicat corpori ut sit unum esse totius compositi, tum etiam quia etsi possit per se subsistere non tamen habet speciem completam, sed corpus advenit ei ad complementum speciei" (Aquinas, *Quaestiones disputatae De anima* 1, ad 1 [Leonine ed. 24.1: 10]); cf. *SCG* 2.68 (Leonine ed. 13: 440). See Etienne Gilson, *The Christian Philosophy of St. Thomas Aquinas*, trans. L.K. Shook (New York, 1956), pp. 196–197; Anton C. Pegis, *St. Thomas and the Problem of the Soul in the Thirteenth Century* (Toronto, 1934; repr. 1978), p. 139.

7. Aquinas, *ST* 1.76.3–4. Gilson, ibid., pp. 194–195.

8. *Quodl.* 2.10 (*OTh* 9: 156.7–8). Cf. Aquinas, *ST* 1.76.3, obj. 3.

desire the same object in two different ways: by an act of the sense appetite and by the will. Hence these acts must proceed from two different forms, one sensory and the other intellectual. Another proof: the same form cannot be both extended and not extended, material and immaterial. Now the person's sensory soul is extended and material while the intellectual soul is not, for it is totally present in the whole person and in every part. It follows that they are really distinct substantial forms.[9]

Ockham acknowledges the difficulty of giving a solid proof either for or against the plurality of substantial forms in the person. However, he clearly believes the weighter arguments support the distinction between the sensory and intellectual forms. Even more convincing are the proofs that prior to the sensory form in both animals and humans there is another substantial form called the "form of corporeity." This form is immediately received by matter, rendering it a body with extension in space and endowed with qualities, such as color and shape. The reason for assuming this bodily form is that the qualities and quantity remain the same in both a living and dead animal or human. Hence they must be based on a subject different from the sensory form, and what can this be but a bodily form?

Theologians have a special reason for assuming the presence of a distinct bodily form in the person. Without it they could not explain the identity of the body of the living Christ with the body in his tomb, or how Christ's body in the tomb could have been an essential part of his human nature, or how the bodies of the saints were the same living and dead and consequently worthy of reverence after death. Thus it is more in keeping with the Christian faith to assume a distinction between the substantial form of "bodiness" and the sensory form.[10]

---

9. Ibid. (*OTh* 9: 158.32–36, 159.62–65); *Rep.* 4.9 (*OTh* 7: 161.8–22).

10. Ibid. 2.11 (*OTh* 9: 163.49–164.58). The matter in the body is not always the same; some can be added and some lost. But it is perhaps impossible for the main parts of the body, like the heart, to be completely different and the body be said to be the same. Matter belongs to the essence of the

We are now in a position to verify that the person is indeed a total being, composed of many parts, all of which count as things (*res*) or beings. The most basic part is primary matter, which lacks all form but is still an actually existing entity (*res*) potential to receiving all substantial forms.[11] The primary matter in the person has the same nature as the matter in all composite substances, though it differs numerically in each of them (it would be superfluous to assume that they are different in nature).[12] The first substantial form received by matter is the form of "bodiness," which gives matter its quantity. Next, the sensory form adds life and sensation to the composite. Some would assign life to a distinct vegetative form prior to the sensory form, but Ockham finds this unnecessary. Finally, the intellectual form is received by the composite, completing it and specifying it as an individual of an intellectual nature.[13]

In proposing a plurality of substantial forms in the human person Ockham aligns himself with the great majority of late medieval masters, including Richard of Middleton, Robert Kilwardby, John Pecham, Henry of Ghent, and Duns Scotus.[14] The contro-

---

composite individual. If the individual increases in size with more matter, it is in a sense a really new individual, but the human person remains numerically the same because of his intellectual soul, which, as a simple form, remains in the whole person and in each part; see *Rep.* 4.13 (*OTh* 7: 264.2–21, 268.14–269.17).

11. "Circa quam est sciendum, quod materia est quaedam res actualiter existens in rerum natura, quae est in potentia ad omnes formas substantiales, nullam habens necessario et semper sibi inexsistentem" (*Sum. phil. nat.* 1.9 [*OPh* 6: 179.5–8]); cf. ibid. 1.10 (*OPh* 6: 181.2–186.152).

12. Ibid. 1.12 (*OPh* 6: 188.3–191.68).

13. *Quodl.* 2.11 (*OTh* 9: 164.64–72).

14. On the dispute over the plurality of forms see Etienne Gilson, *A History of Christian Philosophy in the Middle Ages* (New York, 1955), pp. 416–420; Robert Zavalloni, *Richard de Mediavilla et la controverse sur la pluralité des formes* (Louvain, 1951). Godfrey of Fontaines favored the oneness of form (that is, the rational soul) in the person on the philosophical ground that it best accounts for the substantial unity of the person. Yet he did not clearly see how this was reconcilable with Christian doctrine. In other substances there can be only one form. See John F. Wippel, *The Metaphysical Thought of Godfrey of Fontaines* (Washington, DC, 1981), pp. 314–347.

versy over the subject was heated, chiefly because of the theological issues involved. In 1277 Robert Kilwardby, the Archbishop of Canterbury, condemned the proposition "That the vegetative, sensory, and rational (souls) are one simple form," and in 1286 his successor, John Pecham, repeated the condemnation.[15]

Ockham undoubtedly sided with the pluralists because of the religious aspects of the problem, but the deciding factor was his philosophical views on being and unity, which disposed him to see the person, not in the manner of Thomas Aquinas as strictly one being, but as an ordered totality of really distinct beings whose unity is found in the physical and ontological ordering of the parts of the whole person.

Up to the present Ockham has told us that the intellectual soul is the completing substantial form of the body, and that it is totally in the whole body and in each of its parts. Can this be demonstrated rationally or is it only a matter of faith? Ockham leaves us in no doubt about his answer to this question and others concerning the intellectual soul:

> I assert that if you mean by an intellectual soul an immaterial, incorruptible form that is as a whole in the whole body and in each part, it cannot be evidently known by reason or experience that a form of this sort is present in us, or that the understanding proper to this form exists in us, or that this soul is the form of the body, but these three [propositions] are held only on faith. (I don't care at the moment what the Philosopher thought about this, for he always seems to speak about it as a disputed question).[16]

15. For the condemnations see Daniel A. Callus, *The Condemnation of St. Thomas at Oxford* (Westminster, MD, 1946). It is noteworthy that the proposition, whose condemnation at Oxford was chiefly directed against Thomas Aquinas, was not included among those condemned at Paris in 1277 by Bishop Tempier. Clearly, Thomas had more support at Paris than at Oxford.

16. "[D]ico quod intelligendo per 'animam intellectivam' formam immaterialem, incorruptibilem quae tota est in toto corpore et tota in qualibet parte, nec potest evidenter sciri per rationem vel per experientiam quod talis

Attention should be given to the precise point Ockham is making. He is not denying natural reason's ability to prove that humans have substantial forms which distinguish them from irrational animals. He suggests the following as a possible proof: If a composite of form and matter differs in species from another composite, it differs either by its whole self or by part of itself. Now human beings differ in species from an ass, and not by their whole selves because their matter is essentially the same. So they differ by a part of themselves, and if not by matter then by form. Thus natural reason can show with some credibility that humans have substantial forms specifically different from those of irrational animals. But it cannot be proved beyond doubt that this form is the intellectual soul described above as a spiritual or immortal soul, wholly in the whole body and in every part. We can be certain of this only by faith.

Scotus appealed to experience in order to prove the spirituality of the human soul as the form of the body. We experience within ourselves acts of understanding that transcend matter, such as understanding the universal natures of things, relations between objects of sense and intellect, and between intelligible objects themselves. This would be impossible unless these acts were caused by, and situated in, something within us that transcends matter, and since it is not matter it must be form.[17]

---

forma sit in nobis, nec quod intelligere tali substantiae proprium sit in nobis, nec quod talis anima sit forma corporis, – quidquid de hoc senserit Philosophus non curo ad praesens, quia ubique dubitative videtur loqui –, sed ista tria solum credimus" (*Quodl.* 1.10 [*OTh* 9: 63.39–64.47]). These three properties of the human soul were defined as a matter of faith in the Clementine decretals: see *Clementinae* 1.1.1. #1 (ed. Richter–Friedberg 2: 1133); Aristotle, *De anima* 3.5, 430a14–25.

17. Scotus, *Ord.* 4.43.2 (Vivès ed. 20: 37–38, n. 6). Ockham summarizes Scotus' position in *Quodl.* 1.10 (*OTh* 9: 62.4–10). Thomas Aquinas also argued that the intellectual soul is the form of the body. As the most excellent of all forms, the human soul so far transcends matter that it has an intellectual power and act in which the body in no way shares (*ST* 1.76.1).

In Ockham's opinion our experience does not warrant this far-reaching conclusion. From the point of view of natural reason the understanding we experience is the act of a bodily and destructible form. We have no experience of an act of understanding appropriate to a spiritual substance, by which Ockham seems to mean a purely spiritual act in which the body plays no role. If we do perhaps experience an act of this sort, he thinks it more likely that it is situated in a soul that is the body's mover and not its form.[18]

Granted as a truth of faith that the intellectual soul is the form of the body, is the soul totally in the whole body and totally in every part? This must be so, Ockham contends, for the soul as an indivisible and unextended form exists totally wherever it exists. If it did not exist in some part of the body, that part would not be animated or human. Why then do we seem to experience understanding in our head rather than our feet? This is not so, Ockham says, except that we often experience that our understanding is aided or hindered by the condition of the head more than by that of the feet. But sometimes a condition of the feet can be of more help or hinderance than that of the head, as when our feet hurt badly.[19]

Could we, as a composite of soul and body, be said to understand through the intellectual soul, if it were not the form but only the mover of the body? Ockham thinks this Platonic alternative to the Aristotelian position possible. By the principle of "the transference of names" (*communicatio idiomatum*), we often give a name to a thing owing to its relation to something else to which the name properly belongs, as we call someone a rower (*remigator*) from his oar (*remus*). In the same way we can ascribe something to a moved body because of its mover, without the mover being its form. This was the case with Tobias' angel, who assumed and moved a body, and because of the mover the composite of the assumed body and the angel was said to eat, drink, walk, understand, and judge (Tob 5:5). Thus, even though the soul were only

18. *Quodl.* 1.10 (*OTh* 9: 65.88–97).
19. Ibid. 1.12 (*OTh* 9: 71.54–63).

the mover of the body and not its form, we could still say the
composite understands through the intellectual soul.[20] However,
on the assumption that the intellectual soul is a spiritual and
immortal form within us and our means of understanding – which
faith teaches us – it is more reasonable to hold that it is the form
of the body and not just its mover. If it were its mover, it would
either move the body in place or alter its quality. Not the first, for
then there would be no reason why it would move a young body
more easily than an adult body; nor the second, for other bodily
agents adequately explain all qualitative changes of the body.[21]

2 The Powers of the Soul

The medieval masters commonly considered the soul to be the
primary source of the person's life and vital activities. Being itself
a form and energy (*actus*), it enables the person to act in many
different ways in order to achieve his or her full development and
happiness. The schoolmen, however, did not always agree on the
relation between the soul and its acts. Do the acts issue directly
from the soul or through powers in some way distinct from the
soul and from each other? On this subject Ockham reviews the
opinions of Thomas Aquinas, Henry of Ghent, and Duns Scotus,
forcefully criticizes them, then proposes his own solution.

According to Thomas Aquinas the powers of the soul are not
its very essence but accidents in the category of quality. As such,
they are really distinct from the essence of the soul and from each
other. Ockham is aware that Aquinas closely links this conclusion
to his notion of the act of existing (*esse*) as the actuality of essence.
He formulates Aquinas' argument as follows: the act of existing of
every creature is distinct from its essence and is related to it as act
to potency. And if this is true, by transposing the terms we can
say that as the act of existing is related to action, so essence is
related to potency. Now in God alone is the act of existing the

---

20. *Quodl.* 1.10 (*OTh* 9: 63.22–37).
21. Ibid. (*OTh* 9: 64.67–65.77).

same as his action. It follows that in creatures the power to act is not the same as their essence.[22] Moreover, action and the power to act belong to the same genus. Now the actions of creatures are not in the genus of substance but of accident, and consequently the same must be true of their power. Again, some powers are exercised through bodily organs and others, like the intellect and will, are not. This diversity of actions requires a diversity of powers. Aquinas concludes from these and other arguments that a natural power of soul, like the intellect, will or sensory powers, cannot be the essence or substance of the soul but an accident added to it, more specifically an accident in the second species of quality. Action, then, issues from the essence of the soul through the medium of powers, which, being diverse, diversity the actions.[23]

Thus, in God there is an identity of *esse*, essence, power, and action, whereas in creatures these are always distinct. Aquinas makes it clear, however, that it is not the soul that acts but the composite of soul and body, as it is the composite that exists. The composite has its substantial existence through its substantial form, and it acts through the instrumentality of the powers flowing from that form.[24]

Contrary to Aquinas, Henry of Ghent contended that the powers of the soul add nothing to its essence except relations to different objects. Because the soul is one and undifferentiated in its essence, its actions must be diversified and directed to this or that object, not by different absolute powers as Aquinas thought, but simply by different relations, all of which have a foundation in the soul. In this respect the soul is like primary matter, in which there are different poten-

---

22. "[S]icut se habet esse ad essentiam, sic operari ad potentiam. Igitur, permutatim, sicut se habet esse ad operari, sic essentia ad potentiam. Sed in solo Deo sunt esse et operari idem, igitur etc" (*Rep.* 2.20 [*OTh* 5: 426.1–4]). Ockham has reformulated Thomas' argument in *ST* 1.54.3. Altering the proportionality is valid, as can be seen from the following illustration: as 2 is to 4, so 6 is to 12. From this it follows that as 2 is to 6, so 4 is to 12.

23. *Rep.* ibid. (*OTh* 5: 425.18–426.22). See *ST* 1.77.1–2.

24. *ST* 1.77.1, ad 3.

tialities to different forms, the diversity of potentialities arising solely from relations and not from anything absolute.[25]

Duns Scotus offered a third possible explanation of the powers of the soul. Reacting to Henry of Ghent's doctrine, he denied that they differ only as relations to objects. Rather, they are absolute realities, differing formally from each other and from the soul's essence, while being really identical with the soul and with each other. Once more Scotus brings his famous formal distinction into play, enabling him to affirm a real identity of powers with each other and with the soul's essence, while keeping their formal distinction *a parte rei*. The powers are virtually contained in the soul, not as belonging to its essence but as a subject virtually contains its properties.[26]

Of these three doctrines of the powers of the soul Ockham finds nothing to commend in that of Thomas Aquinas, but he shows some sympathy with the other two. His firm opposition to the Thomist position is hardly surprising, for we have seen his rejection of the metaphysical notions with which it is connected. In Aquinas' view the soul by essence is the first principle of the life of the body; but the soul owes its vital energy to its act of existing (*esse*), which is the actuality even of form or essence.[27] Since the soul's essence is always actualized by its *esse*, it cannot be the immediate principle of its vital actions; otherwise, it would always be exercising them. For example, it would always be knowing and willing. The fact that it is not shows that they have a proximate source within the soul that is not the essence itself but its powers.[28]

According to Ockham, Aquinas' arguments are unfounded and inconclusive; what is more they lead to an unnecessarily com-

----

25. *Rep.* 2.20 (*OTh* 5: 431.17–432.3). See Henry of Ghent, *Quodl.* 3.14 (Paris ed. ff. 66r–71r).

26. *Rep.* 2.20 (*OTh* 5: 433.12–434.4). See Scotus, *Rep. Paris.* 2.16.un. (Vivès ed. 23: 73–75, nn. 14–19).

27. *ST* 1.4.1, ad 3.

28. *ST* 1.77.1. The second argument in the *Responsio* is very briefly indicated (or rather truncated) by Ockham: see *Rep.* 2.20 (*OTh* 5: 426.7–9), and Ockham's reply (*OTh* 5: 428.21–23).

plicated doctrine of the powers of the soul.[29] Where Aquinas sees a real distinction between *esse*, essence, power, and action, Ockham believes a verbal or conceptual distinction between them suffices: they are but different words or concepts signifying the same reality of the soul but in different ways. As often happens with Ockham, a metaphysical explanation gives way to a logical and experiential analysis.

Because of its simplicity, the position of Henry of Ghent is more to Ockham's liking, but he regards it as also erroneous. For Henry, the soul's powers are relations to different objects added to the soul. Ockham counters that these relations would be either conceptual or real. They cannot be conceptual, because this sort of relation is made by the mind, whereas the powers of the soul exist perfectly in it before the mind acts. Neither can the powers be real relations, for a relation of this sort requires a really existing terminus. But there is nothing to prevent God from creating a perfect intellectual soul without an actual extramental object.[30]

Turning to Duns Scotus, Ockham commends him for holding that the powers of the soul are not relative but absolute and really identical with the soul's essence and with each other – at least when it is a question of the intellect and will (the sensory powers are another matter and he will consider them later). But Ockham does not approve of Scotus' applying the formal distinction to the soul's powers. Scotus himself does not justify this distinction on rational grounds but only by appealing to authority. It enables the theologian to account for the trinity of Persons in the unity of the divine essence, which is held on faith, but the distinction is inoperative in philosophical matters.[31]

In order to settle the question of the soul's powers, Ockham distinguishes two meanings of the term. In one sense it means the whole description expressing the nominal definition of the power;

29. For Ockham's lengthy counter-arguments see *Rep.* ibid. (*OTh* 5: 427.7–431.15).

30. *Rep.* 2.20 (*OTh* 5: 432.4–15). For Henry of Ghent see above, note 25.

31. Ibid. (*OTh* 5: 434.6–20).

in another sense it means that which is named by the term or concept. In the first sense the intellect and will are different powers, for they do not have the same nominal definitions. The intellect is defined as "the substance of the soul capable of understanding," while the will is defined as "the substance of the soul capable of willing." These descriptions can be taken as words, concepts or things. If taken as words they are really distinct, for words are really distinct. If taken as concepts they are conceptually distinct. If taken as things they are really distinct – at least in part. For even though it is the same numerical substance of the soul that can understand and will, understanding and willing are really distinct acts; and since these acts are connoted in the whole nominal definitions of the intellect and will, there is a partial real distinction between them. Ockham adds parenthetically that if this is all Henry of Ghent meant by saying that the powers are distinct as relations, Ockham is willing to agree with him.

However, if the words and concepts "intellect" and "will" are taken in the second sense, as that which they name, the intellect and will are distinct neither in reality nor in concept. In short, they are identical, just as God is identical with himself or Socrates with Socrates. The terms designate the one substance of the soul in its capacity to bring forth different acts while remaining one in itself. Only because these acts are connoted in the nominal definitions of intellect and will is there a distinction between these powers. As proof of this Ockham offers the razor: "It is useless to do with more what can be done with fewer." Since there is no cogent reason to assume a real distinction between the powers of the soul and between the powers themselves, the principle of economy cautions us not to affirm their distinction. Before Ockham, Duns Scotus appealed to the razor to enforce the same conclusion. It was Aristotle's principle, Scotus recalls, that nature always strives for what is better, and an economy of means is always preferable: *paucitas sine multitudine est melior in natura, si sit possibile.* Consequently, if the soul can have different acts without a real distinction between its powers, we can be certain that nature has arranged it in this way.[32] Nature, however, is not so parsimonious as to preclude a formal distinction between the soul's substance and its powers. The powers well up and flow from the essence of the soul as its properties, so that there is a formal distinction *a parte rei* between them along with real identity.[33] To Ockham, expressions like "welling up" or "gushing forth" (*ebullitio*), in this connection are only metaphorical. It is the soul's acts of understanding and willing, and not their powers, that flow or spring from it as from their partial and principal cause.[34] It is these acts, when connoted with the essence of the soul in nominal definitions, that give rise to the distinction between intellect and will as distinct powers. There is no real or formal distinction between them when they are taken just in themselves.

Is it not true, however, that different kinds of actions require different kinds of principles or sources? And are not the acts of knowing and willing or desiring so different that they must originate in different powers? Ockham grants that sometimes distinct acts require distinct powers, as sensation and understanding call for distinct powers of sense and intellect, but sometimes they do not. We must call upon experience and rational evidence to know when to assume a plurality of powers and when not. In the cases of sensory knowledge and desire on the one hand and intellectual knowledge and will on the other, we experience that when we apprehend a good object we at once naturally desire or will it, if not in fact at least as a possibility. If the object is evil, we immediately dislike it or flee from it. Since the acts of knowing and desiring or disliking naturally go together, and indeed have the same object, there is no need to assume a real distinction between the intellect and will. Referring to these powers in their reality and not in their nominal definitions, they are really and conceptually the same.[35]

32. Scotus, *Ord.* 2.16.un. (Vivès ed. 13: 38–39, n. 15).
33. *Rep.* 2.20 (*OTh* 5: 437.22–438.1); Scotus, *Rep. Paris.* 2.16.un. (Vivès ed. 23: 75, n. 19).
34. *Rep.* 2.20 (*OTh* 5: 438.1–13).
35. Ibid. (*OTh* 5: 444.2–447.19).

If this is true, it would seem to imply the oxymoron that we understand through the will and will through the intellect. But Ockham sees no problem here. If we think of the soul as an entirely undifferentiated nature efficiently causing both the acts of understanding and willing, we can say that the will wills through the intellect just as it does through the will, for intellect and will mean the same thing. However, if we consider the propositions, "The will is volitional," "The will is able to will," "The intellect is intellectual," "The intellect can understand," we have to say, "The will wills through the will and not through the intellect," because now the term "will" connotes the act of willing, which is not connoted by the term "intellect." Similarly we have to say, "The intellect knows through the intellect and not through the will," for now the term "intellect" connotes the act of knowing, which is not connoted by the term "will."[36]

Is the intellect or will the more excellent human power? There can be no question of their relative nobility if the terms are taken to mean that which they name, for they name exactly the same reality of the soul. From this perspective intellect and will are entirely on the same footing. But if we take both of them with their whole nominal definitions, the will is more excellent than the intellect, because the act of loving connoted by the will is more excellent than the act of understanding connoted by the intellect. The intellect is prior to the will, because the act of understanding is a partial efficient cause of the act of willing and it can naturally exist without that act, but not vice versa. The intellect's priority, however, does not entail that it is more perfect than the will.[37]

In his *Ordinatio* Ockham clarifies that when the will and the intellect are distinguished by their nominal definitions, the will and its acts of love and joy are more excellent than the intellect and its acts of knowing. He is happy to see Thomas Aquinas admit this in his *Scriptum* on the *Sentences*. He quotes Thomas as saying,

36. *Rep.* 2.20 (*OTh* 5: 439.5–25).
37. Ibid. (*OTh* 5: 441.6–442.3).

"The highest part [of the soul] has an intellect and will, the intellect being the loftier according to order and the will according to perfection. And the same order is present in habits and also in acts, namely vision and love. Now joy is the name of the highest activity with regard to perfection." To which Ockham adds, "Truth compelled him to say that joy (*fruitio*), which is an act of the will, is more excellent than the act of the intellect, although in many works he said the opposite – the result of his own mental lapses (*sequens errores proprii capitis*)."[38]

The Muslim philosopher Averroes posited two really distinct intellects, which he called the agent and possible intellects. These he conceived, not as intrinsic perfections of the human person, but only as movers of the body, similar to the Intelligence moving the heavens. But Ockham protests that this is not only contrary to Christian teaching but it assumes a plurality without necessity. One intellect suffices to account for human understanding; hence what are called the agent and possible intellects are the same both in reality and in concept. These terms, however, have different connotations: the agent intellect connotes knowledge actively issuing from the soul and the possible intellect denotes the same soul while connoting knowledge received in it. But it is absolutely the same intellect that produces and receives knowledge.[39]

---

38. "Si tamen distinguerentur, dicerem quod potentia volitiva esset nobilior. Et hoc dicit Thomas, quamvis alibi dixerit oppositum. Unde libro primo, distinctione prima, quaestione prima dicit sic: 'Suprema pars habet intellectum et voluntatem, quorum intellectus est altior secundum ordinem et voluntas secundum perfectionem. Et similis ordo est in habitibus et etiam in actibus, scilicet visione et amore. Fruitio autem nominat altissimam operationem quantum ad sui perfectionem'. Et ita iste, tamquam a veritate coactus, dicit hic fruitionem, quae est actus voluntatis, esse nobiliorem actu intellectus, licet alibi, in multis locis, – sequens errores proprii capitis –, dicat oppositum" (*Ord.* 1.1.2 [*OTh* 1: 402.18–403.6]; cf. Aquinas, *In Sent.* 1.1.1, ad 1 [ed. Mandonnet–Moos 1: 34]). The text reads "originem" for "ordinem," which seems correct (*ST* 1.82.3; *SCG* 3.26). For Aquinas, the will remains relatively superior to the intellect, but in itself intellect is the nobler power: see Gilson, *Christian Philosophy of St. Thomas Aquinas*, pp. 243–244.

39. *Rep.* 2.20 (*OTh* 5: 442.15–443.3); Averroes, *In De anima* 3, com. 18 (ed. Crawford pp. 437–440).

Averroes also made the mistake of holding that all humans have one and the same intellect; their thoughts and ideas vary owing to the different connections between that intellect and the images in the imagination. This can be refuted by experience and reason, because if all humans had the same intellect it would at the same time know and not know, assent and dissent regarding the same object. The intellect in one person would know something and the same intellect in another would not know it. It is clear, then, that two individuals cannot have the same intellect. The joining of the single intellect with images in individual sensory powers cannot explain how contrary notions can exist in the intellect, for images are only efficient causes of these notions.[40]

Some of the powers of the soul – like the intellect and will – are inorganic, that is, they do not act through a bodily organ; others are organic, using bodily organs to act. Organic powers include all those extended in matter, like the sense and motive powers of the soul. Scotus ascribed both organic and inorganic powers to the intellectual soul because he held that it is identical with the sensory soul. Ockham, on the contrary, considers the two souls to be really distinct, the organic powers belonging to the sensory soul and the inorganic powers to the intellectual soul.[41]

We have seen that in themselves the inorganic powers of intellect and will are really identical with each other and with the intellectual soul. Similarly Ockham contends that the organic sense powers in themselves are really identical with each other and with the sensory soul. Thomas Aquinas took the opposite stand, holding that the powers of sense are accidents really distinct from each other and from the essence of the soul, flowing from the soul but existing in the composite of soul and body as in a subject.[42]

40. *Quodl.* 1.11 (*OTh* 9: 67.23–38); Averroes, *In De anima* 3, com. 36 (ed. Crawford pp. 486, 500–501).

41. *Rep.* 4.7 (*OTh* 7: 121.4–17); *Quodl.* 4.14 (*OTh* 9: 369.70–88); cf. Scotus, *Ord.* 4.10.7 (Vivès ed. 17: 276, n. 2).

42. *Rep.* 3.4 (*OTh* 6: 131.2–134.19); cf. Aquinas, *In Sent.* 4.44.3.3, sol. 1 (Vivès ed. 11: 347); *ST* 1.77.5–6.

Ockham sees Aquinas as once again too prodigal in multiplying beings beyond necessity. There is no need, in his view, to posit real distinctions between the sense powers and the sensory soul, treating them like distinct things and essences. The sensory soul can be the single principle of all sensations.

From another point of view, however, the sense powers are really distinguished from each other and from the sensory soul. Ockham explains how this is possible:

> Understand that, although there is only one sensory soul in an animal giving rise to all these actions [of the senses], nevertheless the form itself [that is, the soul] is not indivisible but divisible into parts of the same nature. For as I maintain, the sensory form in each animal is extended with the extension of quantity in matter, so that just as one part of quantity is in one part of matter and another part in another part, so one part of the sensory soul perfects one part of matter and another part – in all respects with the same nature – perfects another part. Thus the part of the sensory form perfecting the organ of sight is the power of sight – in the way we are now speaking of power – and another part of the same nature perfecting the organ of hearing is the power of hearing, and so on.[43]

From this perspective there is a real distinction between the powers of sense as parts of the same sensory soul or form. This is clear enough, because one part of the form that is one power can be completely destroyed while another part that is another power can remain. For example, if an eye is removed, the part of the soul animating the pupil of the eye is destroyed, while the part of the soul animating the organ of hearing remains. It is even possible that we have several really distinct powers of sight, one part of the sensory soul animating one eye and another part the other eye. Because all these parts are parts of the same soul which is uniform in nature, what belongs to one part can equally well belong to

---

43. *Rep.* 3.4 (*OTh* 6: 136.22–137.11).

another. As a consequence, there is nothing to prevent the part of the soul that animates the ear or tongue from animating the eye, so that the part of the soul that previously elicited the act of hearing or tasting can later elicit the act of seeing. The tactile power is unusual, for it is the whole sensory soul as it informs the entire body, enabling it to touch the qualities of bodies, unless some necessary disposition for the sensation is missing. We find this disposition lacking in paralyzed or dying persons, who at first will lose the sense of touch in one part of the body and later in another part.[44]

In proposing his novel notion of the sense powers of the soul Ockham has not forgotten the need for economy of thought. He invoked the razor when arguing against the Thomistic doctrine, that the sense powers are accidents of the soul, really distinct from each other and from the substance of the soul, because it assumes a plurality without necessity: no experience or reason justifies that doctrine. His own views on the subject, however, he regards as both parsimonious and warranted by reason and experience. We experience seeing, hearing, tasting, and so on, as really distinct acts, and we reason that they derive from really distinct powers. The real distinction between the powers, however, need only be the quantitative difference between parts of the sensory soul which is uniform in nature, somewhat as two areas of whiteness are really different while having the same nature. In this way Ockham balances parsimony with the demands of experience and reason.

3 Knowledge

Ockham's epistemology is dominated by his conception of being or reality as radically individual. We have seen him insist that everything real is by that very fact individual; there are no forms or essences in individuals distinct from them either really, formally, or conceptually. An individual is a thing (res), really and essentially distinct from every other individual. Consequently

---

44. *Rep.* 3.4 (*OTh* 6: 139.4–15).

knowledge of the real is *ipso facto* knowledge of the individual. In his early writings Ockham defended the notion of an "objective being," existing only in the mind either as a *fictum* or *figmentum*. This type of being would be different from real being in the categories of substance and quality; its whole being would be its being an object of thought. But in his later writings Ockham dismissed "objective being" as superfluous and held that even beings in the mind like concepts have real "subjective being."[45] Understanding the individual in the latter sense, it is the first object of both the senses and intellect. Knowledge of the universal (which is itself an individual, but signifying many things) comes later. Before examining more closely the primacy and centrality of the individual in our knowledge, it will be well to note certain basic distinctions in our acts of knowing.

Apprehension and Judgment

Apprehension is either the mental act by which we form a proposition or the act by which we know the proposition we have formed. In either sense apprehension is really distinct from the act by which we assent to the proposition or dissent from it. This is shown by the fact that we often entertain a proposition without immediately assenting to it and later for some reason we do assent to it; or we may first deny a proposition and afterward affirm it, all the while apprehending it. Thus apprehension is really different from assent or judgment.[46] The object apprehended may not be a proposition (*complexum*) but only a simple term or that for which the term stands (*incomplexum*); for example "Socrates." Included among simple objects are several terms and their significates that do not form a proposition; for example "white man."[47] In sum, we can apprehend propositions, demonstrations, imposs-

---

45. See below, pp. 504–510.
46. *Quodl.* 5.6 (*OTh* 9: 501.20–503.75); In *Quaest. in Phys.* 6 (*OPh* 6: 409.106–108) the act of apprehending a proposition is said to be nothing but its formation, which is different from knowing the proposition.
47. *Expos. in Periherm.* 1.prooem. (*OPh* 2: 372.3–373.22).

ible and necessary items; in short, everything that can be grasped by the mind.[48]

Judgment is the act by which the mind not only apprehends a proposition but also assents to it or dissents from it. Assent and dissent in the strict sense are limited to propositions, for they alone can be judged to be true or false. Properly speaking we do not assent to things but to propositions about them: we do not assent to a stone or cow but to propositions about them. However, we can judge things, or have knowledge about them equivalent to a judgment, as when we judge that something exists or does not exist, or that something is good or white.[49]

Ockham adds that just as there are two acts regarding a proposition – apprehension and judgment – so there are two habits corresponding to them. One inclines us to acts of apprehension, the other to acts of judgment. Experience shows us that after frequently apprehending a proposition to which we withhold assent we find ourselves more inclined than before to know it. So we have acquired a habit inclining us to this act of apprehension. Similarly, frequent acts of judging a proposition engenders in us a habit of making these acts. In his *Nicomachean Ethics* Aristotle shows that the habits we thus acquire can be distinguished into art, science, philosophy, practical wisdom, and intuitive reason.[50]

It goes without saying that the assent to a proposition presupposes its apprehension, and this in turn presupposes the apprehension of its terms. The immediate and proximate cause of any act of judgment is mental, and not sensory data. "No act of the sensory part [of the soul]," Ockham says, "is the immediate and proximate cause, either partial or total, of any act of judgment on the part of the intellect." He is not denying that the senses are the remote causes of our intellectual judgments, for, as we shall see, all our knowledge begins with the sensory intuition of individual things. What he means is that the proximate cause of the mind's

48. *Ord.* 1.prol.1 (*OTh* 1: 16.6–17.2).
49. *Quodl.* 5.6 (*OTh* 9: 500.16–18).
50. *Ord.* 1.prol.1 (*OTh* 1: 17.3–12); Aristotle, *Eth. Nic.* 6.3, 1139b16–17.

judgment is some datum within the mind itself. Ockham does not believe he can demonstrate this opinion, but he offers a persuasive or dialectical proof based on the principle of the razor. In some cases mental data suffice for an intellectual judgment, and consequently it is unnecessary to assume other causes in other cases.[51] In judging Ockham as an empiricist, his opinion on this subject should be kept in mind.

Ockham constantly stresses that if two items are really distinct, at least by the divine power one can exist without the other.[52] In controversy with his confrere Walter Chatton, this principle leads him to conclude that, because the act of forming a demonstration in the mind really differs from the act of judging it, and there is no formal contradiction (but at best a virtual one) between the act of doubting and the conclusion of a demonstration, there is nothing to prevent a demonstration's existing in a mind, while through the divine power the mind doubts the truth of its conclusion. In this extraordinary case, the mind would form a demonstration within itself (without actually knowing it) and at the same time, through the divine power, doubt its conclusion.[53] We shall presently encounter another remarkable possibility through the divine power: the intuition of something that does not exist.

Intuitive and Abstractive Knowledge

Ockham divides knowledge into two kinds: incomplex and complex. Incomplex knowledge has for its object terms and the simple objects for which they stand. Examples are "Socrates," "man," "white." Complex knowledge has for its object propositions formed from terms; for example, "Socrates is a white man." Incomplex knowledge in turn is divided into intuitive and abstractive. The terms "intuitive" and "abstractive" knowledge probably originated with Duns Scotus at the end of the thirteenth century. Robert Holcot, writing a few decades later, remarks that these

---

51. *Ord.* 1.prol.1 (*OTh* 1: 17.15–22.15).
52. See above, pp. 131–132 and below, pp. 481–482.
53. *Quodl.* 5.6 (*OTh* 9: 503.76–81).

expressions were not used by the saints or philosophers but appear to have been coined by Scotus, adding that for this reason one is free either to use them or not.[54] In fact they became part of the common vocabulary of the schoolmen in the late Middle Ages, whether they were Scotists, Thomists or Ockhamists. Mastrius de Meldula, one of the principal commentators on Scotus, called the distinction between intuitive and abstractive knowledge the best known and most frequently used division of knowledge.[55]

As the possible initiator of the distinction, Scotus was never far from the minds of those who later used his terms, even when they interpreted them in ways he would never have accepted. He described intuitive knowledge as the cognition of something actually existing and present to the knower, in opposition to abstractive knowledge which abstracts from the actual existence or nonexistence of its object.[56] According to Scotus the whole difference between these two kinds of cognition lies in the way the object is present to the knower. In intuitive knowledge the object is present in itself, in its actual existence; in abstractive knowledge the object is present in its image or likeness, which can represent it as either

---

54. Robert Holcot, "Utrum theologia sit scientia," ed. Joseph T. Muckle, *Mediaeval Studies* 20 (1958): 127–153, at p. 130. Ockham also refers to Scotus for the distinction between intuitive and abstractive cognition: see *Ord.* 1.prol.1 (*OTh* 1: 44.8–46.24); cf. ibid. 4.14 (*OTh* 7: 287.13–289.16).

55. "De cognitione intuitiva et abstractiva ... inter alias cognitionis nostrae divisiones haec est famosior et frequentissima" (Mastrius de Meldula, *Cursus philosophicus: In De anima* 6.11 [Venice, 1708], 3: 204a).

56. Scotus, *Ord.* 2.3.2.9 (Vatican ed. 7: 552–553, nn. 318–322); *Quodl.* 6 and 13 (Vivès ed. 25: 243–244, nn. 7–8 and 25: 521, n. 8), trans. Felix Alluntis and Allan B. Wolter, in *John Duns Scotus, God and Creatures: The Quodlibetal Questions* (Princeton, NJ, 1975), pp. 135–137 and 290–296. For Scotus' doctrine of intuitive and abstractive knowledge see Gilson, *Jean Duns Scot* (Paris, 1952), pp. 544–555; Sebastian J. Day, *Intuitive Cognition: A Key to the Significance of the Later Scholastics* (St. Bonaventure, NY, 1947), pp. 39–139; and Allan B. Wolter, "Duns Scotus on Intuition, Memory and Knowledge," in *History of Philosophy in the Making: A Symposium of Essays to Honor Professor James D. Collins on His 65th Birthday*, ed. Linus J. Thro (Washington, DC, 1982), pp. 81–104, repr. in his *The Philosophical Theology of John Duns Scotus*, ed. Marilyn M. Adams (Ithaca, NY, 1990), pp. 98–122.

existing or nonexisting. The likeness by itself is not sufficient to cause intuitive knowledge of a thing; for this kind of knowledge the thing must actually exist and be present to the knower.[57] Hence for Scotus the intuition of a nonexisting thing is a contradiction in terms; but more about this later.[58]

Scotus explains further that both the senses and intellect can know an object both intuitively and abstractively. We can see an existing person present to our sight and we can also imagine him or her in their absence. In the first case we have sensory intuitive knowledge of the person, in the second sensory abstractive knowledge. Scotus argues that if this twofold cognition is possible for the senses, it must also be possible for the higher power of the intellect. We can have intellectual intuition of an object as existing and present to the mind and intellectual abstractive knowledge of the same object as represented in an intelligible likeness. The intuitive cognitions just described are called perfect, because their object is something known as present and actually existing. There is also an imperfect intuitive knowledge of an object that existed in the past or will exist in the future but which is not actually present to the knower.[59]

Intuitive and abstractive cognition do not differ because the object of the former is an individual and the object of the later is a universal. Intuitive knowledge opens upon existing things as present and existing, and yet it is not only a perception of individuals; like abstractive cognition, it can also grasp the natures of things. In Scotus' words, "By both cognitions we can know both the nature [of an individual] as preceding individuality and the individual as this [individual]."[60] However, in this life we cannot have in-

---

57. Scotus, *Ord.* 4.10.8 (Vivès ed. 17: 285, n. 5).

58. Scotus, *Rep. Paris.* 3.14.3 (Vivès ed. 23: 359). Scotus qualifies this by granting that in God's vision of creatures in the divine essence the object need not be present with its own presence; see *Ord.* 4.10.8 (Vivès ed. 17: 287).

59. Scotus, *Ord.* 3.14.3 (Vivès ed. 14: 527, n. 6).

60. "[U]traque cognitione potest cognosci tam natura ut praecedit singularitatem quam singulare ut hoc" (Scotus, *Ord.* 3.14.3 [Vivès ed. 14: 524, n. 4]). "[C]ognitio intuitiva potest esse universalis et naturae et ipsius singularis" (*Rep. Paris.* 3.14.3 [Vivès ed. 23: 358, n. 11]).

tuitive knowledge of the mysterious singularity or individual difference of the individual; this can be intuited only in the future life.

As noted above, Ockham adopted from Scotus the terms "intuitive" and "abstractive" knowledge but he radically transformed their meaning. The transformation was inevitable, for after Ockham rejected the Scotist absolute nature and individual difference as formally distinct features in the structure of reality, he had to rethink the distinction between these cognitions. This he did in the light of his own notion of reality as radically individual and the revealed doctrine of the divine omnipotence. The Ockhamist concept of the individual along with the Christian belief in the divine omnipotence combined to overturn Scotus' concept of intuitive knowledge.

Ockham begins by showing that "our intellect, even in this life, can have two specifically distinct kinds of noncomplex knowledge even when it is concerned with the same object under the same aspect. The one may be called intuitive, the other abstractive cognition."[61] He appeals to experience to prove this. We can know the simple objects Socrates and whiteness in such a way that we cannot know evidently whether or not Socrates is white. In another way we can know evidently that Socrates is white, if he is white. Thus the intellect can have two specifically distinct noncomplex cognitions of these objects: one is intuitive and can cause an evident assent to the contingent proposition "Socrates is white"; the other is abstractive and cannot cause this assent.

This proves that our intellect can know sensible things both abstractively and intuitively. It can also be shown that the intellect is capable of both kinds of cognition regarding purely intelligible objects, such as acts of knowing and loving. I can know intuitively my own knowing and loving, and thus assent to the proposition "I know" or "I love." Indeed, our knowledge about these intelli-

---

61. "[P]rimo ostendam quod intellectus noster etiam pro statu isto respectu eiusdem obiecti sub eadem ratione potest habere duas notitias incomplexas specie distinctas, quarum una potest dici intuitiva et alia abstractiva" (*Ord.* 1.prol.1 [*OTh* 1: 15.14–17]); trans. Philotheus Boehner, in *Philosophical Writings*, rev. Stephen Brown (1957; Indianapolis/Cambridge, MA, 1990), p. 18.

gible facts is most evident and certain. This is clear from experience and also from Augustine, who states that, even though we could doubt about the objects of our senses, as the Academics [that is, ancient Skeptics] do, we cannot doubt that we live and know. In the presence of another person I can also be intuitively aware of his or her knowing or loving. In their absence, however, I cannot be certain that the person still knows or loves, though the person's knowing and loving can remain in my mind and be known abstractively. Hence there can be both intuitive and abstractive knowledge of the same simple object.[62]

As used here, the term "abstractive knowledge" does not mean the cognition of a universal abstracted from individuals. We shall discuss this notion of abstraction when we consider the nature of the concept. In the present context, abstractive knowledge is the cognition of an incomplex object in abstraction from existence and nonexistence and other contingent and temporal conditions that might attach to it. This knowledge does not permit us to know with evidence whether a contingent thing exists or does not exist. In contrast, intuitive knowledge is defined precisely as follows:

> Intuitive cognition of a thing is cognition that enables us to know whether the thing exists or does not exist, in such a way that, if the thing exists, then the intellect immediately judges that it exists and evidently knows that it exists, unless the judgment happens to be impeded through the imperfection of the cognition. And in the same way, if the divine power were

---

62. *Ord.* 1.prol.1 (*OTh* 1: 28.5–30.4, 43.7–23). Augustine, *De Trinitate* 15.12 (CCL 50A: 490–493, n. 21). In *Quodl.* 1.14 (*OTh* 9: 78–82) Ockham argues that in its present state the mind can know its own acts intuitively. Walter Chatton counters that the mind of a *viator* does not naturally have an intuitive knowledge by which it sees its own acts. He argues that an intuition of one's acts is unnecessary and thus contrary to the razor. All that is needed to verify the proposition "the soul experiences its act" is the reception of the actual knowledge in the mind. Moreover, Ockham's position leads to an infinity of intuitive acts: see Walter Chatton, *Reportatio et Lectura super Sententias*, prol.2.5 (ed. Wey pp. 117–129). Ockham replies that the intuitive power is so limited that it does not extend to an infinity of acts (ibid. [ed Wey p. 80.42–47]).

to conserve a perfect intuitive cognition of a nonexistent thing, in virtue of this noncomplex knowledge the intellect would know evidently that the thing does not exist.[63]

By means of intuitive cognition we also have immediate and evident knowledge of other contingent truths about a thing; for example, that it has a particular property or that it is at a given distance from another thing. In general, "every noncomplex cognition of one or more terms or things is an intuitive cognition if it enables us to know a contingent truth with evidence, especially relating to the present."[64] Abstractive cognition, on the contrary, cannot give us evident knowledge of a thing's existence or nonexistence or any of its contingent properties. Thus, knowing Socrates and his whiteness in his absence, we cannot be sure that he is or is not white, or whether he is or is not at a given distance from something else.

Since we clearly know contingent truths, we must be able to know things intuitively. Indeed, we have sensory intuitive cognition of sensible things, immediately followed by intellectual intuitive cognition of the same things. We also have intellectual intuitive cognition of intelligible objects, such as our acts of knowing and willing, and of mental states such as joy and sadness. Thus intuition, either sensory or intellectual, is at the origin of all our experiential knowledge of contingent truths, and all our abstractive and scientific knowledge of necessary truths derives from previous intuitive cognition.[65]

---

63. "[N]otitia intuitiva rei est talis notitia virtute cuius potest sciri utrum res sit vel non, ita quod si res sit, statim intellectus iudicat eam esse et evidenter cognoscit eam esse, nisi forte impediatur propter imperfectionem illius notitiae. Et eodem modo si esset perfecta talis notitia per potentiam divinam conservata de re non exsistente, virtute illius notitiae incomplexae evidenter cognosceret illam rem non esse" (*Ord.* 1.prol.1 [*OTh* 1: 31.10–16]); trans. Boehner, in *Philosophical Writings*, p. 23 (slightly modified).

64. "Et universaliter omnis notitia incomplexa termini vel terminorum, seu rei vel rerum, virtute cuius potest evidenter cognosci aliqua veritas contingens, maxime de praesenti, est notitia intuitiva" (ibid. [*OTh* 1: 31.25–32.3]).

65. Ibid. (*OTh* 1: 32.4–33.12). In *Quodl.* 1.14 (*OTh* 9: 78–82) Ockham contends that in the present life our intellect knows its own acts of knowing

Intuitive Cognition of Nonexistents

While taking the terms "intuitive" and "abstractive" cognition from Duns Scotus, Ockham criticizes the way he distinguished between them. As we have seen, for Scotus the object of intuitive cognition is always something really existing and present to the knower, whereas the object of abstractive cognition may be either existing or nonexisting, either present in reality or absent. Furthermore, the object of intuitive cognition is present in its own existence, while the object of abstractive cognition is present in a representative image or likeness (*species*) that virtually contains the thing whose likeness it is. Consequently intuitive cognition reaches its object in itself and from a perfect perspective; abstractive cognition contacts it only in a sort of "diminished" likeness.[66]

Neither of these ways of distinguishing between the two kinds of cognition is acceptable to Ockham. Their difference cannot lie in their objects, because "absolutely the same thing, under the same aspect on the side of the object, is the object of both intuitive and abstractive [cognition]."[67] Ockham justifies this revolutionary statement by claiming that there is nothing that we can know intuitively, especially in this world of ours, under any aspect proper to it, that we cannot doubt whether it exists or not, and hence that we can know it abstractively. Ockham's rationale for this unsettling statement is that in our present state we have no

---

and willing intuitively without any preceding sensory intuition. We form a contingent proposition about the intellect's knowing and our willing, for example "I am knowing" and "I am willing." This proposition, which the intellect knows with evidence, is known either by means of intuitive or abstractive intellectual cognition. Not by abstractive cognition, for this abstracts from actual existence; therefore by intuitive cognition (*OTh* 9: 79.11–16).

66. Ibid. (*OTh* 1: 33.15–35.2). See Scotus, *Ord.* 2.3.2.2 (Vatican ed. 7: 552–553, nn. 318–322); cf. Scotus, *Quodl.* 6 and 13 (Vivès ed. 25: 244, n. 8 and 25: 525, n. 11, 539–541, n. 13), trans. Alluntis and Wolter, pp. 135–137 and 292–293.

67. "[I]dem totaliter et sub eadem ratione a parte obiecti est obiectum intuitivae et abstractivae" (*Ord.* 1.prol.1 [*OTh* 1: 36.15–16]). Cf. ibid. 1.27.3 (*OTh* 4: 242.10–12).

perfectly clear intuitions of anything.[68] If one objects that by intuitive knowledge we do in fact know the existence of things, Ockham replies that "existence itself can be known abstractively." Neither can the difference between these types of cognition lie in their causes. In the natural course of events, intuitive cognition is caused immediately by the real existence of its object, with God acting as the intuition's primary cause. But the real existence of the object is not absolutely required as an essential cause of intuitive cognition. Being omnipotent, God can always dispense with creaturely causes and do by himself what he ordinarily does through them. Hence, by the divine power there can be an intuitive cognition without the real existence and causality of the object. In this case the object is not a real being but nonbeing. Ockham's conclusion decisively negates the position of Scotus:

> Consequently I say that intuitive and abstractive cognition differ by themselves and not by reason of objects nor by reason of any causes whatsoever, though naturally there cannot be intuitive cognition without the thing's existence, which is truly the mediate or immediate efficient cause of intuitive cognition, as will be said elsewhere. But there can naturally be abstractive cognition when the thing known is completely destroyed.[69]

68. "Secundum patet, quia idem totaliter et sub eadem ratione a parte obiecti est obiectum intuitivae et abstractivae. Hoc patet, quia nulla res est, saltem in istis inferioribus, nec aliqua ratio sibi propria sub qua potest res intuitive cognosci quin illa cognita ab intellectu possit intellectus dubitare utrum sit vel non sit, et per consequens quin possit cognosci abstractive" (*Ord.* 1.prol.1 [*OTh* 1: 36.15–20]). This is difficult, if not impossible, to reconcile with Ockham's later statement (*OTh* 1: 70.18–20) that by its nature intuitive knowledge enables us to make a correct judgment of the existence or nonexistence of things. It would seem that the judgment would be correct only if the intuition were perfect and evident and not obscure or otherwise impeded. In fact, Ockham denies that in our present life our mind has a perfect and clear intuitive knowledge of anything: "Intellectus autem noster pro statu isto nihil cognoscit intuitive clare et perfecte" (*OTh* 1: 68.17–19).

69. "Ideo dico quod notitia intuitiva et abstractiva se ipsis differunt et non penes obiecta nec penes causas suas quascumque, quamvis naturaliter notitia intuitiva non possit esse sine exsistentia rei, quae est vere causa efficiens

Again, Ockham says:

> Thus intuitive knowledge, taken in itself and necessarily, has no more to do with an existing thing than with a nonexisting thing, nor does it concern existence any more than nonexistence. Rather, it concerns both the existence and nonexistence of a thing as stated above.[70]

Ockham sends us back a few pages for a clarification of this statement. Intuitive knowledge, he says, differs from abstractive knowledge because the intuitive knowledge of a thing enables us to know whether it exists or not; so that if the thing exists, the mind at once judges that it exists and knows with evidence that it exists, unless it is impeded because of some imperfection in the knowledge. Similarly, if the intuition were perfect and caused by the divine power, the mind would know with evidence that the object does not exist.[71]

Ockham's conclusion that there can be both a sensory and intellectual intuitive cognition of a nonexisting object is reinforced by an argument drawn from metaphysics. We have seen that everything real is an individual, so distinct from every other individual that it can exist apart from it, if not naturally at least by the divine power. Now an intuitive cognition is one real thing and its object is another, existing in a different place and subject than the intuitive cognition. Hence by his absolute power God can make one of them exist

---

notitiae intuitivae mediata vel immediata, sicut alias dicetur. Notitia autem abstractiva potest esse naturaliter ipsa re nota simpliciter destructa" (*Ord.* 1.prol.1 [*OTh* 1: 38.5–10]). Ockham refers to *Rep.* 2.12–13 (*OTh* 5: 256–261). For God's power in this case to produce an effect immediately without using secondary causes see *Quodl.* 6.6 (*OTh* 9: 604.18–605.24).

70. "Et ita notitia intuitiva, secundum se et necessario, non plus est exsistentis quam non exsistentis, nec plus respicit exsistentiam quam non-exsistentiam, sed respicit tam exsistentiam quam non-exsistentiam rei, per modum prius declaratum" (*Ord.* 1.prol.1 [*OTh* 1: 36.8–12]). This statement was censured by the papal commission examining Ockham's doctrine at Avignon in 1326; see J. Koch, "Neue Aktenstücke zu dem gegen Wilhelm Ockham in Avignon geführten Prozess," *Recherches de théologie ancienne et médiévale* 8 (1936): 79–93, 168–197, at p. 92.12–93.14, and *Extracta*, p. 197.15–21.

71. See above, note 63.

without the other. For example, if we see a star in the sky, that sight or intuition, whether sensory or intellectual, is in a different place and subject from the star. Hence God can bring it about that the sight of the star remains even though the star does not exist.[72]

At first sight Ockham's claim that we can see intuitively something that does not exist is surprising. But we have already encountered a prime case of this sort of intuition. Studying the divine knowledge, we saw that God knows all his creatures intuitively, both when they exist and when they do not. Thus he has intuitive cognition of nonexistents, just as he has of existents. From all eternity he sees everything creatable, and yet from eternity they are nothing (*nihil*).[73] Ockham is saying that through the divine power we can share in this ability to see intuitively both what actually exists and does not exist. This must be qualified, however, for the objects God sees from eternity are not purely nothing but possible objects of creation. So too the nonexistents we could intuitively see either actually or possibly exist. God cannot give us an intuition of something that neither actually exists not can exist; for example, an intuition of a chimera. This mythical animal cannot exist, and so it would be contradictory for God to give us an intuition of it by which we would judge that it exists. In short, the objects of intuitive cognition must either actually or possibly exist.[74] In this respect they resemble the divine ideas, which are nonbeings eternally

---

72. "Ex istis sequitur quod notitia intuitiva, tam sensitiva quam intellectiva, potest esse de re non exsistente. Et hanc conclusionem probo, aliter quam prius, sic: omnis res absoluta, distincta loco et subiecto ab alia re absoluta, potest per divinam potentiam absolutam exsistere sine illa, quia non videtur verisimile quod si Deus vult destruere unam rem absolutam exsistentem in caelo quod necessitetur destruere unam aliam rem exsistentem in terra. Sed visio intuitiva, tam sensitiva quam intellectiva, est res absoluta, distincta loco et subiecto ab obiecto. Sicut si videam intuitive stellam exsistentem in caelo, illa visio intuitiva, sive sit sensitiva sive intellectiva, distinguitur loco et subiecto ab obiecto viso; igitur ista visio potest manere stella destructa" (*Ord.* 1.prol.1 [*OTh* 1: 38.15–39.6]). See also *Quodl.* 6.6 (*OTh* 9: 605.25–28).

73. *Ord.* 1.prol.1 (*OTh* 1: 39.7–10); *Quodl.* 6.6 (*OTh* 9: 607.67–68).

74. *Quodl.* 6.6 (*OTh* 9: 606.61–607.66).

seen by God, some of which he creates, but all of which are at least possible objects of creation. If God gave us an intuition of a nonexistent thing, it would be an intuition of a "nothing" in the sense in which God's ideas are "nothings."[75]

Even within his lifetime Ockham met opposition to his notion of intuitive cognition. Walter Chatton objected to Ockham's position that intuitive cognition can be the means of knowing not only that a thing exists and is present but also that something does not exist and is absent. For Ockham, the difference between these two cases lies in their causes. The intuitive cognition of a thing, along with the thing itself, cause the judgment that the thing exists. But when the thing is absent, the intuitive cognition without the object will cause the opposite judgment, namely that it does not exist.[76] But Chatton protests that we know intuitively the presence of an object but not its absence. How could a nonexistent or absent object cause an intuition of the senses or intellect? It is not by intuition that we know something is not present, as Ockham thought, but by a process of reasoning (*arguitive*). We can be aware that we do not see something or have an intuitive knowledge of it, and so we conclude that it is not present.[77]

Chatton also thought Ockham misguided in thinking that if God gave us a perfect intuition of a nonexistent object it would represent the object as nonexisting. If this were the case, Chatton contends, God could not give us an act of knowing that would represent an absent object as present, though this is not contradictory and hence comes within the divine power. The act cannot be intuitive according to Ockham, for he describes intuitive cognition as the knowledge by which a thing appears to exist when it exists and not to exist when

75. For the divine ideas see above, pp. 220–225.

76. *Ord.* 1.prol.1 (*OTh* 1: 70.21–71.9).

77. Chatton, *Reportatio et Lectura*, prol.2.3 (ed. Wey pp. 103.149–158). On Chatton's criticism of Ockham on this subject see Katherine H. Tachau, "The Problem of the *species in medio* at Oxford in the Generation after Ockham," *Mediaeval Studies* 44 (1982): 406–413. See also Anneliese Maier, "Das Problem der 'Species Sensibiles in Medio' und die neue Naturphilosophie des 14 Jahrhunderts," *Freiburger Zeitschrift für Philosophie und Theologie* 10 (1963): 3–32.

it does not. Neither can it be an act of abstractive cognition, for in Ockham's view (and here, Chatton adds, he speaks the truth), this kind of knowledge abstracts from existence and nonexistence and thus does not make an object appear to be present.[78]

Replying to Chatton in his *Quodlibeta*, Ockham adds a clarification of his views on intuitive cognition. First, he insists that God cannot cause in us a cognition such that by means of it a thing would *evidently* appear to be present when it is absent because this would be contradictory. His reason is that evident knowledge implies that the facts are such as stated by the proposition to which we assent. Thus, since the evident knowledge of the proposition "The thing is present" implies that it is present, it must be present, and not even God could alter the fact. Nevertheless God can make us *believe* that a thing is present when it is absent. This would be an act of faith, and it would not be intuitive but abstractive, and because it lacks evidence it could make a thing appear to be present when it is absent.[79] Ockham continues that "God can make an assent of the same kind as the evident assent to the contingent proposition 'This whiteness exists' when the whiteness does not exist; but that assent is not evident, because the facts are not such as implied by the proposition to which we give assent."[80]

---

78. Chatton, *Reportatio et Lectura*, prol.2.3 (ed. Wey pp. 98.21–99.28), reported by Ockham, *Quodl.* 5.5 (*OTh* 9: 496.30–36).

79. "Tamen Deus potest causare actum creditivum per quem credo rem esse praesentem quae est absens. Et dico quod illa cognitio creditiva erit abstractiva, non intuitiva; et per talem actum fidei potest apparere res esse praesens quando est absens, non tamen per actum evidentem" (*Quodl.* 5.5 [*OTh* 9: 498.73–76]). Ockham defines an act of faith as an assent without evidence commanded by the will (*Ord.* 1.prol.7 [*OTh* 1: 186.5–6]). In this context the term "abstractive" does not have its usual meaning of abstracting from existence and nonexistence, but it has the sense of an imperfect and nonevident intuition. See below, note 81. To the best of my knowledge only once (in *Quodl.* 5.5) Ockham refers to an abstractive act of belief by which we would judge an absent thing to be present. When he takes up the question of the possibility of an intuition of a nonexistent object later, in *Quodl.* 6.6, he does not mention it.

80. "Concedo tamen quod Deus potest facere assensum eiusdem speciei cum illo assensu evidenti respectu huius contingentis 'haec albedo est' quando albedo

This is an astute reply to Chatton's contention that God could give us an act of knowing that would represent an absent object as present. Ockham grants this possibility, but he denies that the act would be a perfect intuition; rather it would be an act of faith, and in this sense an instance of abstractive knowledge. Lacking evidence, it would not be a perfect but an imperfect intuition.[81] Ockham's rejoinder to Chatton accomplishes its purpose in debate, but it leaves him open to the objection that God can deceive us through abstractive or imperfect intuition, though not through perfect or evident intuition. Critics of Ockham have pointed out that he offers no way of distinguishing perfect intuitive cognitions from possible deceptive acts of belief. Léon Baudry writes:

> Ockham says that God can produce in us an act of knowledge by which we affirm that what does not exist exists, but that we have to do here with a belief and not with an evident judgment, with an abstractive and not with an intuitive cognition. Unfortunately he does not tell us how we can know that in this case it is a question of an abstractive knowledge and a simple belief. And this, it must be granted, is a serious lacuna in his doctrine.[82]

---

non est; sed ille assensus non est evidens, quia non est ita in re sicut importatur per propositionem cui fit assensus" (*Quodl.* 5.5 [*OTh* 9: 499.100–104]).

81. For the distinction between perfect and imperfect intuitive cognition see *Rep.* 2.12–13 (*OTh* 5: 261–267). Memory is an instance of imperfect intuitive cognition, enabling us to judge that something was or was not in the past. Immediately after a perfect intuitive cognition, when the object has been destroyed or removed from sight, the mind can think about the thing it saw before intuitively and form the proposition 'this thing once existed' and assent with evidence to it. This imperfect intuitive cognition is also called abstractive. In this case, too, God could produce in us a habit inclining us to a false memory of a past event, though this would not happen naturally (*Rep.* 4.14 (*OTh* 7: 311.15–19).

82. "Ockham affirme que Dieu peut causer en nous un acte de connaissance par lequel nous affirmons que ce qui n'est pas existe, mais que nous avons alors une croyance et non un jugement évident, une connaissance abstractive et non une connaissance intuitive. Malheureusement il ne nous dit

It should be emphasized that Ockham's doctrine of an intuition of a nonexistent object does not concern our natural knowledge, but possible knowledge in the supernatural order through the divine power. Ockham wants to show the contingency of our present ways of knowing and the possibility of other ways through the absolute power of God. Ockham gives us no reason to think that intuitions of nonexistents actually occur through the divine power, or that God can deceive us through them, at least if the intuitions are evident. Indeed, he insists that whether they are caused supernaturally or naturally, intuitions and the judgments following upon them in no way lead the mind into error: *Et sic nullo modo ponit intellectum in errore.*[83]

Peter Aureol argued from experience that even naturally an intuitive cognition can be caused and conserved while the object does not exist. If someone looks at the sun and then enters a dark room, he appears to see the sun in the same place and with the

---

pas comment nous pouvons savoir que c'est, dans ce cas, d'une connaissance abstractive et d'une simple croyance qu'il s'agit. Et c'est, il faut l'avouer, une grave lacune dans sa doctrine" (Léon Baudry, *Lexique philosophique de Guillaume d'Ockham* [Paris, 1958] p. 177). On the same subject see Etienne Gilson, *The Unity of Philosophical Experience* (New York, 1941), pp. 80–81; John Boler, "Intuitive and Abstractive Cognition," in *The Cambridge History of Later Medieval Philosophy*, ed. Norman Kretzmann et al. (Cambridge, 1982), p. 471. Marilyn Adams ("Intuitive Cognition, Certainty, and Scepticism in William Ockham," *Traditio* 26 [1970]: 389–398) argues convincingly against Philotheus Boehner's suggestion that intuitive and abstractive cognitions can be distinguished by introspecting their characteristics. Ockham consistently bases the distinction on whether the resulting proposition is true.

Since Gilson's views on Ockham's alleged skepticism have sometimes been misrepresented, it will not be out of place to remark that, for philosophical reasons, he says that Ockham's doctrine of the intuition of nonexistents is on the road to skepticism, but that it "cannot be described as a scepticism" (*Unity*, p. 86). It is true that in his *La philosophie au moyen âge* (Paris, 1944), p. 655, he speaks of Ockhamism, especially its natural philosophy, as a veritable and metaphysical skepticism; but it should be noted that in his later *History of Christian Philosophy in the Middle Ages*, pp. 498–499, he omits these expressions.

83. *Rep.* 2.12–13 (*OTh* 5: 287.6–7).

same size. Thus the sight of the sun remains when it is absent, and it would remain even if the sun did not exist. In reply, Ockham contends that a real effect cannot be brought into being and conserved by nothing. Naturally speaking, therefore, intuitive cognition needs both a created efficient and conserving cause. In the above example, it is not the sun that is seen in a dark room, but a certain quality, namely the light impressed on the eye. Ockham concludes that in the natural order intuitive cognition cannot be produced or conserved by a nonexistent object, but only through the divine power.[84]

84. *Quodl.* 6.6 (*OTh* 9: 604–609). See Peter Aureol, *Scriptum super Sent.* 1.prooem.2.3 (ed. Buytaert 1: 198–199, n. 82). On this theme see Philotheus Boehner, "*Notitia Intuitiva* of Non-Existents according to Peter Aureoli, OFM (1322)," *Franciscan Studies* 8 (1948): 388–416. Ockham quotes Aureol at length and criticizes his doctrine in *Ord.* 1.27.3 (*OTh* 4: 230–258) and in *Rep.* 2.12–13 (*OTh* 5: 286.10–287.7). Like Ockham, Chatton argues against Aureol's notion of a naturally produced intuitive cognition of a nonexisting object (*Reportatio et Lectura*, prol.2.2 [ed. Wey pp. 86–94]). On this subject see Katherine H. Tachau, "The Response to Ockham's and Aureol's Epistemology (1320–1340)," in *English Logic in Italy in the 14th and 15th Centuries* (Naples, 1982), pp. 185–217. Francis of Meyronnes (*fl* 1323), a follower of Scotus, defended his master's position on this subject against the criticism of Aureol: see Armand Maurer, "Francis of Meyronnes' Defense of Epistemological Realism," *Studia Mediaevalia et Mariologica in Honour of P. Carolo Balić* (Rome, 1971), pp. 203–225, repr. Maurer, *Being and Knowing*, pp. 311–331.

There is an extensive bibliography on the subject of the intuition of a nonexistent. See especially Erich Hochstetter, *Studien zur Metaphysik und Erkenntnislehre Wilhelms von Ockham* (Berlin, 1927); Gilson, *Unity of Philosophical Experience*, pp. 78–83; Day, *Intuitive Cognition*; Boehner, "The *Notitia Intuitiva* of Non-Existents according to William Ockham," *Traditio* 1 (1943): 223–275, repr. in his *Collected Articles on Ockham*, ed. Eligius M. Buytaert (St. Bonaventure, NY, 1958), pp. 268–319; Anton C. Pegis, "Concerning William of Ockham," *Traditio* 2 (1944): 223–275, and "Some Recent Interpretations of Ockham," *Speculum* 23 (1948): 452–463; Theodore K. Scott, "Ockham on Evidence, Necessity, and Intuition," *Journal of the History of Philosophy* 7 (1969): 27–49; Marilyn M. Adams, *William Ockham* (Notre Dame, IN, 1987), 1: 501–506, 588–629, and "Intuitive Cognition, Certainty, and Skepticism"; Katherine Tachau, *Vision and Certitude in the Age of Ockham* (Leiden, 1988); Rega Wood, "Intuitive Cognition and Divine Omnipotence: Ockham in Fourteenth-Century Perspective," in *From Ockham to Wyclif*, ed. Anne Hudson and Michael Wilks (Oxford, 1987), pp. 51–61.

The theme of an intuition of a nonexistent object appears in several works of Ockham, written at different times and under different circumstances. Certain constants, however, appear in all his presentations of the doctrine. One of the most important is the principle of the divine omnipotence, held on faith, that God can do anything whose doing does not include a clear contradiction. Another constant is the truth of evident experience. Ockham never deviates from his conviction that a judgment based on evident intuition is always true; only one based on abstractive cognition can be false, for it lacks the evidence of the object's existence or non-existence. In this way Ockham brings together the two principles of the divine omnipotence and the truth of evident cognition and thereby establishes an equilibrium in his noetic.

This is a good illustration of the observation ascribed to Victor Delbos (1862–1916), a professor of philosophy at the Sorbonne, "that every philosophical doctrine is the result not of one principle but of a compromise among a number of principles, some of which serve to prevent any one of the others from developing the whole train of its consequences."[85] Like other scholastics, Ockham regards the divine power as limited by the principle of non-contradiction: the divine omnipotence is defined as the power to do or make anything that does not include an evident contradiction.[86] In his noetic he insists that it would be clearly contradictory for God to give us an evident intuition that would result in a

---

85. "Victor Delbos avait coutume de dire que toute doctrine philosophique résulte, non d'un principe, mais d'un compromis entre plusieurs principes, dont les uns ont pour fonction d'empêcher aucun des autres de développer la suite entière de ses conséquences" (Etienne Gilson, "Remarques sur l'expérience en métaphysique," in *Proceedings of the XIth International Congress of Philosophy* [Amsterdam, 1953], 4: 5–10; trans. Armand Maurer as "Remarks on Experience in Metaphysics," in Maurer, "Gilson's Use of History in Philosophy," *Thomistic Papers* 5 [1990]: 25–48, at pp. 40–48). Gilson expresses Delbos' thesis in *The Unity of Philosophical Experience*, p. 301: "Each particular philosophy is, therefore, a co-ordination of self and mutually limiting principles which defines an individual outlook on the fullness of reality."

86. See above, pp. 131, 246–247, 257–258.

false judgment. The divine power is held in check by the principle of the truth of evident knowledge. As we have seen, God can give us an intuition of something that does not exist, but if the intuition is evident it would not cause us to judge that the thing exists but that it does not exist. In this way Ockham achieves a balance in his principles, assuring us of the truth of both God's omnipotence and the veracity of evident intuitive cognition.

This equilibrium of principles, however, was precarious, and it was almost at once upset by Ockham's followers who emphasized the divine omnipotence at the expense of the certainty of evident knowledge. This is not the place to enlarge on the subject, but the example of Adam of Wodeham will help to illustrate it.

Adam of Wodeham, Ockham's friend and first disciple,[87] contradicted his master's claim of the certitude of intuitive knowledge, caused either naturally or supernaturally by God. Adam could see no reason that a judgment of a contingent truth about an extramental thing should exclude every possible doubt. Expanding on this topic, he writes:

> For it is compatible with God's or nature's causing any cognition or possible judgment in the mind that, by God's absolute power, things are not the way the intuitive apprehension signifies them to be. And I grant that every intellect that can be created is of a diminished nature, in the sense that it can be deceived about any contingent truth about extramental things, if it categorically asserts that they are or are not thus.

As a consequence Wodeham believed that no cognition is so certain that we cannot be deceived by God:

> Against Ockham's claims and in behalf of my own reply, I argue as follows: for it would not be possible to have any certain judgment that a thing which exists exists or that it

---

87. William J. Courtenay, *Adam Wodeham: An Introduction to His Life and Writings* (Leiden, 1978).

does not exist when it does not exist. Therefore, it would be contradictory for God to make us certain about a contingent truth. Proof of the inference: just as God could conserve the vision without the existence of the object, so also he could conserve any other mental cognition, whether noncomplex or complex without its existing. Therefore, he could not make us certain by any mental cognition. I grant that there is no cognition by means of which we can be so certain that we could not be deceived by him, if he wished it.[88]

Ockham avoids skepticism in his doctrine of the intuition of nonexistent objects by showing that if our cognition is truly intuitive, not even by the divine power can the mind be led into error. Wodeham, for his part, deserves the name of skeptic, for he denies our capacity to have any certain knowledge owing to the possibility of divine deception.

The Primacy of the Individual in Knowledge

Having seen the central position of the individual in Ockham's metaphysics, we can hardly be surprised to find it holding a similar place in his noetic. Every real being in his view is an individual; universals are only verbal or conceptual terms explainable by individuals. As a consequence all our knowledge has its origin in our knowledge of the individual, more precisely in individual sensory and intellectual intuitive cognition.

We should not overlook the historical significance of Ockham's shift of focus from the universal to the individual as the primary and direct source of all our knowledge, including the knowledge of our own mind. According to Aristotle the intellect apprehends universals but the senses individuals: *Intellectus est uni-*

---

88. I am indebted to Marilyn M. Adams (*William Ockham* 1: 605–606), for these quotations from Adam of Wodeham. Her translations were made from Wodeham's *Quaest. in 1 librum Sent.* prol., q. 2 in Cambridge, Gonville and Caius, MS Cod. 281/674, fol. 109va (transcribed by Gedeon Gál). For Wodeham's doctrine see Rega Wood, "Adam Wodeham on Sensory Illusions, with an Edition of 'Lectura secunda,' Prologus, Quaestio 3," *Traditio* 38 (1982): 213–252.

versalium, sensus autem particularium.[89] In the Middle Ages this was often taken to mean that the intellect directly knows only universals; it knows individuals indirectly by reflecting on their individual images in the interior senses.[90] The reason given was that, as an immaterial power, the intellect could only directly know what is immaterial, and that is a universal nature and not a sensible individual. In the twelfth century Abelard made an effort to install the individual and its knowledge in the first place, but "Ockham was the first thinker to incorporate universal knowledge into an individual ontology, systematically reducing ... concepts, terms and propositions to their individual import."[91]

What is the first object of the intellect from the point of view of the origin of its knowledge? Does the intellect first know an individual, or a common or universal object and only later arrive at a knowledge of the individual? It is not difficult to surmise what Ockham's answer will be. He has told us that there is nothing common or universal in reality but only individuals; universals are nothing but concepts or words functioning as signs of individual things. Hence, through our senses and intellect we know a real world of individuals before becoming aware of the terms and concepts we use to signify them. We have seen that our first cognition is sensory and intellectual intuition, and the object of intuition is always an individual. On this score, too, it is not the universal but the individual that is the primary object of both our senses and

89. Aristotle, *De anima* 2.5, 417b22–23.

90. *ST* 1.86.1. Aquinas holds that the individual is not unintelligible insofar as it is individual but insofar as it is material. Ockham argues against his position that universals are better known to us than individuals, and that they are known by the intellect prior to individuals; see *Ord.* 1.3.5 (*OTh* 2: 464.2–471.10). He criticizes both the Thomist doctrine and that of Henry of Ghent; see ibid. 1.3.6 (*OTh* 2: 483.16–492.13). He also opposes Scotus' doctrine that the first object of the intellect is not what is most universal but "the ultimate species (*species specialissima*) of the individual that most strongly impresses the senses" (ibid. 1.3.5 [*OTh* 2: 453.18–24]; cf. Scotus, *Ord.* 1.3.1.3 [Vatican ed. 3: 113–114, n. 187]).

91. Gordon Leff, *William of Ockham* (Manchester, 1975), p. 2. For Abelard see Martin M. Tweedale, *Abailard on Universals* (Amsterdam, 1976).

intellect, if by "primary" we mean what comes first in the process of acquiring knowledge.[92]

If this is true, the first object of our knowledge is not just any kind of individual, but something one in number that is not a natural or conventional sign common to many individuals. This excludes concepts and written or spoken words as our first objects of knowledge. A precision can also be made regarding the meaning of knowledge in this context. Ockham is not talking about general or universal knowledge but proper and incomplex individual knowledge. Even our general knowledge is a knowledge of individuals, for it is not restricted to any one in particular but includes many individuals. For example, by knowing man in general we know all men. Proper knowledge is restricted to the one individual. The knowledge in question is also called incomplex because its object is one item and not several; for example, whiteness and not white man.[93]

An object of knowledge may be called primary in other senses than first in the acquisition of knowledge (*primitas generationis*). It may be primary because it satisfies the knowing power (*primitas adaequationis*). This can have two meanings. First, it can mean the most general notion the intellect can form, predicable essentially of everything the intellect can naturally know in its present state. Second and more profoundly, it can mean the object that contains everything knowable in its singularity and proper nature. In the first sense we can naturally know that being is the adequate object

---

92. *Ord.* 1.3.6 (*OTh* 2: 483–521); *Quodl.* 1.13 (*OTh* 9: 72–78). Is the individual primarily known intuitively as a substance or quality or the two together? Ockham speaks of intuiting Socrates, a lamb or a sheep, giving the reader the impression that we have intuitive cognition of substances. He makes it clear, however, that naturally we do not have intuitive cognition of material substances in themselves, but only through their accidents. See *Ord.* 1.3.2 (*OTh* 2: 412.19–22), *Quodl.* 1.13 and 3.6 (*OTh* 9: 77.122–128 and 9: 227.53–54). But Ockham does not explain how a knowledge of one thing (a quality) can be the means of knowing another thing (a substance). For a discussion of this problem see T.K. Scott, "Ockham on Evidence, Necessity, and Intuition," *Journal of the History of Philosophy* 7 (1969): 27–49; and Adams, *William Ockham* 1: 539–547.

93. *Quodl.* 1.13 (*OTh* 9: 72.13–73.36).

of the intellect, for it is the most general concept it can form and predicate essentially of everything naturally accessible to it. In the second sense, however, we cannot know by natural reason that being is the adequate object of our intellect, for in its present state it cannot grasp everything in its individuality and proper nature; for example, all material and immaterial substances, many accidents, and God, the most perfect being.

Ockham criticizes Scotus for holding that we can naturally know that being is the primary object of the intellect in the second sense; that is, by natural reason we can know distinctly the unlimited range of things contained under being, including God. But Ockham here ascribes to Scotus a position he himself did not accept but attributed to his opponent.[94] Actually, Scotus, like Thomas Aquinas, thought that in its present fallen state the mind's adequate object is the essence of a material, or more particularly, a sensible thing and what is essentially or virtually contained in that thing. In the opinion of Scotus, however, the natural and adequate object of the human mind, taken just in itself as a natural power and abstracting from its present state, is as unlimited as the angelic mind. Its object is being, in its full range of material and immaterial beings, including God. But he did not believe that human reason could know this with its own resources without divine revelation.[95]

Originating in the sensory intuition of individual things, followed by the intellectual intuition of the same things, our knowledge progresses as the mind grasps them with an abstractive and

---

94. *Rep.* 4.16 (*OTh* 7: 348.21–349.22), *Ord.* 1.1.4 (*OTh* 1: 432.5–437.20). The latter text reverses the order of the two meanings of adequate object. Ockham criticizes Scotus for holding that we can naturally know that being is the natural and adequate object of the intellect in the second sense. But Ockham's editors point out that Scotus firmly denies what Ockham attributes to him; see *OTh* 7: 348 n1 and *OTh* 1: 432 n1. Ockham takes arguments that Scotus levels against his opponent to be Scotus' own; see Scotus, *Ord.* prol.1.un. (Vatican ed. 1: 19, n. 33).

95. Scotus, *Quodl.* 14 (Vivès ed. 26: 46–47, n. 12). See Gilson, *Jean Duns Scot*, pp. 30–32. For Aquinas see *ST* 1.84.7.

universal cognition. This is truly an advance in knowledge, for science is possible only on this level. As we have seen in Chapter 2, science does not directly have to do with individuals but with universals abstracted from individuals and used in propositions and syllogistic reasoning. The mind is not satisfied with knowing individuals; it presses on and finds its adequate object in the abstractive and universal knowledge of science.

The abstraction that makes science possible is not the grasping of the essences of individuals apart from their individual conditions, as was commonly thought. The agent intellect does not abstract the likenesses of things by acting upon phantasms and the possible intellect, "purifying, illuminating, irradiating, removing, abstracting, or separating."[96] We have seen that in Ockham's view things do not have essences at all; each individual is an essence by itself. Rather, abstraction is the mind's forming universal concepts of individual things, which the concepts then stand for and signify.[97]

How the mind forms universal concepts Ockham left rather unclear. When Ockham first wrote the commentary on the *Sentences* he favored the view that a concept has a special kind of being called "objective." In a later revision of book 1 he added the possibility that the concept is nothing but the act of understanding. In support of the first version of the concept, he contends that the mind is not active in forming universal concepts. They are

---

96. *Rep.* 2.12–13 (*OTh* 5: 308.15–18). Cf. Aquinas, *ST* 1.85.1.

97. Abstraction has several meanings for Ockham. In one sense it is the mind's grasping one thing without another with which it is joined, for example the whiteness in milk without its sweetness. Even the senses abstract in this way. In another sense the mind abstracts a universal from individuals. The universal is not really identical with the individual but it discloses and stands for it. This kind of abstraction is found in all the sciences. Again, the mind abstracts when it forms one proposition about a thing and not another about the same thing. In this way mathematics abstracts from matter and motion, forming propositions about the quantitative aspects of a thing and not about its material and mobile aspects; see *Expos. in Phys.* 2.3 (*OPh* 4: 263.151–265.194).

naturally caused, he says, by the incomplex knowledge of terms without any act of the intellect or will. Thus, someone seeing one or two whitenesses intuitively naturally abstracts from them the specific concept of whiteness, so that whiteness now exists in the mind with "objective" being corresponding to its extramental existence in "subjective" being.[98] Borrowing a phrase from the twelfth-century *Liber sex principiorum*, Ockham says "nature works secretly in the matter of universals."[99] He later seems to have dismissed the idea that universals have "objective" being, arguing that they are general acts of knowledge. But more about this shortly.

However the mind may form its general concepts, it always does so attending to the likenesses of things, the generality of the concept depending on the degree of their likeness. Beings most resembling each other, like all humans, give rise to ultimate specific concepts; those less like each other, for example a human being and an ox, cause generic concepts. All things have the most tenuous likeness of being, giving rise to the most universal concept of being. Ockham insists that this explanation of universal concepts has the advantage of simplicity, avoiding as it does the positing of many different realities in things as the bases of the various degrees of universality of concepts.[100]

---

98. *Quaest. variae* 5 (*OTh* 8: 175.402–419). At the end of this Disputed Question Ockham says he has taken the occasion to refute all the arguments proving the mind and will are active in producing universals. But bowing to the authority of the Church fathers and the philosophers, he holds the opposite opinion. He grants there are probable arguments in support of it; see ibid. (*OTh* 8: 191.730–736).

99. "Sed natura occulte operatur in universalibus, nam producendo singularia producit universalia" (*Ord.* 1.2.7 [*OTh* 2: 231.21–22]). The phrase is "Natura igitur occulte in his operatur" in *Liber sex principiorum* 1 (ed. Minio-Paluello p. 37.2). See Ockham, *Rep.* 2.12–13 (*OTh* 5: 304.24–305.3).

100. *Ord.* 1.8.2 (*OTh* 3: 188.14–191.9). Ockham suggests that the only concepts naturally abstracted from individuals may be the concept of an ultimate species (*species specialissima*) – that is, a species that is not divisible into higher species – and the concept of being. The concept of a genus may not be natural but arbitrary and conventional (*OTh* 3: 194.8–25).

Ockham suggests that the intuitive or abstractive cognition of one man or one whiteness suffices for the formation of a specific concept such as man or whiteness.[101] This is possible, because even though I may actually know only one individual, I know that other similar individuals may exist. A generic concept, such as color, can be abstracted from the knowledge of two species of color, such as white and black.[102] The concept of a genus cannot be abstracted from one individual. Thus, if I see something coming from a distance, on the basis of my perception of the thing I cannot judge it to be an animal. I must first possess the concept of animal and call it to mind in order to judge "This is an animal." If I did not previously have the concept of animal, I would only judge that what I perceive is something.[103]

The Nature of the Concept

We treated briefly of the nature of the concept when considering universal terms in Chapter 1.[104] Because of the importance and complexity of the topic, however, it deserves a fuller and closer examination.

Ockham's notion of a concept underwent significant development from his earlier to his later works. In this connection the chronology of his writings raised problems for historians of Ockham's thought, but most of them have been solved, especially with the help of the critical edition of his theological and philosophical works. It is now accepted that his first work was the magistral commentary on the *Sentences* of Peter Lombard, dated about 1317–1319.[105] Ockham prepared book 1 for publication, making it an authoritative *ordinatio*. The other three books exist only in student reports called *reportationes*. The editors have shown that when revising book 1 for publi-

---

101. *Sum. log.* 3–2.29 (*OPh* 1: 557.7–25).
102. *Ord.* 1.3.6 (*OTh* 2: 501.6–9).
103. *Quodl.* 1.13 (*OTh* 9: 77.135–78.141).
104. See above, pp. 86–87.
105. See the editor's introduction *OTh* 1: 36*.

cation, Ockham made significant corrections and additions, some of which are vital for his notion of the concept.[106]

In his *Ordinatio* and subsequent works he was engaged in a lively controversy with his contemporaries and immediate predecessors over the nature of the concept and, more generally, about the meaning of human knowledge. At first hesitant to make a definite choice among various possible notions of the concept and willing to weigh their pros and cons, in his later works, he settles upon the one most conformable to his basic principles and insights: the notion that a concept is nothing but the act of understanding.

In his final version of the *Ordinatio*, as published in the critical edition, Ockham describes four opinions about the nature of universal concepts, points out their weaknesses or falsity, without choosing one as his own.[107] According to the first opinion, a universal concept is identical with the act of understanding (*intellectio*). In this account a universal concept would be a confused and indistinct understanding of something, but not of one thing more than of another similar to it. Hence it would be indifferent and common to many individuals, the degree of its universality depending on its indistinctness. Calling the universal a confused knowledge of a thing means that it is not a knowledge of one thing alone but includes one or more things similar to it.[108]

In informative notes Ockham's editors point out that this notion of the concept was well known to masters at the end of the thirteenth century and it was accepted by some, notably Henry of

106. See *OTh* 1: 19*–31*. Philotheus Boehner thought Ockham made two redactions of the *Ordinatio*: see "The Text Tradition of Ockham's Ordinatio," *The New Scholasticism* 16 (1942): 203–241, and "The Relative Date of Ockham's Commentary on the *Sentences*," *Franciscan Studies* 2 (1951): 305–316, repr. in his *Collected Articles on Ockham*, pp. 96–110, and 110–127. The editors of volume 1 of Ockham's works conclude that Ockham did not produce two redactions of the *Ordinatio*, but an incomplete and a complete redaction (*OTh* 1: 19*–23*).

107. See above, p. 86. Ockham usually raises the question not in terms of the individual but universal concept, because the latter functions as a term in scientific propositions.

108. For meanings of confused knowledge see *Ord.* 1.3.5 (*OTh* 2: 472.11–20).

Ghent, Godfrey of Fontaines, Duns Scotus, and William of Nottingham.[109] But Ockham has serious difficulties with it. What, he asks, is the object of the act of understanding a universal? The act must have an object, and it does not seem to be any one individual more than another, or an existing thing any more than a nonexisting thing. Furthermore, a universal concept that is an act of understanding would be the concept of an infinite number of things. Another difficulty is that the concept is commonly thought to terminate the act of knowing, and if the concept is identical with that act, the act would terminate itself.[110]

In his *Ordinatio* Ockham does not attempt to answer these difficulties, but he does in his commentary on Aristotle's *Perihermenias*, written between the first and second versions of the *Ordinatio* (c. 1321).[111] Now he calls the mental act theory of the concept more probable than any of the other theories that define the concept as a real quality of the mind. According to this theory, he says, an individual concept is an act of the mind knowing one individual, for example Socrates, so that by its nature the concept signifies that individual and it can stand for it in a proposition. If the concept is universal or general, it is formed by the mind as a natural sign of many individuals, as the concept "man" naturally signifies all humans. The more general concept "animal" is an act of the mind by which it naturally knows all animals and stands for them in propositions.

Once again, Ockham raises the serious objection that if the concept is nothing but an act of knowing, a general concept would seem to lack an object. What do I know when I know man, tree, or dog? Either something is known or nothing. It cannot be nothing, for there cannot be a seeing with nothing seen. Clearly something is known, but is it something in reality or in the mind? Not

---

109. *Ord.* 1.2.8 (*OTh* 2: 267 n3); *Expos. in Periherm.* 1.prooem. (*OPh* 2: 351 n1).

110. *Ord.* 1.2.8 (*OTh* 2: 268.7–19).

111. Ockham's lectures on the *Ars vetera*, containing the commentary on the *Perihermenias*, probably began in 1321; see the editor's introduction to *OPh* 2: 14*.

in reality, for everything real is individual. There is no universal man in reality, serving as the object of my act of knowing man. As we have seen in Chapter 1, there is no essence or nature in individuals that can be abstracted from them and serve as the object of universal concepts. Can individuals be the object of my general act of knowing? But by this act I do not know one individual any more than another. Hence, if they were the object of my act of knowing a species or genus, it would have to include all the individuals in the species or genus. By knowing man, for example, I would know every man, even those I have never met or thought about, which seems absurd. Suppose, on the other hand, that by a general act of knowing I know something in my mind. According to the present theory my object could only be my act of knowing. This also seems absurd.[112]

In the commentary on the *Perihermenias*, however, Ockham does not leave the proponent of this opinion reduced to silence, as he did in the *Ordinatio*. He can reply, Ockham says, that by a confused or indeterminate act of knowing we can know extramental individual things. In short, they can be the object of universal concepts, understood as indeterminate acts of knowing. For instance, we can have a confused or indeterminate knowledge of man which is one single act of knowing by which we know all men – not one more than any other; and yet this gives us a knowledge of a man rather than an ass. And the reason is that a knowledge of this sort in some way bears a greater resemblance to a man than to an ass, and not more to this particular man than to another. In this way we can even know an infinite number of individuals, as by one act of loving or desiring we can love or desire an infinity of things; for example, all possible human beings or the infinite parts of a continuum. Ockham continues:

> And so it could be said that one and the same cognition refers to an infinite number of singulars without being a cognition proper to any one of them, and this is so because of some

---

112. *Expos. in Periherm.* 1.prooem. (*OPh* 2: 352.33–353.51).

specific likeness between these individuals that does not exist between others. However, no singular thing can be distinguished from another by such a cognition.[113]

On the hypothesis, however, that the concept is the act of knowing, how can we account for the knowing of universals such as chimera, goatstag or even nonbeing? In their case, at least, the object seems to be a figment of the mind with objective being. Ockham replies that the mind's production of such objects as gold mountains could be nothing but the eliciting of an act of knowing (which is a real quality of the mind), to which nothing corresponds in reality. It could be called a *fictum*, but nonetheless it would be a real being: a quality identified with the act of knowing. It would differ from other acts of knowing only because nothing corresponds to it in reality. Suppose someone retorts that then it is true to say "A chimera exists in reality." Ockham replies with a distinction. If the term "chimera" has personal supposition in this proposition, the proposition is false, for no individual chimeras exist in reality. But the proposition is true if "chimera" has simple or material supposition, for both the word "chimera" and its concept really exist.[114]

What is a proposition if the concept is the act of knowing? Ockham offers two possibilities. (1) It is a composite made up of many acts of knowing. Thus the proposition "Man is an animal" would be composed of the act by which all humans are confusedly known, the act by which all animals are likewise confusedly known, and one act corresponding to the copula. (2) The proposition is one act of knowing equivalent to the above composite of three acts.[115]

Both in the *Ordinatio* and commentary on the *Perihermenias* Ockham discusses two other theories of the concept that, like the

---

113. "Sic igitur posset dici quod eadem cognitio potest esse infinitorum, non tamen erit cognitio propria alicui illorum, nec ista cognitione potest unum distingui ab alio, et hoc propter aliquam similitudinem specialem istius cognitionis ad individua illa et non alia" (*Expos. in Periherm.* 1.prooem. [*OPh* 2: 355.105–109]); trans. Boehner, in *Philosophical Writings*, p. 45.

114. Ibid. (*OPh* 2: 366.87–367.116).

115. Ibid. (*OPh* 2: 355.110–356.119).

mental act theory, hold it to be a real being in the category of quality. The first maintains that a concept is a natural likeness (*species*) of things, existing in the intellect as a real individual quality naturally representing one or more things, as a written or spoken word signifies them by convention. If it represents one thing, it is an individual concept; if more, it is a universal concept.[116]

The notion of a mental likeness or representation, distinct from the act of knowing and the means by which we know things, is firmly rejected by Ockham. In the same spirit he strongly argues against the need, or even possibility, of a sensible likeness in the sensory powers or organs in order to account for sense perception.[117] In both cases the razor comes into play, cautioning against the positing of entities beyond necessity. A more telling argument against intelligible and sensible likenesses mediating between the object known and the knowing power is that they would stand in the way of knowing or perceiving things themselves. They would have to be known before they could function as representations of other things, and in order to know them other representations would be needed, and so on ad infinitum. How could a likeness enable me to know something I did not previously know? Seeing a statue of Hercules, I would never come to know him unless I had seen him before. Mental and sensible likenesses are said to be necessary in order to assimilate the knowing power to the thing known and thus effect the union of knower and the known thing; but *species* are accidents in the category of quality, and so they could hardly liken the knower to a

---

116. *Ord.* 1.2.8 (*OTh* 2: 269.2-4), *Expos. in Periherm.* 1.prooem. (*OPh* 2: 350.2-7).

117. *Rep.* 3.3 (*OTh* 6: 98-129). Ockham also opposes the notion of *species* existing in any medium, such as the air or a mirror. See ibid. 3.2 (*OTh* 6: 43-97). On this subject see Katherine H. Tachau, "The Problem of the *Species in Medio* at Oxford in the Generation after Ockham," *Mediaeval Studies* 44 (1982): 394-443, and *Vision and Certitude in the Age of Ockham*, pp. 113-153; Robert Pasnau, *Theories of Cognition in the Later Middle Ages* (Cambridge, 1997), pp. 76-85, 162-167, 247-253.

substance. The likening of knower to thing known is adequately accounted for by the act of knowing directly caused by the object. If someone objects that this would require action at a distance, and this is impossible, Ockham points out that even in the hypothesis of an intermediary likeness there would be a distance between the object and the likeness. Hence it is more reasonable to hold that the thing known causes the act of knowing without any previous representative likeness. Since neither reason nor experience requires us to posit these likenesses, we must conclude that they are not needed for intuitive cognition: the intellect and the thing known suffice. In abstractive cognition, following upon intuition, a habit (*habitus*) is left, enabling the knower to recall the object previously known, but the habit is not a cause of the initial knowledge of the object; for this, all that is needed as partial causes are the object and intuitive cognition.[118] Knowledge presupposes the presence of the object to the knowing subject, but the presence of the object itself suffices both in intuitive and abstractive knowledge, which are perfect likenesses of the object, and also in habitual knowledge. The distance between the object and the knower is no impediment to knowledge, as long as the distance does not exceed the efficacy of the cognitive power and the object. Thus Aristotle was right: the soul is in a way all things through our knowledge of them. Through sense knowledge it is all sensible things and through intellectual knowledge it is all intelligible things. Each of these knowledges is a perfect likeness of the object and more perfect than a *species*.[119]

The main burden of Ockham's criticism of *species* in the cognitive powers as means of knowing extramental things is that in fact they would prevent our knowing them.[120] The *species* themselves would be known objects, standing in the way of the mind's reaching out to extramental reality. Thomas Aquinas and Duns

118. *Rep.* 2.12–13 (*OTh* 5: 268–277).
119. Ibid. (*OTh* 5: 309.1–18).
120. See Philotheus Boehner, "The Realistic Conceptualism of William Ockham," *Traditio* 4 (1946): 307–335, repr. in his *Collected Articles on Ockham*, pp. 156–174.

Scotus could admit sensible and intelligible *species* precisely because, in their philosophies, they are not known objects but pure means by which things are known. According to Aquinas, *species* are means *by which* (*id quo*) we know, not *that which* (*id quod*) we know, except when we reflect on the condition of our knowing.[121] *Species*, in this account, are the forms of things existing immaterially or "intentionally" in the knowing subject: not their representations or images but their very forms, determining the mind and making it one with the known thing. But this way of thinking of *species*, in terms of forms and modes of existing, was foreign to Ockham. If there were sensible and intelligible species, he could only conceive them as things (*res*) in their own right, or beings with "objective" existence. It is hardly surprising, then, that among all the opinions of the concept as a real quality of the mind he rejects this one as false.[122]

Another probable opinion of the concept is that it is a real being in the mind following upon the act of knowing, serving as a likeness of the known thing and universal because it is equally a likeness of many things. This resembles Thomas Aquinas' notion of the concept or mental *verbum*, engendered by the mind after being fecundated by the species of the object.[123] Duns Scotus in his own way also held this notion of the concept, calling it an *intentio* formed by the mind.[124] Ockham gives short shrift to it, however, for he finds no

---

121. *ST* 1.85.2; see Pasnau's discussion of Aquinas' notion of species in *Theories of Cognition*, pp. 11–18, 195–219. He cites (201 n12) Aquinas' *In Sent.* 1.35.1.2 (ed. Mandonnet-Moos 1: 814–815), which contains the unusual statement that species are that which are first seen and understood. This should be taken in its context of the order in which God knows himself and creatures. As Pasnau say, in Aquinas' mature works he makes it clear that species is a means of knowing, not an object known, except by reflecting on our way of knowing. Perhaps species may be said to be known with the external object because they are similar in form.

122. *Ord.* 1.2.8 (*OTh* 2: 269.6); *Expos. in Periherm.* 1.prooem. (*OPh* 2: 350–351).

123. See *SCG* 4.11 (Leonine ed. 15: 32–33).

124. Scotus, *Super universalia Porphyrii* 4 (Vivès ed. 1: 96–97).

purpose for it in knowledge. Moreover, it has no basis in Aristotle's noetic, which admits only acts, passions, and habits in the mind.[125]

Still another probable opinion of the concept, described by Ockham at length in his *Ordinatio* and more briefly in his commentary on the *Perihermenias*, proposes that it is a construct (*fictum*) in the mind.[126] In the language of the medieval schoolmen, the concept would have objective, not subjective being. "Subjective" in this context (contrary to its modern meaning) denotes real being in the categories of substance or quality. Something with objective being has no reality outside or inside the mind, but only the being of an object of thought, similar or proportionate to the being of a corresponding extramental reality. To have objective being is simply to be an object of thought. For items with being of this sort, "their being is their being known (*eorum esse est eorum cognosci*).[127] In short, their being consists in pure objectivity. The notion of an *ens fictum* applies to universals: it is that which immediately terminates the act of cognition when no individual is known. As a likeness of many individuals, by its nature it can stand for them in propositions.[128]

Henry of Harclay, an immediate predecessor of Ockham, seems to have introduced the notion of a concept as a mental *fictum*. We have already encountered his notion of a universal and Ockham's criticism of it,[129] but he was more receptive of Harclay's doctrine of the concept. Harclay devised the notion of a *fictum* as the answer to the problem of definition. What indeed is

---

125. *Ord.* 1.2.8 (*OTh* 2: 269.18–270.4); Aristotle, *Eth. Nic.* 2.5, 1105b19–21.

126. *Ord.* 1.2.8 (*OTh* 2: 271.14–289.10); *Expos. in Periherm.* 1.prooem. (*OPh* 2: 359.3–361.60; 370.4–371.40).

127. *Ord.* ibid (*OTh* 2: 273.21); *Expos. in Periherm.* ibid. (*OPh* 2: 359.10–11).

128. *Ord.* ibid. (*OTh* 2: 274.13–19). Francis Kelley points out that Ockham uses *ens fictum* only to explain knowledge of the universal. A *fictum* has objective being, but the two notions are not synonymous. An individual object can exist in the knowing power with objective being without being a *fictum*. But he grants this is an unusual use of language; see "Some Observations on the 'Fictum' Theory in Ockham and Its Relation to Hervaeus Natalis," *Franciscan Studies* 38 (1978): 260–282, at p. 276.

129. See above, pp. 82–84.

the object of a definition? Harclay opposed the Scotist reply, that it is a real quiddity or essence existing in individual things. In his view the only realities outside the mind are individuals. But in thinking about them and recognizing their likenesses, the mind can construct (*fingit*) one concept from them. The resultant concept or *fictum* exists only in the mind, and it is that which we define. In a sense we define the individual, not in itself but as it is conceived. A *fictum* of this sort is not a poetical fiction (*figmentum poeticum*), but rather a philosophical fiction (*figmentum philosophicum*), existing in the mind not subjectively but objectively.[130]

In support of the notion of the concept as a *fictum*, Ockham appeals to experience to show that we can produce in our imaginations and minds a likeness, picture or image of something we have perceived, or even of something we have never perceived, or which may not even be real. A workman seeing a house can form a sense and mental image of the house and then build a house resembling the original house and differing from it only in number. So too, the mind can construct an exemplar of anything whatsoever that equally resembles many real things; and because of its resemblance to them in objective being, it can be a term in a proposition and stand for all of them. The notion of the concept with objective being would explain our knowledge of unreal and impossible things, such as chimeras or goatstags. But these would be figments (*figmenta*) of the mind rather than *ficta*, which are resemblances of real things. Logical entities, such as propositions and syllogisms, could also be explained as having objective being and not real subjective being.[131]

---

130. See Gedeon Gál, "Henricus de Harclay: Quaestio de significato conceptus universalis," *Franciscan Studies* 31 (1971): 178–234, "Gualteri de Chatton et Guillelmi de Ockham controversia de natura conceptus universalis," *Franciscan Studies* 27 (1967): 191–199; Mark G. Henninger, "Henry of Harclay," in *Individuation in Scholasticism: The Later Middle Ages and the Counter-Reformation (1150–1650)*, ed. Jorge J.E. Gracia (Albany, NY, 1994), pp. 333–346.

131. *Ord.* 1.2.8 (*OTh* 2: 271.14–273.22). The distinction between *figmenta* and *ficta* is found in Henry of Harclay, "Quaestio de significato conceptus universalis," ed. Gál, p. 225.

Ockham finds precedents for the notions of *ficta* and objective being. Aristotle divided being primarily into being in the mind and being outside the mind, the latter divided into the ten categories.[132] Aristotle's mental being, or being in the sense of the true, would, in the present theory, be an instance of objective being. The language of *fictum* came with the authority of Augustine, who speaks of the mind being able to construct (*fingere*) the image of the great city of Alexandria from the reports of those who have seen it.[133]

The notion of objective being was in common use in the late thirteenth and early fourteenth centuries. It appears in Scotus' doctrine of the divine ideas, which he conceived as so many intelligible beings existing objectively in the divine mind.[134] It is also found in the noetic of Peter Aureol, who, writing slightly before Ockham, proposed that in every act of knowing the thing known takes on an objective or apparent being (*esse apparens*) which, along with the thing, is the object of our knowledge.[135] The concept of a rose, for example, is the rose itself, not with its real being but with the objective being the mind gives to it. This accounts for the universality of the concept of a rose. When known, the rose has apparent and intentional being; and although real roses are distinct from each other, in intentional being they coalesce to form "one total rose." That apparent rose is really the same as all roses, for when it is seen all roses appear, not as distinct but as one.[136] Aureol cites many experiences to show that the external senses perceive things not as they really exist but as they appear to the senses. An example is the movement of trees on the bank of a river as seen by someone moving on the water. On the analogy of this and many other experiences,

---

132. Aristotle, *Metaph.* 5.7, 1017a7–b9.

133. Augustine, *De Trinitate* 8.6 (CCL 50: 281, n. 9).

134. See above, p. 225.

135. "Hic videndum quod in actu intellectus de necessitate res intellecta ponitur in quodam esse intentionali conspicuo et apparenti" (Peter Aureol, *Scriptum super Sent.* 1.3.14 [ed. Buytaert 2: 696 n. 31]). For Aureol's doctrine see Boehner, "*Notitia Intuitiva* of Non-Existents according to Peter Aureoli."

136. *Ord.* 1.27.3 (*OTh* 4: 237.15–22).

Aureol argues that the mind gives to its objects an objective or apparent being when it forms concepts of them.[137]

Ockham quotes long passages from Aureol's commentary on the *Sentences* setting forth his novel opinion of sense perception and concept formation, then subjects it to serious criticism. In fairness to Aureol, he acknowledges that he has spent only twenty-four hours reading his work, but on the face of it he thinks his position is wrong. His main objection to it is that it makes all knowledge of the senses and intellect productive, so that their objects are not simply real but include a new being imparted to them by the cognitive faculty. To Ockham, the addition of an apparent being to the real thing is not only unnecessary but it stands in the way of knowing reality as it is. He asks: does whiteness itself appear to the sense of sight or does it not? If it does, and along with it an apparent being appears, then two things appear. If the whiteness needs an apparent being in order to appear, then the apparent being needs another apparent being in order to appear, and the process goes on to infinity.[138] In fact, no medium between the real thing and the act of knowing is needed in either sense or intellectual intuition. Rather, "the thing itself is seen and apprehended immediately, without any intermediary between it and the act [of knowing]."[139]

The saying of the ancient skeptics, that everything is as it appears, is false. Mistakes can be made, judgments may be faulty, something can appear to be what in fact it is not; but this is not because of some intermediary between the thing itself and its appearance. When someone is moving on the water and seems to see the trees move, this is not because seeing them gives them a new apparent or (to use a modern term) phenomenal being. The illusion can be accounted for by the fact that the trees are seen

---

137. Ibid. (*OTh* 4: 231.1–233.11).

138. Ibid. (*OTh* 4: 240.11–20).

139. "Unde dico primo quod in nulla notitia intuitiva, nec sensitiva nec intellectiva, constituitur res in quocumque esse quod sit aliquod medium inter rem et actum cognoscendi. Sed dico quod ipsa res immediate, sine omni medio inter ipsam et actum, videtur vel apprehenditur" (ibid. [*OTh* 4: 241.19–23]).

successively at a different distance and from a different perspective by the eye moving with the motion of the boat.[140] Ockham solves the other so-called illusions of the senses in a similar way, showing that they do not involve any apparent or intentional being imparted to real things through the actions of the senses.

Up to now we have been following Ockham as he tries to discern the true nature of the concept in his earlier works: the *Ordinatio* and commentary on the *Perihermenias*. He has eliminated some views of the concept as unreasonable or downright fallacious; to others he has granted some probability; but he has chosen none as his own and as true. However, the complete version of the *Ordinatio* and the commentary indicate that he was inclining toward the opinion that the concept is a real being existing in the mind as in a subject, rather than a mental being with only objective existence. He still regarded the *fictum* theory as probable, but he was dissuaded from it because of the difficulty of imagining that something that is not in any way real can be known by a real act of the mind. Furthermore, knowing is an assimilation of the mind to what is known, and it is more reasonable to think that this assimilation takes place between reality and the mind by means of a concept that is itself a real entity, rather than by means of a non-real *fictum* with only objective being.[141]

Ockham may have been influenced to move in this direction by his Franciscan confrere, Walter Chatton, who argued that *ficta* are unnecessary, and that the act of understanding suffices to account for everything *ficta* were introduced to explain. He concluded that both the individual and universal concept are nothing but the act of knowing.[142]

---

140. *Ord.* 1.27.3 (*OTh* 4: 245.18–246.2).

141. *Expos. in Periherm.* 1.prooem. (*OPh* 2: 351–361).

142. Chatton, *Rep.* 1.3.2 (ed. Gál, "Gualteri de Chatton controversia de natura conceptus universalis," pp. 192–212). As Gál observes, Chatton here seems to be arguing against Ockham, knowing at the time only the incomplete redaction of his *Ordinatio*, in which he defends the *fictum* theory as probable. Gál also shows that Chatton adopted the Scotist view that a universal concept *per se* has a quiddity or essence, and not an individual, for its object (ed. Gál p. 195).

In his later works Ockham no longer defended the *fictum* theory of the concept, but like Chatton, and with similar arguments, he accepted as his own the position that concepts or intentions, both individual and universal, are simply acts of knowing. He concludes in his *Quodlibeta*:

> Consequently I assert that both a first and second intention are truly an act of knowing, because whatever can be solved by a *fictum* can be solved by an act [of knowing]; for just like a *fictum*, an act is the likeness of the object, it can signify and stand for extramental things, it can be the subject and predicate in a proposition, it can be a genus, species, etc.[143]

Ockham also favored this position in his *Summa logicae*, and he adopted it in his *Quaestiones in libros Physicorum*.[144]

The question remains whether Ockham believed that he had strictly demonstrated this conclusion. The editors of volume 3 of the *Ordinatio* believe the reader should be cautious in interpreting Ockham's opinion. How much weight should be given to the argument against *ficta* on the ground that they would stand between the knower and reality? According to Ockham, whatever he says about *esse fictum* is by way of reporting (*recitative*), though he does not always make this clear.[145] By reporting, he means that he is not necessarily speaking his own mind and giving his own opinion. Now if Ockham is only speaking *recitative* about *ficta*, might he not be doing the same in *Quodlibet* 4, q. 35, as

---

143. "Ideo dico quod tam intentio prima quam secunda est vere actus intelligendi, quia per actum potest salvari quidquid salvatur per fictum, eo quod actus est similitudo obiecti, potest significare et supponere pro rebus extra, potest esse subiectum et praedicatum in propositione, potest esse genus, species etc., sicut fictum" (*Quodl.* 4.35 [*OTh* 9: 474.115–120]). For the meaning of first and second intentions see above, pp. 22–23.

144. *Sum. log.* 1.12 (*OPh* 1: 42.30–43.39); *Quaest. in Phys.* 1 (*OPh* 6: 397.10–398.35). Questions 1–7 are devoted to the nature of concepts. For Ockham's abandonment of *ficta* see Robert Pasnau, *Theories of Cognition in the Later Middle Ages*, pp. 76–85, 277–289.

145. *Ord.* 1.27.3 (*OTh* 4: 242.15–243.5).

quoted above, when using a similar argument in behalf of the concept as the act of knowing?[146] However this may be, it is clear that Ockham's use of the razor to disprove the *fictum* theory is not intended to be demonstrative. As was shown above, Ockham thought the razor yields conclusions that are persuasive or highly probable. They may be true, but on the strength of the razor their truth is not demonstrated.[147]

What is certain is that Ockham's abandonment of *ficta*, with their objective being, considerably simplified his noetic. He no longer had to find a place in it for Aristotle's "being of reason" (*ens rationis*) distinct from real being, nor for Aureol's fictive being. What remained was the real individual, both intra- and extramental, around which Ockham could now more securely center his philosophy.

4 The Freedom of the Will

The dignity of persons is nowhere more evident than in their freedom – an innate quality that reflects God's own freedom. The root of the person's freedom is found in the will. In distinction to a natural active principle, which is determined to one course of action, such as fire to burning, the will is endowed with a freedom of action, enabling it to produce an effect in such a way that, without any variation on the part of the will or of anything else, it is equally open to producing or not producing an effect, or to produce a certain effect or its opposite. By its very nature it is not determined to either course of action, or indeed to will at all.[148] Thus freedom can be defined as "the power by which I can indif-

---

146. See the editors' introduction *OTh* 4: 16*.

147. See above, pp. 122–123. Adams (*William Ockham* 1: 73 n9) reports that according to Gedeon Gál the latest works in which Ockham discusses this issue – the *Quodlibeta* and the *Quaestions* on Aristotle's *Physics* – are records of school debates in which Ockham may have defended an opinion with which he did not entirely agree. So they do not conclusively prove that he gave his full support to the mental act theory of the concept.

148. *Ord.* 1.1.6 (*OTh* 1: 501.2–22).

ferently and contingently produce different effects, in such a way that I can cause an effect or not cause it without any change taking place outside that power."[149]

A natural cause will always act unless some change takes place in it, like losing energy, or an impediment prevents it from acting, or a cause acting along with it is removed. But besides these ways in which an action can cease, there is another peculiar to the will: it can stop acting just by itself, even if none of the above causes of inaction are present. This, Ockham insists, is precisely what is meant when we say the will causes its effect contingently.[150]

Not only can the will stop acting on its own initiative, but it can begin to act after not acting for a time and being only potentially active. At first sight this would seem to be impossible, for according to Aristotle nothing can reduce itself from potency to act without an external cause. This is true of natural agents, Ockham says, whether they are material or spiritual. If for some time they are simply capable of acting, there must be some external cause concurring with them to bring them into act. For example, if the intellect is not acting for a while but then begins to act, some external cause is needed to bring it into action. The cause may be an object that the intellect begins to think about, or the will moving the intellect to consider it. But this is not the case with a free agent like the will. The object can be known and presented by the intellect to the will, and all the conditions required for the act of the will can be present, such as the concurrence of God as a partial cause of the act, without the will eliciting its act. Then the will can elicit its act without being determined to do so by any extrinsic cause whatsoever. And all this is possible because the will is free.[151]

149. "[V]oco libertatem potestatem qua possum indifferenter et contingenter diversa ponere, ita quod possum eumdem effectum causare et non causare, nulla diversitate existente alibi extra illam potentiam" (*Quodl.* 1.16 [*OTh* 9: 87.12–15]).

150. *Ord.* 1.38, q. u. (*OTh* 4: 580.14–581.8).

151. *Quodl.* 1.16 (*OTh* 9: 89.39–51), *Rep.* 4.15 (*OTh* 7: 332.7–334.5); Aristotle, *Phys.* 8.4, 254b7–256a3. We have seen that self-movement is not limited to the will and living bodies. Inanimate bodies can also cause their own movement, as in gravitational and projectile movement. See above, pp. 431–435.

In stressing the autonomy of the will and its preeminence in relation to the intellect, Ockham follows in the path of his Franciscan predecessors, Peter Olivi and Duns Scotus.

Olivi broke with the Aristotelian and Averroist notion that the will is a partially passive power moved by the intellect. Appealing to Augustine, he stressed that the will is totally active and self-moving. He writes:

> Therefore the first things about which Catholics differ from certain pagans and Saracens, namely that free acts are totally produced by the will, or that free choice, or the will insofar as it is free, is totally an active power, must be held both in accordance with the Catholic faith and right reason.[152]

Olivi granted that the will needs the intellect for the presentation of an object, but he denied that the intellect or the object is an efficient cause of willing.

For Scotus, the will is so independent that it cannot be necessitated by anything, either without or within, either created or divine. In fact, the will is the total efficient cause of its volition; the object of the will and the knowledge of the intellect are not properly causes of the will but only causes *sine qua non*.[153] Con-

---

152. "Primum igitur in quo catholici a quibusdam paganis et Saracensis dissentiunt, quod scilicet actus liberi sint totaliter producti a voluntate seu quod liberum arbitrium vel voluntas, in quantum est libera, sit totaliter potentia activa, est necessario tenendum tam secundum fidem catholicam quam secundum rationem rectam" (Peter Olivi, *Quaestiones in secundum librum Sententiarum* 58 [ed. Jansen 2: 410]). On this subject see Bonnie Kent, *Virtues of the Will: The Transformation of Ethics in the Late Thirteenth Century* (Washington, DC, 1995), p. 134; Calvin G. Normore, "Picking and Choosing: Anselm and Ockham on Choice," *Vivarium* 36 (1998): 23–39, at pp. 29–30, and "Ockham, Self-Motion, and the Will," in *Self-Motion from Aristotle to Newton*, ed. Mary Louise Gill and James G. Lennox (Princeton, NJ, 1994), pp. 291–303, at p. 295.

153. "Dico ergo ad quaestionem quod nihil aliud a voluntate est causa totalis volitionis in voluntate" (Scotus, *Ord*. 2.25.un. [Vivès ed. 13: 221, n. 22]; cf. ibid. [p. 213, n. 20]). An adequate account of the dispute over the freedom of the will at the turn of the century would include the position of Henry of Ghent. According to Henry, the will is the efficient cause of its

trary to Thomas Aquinas, who held that the will necessarily wills its final end or beatitude and is free only with regard to particular means to it,[154] Scotus denied that the will necessarily wills its final end or beatitude. Rather, the will enjoys the same freedom with regard to it as it does with regard to the means to it. Furthermore, in a passage summarized by Ockham, Scotus contends that the will does not necessarily enjoy its ultimate end or beatitude when presented to it in general, in particular but obscurely, or in particular and clearly.[155]

Ockham has no quarrel with Scotus on the latter subject (though he thinks Scotus' arguments for it are weak), but in contradiction to the Subtle Doctor he contends that the act of the will has partial causes, including God, the object of the will, and the intellect's presentation of the object to the will. Nevertheless, he insists that the act of the will is not necessitated by them, but retains its freedom to act or not to act, to will this particular object or its opposite.

In some cases, however, the act of the will is not free. For example, if I love God and all that God wants me to love, and I know that God wants me to love a certain person, I necessarily have to love that person. But loving the person is only indirectly in the will's power, because I can always not will to love God.

---

own acts, capable of reducing itself from virtual act to formal act. The intellect moves the will by presenting to it an object as good, and hence moves it as a final cause, but not as a formal or efficient cause (*Quodl.* 1, q. 17. resp. [ed. Macken et al. 5: 125–127]). Godfrey of Fontaines opposed Henry's view on the ground that nothing can reduce itself from potency to act. For the position of Henry of Ghent see Kent, *Virtues of the Will*, pp. 144–145. Godfrey assigned efficient causality in volition to the object (John F. Wippel, *The Metaphysical Thought of Godfrey of Fontaines*, pp. 180–202). For a general study of the problem of free will at this period see Odon Lottin, *Psychologie et morale aux XIIe et XIIIe siècles* (Louvain, 1942–1949), 1: 225–389; and Kent, *Virtues of the Will*, pp. 94–198.

154. *ST* 1.82.1–2. According to Aquinas the will necessarily wills beatitude with a teleological necessity (*necessitas finis*), which is a natural but not an absolute necessity.

155. Ockham, *Ord.* 1.1.6 (*OTh* 1: 486.17–490.17); Scotus, *Ord.* 1.1.2.2 (Vatican ed. 2: 96–97, nn. 143–145).

Sometimes the will produces an act under the influence of a habit that constrains the will to elicit it. Seeing something desirable and having the habit of "going for it," we experience a first movement of the will, prior to deliberation, that is not in our power to suppress. Since this act is not under our control, it is not blameworthy.[156] Again, if the will wills to do everything that right reason dictates, and if it is known that it dictates that one should practice self-restraint in sexual matters, the will necessarily wills to do so.[157] But for Ockham the will still remains free, because it can always reverse its initial will to follow the dictates of right reason.

The interior act of the will, then, remains in the power of the will; but this does not mean that it cannot be obstructed under any circumstance. Aristotle would have to say that there is no way the will can be impeded, for he did not know that God acts intimately in our world and could prevent the will from acting. But the Christian, who believes that God immediately acts along with every action of his creatures, knows that unless God is a coagent with the will it cannot produce its act, for it would lack one of its required partial causes. Nevertheless the act of the will is in the will's power in such a way that nothing created can completely obstruct it.[158]

Is the possibility of doing evil or sinning necessary for freedom? Freedom does not exclude the possibility, but neither does it include it. The possibility of sinning is not freedom itself nor a part of freedom; and yet, as Anselm says, in a way it diminishes freedom by making one a slave of sin: one is freer in heaven when sinning is impossible. But it does not lessen the will's native freedom from coercion as regards its intrinsic acts of willing or not willing.[159]

---

156. *Rep.* 3.7 (*OTh* 6: 210.17–212.12).

157. *Quaest. variae* 7.3 (*OTh* 8: 353.293–301). Other examples of the will acting necessarily are given in Marilyn McCord Adams, "The Structure of Ockham's Moral Theory," *Franciscan Studies* 46 (1986): 1–35, at pp. 11–12.

158. *Rep.* 3.7 (*OTh* 6: 206.4–13). On the opposition between Aristotle and Christianity regarding God's direct action in our world see ibid. 3.6 (*OTh* 6: 186.18–189.16).

159. *Ord.* 1.10.2 (*OTh* 3: 342.25–343.20). See Anselm, *De libero arbitrio* 1 (*Opera omnia* 1: 209).

Ockham does not believe that the freedom of the will can be rationally proven. All the arguments advanced to prove it, he says, contain propositions as doubtful or obscure – or even more so – than the conclusion. Nevertheless experience assures us of the freedom of the will. Everyone experiences that no matter what reason tells us to do, the will can either will it or not.[160] Another indication of the will's freedom is the fact that we praise or blame persons for at least some of their actions, showing that we think them to be done freely and under their control. Ockham cites Aristotle to the effect that "No one blames a man born blind for his blindness, but he is blamed if he is blind through his own sinful conduct."[161]

Ockham cautions his readers not to think of freedom as having a reality of its own, in some way distinct *ex natura rei* from the will – a mistake he believes Scotus made. The word "freedom" does not denote anything but the will itself or our intellectual nature, while connoting its ability to bring about effects contingently.[162] It has been Ockham's constant complaint that philosophers are prone to hypothesize terms like "motion," "relation," and "time," as though there were distinct realities corresponding to them. In the spirit of Wittgenstein we could say that these philosophers are deceived by language. Ockham is well aware of this danger, and once again warns us against it in using the language of freedom. His own analysis of the term, moreover, is in accord with his often-used principle of parsimony, which enjoins us not to assume unnecessary entities. On this score too there is no need to regard freedom as a perfection added to the substance of the will.

160. *Quodl.* 1.16 (*OTh* 9: 88.23–28), *Ord.* 1.1.6 (*OTh* 1: 499.18–22).

161. *Rep.* 3.11 (*OTh* 6: 366.5–9); Aristotle, *Eth. Nic.* 3.1, 1109b30–31 and 6, 1114a26–27.

162. "Unde illa ratio et sequens procedunt ex falsa imaginatione. Imaginatur enim ac si libertas esset aliquid unum reale distinctum aliquo modo ex natura rei a voluntate, vel non omnino idem cum voluntate, quod tamen non est verum. Sed est unum nomen connotativum importans ipsam voluntatem vel naturam intellectualem connotando aliquid contingenter posse fieri ab eadem" (*Ord.* 1.10.2 [*OTh* 3: 344.11–17]). Ockham here counters arguments of Scotus implying that freedom is a perfection compatible with necessity; see ibid. (*OTh* 3: 331.12–335.5).

5 Morality

Ockham did not write a special treatise on ethics or even a commentary on Aristotle's *Nicomachean Ethics*, so we must glean his views on moral topics from discussions scattered throughout his works. Numerous attempts have been made to interpret his moral doctrine, with widely different and even contradictory results. It has often been called a voluntarism or an ethics of obligation or duty, with the goodness or evil of a human act depending on the person's free acceptance or rejection of divine commands. In this view human acts are not good or bad in themselves, but only because they are commanded or prohibited by God. In recent years more attention has been given to the role right reason plays in Ockham's ethical theory. Two moral doctrines, on two distinct tiers, are said to be at play in his works: one, an authoritarian conception of the moral law; the other, an ethics of right reason that would give natural reason the ability to distinguish between right and wrong. It has even been suggested that Ockham's doctrine should be called a modified right reason ethical theory.[163]

It is beyond the scope of this book to deal with all the problems raised by Ockham's moral doctrine. We would suggest, however, that many of them would disappear, or at least be less acute, if his ethics were seen as an attempt to balance the consequences of several of his basic principles: the divine omnipotence and will on the one hand and evident experience on the other. We have found that the interpretive principle described above: that a philosopher's doctrine is the result not of one principle but of a com-

---

163. Adams, "Structure of Ockham's Moral Theory," pp. 1–4. See Lucan Freppert, *The Basis of Morality according to William Ockham* (Chicago, 1988); Anita Garvens, "Die Grundlagen der Ethik Wilhelms von Ockham," *Franziskanische Studien* 21 (1934): 243–273; 360–408; David W. Clark, "Voluntarism and Rationalism in the Ethics of Ockham," *Franciscan Studies* 31 (1971): 72–87 and "William of Ockham on Right Reason," *Speculum* 48 (1973): 13–36; Linwood Urban, "William of Ockham's Theological Ethics," *Franciscan Studies* 33 (1973): 310–350; Frederick Copleston, *A History of Philosophy* (Garden City, NY, 1963), 3.1: 115–122; Vernon Bourke, *History of Ethics* (Garden City, NY, 1970), pp. 104–106.

promise among a number of principles, helped us to understand Ockham's doctrine of the intuition of nonexistents.[164] Perhaps it can also throw light on Ockham's thorny ethical theory.

Moral Science

Ockham describes the science of morals as a practical science, regulating the actions within our power so that we might become morally good (*ut boni fiamus*). Every practical science aims at doing or making something; the objective of moral science is not to produce an effect outside moral agents but within them, such as moral virtues, and especially prudence, which enable them to pursue the good and avoid evil.

In one sense moral science is purely practical, dealing strictly with human actions within our control and directing them for our good, without speculating about truths outside the practical order. In this meaning of the term, moral science would not contain speculative truths such as, "Everything in the soul is either a passion, a faculty, or a state of character," or "The soul is divided into practical and speculative parts," and yet these truths are found in Aristotle's *Nicomachean Ethics*. They are not out of place there, because he, like other philosophers and the fathers of the Church (*sancti*), conceived moral science in a broader sense, as having both speculative and practical parts, the speculative part providing principles from which practical conclusions can be drawn. The science is called moral because it ends with practical moral conclusions. Concurring with these authorities in moral theory, Ockham does not envisage it as exclusively practical and autonomous, without a foundation in speculative philosophy. Unlike some modern moralists, he would not think it incongruous to derive an "ought" from an "is"![165]

The above description of moral science is taken from Ockham's treatment of the question whether theology is speculative or practical in his commentary on the *Sentences*. The account of moral

---

164. See above, pp. 488–489.

165. *Ord.* 1.prol.12 (*OTh* 1: 359.16–361.4); Aristotle, *Eth. Nic.* 2.5, 1105b19–21 and 6.2, 1138b35–1139a17.

science is accordingly in the context of theology, but it embraces all knowledge whose practical aim is to make us good, including the ethical teachings of philosophers like Aristotle, as well as those handed down to us by the Church fathers such as Augustine. Another division of moral science is contained in one of Ockham's last theological works, the *Quodlibeta septem*, while debating the question whether there can be a demonstrative science of morals.

In the latter work he begins by explaining that the term "moral" in a broad sense describes human acts simply as falling under the power of the will, whether the acts are good or bad. More strictly, the term denotes human conduct or acts under the control of the will in accord with the natural dictates of reason and other circumstances.[166] After this preliminary distinction he proceeds to divide moral doctrine into two parts: positive and nonpositive. Positive moral science contains human and divine laws obliging us to pursue what is good or avoid what is evil simply because they are forbidden or ordered by a superior whose business it is to make laws. An example is the science of the jurists, or jurisprudence. Positive moral science, Ockham continues, is not itself a demonstrative science, although it is often regulated by the nonpositive demonstrative part of moral science. But in itself the positive part of morals is not demonstrative, for the jurists base their arguments on human positive laws, and they do not contain evidently known principles required for demonstrative knowledge.[167]

166. "Circa primum dico quod 'morale' accipitur large pro actibus humanis qui subiacent voluntati absolute. Et sic accipitur in *Decretis*, d. 1, c. *mos*. Et patet in *Glossa*. Aliter accipitur magis stricte pro moribus sive actibus subiectis potestati voluntatis secundum naturale dictamen rationis et secundum alias circumstantias" (*Quodl.* 2.14 [*OTh* 9: 176.11–177.16]). The reference is to Gratian's *Decretum* 1.4 (Lyons ed. 3: 39–40).

167. "Circa secundum sciendum quod moralis doctrina habet plures partes, quarum una est positiva, alia non positiva. Scientia moralis positiva est illa quae continet leges humanas et divinas, quae obligant ad prosequendum vel fugiendum illa quae nec sunt bona nec mala nisi quia sunt prohibita vel imperata a superiore, cuius est leges statuere. ... Circa tertium dico quod moralis scientia positiva, cuiusmodi est scientia iuristarum, non est scientia demonstrativa, quamvis sit a

In contrast to positive moral science, nonpositive moral science does not direct human acts by precepts laid down by a superior but by principles that are known through experience or are self-evident, such as, Good should be done and evil avoided. Ockham's remark that Aristotle speaks of these principles in moral philosophy makes it clear that he has Aristotelian ethics in mind when describing nonpositive moral science. This science, Ockham continues, is truly demonstrative, for it deduces conclusions by means of syllogisms from principles that are self-evident or known through experience. There is no doubt that there are many self-evident principles in moral science, such as, The will ought to conform itself to right reason, and Every reprehensible evil should be avoided. Many moral principles are also known through experience, as is clear to those who use the experiential method.[168]

Ockham concludes his account of positive and nonpositive moral science with the intriguing remark that this science is more certain than many others, because we can have more experience of our own acts than we can of anything else. Moral science is accordingly very exact, useful, and evident. In other words, we are closer to ourselves than to anything else, and hence we know

---

scientia demonstrativa ut in pluribus regulata; quia rationes iuristarum fundantur super leges humanas positivas, quae non accipiunt propositiones evidenter notas" (*Quodl.* 2.14 [*OTh* 9: 177.18–23, 30–34]). Having previously referred to the *Decretum* of Gratian (*OTh* 9: 176.13), Ockham probably has this jurist in mind.

168. "Scientia moralis non positiva est illa quae sine omni praecepto superioris dirigit actus humanos; sicut principia per se nota vel nota per experientiam sic dirigunt, sicut quod omne honestum est faciendum, et omne inhonestum est fugiendum, et huiusmodi, de quibus loquitur Aristoteles in morali philosophia. ... Sed disciplina moralis non positiva est scientia demonstrativa. Probo, quia notitia deducens conclusiones syllogistice ex principiis per se notis vel per experientiam scitis est demonstrativa; huiusmodi est disciplina moralis; igitur etc. Maior est manifesta. Minor probatur, quia multa sunt principia per se nota in morali philosophia; puta quod voluntas debet se conformare rectae rationi, omne malum vituperabile est fugiendum, et huiusmodi. Similiter per experientiam sciuntur multa principia, sicut manifeste patet sequenti experientiam" (Ibid. [*OTh* 9: 177.24–178.43]). For examples of conclusions drawn from self-evident moral principles and experience see *Quaest. variae* 6.10 (*OTh* 8: 281.219–282.232).

ourselves best.[169] This high praise of moral science is in keeping
with Ockham's conviction that we are able to have an evident
intuition of the soul's interior acts.[170]

It is not difficult to recognize the Aristotelian character of
Ockham's nonpositive moral science. Its bases and norms are philosophical: self-evident moral truths and moral experience. Positive
moral science, on the other hand, is founded on the decrees of
legitimate superiors, whom one is obliged to obey. Ockham
mentions as an eminent example the jurists "whose arguments are
based on human positive laws." This refers to jurists or canon
lawyers like Gratian, who in the twelfth century codified precepts
of the Church and its councils. But Ockham's mention of divine
laws in positive moral science indicates that he does not intend to
identify positive moral science with jurisprudence, as has been
claimed.[171] He simply uses jurisprudence as an obvious example
of this part of moral science. This part includes the positive laws
of any legitimate superior, including the many positive laws laid
down by God for the Jewish people and recorded in their scriptures. If this is so, moral science embraces an ethics of obligation
that commands us to follow the laws of legitimate superiors, both
human and divine, and a philosophical ethics based on moral
experience and right reason. Both are essential to Ockham's moral
science, the claims of one tending to balance – and sometimes to
conflict with – the claims of the other. We shall return to this
subject in a later section.

Moral Virtues

Our will being free, it can act either well or badly. Hence it is not
virtuous by itself, but there is need for an external rule directing

---

169. "Et ultra dico quod ista scientia est certior multis aliis, pro quanto
quilibet potest habere maiorem experientiam de actibus suis quam de aliis. Ex
quo patet quod ista scientia est multum subtilis, utilis, et evidens" (*Quodl.*
2.14 [*OTh* 9: 178.44–47]).

170. See above, pp. 476–477.

171. "This part of moral science is the science of the jurists, the science
of jurisprudence" (Freppert, *Basis of Morality*, p. 16).

it to good actions. It is different with the divine will: being the primary rule of action and accordingly unable to act badly, it does not need something else to regulate it. Our will, on the contrary, has to be regulated by right reason and the moral virtues.[172]

Ockham cites Aristotle's definition of virtue: "Virtue is a habit (*habitus*) concerned with choice, lying in a mean, that is, the mean relative to us, this being determined by a rational principle, and by that principle by which the person of practical wisdom would determine it."[173] We know by inner experience that our wills are habituated to act in determined ways. After having willed something many times, we are inclined afterward to will it with greater ease, intensity, and pleasure. If we act against the inclination we experience displeasure. This shows that the will now possesses a new quality or stable disposition to will that object.

There are other habits than those in the will. The body can acquire habits enabling us to perform with ease acts we could not perform before, such as writing and weaving. There are also habits in the sensory appetite, as is evident from the fact that after many acts of desiring something we experience a stronger inclination to it. The imagination can also be habituated to act promptly in definite ways, and so too can the intellect, especially in thinking abstractly in the absence of its object. Of course there are also habits in the will, and these are our immediate concern, because with them alone we encounter a habit that can be virtuous.[174]

The question was widely debated at the time whether there are moral virtues in the sensory appetites of the soul. Thomas Aquinas thought that insofar as the sensory appetites participate in reason

---

172. In *Ockham on the Virtues* (West Lafayette, IN, 1997) Rega Wood provides the Latin text of Ockham's *De connexione virtutum* with a translation and an illuminating commentary.

173. *Quaest. variae* 8 (*OTh* 8: 409.16–410.29); cf. Aristotle, *Eth. Nic.* 2.6, 1107a1–3 (Oxford translation, slightly modified).

174. *Quodl.* 3.20 (*OTh* 9: 281.10–283.56). "[N]ullus alius habitus ab habitu voluntatis est intrinsece et perfecte virtuosus, quia quilibet alius inclinat indifferenter ad actus laudabiles et vituperabiles" (*Quaest. variae* 7.2 [*OTh* 8: 330.158–160]).

they can acquire virtues, disposing them to good acts; an example is temperance in the concupiscible appetite.[175] Scotus was of the same opinion.[176] But Ockham contends that only an act of the will can be strictly virtuous or evil, because it alone is under our control and consequently worthy of praise or blame.[177] No doubt a habit is formed in the sensory appetites after repeated acts, but it is not a virtue or vice in itself but a quality of the body that can be present even when it is not under the control of the will. It is called a virtue or vice only by extrinsic denomination; that is, because it inclines us to act well or badly.[178]

Since only an act of the will is properly virtuous or evil, external acts cannot have their own morality; rather, they are said to be good or bad only by extrinsic denomination, by reference to a good or bad will. Scotus was of the contrary opinion, arguing that because there are distinct prohibitions against internal and external acts they must have their own distinct malice.[179] Ockham counters that an external act cannot have a moral value in itself, for the same act can be good at one time and bad at another. Thus, walking to church is good if done for the glory of God but bad if done out of vainglory. The act in itself is morally neutral. Suppose a person commits suicide by jumping off a cliff. On the way down

175. *ST* 1-2.56.4, reported by Ockham, *Rep.* 3.11 (*OTh* 6: 352.2–354.7).

176. Scotus, *Quodl.* 18 (Vivès ed. 26: 246–247, n. 12 and 254–255, n. 17), reported by Ockham, *Rep.* 3.11 (*OTh* 6: 370.11–18).

177. *Rep.* 3.11 (*OTh* 6: 366.1–9).

178. *Quodl.* 2.16 (*OTh* 9: 182.9–183.35). By "extrinsic denomination" Ockham means giving something another name because of something extrinsic to it: "quando aliquid praecise denominat aliud propter aliquid extrinsecum" (*Ord.* 1.2.7 (*OTh* 2: 241.2–5). Ockham understands a passion to be a form existing in an appetitive power that can be regulated by right reason. It is not actual knowledge but requires it for its very existence. Passions include acts of the sensory appetite and the will, such as joy and sorrow in the will; see *Quodl.* 2.17 (*OTh* 9: 186.10–187.25). See Girard J. Etzkorn "Ockham's View of the Human Passions in the Light of his Philosophical Anthropology," in *Die Gegenwart Ockhams*, ed. Wilhelm Vossenkuhl and Rolf Schönberger (Weinheim, 1990), pp. 265–287.

179. Scotus, *Quodl.* 18 (Vivès ed. 26: 246–247, n. 12), reported by Ockham, *Quodl.* 1.20 (*OTh* 9: 99.11–100.15).

he repents and would rescind his act if he could. The act of falling, which before was bad, is not bad after his repentance, for it is not in the control of his will. External acts have a natural or physical goodness, but they are morally good only by reason of the goodness of the interior act of the will.[180]

From antiquity the chief acquired virtues have been called cardinal virtues because they are, so to speak, the hinges (*cardines*) on which the other virtues turn. They are prudence, fortitude, justice, and temperance.[181] According to tradition, prudence plays an essential unifying role in all the other virtues, since without it there can be no moral virtue or virtuous act. This is because every virtuous act must conform to right reason, and prudence dictates what should be done in accord with right reason. Aristotle defines prudence as "a reasoned and true state of capacity to act with regard to human goods."[182]

Ockham follows the classical tradition of the cardinal virtues and the central, unifying role prudence plays in all the virtues, but he interprets these themes in his own way. Of special importance is his understanding of prudence and its relation to the moral virtues. He distinguishes between four meanings of prudence as directive of moral actions in various ways.[183] We shall limit our discussion here to the third meaning, which Ockham says is its proper meaning according to Aristotle. It is the knowledge of a particular proposition that is known only through experience and not by deduction from a self-evident proposition, and it is directive and dictative of some particular act to be done. He gives as an example: "This angry man should be placated by soft words." Now

180. "[A]ctus exterior est bonus bonitate sua propria, quae est ipse actus naturalis; sed moraliter et causaliter est bonus bonitate actus interioris, quia solum est bonus quadam denominatione extrinseca" (ibid. [*OTh* 9: 106.152–155]; cf. *Quaest. variae* 6.9 [*OTh* 8: 262.248–264.276]).

181. This is the traditional listing of the cardinal virtues; Aristotle mentions justice, fortitude, liberality, and temperance: see *Eth. Nic.* 10.8, 1178b10–15.

182. Ibid. 6.5, 1140b20.

183. *Quaest. variae* 7.2 (*OTh* 8: 330.162–331.33). See Freppert, *Basis of Morality*, pp. 20–22.

according to Ockham (who here follows Scotus), this prudential knowledge is not under the control of the will, nor are we praised or blamed for it; hence it is not a virtue or virtuous act but a natural act like seeing.[184] Prudence comes before a virtuous act, and it is a partial efficient cause of the act along with the act of the will and God, but it is not itself virtuous. This is shown by the fact that there can be an act of prudence, dictating that a certain act should be done or avoided, and yet the will can act against reason and will the opposite, or the will can suspend its act and not will at all.[185] However, there can be no virtuous act without prudence, for an act can be virtuous only if it in accord with right reason and done under suitable circumstances.[186] To be more precise, conformity with right reason by itself does not make an act virtuous, for if God, being omnipotent, produced in my will an act conforming to right reason without my will taking any part in it, that act would not be virtuous or meritorious. The goodness of the act requires that it be done under the control of the will.[187]

Right reason, or prudence, is accordingly needed for a perfectly virtuous act. It is in a special way a necessary circumstance or object of the act, since the act must conform to right reason to be perfectly virtuous. Besides right reason, place, time, and intention are also necessary circumstances or partial objects of the act. The intention or end for which the virtue is acquired is of special significance, for it is the basis for distinguishing between the moral virtues of philosophers and Christians. Good Christians acquire moral virtues and avoid immoral acts out of love of God and because of his commands. Philosophers may acquire the same virtues and abstain

---

184. *Quaest. variae* 7.4 (*OTh* 8: 380.96–104); Scotus, *Ord.* 2.40.un. (Vivès ed. 13: 427, n. 4 ad 2). Thomas Aquinas places prudence not only among the intellectual virtues but also among the moral virtues, because through prudence we not only know what is right to do in a particular case but we also apply the knowledge to the act, and this implies a rectified will (*ST* 2–2.47.4).

185. *Rep.* 3.12 (*OTh* 6: 421.9–22).

186. *Quaest. variae* 8 (*OTh* 8: 409.16–410.35); *Rep.* 3.12 (*OTh* 6: 422.1–21).

187. *Rep.* 3.11 (*OTh* 6: 389.18–22).

from the same bad acts but for a totally different motive. They may be virtuous for the sake of health, proficiency in science, peace, or simply because it is good in itself. Their virtues, however, will not be perfect, since they are not directed to the love of God above everything else. Since the intentions of the good Christian and non-Christian are different, their virtues may appear to be the same but in fact they are specifically different.[188]

Besides acquired moral virtues, Christians through Baptism have supernatural virtues directly infused in the soul by God. They do not result from experience nor are they increased by repeated acts. The three most important are the theological virtues of faith, hope, and love – so-called because they have God as their object. Nonbelievers can have theological virtues but not strictly, since they are not infused by God but acquired by experience, just like other natural virtues. Instructed in Christian doctrine, nonbelievers may learn to love God above all things and even to sing God's praises, but their love of God is acquired and not God-given.[189]

Moral Acts and the Divine Omnipotence

As we have seen, Ockham uses two norms by which to judge whether an act is good or bad: the command of God and right reason. He divides moral acts into those that are intrinsically good, those that are intrinsically evil, and those that are morally indifferent. It should be noted that by "intrinsically" Ockham does not mean that these acts have natures of their own, describable as good, bad or indifferent just in themselves. We have seen him deny that things have natures or essences of any sort. Rather, he means that an act is intrinsically good or bad in contrast to one that is extrinsically such. We have seen that only acts of the will qualify as intrinsically moral. On the other hand, exterior acts commanded by the will are extrinsically moral, for their morality depends on the morality of the acts of the will. An example of an intrinsically

---

188. *Quaest. variae* 7.4 (*OTh* 8: 402.634–403.652); *Rep.* 4.5 (*OTh* 7: 58.5–19).
189. *Rep.* 3.9 (*OTh* 6: 281.6–17); *Quaest. variae* 7.2 (*OTh* 8: 338.194–198).

morally good act is to will to pray in order to give honor to God and because he has commanded it according to right reason. An example of an intrinsically morally bad act is to will to pray out of vainglory and contrary to the command of God and right reason. An example of a morally indifferent act is to will to pray, but without giving attention to what one is doing, having neither a good nor a bad intention. An act of this sort, whether interior or exterior, is said to be good only by extrinsic denomination and in no sense intrinsically such nor evil.[190]

Ockham adopts from Duns Scotus another division of moral acts. Acts can be good or bad either in themselves (*ex genere*) or from the circumstances that accompany them; furthermore, they can be good and meritorious if done with a supernatural intention. The three divisions of moral acts can be exemplified as follows: Wanting to pray and give alms are good in themselves, abstracting from the circumstances. Wanting to steal or fornicate are evil in themselves, quite apart from the circumstances. Taking into account circumstances dictated by right reason, it would be a good act to want to abstain from certain things in order to conserve nature or just because it is something good to do, as a pagan philosopher might intend. Wanting to fornicate, contrary to right reason, in an improper place and for the sake of pleasure, would be a bad act. It would be a good act to wish to be continent according to right reason and the other circumstances and for the honor of God, because he accepts this act.[191]

Are there human acts that are necessarily good and not bad under any circumstances? Strictly speaking, Ockham does not believe any act is necessarily good, for the simple reason that it is not necessary for any human acts to exist at all. God alone is a necessary being; the existence of everything else is contingent, depending on his will for its existence. Hence human acts are only contingently virtuous. Furthermore, since God can do by himself

190. *Quaest. variae* 7.2 (*OTh* 8: 338: 200–210). Since the act is not intended, it is not a human act.
191. Ibid. (*OTh* 8: 338.200–339.229). On the subject of the nature of morality see Freppert, *Basis of Morality*, pp. 141–170.

everything he does by secondary causes, he can be the sole cause of every act; and if he were, the act would not be necessarily virtuous because it would not be under the control of the human will.

From another, less strict, perspective a human act can be necessarily virtuous, so that as long as the divine command remains (*stante praecepto divino*) it cannot be bad; if caused by the created will, it can only be virtuous. Ockham proves this as follows: Consider a contingently virtuous act such as walking – contingently virtuous because it can be either good or bad, depending on the circumstances. It becomes definitely good only by conforming to another act, such as the act of intending to go to church. If the latter act is also contingently virtuous, it must be made definitely good by another virtuous act; and this process either goes on to infinity or it ends with some act that is necessarily virtuous. An act meeting this condition is the first of all good acts: the love of God above everything else. This act is so virtuous that it cannot be bad, nor can it be caused by a creature's will without being virtuous. Taking into account time and place, we are obliged to love God for himself and above all things.[192] Moreover, our love of God ought to be a love of friendship, not a love of desire, for then we would love something more than God.[193]

In a parallel passage in the treatise *The Connection of the Virtues*,[194] Ockham uses the same proof that some act is necessarily and intrinsically virtuous, but now his example is not the love of God

192. *Quodl.* 3.14 (*OTh* 9: 254.36–256.67). Circumstances must be taken into account, because we are not obliged to love God at every moment and in every place, as when sleeping or at study.

193. "Ad secundam dico quod fruitio non est amor concupiscentiae, non plus fruitio patriae quam fruitio viae. Cuius ratio est quia omnis amor concupiscentiae, qui est praecise concupiscentiae, praesupponit amorem amicitiae, ita quod quando aliquid diligitur amore concupiscentiae est aliquid magis dilectum amore amicitiae. Igitur si Deus praecise diligeretur amore concupiscentiae esset aliquid magis dilectum quam Deus, quod est inconveniens. Ideo dico quod fruitio est amor amicitae" (*Ord.* 1.1.4 [*OTh* 1: 444.14–21]).

194. On the connection of the virtues, the history of the subject, and the role of prudence, see Othmar Suk, "The Connection of Virtues according to Ockham," *Franciscan Studies* 10 (1950): 9–32, 91–113; and Wood, *Ockham on the Virtues*.

but willing to do something because God has commanded it. While the divine command remains (*stante praecepto divino*), he says, the act of obeying God is so virtuous that it cannot become evil.[195] Thus both the love of God above all things and the willingness to obey him are necessarily virtuous as along as the divine law stands.

It should be noted that this account of moral acts remains on the level of God's ordained power without touching upon his absolute power. It concerns what God in fact has willed and obliged us to do, not absolutely speaking what he can, will and oblige us to do. The acts mentioned are necessarily virtuous *while the divine decree remains in force*. What human morality would be like under divine decrees different from those in the present moral order is another question.

Ockham gives us a glimpse of what such a morality could be, given God's freedom to legislate as he wills. By common law, he says, acts of hatred, theft, and adultery are evil because they are connected with the evil fact that they are done in defiance of the divine law commanding the opposite. But if these acts are considered just in themselves, without the added qualification of being contrary to the divine precept, there is no reason why they cannot be done by God or a human being. Indeed, if these acts were commanded by God they would be good and even meritorious for eternal life. These acts have bad sounding names because they are opposed to God's law; but if commanded by God they would be given new names and no longer be called theft or adultery.[196] Thus, when the Israelites leaving Egypt despoiled the Egyptians of their possessions, they were not really stealing but doing a good deed because it was commanded by God. The only Jews who sinned in taking the Egyptians' property were those who did so with a bad will and not precisely in obedience to God's precept.[197]

In an oft-quoted passage Ockham boldly asserts that God can order a creature to hate him, and if the creature does so the act

195. *Quaest. variae* 7.1 (*OTh* 8: 327.99–328.128).
196. *Rep.* 2.15 (*OTh* 5: 352.3–353.2). The *Tractatus de principiis theologiae* 1 (*OPh* 7: 509, nn. 7–8) confirms that a creature can meritoriously hate God.
197. *Ord.* 1.47.un. (*OTh* 4: 685.8–12).

would be good not only on earth but in heaven.[198] Obviously this command is possible by God's absolute power and not by his ordered power, for in the present moral dispensation creatures are commanded to love God above everything else, and this would be incompatible with hating him. "The created will," Ockham writes, "is obliged by divine precept to love God; accordingly while this precept is in force the will cannot virtuously hate God or cause the act of hating, but necessarily causes it in an evil and malicious way, and this because it is obliged by God's precept to the opposite act."[199]

Not only can God command us to hate him but he himself can be the total cause of our act of hating him. Normally God is the first cause of our acts, but he can dispense with us as secondary causes and cause the effect by himself. Hence he can be the total cause of both our loving or hating him. In either case, Ockham adds, God would always act for a good purpose, for unlike creatures he cannot act for an unsuitable end.[200]

It is shocking to hear that God might order us to hate him and even to cause our act of hating him. It is no less scandalous to read that "hatred is not formally a sin."[201] Light is thrown on these disturbing statements of Ockham by the special sense in which he

---

198. "Praeterea, omnis voluntas potest se conformare praecepto divino. Sed Deus potest praecipere quod voluntas creata odiat eum, igitur voluntas creata potest hoc facere. Praeterea, omne quod potest esse actus rectus in via, et in patria. Sed odire Deum potest esse actus rectus in via, puta si praecipiatur a Deo, igitur in patria" (*Rep.* 4.16 [*OTh* 7: 352.5–10]). This passage was censured at Avignon in 1326; see A. Pelzer, "Les 51 articles de Guillaume Occam censurés en Avignon en 1326," *Revue d'histoire ecclésiastique* 18 (1922): 240–270, at p. 254.

199. "[V]oluntas creata obligatur ex praecepto Dei ad diligendum Deum, et ideo stante illo praecepto non potest bene odire Deum nec causare actum odiendi, sed necessario male causat malitia moris. Et hoc quia obligatur ex praecepto Dei ad actum oppositum" (*Rep.* 2.15 [*OTh* 5: 353.6–10]). The love and hatred of God are formally opposed and contrary acts: "Si quaeras utrum conversio ad Deum actu caritativo et aversio ab eo actu odiendi Deum opponuntur formaliter, dico quod sic, quia diligere Deum super omnia et odire Deum sunt actus contrarii" (*Quaest. variae* 7.4 [*OTh* 8: 391.349–352]).

200. *Rep.* 2.15 (*OTh* 5: 353.10–354.2; 342.22–343.2).

201. "[O]dium non est formaliter peccatum" (Ibid. [*OTh* 5: 343.3]).

uses the word "hatred" (*odium*). In one sense, he says, it means an absolute act of the will with no connotation of being morally good or evil. In another sense it connotes a deformity in the act. Now, when Ockham says that hatred is not formally a sin, the term "hatred" means an act of the will understood absolutely, without the connotation of being contrary to the decree of a superior or to right reason. Hatred has the same meaning when he says that God could command us to hate him, or that he himself could cause the act. Ockham writes:

> The act of hating God, as regards everything that is absolute in it, is not the same as with the deformity and evil in the act, and consequently God can cause whatever is absolute in the act of hating God or not willing him, by not causing any deformity or malice in the act.[202]

This makes it clear that Ockham's use of the word "hatred" in the above context abstracts from any moral connotation. In its moral sense the act of hatred includes the notion of an act done contrary to what a person is obliged to do. Taken in its absolute sense it lacks this moral connotation, and it is with this meaning that Ockham can say that hatred is not formally (that is, as an absolute term) sinful, and that God can cause us to hate him.

Ockham is here speaking according to positive moral doctrine, in which the morality of human acts is determined by the will of a superior, especially God. From the perspective of positive morality, acts are morally good if they conform to God's decrees; they are morally bad if they are contrary to these decrees. In the present moral dispensation we are commanded to love God above everything

---

202. "Et quod Deus possit causare actum odiendi Deum quantum ad omne absolutum in actu in voluntate creata probatur, quia Deus potest omne absolutum causare sine omni alio quod non est idem cum illo absoluto. Sed actus odiendi Deum quantum ad omne absolutum in eo non est idem cum deformitate et malitia in actu, igitur Deus potest causare quidquid absolutum est in actu odiendi Deum vel nolendi, non causando aliquam deformitatem vel malitiam in actu, igitur etc." (*Rep.* 2.15 [*OTh* 5: 342.8–15]).

else and for his own sake, and since the love of God is the first of all moral acts it is the basis of our whole moral life. However, by his absolute power God can decree otherwise and command a creature to hate him.[203]

This is Ockham's teaching in his *Reportatio,* an early work that is part of his *Sentences* written between 1317–1319. But Lucan Freppert claims that Ockham later made an important change in his doctrine. According to Freppert, in the *Quodlibeta* Ockham asserts that the act of loving God above everything else and for his own sake is necessarily virtuous and cannot be otherwise, without mentioning any divine precept. Whereas in the *Reportatio* the love of God above all and for himself is said to be a good act because it is commanded by God, in the *Quodlibeta* it is said to be a good act "that would hold in any possible [moral] order."[204] In support of this Freppert cites the following words of Ockham:

> [T]his act [by which God is loved above everything and for his own sake] is so virtuous that it cannot be evil, nor can this act be caused by a created will unless it be virtuous, both because everyone is obliged in a given place and time to love God above everything, and consequently this act cannot be evil.[205]

However, when these words are placed in their context they do imply a reference to the divine precept. Ockham says that the act of loving God above everything is necessarily virtuous *"in the way described above"* ("modo praedicto"), referring to the preceding phrase

---

203. See above, note 198.
204. Freppert, *Basis of Morality,* p. 176.
205. "[N]am iste actus [quo Deus diligitur super omnia et propter se] sic est virtuosus quod non potest esse vitiosus, nec potest iste actus causari a voluntate creata nisi sit virtuosus; tum quia quilibet pro loco et tempore obligatur ad diligendum Deum super omnia, et per consequens iste actus non potest esse vitiosus" (*Quodl.* 3.14 [*OTh* 9: 255.62–66]); cited by Freppert, *Basis of Morality,* p. 121 n124. "Here in the *Quodlibeta,"* Freppert observes, "there is no reference to any dependence on the precept of God remaining in force" (p. 148).

"while the divine precept is in force" ("stante praecepto divino").[206] Ockham's thought on this subject seems to have been consistent throughout his life. There is no reason to believe he abandoned his view that the created will is bound to love God above everything and for his own sake because of his present divine decree and not because humankind by its nature inclines to this goal in life.[207]

The consequence of this situation is well summed up by Calvin Normore:

> [Ockham] thinks that God in fact set up a world which has the actual teleological features someone like Aquinas would think essential to any created world. But Ockham does not think these features essential to any created world. And so it is no part of the essence of God or creature that the world be in this way.[208]

What is true of Ockham's moral world is also true of his physical universe. He accepts the main features of the Aristotelian description of that universe, with its unity, structure, elements and their movements. He simply refuses to grant that they are essential to a created world but depend on the will of God. Nothing stands

206. The passage reads: "Tertio dico quod ille actus necessario virtuosus modo praedicto est actus voluntatis, quia actus quo diligitur Deus super omnia et propter se, est huiusmodi; nam iste actus sic est virtuosus quod non potest esse vitiosus, nec potest iste actus causari a voluntate creata nisi sit virtuosus; tum quia quilibet pro loco et tempore obligatur ad diligendum Deum super omnia, et per consequens iste actus non potest esse vitiosus; tum quia iste actus est primus omnium actuum bonorum" (*Quodl.* 3.14 [*OTh* 9: 255.60–67]). The editor notes (ibid. [*OTh* 9: 255 n8]) that "modo praedicto" refers to line 44 above: "stante praecepto divino."

207. Granted that God by his absolute power could command a creature to hate him, could this act possibly be carried out? It seems that it would be impossible, because by obeying the divine command the creature would love God, leading to the contradictory situation of the creature's both loving and hating God at the same time. On this antinomy see Freppert, *Basis of Morality*, p. 122; Boehner, introduction to Ockham, *Philosophical Writings*, pp. xlix–l. The reasoning is sound, but it presupposes that love and obedience are equivalent notions: to obey God is to love him. But there are other motives for obeying a superior than love.

208. Normore, "Picking and Choosing," p. 38.

in the way of his creating a different and more perfect world, and more worlds than our own.[209] Thus we find at play in both Ockham's ethics and physics the same contingency of nature and the absolute freedom and power of God.

But if God ordered us to hate him, would he not will and do something evil and contrary to the teaching of the fathers of the Church? Ockham replies with a distinction. It is one thing to will or do something evil and another to will or do it maliciously. As Aristotle says, not everyone who does a just act is just, but only one who does it in a just manner. It follows that not everyone who does something evil is evil, but only a person who does it maliciously. Now a person does an evil act evilly if he does something he is obliged not to do. But it is completely absurd to say that God can will or do what he is obliged not to do, for he is not under any obligation whatsoever. So he can do something evil but he himself is not evil. Of course the Church fathers would not say that God wills or does evil, but what they mean is that he does not do anything wrong maliciously or unjustly.[210]

Ockham suggests that there is only a difference of language between himself and traditional Christian theologians on this subject, but in fact he is saying something new, in accord with his nominalist principles. He is denying that human acts have natures that qualify them as either good or bad in themselves. In opposition to Scotus, he asserts that the evil of an act is not the lack of a rightness that ought to be in the exterior act or in the will, but it is precisely the act of the will itself elicited contrary to the divine precept.[211] In other words, the moral qualities of acts do not belong to the acts in themselves, but to the acts in their conformity or nonconformity with the divine will and right reason.

209. See above, pp. 326–338.

210. *Ord.* 1.47.un. (*OTh* 4: 682.20–685.6). Ockham presents these views tentatively and by way of reporting an opinion that may or may not be orthodox. See Aristotle, *Eth. Nic.* 2.3, 1105b5–9.

211. *Quaest. variae* 7.4 (*OTh* 8: 387.256–269); Scotus, *Ord.* 2.37.1 (Vivès ed. 13: 356–357, n. 6), *Quodl.* 18 (Vivès ed. 26: 249, n. 16).

We are here at a dividing line between Ockham and Scotus. According to Scotus, God has freely chosen to create things with certain natures which we must respect when making judgments about them. This is also true when it is a question of our moral judgments about what we ought to do or not do. There is a natural law inscribed in the nature of things, expressing both the divine knowledge and will, which is accessible to human reason, though not always without difficulty. As interpreted by Scotus, St. Paul's statement that the law of nature is written in our heart (Rom 2:15) means that its precepts are within nature itself (*ex natura rei*), so that by natural reason we can see that each precept thereof must be observed.[212] More clearly, Scotus says that to know whether an action is morally good we have only to know the nature of the agent, the nature of the faculty by which the agent acts, and the essential character (*ratio quidditativa*) of the action itself.[213] Though the moral goodness of an act, and the moral law itself, is thus rooted in nature and shares in its necessity, it is not absolutely necessary, because God freely chose to create nature as he did, and he could have created it otherwise. Then he would have established other laws, which would be right and just because they would be in accord with nature as actually created and willed by God. Accordingly there is contingency in the moral order as there is in God's whole creation – a contingency flowing from the divine freedom.

Indeed, Scotus sees an element of contingency even in the ten commandments, which are an expression of the natural law actually in force. God can dispense – and in fact has already dispensed in certain cases – from the last seven commandments,

---

212. Scotus, *Ord.* prol.2.un (Vatican ed. 1: 70, n. 108); *Ord.* 2.28.un. (Vivès ed. 13: 262, n. 8). For Scotus' doctrine of moral law in relation to will and reason see Wolter, *Philosophical Theology of John Duns Scotus*, pp. 148–162; Gilson, *Jean Duns Scot*, 603–624; and the essays in *John Duns Scotus: Metaphysics and Ethics*, ed. Ludger Honnefelder et al. (Leiden, 1996).

213. Scotus, *Quodl.* 18 (Vivès ed. 26: 236, n. 5), trans. Alluntis and Wolter, p. 402.

which define our relations to our neighbor, and consequently they cannot strictly belong to the natural law. An example is God's allowing the Israelites to take the possessions of the Egyptians when fleeing their country (Ex 12: 35–36). But he cannot dispense from the first three commandments, which define our duties toward God and which are necessary for attaining our ultimate end. Scotus here takes issue with Thomas Aquinas, who taught that none of the precepts of the decalogue is dispensable. Thus the two theologians agreed that God cannot dispense anyone from observing the natural law, but from this Aquinas concluded that, in spite of appearances, God has never dispensed anyone from the commandments; whereas Scotus contended that, since God did dispense certain persons from some commandments of the decalogue, they do not belong to the natural law.[214]

Having seen Ockham's opposition to both the Thomist and Scotist views of nature, we will hardly be surprised to find him going his own way when treating of natural law and the decalogue. Some of Ockham's most illuminating comments on natural law are to be found in his *Opus nonaginta dierum*, a work written after fleeing from Avignon and joining the anti-papal party under the protection of the Emperor Louis of Bavaria. Ockham divides law (*ius*) into positive law (*ius fori*) and natural equity or law (*ius poli*). Positive law, which includes both human and divine laws, is established by agreement or covenant (*pactio*) between humans or between God and humankind, at some times in conformity with right reason and at other times not. It can also be called customary law in a broad sense. In contrast, natural equity or law (*ius poli*) is in conformity with right reason, without involving any human or divine positive covenant. Right reason can be either pure right reason whose dictates are accessible to natural reason, and revealed right reason whose dictates or

---

214. *ST* 1–2.100.8. In reply to objection 3, Aquinas makes it clear that for a good reason God can permit an act against the letter of the law but not against its intent, as when he allowed the Israelites to despoil the Egyptians. This was not theft, as forbidden by the commandment, which is taking someone's property unjustly or unduly.

prudential acts have been revealed in scripture. In the latter case natural equity or law can rightly be called divine law.[215]

This description of natural law is in terms of right reason, which we already know to be prudence in acting or in habit. Since no agreement or covenant is needed for natural law in either sense, there seems to be no place in it for the will. It appears to come solely within the orbit of reason.

In another political treatise, entitled *Dialogus*, Ockham divides natural law into absolute natural law, which is unconditional, immutable, and (contrary to Scotus) admitting of no dispensation, and natural law that admits of modification and specification. Examples of the first are: You shall not worship another god, and You shall not commit adultery. An example of the second is: If necessary, cut off one of your members in order to conserve the health of your body.[216]

Reading these political works of Ockham, one can readily come to the conclusion that there is no voluntarism in his doctrine of natural law. It appears that reason, not will, is at its center. Thus Thomas Callahan concludes that "there is no textual evidence to substantiate the claim that Ockham proposed either a voluntarist theory of law or of natural law or ever intended to do so." Neither does George Knysh find Ockham a voluntarist, but "per-

215. "Ius autem poli non est aliud quam potestas conformis rationi rectae absque pactione; ius fori est potestas ex pactione aliquando conformi rationi rectae, et aliquando discordanti" (*Opus nonag. dierum* 65 [*OP* 2: 579.273-276]). For Ockham's notion of law see Thomas G. Callahan, "William Ockham and Natural Law" (PhD dissertation, Michigan State University, 1975), pp. 91-92; Wilhelm Kölmel, "Das Naturrecht bei Wilhelm Ockham," *Franziskanische Studien* 35 (1953): 39-85; Georges de Lagarde, *La naissance de l'esprit laïque au déclin du moyen âge*, nouv. éd. (Louvain and Paris, 1956-1970), esp. 4: *Guillaume d'Ockham: Défense de l'empire*; 5: *Guillaume d'Ockham: Critique des structures ecclésiales*. For Ockham's doctrine of natural law and rights see Brian Tierney, *The Idea of Natural Rights: Studies in Natural Rights, Natural Law and Church Law, 1150-1625* (Atlanta, GA, 1997).

216. *Dialogus* 3.2.1, ch. 10 and 3.2.3, ch. 6, ed. M. Goldast, *Monarchia Sancti Romani Imperii* (Frankfurt, 1668), pp. 878 and 932. See Callahan, "William Ockham and Natural Law," pp. 146-147.

haps the most rationalist of rationalists." Alan Gewirth also doubts the extent of the legal voluntarism and irrationalism that other writers attribute to Ockham.[217]

It should be pointed out, however, that the question of Ockham's possible voluntarism in law cannot be settled by examining his political works alone. They must be read along with his theological writings, which specifically treat of the relation of reason and will in the moral act and in law. We have seen that Ockham gives an essential role to right reason in a virtuous act. Indeed, he takes it as self-evident that the will ought to conform itself to right reason, which is nothing else than prudence. He insists that we should follow the dictates of reason just because reason dictates them. On the other hand, Ockham makes it clear that right reason dictates what ought to be willed because God wills it.[218] It appears that the divine will is thus at the origin of right reason and

217. Callahan, ibid., pp. 264–265; George Knysh, *Political Ockhamism* (Winnipeg, 1996), p. 83; Alan Gewirth, "Philosophy and Political Thought in the Fourteenth Century," in *The Forward Movement of the Fourteenth Century*, ed. Francis Lee Utley (Columbus, OH, 1961), pp. 125–164, at p. 158 n22. In addition to Gewirth, Callahan (pp. 85, 103) cites other authors who are quite convinced that Ockham was a legal voluntarist: Georges de Lagarde, *La naissance de l'esprit laïque au déclin du moyen âge* (Saint-Paul-Trois-Châteaux and Paris, 1934–1946), 6: 140–163; Francis Oakley, "Medieval Theories of Natural Law: William of Ockham and the Significance of the Voluntarist Tradition," *Natural Law Forum* 6 (1961): 65–83; Otto von Gierke, *Political Theories of the Middle Ages*, trans. F.W. Maitland (Boston, 1958), p. 173 n256.

218. Replying to the argument that, since every right will conforms to right reason, and the will by which God predestines one person and not another is right, therefore it conforms to right reason, Ockham replies: "Since this proves that in general there is some reason and cause in both the predestined and reprobated, it can be said that every right will conforms to right reason. But it does not always conform to the *previous* right reason which gives the cause why the will ought to will this. But by the very fact that the divine will wills this, right reason dictates that it should be willed: "Sed eo ipso quod voluntas divina hoc vult, ratio recta dictat quod est volendum" (*Ord.* 1.42.un. [*OTh* 4: 609.22–610.5]). This neatly explains the status of right reason vis-à-vis right will: A right will is generally in conformity with right reason, but not in every case. Ultimately right reason depends on the divine will.

natural law. The natural law is absolute and immutable because God has willed it to be so, following his ordered power (*potentia ordinata*). With his absolute power, however, he can alter the precepts of the natural law as he wills. Scotus thought this could be done, but it would necessitate a change in the natures God creates. Ockham requires nothing but a change in the name of the precepts. We can conclude that there is a strong element of rationality in Ockham's ethics, but there is even a stronger element of volition. For this reason it seems inappropriate to label Ockham's doctrine simply voluntarist or rationalist. It does not fall neatly into either category but has a place in both.[219]

Justice can be done to both sides of Ockham's ethical theory if we view it as an attempt to balance the consequences of several of his first principles: the divine omnipotence and absolute divine will on the one hand, and evident experience and reason on the other. Since God is all-powerful and free, he is not constrained to create anything or, if he does, to create it in a specific way. What he creates, and the laws he lays down for his creatures, are in his regard wholly contingent and free. But once he has created the world and legislated how it ought to operate, in accord with his ordered power, its laws are conditionally necessary. Only by his absolute power can they be changed, and this will happen only if the change comes within his ordered power; that is to say, if the change is foreseen and willed. Rational creatures, whose prerogative it is to know themselves, experience the demands of the moral laws within themselves. Some of these laws are primary and self-evident; others are consequences drawn from them. Together they comprise a rational or philosophical ethics shared alike by pagans and Christians. The latter, however, have the added advantage of knowing precepts and laws revealed in sacred scripture.

---

219. David Clark has argued this persuasively in his articles, "Voluntarism and Rationalism in the Ethics of Ockham" and "William of Ockham on Right Reason."

Interpreters of Ockham's ethics point out its apparent dualism and the antinomy between its parts, but both have a place in his ethics, and neither should be neglected in presenting a balanced account of it. There are two sides of that doctrine, each preventing the other from taking over the whole theory and developing all its consquences. If the theory were based solely on right reason, it would become a full-blown rationalist ethics and its theological input would be forgotten or dismissed. In fact, this is what happened after Ockham in the rationalist ethical doctrines of the Renaissance. If Ockham's ethics were solely voluntarist and dependent on the divine will, it would lose its rationality and become purely authoritarian, anticipating the theological positivism of the Reformation.[220] Ockham's own ethics avoided these extremes by including the principles of both right reason and the divine omnipotent will, however uneasy the equilibrium between them might be.

220. Clark, "William of Ockham on Right Reason," pp. 14–15 nn5–6.

Conclusion

MARTIN HEIDEGGER ONCE MADE the perceptive observation: "Every thinker thinks but one single thought."[1] Of course, he was well aware of the complexity of every great philosophy, but he suggests that every one has a dominant theme, like "the eternal recurrence of the same" in Nietzsche's philosophy. If we were to choose a single thought that plays this role in Ockham's philosophy, what would it be? The divine omnipotence and the razor are likely candidates because of their prominence in shaping his philosophy. But neither was original with him, nor was he the only one who used them; they were common coin for the schoolmen. It is true that he interpreted them in his own way, but always under the influence of his new notion of the individual. The evidence presented here leads to the conclusion that the central theme of Ockham's philosophy is the singular or individual thing (*res singularis*), as common nature (*natura communis*) is the focal point of Scotism and the act of existing (*esse*) is at the heart of Thomism. Ockham takes his place among the great philosophers of the Western world because, like all of them, he followed out the implications of his initial insight to the very end.[2]

---

1. "Jeder Denker denkt nur einen einzigen Gedanken" (*Was Heisst Denken?* [Tübingen, 1954], p. 20; *What is Called Thinking?*, trans. F.D. Wieck and J.G. Gray [New York, 1968], p. 50).

2. Pierre Alféri (*Guillaume d'Ockham: Le singulier* [Paris, 1989]) presents Ockham's philosophy as centered around the notion of the individual or singular. The present book, completed before Alféri's book came to my notice, agrees with his thesis. Marilyn M. Adams ("Ockham's Individualisms," in *Die Gegenwart Ockhams*, ed. Wilhelm Vossenkuhl and Rolf Schönberger [Weinheim, 1990], pp. 3–24) grants that Ockham "does bring individuals into prominence in a variety of theoretical connections," but questions "that the individual is an integrating symbol in Ockham's thought" or "that he started us down the road to 'the

In the beginning Ockham entertained the notions of an objective being (*esse objectivum*) and mental construct (*fictum*) that were not reducible to the notion of an individual thing (*res singularis*); but he finally found them unnecessary to account for knowledge, and indeed intrusive for this purpose. With serene simplicity, he reduced words and concepts to individual things, with the unique character of being signs of other things. In the end there remained as a positive entity only real individual things, each of which is so self-contained and one that it shares nothing with anything else. Being individual by essence, it has no need of a principle of individuation other than the causes that bring it into existence.

The uniqueness of each individual assures its separability from every other individual, at least by the divine power. Some individuals are naturally separable, like substances and certain accidents that can be removed without destroying their subject, as blackness can be removed from Socrates without destroying Socrates. Other accidents are naturally inseparable from their subjects, like the blackness of a crow, which cannot survive without it. But by the divine power any accident can be removed from its subject.[3] The substantial form and primary matter of a material substance are also inseparable by nature; but since they are real individuals it would not be contradictory for God to separate them so that they can exist apart.[4] The separability of individuals inevitably leads to the denial that the simple knowledge (*notitia incomplexa*) of any one thing can give us the simple and proper knowledge of any other. In other words, the intuition of one thing is not the intuition of another thing.[5]

---

individualism' of the modern period" (p. 18). Though her caution against vaguely "placing Ockham in any grand historical sweep" is salutary, there is evidence (some provided by herself in the areas of morality and political philosophy) for calling Ockham's philosophy "a philosophy of the singular." For Scotus' notion of essence and Thomas Aquinas' notion of existence see Etienne Gilson, *Being and Some Philosophers*, 2nd ed. (Toronto, 1952), pp. 84–94, 159–188.

    3. *Sum. log.* 1.25 (*OPh* 1: 82.44–59).

    4. For this divine ability see above, pp. 131–132.

    5. See above, p. 408 and n106.

Things are radically diverse and incommunicable, each being different from every other not only in number but in essence. An individual thing does not *have* an essence; rather, it *is* an essence. We may speak of the essence or existence of the individual, as Ockham speaks of the entity of a thing (*entitas rei*), but this does not imply a real distinction between the existence or essence of a thing and the thing itself. It has been well said that, with Ockham, "the great concepts of traditional ontology: 'essence,' 'being,' 'existence,' 'entity,' or 'a being,' all of which are derived from the verb 'to be,' come to signify the singular thing, the *res singularis* in its irreducible simplicity, in its numerical unity, which is also the pure transparency of being."[6] This does not mean that these terms denoting an individual thing are always synonyms: essence denotes it as intelligible in itself, existence as proceeding from its cause.

We already know that for Ockham the notion of being is univocal. As his philosophy developed, it progressed to a more unitary concept of being as simply a singular thing (*res singularis*). This did not admit of an analogy of being or modes of being in the traditional scholastic sense. There is just one mode of being, so to speak, and that is the numerical unity of the individual. Generic and specific unity attach to concepts in their values as signs of a greater or lesser range of individual things. There are logical modes, like actual and possible, but they do not count as real. We should not think, for example, that essence is indifferent to being and nonbeing, and hence essence is really potential to actual existence. Actuality and possibility are modes of predication, not of being. In short, things are not modal, but propositions containing the notes of necessary, possible, impossible, and the like.[7]

---

6. "Par la réduction ainsi entamée, les grands concepts de l'ontologie traditionnelle, 'essence,' 'être,' 'existence,' 'entité,' ou 'étant,' tous les dérivés du verbe 'être,' en viennent à signifier la chose singulière, la *res singularis* dans son irréductible simplicité, dans son unité numérique qui est aussi la pure transparence de l'être" (Alféri, *Guillaume d'Ockham: Le singulier*, p. 73).

7. *Sum. log.* 2.1 (*OPh* 1: 242–243); *Quodl.* 2.7 (*OTh* 9: 142–143). On this topic see Alféri, ibid., pp. 71–74.

Though things do not display modes of being, they do have degrees of unity (which is really the same as being). Some things are simple or incomplex, such as an angel or a human soul. Others are complex, being composed to several things, as a human being is made up of several forms and matter, each of which qualifies as a distinct *res*. Among complex things, some have an essential (*per se*) unity, like those composed of matter and form, while others have only the unity of an aggregate, like a heap of stones. An aggregate, however, is not one in the strict sense.[8]

In this view, community and universality are not features of the real world but of the way we think and speak about it. It is true that things are really related, for example as cause and effect or as similar to each other, but their relations derive from what they are in themselves, as absolute, individual entities. Moreover, an individual is so radically one that it is impervious to any distinction the mind may make regarding it (*distinctio rationis*). In other words, there is no distinction of reason with a foundation in one thing. A distinction of reason has to do with descriptions we make of it and only improperly with the thing itself.[9]

Ockham's notion of the individual plays a pivotal role in every area of his thought. It undergirds his innovations in logic, as is clear in his doctrines of the signification and supposition of terms. It is the centerpiece of his noetic, with its primacy of the intuition of the individual. It dominates his notion of science as an organized collection of individual mental habits and propositions. It is found in his new concepts in physics like motion and quantity. It influences even his social and political thought: if nothing is real save the individual, there can be no social or communal reality. A society is nothing but the sum of the individuals that compose it. The Church and his own Franciscan Order can have no reality but that of the individuals of which they are made up. The common good is simply a concept bringing together all individual goods.[10]

8. See above, p. 58 n138.

9. See above, pp. 197–199.

10. Ockham is intent on showing that societies have no personality, real, imaginary, or fictitious: see *Opus nonag. dierum* 62 (*OP* 2: 568–570). See also

With his new conception of reality or being as radically individual, Ockham elaborated a conceptualist philosophy whose influence was to last for centuries, indeed to our own day. It attracted Leibniz, whose monads are similarly individuals, each perfectly one, endowed with its own essence. It is hardly surprising, then, to find him praising Ockham as "a man of the highest genius and of outstanding erudition for his time." To Leibniz the nominalist sect was "the one most in harmony with the spirit of modern philosophy."[11]

Charles S. Peirce criticized the individualism of Ockham's thought. He preferred the realism of Duns Scotus because he believed it offered a sounder basis for the generality of scientific laws and prediction. Ockham's individuals resemble each other, he conceded, but he did not think resemblance can be a solid foundation for the real generality found in science. In his view the Scotist common nature provided a more adequate foundation for science and philosophy. He admired Ockham, however, as a very radical and profound thinker: "truly the *venerabilis inceptor* of a new way of philosophizing which has now broadened, perhaps deepened also, into English empiricism. England never forgot these teachings."[12] While acknowledging that Ockham's influence is very complex, Julius Weinberg expresses the widely held view that

---

Georges de Lagarde, *La naissance de l'esprit laïque au déclin du moyen âge* nouv. éd. (Louvain and Paris, 1956–1970), 5: 38. On the common good see Léon Baudry, *Lexique philosophique de Guillaume d'Ockham* (Paris, 1958), p. 32.

11. Leibniz, *Dissertatio de stilo philosophico Nizolii* 28, in *Opera philosophica*, ed. Johann Eduard Erdmann (Berlin, 1840), pp. 55–71, at p. 69. This is not to say that Leibniz' monads are equivalent to Ockham's individuals: the former are metaphysical points without extension and Ockham's material substances are really identical with their extension. However, Ockham thought that by the divine power a material individual could be reduced to a point without parts arranged in place; see *Quodl.* 4.18 (*OTh* 9: 391.78–85).

12. "Fraser's Edition of *The Works of George Berkeley*" (1871), in *Collected Papers of Charles Sanders Peirce* (Cambridge, MA, 1958), 8: 9–38, at p. 24. See John F. Boler, *Charles Peirce and Scholastic Realism: A Study of Peirce's Relation to John Duns Scotus* (Seattle, WA, 1963), pp. 145–165.

"[Ockham's] conceptualism had a lasting influence into the seventeenth and eighteenth centuries; indeed, it is no exaggeration to say that the British Empirical philosophers from Hobbes to Hume owe their conceptualism to Ockham directly or indirectly."[13]

Ockham's possible impact on the English empiricists has not yet been adequately studied, and until this has been done it is premature to make confident general statements about it.[14] In all probability Ockham (and other late medieval conceptualists) did influence the development of English empirical philosophy, as attested by their similarities and the availability of Ockham's works. Note that Ockham's *Summa logicae* (first printed in Paris in 1488) was reprinted at Oxford in 1675, during Locke's lifetime.[15]

Throughout the book we have seen Ockham's preoccupation with logic and language. When his opponents offered the solution of a problem in terms of realities, Ockham often countered with a logical or linguistic solution in terms of concepts or words. This is clear enough in his treatment of the problems of supposition and universals, and in his analysis of notions in physics, such as motion, action, and place. Not that Ockham denied the importance of realities; but he was acutely aware that we cannot know or talk about them without concepts or words, and that it is wrongheaded to confuse them with the things they are designed to signify. Before modern linguistic analysis Ockham was practicing a sort of proto-analysis that tended to reduce problems of physics

---

13. Julius R. Weinberg, *A Short History of Medieval Philosophy* (Princeton NJ, 1964), p. 265.

14. Richard I. Aaron (*John Locke*, 3rd ed. [Oxford, 1971], p. 8 n1), cites two studies on the subject of Locke's relation to scholasticism, published in the early decades of the century, but dismisses them as unsatisfactory, concluding that "much work remains to be done in this field." For a more recent study see E. Jennifer Ashworth, "'Do Words Signify Ideas or Things?': The Scholastic Sources of Locke's Theory of Language," *Journal of the History of Philosophy* 19 (1981): 299–326.

15. For the editions of this work see editors' introduction to *Sum. log.* (*OPh* 1: 33*–34*).

and metaphysics to problems of grammar or logic.[16] Conscious of the difficulties and mistakes in philosophy occasioned by the use of terms, especially abstract terms, he tried to remove them by a correct semantic analysis. This ran counter to modistic logic that somehow grounded the structure of human language in nature and independent of human convention, but it was congenial to terminist logic that viewed these structures as basically human creations.[17] Ockham's interest in language, mental, oral, and written, is consistent with his view of science or philosophy as properly speaking concerned with propositions and their universal terms, and only improperly and metaphorically with the real individuals of which they are the signs.[18] In its own way Ockham's philosophy can be called a philosophy of language.

Ockham can be seen from the perspective of his influence on later generations, but he can only be understood in the context of

16. For differences and similarities between Ockham and Wittgenstein see Graham White, "Ockham and Wittgenstein," in *Die Gegenwart Ockhams*, ed. Vossenkuhl and Schönberger, pp. 165–188.

17. For the distinction between these two logics see William J. Courtenay, "*Antiqui* and *Moderni* in Late Medieval Thought," *Journal of the History of Ideas* 48 (1987): 3–10, at p. 7.

18. See above, pp. 66–67, 142. Writing about natural science, Ockham says: "Tamen metaphorice et improprie loquendo dicitur scientia naturalis esse de corruptibilibus et mobilibus, quia est de illis terminis qui pro talibus supponunt" (*Expos. in Phys.* prol. [*OPh* 4: 11.24–26]). The words *metaphorice* and *improprie* are here used as synonyms. Ockham says that a word is used metaphorically when it is transferred from its proper to an improper meaning; see *Sum. log.* 3–4.3 (*OPh* 1: 758.61–62).

Ockham's doctrine that science or philosophy is properly concerned with terms and propositions and improperly said to concern extramental reality was censured at Avignon as contrary to philosophy and heretical if applied to some theological issues; see J. Koch, "Neue Aktenstücke zu dem gegen Wilhelm Ockham in Avignon geführten Prozess," *Recherches de théologie ancienne et médiévale* 8 (1936): 79–93, 168–197, at pp. 171–172. Though their judgment appears to be temerarious, the censors clearly realized that Ockham was proposing a radically new conception of philosophy with serious consequences for theology. A thorough study of this censored article, and of all the censored articles, would be highly desirable.

his own time, as growing out of a tradition that he inherited and shaped to his own liking. Ockhamism was a novelty in the fourteenth century. It epitomized the *via moderna*; but it was an answer to a centuries-old problem of how to use Aristotelianism and other non-Christian philosophies for the understanding of the Faith. It was also a Franciscan answer, the last significant medieval one in a long line that began with Alexander of Hales and Bonaventure and extended to Scotus and Ockham. Like his fellow Franciscans, Ockham had no intention of compromising the omnipotence and freedom of God by making undue concessions to the pagan and Muslim philosophers. Above all, he wanted to safeguard the first article of the Creed: "I believe in one God, the Father almighty." As he saw it, Aquinas, Henry of Ghent, and even Scotus failed to uphold the complete contingency of creatures and the absolute liberty of God with regard to them. Working creatively within the Franciscan tradition, he devised his theology and philosophy as his answer to this question.[19]

19. The substance of the foregoing paragraph is adapted from my article "Some Aspects of Fourteenth-Century Philosophy," *Mediaevalia et Humanistica*, new series, 7 (1976): 175–188, repr. *Being and Knowing* (Toronto, 1980), pp. 447–460, at p. 460. For the history of Ockhamism in the fourteenth century see William J. Courtenay (with Katherine H. Tachau), "Ockham, Ockhamists, and the English-German Nation at Paris, 1339–1341," *History of Universities* 2 (1982): 53–96; Courtenay, "The Reception of Ockham's Thought at the University of Paris," in *Preuve et raisons à l'Université de Paris: Logique, ontologie, et théologie au XIVe siècle*, ed. Zénon Kaluza and Paul Vignaux (Paris, 1984), pp. 43–64, and "The Reception of Ockham's Thought in Fourteenth-Century England," *From Ockham to Wyclif*, ed. Anne Hudson and Michael Wilks (Oxford, 1987), pp. 89–107; and Ernest Moody, "Ockham, Buridan, and Nicholas of Autrecourt," *Franciscan Studies* 7 (1947): 113–146, repr. in his *Studies in Medieval Philosophy, Science, and Logic* (Berkeley, 1975), pp. 127–160. For the spirit of Ockhamism and the nominalist movement initiated by Ockham see Etienne Gilson, *A History of Christian Philosophy in the Middle Ages* (New York, 1955), pp. 498–520; Frederick Copleston, *A History of Philosophy* 3, part 1: *Ockham to the Speculative Mystics* (Garden City, NY, 1963), pp. 134–164.

Bibliography

REFERENCE WORKS

Baudry, Léon. *Lexique philosophique de Guillaume d'Ockham: Étude des notions fondamentales*. Paris: Lethielleux, 1958.

Beckmann, Jan P. *Ockham-Bibliographie 1900–1990*. Hamburg: Felix Meiner, 1992.

Forcellini, Egidio. *Totius latinitatis lexicon: consilio et cura Jacobi Facciolati, opera et studio Ægidii Forcellini ... .* 4 vols. Prati: Ex officina Fratri Giachetti, 1839–1845.

Heynck, Valens. "Ockham-Literatur 1919–1949." In *Franziskanische Studien* 32 (1950): 164–183; continued by James P. Reilly in *Franciscan Studies* 28 (1968): 197–214.

THE WORKS OF WILLIAM OF OCKHAM

Collected Works

William of Ockham. *Opera Philosophica*. Ed. Philotheus Boehner et al. 7 vols. St. Bonaventure, NY: Franciscan Institute, 1974–1988.

—. *Opera Politica*. Ed. H.S. Offler et al. 4 vols. Manchester: Manchester University Press, 1940–1997.

—. *Opera Theologica*. Ed. Gedeon Gál et al. 10 vols. St. Bonaventure, NY: Franciscan Institute, 1967–1988.

Individual Works

William of Ockham. *Brevis summa libri Physicorum, Summula philosophiae naturalis, et Quaestiones in libros Physicorum Aristotelis*. Ed. Stephen F. Brown. *Opera Philosophica* 6. 1984.

—. *Dialogus de imperio et pontificia potestate*. In *Monarchia Sancti Romani Imperii*. Ed. M. Goldast. Frankfurt, 1668.

—. *Expositio in libros Physicorum*. Prologus et libri 1–3. Ed. Vladimir Richter and Gerhard Leibold. *Opera Philosophica* 4. 1985.

—. *Expositio in libros Physicorum*. Libri 4–8. Ed. Rega Wood, Romualdus Green, Gedeon Gál, J. Giermek, Francis E. Kelley, Gerhard Leibold, and Girard J. Etzkorn. *Opera Philosophica* 5. 1985.

—. *Expositio in librum Perihermenias Aristotelis.* Ed. Angelus Gambatese and Stephen F. Brown. *Opera Philosophica* 2. 1978.

—. *Expositio in librum Praedicamentorum Aristotelis.* Ed. Gedeon Gál. *Opera Philosophica* 2. 1978.

—. *Expositio super libros Elenchorum.* Ed. Francesco del Punta. *Opera Philosophica* 3. 1979.

—. *Expositionis in libros artis logicae prooemium. Expositio in librum Porphyrii De praedicabilibus.* Ed. Ernest A. Moody. *Opera Philosophica* 2. 1978.

—. *Opera dubia et spuria: Tractatus minor et Elementarium logicae.* Ed. E.M. Buytaert, Gedeon Gál and J. Giermek; *Tractatus de praedicamentis.* Ed. Girard J. Etzkorn; *Tractatus de principiis theologiae.* Ed. Léon Baudry and Francis E. Kelley. *Opera Philosophica* 7. 1988.

—. *Opus nonaginta dierum.* Ed. R.F. Bennett and H.S. Offler. *Opera Politica* 2. 1963. 2nd rev. ed. 1974.

—. *Ordinatio:* see *Scriptum in librum primum Sententiarum.*

—. *Quaestiones in ... Sententiarum (Reportatio). Librum secundum:* Ed. Gedeon Gál and Rega Wood. *Opera Theologica* 5. 1981. *Librum tertium:* Ed. Francis E. Kelley and Girard J. Etzkorn. *Opera Theologica* 6. 1982. *Librum quartum:* Ed. Rega Wood, Gedeon Gál, et al. *Opera Theologica* 7. 1984.

—. *Quaestiones variae.* Ed. Girard J. Etzkorn, Francis E. Kelley, and Joseph C. Wey. *Opera Theologica* 8. 1984.

—. *Quodlibeta septem.* Ed. Joseph C. Wey. *Opera Theologica* 9. 1980.

—. *Reportatio:* see *Quaestiones in ... Sententiarum.*

—. *Scriptum in librum primum Sententiarum (Ordinatio).*
   Ed. Gedeon Gál and Stephen F. Brown. *Opera Theologica* 1. 1967.
   Ed. Stephen F. Brown and Gedeon Gál. *Opera Theologica* 2. 1970.
   Ed. Girard J. Etzkorn. *Opera Theologica* 3. 1977.
   Ed. Girard J. Etzkorn and Francis E. Kelley. *Opera Theologica* 4. 1979.

—. *Summa logicae.* Ed. Philotheus Boehner, Gedeon Gál, and Stephen F. Brown. *Opera Philosophica* 1. 1974.

—. *Tractatus contra Benedictum.* Ed. H.S. Offler and J. Sikes. 3 vols. *Opera Politica* 3. 1944-1956.

—. *Tractatus de praedestinatione et de praescientia Dei respectu futurorum contingentium.* Ed. Philotheus Boehner and Stephen F. Brown. *Opera Philosophica* 2. 1978.

—. *Tractatus de quantitate et Tractatus de corpore Christi.* Ed. Carlo A. Grassi. *Opera Theologica* 10. 1986.

Translations

William of Ockham. "Five Questions on Universals from His *Ordinatio*, d. 2, qq. 4–8." Trans. Paul Vincent Spade. In *Five Texts on the Mediaeval Problem of Universals: Porphyry, Boethius, Abelard, Duns Scotus, Ockham*, ed. Spade, pp. 114–231. Indianapolis/Cambridge: Hackett, 1994.

—. *Ockham's Theory of Propositions: Part II of the Summa logicae.* Trans. Alfred J. Freddoso and Henry Schuurman. Notre Dame, IN: University of Notre Dame Press, 1990.

—. *Ockham's Theory of Terms: Part I of the Summa logicae.* Trans. Michael J. Loux. Notre Dame, IN: University of Notre Dame Press, 1974.

—. "On Possibility and God [*Ord.* 1.43]." Trans. Allan B. Wolter. In *Medieval Philosophy: From St. Augustine to Nicholas of Cusa*, ed John F. Wippel and Wolter, pp. 447–454. New York: Free Press; London: Collier–Macmillan, 1969.

—. *Philosophical Writings: A Selection.* Ed. and trans. Philotheus Boehner. Edinburgh: Nelson, 1957. Rev. ed. Stephen F. Brown. Indianapolis/Cambridge: Hackett, 1990.

—. *Predestination, God's Foreknowledge, and Future Contingents.* Trans. with an introduction, notes, and appendices by Marilyn McCord Adams and Norman Kretzmann. New York: Appleton-Century-Crofts, 1969. New ed. with a new intro. by M.M. Adams. Indianapolis, IN: Hackett, 1983.

—. *Quodlibetal Questions.* Vol. 1: qq. 1–4. Trans. A.J. Freddoso and Francis E. Kelley. Vol. 2: qq. 5–7. Trans. A.J. Freddoso. New Haven: Yale University Press, 1990.

OTHER PRIMARY SOURCES

Abelard, Peter: *see* Peter Abelard.

Albert the Great. *Opera omnia.* Ed. Auguste Borgnet. 38 vols. Paris: Vivès, 1890–1899.

—. *Commentarii in Sententiarum. Opera omnia* 25–30. 1893–1894.

—. *Liber de Praedicabilibus. Opera omnia* 1. 1890.

Alexander of Hales. *Summa theologica.* Studio et cura PP. Collegii S. Bonaventurae. 4 vols. Quaracchi: Collegium S. Bonaventurae, 1924–1948.

Anonymi auctoris franciscani Logica "Ad Rudium." Edited from the MS Vat. lat. 946 with a short introduction, notes and indices by L.M. de Rijk. Nijmegen: Ingenium Publishers, 1981.

Anselm of Canterbury. *Opera omnia.* Ed. Francis S. Schmidt. 6 vols. Seckau: Ex officina abbatiae Seccoviensis; Edinburgh: Nelson, 1938–1961.

Aquinas: *see* Thomas Aquinas.

Aristotle. *The Works of Aristotle Translated into English.* Ed. W.D. Ross. 12 vols. Oxford: Clarendon Press, 1928–1952.

Augustine. *Confessiones.* Ed. L. Verheijen. CCL 27. 1981.

—. *De diversis quaestionibus octoginta tribus.* CCL 43A. Ed. Almut Mützenbecker. 1975.

—. *De doctrina christiana.* Ed. Joseph Martin. CCL 32. 1962.

—. *De Genesi ad litteram.* Ed. Josephus Zycha. CSEL 28. 1894.

—. *De Genesi contra Manichaeos.* PL 34: 15–220.

—. *De immortalitate animae.* PL 32: 1024–1034.

—. *De symbolo.* PL 40:1189–1202.

—. *De Trinitate.* Ed. W.J. Mountain. CCL 50–50A. 1968.

Averroes. *Aristotelis opera cum Averrois commentariis.* Venice: apud Juntas, 1562–1574. 10 vols. Repr. Frankfurt: Minerva, 1962.

—. *Commentarium magnum in Aristotelis De anima libros.* Ed. F.S. Crawford. Cambridge, MA: The Medieval Academy of America, 1953.

Avicenna. *Liber de philosophia prima sive scientia divina.* Ed. S. Van Riet. Avicenna Latinus. 3 vols. Louvain: Peeters; Leiden: Brill, 1977–1983.

Bede, Venerable (Pseudo-). *Sententiae sive axiomata philosophica ex Aristotele et aliis praestantibus collecta.* PL 90: 966–1054.

Boethius. *Commentariorum libri sex in Topica Ciceronis.* PL 64: 1039–1174.

—. *De hebdomadibus.* PL 64: 1311–1314.

—. *Liber de persona et duabus naturis* PL 64: 1355–1412.

—. *De topicis differentiis.* PL 64: 1173–1218.

—. *In Isagogen Porphyrii commenta.* Ed. Samuel Brandt. CSEL 48: 1–132 (editio prima), 133–348 (editio secunda). 1906. "The Second Edition of the Commentaries on the Isagoge of Porphyry." In *Selections from Medieval Philosophers,* ed. and trans. Richard McKeon, 1: 70–99. 2 vols. New York: Charles Scribner's Sons, 1929–1930.

—. *In librum Aristotelis De interpretatione.* Ed. prima et secunda. PL 64: 293–392.

—, trans. *Topica.* Ed. Lorenzo Minio-Paluello. In *Aristoteles Latinus* 5.1–3: 1–179. Brussels: Desclée de Brouwer; Leiden: Brill, 1969.

Boethius of Dacia. *De aeternitate mundi; De summo bono; De somniis.* In *Boethii Daci opera: Opuscula.* Ed. N.J. Green-Pedersen. Copenhagen: G.-E.-C. Gad, 1976. Trans. John F. Wippel. *On the Supreme Good;*

On the Eternity of the World; On Dreams. Mediaeval Sources in Translation 30. Toronto: Pontifical Institute of Mediaeval Studies, 1987.

Bonaventure. *Commentaria in quatuor libros Sententiarum Petri Lombardi.* In *Opera omnia* 1–4. 10 vols. Quaracchi: Collegium S. Bonaventurae, 1882–1902.

Chartularium universitatis parisiensis. Ed. Heinrich Denifle and Émile Chatelain. 4 vols. Paris: Delalain, 1889–1897.

Chatton, Walter: *see* Walter Chatton.

Clementinae (Clementis papae V constitutiones). In *Corpus iuris canonici* 2: cols. 1130–1200. Ed. Aem. Richter and Aem. Friedberg. Leipzig: Bernhard Tauchnitz, 1881.

Damascene, John. *Dialectica.* PG 94.

Dante. *The Divine Comedy.* Trans. with commentary by Charles S. Singleton. 3 vols in 6. Princeton: Princeton University Press, 1970.

Dionysius, the Pseudo-Areopagite. *De caelestia hierarchia.* PG 3.

Gilbert of Poitiers. *The Commentaries on Boethius by Gilbert of Poitiers.* Ed. Nikolaus M. Häring. Studies and Texts 13. Toronto: Pontifical Institute of Mediaeval Studies, 1966.

Giles of Rome. *Egidii Romani Commentaria in octo libros Phisicorum Aristotelis.* Venice, 1502. Repr. Frankfurt: Minerva, 1968.

—. *Theoremata de esse et essentia.* Ed. Edgar Hocedez. Louvain: Museum Lessianum, 1930.

Godfrey of Fontaines. *Quodlibet 7.* In *Les Quodlibet cinq, six et sept de Godefroid de Fontaines.* Ed. M. de Wulf and J. Hoffmans. Philosophes belges, Textes et études 3. Louvain: Institut supérieur de philosophie de l'Université, 1914.

Gratian. *Decretum.* Lyons: Hugo a Porta, 1560.

Grosseteste, Robert: *see* Robert Grosseteste.

Henry of Ghent. *Opera omnia.* Ed. Raymond Macken et al. Louvain: University Press; Leiden: Brill, 1979– .

—. *Quodlibet 1.* Ed R. Macken. *Opera omnia* 5. 1979.

—. *Quodlibet 2.* Ed R. Wielockx. *Opera omnia* 6. 1983.

—. *Quodlibet 6.* Ed G.A. Wilson. *Opera omnia* 10. 1987.

—. *Quodlibet 7.* Ed G.A. Wilson. *Opera omnia* 11. 1991.

—. *Quodlibet 10.* Ed R. Macken. *Opera omnia* 14. 1981.

—. *Quodlibet 12.* Ed J. Decorte. *Opera omnia* 16–17. 1987–1989.

—. *Quodlibeta.* Paris, 1518. Repr. 2 vols. Louvain: Bibliothèque S.J., 1961.

—. *Summa (Quaestiones ordinariae)* 31–34. Ed. R. Macken. *Opera omnia* 27. 1991.

—. *Summa (Quaestiones ordinariae)* 35–40. Ed. G.A. Wilson. *Opera omnia* 28. 1994.

—. *Summa (Quaestiones ordinariae)* 41–46. Ed. L. Hödl. *Opera omnia* 29. 1998.

—. *Summae quaestionum ordinariarum.* Paris, 1520. 2 vols. Repr. St. Bonaventure, NY: Franciscan Institute, 1953.

Henry of Harclay. "Henricus de Harclay: Quaestio de significato conceptus universalis." Ed. Gedeon Gál. *Franciscan Studies* 31 (1971): 178–234.

—. "Henry of Harclay's Disputed Question on the Plurality of Forms. Ed. Armand Maurer. In *Essays in Honour of Anton Charles Pegis,* ed. J. Reginald O'Donnell, pp. 125–159. Toronto: Pontifical Institute of Mediaeval Studies, 1974.

—. "Henry of Harclay's *Quaestio* on Relations in His *Sentences* Commentary: An Edition." Ed. Mark G. Henninger. In *Greek and Medieval Studies in Honor of Leo Sweeney, S.J.,* ed. William J. Carroll and John J. Furlong, pp. 237–254. New York: Peter Lang, 1994.

—. "Henry of Harclay's Question on Relations." Ed. Mark G. Henninger. *Mediaeval Studies* 49 (1987): 76–123.

—. "Henry of Harclay's Questions on the Divine Ideas." Ed. Armand Maurer. *Mediaeval Studies* 23 (1961): 163–193.

—. *Quaestiones utrum aliud a Deo sit simpliciter necesse esse, Utrum anima intellectiva sit immortalis.* Ed. Armand Maurer. In Maurer, "Henry of Harclay's Questions on Immortality." *Mediaeval Studies* 19 (1957): 79–107. Repr. Maurer, *Being and Knowing,* pp. 229–271.

Holcot, Robert: *see* Robert Holcot.

Hume, David. *An Enquiry Concerning Human Understanding.* Ed. L.A. Selby-Bigge. La Salle, IL: Open Court Publishing Co., 1963.

—. *A Treatise of Human Nature.* Ed. L.A. Selby-Bigge. 2nd ed. Oxford: Clarendon Press, 1978.

John Duns Scotus. *Opera omnia.* 26 vols. Paris: Vivès, 1891–1895. Vol. 7: *Quaestiones super libros Metaphysicorum.* Vols. 8–21: *Quaestiones super libros Sententiarum (Ordinatio,* also known as *Opus Oxoniense).* Vols. 22–24: *Reportata Parisiensia.* Vols. 25–26: *Quodlibeta.*

—. *Opera omnia, studio et cura Commissionis Scotisticae ad fidem codicum edita praeside Carolo Balic.* 19 vols. to date. Vatican: Typis Polyglottis Vaticanis, 1950– . Vols. 1–7: *Ordinatio.* Vols. 16–19: *Lectura.*

—. *Duns Scotus, Metaphysician.* Ed. and trans. William A Frank and Allan B. Wolter. West Lafayette, IN: Purdue University Press, 1995. Contains Latin texts with translations.

—. *God and Creatures: The Quodlibetal Questions.* Trans. with introduction and notes by Felix Alluntis and Allan B. Wolter. Princeton and London: Princeton University Press, 1975.

—. *Philosophical Writings: A Selection.* Trans. with Introduction and Notes, by Allan B. Wolter. Indianapolis: Hackett, 1987.

—. *Six Questions on Individuation from the Oxford Lectures*, Book 2, d. 3. Trans. Allan B. Wolter. Washington, DC: Catholic University of America Press, 1981.

—. *A Treatise on God as the First Principle.* A revised Latin text of the *De primo principio.* Trans. Allan B. Wolter. Chicago: Franciscan Herald Press, 1966. Rev. ed. with commentary, 1983.

John of Bassolis. *In quartum Sententiarum opus.* Ed. Oronce Fine. Paris: Nicolas Des Prez, Jean Frellon, François Regnault, 1517.

John of Reading. *Quaestio Ioannis de Reading de necessitate specierum intelligibilium. Defensio doctrinae Scoti.* Ed. Gedeon Gál. *Franciscan Studies* 29 (1969): 66–156.

John of Salisbury. *Ioannis Saresberiensis episcopi carnotensis Metalogicon libri IIII.* Ed. Clemens C.I. Webb. Oxford: Clarendon Press, 1929.

Leibniz, G.W. *Dissertatio de stylo philosophico Nizolii* (1670). In *Opera philosophica,* ed. Johann Eduard Erdmann, pp. 55–70. Berlin: G. Eichleri, 1840.

Liber de causis. Ed. Adriaan Pattin. *Tijdschrift voor Filosofie* 28 (1966): 90–203.

Liber sex principiorum. Ed. Lorenzo Minio-Paluello. In *Aristoteles Latinus* 1.6–7: 33–59. Bruges/Paris: Desclée de Brouwer, 1966.

Lombard, Peter: see Peter Lombard.

Mastrius de Meldula. *Cursus philosophicus: In De anima.* Venice: Hertz, 1708.

Matthew of Aquasparta. *Quaestiones disputatae de fide et de cognitione.* 2nd ed. Quaracchi: Collegium S. Bonaventurae, 1957.

Michael Scot. *Super auctore Spherae.* Venice, 1518.

Newton, Isaac. *Principia philosophiae naturalis.* 2 vols. 3rd ed. Ed. Alexandre Koyré and I. Bernard Cohen. Trans. Andrew Motte and Florian Cajori. Cambridge, MA: Harvard University Press, 1972.

Peter Abelard. *Apologia seu fidei confessio.* PL 178.

—. *Theologia christiana.* Ed. E.M. Buytaert. CCL Continuatio medievalis 12. 1969.

—. *Theologia "Scholarium."* PL 178.

Peter Aureol. *Commentaria in libros Sententiarum.* 2 vols. Rome: Ex typographia Vaticana; A. Zannetti, 1596–1605.

—. *Scriptum super primum Sententiarum* [to Liber 1, d. 8, sec. 24]. Ed. E.M. Buytaert. 2 vols. St. Bonaventure, NY: Franciscan Institute, 1952–1956.

Peter Lombard. *Sententiae in IV libris distinctae.* Spicilegium Bonaventurianum 4. 2 vols. in 3. Grottaferrata (Rome): Collegium S. Bonaventurae, 1971–1981.

Peter of Candia. *Sententiae.* Vatican City, Biblioteca Apostolica Vaticana, MS Vat. lat. 1081.

Peter of Spain. *Tractatus: called afterwards Summulae logicales.* Ed. L.M. de Rijk. Philosophical Texts and Studies 22. Assen: Van Gorcum, 1972.

Peter Olivi. *Quaestiones in secundum librum Sententiarum.* Ed. Bernhard Jansen. 3 vols. Quaracchi: Collegium S. Bonaventurae, 1922–1926.

Petrus de Trabibus. "Petrus de Trabibus on the Absolute and Ordained Power of God." Ed. Gedeon Gál. In *Studies Honoring Ignatius Charles Brady, Friar Minor*, ed. Romano Stephen Almagno and Conrad L. Harkins, pp. 283–292. St. Bonaventure, NY: Franciscan Institute, 1976.

Porphyry. *Isagoge.* Trans. Boethius. Ed. Lorenzo Minio-Paluello. In *Aristoteles Latinus* 1.6–7: 1–31. Bruges/Paris: Desclée de Brouwer, 1966.

(Pseudo) Richard of Campsall. *Logica Campsale Anglicj, valde utilis et realis contra Ockham.* In *The Works of Richard of Campsall* 2. Ed. Edward A. Synan. Studies and Texts 58. Toronto: Pontifical Institute of Mediaeval Studies, 1982.

Richard of Middleton [Ricardus, de Mediavilla]. *Super quatuor libros Sententiarum Petri Lombardi quaestiones subtilissimae.* Brescia, 1591. 4 vols. Repr. Frankfurt: Minerva, 1963.

Richard of St. Victor. *De Trinitate.* PL 196.

Robert Grosseteste. *Commentarius In Posteriorum Analyticorum libros.* Ed. Pietro Rossi. Florence: Olschki, 1981.

Robert Holcot. "Utrum theologia sit scientia: A Quodlibet Question of Robert Holcot, O.P." Ed. Joseph T. Muckle. *Mediaeval Studies* 20 (1958): 127–153.

Roger Bacon. *The Opus Majus of Roger Bacon.* Trans. R.B. Burke. 2 vols. Philadelphia: University of Pennsylvania Press, 1928.

Scotus, John Duns: *see* John Duns Scotus.

Seneca. *Ad Lucilium epistulae morales.* Trans. R.M. Gummere. Loeb Classical Library. 3 vols. Cambridge, MA: Harvard University Press; London: William Heinemann, 1917–1934.

Thomas Aquinas. *Opera omnia.* Ed. S.E. Fretté and Paul Maré. 34 vols. Paris: Vivès: 1871–1880.

—. *Opera omnia*. Rome: Commissio Leonina; Paris: Vrin; etc., 1882– .

—. *Commentaria in librum De caelo et mundo*. Leonine ed. 3. 1886.

—. *Commentaria in Metaphysicam Aristotelis*. Ed. M.R. Cathala and R. Spiazzi. Turin: Marietti, 1971.

—. *Commentaria in octo libros Physicorum*. Leonine ed. 2. 1884.

—. *De aeternitate mundi*. Leonine ed. 43. 1976.

—. *De ente et essentia*. Leonine ed. 43. 1976. *On Being and Essence*. Trans. A. Maurer. 2nd ed. Mediaeval Sources in Translation 1. Toronto: Pontifical Institute of Mediaeval Studies, 1968.

—. *De potentia*. Ed. Paulus M. Pession. In *Quaestiones disputatae*, ed. R. Spiazzi, 2: 1–276. 9th ed. Turin and Rome: Marietti, 1953.

—. *De physico auditu sive Physicorum*. Ed. Fr. Angeli and M. Pirotta. Naples: D'Auria Pontificius, 1953.

—. *De spiritualibus creaturis*. Ed. Leo W. Keeler. Rome: Gregorianum, 1946.

—. *De veritate*. Leonine ed. 22. 1970.

—. *Expositio libri Peryermenias*. Leonine ed. 1.1. 2nd rev. ed. 1989.

—. *Expositio libri Posteriorum*. Leonine ed. 1.2. 2nd rev. ed. 1989.

—. *Expositio super librum Boethii De Trinitate*. Ed. Bruno Decker. Leiden: Brill, 1955. *The Division and Methods of the Sciences. Questions v and vi of His Commentary on the De Trinitate of Boethius*. 4th rev. ed. Mediaeval Sources in Translation 3. Toronto: Pontifical Institute of Mediaeval Studies, 1986.

—. *Quaestiones disputatae De anima*. Leonine ed. 24.1. 1996.

—. *Scriptum super libros Sententiarum*. Ed. Pierre Mandonnet and Maria F. Moos. 4 vols. Paris: Lethielleux, 1929–1947.

—. *Summa contra Gentiles*. Leonine ed. 13–15. 1918–1930.

—. *Summa theologiae*. Leonine ed. 4–12. 1888–1906.

—. *Summa theologiae*. 5 vols. Ottawa: Dominican College, 1941–1945.

Walter Burley. *De puritate artis logicae tractatus longior*. Ed. Philotheus Boehner. St. Bonaventure, NY: Franciscan Institute, 1955.

—. *In Physicam Aristotelis expositio et quaestiones*. Venice, 1501. Repr. Hildesheim/New York: Olms, 1972.

—. *Questions on the De anima of Aristotle by Magister Adam Burley and Dominus Walter Burley*. Ed. Edward A. Synan. Studien und Texte zur Geistesgeschichte des Mittelalters 55. Leiden/New York: Brill, 1997.

—. *Super artem veterem Porphirii et Aristotelis*. Venice, 1497. Repr. Frankfurt: Minerva, 1967.

—. "Walter Burley's Text, *De Diffinitione*." Ed. Herman Shapiro and Frederick Scott. *Mediaeval Studies* 27 (1965): 337–340.

Walter Chatton. *Commento alle Sentenze: Prologo – Questione Terza.* Ed. Luciano Cova. Rome: Edizioni dell' Ateneo, 1973.

—. *Reportatio et lectura super Sententias: Collatio ad librum primum et prologus.* Ed. Joseph C. Wey. Studies and Texts 90. Toronto: Pontifical Institute of Mediaeval Studies, 1989.

William of Alnwick. *Quaestiones disputatae de esse intelligibili et de quodlibet.* Ed. Athanasius Ledoux. Bibliotheca franciscana scholastica medii aevi 10. Quaracchi: Collegium S. Bonaventurae, 1937.

William of Sherwood. *Introduction to Logic.* Trans. with introd. and notes by Norman Kretzmann. Minneapolis: University of Minnesota Press, 1966.

William of Ware. "Quaestio inedita De unitate Dei." Ed. P. Muscat. *Antonianum* 2 (1927): 335–350.

SECONDARY SOURCES

Ackrill, J.L. *Aristotle's "Categories" and "De Interpretatione."* Oxford: Clarendon Press, 1963.

Adams, Marilyn McCord. "Intuitive Cognition, Certainty, and Scepticism in William Ockham." *Traditio* 26 (1970): 389–398.

—. "Ockham on Identity and Distinction." *Franciscan Studies* 36 (1976): 5–74.

—. "Ockham on Truth." *Medioevo* 15 (1989): 143–172.

—. "Ockham's Individualisms." In *Die Gegenwart Ockhams,* ed. Vossenkuhl and Schönberger, pp. 3–24.

—. "Ockham's Nominalism and Unreal Entities." *Philosophical Review* 86 (1977): 144–176.

—. "Ockham's Theory of Natural Signification." *The Monist* 61 (1978): 444–459.

—. "The Structure of Ockham's Moral Theory." *Franciscan Studies* 46 (1986): 1–35.

—. "Universals in the Early Fourteenth Century." In *The Cambridge History of Later Medieval Philosophy,* ed. Kretzmann et al., pp. 411–439.

—. "What Does Ockham Mean by 'Supposition'?" *Notre Dame Journal of Formal Logic* 17 (1976): 375–391.

—. *William Ockham.* Notre Dame, IN: University of Notre Dame Press, 1987. Repr. paperback ed. 1989.

—, trans.: *see* THE WORKS OF WILLIAM OF OCKHAM: Translations.

Alféri, Pierre. *Guillaume d'Ockham: Le singulier.* Paris: Minuit, 1989.

Ariew, Roger. "Did Ockham Use His Razor?" *Franciscan Studies* 37 (1977): 5–17.

Ashworth, E. Jennifer. "'Do Words Signify Ideas or Things?': The Scholastic Sources of Locke's Theory of Language." *Journal of the History of Philosophy* 19 (1981): 299–326.

Bannach, Klaus. *Die Lehre von der doppelten Macht Gottes bei Wilhelm von Ockham.* Wiesbaden: Franz Steiner, 1975.

Barth, Timotheus. "Being, Univocity, and Analogy according to Duns Scotus." In *John Duns Scotus, 1265–1965*, ed. John K. Ryan and Bernardine M. Bonansea, pp. 210–262. Washington, DC: Catholic University of America Press, 1965.

Baudry, Léon. "En lisant Jean le chanoine. Les rapports de Guillaume d'Ockham et de W. Burley." *Archives d'histoire doctrinale et littéraire du moyen âge* 9 (1934): 175–197.

—. "Guillaume d'Occam, critique des preuves scotistes de l'unicité de Dieu." *Archives d'histoire doctrinale et littéraire du moyen âge* 20 (1953): 99–112.

—. *Guillaume d'Occam: Sa vie, ses oeuvres, ses idées sociales et politiques.* 1: *L'homme et les oeuvres.* Paris: Vrin, 1949.

—. "Les rapports de la raison et de la foi selon Guillaume d'Occam." *Archives d'histoire doctrinale et littéraire du moyen âge* 29 (1962): 33–92.

—. *See also* REFERENCE WORKS.

Beckmann, Jan P. "Ontologisches Prinzip oder methodologische Maxime? Ockham und der Ökonomiegedanke einst und jetzt." In *Die Gegenwart Ockhams*, ed. Vossenkuhl and Schönberger, pp. 191–207.

—. *Wilhelm von Ockham.* Munich: C.H. Beck, 1995.

—. *See also* REFERENCE WORKS.

Bérubé, Camille. *La connaissance de l'individuel au moyen âge.* Montréal: Presses de l'Université; Paris: Presses Universitaires de France, 1964.

Bird, Otto. "Topic and Consequence in Ockham's Logic." *Notre Dame Journal of Formal Logic* 2 (1961): 65–78.

Blanchette, Oliva. *The Perfection of the Universe according to Aquinas.* University Park, PA: University of Pennsylvania Press, 1992.

Boehner, Philotheus. *Collected Articles on Ockham.* Ed. Eligius M. Buytaert. St. Bonaventure, NY: Franciscan Institute, 1958.

—. "In Propria Causa: A Reply to Professor Pegis' 'Concerning William of Ockham.'" *Franciscan Studies*, new ser. 5 (1945): 37–54. Repr. *Collected Articles on Ockham*, pp. 300–319.

—. "The Metaphysics of William Ockham." *The Review of Metaphysics* 1 (1947): 59–86. Repr. *Collected Articles on Ockham*, pp. 373–399.

—. "Ockham's Theory of Signification." *Franciscan Studies* 6 (1946): 143–170. Repr. *Collected Articles on Ockham*, pp. 201–232.

—. "*Notitia Intuitiva* of Non-Existents according to Peter Aureoli, OFM (1322)." *Franciscan Studies* 8 (1948): 388–416.

—. "The *Notitia Intuitiva* of Non-Existents according to William Ockham." *Traditio* 1 (1943): 223–275. Repr. *Collected Articles on Ockham*, pp. 268–319.

—. "The Realistic Conceptualism of William Ockham." *Traditio* 4 (1946): 307–335. Repr. *Collected Articles on Ockham*, pp. 156–174.

—. "The Relative Date of Ockham's Commentary on the Sentences." *Franciscan Studies* 11 (1951): 305–316. Repr. *Collected Articles on Ockham*, pp. 96–110.

—. "The Text Tradition of Ockham's Ordinatio." *The New Scholasticism* 16 (1942): 203–241. Repr. *Collected Articles on Ockham*, pp. 110–127.

—. "Zu Ockhams Beweis der Existenz Gottes." *Franziskanische Studien* 32 (1950): 50–69. Repr. *Collected Articles on Ockham*, pp. 399–420.

—, ed. and trans.: *see* THE WORKS OF WILLIAM OF OCKHAM: Translations; OTHER PRIMARY SOURCES: Walter Burley.

Boh, Ivan. "Divine Omnipotence in the Early *Sentences*." In *Divine Omniscience and Omnipotence in Medieval Philosophy*, ed. Tamar Rudavsky, pp. 185–211.

—. "Walter Burley." In *Individuation in Scholasticism*, ed. Gracia, pp. 347–372.

Boler, John Francis. *Charles Peirce and Scholastic Realism: A Study of Peirce's Relation to John Duns Scotus.* Seattle: University of Washington Press, 1963.

—. "Intuitive and Abstractive Cognition." In *The Cambridge History of Later Medieval Philosophy*, ed. Kretzmann et al., pp. 460–478.

—. "Ockham's Cleaver." *Franciscan Studies* 45 (1985): 120–144.

Bolton, Robert. "The Problem of Dialectical Reasoning (Συλλογισμός) in Aristotle." In *Logic, Dialectic, and Science in Aristotle*, ed. Bolton and Robin Smith, special issue of *Ancient Philosophy* 14 (1994): 99–132.

Boulnois, Olivier. "Réelles intentions: nature commune et universaux selon Duns Scot." *Revue de métaphysique et morale* 97 (1992): 3–33.

Bourke, Vernon J. *History of Ethics.* Garden City, NY: Doubleday, 1968.

Brampton, C.K. "Nominalism and the Law of Parsimony." *The Modern Schoolman* 41 (1963–1964): 273–281.

—. "Ockham and His Authorship of the *Summulae Physicorum*." *Isis* 55 (1964): 418–426.

—. "Traditions Relating to the Death of William of Ockham." *Archivum Franciscanum Historicum* 53 (1960): 442–449.

Brown, Stephen F. "A Modern Prologue to Ockham's Natural Philosophy." In *Sprache und Erkenntnis im Mittelalter*, ed. J.P. Beckmann et al., Miscellanea Mediaevalia 13.1-2, pp. 107–129. Berlin/New York: de Gruyter, 1981.

—. "Ockham and Final Causality." In *Studies in Medieval Philosophy*, ed. John F. Wippel, pp. 249–272. Washington, DC: Catholic University of America Press, 1987.

—. "Sources for Ockham's Prologue to the *Sentences* – Part II." *Franciscan Studies* 5 (1967): 39–107.

—. "Walter Burleigh's Treatise *De Suppositionibus* and its Influence on William of Ockham." *Franciscan Studies* 32 (1972): 15–64.

Buescher, Gabriel. *The Eucharistic Teaching of William Ockham*. St. Bonaventure, NY: Franciscan Institute, 1950.

Burr, David. "Quantity and Eucharistic Presence: The Debate from Olivi through Ockham." *Collectanea Franciscana* 44 (1974): 5–44.

Buytaert, E.M., ed.: *see* Boehner, Philotheus.

Callahan, Thomas G. "William Ockham and Natural Law." PhD dissertation. Michigan State University, 1975.

Callus, Daniel A. *The Condemnation of St. Thomas at Oxford*. Westminster, MD: The Newman Bookshop, 1946.

Chenu, Marie-Dominique. "*Authentica* et *magistralia*: Deux lieux théologiques aux XII–XIII siècles." *Divus Thomas* (Piacenza) 28 (1925): 257–285.

—. "Aux origines de la 'science moderne'." *Revue des sciences philosophiques et théologiques* 29 (1940): 206–217.

—. *Is Theology a Science?* Trans. A.H.N. Green-Urmtase. New York: Hawthorn Books, 1959.

—. *La théologie comme science au XIIIe siècle*. 3rd ed. Paris: Vrin, 1969.

Clagett, Marshall. *Science of Mechanics in the Middle Ages*. Madison, WI: University of Wisconsin Press, 1959.

Clark, David W. "Voluntarism and Rationalism in the Ethics of Ockham." *Franciscan Studies* 31 (1971): 72–87.

—. "William of Ockham on Right Reason." *Speculum* 48 (1973): 13–36.

Congar, Yves M.-J. *A History of Theology*. Trans. and ed. Hunter Guthrie. Garden City, NY: Doubleday, 1968.

Copleston, Frederick. *A History of Philosophy*. 3: *Late Mediaeval and Renaissance Philosophy*, part 1. Garden City, NY: Doubleday, 1963.

Courtenay, William J. *Adam Wodeham: An Introduction to His Life and Writings.* Leiden: Brill, 1978.

—. "*Antiqui* and *moderni* in Late Medieval Thought." *Journal of the History of Ideas* 48 (1987): 3–10.

—. *Capacity and Volition: A History of the Distinction of Absolute and Ordained Power.* Bergamo: Pierluigi Lubrina, 1990.

—. "Covenant and Causality in Pierre d'Ailly." *Speculum* 46 (1971): 94–119. Repr. in his *Covenant and Causality in Medieval Thought*, essay IX. London: Variorum, 1984.

—. "The Dialectic of Omnipotence in the High and Late Middle Ages." In *Divine Omniscience and Omnipotence in Medieval Philosophy*, ed. Tamar Rudavsky, pp. 243–269.

—. "John of Mirecourt and Gregory of Rimini on Whether God Can Undo the Past." *Recherches de théologie ancienne et médiévale* 39 (1972): 224–256; 40 (1973): 147–174.

—. "Nominalism and Late Medieval Religion." In *The Pursuit of Holiness in Late Medieval and Renaissance Religion*, ed. Charles Trinkaus and Heiko A. Oberman, pp. 26–59. Leiden: Brill, 1974.

—. "Ockham, Chatton, and the London *Studium*: Observations on Recent Changes in Ockham's Biography." In *Die Gegenwart Ockhams*, ed. Vossenkuhl and Schönberger, pp. 327–337.

—. "The Reception of Ockham's Thought at the University of Paris." In *Preuve et raisons à l'Université de Paris: Logique, ontologie, et théologie au XIVe siècle*, ed. Zénon Kaluza and Paul Vignaux, pp. 43–64. Paris: Vrin, 1984.

—. "The Reception of Ockham's Thought in Fourteenth-Century England." In *From Ockham to Wyclif*, ed. Hudson and Wilks, pp. 89–107.

—. *Schools and Scholars in Fourteenth-Century England.* Princeton, NJ: Princeton University Press, 1987.

—, and Katherine H. Tachau. "Ockham, Ockhamists, and the English-German Nation at Paris, 1339–1341." *History of Universities* 2 (1982), pp. 53–96.

Cova, Luciano. "L'unità della scienza teologica nella polemica di Walter Chatton con Guglielmo d'Ockham." *Franciscan Studies* 45 (1985): 189–230.

—, ed.: *see also* OTHER PRIMARY SOURCES: Walter of Chatton.

Crombie, Alistair C. *Medieval and Early Modern Science.* 2 vols. Garden City, NY: Doubleday, 1959.

Damiata, Marino. *I Problemi di G. d'Ockham.* 1: *La Conoscenza*; 2: *Dio.* Florence: Edizioni "Studi francescani," 1996, 1998.

—. "Ockham e San Tommaso d'Aquino." *Studi francescani* 91 (1994): 21–88.

Day, Sebastian J. *Intuitive Cognition: A Key to the Significance of the Later Scholastics.* St. Bonaventure, NY: Franciscan Institute, 1947.

Deman, Thomas. "*Probabilis.*" *Revue des sciences philosophiques et théologiques* 22 (1933): 260–290.

Denzinger, Heinrich, and A. Schönmetzer, eds. *Enchiridion Symbolorum.* 36th ed. Freiburg-i.-Br.: Herder, 1976.

Duhem, Pierre. *Études sur Léonard de Vinci.* 3 vols. Paris: A. Herman, 1906–1913.

—. *Le système du monde.* 10 vols. Paris: A. Hermann, 1913–1959.

Dumont, Stephen D. "The Origin of Scotus's Theory of Synchronic Contingency." *The Modern Schoolman* 72 (1995): 149–167.

—. "The *Propositio Famosa Scoti*: Duns Scotus and Ockham on the Possibility of a Science of Theology." *Dialogue* 31 (1992): 415–429.

—. "Theology as a Science and Duns Scotus's Distinction between Intuitive and Abstractive Cognition." *Speculum* 64 (1989): 579–599.

—. "Time, Contradiction and Freedom of the Will in the Late Thirteenth Century." *Documenti e studi sulla tradizione filosofica medievale* (Rivista della Società internazionale italiano per lo Studio del Medioevo Latino) 3 (1992): 561–597.

—. "The Univocity of the Concept of Being in the Fourteenth Century: John Duns Scotus and William of Alnwick." *Mediaeval Studies* 49 (1987): 1–75.

Dunphy, William B. "St. Albert and the Five Causes." *Archives d'histoire doctrinale et littéraire du moyen âge* 41 (1966): 7–21.

Effler, Roy R. *John Duns Scotus and the Principle "Omne quod movetur ab alio movetur."* St. Bonaventure, NY: Franciscan Institute, 1962.

Élie, Hubert. *Le complexe significabile.* Paris: Vrin, 1936.

Etzkorn, Girard J. "Ockham's View of the Human Passions in the Light of his Philosophical Anthropology." In *Die Gegenwart Ockhams*, ed. Vossenkuhl and Schönberger, pp. 265–287.

Freppert, Lucan. *The Basis of Morality according to William Ockham.* Chicago: Franciscan Herald Press, 1988.

Funkenstein, Amos. *Theology and the Scientific Imagination from the Middle Ages to the Seventeenth Century.* Princeton: Princeton University Press, 1986.

Gabriel, Astrik L. "*Via Antiqua* and *Via Moderna* and the Migration of Paris Students and Masters to the German Universities in the Fifteenth Century." In *Antiqui und Moderni: Traditionsbewußtsein und Fortschrittsbewußtsein im späten Mittelalter*, ed. Albert Zimmermann, pp. 439–483. Berlin/New York: de Gruyter, 1974.

Gál, Gedeon. "Adam of Wodeham's Question on the *Complexe Significabile* as the Immediate Object of Scientific Knowledge." *Franciscan Studies* 37 (1977): 66–102.

—. "Gualteri de Chatton et Guillelmi de Ockham controversia de natura conceptus universalis." *Franciscan Studies* 27 (1967): 191–199.

—. "William of Ockham Died 'Impenitent' in April 1347." *Franciscan Studies* 42 (1982): 90–95.

—, ed.: *see* OTHER PRIMARY SOURCES: Henry of Harclay; John of Reading; Petrus de Trabibus.

Garvens, Anita. "Die Grundlagen der Ethik Wilhelms von Ockham." *Franziskanische Studien* 21 (1934): 243–273, 360–408.

Geach, Peter. "Nominalism." In *Aquinas: A Collection of Critical Essays*, ed. Anthony Kenny, pp. 139–154. Garden City, NY: Doubleday, 1969.

Geiger, L.B. "Les idées divines dans l'oeuvre de S. Thomas." In *St. Thomas Aquinas 1274–1974: Commemorative Studies*, ed. Armand Maurer, 1: 175–209. Toronto: Pontifical Institute of Mediaeval Studies, 1974.

Gelber, Hester, G. "I Cannot Tell a Lie: Hugh of Lawton's Critique of Ockham on Mental Language." *Franciscan Studies* 44 (1984): 141–179.

—. "Logic and the Trinity: A Clash of Values in Scholastic Thought, 1300–1335." 2 vols. PhD dissertation. University of Wisconsin, 1974.

Gewirth, Alan. "Philosophy and Political Thought in the Fourteenth Century." In *The Forward Movement of the Fourteenth Century*, ed. Francis Lee Utley, pp. 125–164. Columbus, OH: Ohio State University Press, 1961.

Gierke, Otto von. *Political Theories of the Middle Ages*. Trans. F.W. Maitland. Boston: Cambridge University Press, 1958.

Gilbert, Neal W. "Ockham, Wyclif, and the 'via moderna.'" In *Antiqui und Moderni: Traditionsbewußtsein und Fortschrittsbewußtsein im späten Mittelalter*, ed. Albert Zimmermann, pp. 85–125. Berlin/New York: de Gruyter, 1974.

Gilson, Etienne. "Avicenne et les origines de la notion de cause efficiente." In *Atti del XII Congresso internazionale di filosofia* 9: 121–130. 12 vols. Florence: Sansoni, 1958–1961.

—. *Being and Some Philosophers*. 2nd ed. Toronto: Pontifical Institute of Mediaeval Studies, 1952.

—. *Christian Philosophy*. Trans. Armand Maurer. Etienne Gilson Series 17. Toronto: Pontifical Institute of Mediaeval Studies, 1993.

—. *The Christian Philosophy of Saint Augustine*. Trans. Lawrence E.M. Lynch. New York: Random House, Vintage Books, 1960.

—. *Elements of Christian Philosophy*. Garden City, NY: Doubleday, 1960.

—. *History of Christian Philosophy in the Middle Ages*. New York: Random House, 1955.

—. *Jean Duns Scot*. Paris: Vrin, 1952.

—. "Notes pour l'histoire de la cause efficiente." *Archives d'histoire doctrinale et littéraire du moyen âge* 37 (1962): 7–31.

—. *La philosophie au moyen âge*. Paris: Vrin, 1944.

—. *The Philosophy of St. Bonaventure*. Trans. Illtyd Trethowan and Frank Sheed. 1938. Repr. Paterson, NJ: St. Anthony Guild Press, 1965.

—. "Remarques sur l'expérience en métaphysique." *Proceedings of the XIth International Congress of Philosophy/Actes du XIe Congrès international de philosophie* (Brussels, August 20–26, 1953), 4: 5–10. 14 vols. Amsterdam: North–Holland Publishing, 1953. Trans. Armand Maurer as "Remarks on Experience in Metaphysics." In Maurer, "Gilson's Use of History in Philosophy," *Thomistic Papers* 5 (1990): 25–48, at pp. 40–48.

—. *The Spirit of Mediaeval Philosophy*. Trans. A.H.C. Downes. New York: Charles Scribner's Sons, 1936.

—. *Le thomisme*. 6th ed. Paris: Vrin, 1965. 5th ed. trans. Laurence K. Shook. *The Christian Philosophy of St. Thomas Aquinas*. New York: Random House, 1956.

—. *The Unity of Philosophical Experience*. New York: Charles Scribner's Sons, 1937.

Goddu, André. *The Physics of William of Ockham*. Leiden/Cologne: Brill, 1984.

Gracia, Jorge J.E. *Individuality: An Essay on the Foundations of Metaphysics*. Albany, NY: State University of New York Press, 1988.

—. *Introduction to the Problem of Individuation in the Early Middle Ages*. Munich: Philosophia Verlag, 1984. 2nd ed. 1988.

—, ed. *Individuation in Scholasticism: The Later Middle Ages and the Counter-Reformation (1150–1650)*. Albany, NY: State University of New York Press, 1994.

Grajewski, Maurice. *The Formal Distinction of Duns Scotus*. Washington, DC: Catholic University of America Press, 1944.

Green–Pedersen, N.J. *The Tradition of the Topics in the Middle Ages: The Commentaries on Aristotle's and Boethius' "Topics."* Vienna: Philosophia, 1984.

Guelluy, Robert. *Philosophie et théologie chez Guillaume d'Ockham.* Louvain: Nauwelaerts; Paris: Vrin, 1947.

Henninger, Mark G. "Henry of Harclay." In *Individuation in Scholasticism*, ed. Gracia, pp. 333–346.

—. "Some Late Medieval Theories of the Category of Relation." PhD dissertation. University of California, Los Angeles, 1984.

—, ed.: *see* OTHER PRIMARY SOURCES: Henry of Harclay.

Henry, Desmond P. "Ockham and the Formal Distinction." *Franciscan Studies* 25 (1965): 285–292.

Hochstetter, Erich. *Studien zur Metaphysik und Erkenntnislehre Wilhelms von Ockham.* Berlin: de Gruyter, 1927.

Hoffmann, Fritz. *Ockham-Rezeption und Ockham-Kritik im Jahrzehnt nach Wilhelm von Ockham in Oxford 1322–1332.* Beiträge zur Geschichte der Philosophie und Theologie des Mittelalters, neue Folge 50. Münster: Aschendorff, 1998.

Honnefelder, Ludger. *Ens inquantum ens: Der Begriff des Seienden als solchen als Gegenstand der Metaphysik nach der Lehre des Johannes Duns Scotus.* Beiträge zur Geschichte der Philosophie und Theologie des Mittelalters, neue Folge 16. Münster: Aschendorff, 1979.

—, Rega Wood, and Mechthild Dreyer, eds. *John Duns Scotus: Metaphysics and Ethics.* Leiden/New York: Brill, 1996.

Hübener, Wolfgang. "*Oratio mentalis* and *oratio vocalis* in der Philosophie des 14. Jahrhunderts." In *Sprache und Erkenntnis im Mittelalter*, ed. Jan P. Beckmann et al., 1: 488–497. 2 vols. Berlin/New York: de Gruyter, 1981.

Hudson, Anne, and Michael Wilks, eds. *From Ockham to Wyclif.* Oxford: Blackwell, for the Ecclesiastical History Society, 1987.

Jordan, Michael. "What's New in Ockham's Formal Distinction?" *Franciscan Studies* 45 (1985): 97–110.

Kelley, Francis E. "Ockham: Avignon, Before and After." In *From Ockham to Wyclif*, ed. Hudson and Wilks, pp. 1–18.

—. "Some Observations on the 'Fictum' Theory in Ockham and its Relation to Hervaeus Natalis." *Franciscan Studies* 38 (1978): 260–282.

Kennedy, Leonard A. *Peter of Ailly and the Harvest of Fourteenth-Century Philosophy.* Lewiston, NY: Edwin Mellen Press, 1986.

Kenny, Anthony. *The Five Ways: Saint Thomas Aquinas' Proofs of God's Existence.* London: Routledge & Kegan Paul, 1969.

Kent, Bonnie. *Virtues of the Will: The Transformation of Ethics in the Late Thirteenth Century.* Washington, DC: Catholic University of America Press, 1995.

King, Peter. "Duns Scotus on the Reality of Self-Change." In *Self-Motion from Aristotle to Newton,* ed. Mary Louise Gill and James G. Lennox, pp. 227–290. Princeton, NJ: Princeton University Press, 1994.

Kneale, William and Martha. *The Development of Logic.* Oxford: Clarendon Press, 1962.

Knysh, George. *Political Ockhamism.* Winnipeg: WCU Council of Learned Societies, 1996.

Koch, J. "Neue Aktenstücke zu dem gegen Wilhelm Ockham in Avignon geführten Prozess." *Recherches de théologie ancienne et médiévale* 7 (1935): 353–380; and 8 (1936): 79–93, 168–197.

Kölmel, Wilhelm. "Das Naturrecht bei Wilhelm Ockham." *Franziskanische Studien* 35 (1953): 39–85.

Kossel, Clifford. "Principles of St. Thomas's Distinction between *Esse* and *Ratio* of Relation." *The Modern Schoolman* 24 (1946): 19–36; and 25 (1947): 93–107.

Kretzmann, Norman. "Ockham and the Creation of the Beginningless World." *Franciscan Studies* 45 (1985): 1–31.

— et al., eds. *The Cambridge History of Later Medieval Philosophy: From the Rediscovery of Aristotle to the Disintegration of Scholasticism, 1100–1600.* Cambridge: Cambridge University Press, 1982.

—, trans.: *see* THE WORKS OF WILLIAM OF OCKHAM: Translations.

Lagarde, Georges de. *La naissance de l'esprit laïque au déclin du moyen âge.* Original edition. 6 vols. Saint-Paul-Trois-Châteaux (Drôme): Éditions Béatrice; Paris: Droz, 1934–1946. Nouvelle édition, refondue et complétée. 5 vols. Louvain: Éditions Nauwelaerts; Paris: Béatrice Nauwelaerts, 1956–1970. 1: *Bilan du XIIIe siècle* (3rd ed., 1956); 2: *Secteur social de la Scholastique* (2nd ed., 1958); 3: *Le Defensor Pacis* (1970); 4: *Guillaume d'Ockham: Défense de l'empire* (1962); 5: *Guillaume d'Ockham: Critique des structures ecclésiales* (1963).

Leff, Gordon. *William of Ockham: The Metamorphosis of Scholastic Discourse.* Manchester: Manchester University Press, 1975.

Lewry, P. Osmund, ed. *The Rise of British Logic.* Acts of the Sixth European Symposium on Medieval Logic and Semantics, Balliol College,

Oxford, 19–24 June, 1983. Papers in Mediaeval Studies 7. Toronto: Pontifical Institute of Mediaeval Studies, 1983.

Lottin, Odon. *Psychologie et morale aux XIIe et XIIIe siècles*. 6 vols. Louvain: Abbaye du Mont César, 1942–1949.

Loux, Michael J., ed. and trans.: *see* THE WORKS OF WILLIAM OF OCKHAM: Translations.

Macken, Raymond. "La temporalité radicale de la créature selon Henri de Gand." *Recherches de théologie ancienne et médiévale* 38 (1971): 211–272.

—, ed: *see also* OTHER PRIMARY SOURCES: Henry of Ghent.

Maier, Anneliese. *An der Grenze von Scholastik und Naturwissenschaft*. 2nd ed. Rome: Edizioni di Storia e Letteratura, 1952.

—. "Das Problem der Quantität oder der räumlichen Ausdehnung." In her *Metaphysische Hintergründe der spätscholastischen Naturphilosophie*, pp. 141–223. Rome: Edizioni di Storia e Letteratura, 1955.

—. "Das Problem der 'Species Sensibiles in Medio' und die neue Naturphilosophie des 14 Jahrhunderts." *Freiburger Zeitschrift für Philosophie und Theologie* 10 (1963): 3–32. Repr. in her *Ausgehendes Mittelalter: gesammelte Aufsätze zur Geistesgeschichte des 14. Jahrhunderts*, 2: 419–451. 2 vols. Rome: Edizioni di Storia e Letteratura, 1964–1977.

—. "Diskussionen über das aktuell Unendliche in der ersten Hälfte des 14 Jahrhunderts." *Divus Thomas* (Freiburg) 25 (1947): 147–166; 317–337.

—. "'Ergebnisse' der spätscholastischen Naturphilosophie." *Scholastik* 35 (1960): 161–187.

—. *Zwei Grundprobleme der scholastischen Naturphilosophie*. Rome: Edizioni di Storia e Letteratura, 1951.

—. *Zwischen Philosophie und Mechanik*. Rome: Edizioni di Storia e Letteratura, 1958.

Maritain, Jacques. "The Conflict of Methods at the End of the Middle Ages." *The Thomist* 3 (1941): 527–538.

—. *Philosophy of Nature*. Trans. Imelda Byrne. New York: Philosophical Library, 1951.

Maurer, Armand. *Being and Knowing. Studies in Thomas Aquinas and Later Medieval Philosophers*. Papers in Mediaeval Studies 10. Toronto: Pontifical Institute of Mediaeval Studies, 1990.

—. "Form and Essence in the Philosophy of St. Thomas." *Mediaeval Studies* 13 (1951): 165–176. Repr. *Being and Knowing*, pp. 3–18

—. "Francis of Meyronnes' Defense of Epistemological Realism." In *Studia Mediaevalia et Mariologica in Honour of P. Carolo Balić*, pp.

203–225. Rome: Pontificium Athenaeum Antonianum, 1971. Repr. *Being and Knowing*, pp. 311–331.

—. *Medieval Philosophy*. Étienne Gilson Series 4. Toronto: Pontifical Institute of Mediaeval Studies, 1962. 2nd rev. ed. 1982.

—. "Method in Ockham's Nominalism." *The Monist* 61 (1978): 426–443. Repr. *Being and Knowing*, pp. 403–421.

—. "Ockham on the Possibility of a Better World." *Mediaeval Studies* 38 (1976): 291–312. Repr. *Being and Knowing*, pp. 383–402.

—. "Ockham's Conception of the Unity of Science." *Mediaeval Studies* 20 (1958): 98–112.

—. "Ockham's Razor and Chatton's Anti-Razor." *Mediaeval Studies* 46 (1984): 463–475. Repr. *Being and Knowing*, pp. 431–443.

—. "Ockham's Razor and Dialectical Reasoning." *Mediaeval Studies* 58 (1996): 52–65.

—. "The Role of Divine Ideas in the Theology of William of Ockham." *Studies Honoring Ignatius Charles Brady, Friar Minor*. Ed. R.S. Almagno and C.L. Harkins. St. Bonaventure, NY: Franciscan Institute, 1976, pp. 357–377. Repr. *Being and Knowing*, pp. 363–381.

—. "The Unity of a Science: St. Thomas and the Nominalists." *St. Thomas Aquinas 1274–1974: Commemorative Studies*, ed. A. Maurer, 2: 269–291. Toronto: Pontifical Institute of Mediaeval Studies, 1974. Repr. *Being and Knowing*, pp. 71–93.

—. "William of Ockham." In *Individuation in Scholasticism*, ed. Gracia, pp. 373–396.

—. "William of Ockham on Logic and Reality." In *Sprache und Erkenntnis im Mittelalter*, ed. J.P. Beckmann et al., pp. 795–802. Miscellanea Mediaevalia 13.1–2. Berlin/New York: de Gruyter, 1981. Repr. *Being and Knowing*, pp. 423–430.

—, and Alfred P. Caird. "The Role of Infinity in the Thought of Francis of Meyronnes." *Mediaeval Studies* 33 (1971): 201–227. Repr. *Being and Knowing*, pp. 333–359.

—, ed.: *see* OTHER PRIMARY SOURCES: Henry of Harclay; Thomas Aquinas.

McGrade, Arthur S. "Plenty of Nothing: Ockham's Commitment to Real Possibles." *Franciscan Studies* 45 (1985): 145–156.

McGuire, J.E. "Natural Motion and Its Causes: Newton on the *vis insita* of Bodies." In *Self-Motion from Aristotle to Newton*, ed. Mary Louise

Gill and James G. Lennox, pp. 305–329. Princeton, NJ: Princeton University Press, 1994.

McMullin, Ernan, ed. *The Concept of Matter*. Notre Dame, IN: University of Notre Dame Press, 1963.

Menges, Matthew C. *The Concept of Univocity regarding the Predication of God and Creatures according to William Ockham*. St. Bonaventure, NY: Franciscan Institute, 1952.

Moody, Ernest A. *The Logic of William of Ockham*. New York: Sheed & Ward, 1935. 2nd ed. 1965.

—. "Ockham, Buridan, and Nicholas of Autrecourt." *Franciscan Studies* 7 (1947): 113–146. Repr. in his *Studies in Medieval Philosophy, Science, and Logic*, pp. 127–160. Berkeley: University of California Press, 1975.

Moore, Walter L. "Via Moderna." In *Dictionary of the Middle Ages*, ed. in chief, Joseph R. Strayer, 12: 406–409. 13 vols. New York: Charles Scribner's Sons, 1982–1989.

Moorman, John. *A History of the Franciscan Order: From Its Origin to the Year 1517*. Oxford: Clarendon Press, 1968.

Muckle, Joseph T., ed.: *see* OTHER PRIMARY SOURCES: Robert Holcot.

Normore, Calvin, G. "Divine Omniscience, Omnipotence, and Future Contingents: An Overview." In *Divine Omniscience and Omnipotence in Medieval Philosophy*, ed. Tamar Rudavsky, pp. 3–22.

—. "Ockham on Mental Language." In *Historical Foundations of Cognitive Science*, ed. J.C. Smith, pp. 53–70. Dordrecht: Reidel, 1990.

—. "The Tradition of Medieval Nominalism." In *Studies in Medieval Philosophy*, ed. John F. Wippel, pp. 201–217. Washington, DC: Catholic University of America Press, 1987.

Nuchelmans, Gabriel. "The Semantics of Propositions." In *The Cambridge History of Later Medieval Philosophy*, ed. Kretzmann et al., pp. 197–210.

Oakley, Francis. "Medieval Theories of Natural Law: William of Ockham and the Significance of the Voluntarist Tradition." *Natural Law Forum* 6 (1961): 65–83.

Oberman, Heiko A. *The Harvest of Medieval Theology: Gabriel Biel and Late Medieval Nominalism*. Cambridge, MA: Harvard University Press, 1963.

Owen, G.E.L. "Tithenai ta phainomena." In *Aristote et les problèmes de méthode: Communications présentées au Symposium Aristotelicum*, ed. S. Mansion, pp. 83–103. Louvain: Institut Supérieur de Philosophie, 1961. Repr. in his *Logic, Science, and Dialectic: Collected Papers in Greek Philosophy*, ed. Martha Nussbaum, pp. 239–251. Ithaca, NY: Cornell University Press, 1986.

—, ed. *Aristotle on Dialectic: The Topics*. Proceedings of the Third Symposium Aristotelicum. Oxford: Clarendon Press, 1968.

Owens, Joseph. "Common Nature: A Point of Comparison between Thomistic and Scotistic Metaphysics." *Mediaeval Studies* 19 (1957): 1–14.

—. "Diversity and Community of Being in St. Thomas Aquinas." *Mediaeval Studies* 22 (1960): 257–302.

—. *The Doctrine of Being in the Aristotelian Metaphysics: A Study in the Greek Background of Mediaeval Thought*. 3rd ed. Toronto: Pontifical Institute of Mediaeval Studies, 1978.

—. *An Elementary Christian Metaphysics*. Milwaukee: Bruce Publishing, 1963.

—. "Thomas Aquinas." In *Individuation in Scholasticism*, ed. Gracia, pp. 173–194.

—. "Unity and Essence in St. Thomas Aquinas." *Mediaeval Studies* 23 (1961): 240–259.

Panaccio, Claude. "From Mental Word to Mental Language." *Philosophical Topics* 20 (1992): 125–147.

—. "Intuition, abstraction et langage mental dans la théorie occamiste de la connaissance." *Revue de métaphysique et morale* 97 (1992): 61–81.

—. *Les mots, les concepts et les choses: La sémantique de Guillaume d'Occam et le nominalisme d'aujourd'hui*. Montréal: Bellarmin; Paris: Vrin, 1991.

Pasnau, Robert. *Theories of Cognition in the Later Middle Ages*. Cambridge: Cambridge University Press, 1997.

Pater, W.A. de. *Les Topiques d'Aristote et la dialectique platonicienne: La méthodologie de la définition*. Fribourg: Éditions St-Paul, 1965.

Paulus, Jean. *Henri de Gand: Essai sur les tendances de sa métaphysique*. Paris: Vrin, 1938.

Pegis, Anton C. "Concerning William of Ockham." *Traditio* 2 (1944): 465–480.

—. "The Dilemma of Being and Unity." *Essays in Thomism*. Ed. R.E. Brennan. New York, 1942, pp. 151–183.

—. "Matthew of Aquasparta and the Cognition of Non-Being." In *Scholastica ratione historico-critico instauranda*. Congressus Scholasticus Internationalis, pp. 461–480. Rome: Bibliotheca Pontificium Athenaeum Antonianum, 1951.

—. "Necessity and Liberty: An Historical Note on St. Thomas Aquinas." *The New Scholasticism* 15 (1941): 18–45.

—. "Some Recent Interpretations of Ockham." *Speculum* 23 (1948): 452–463.

—. *St. Thomas and the Problem of the Soul in the Thirteenth Century*. Toronto: Pontifical Institute of Mediaeval Studies, 1934. Repr. 1978.

Peirce, Charles Sanders. *Collected Papers of Charles Sanders Peirce.* Gen. ed. Charles Hartshorne. Vol. 8: ed. Arthur W. Burks. Cambridge, MA: Harvard University Press, 1958.

Pelletier, Yves. *La dialectique aristotélicienne: Les principes clés des "Topiques."* Montreal: Éditions Bellarmin, 1991.

Pelzer, A. "Les 51 articles de Guillaume Occam censurés en Avignon en 1326." *Revue d'histoire ecclésiastique* 18 (1922): 240–270.

Pinès, Shlomo. "Les précurseurs musulmans de la théorie de l'*impetus.*" *Archeion* (Argentina) 21 (1938): 294–300. Repr. in his *Studies in Arabic Versions of Greek Texts and in Mediaeval Studies*, pp. 409–417. The Collected Works of Shlomo Pinès 2. Jerusalem: Magnes Press, The Hebrew University; Leiden: Brill, 1986.

Quinn, John F. *The Historical Constitution of St. Bonaventure's Philosophy.* Studies and Texts 23. Toronto: Pontifical Institute of Mediaeval Studies, 1973.

Rudavsky, Tamar, ed. *Divine Omniscience and Omnipotence in Medieval Philosophy: Islamic, Jewish and Christian Perspectives.* Synthese historical library 25. Dordrecht: Reidel, 1985.

Schmidt, Robert W. *The Domain of Logic according to Saint Thomas Aquinas.* The Hague: Nijhoff, 1966.

Schönberger, Rolf. "Realität und Differenz: Ockhams Kritik an der *distinctio formalis.*" In *Die Gegenwart Ockhams*, ed. Vossenkuhl and Schönberger, pp. 97–122.

Scott, T.K. "Ockham on Evidence, Necessity, and Intuition." *Journal of the History of Philosophy* 7 (1969): 27–49.

Shapiro, Herman. *Motion, Time and Place according to William Ockham.* St. Bonaventure, NY: Franciscan Institute, 1957.

Shircel, Cyril L. *The Univocity of the Concept of Being in the Philosophy of John Duns Scotus.* Washington, DC: Catholic University of America Press, 1942.

Simon, Yves. *The Great Dialogue of Nature and Space.* Albany, NY: State University of New York Press, 1970.

Spade, Paul Vincent. "Ockham's Distinctions between Absolute and Connotative Terms." *Vivarium* 13 (1975): 55–76.

—. "Ockham's Rule of Supposition: Two Conflicts in His Theory." *Vivarium* 12 (1974): 63–73.

—. "The Semantics of Terms." In *The Cambridge History of Later Medieval Philosophy*, ed. Kretzmann et al., pp. 188–196.

—. "Synonymy and Equivocation in Ockham's Mental Language." *Journal of the History of Philosophy* 18 (1980): 9–22.

—. "The Unity of a Science according to Peter Aureol." *Franciscan Studies* 32 (1972): 203–217.

—, trans: *see* THE WORKS OF WILLIAM OF OCKHAM: Translations.

Stump, Eleonore. *Boethius's "De topicis differentiis."* Ithaca, NY: Cornell University Press, 1978.

—. "Boethius's Works on the Topics." *Vivarium* 12 (1974): 77–93.

—. *Dialectic and Its Place in the Development of Medieval Logic.* Ithaca, NY: Cornell University Press, 1989.

—. "Topics: Their Development and Absorption into Consequences." In *The Cambridge History of Later Medieval Philosophy*, ed. Kretzmann et al., pp. 273–299.

Suk, Othmar. "The Connection of Virtues according to Ockham." *Franciscan Studies* 10 (1950): 9–32, 91–113.

Swiniarski, John. "A New Presentation of Ockham's Theory of Supposition with an Evaluation of Some Contemporary Criticisms." *Franciscan Studies* 30 (1970): 181–217.

Synan, Edward A., ed: *see* OTHER PRIMARY SOURCES: (Pseudo) Richard of Campsall; Walter Burley

Tachau, Katherine, H. "The Problem of the *Species in Medio* at Oxford in the Generation after Ockham." *Mediaeval Studies* 44 (1982): 394–443.

—. "The Response to Ockham's and Aureol's Epistemology (1320–1340)." In *English Logic in Italy in the 14th and 15th Centuries*, ed. Alfonso Maierù, pp. 185–217. Naples: Bibliopolis, 1982.

—. *Vision and Certitude in the Age of Ockham: Optics, Epistemology, and the Foundation of Semantics 1250–1345.* Leiden and New York: Brill, 1988.

—.: *see also* Courtenay, William J.

Thro, Linus J., ed. *History of Philosophy in the Making: A Symposium of Essays to Honor Professor James D. Collins on His 65th Birthday.* Washington, DC: Catholic University of America Press, 1982.

Tierney, Brian. *The Idea of Natural Rights: Studies in Natural Rights, Natural Law and Church Law, 1150–1625.* Atlanta, GA: Scholars Press, 1997.

Todisco, Orlando. "Il primato del singolare e l'onnipotenza divina secondo Guglielmo d'Ockham." *Collectanea Franciscana* 60 (1990): 539–576.

Trentman, John. "Ockham on Mental." *Mind* 79 (1970): 586–590.

Tweedale, Martin. *Abailard on Universals.* Amsterdam: North-Holland Publishing Co., 1976.

—. "Ockham's Supposed Elimination of Connotative Terms and His Ontological Parsimony." *Dialogue* 31 (1992): 431–443.

Uña Juarez, Agustin *La filosofia del siglo xiv: contexto cultural de Walter Burley.* Biblioteca Ciudad de Dios 1, Libros 26. Madrid: Real Monasterio, 1978.

Urban, Linwood. "William of Ockham's Theological Ethics." *Franciscan Studies* 33 (1973): 310–350.

Van Ackeren, Gerald F. *Sacra Doctrina: The Subject of the First Question of the Summa Theologica of St. Thomas Aquinas.* Rome: Catholic Book Agency, 1952.

Van Steenberghen, Fernand. *Maître Siger de Brabant.* Louvain: Publications Universitaires, 1977.

—. *La philosophie au XIIIe siècle.* Louvain: Publications Universitaires, 1966.

Vignaux, Paul. *Justification et prédestination au XIVe siècle: Duns Scot, Pierre d'Auriole, Guillaume d'Occam, Grégoire de Rimini.* Paris: E. Leroux, 1934.

—. *Luther, commentateur des Sentences.* Paris: Vrin, 1935.

—. "Nominalisme." In *Dictionnaire de théologie catholique,* ed. Alfred Vacant, et al., 11 [1931]: 717–784. 15 vols. in 23. Paris: Letouzey et Ané, 1903 [i.e., 1899]–1950.

—. *Nominalisme au XIVe siècle.* Montréal: Institut d'études médiévales, 1948.

Vossenkuhl, Wilhelm, and Rolf Schönberger, eds. *Die Gegenwart Ockhams.* Weinheim: VCH Acta Humaniora, 1990.

Wallace, William A. "Albert the Great's Inventive Logic: His Exposition of the *Topics* of Aristotle." *American Catholic Philosophical Quarterly* 70 (1996): 11–39.

—. *Causality and Scientific Explanation 1: Medieval and Early Classical Science.* Ann Arbor: University of Michigan Press, 1972.

Webering, Damascene. *Theory of Demonstration according to William Ockham.* St. Bonaventure, NY: Franciscan Institute, 1953.

Weinberg, Julius R. *A Short History of Medieval Philosophy.* Princeton: Princeton University Press, 1964.

Weisheipl, James A. "The Concept of Matter in Fourteenth Century Science." In *The Concept of Matter in Greek and Medieval Philosophy.* Ed. Ernan McMullin. Notre Dame, IN: University of Notre Dame Press, 1963, pp. 328–334.

—. *The Development of Physical Theory in the Middle Ages.* London and New York: Sheed & Ward, 1960. Repr. Ann Arbor: University of Michigan Press, 1971.

—. "The Interpretation of Aristotle's Physics and the Science of Motion." In *The Cambridge History of Later Medieval Philosophy*, ed. Kretzmann et al., pp. 530–536.

—. "The Meaning of *Sacra Doctrina* in *Summa Theologiae* 1, q. 1." *The Thomist* 38 (1974): 49–80.

—. "Medieval Natural Philosophy and Modern Science." In James A. Weisheipl. *Nature and Motion in the Middle Ages*, pp. 261–276.

—. "Natural and Compulsory Movement." *The New Scholasticism* 29 (1955): 50–81. Repr. *Nature and Motion in the Middle Ages*, pp. 25–48.

—. *Nature and Motion in the Middle Ages*. Ed. W.E. Carroll. Washington, DC: Catholic University of America Press, 1985.

—. "Ockham and some Mertonians." *Mediaeval Studies* 30 (1968): 163–213.

—. "The Principle *Omne quod movetur ab alio movetur* in Medieval Physics." *Isis* 56 (1965): 26–45. Repr. *Nature and Motion in the Middle Ages*. Ed. Carroll, pp. 75–97.

—. "The Specter of *motor coniunctus* in Medieval Physics." In *Studi sul XIV secolo in memoria di Anneliese Maier*, ed. A. Maierù and A. Paravicini Bagliani, pp. 81–104. Rome: Edizioni di Storia e Letteratura, 1981. Repr. *Nature and Motion in the Middle Ages*, pp. 99–120.

Westfall, Richard S. *Force in Newton's Physics: The Science of Dynamics in the Seventeenth Century*. New York: American Elsevier, 1971.

Wey, Joseph C., ed.: *see* OTHER PRIMARY SOURCES: Walter Chatton.

White, Graham. "Ockham and Wittgenstein." In *Die Gegenwart Ockhams*, ed. Vossenkuhl and Schönberger, pp. 165–188.

Wippel, John F. "Did Thomas Aquinas Defend the Possibility of an Eternally Created World? (The *De aeternitate mundi* Revisited)." *The Journal of the History of Philosophy* 19 (1981): 21–37. Repr. as "Thomas Aquinas on the Possibility of Eternal Creation" in his *Metaphysical Themes in Thomas Aquinas*, pp. 191–214. Washington, DC: Catholic University of America Press, 1984.

—. *The Metaphysical Thought of Godfrey of Fontaines*. Washington, DC: Catholic University of America Press, 1981.

Wolter, Allan B. "Duns Scotus and the Existence and Nature of God." *Proceedings of the American Catholic Philosophical Association* 28 (1954): 94–121. Repr. *The Philosophical Theology of John Duns Scotus*. Ed. M.M. Adams. Ithaca, NY: Cornell University Press, 1990, pp. 254–277.

—. "Duns Scotus on Intuition, Memory, and our Knowledge of Individuals." In *History of Philosophy in the Making: A Symposium of Essays to Honor*

Professor James D. Collins on His 65th Birthday. Ed. Linus J. Thro. Washington, DC: Catholic University of America Press, 1982, pp. 81–104. Repr. *The Philosophical Theology of John Duns Scotus*, pp. 98–122.

—. "The Formal Distinction." *John Duns Scotus, 1265–1965*, ed. John K. Ryan and Bernardine M. Bonansea, pp. 45–60. Washington, DC: Catholic University of America Press, 1965. Repr. *The Philosophical Theology of John Duns Scotus*, pp. 27–41.

—. "Is Existence for Scotus a Perfection, Predicate, or What?" In *The Philosophical Theology of John Duns Scotus*, pp. 278–284.

—. "John Duns Scotus." In *Individuation in Scholasticism*, ed. Gracia, pp. 271–298.

—. "The Ockhamist Critique." In *The Concept of Matter*, ed. Ernan McMullin, pp. 124–146. Notre Dame, IN: University of Notre Dame Press, 1965.

—. *The Philosophical Theology of John Duns Scotus.* Ed. Marilyn M. Adams. Ithaca, NY: Cornell University Press, 1990.

—. "The Realism of Scotus." *The Journal of Philosophy* 59 (1962): 725–736. Repr. *The Philosophical Theology of John Duns Scotus*, pp. 42–53.

—. *The Transcendentals and Their Function in the Metaphysics of Duns Scotus.* St. Bonaventure, NY: Franciscan Institute, 1946.

—, ed. and trans.: *see* THE WORKS OF WILLIAM OF OCKHAM: Translations; *and* OTHER PRIMARY SOURCES: John Duns Scotus.

Wood, Rega. "Adam Wodeham on Sensory Illusions, with an Edition of 'Lectura secunda', Prologus, Quaestio 3." *Traditio* 38 (1982): 213–252.

—. "Intuitive Cognition and Divine Omnipotence. Ockham in Fourteenth-Century Perspective." In *From Ockham to Wyclif*, ed. Hudson and Wilks, pp. 51–61.

—. "Ockham on Essentially-Ordered Causes: Logic Misapplied." *Die Gegenwart Ockhams*, ed. Vossenkuhl and Schönberger, pp. 25–50.

Zavalloni, Robert. *Richard de Mediavilla et la controverse sur la pluralité des formes.* Louvain: Éditions de l'Institut supérieur de philosophie, 1951.

Index of Names

This index of names lists medieval and modern authors, including anonymous works. Entries for frequently cited authors such as Thomas Aquinas, Duns Scotus, and Henry of Ghent, provide a conspectus of significant topics discussed, not an exhaustive, mechanical listing of citations. References to modern scholars exclude citations to editions and translations.

Index of Subjects

This index refers principally to Ockham's own doctrines. The views of his predecessors are mentioned here only when they have a significant bearing on his own; for a complete overview readers should also consult the Index of Names.